ACCOUNTING CLASSICS SERIES

Editor

ROBERT R. STERLING
University of Kansas

Publication of this Classic was made
possible by a grant from the
PRICE WATERHOUSE FOUNDATION

Suggestions of titles to be included in the Series
are solicited and should be addressed to the Editor.

Publications of Scholars Book Co.

TWENTY-FIVE YEARS
OF ACCOUNTING
RESPONSIBILITY

1911-1936

VOLUME ONE

GEORGE OLIVER MAY

TWENTY-FIVE YEARS OF ACCOUNTING RESPONSIBILITY

1911-1936

ESSAYS AND DISCUSSIONS

Edited by

BISHOP CARLETON HUNT

SCHOLARS BOOK CO.

Box 3344

Lawrence, Kansas 66044

FOREWORD

THE *essays and discussions gathered together in these volumes on the occasion of their author's twenty-fifth anniversary as senior partner of Price, Waterhouse & Co. are published as a mark of the regard and affection of his colleagues, and in appreciation of his distinguished contribution to their profession and his great services to their firm.*

Written at intervals and without thought of collective publication, these papers yet reveal a consistency of thought and a unity of purpose in dealing with the problems which have confronted the public accountant over the last quarter-century: staunch advocacy of considerations of public welfare; unwillingness to be bound by tradition; insistence upon the maintenance of freedom from those fetters which would bar the exercise of individual judgment. They reflect not merely a grasp of the more immediate questions of practice; they reveal an understanding of external factors—of the implications of economic change.

With that devotion to his calling without regard to self which marks the truly professional man, he has always treasured the advancement of his profession above the immediate interests of his own firm; he has always subordinated his own private interests to those of his associates. Indeed, Twenty-five Years of Accounting Responsibility *is at once an epitome of his ideals, and a symbol of the obligations that inhere in the ever-widening province of public accounting.*

Conscious of the privilege of having worked by the side of a gifted and trusted leader, his colleagues rejoice to honor George Oliver May, for nearly forty years associated with Price, Waterhouse & Co.; a partner for thirty-five years; their senior partner for twenty-five years:

> *"Such earnest natures are the fiery pith,*
> *The compact nucleus, 'round which systems grow!*
> *Mass after mass becomes inspired therewith,*
> *And whirls impregnate with the central glow."*

New York
May 8, 1936

ACKNOWLEDGMENT

For permission to reprint material first published elsewhere, we wish to express our thanks to the editors and publishers of the *American Bar Association Journal, The Atlantic Monthly, The Encyclopædia Britannica, Foreign Affairs, Harvard Business Review, The Journal of Accountancy, Journal of the American Statistical Association, The Sun* (New York), *Proceedings, Academy of Political Science,* and *The Quarterly Journal of Economics;* and to Northwestern University and the Ronald Press Co.

CONTENTS

PART V

Taxation

A. General

PART I
THE PROFESSION OF ACCOUNTING

I

THE ACCOUNTANT AND THE INVESTOR *

(1932)

WHEN I was invited to be one of the lecturers in this series, I hesitated on account of a conflict of feelings. I was gratified by an invitation to lecture at an institution which means so much as Northwestern has come to mean in the field of business education, but I felt that ethics should be practiced rather than preached; and I was dismayed at the thought of contributing one of several lectures on the ethics of a single profession. When, however, Professor Custis suggested that I talk on the ethical obligations of the accountant to the investor, my doubts were resolved, because the suggestion offered an opportunity to discuss before a sympathetic audience some of those phases of accounting practice which make it, to me, the most attractive of the professions which are closely allied with business; and an opportunity, also, to discuss some questions possessing a broader interest.

Before discussing the ethical questions which arise between the accountant and the investor, it seems desirable to consider briefly the nature of the investor's interest in the work of the accountant and the conditions under which that work is ordinarily done. Accountancy today has become an important profession, the work of which varies greatly in character and purpose. Its work may, perhaps, be divided into three broad classes: first, the constructive work, such as the formulation and installation of systems of accounting; second, the detailed auditing of cash and other transactions; and third, the preparation and verification of financial statements.

* A lecture given at Northwestern University, Chicago, Illinois, on January 11, 1932, under the auspices of the William A. Vawter Foundation on Business Ethics. Published in *The Ethical Problems of Modern Accountancy,* Ronald Press Co. (1933), pp. 26-54.

3

It is with this third class of work that the investor is more particularly concerned.

Investors are interested in the reports of accountants on the affairs of businesses in which they already are, or contemplate becoming, security holders. If they already hold securities of a corporation carrying on a business, they are concerned with the annual reports presented by the directors to keep them informed of the progress of the enterprise. These reports contain, among other things, annual accounts, which may be certified by accountants. If investors are only potentially interested in any securities, they may turn either to the annual reports or, if the securities are newly created, to the "offering" or prospectus issued by the banking house sponsoring them. This prospectus is likely to contain financial statements made by or on the authority of accountants.

It is interesting to note that the development of the work of the accountant in relation to annual reports and prospectuses dates from the last great period of depression which, beginning in 1893, came to an end with the sound money victory of 1896. My own experience in Wall Street began just as that period ended; and the memory of the disastrous losses shown year after year in the middle 90's, and of the successes subsequently achieved around the end of the century by the same companies, enables me to take heart of grace in even this distressing time.

The practice of having annual accounts audited, which began to make headway in the late 90's, has grown so that today about eighty to ninety per cent of all industrial companies whose securities are listed on the New York Exchange publish audited accounts.

In the early days of my experience, representations in prospectuses as to earnings and assets were usually based on information furnished to the bankers by the officers of the company, and were made by the issuing house itself. Later, it became more and more customary for the issuing houses to secure confirmation of the accounts by accountants, but they continued to make the representations themselves.

More recently the practice has developed (which has long been customary and is now compulsory in England) of publishing the results of the accountants' investigations in the form of a report from the accountants themselves, embodied in the prospectus.   Some concerns, however, still cling to the old procedure and rely on accountants' reports only to support their own representations should those representations later be challenged.

With the rapid development of this field of accountancy, it is not to be expected that standards either of practice or of ethics should be uniform throughout the profession or uniformly satisfactory.   It is in times of depression such as we are now passing through that reforms are most easily initiated, and it is timely, therefore, to consider now what standards of ethics the profession of accountancy can fairly be asked to accept and adhere to.

It will be well, next, to consider the nature of the accountant's responsibility in respect of financial statements which are embodied either in a prospectus or in the annual report of a corporation.   As a preliminary to a consideration of this question, I should like to emphasize the fact that the accounts of a corporation carrying on a complex modern business are not, and cannot be, statements of absolute fact.   They are necessarily based largely on conventions, on estimates, and on opinions.   I shall return later to a further discussion of this point, but think it desirable to mention it early in my address, as I have found from experience that it is by no means always fully appreciated even by people who might be supposed to be well versed in financial affairs.

The character of the accountant's responsibility in respect of accounts embodied in a prospectus or in an annual report rests naturally on the nature and purpose of those documents.   The prospectus is a document issued by a vendor of securities, and is frankly designed to induce investors to purchase securities.   An annual report is a document addressed by the directors to shareholders, reporting on their administration of the affairs of the company for the year and the financial results thereof.

A number of differences between the two cases at once suggest themselves. The banker, who is offering securities, is not expected himself to be informed regarding the financial status and past earnings of a corporation. He must make his representation on the authority of others. He may conceivably rely on the representations of the officials of the company, but obviously this course involves a certain danger, since they are interested parties. Therefore, he is likely to have recourse, instead, to the accountant, who can furnish a disinterested report. In such a case, the full responsibility is put squarely on the shoulders of the accountant.

In the case of the annual report, however, the primary responsibility for the financial statements submitted to shareholders rests with the officers and directors, and the function of the accountant is to advise the shareholders whether, in his opinion, the statements so submitted fairly present the position of the company and the results of its operations. The investor has the right to assume that the figures, let us say, of earnings, presented by an accountant in a prospectus represent the accountant's own best judgment of the results for the period which they cover. In the case of similar figures appearing in the annual report of a corporation, not quite the same assumption can properly be made. In that case, the figures should represent the best judgment of the officers and the directors—a judgment, however, which the auditor either concurs in or regards as being within the reasonable limits of a legitimate difference of opinion, unless the contrary is indicated by his certificate.

Every balance sheet is, as judicial authorities have recognized, necessarily a matter of estimate and opinion, and in some cases the limits of a reasonable difference of opinion may be fairly wide. I do not wish to make too much of the point, but the investing public generally fails to appreciate that there is any distinction at all, and therefore it is essential to mention that it does exist, and that it must exist.

Often, perhaps usually, the accounts presented in an annual report are the results of discussion between the officers or directors of the corporation and its independent auditors, and represent their combined judgment. But the representatives of the corporation, on the one hand, and the accountant, on the other, may not entirely agree, and in such a case the accountant can properly accept the judgment of the corporation's representatives if he is satisfied that it is honestly formed and inherently reasonable.

Suppose, for instance, the question to be what provision for depreciation is required; and suppose that the directors, if left to themselves, would consider a provision of $50,000 as adequate, while the auditor would favor the provision of from $80,000 to $100,000. The directors may agree to provide $70,000 if thereby they can secure the auditor's unqualified certificate to the accounts. For the purposes of an annual report, the auditor would be quite justified in accepting this solution, perhaps saying in his certificate that the provision made is reasonable. But if he were preparing figures for a prospectus, the sole responsibility for which would be his, he would be bound to give expression to his own final judgment, though in reaching that judgment he would naturally give full consideration to the views of the company's representatives.

Another and perhaps more important distinction between the prospectus and the annual report is that the annual report is essentially historical in its character, whereas the prospectus, even when it deals with events in the past, does so solely for the bearing that they have on the prospects for the future. For, obviously, the intending investor has no interest in what has happened in the past merely because it has happened; he is interested only to the extent that the past is a guide to the probable future.

I should like to emphasize this point particularly, because in recent years there has, to my mind, grown up a tendency to attach an altogether exaggerated importance to the earnings reported annually by corporations as an index of future earning capacity and, consequently, of the value of the business. This tendency has, I think, incidentally had the effect of magnifying the swings in the market prices of stocks. In passing, I might express the opinion that the habit of valuing stocks at ten, twelve or any other number of times the annual earnings applicable thereto, and using for the purpose of the calculation the earnings of a single year, has tended to bring about excessive valuations for stocks in periods of great prosperity and correspondingly inadequate values in times of depression such as we are now passing through.

Perhaps I can sum up the position by saying that the investor should be entitled to regard an accountant's statement in a prospectus as a little more objective and more clearly indicative of earning capacity than a statement made in an annual report primarily by the directors but with the concurrence and approval of the auditor.

I should like, now, to consider in more detail the position of the accountant in relation to the prospectus and the annual report of a corporation. I will take the prospectus first because, as I have already pointed out, the accountant assumes the greater responsibility in respect of such a document.

When a banker contemplates an issue of securities of, let us say, an industrial company, he is likely to take steps to secure the report of an accountant on the financial position and past earnings of the business. In doing so, he has two purposes in mind: first, to decide whether the proposed issue is one that he cares to undertake; secondly, to ascertain what sort of a presentation of facts he is likely to be able to secure for the purpose of influencing the judgment of potential investors. Very commonly he will ask the corporation proposing the issue to cause an examination to be made by accountants satisfactory to him. In such work, the accountant is retained at the request of one party, but is actually employed and paid by another, and the purpose of his work is ultimately to influence the attitude of third parties with

whom he never comes into contact. It is apparent at once
that he owes an obligation to each of three groups or parties,
and that the interests of these groups are by no means
identical.

Now, the most difficult ethical problems generally arise
from conflicts of interests and conflicts of loyalties. The
simplest case is that in which the personal interest of the
accountant conflicts with the interest of his client; but obviously no one can claim to be a member of a profession, or
expect to succeed in one, unless he is prepared, when necessary, to subordinate his own interest to that of his client.

More difficult problems arise in cases such as the one I
have just outlined, in which the accountant owes an obligation or a loyalty to more than one individual or group of
individuals, and the interests of the different parties conflict.
Naturally, the problem is not made any less delicate by the
fact that the accountant is dealing with matters of opinion
in relation to operations with which one of the parties (the
corporation) through its officials should be more completely
informed than he can be.

Frequently, the first stage of his work is an investigation
and report to the issuing house upon representations previously made to it by the corporation, and upon his report
the issuing house decides whether those representations have
been borne out and whether the issue is one which it is willing to sponsor. During this stage, the corporation and the
issuing house are on the opposite sides of the table. If this
stage is successfully completed, and mutually satisfactory arrangements are agreed upon by the corporation and the
issuing house, the questions arise what is to be shown in the
prospectus, and in what form, and from this point onwards
the interests of the issuing house and the corporation are,
broadly speaking, identical.

The accountant is apt to encounter difficult ethical problems at both stages of the procedure, but those encountered
in the later stage are by far the more difficult and are the
only ones with which we are concerned today. In the first

stage, the issuing house is trading with the corporation and has an interest in stressing any weaknesses in the corporation's position in order to secure more favorable terms. The accountant is frequently under pressure from two parties advancing conflicting views on the question at issue, and owing a duty to each party. He has, however, the advantage of hearing fully the arguments on both sides and reaching his decision with due regard thereto.

In the second stage—when the prospectus is being prepared —the banker and the corporation are, as I have said, united in presenting their views. The banker is sometimes found to be minimizing at this stage weaknesses which he had stressed in the first stage. The accountant must recognize that his paramount obligation is to the investor, to whom his report is in reality to be addressed; and that the investor is someone with whom the accountant in the nature of things is not in touch, and who is incapable of presenting arguments counter to those presented on behalf of the banker and the corporation. The problem is made the more difficult because the importance of the accountant's report often lies as much in what it implies as in what it says, and because the differences relate almost universally to questions, not of right or wrong, but of judgment.

To illustrate my point—the fact that a corporation has made money in the past has absolutely no significance to the potential investor except for its bearing on the probable earnings of the future. Therefore, neither the issuing house nor the accountant has any ethical right to put forward a statement of past earnings if to their knowledge it is calculated to mislead the investor as to the reasonable prospects for the future. On the other hand, what has been accomplished in the past is usually the main factual basis for estimating future prospects, and it is certainly no part of the work of the accountant to make estimates for the future; so that if he is to make any contribution at all to the knowledge of the investor, it must be in the form of a report on what has taken place in the past.

What position, then, ought the accountant to take if either general conditions or the conditions specifically affecting the business under consideration have changed since the profits proposed to be reported were earned?   This is a question which has occasioned conscientious accountants much concern.   Conditions are never exactly the same from one year to another, and investment must, as a practical matter, always be based on imperfect knowledge and approximations.

I suggest that the auditor should always consider how far conditions at the time of issue differ from those obtaining during the period covered 'by his report, and particularly how far any changes are a matter of common knowledge. He may, for instance, properly certify accounts covering a period of five years even though in his judgment general business conditions are as a whole less favorable than the average during the period covered by his report. He might conceivably justify certifying profits earned during the boom period which culminated in 1929, after the collapse of that year, upon the ground that the change of conditions was a matter of common knowledge and that everyone must judge for himself how far-reaching its effects would be.   He certainly would not be entitled to certify figures for a prospectus if to his knowledge, but not to the knowledge of the public, new conditions had arisen within the corporation itself which practically negatived the possibility of a continuance of any such earnings in the future, or made earnings dependent upon entirely different considerations.

An accountant would not, for instance, be justified in giving a certificate which he knew to be desired for use in a prospectus in circumstances such as came to my notice (not in this country) recently.   A corporation had conducted a very satisfactory and profitable general investment business for a number of years.   Control of it was acquired by a financier of somewhat doubtful reputation, who proceeded at once to dispose of the investments previously held and to reinvest the proceeds in a series of companies controlled by himself.   He also put out a prospectus in which he invited subscriptions to new securities of the investment company on the basis of the results obtained in the past under conditions entirely different from those existing when the issue was made.

Obviously, problems of great nicety must constantly arise, and in order to solve them properly the accountant must possess good judgment and be willing and able to exercise that judgment objectively and dispassionately. The investor must rely on the judgment and ethical standards of the accountant, and except in cases so flagrant as to be fraudulent, the community will be wiser to leave the penalty for failure to justify such confidence to be inflicted through the loss of standing in business which is likely to follow upon it, than to attempt to impose legal penalties.

To be willing to exercise his judgment objectively and dispassionately the accountant must be a man of high character, prepared to recognize and observe high ethical obligations even to his own immediate disadvantage. To be able to do so he must be free from any relation to the subject matter or to the parties in interest which might cloud his judgment or impair his loyalty to the investors to whom his paramount duty is owed. As I have indicated, he necessarily stands in some business relation to the corporation creating the securities and the banking house undertaking their issue, but he should be careful to keep those relations on such a footing as to insure that his freedom of action and independence of judgment will not be affected.

It might be a counsel of perfection to suggest that no accounting firm should give a report or certificate if any member of the firm has any interest, however slight, in the corporation creating the securities to be sold. On the other hand, it would seem unnecessary to say that an accountant should regard himself as disqualified from giving any certificate or opinion if he has any substantial interest in the corporation whose securities are to be sold. Yet I have encountered at least one case in which this principle has been ignored by accountants carrying on a large business and claiming a good standing. As a practical rule, an accountant should run no risk of putting himself in a position where his interest might with any reason be thought to be large enough to affect his judgment, and it is the part of wisdom to resolve all doubts on such a question conservatively by declining the doubtful appointment.

Similarly, the accountant should be extremely careful not to put himself at any time in the position of accepting from the issuing house any favor, or of buying securities from it on any terms more favorable than those offered to the general public. His compensation for services should be fixed, so as to make it as nearly as possible a matter of indifference to him whether the issue is or is not made, or whether if made it is or is not successful. Any agreement in advance whereby the compensation to be received is directly dependent on the success or failure of the financing destroys the disinterestedness of the accountant and is wholly objectionable.

These general considerations seem to me to offer little difficulty. The really difficult ethical problems of the accountant arise when differences of opinion develop between him and the officers of the corporation or the representatives of the issuing house, and when actual or potential weaknesses in the position of the issuing corporation are disclosed. Frequently, the facts of an industrial situation are uncertain, and the most correct accounting treatment of them is a matter of opinion. The officials of the corporation may represent the situation forcefully, and the accountant, while taking a different view, may believe them to be honest and may be conscious of the fact that their familiarity with the subject and knowledge of the details are necessarily greater than his own. He should, however, remember that as against their advantage of greater familiarity he possesses the important advantage of greater objectivity, and though he should always be open to conviction by sound reasoning, he should never allow his judgment to be overborne by the mere authority of interested parties.

Perhaps I might illustrate the difficulties of the situations which arise by an actual case, where the differences of opinion became a matter of public record. In connection with an important recent issue, the accountants, after listening to the views of the management, felt compelled to formulate their conclusions on a basis different from that which the management thought appropriate. In the prospectus it was explained that the earnings, as reported by the accountants employed in that connection, were based on amortization tables which differed "drastically" from those theretofore accepted by the corporation on the advice of accountants, and the following statement was made: "The management believes that the adjustment, which accounts in large measure for the variation between the figures shown above and the interim figures reported by the Corporation, is extremely conservative and in the light of subsequent experience, may prove to be excessive."

It is easy to realize how embarrassing the situation in this case must have been. The question was purely one of opinion, the correct answer to which only time could determine. The management was, as the prospectus indicated, very definite in the expression of its opinion, and had the support of other accountants. The financial issues at stake were important. No doubt the accountants engaged in connection with the prospectus could have framed a form of statement which would have conformed to the views of the management, and which would have left them in a position legally secure. But ethically they were bound to give effect to the judgment which, whether right or wrong, they had honestly and definitely formed.

It is painful to have to disagree with those by whom one has been retained, and the person in whose interest one does so is unlikely ever to know what has been done or to appreciate the stand that has been taken on his behalf. But in the long run, the willingness of an accountant to do what he conceives to be his duty to the unknown investor, even if by so doing he alienates a client and suffers a present loss of business, brings a rich reward both in self-respect and in a professional reputation which, in turn, brings a pecuniary benefit.

Fortunately, in recent years a clearer recognition on the part of issuing houses of their own true interests has tended to make such controversies less frequent and less acute. The wise issuing house today recognizes that the prospectus is the basis of its contract with the investor and that all questions of ethics apart, it is not even expedient to issue a prospectus in which material facts are unfairly or inaccurately stated or suppressed. Such a course may help the sale of securities at the moment, but that is of little worth if it creates possible ground of action against the banker later, should the securities for any reason involve the investor in loss. It is to the interest of the issuing house to see that no pretext is afforded for a later claim for rescission or damages. Here, again, an illustration may be helpful.

A few years ago, in discussion of a proposed issue, the accountants insisted that the existence of certain litigation should be disclosed. The junior representatives of the issuing house strongly opposed this suggestion, saying that it would be fatal to the issue, and the lawyers seemed disposed to agree with them. The matter was, however, taken by the accountants to the head of the firm, who instantly decided that the existence of the litigation must be disclosed so clearly as to preclude any possibility of a claim being made against his firm later in the event that the litigation should result adversely to the corporation. He further expressed the opinion that such frank disclosure would affect the issue favorably, not unfavorably; and events seemed to bear out his judgment, the issue being extremely successful.

I believe that every high-minded accountant has accepted the principle that, once his conclusions are reached, the report or certificate which he issues, and which is designed to influence action, must be so worded that not only will every statement made therein be literally true, but every inference which could legitimately be drawn from the language will be warranted by the facts. There is no place in accountants' certificates for what President Roosevelt once called "weasel words."

In England, it would appear that what has heretofore been regarded as a canon of ethics may sometimes be a legal obligation, enforcible, possibly, under the criminal law. As long ago as 1884, Lord Blackburn, in the House of Lords, in a civil case expressed admirably his view of the position of those concerned in the issue of a prospectus: "If," he said, "with intent to lead the plaintiff to act upon it, they put forth a statement which they know may bear two meanings, one of which is false to their knowledge, and thereby the plaintiff putting that meaning on it is misled, I do not think they can escape by saying he ought to have put the other. If they palter with him in a double sense, it may be that they lie like truth, but I think they lie, and it is a fraud. Indeed, as a question of casuistry, I am inclined to think the fraud is aggravated by a shabby attempt to get the benefit of a fraud without incurring the responsibility." Since that time, many an embittered victim of a disingenuous prospectus has no doubt echoed the outburst of Macbeth which Lord Blackburn had in mind:

> "And be these juggling fiends no more believ'd,
> That palter with us in a double sense;
> That keep the word of promise to our ear
> And break it to our hope."

In the case against Lord Kylsant, which attracted attention here as well as in England and which was recently decided adversely to him both on his trial and in the Court of Criminal Appeal, it was admitted by the Crown that every statement in the prospectus was literally true. Nevertheless, the Judge charged the jury that if they believed that when the language was used the defendant knew that it was calculated to induce investors to draw entirely false inferences and intended that it should have this effect, they should convict him of the charge, which was that he had issued a prospectus which he knew to be "false in a material particular" with intent to induce persons to subscribe for the debentures offered.

Unfortunately, the precise grounds on which the prospectus was held to come within the statute are not entirely clear. Two paragraphs were specified in the indictment— one, giving average profits for ten years, the other, which followed immediately, containing a statement of dividends which showed that dividends had been paid in all but one of the last seventeen years. On the trial, the Crown in stating its case and the Judge in summing up seemed to take the view that the statement of an average for ten years, when in fact all, or substantially all, of the profits were earned in the first four of the ten years and the operations in some of the later years resulted in losses, was a statement false in a material particular, even though the average was authentically true. In sustaining the verdict, however, the Court of Appeal pointed to the statement of dividends paid as being ʻhe portion of the prospectus that was particularly deceptive by reason of the false inferences it was likely and intended to create.

To justify a criminal conviction on the ground that a statement of dividends created a natural inference as to earnings, when there was, in fact, a separate paragraph dealing with earnings, might seem to be straining the law. Possibly, however, what the Court had in mind was that the statements made in successive paragraphs regarding earnings and dividends were together so misleading as to justify a jury in finding a criminal intent. Fortunately, no accountant was chargeable with responsibility for the language used in the Royal Mail prospectus; and I think most accountants would refuse to certify an average alone where the figures for individual years were ascertainable.

This is not the place in which to pursue the particular question before the courts in the Kylsant case. For the present it is sufficient to say that all questions of criminality or even civil liability apart, the ethical obligation of the accountant is clearly to see that no statement is put forward

which is a half truth or which he realizes will probably give
rise to inferences which would, in fact, be ill founded. Of
course, he cannot be held responsible for every inference,
however unwarranted, which the ignorant or careless investor may draw from the appearance of his name in a prospectus. Every accountant with any considerable practice has
probably, after a company with which he has been associated
has come to grief, been told in aggrieved tones: "I took it
for granted that if your name was on the document it was
all right; I didn't trouble to read just what you said." Such
an attitude is wholly unreasonable; but if a statement carries
a natural and almost irresistible inference, the accountant
is ethically and perhaps legally as responsible for that inference as for the literal truths of the words he uses.

The question of phraseology assumes a different form
when we come to consider accounts embodied in annual reports. As I have pointed out, the figures and the language
of an accountant's report or certificate, given for use in a
prospectus, are his own. Others may make suggestions, but
the final decision is entirely in his hands. The annual accounts of a corporation, on the other hand, are those of its
officers and directors, and the primary responsibility is shared
between them. In this case, it is the accountant who makes
suggestions and the directors who must make the final decisions. When they have done so, the accountant must consider what report he will make to the shareholders on the
accounts which the directors have adopted.

Clearly it is not desirable that he should insist on register-
ing every difference of opinion, however slight, that may arise
between the directors and himself. His power to render
service to the shareholders, and his ability to influence directors towards sound decisions, will be impaired if he adopts a
too pedantic or too captious attitude. But when he differs
with the directors on a point which he deems really important, he should indicate his dissent and express it clearly.

There is probably considerable justice in the criticism that
qualifications of accountants' reports are frequently inade-

quate to convey to the average shareholder the precise nature and extent of the accountant's reservation. Those versed in financial affairs regard any sort of a qualification as a danger signal and refuse to pass it until they are satisfied just what danger threatens. But it would be a distinct forward step if auditors would aim to express their qualifications in clear, non-technical as well as unambiguous language. This point may be elaborated by a future lecturer, as Mr. Hoxsey of the New York Stock Exchange is taking a keen and active interest in such questions.

In relation to annual accounts, a conflict of interests, which I have not heretofore mentioned, may arise between those who are already shareholders and those who may become so. The auditor's primary ethical duty is clearly to existing shareholders, but since he knows his report is likely to influence others to become shareholders, he must recognize some obligation to that class of investors. At the same time, annual accounts are historical in their nature. They are not intended to be and cannot properly be regarded as designed to indicate earning capacity. And if accounts are fair as an historical record, no one can justly assert a grievance against the accountant on the score that they led him to draw inferences as to future earning prospects which the accountant with his greater knowledge might have known to be unwarranted.

To illustrate the point—suppose a company to have been operating during a year on the basis of a sales contract covering the bulk of its output at a high price, which at the end of the year has expired and been replaced by a contract at a substantially lower price. An accountant would not be justified ethically in giving a certificate of the profits for the year for use in a prospectus, without referring to the expiration of the old contract and the making of the new one. It would, however, be no part of his duty to refer to the contract situation in his certificate to the annual accounts, though it might be a part of the ethical duty of the directors to do so in their report.

While everyone experienced in corporation finance must recognize the impossibility of giving to annual accounts all the significance as indices of earning capacity which investors (and those who undertake to advise investors) too often attribute to them, neither directors nor auditors can completely ignore the fact that the history of the past is commonly regarded as some guide to the prospects for the future. The obligation of directors is, it would seem, greater if they have caused the securities of their company to be listed on a public exchange, for in doing so they have invited the public to trade in those securities. They have endeavored to secure for their shareholders the advantage which a broader market sometimes affords; and both they and the shareholders should be willing to pay the fair price for this benefit.

That fair price seems to me to be a sufficient disclosure of the affairs of the corporation to enable the public to deal in its securities with a reasonable degree of understanding. I have heard it argued that it is impossible to throw the full light of day on the affairs of a corporation, and that it is therefore unwise for a body like the New York Stock Exchange to exert its influence actively to secure more disclosure than corporations would otherwise undertake. The suggestion is, that as a result of such efforts the public is deceived because it is led to believe that it is trading in the full light of day when it is trading only in the twilight. Personally, I have no sympathy with this point of view, but favor a liberal standard of disclosure. Inasmuch as Mr. Hoxsey has been one of the most persistent and effective campaigners in favor of publicity, I trust that he, when he comes to lecture to you, will discuss the question more fully than I can now attempt to do.

The difficult questions in this field revolve largely around two classes of items frequently referred to as "non-recurring items" and "secret reserves." The term "non-recurring items" is applied to those items, whether of income or outgo, which, although relating to the business and properly finding their way into the income account, are in character quite exceptional and not likely to be repeated at all regularly. Illustrations may be found in the case of recovery of insurance on the life of the president of the company, or a loss through fire of an important plant. "Secret reserves" is the term applied to amounts set aside out of income purely as a precaution and not in respect of any losses presently known or anticipated. The amounts so set aside may be used to meet totally unexpected losses in the future, or may be restored at a later date to the income account.

It is obvious that both classes of items require either to be eliminated or given special consideration in any study of the income account which is designed to determine the normal earning capacity of the business; but how these items should be treated in the regular annual reports of corporations is a question on which there is considerable divergence of opinion and practice. I think the minimum which a reasonable standard of ethics calls for on the part of directors and auditors of companies whose securities are listed on exchanges is that when any important non-recurring items are included in the income of the year, the fact that they are so included shall be clearly stated; and that where secret reserves are drawn upon to improve the profits of the year, this fact, also, shall be disclosed. I do not think there is room, thus far, for any serious disagreement. Differences, however, would arise on the further suggestion which I would make, that the amounts involved should in all cases be indicated.

There remains for consideration the attitude of the accountant towards the original establishment of secret reserves, the result of which is, of course, that the profits for the period in which they are established are understated. This is a particularly difficult problem because of the varied ways in which what are substantially secret reserves can be established. There is the simple case of a general reserve for contingencies; but there are more difficult cases, such as the under-valuation of inventories or securities, which have precisely the same effect.

One view of the question is that the directors should always submit accounts that represent as accurately as possible their best judgment of the true profits for the year, according to the general method of accounting adopted by the corporation. Others take the position that all businesses are subject to many hazards which cannot be accurately measured; that the attribution of profits to years is at best largely conventional; that business moves in cycles; and that a certain amount of deliberate understatement in good years is warranted and in the interests of the shareholders.

The question is partly a practical and partly an ethical one, and my own judgment is that directors would usually be well advised to follow their own judgment in regard to the establishment of precautionary reserves, but to disclose to shareholders the fact that the reserves have been made. Whether they should give general publicity to the amount of the reserves established is a matter of judgment. Their ethical obligation is probably discharged if they tell shareholders explicitly that reserves have been made, and give them the opportunity to make further inquiries if they so desire. Drawing on reserves to supplement current profits is, as I have indicated, an entirely different matter, and should be fully disclosed.

So far as the accountant is concerned, I do not think that in the present state of public opinion and general practice he can be charged with an ethical duty to insist on the disclosure even of the fact that a secret reserve has been created, if he believes that the action was taken in good faith and if the amount involved is not so large that ignoring it completely distorts the earnings picture. Cases occasionally arise in which the accountant may be convinced that earnings are being deliberately understated in order that one group, often referred to colloquially as the "insiders," may profit at the expense of the general body of shareholders. There can be no question of his ethical obligation to the shareholders as a whole in such a situation. His position at such times would be greatly strengthened if he were elected by the shareholders and directly responsible to them instead of being appointed by and responsible to the officers or directors as is the common case in our country.

I hope that this discussion of the ethical obligations of the accountant to the investor will be sufficient to convince you that the high-minded accountant who undertakes to practice in this field assumes high ethical obligations, and it is the assumption of such obligations that makes what might otherwise be a business, a profession. Of all the group of professions which are closely allied with business, there is none in which the practitioner is under a greater ethical obligation to persons who are not his immediate clients; and it is for this reason that I believe accounting ought, and can be made, to take an outstanding position in this group.

I would not have you think that because the investor is not his immediate client the accountant owes nothing to the investor except legal duties and ethical obligations. This is not, of course, the fact. It is to the investor that he owes his entire practice in the field of financial auditing, and it is only because the investor exists and attaches weight to an accountant's report that the banker employs the accountant's services in this field. And the continued success of the accountant is dependent on his retaining the confidence of the investing public. An enlightened self-interest, therefore, as well as self-respect calls for the maintenance of a proper ethical standard by the practitioner.

The young accountant may find it hard to take the first stand for the principles that have been suggested for his observance, but he will find that this is essentially a case in which "it is the first step that costs." Perhaps, therefore, I may, in bringing this discussion to a close, indulge in a personal reminiscence which bears on this point and which as it happens relates, also, to the question of showing average profits, which arose in the Kylsant case.

A good many years ago—as a matter of fact, in 1899—owing to the death of one of the senior partners, I was called upon to settle with an important New York banker the form of a certificate for use in connection with a prospectus. As the issue was to be made on both sides of the Atlantic, it was planned to print the accountants' certificate in the prospectus as was and is customary in England.

The profits of the company showed a fairly steady decline over a period of ten years except that in 1898, owing to the Spanish-American War, they rose considerably to a point higher than the average of the ten years. The banker desired the certificate to show only the average for the ten years and the profits for the last year. I demurred to this suggestion on two grounds: first, that it was contrary to the practice of my firm to show only averages where the profits for separate years were readily ascertainable; and, secondly, that the information proposed to be given would create a natural but erroneous impression as to the trend of profits.

The discussion became difficult, and it was indicated to me that if we adhered to the position I had taken there would be no possibility of any similar differences with that particular banker in the future. However, I refused to modify the stand I had taken and was supported by the senior partner, with the result that no certificate was printed in the prospectus, but a statement was made by the banker on his own responsibility. I felt that I was right, but I could not fail to be conscious of the fact that my first important interview with a banker had not been a success and promised to result in the loss of an important client.

There was, however, a sequel. Some six months later, the same banker was contemplating the purchase of a business and desired a full and reliable report on its operations. His lawyers approached the firm saying that while he still thought we were entirely wrong in the stand we had taken six months earlier, he believed that we had taken it in perfect good faith and that the incident should not, therefore, be a bar to friendly relations between us. They thereupon gave us instructions to make the investigation, and further intimated that the banker desired that I should personally take charge of it; and I may add that the banker is today a valued client of the firm.

This sequel made the whole incident one of the most helpful of my experiences, and I hope it may also be of service in encouraging those of you who may be about to start practice, or are in the early days of practice, to take a firm stand for sound ethical principles, which I am sure will ultimately tend to bring you professional success as well as a consciousness of professional integrity.

II

QUALIFICATIONS IN CERTIFICATES *

(1915)

FIRST of all, the fact that the qualified certificate has been selected by the authorities of the association as a suitable topic for discussion is evidence of the progress our profession is making, for it is not so many years since the qualified certificate was not sufficiently common for the subject to be of importance.

Twenty years ago an audit certificate seldom assumed any special importance. It was regarded rather as a frame which helped to set off the financial picture. Obviously it is better to present a picture unframed than in a frame showing bare spots from which the gilt has disappeared; and so the demand was for an unqualified certificate or none at all. This condition is at least in part responsible for the opinion sometimes expressed that an accountant should give no certificate but an unqualified one, though often the opinion is the result of a failure to read a certificate properly and a desire to blame the accountant for subsequent failure of the enterprise, possibly due to the very causes which necessitated a qualification in the certificate. We too frequently hear investors say: "Oh, well, I didn't read every word of the certificate; I saw it was signed by so and so and I thought that was good enough." Of course, the position is unreasonable, but if we remember that there was a time when practically all certificates printed were unqualified because qualified certificates were wrongly regarded as valueless and promptly suppressed, we may find for those who take the position some

* An Address at the annual meeting of the American Association of Public Accountants, Seattle, Washington, September 21, 1915. Cf. *The Journal of Accountancy*, Vol. XX (October, 1915), pp. 248-59.

better excuse than mental laziness or an unfair desire to make the accountant the scapegoat.

The impracticability of the suggestion that only unqualified certificates should be given is apparent. A client retains an auditor to audit his accounts, with a view to certifying a balance sheet. The auditor dissents from the treatment of an item in the balance sheet but finds the books and accounts in all other respects correct. Clearly the client is entitled to a certificate as to their correctness subject to the one point; and it is desirable too, as a matter of broad policy, that he should get it, otherwise one of two things would be likely to happen —either an exaggerated impression as to the unreliability of the accounts would be created by the refusal of a certificate, or the auditor to avoid that serious result would waive or sink his convictions and sign an unqualified certificate. Moreover, every balance sheet, as has been judicially pointed out, is necessarily to some extent a matter of estimate and opinion, and qualifications often represent an honest difference of opinion between directors and auditors. What more effective disposition can be made of such a case than for the stockholders to have placed before them the two views—the one perhaps possessing the advantage of greater familiarity with the subject matter, the other the advantage of a more detached viewpoint, and then for the final disposition of the question to be determined by the stockholders?

Before leaving this question it may not be amiss to point out that among the things to be done by investors and bankers to make audit certificates attain their full value (what accountants have to do is not now discussed) are these:

(1) Use every opportunity to extend the practice of having auditors appointed by and report to stockholders;

(2) Note and require explanations where companies which present audited accounts one year present unaudited accounts the next or change their auditors.

The next question to be considered is the more difficult one as to the form and character of qualifications. In the consideration of this question, qualifications may be divided into two groups—those that merely limit responsibility without expressing or implying disapproval of the accounts (as, for instance, where branch accounts have been accepted without audit) and those that constitute criticisms of the accounts (as, for instance, where proper provision for depreciation has not been made).

The great essential of any proper qualification is, of course, that it shall be clear and readily understandable by anyone not expert in accounts, and shall be expressed directly and not implied by subtle refinements in wording which may easily escape the notice of many who read the certificate. An accountant who relies on fine distinctions of language, or the assignment of wider meaning to a word or phrase than it would ordinarily be given, to limit his responsibility for accounts he has certified, may succeed in avoiding any legal liability therefor but prejudices the interests of the whole profession. This is not to say that great care in the choice of words in a certificate is undesirable or superfluous; on the contrary, the ideal certificate is the one that conveys precisely the right shade of meaning to anyone who carefully studies its every word and at the same time creates the correct general impression in the mind of anyone who reads it hurriedly and with no more than ordinary care.

Qualifications which limit responsibility should not only indicate the extent of the limitations but their importance; at least, if the limitation is of marked importance, that fact should be made clear. Thus, in the illustrative case above cited, it should not be considered sufficient to state that the branch accounts have been accepted without audit if the branch assets constitute, say, 75% or more of the total so that only a small proportion of the total has been really verified.

As to qualifications which are in the nature of criticisms of the accounts, it would clearly be desirable that they should show the exact or approximate effect on the accounts of the adoption of the auditor's view; but such an ideal is not always attainable, and it cannot be said that any qualification which falls short of this standard is defective. The generally accepted rule is that a qualification is adequate if it is sufficient to put the reader on notice and afford him a basis for investigation if he desires to carry the matter further. Thus, a qualification "subject to the fact that no provision has been made for depreciation" is regarded as sufficient without any statement by the auditor as to what provision he thinks should be made.

Although in some cases a more specific qualification which would indicate the precise amount involved might be undesirable from the business standpoint in a certificate receiving wide publicity, yet there is some justice in the demand for less general qualifications, which is sometimes heard. So long as audits are not compulsory, however, progress in the desired direction can be made only with the assistance of bankers and investors—particularly the former, since the investors are not organized and are not in so advantageous a position for making their wishes effective as the bankers. Accountants gladly recognize the help which bankers have given in recent years, and the resulting improvements in the form of accounts and certificates is apparent. Continued coöperation will produce continued improvement.

So long as the discontinuance of audits or change of auditors passes without comment from stockholders or creditors, the auditors are hampered in their efforts to make accounts as accurate and their certificates as complete and informative as possible. If auditors take too rigid a stand the directors will simply publish unaudited accounts or perhaps seek some more amenable auditors. It is not the financial effect on themselves of such a course that influences those auditors who view their responsibility most seriously to modify their position so as to reach an agreement with directors if possible; it is the knowledge of the fact that too rigid an attitude will defeat the very purpose they are seeking to accomplish. They realize that it is to the public interest that they should concede something in the language of a certificate or that they should bring the accounts nearer to the correct standard

even though that standard be not quite attained, rather than
that the accounts should be published entirely uncorrected
and unexplained. There are many accountants who would
never pass accounts they did not thoroughly approve for the
sake of retaining the audit, who have done so for the reason
just given. Of course, there can be no compromise on really
vital questions, and the determination of the proper limit of
concessions calls for the nicest judgment. Extended experience convinces, however, that the policy has in the long run
resulted in greater improvement in accounting standards
than a more drastic policy would have produced and has
been beneficial to the business and financial community.

Turning now to the consideration of specific forms of
qualification, it should perhaps be pointed out that in the
ordinary certificate that "in our opinion the balance sheet is
properly drawn up so as to set forth the true financial position of the company as shown by the books and accounts,"
neither of the expressions "in our opinion" and "as shown
by the books and accounts" should be regarded as a qualification. The insertion of the words "in our opinion" is an
honest recognition of the fact that the certificate can be but
an expression of opinion, as indeed a balance sheet itself
is in a large measure. The use of the expression "as shown
by the books and accounts" does not justify the certification
of accounts which are in accord with the books if the auditor has reason to believe that the books are not correct or has
not satisfied himself that they are correct. It is suggested,
however, that the phrase is so frequently regarded as a limitation, or in some cases an attempted evasion of responsibility, that it would be well to omit it. The statement that
"the balance sheet is in accord with the books and in our
opinion, etc.," is suggested as a preferable form.

The insertion of limiting phrases should not be regarded
as absolving the auditor from all duty and responsibility
in regard to the assets or liabilities to which the phrases
apply. Thus, before issuing a certificate containing a statement that the branch accounts have been accepted without

audit, the auditor should look into the way in which the branch accounts are prepared and satisfy himself as far as is possible without auditing the branch accounts that he is justified in accepting them, and that there is no evidence tending to show that they are unreliable.   In the same way a statement that valuations of certain assets by persons indicated have been accepted should not be embodied in a certificate if the auditor suspects the good faith or qualifications of the valuers.

It is, naturally, the qualification which constitutes a criticism that offers the greatest difficulty.   Much of the objection offered by directors to qualifications seems shortsighted. For instance, if it is apparent on the face of a company's accounts that no provision has been made for depreciation where a provision is ordinarily regarded as necessary, it would seem wise for the directors to accept a certificate with that one qualification, and to offer an explanation of the omission if they deem it proper to do so.   If an unqualified certificate is given, any competent person examining the accounts and finding that no depreciation is provided and no comment on the fact is made by the auditors will begin at once to suspect other defects in both the accounts and the auditors.   No doubt there are many less careful or competent recipients of reports who would not carry their analysis so far, but of these a large part probably would not read the certificate at all and others would take the qualification lightly, perhaps dismissing the requirement of a provision for depreciation as one of the accountant's fetishes. The readers whose impressions are of most importance to the directors issuing the report are, it is believed, more likely to be unfavorably impressed by the unqualified than by the qualified certificate in such a case.   That this is so is perhaps indicated by a growing tendency to discard the ostrich-like policy in such matters and to aim rather to minimize the effect of unfavorable features in accounts and reports by stating them boldly.

An amusing feature of the continual discussion of the form

of qualification is the way in which an expression, such, for instance, as "subject to," acquires an evil significance, and great effort is expended in finding a more acceptable equivalent. The equivalent in time falls into disrepute, and a fresh search is instituted. The attitude of those to whom the qualified certificate is given is perhaps natural—no great harm results—and possibly in so far as the attitude stimulates the ingenuity of the auditor, widens his vocabulary and tends away from stereotyped forms of expression, it may be said to be positively beneficial.

An interesting question arises as to how far an exposition of the views of directors may properly be appended to a qualification. In general the more detached the attitude of the auditor, the more his certificate creates the impression that it was designed to benefit his ultimate clients to whom the certificate is to be presented, rather than his immediate clients—those by whom the certificate is sought—, the greater weight his audit will carry. But where an auditor in a certificate intended for stockholders criticizes the accounts in any particular, the directors may reasonably desire to be sure of having their point of view put before the stockholders, and that at as nearly as possible the same time as the criticism. Hence, such expresisons as "no provision has been made for ————, the directors considering, etc." It is suggested, however, that this practice should be resorted to only very sparingly. The comment that no provision has been made for something implies that the auditor thinks some provision should have been made. If the auditor then proceeds to state the directors' reasons for not making the provision, it may be urged that he should logically go on to show why these reasons were not accepted by him as conclusive. There are, of course, cases where the value of certain assets or the amount of certain liabilities is so uncertain that neither auditors nor directors can form definite opinions. If in such cases the best judgment of the auditor differs from that of the directors, or if the auditor is not prepared either to endorse the directors' opinions or express one of his own, a statement of the facts and of the directors' views thereon may, it would seem, properly be embodied in the audit certificate. An alternative course which has often proved convenient and satisfactory to all concerned is for the auditor to agree with directors on a statement to be made by the latter in their report to stockholders regarding the special point involved, and for the auditor then to certify that the accounts, "read in conjunction with the explanation regarding ———— contained in the directors' report, set forth, etc."

One note of warning may be sounded. It must be remembered that some rules of accounting are rules of conservatism, not of law, and an auditor cannot compel his client to be conservative under penalty of receiving only a qualified certificate. If accounts clearly state the method of treating certain items and that method is not improper, though not the most conservative, the auditor is not justified in giving his certificate a qualified form.

In general where facts are fully disclosed in the accounts in such a way as to be readily understood, one of the great objects for which auditors are constantly striving is attained, and the references to features which are not treated precisely in accord with the auditor's view may be made less severe than where suppression of material fact aggravates error in treatment.

Pursuing this line of thought, it is suggested that comments, not really critical, but which clients will nevertheless resent as being likely to be regarded by the public as qualifications, may often be obviated by embodying the equivalent explanation in the accounts. Suppose, for instance, that during the year the basis of valuation of capital assets has been changed with a resulting large credit to surplus: if the accounts do not disclose these facts the auditor must bring them out in his certificate. The change may be perfectly proper, and the client may object to the reference in the certificate on the ground that it implies—or will be regarded by many as implying—a doubt as to the propriety of the change. The natural solution of such a difficulty is to amplify the accounts so as to bring out the facts, and the reference in the certificate can then be omitted. Experience suggests that this alternative is not used so freely as it might properly be, and that, consequently, much friction that could easily be avoided occurs between auditors and clients.

It may be well now to consider briefly some of the points on which qualifications are more commonly necessary, and in doing so the balance sheet items may be taken in the usual order: capital assets, investments, inventories, accounts receivable, deferred charges, capital and current liabilities, surplus.

Qualifications as to capital assets are perhaps the most frequent, the reasons being partly that there is more room for difference of opinion as to capital assets than as to current assets or liabilities and that capital assets are not of great importance for credit purposes, and directors are, therefore, willing to accept qualifications as to capital assets where they would prefer to adjust current items rather than have any qualification in regard to them.

Depreciation and discount on bonds charged to capital are time-honored subjects of qualification. Fortunately, the auditor's position as to both has been made easier by the growing insistence of courts and regulating authorities upon their correct treatment. Those who urged ten years ago that discount was not a proper charge to capital were faced by interstate commerce regulations providing for its charge to cost of property, but the rule has since been changed, and other regulating bodies have followed the Interstate Commerce Commission. Today an auditor comparatively seldom has difficulty in securing acceptance of the sound accounting principles regarding depreciation and discount, and the issue is usually only as to the amount to be written off—an issue that must always be open for discussion.

Another question as to capital assets concerns the adoption of valuations in lieu of previous book figures. In such cases, unless the auditor has reason to doubt the good faith of the valuation, the question is, as already suggested, best dealt with by clear explanations in the accounts.

Investments frequently offer difficulty where values have depreciated or are not well established. The auditor's contention that provision should be made for a fall in value of marketable securities, though appreciation should not be taken up until realized, is attacked as illogical, though it obviously is the one safe rule. An explanation or qualification in the certificate is desirable where the rule is not followed, unless the amounts involved are relatively small and the facts are clear in the face of the accounts as, for instance,

> Marketable investments at cost $........
> (market value $.......)

In the case of investments the value of which is uncertain (which include securities the quoted prices of which are nominal), the basis of valuation should be made clear either in the accounts or certificate; and where the amount is at all material and the valuation is not at cash cost, a reference to the item in the certificate is always desirable. If the auditor regards the securities as not being worth the value at which they are taken, a qualification is required such as: "Subject to the value of the investments, we certify, etc." If the auditor has no reason to dissent from the valuation and yet is unable fully to confirm it independently, the certificate may read: "Accepting the valuation placed on the investments by ————, I certify, etc." Where the auditor is unwilling to go so far as to "accept" the valuation he can state the basis and say: "Upon this basis, I certify, etc.," leaving every reader to decide for himself as to the propriety of the basis.

Inventories may probably be valued legally at a figure not exceeding their net realizable value (*i.e.*, their selling value, less costs of realization), but the "cost or market, whichever is lower" basis is so obviously sound and so generally adopted that a departure from this basis should be indicated either in the accounts or certificate; except, perhaps, in certain industries, such as the leather or packing-house businesses, where it is a matter of common knowledge that costs are practically unobtainable for finished products, and that it is a trade custom to adopt a valuation based on selling prices with conservative deductions.

Differences of opinion as to the necessary reserves for bad debts sometimes give rise to qualifications, and even more generally the necessity for reserves for collection expenses on debts where collection cost is an important item (as, for instance, in instalment businesses) is or should be the subject of comment in the auditor's certificate. The necessity for such reserves is not yet fully recognized, and the practice of establishing them is by no means universal. The position regarding future collection expenses now is similar to the position regarding depreciation a few years ago, and it is to be hoped that the coming years will furnish a parallel to the steady growth of sounder opinion on that question.

Deferred charges are a fruitful source of qualifications: officers who are anxious to avoid showing a deficit but are unwilling to overstate "real" assets are tempted sometimes to solve the difficulty by carrying as deferred charges items which ought to be charged to profit and loss and would have been so charged without question if operating results had been more favorable. The particular forms of qualification are so varied that no general comment is possible.

Qualifications as to liabilities usually relate to liabilities unascertained in amount or contingent, which exist and are not noted on the balance sheet, or to such special liabilities as indebtedness for goods in transit, or for goods intended for sale in a future season, the invoices for which are post-dated. In such cases both the asset and the liability are sometimes omitted, but they should be disclosed or the fact of their being omitted clearly brought out.

In addition to the questions which have been already discussed and which indirectly affect the amount of the surplus, questions arise as to the manner of stating the surplus. These questions include the proper disclosure of extraor-

dinary profits, the separation of earned surplus from surplus
arising in other ways, and the treatment of losses which it
is claimed are chargeable against prior surplus instead of
against current operations. These questions often give rise
to serious differences between client and auditor, the client
arguing that "it is all the same in the end and that there
is nothing in the balance sheet that is not literally true."
The auditor's position must be that to receive a clear certificate accounts must be fair as well as literally true. Accounts are often more important on account of the inferences that may be drawn from them than as mere statements
of a past condition. We all know how easy it is to join together a series of statements, each of which is literally true,
in such a way that an inference will naturally be drawn
which is in reality incorrect. The auditor aims to ensure
not only that statements he makes or certifies shall be true,
but that every legitimate inference drawn from them shall
also be correct. Of course, he can accept no responsibility
as to unwarranted inferences, though it is often sought to
impose such a responsibility on him.

Qualification is sometimes necessary as to the general form
of accounts submitted to the auditor, especially in the case
of holding companies. While the general adoption of the
practice of publishing consolidated balance sheets affords the
auditor a strong argument in favor of that form of statement, clients who desire to publish a holding company balance sheet have the legal position in their favor. The auditor can, however, meet such cases by insisting that while
the balance sheet is a correct balance sheet of the holding
company, it does not adequately disclose the financial position unless supplemented by a consolidated balance sheet of
the subsidiaries or its equivalent.

Questions also arise where extraordinary transactions such
as the declaration of a large dividend which very materially
affects the financial position, have taken place shortly after
the date of a balance sheet and before the certificate is
signed. These questions are of great importance where the

balance sheet is likely to be used for the purpose of securing credit. Irrespective of any technical view of such a question, which might seem to justify a clear certificate, the auditor should take a broader view; and if he feels that there is danger that the statement prove seriously misleading, he should take adequate steps to avoid that result.

Another general question which it may be well to touch upon is the position where an auditor is appointed by a company long in existence to make an audit of its accounts for one year. Is a specific disclaimer of responsibility as to the accounts prior to the year under audit necessary? The correctness of current assets and liabilities can be determined without delving into the past to any great extent, but capital assets carried at cost are not so easily verified. Where the balance sheet shows the figures of capital assets at the beginning of the year and the charges during the year, and the auditor states that he has audited the accounts for the year, he is justified in accepting the opening balance, unless he has reason to believe it to be incorrect, because the capital assets could only be verified by auditing, at least in part, the accounts of a prior period. Taking into consideration the fact that capital assets are not usually stated on the basis of present values, the magnitude of the task involved in a complete verification of the capital assets, and the clear indication on the face of the balance sheet that the opening balances have been accepted, no one would be justified in assuming that the auditor had in such a case done more in connection with capital assets than verify the changes during the year. This is especially true where the long form of certificate is given, stating specifically that the changes during the year have been examined and found to be proper, the inference clearly being that the auditor is not prepared to accept responsibility for the treatment of the accounts in the past, though in practice auditors usually look cursorily over the past history of capital asset accounts with a view to detecting any gross inflation or special adjustments thereof.

This discussion of specific qualifications has been limited to those arising on the certification of annual balance sheets. The questions arising on certificates of profits for prospectuses and other special work are to a large extent similar and will offer no difficulty to anyone who has a clear idea of the principles which govern the issue of certificates as to annual accounts.

In granting certificates the accountant stands between his client and the public, and the decision as to how far he can go to meet his client's wishes and still do his full duty to the public is often difficult to make. Upon his ability to decide such questions rightly his ultimate standing and success largely depend. He should err, if at all, on the side of the public, for undue laxity will damage the profession and himself; at the same time excessive rigidity, as has been suggested, will often defeat the purpose he is seeking. As in most walks of life, success lies in finding the happy mean.

III

A PROPER COURAGE IN THE ASSUMPTION OF RESPONSIBILITY BY THE ACCOUNTANT *

(1926)

WHEN your Committee invited me to speak tonight, they suggested that I should, if possible, select a topic which would possess not only a professional but a more general interest. Since that invitation was extended, the article by Professor Ripley on corporate publicity, which has received such general notice, has appeared in the *Atlantic Monthly,* and it has seemed to me to raise questions of great professional importance which affect also the whole financial community. In speaking before the American Institute of Accountants at Atlantic City recently, I drew attention to the significance of the movement initiated by Professor Ripley as affecting accountants, and with your permission I should like to develop more fully some of the thoughts then briefly expressed.

It is not perhaps inappropriate to do so in the State of New Jersey, as, though your State is no longer a pennant holder in what has become a somewhat undignified competition for new incorporations, some of the country's most important industries are still conducted by corporations organized under your laws.

At Atlantic City I suggested that an extension of the practice of having accounts audited annually, which has now become almost universal among the important industrial companies, might do much, perhaps more than supervision by the Federal Trade Commission, to bring about improved standards of corporate publicity. I may say that I have since received, with much gratification, a very cordial letter from

---

* An address delivered to the Society of Certified Public Accountants of the State of New Jersey, Newark, N. J., October 19, 1926.

40

Professor Ripley welcoming the suggestions I then put forward.

At that time I expressed the view that if the desired end were to be accomplished it would be necessary that the responsibilities of auditors should be made more real and definite, and that as a necessary corollary auditors would have to be given fuller and more clearly defined authority and be reasonably assured of an opportunity to present their views to stockholders if they should unfortunately come into serious disagreement with the directors or officers of the corporation under audit.

The status and responsibilities of an auditor who certifies or reports upon the annual accounts of a corporation are at present vague and indefinite; some accountants, I believe, would be glad to have them remain so. Why, they would ask, should we add to our responsibilities? The answer is, of course, simple. We cannot expect, for any length of time, to get something for nothing; and if we wish to see the prestige and authority of the profession, or for that matter its financial rewards, continue to increase, we must be prepared to assume correspondingly greater responsibilities. We should, nevertheless, be careful what responsibilities we assume; a rash assumption of responsibility in matters beyond our competence would be as disastrous to the profession as unwillingness to assume it in matters which are within our competence.

From time to time we see corporations which have been audited fail as a result of conditions which were either not discovered or not brought out by the auditors; in connection therewith we hear comments on the uselessness of audits. As well might we complain of the uselessness of doctors because people die of complaints other than old age. Sometimes no doubt the auditor is fairly subject to criticism—just as doctors sometimes are; in other cases no such criticism is warranted.

The position is simply that an audit is not a complete safeguard and insurance against all financial ills any more than the doctor's services are against all bodily ills. Quacks there are of course in both professions who assert extravagant pretensions, and they are a menace to both the professions and the general public. Few people are so foolish as to reject medical advice entirely because it sometimes proves defective; it would be equally foolish to deny the value of audits on similar grounds. Fortunately this elementary fact seems to be generally recognized if we may judge from the rapid and widespread growth of the practice of having accounts audited. This growth is the more remarkable when we recall that in the early years little support was given to the movement by bankers and others who should have been the first to recognize the possibilities of the development.

I believe, however, the time has come for a great step forward in the interests both of the financial community and of the profession. Unless some effective steps are taken to meet criticisms such as those voiced by Professor Ripley, the result will be some sort of bureaucratic control, and I am satisfied that through proper coöperation methods can be devised, without resort to government, which will be more effective and at the same time less burdensome and vexatious than control by a governmental body is likely to be.

It may be said, and we should have to admit, that there is not in the profession as it now exists a body of men capable of dealing adequately with the problem of securing full and fair publicity in corporation matters, laying down proper standards and seeing that they are duly observed. It is, however, even clearer that there is no such body outside the profession, and the extent to which corporations are already audited shows that at least we have an adequate nucleus about which we can build.

As I have already suggested, it seems to me that if the profession is to take its proper place in this development two things are essential: first, that it should squarely face its responsibilities; secondly, that it should strenuously resist any attempt to impose on it responsibilities beyond its ability to bear. I think the profession as a whole will gladly assume its proper responsibilities if those responsibilities are reasonably defined and if commensurate powers are given to it.

When I say the responsibilities of the auditor should be defined I do not mean that a fixed code of procedure must be laid down; that is not possible; much must always be left to the judgment of the individual auditor. Such general guides as, for instance, the memorandum on balance sheet audits which was drafted by the American Institute of Accountants in the first year of its existence, and provisionally adopted and circulated by the Federal Reserve Board, are of very great value, and much more might be done along similar lines.

Useful work has since been done by the Institute's Committee on Coöperation with Bankers and by other committees of the Institute or State Societies; and similar coöperation with such bodies as the Listing Committee of the New York Stock Exchange might lead to the formulation of other standards with which it would be the duty of every practicing accountant to be familiar.

In any such work we must be practical; it is no use laying down counsels of perfection or attempting to extend the scope of an audit unduly. An audit is a safeguard; the maintenance of this safeguard entails an expense; and this expense can be justified only if the value of the safeguard is found to be fully commensurate with its cost. The cost of an audit so extensive as to be a complete safeguard would be enormous and far beyond any value to be derived from it. A superficial audit is dangerous because of the sense of false security which it creates. Between the two extremes there lies a mean, at which the audit abundantly justifies its cost.

The problem is to determine this happy mean, to ensure that the auditor does not fall short of a reasonable discharge of his duties, and that the investor or lender does not attribute to the audit a greater significance than it can as a practical matter possess. And it must be recognized that skilled dishonesty, especially collusive dishonesty, may at times and for a time deceive even the auditor who conducts what is regarded as a reasonable audit, and that this should be so is not to be regarded as a defect of the system, since, as I have said, audit procedure represents a balancing of the consideration of risks on the one side and cost on the other. As a matter of fact, investors and lenders need protection against deliberate dishonesty less than protection against unsound practices and undue optimism. In the experience of my firm, and probably it is also the experience of other firms, cases of deliberate dishonesty are trivial in number in comparison with cases where misrepresentations have been made on the basis of excessive hopes, or as the result of unwillingness to face unpleasant facts, or through an incorrect treatment of facts which there was no attempt to conceal, or which the ordinary procedure of an audit would readily disclose.

To illustrate the point I am attempting to make, I might refer to the demand which has sometimes been made, as for instance by a banker in an address before the New York Society of Certified Public Accountants some time ago, that auditors should assume complete responsibility for the correctness of inventories. Now, every banker no doubt would be glad to have the auditor assume such a responsibility if he would be willing to do so without any increase in his fee, but I do not believe one banker in a thousand would advocate such an extension of responsibility at the price of the increase of the cost of auditing which would be necessary if the auditor were to undertake the work which would justify acceptance of so great a responsibility. I will not undertake to say how many times the present cost of auditing would be multiplied if this suggestion were universally adopted, but it would clearly be a case of multiplication, not one of relatively simple addition.

I am whole-heartedly opposed to any such proposition. In the first place, I do not believe the verification of physical inventories is within the competence of auditors; in the second place, I do not think any case has been made out for the verification of inventories in the manner suggested either by auditors or by any other independent experts.

As in most other financial matters, the problem presents different phases in the case of the large and small corporations respectively. In the case of the large companies the loss to an individual grantor of credit in a particular case might be substantial and very serious. In such companies, however, if a reasonable system of inventory is in force (and it is a part of the ordinary procedure of audit to see whether such a method is employed), then the collusion necessary to perpetrate an inventory fraud on any large scale is so extensive that only the most desperate of dishonest executives would ever think of resorting thereto.

In the case of smaller companies, deliberate falsification is no doubt more easily effected, but unless and until experience shows it to be a common occurrence, grantors of credit should find their protection in the distribution of risks and rely on the law of averages rather than attempt to enforce safeguards involving an expense wholly out of proportion to the demonstrated risks.

The conclusions thus reached by reasoning are confirmed by experience. Going back over that of my own firm in the last thirty years I find it difficult to recall more than, at most, a single case in which material overstatement of inventories occurred that would not have been disclosed by the work done in an ordinarily efficient audit, but which independent inventory checkers might reasonably have been expected to detect. In the course of this period we have by ordinary audit methods in very many cases found that inventories were overstated either in quantities, as the result of incorrect methods of inventory determination, or in valuation.

I think those who advocate a complete change in the auditor's work and responsibilities in relation to inventories both overlook the great practical value of the work now done by auditors in relation to inventories, and also greatly exaggerate the value and importance of the further verification which they would like auditors to undertake.

Some bankers appear to think that auditors at present do practically nothing to ascertain whether the inventories are correctly stated, and are surprised when confronted with a statement of what the auditor can and should do—such, for instance, as is set forth in the *Federal Reserve Bulletin* on the audit of credit statements. It is only fair to say that others are very appreciative of the auditor's work, and such publications as the Institute's bulletin in 1921, when prices were crumbling and inventories and commitments were matters of vital importance, have elicited warm expressions of approval from well-informed bankers.

If the question be considered, as I think it should be, from the standpoint of a comparison between the risks involved and the costs of eliminating, or materially reducing, those risks, then I am satisfied that the independent verification of annual inventories will be found not to be a practical suggestion.

The demand has arisen, I think, as a result of a few sporadic cases, and I feel sure there will always be enough experienced men in both the banking and the accounting worlds to appreciate the unwisdom of adding to the general credit system an expensive piece of machinery, the need for which seldom arises. No doubt, however, special inventory verification should and will be made where suspicions are aroused or unusual conditions seem to make them necessary.

Returning to my main subject, I have said that if auditors are to assume greater responsibilities they not only should be given adequate powers but should also be put in a stronger position in the event of their finding themselves in serious disagreement with the directors or officers of a company which they audit. At the present time auditors hold office usually at the pleasure of the officers of the company. We have all known cases in which the auditor, possibly towards the end of his audit, finds himself unable to approve of the accounts which the officials of the company have prepared, and on informing them of his position, is told, politely or otherwise, to discontinue his work, and later finds a statement issued by the company signed by more subservient auditors. To meet this situation it seems to me that the auditor should be assured of a right to report to the stockholders the results of an audit once he has been commissioned to make it.

I think also that he should not be liable to be superseded without having an opportunity to state his case to the stockholders. I have, therefore, suggested that auditors should be elected by, and should report to, stockholders, and that no auditors other than the retiring auditors should be eligible for appointment unless due notice should have been given to the stockholders and the retiring auditors of the intention to nominate such new auditors. This, as you know, is the rule under the English law.

I have heard some objection to this suggestion on the ground that it would operate to the advantage of large firms of accountants, but I do not believe that it would operate in any such way. I believe that where auditors are changed the change is more frequently from a small firm to a large firm than the reverse, and the suggestion that I have made seems, therefore, to be calculated to protect the smaller firms in the retention of the business which they have or may secure. Certainly nothing would be farther from my wish than that the provision should operate to deprive small firms of business.

Since the question has been raised I should like, by way of conclusion, to say just a few words on the relationship between the large and small firms. I believe the large firm with numerous offices is a natural result of the form our industrial and financial development has taken; but I think there is room and need for both types of organizations, and that they should be able to practice side by side in amity and with mutual respect. Many of our ablest practitioners are connected with relatively small organizations. I recognize that the large firms must attract some business from smaller ones, but I feel very strongly that the larger firms should do nothing to encourage such transfers, and personally try to discourage them when I have the opportunity. My firm is altogether unwilling to build up its practice at the expense of other firms of good standing, large or small.

I believe that the existence of the large firms has created a greatly increased demand for accounting services, and I suggest that the smaller firms should regard the indirect benefits resulting to them from this source as an offset to the direct losses to which I have referred, and which are naturally galling to them. The large firms also provide a training school for young accountants, and in other ways by mere size they are able to do for the profession things which smaller organizations could scarcely undertake to do.

I think, however, that the larger firms have a further duty as a result of their position in the profession. That duty is to take the lead in correcting defects in practice, and to take a strong stand with their clients where necessary in order to maintain sound principles. They can do so more easily and at the risk of relatively less important sacrifices than smaller organizations, and the precedents they establish have more far-reaching effects. The large firms owe it to themselves and to the profession at large that the precedents they set should always tend to advance the standing of the profession; should make the work of the large body of thoroughly conscientious, though less conspicuous, members constantly easier; and, above all, should never by laxity or want of courage create embarrassment for others.

We are sometimes told that some firms can afford to adopt such policies—the implication being that others less fortunate cannot. But I believe everyone can afford to do so because, apart from every other argument in favor of such policies, experience shows that they pay; not only in our own, but in other fields we constantly see that fairness, courage and honesty do really pay. It is not necessary to attribute to the business world of today a higher natural morality than past generations possessed. The undoubted improvement in methods can be quite adequately explained by a constantly increasing recognition of this heartening fact.

IV

PUBLICITY OF ACCOUNTS *

Professor Ripley's Position

(1926)

THE contention of Professor Ripley that stockholders are entitled to receive reasonably full information regarding the affairs of a company in which they are interested can scarcely be questioned.

It is, however, wholly unfortunate that he should in his enthusiasm for his objective have allowed himself to be betrayed into inaccuracy and injustice of statement, more especially as his cause is so obviously good. It is because I fear that the movement toward fuller and fairer information to stockholders, which has been making great progress in recent years, may be injured by this unwise advocacy that I venture to write to you.

Only reference to annual reports is necessary to demonstrate the inaccuracy of such statements as that the Bethlehem Steel Company does not disclose the method of inventorying its assets, whether the reference be to fixed assets or to inventories in the narrower sense of the term. Similarly, while Professor Ripley states that the word depreciation might just as well not exist for the National Cash Register Company under its present management, the only annual report issued since the recent financing not only states that depreciation has been provided for but states the precise amount.

In the same way, references to the prospectuses which one receives daily will prove the inaccuracy of the statement that appraisals contained in such prospectuses "are invariably made up not by experts of independent status, but by those

* A Letter to the *New York Times* (August 27, 1926).
49

whose prospects and emoluments are directly dependent upon the existing management."

Anyone familiar with British practice will be amused or amazed at the statement that in England questions such as whether a given item should be charged to capital or income account "would be referred for decision to an independent executive committee of the shareholders."

Moreover, Professor Ripley's criticisms are neither consistent nor judicial. We find him criticizing one company for a given procedure, while for another which has followed substantially the same procedure he has nothing but praise. He is so convinced of the inequities of Dodge Brothers, Inc., that he devotes a substantial part of his article to them, though the one virtue he is prepared to concede is the complete frankness of disclosure for which his whole article is a plea. And, as he himself points out, disclosure is the vital thing; the form of disclosure is of minor importance.

Professor Ripley seems more concerned to heighten the color of his picture than to secure either accuracy of detail or justness of proportion—else why cite as illustrative of the attitude of men in executive positions today a foolish utterance of more than a quarter of a century ago?

It is impossible here to deal fully with his comments on corporate accounting, but as an accountant of many years' standing I may perhaps be permitted to say that his statements do not seem to me to indicate a grasp of the problems. For instance, he begins his criticism of no par value stocks with the statement that under the old par value stock laws the accounts started from "a bench mark solidly established—theoretically, at least." The belief that bench marks established (however solidly) only in theory were useless, if not dangerous, was one of the reasons why such practical men as Francis Lynde Stetson advocated no par value stock laws.

That these laws have brought new problems and dangers is realized by no one more fully than by the accountants. Indeed, the American Institute of Accountants offered $10,-

ooo in prizes for the best discussion of the various aspects—legal, financial, economic and accounting—of the question, though, unfortunately, the offer elicited no adequate response. One looks in vain in Professor Ripley's article for either sympathetic appreciation of the difficulty of these problems or constructive suggestions for their solution.

While the subtitle of Professor Ripley's article is "The Shareholder's Right to Adequate Information," the article itself is wider in its scope, and the demand for publicity is urged also in the interests of the speculator, as an adjunct to industrial efficiency, and on other grounds. This results in confusion. Everyone will recognize the claim of the investor-stockholder who is in a real sense an owner of the business. The information best calculated to further his interests is by no means identical with that desired by the speculator for a turn who never assumes the full responsibility of ownership.

In any consideration of this subject it must be borne in mind, first, that stock values are usually influenced more by prospects than by past events; and, second, that, as a distinguished English judge has pointed out, every balance sheet and income account is necessarily in large measure a matter of estimate and opinion. If those on the inside in a corporation desire to profit at the expense of those on the outside, it is often as easy for them to achieve their purpose by issuing statements which are adequate and correct according to every accepted canon as in any other way. No amount of regulation will make a dishonestly managed company a satisfactory investment.

I suggest that Professor Ripley's article presents a picture of the present situation which is unfair both in detail and in the large. I believe his perspective is wrong. While much remains to be done, American stockholders today in general get fairly adequate information—certainly far more than the average English stockholder, though Professor Ripley compares our practice to the British to our detriment. Indeed, British practice after years of experience and numerous investigations has come to rely for the protection of stockholders less upon detailed disclosure than upon the integrity, competence and judgment of the auditors, whose position has been made stronger in every recent revision of the Companies Acts.

V

CORPORATE PUBLICITY AND THE AUDITOR *

(1926)

My presence here tonight is a direct result of the publication by Professor Ripley of his article in the September *Atlantic Monthly* on the subject of publicity of corporation accounts.

Soon after that article appeared I wrote to a leading New York newspaper, drawing attention to certain inaccuracies in it and suggesting that it did not constitute an altogether fair presentation of the situation which exists today. Your committee then invited me to speak at this meeting, and, as the regular business programme was filled, they suggested that I might take this occasion to make a few remarks on the subject of publicity of accounts from the standpoint of directors and auditors.

I do not propose to discuss Professor Ripley's article in detail. I dissent from him on some of his facts and on some of his arguments, and I entirely disagree with his suggestion as to the rôle which should be played by the Federal Trade Commission. But I do not wish tonight to discuss these disagreements; I would rather express my gratification at the success with which he has attracted the attention of the public to the subject, and consider what we, as accountants, can do to bring about that improvement in the information furnished to stockholders and potential stockholders of corporations for which his article is a plea. No doubt the primary responsibility for furnishing the stockholders adequate information rests on the directors, but the auditor ought to use his best efforts to ensure that the directors publish ac-

* An address at the annual meeting of the American Institute of Accountants, Atlantic City, New Jersey, September 22, 1926. Cf. *The Journal of Accountancy,* Vol. XLII (November, 1926), pp. 321-26.

counts which conform to the highest established standards, and ought to be able to advise directors what these standards are.

I am not sure that auditors have done their full duty in this respect in the past. To some extent this may have been due to the limitations of their authority and the rather precarious tenure of their appointments. I think the time has come when auditors should assume larger responsibilities, and their positions be more clearly defined.

The practice of having independent audits has become so general that it is no longer necessary to demonstrate its value. In discussing the subject, therefore, we are now free from any imputation that we are crying up our own wares.

After undertaking to speak tonight I caused an examination to be made to ascertain what percentage of the companies whose stocks were dealt in on a given day on the New York Stock Exchange had their accounts audited annually, and I was myself surprised to find that in the case of industrial companies the practice had become almost universal; certainly over ninety per cent of all the industrial companies on the list were audited.

In these circumstances it seems to me that the extension of the independent audit, accompanied by a clearer definition of the authority and responsibility of the auditors, is one of the most valuable remedies to be found for the defects of which Professor Ripley complains; and I think the Institute should consider very seriously—and should invite the coöperation of other bodies in considering—what are the proper responsibilities of auditors and what can be done to hold them to such responsibilities and to put them in a position to assume all the responsibilities which they ought to assume.

In England, to which country Professor Ripley pointed, the situation is now fairly clearly defined by statute. I recognize, of course, that owing to the fact that incorporation is a state question it is not readily possible here to define audit standards by legislation, but a reference to the English statutes may at least be helpful in suggesting the objectives at which we ought to aim.

Under the English law the independent audit has for many years been compulsory, the auditors sharing with the directors the responsibility for the accounts as published.

Auditors have been held liable for damages, and have even been subjected to criminal prosecution, for participation in the issue of false accounts. As a necessary corollary they have been given adequate powers. The language of the English Companies Act is simple:

> Every auditor of a company shall have a right of access at all times to the books and accounts and vouchers of the company, and shall be entitled to require from the directors and officers of the company such information and explanation as may be necessary for the performance of the duties of the auditors.

The following clause provides that the auditors shall make a report to the shareholders on every balance sheet laid before a shareholders' meeting during their term of office and shall state whether or not they have obtained all the information and explanations they have required and whether the balance sheet is properly drawn up so as to exhibit a true and correct view of the state of the company's affairs. It is made a misdemeanor to circulate a balance sheet which has not been audited and which does not bear a copy of the auditor's report or a sufficient reference thereto.

Finally, the position of the auditor is strengthened by a provision that no auditor other than the retiring auditor shall be eligible for election at an annual meeting of shareholders unless due notice has been given in advance of the intention to nominate a new auditor, and this notice must be given to every shareholder and also to the retiring auditor. If, therefore, directors are disposed to seek new auditors because of differences of opinion with the existing auditors, ample opportunity is afforded for the shareholders to become informed of the merits of the case and act accordingly.

A government committee which recently reviewed the English company law in the light of developments during the last twenty years felt able to report:

We are of the opinion that in general the law as it stands with regard to the powers and duties of auditors is satisfactory.

and also:

Cases in which auditors fall below the level of their duty are few and far between.

Now, while it is doubtless impracticable to bring about through legislation in this country a development similar to that which has proved so satisfactory in England, I see no reason why this should not be done in a large measure through the coöperation of such bodies as the leading stock exchanges, the investment bankers and the banks which grant credit, and I suggest that the Institute should endeavor to bring about coöperation to this end. Every member of the Institute, I believe, appreciates the value to its membership, to the banks and to the business of the country, of the coöperation with bankers in regard to credit statements which has been developed in recent years. I think the Institute should seek to extend such coöperation to the field with which Professor Ripley's article deals. The New York Stock Exchange, for instance, could readily bring about through its listing agreements a situation as respects companies listed on its exchange similar to that which exists in England. In recent years the Stock Exchange has given various indications that it attaches constantly greater importance to the work of accountants and it has also shown a disposition to examine sympathetically any proposal which may tend to protect those who deal in the securities which it lists. It would, I think, therefore be receptive to a suggestion such as I have put forward.

As I have said, the accounts of a very large proportion of the industrial companies whose stocks are listed (and I limit for the present the suggestion to industrial companies and exclude railways, public utilities and other companies which are under some form of public supervision) are now audited; the public would welcome a clearer definition of the significance of such audits and of the responsibilities of auditors. Such clearer definition, though it might increase the accountant's obligation, would also in the long run be of advantage to the members of the profession and give them enhanced importance in the business world, just as it has done in England.

By similar coöperation, standards might be established for balance sheets and income accounts which would be welcomed by many corporation executives and accountants who desire to be guided by the best practice, if they can be assured what that practice is.

As regards balance sheets, the essential points are fairly well established and observed by the leading companies. A clear statement of the way in which the capital assets are valued is one requirement of an adequate disclosure which is not now generally observed, and there might be some discussion as to the form of statement of surplus. The object should be so to state the surplus as to indicate what part of it is legally available for dividend distributions and what part is not so available; but in the present state of the law, particularly in the case of companies with stock of no par value, this is not always easy, and it is impossible to lay down hard and fast rules.

The practice in regard to the income account is not so well established, and there is probably room for more difference of opinion as to what would constitute a proper disclosure. The difficulties arise largely from two facts which are not at all times adequately appreciated. The first is, that the significance of an income account is two-fold: it shows what amounts have been earned and are available for distribution in dividends if the directors see fit to make the distribution. The income account of the past is also in a measure a guide to the expectations of income in the future. In many cases this second use is the more important because it is the reasonable expectation of yield in the future which determines the value of any property today. This economic truism, which incidentally makes much of the discussion of the values of capital assets from the standpoint of reproduction cost irrelevant and meaningless, should never be lost sight of or obscured.

The second difficulty is that the attribution of income to particular periods of time is at best in a large measure arbitrary and based on conventions. While we accountants recognize this fact more fully the longer we practice, it is by no means properly appreciated by the general public, and far too much significance is commonly attached to the figure of income for a particular year or other period.

Bearing in mind these two points, it seems to me that fairness in the presentation of an income account is even more important than fulness. Much of the information that is contained in more elaborate reports is no doubt interesting to stockholders and appeals to their sense of proprietorship, but is of little practical value to them. The vitally important requirements are that, if the profits of the year include extraordinary or extraneous profits which render the figures useless as a guide to earning capacity, these should be clearly disclosed; and, second, that where the accounts are based on any conventions other than those commonly accepted, that fact should also be clearly disclosed. I have in mind such departures from accepted convention as the valuing of inventories on a basis other than cost or market, or the failure to provide for depreciation or depletion. Probably discussion would arise as to whether the amount of depreciation provided should be shown separately; probably on the whole it should, although the precise amount set aside for depreciation or the amount expended for maintenance is of less real significance to a stockholder than the statement of a competent and disinterested person who is familiar with the details of the business that the amount provided or expended is in his judgment adequate for the purpose.

Undoubtedly there would be differences of opinion on the question whether gross sales should be disclosed. Viewing the matter solely from the standpoint of the stockholder it seems to me this is a question of expediency. Where the percentage of gross profit is high, the profit is apt to be regarded as unreasonable, although in judging its reasonableness many factors besides the percentage it bears to sales ought really to be taken into account. A packing company which can earn a fair return on its investment with a relatively small percentage of profit on a large turnover can very well afford to publish its sales and to point to the small percentage of profits with an expression of surprise at its own moderation. On the other hand, an agricultural-implement company with a large investment and a relatively small turnover might be merely inviting ill-informed criticism by a similar disclosure.

Undoubtedly many of the objections to fuller disclosure are based on unsubstantial grounds and would be cleared up by frank discussion. Many corporations, as Professor Ripley points out, disclose in their listing applications information which they do not give in their reports to their stockholders.

I have been able to touch only briefly tonight on some of the important phases of the question of publicity of corporation accounts; my main purpose is to urge that coöperation between interested bodies should do much to improve the existing situation and that the American Institute of Accountants might well take the initiative in an effort to bring about such coöperation. I think the Institute has reason to be proud of its accomplishments in the single decade of its existence, but I believe that there is here a field in which the Institute could do still greater service and in doing so could help its members to render a higher service to the community.

VI

EXTERNAL INFLUENCES AFFECTING ACCOUNTING PRACTICE *

(1929)

In any attempt to deal with a subject such as has been assigned to me, the first necessity is to place limitations upon its scope, and on such an occasion as this the limits must be narrow. I purpose, therefore, to limit the discussion to the United States and to the period of one generation, which is about the time that has elapsed since I began accounting work in New York. Further, I shall deal only with business accounting, and not with governmental, institutional, or professional accounts. In drawing the line between external and internal influences, I shall consider accounting as a service department of business; and all increases in its efficiency as an aid to business I shall regard, therefore, as created by internal influences even though they may be attributable in part to external causes, such as the growing pressure of competition in business.

The external influences I propose to consider include regulation, official or unofficial; new taxation; changes in the form and distribution of the ownership of business; radical changes in price levels and the like. I shall not attempt to deal with any phases of the question exhaustively, but shall try to draw your attention to some of the less obvious as well as some of the more important of the effects of the external influences with which I shall deal. The first is the regulation of the accounting of public service corporations which began to be effective about the beginning of the present century.

In general the effect of regulation has been to produce

---

* An address to the International Congress on Accounting, New York, 1929. Cf. *Proceedings,* pp. 686-97.

more precise but, I believe, less conservative accounting. To the economist this is probably an improvement; to the accountant and the business man the gain may not be so assured. Certainly under regulation there has been a far more extensive capitalization of minor betterments and of interest and expense items, and to some extent this influence has extended to other fields of business. I admit that in past times I have felt that the tendency was regrettable and the regulating bodies to blame. But at least on the second point I have been compelled to change my view. The tendency seems to me now to be the inevitable result of our constitution as interpreted by the Supreme Court.

The position seems to be as follows. Whether a rate structure is compensatory or confiscatory is determined broadly by a comparison between the earnings it produces and the sum of three things: (1) the cost of rendering the service, exclusive of property consumption; (2) a fair allowance for property consumption; and (3) a fair return on the value of the property employed in rendering service. The value of the property employed must be its *fair present value,* and the determination thereof seems under the Federal decisions to be almost if not quite unrelated to the determination of the other elements in the comparison.

It follows that if a minor betterment is charged off as an operating cost but remains in existence, it is also included at present value in the capital sum on which a return is allowed—the rate base, as it is termed—and the public is thus charged twice. Obviously the only way in which the regulating bodies could protect patrons of the utilities against such results was by insisting on the exclusion from operating charges of expenditures for property which was still in existence and therefore included in the rate base. This they have fairly generally done.

A similar question has arisen in regard to depreciation. The Supreme Court has held that in fixing the rate base only "observed depreciation" may be deducted from new value. While neither the Court nor the engineers have made very clear just what observed depreciation is (what, for instance, is the observed depreciation on an installation of electric light bulbs?) they have made it clear that it is something quite different from and less than the depreciation which is computed on the basis of distributing the new value over the useful life upon some regular plan—a basis which has been regarded by many regulating bodies and most accountants as the proper and prudent one.   Upon this point varying policies have been followed by regulating bodies.   Some classifications, such as those for gas and electrical utilities promulgated by the National Association of Railway and Utilities Commissioners and adopted in the State of New York, appear to accept the Court's decisions regarding the deduction to be made from new value for depreciation in fixing the rate base, and to limit the income charge correspondingly. The Interstate Commerce Commission has taken the opposite course and has tried to insist on more liberal depreciation charges against operations, evidently hoping eventually to secure harmony in treatment for the two purposes by a reversal of the attitude of the courts on the valuation aspect of the question.   In other jurisdictions some utilities at least have been fairly successful in securing the allowance of depreciation as an operating charge on a higher scale, and limiting the deduction therefor in valuation to a lower scale, to their obviously great advantage.

Before passing from this question, I would like to point out that the differing degrees of conservatism which undoubtedly exist are a material consideration when the capitalization of values on an earning basis for utilities and other business activities is under consideration.   If the ratio of capital value to earnings of utilities is being compared, for instance, with that of banks, it is necessary to take into account not only the comparative risks and opportunities in the two fields, but also the fact that if an accountant were adjusting the earnings so as to make them fairly comparable his adjustments of the utility figures (if any) would probably be downward, while there would probably be substantial upward adjustments of the bank figures. This point is not, I think, so widely appreciated as it should be.

The tendency towards less conservative accounting which regulation produced was counteracted in general business, at least for a time, by the development of the income tax as a part of the fiscal machinery of the Federal and of many state governments.

It was surprising to note how immediate was the effect of even such a small tax as the one per cent corporation excise tax of 1909 in inducing a conservative view of debatable questions. And all of us who were practicing in the war years will be able to recall instances of taxpayers seeking to anticipate deductions in 1916 in order to reduce their taxes at the 2% rate then in force. Some of us can also recall cases in which the Bureau of Internal Revenue insisted on the postponement of the deduction to the year 1917 or 1918 in which the taxpayers, as it turned out, became subject to tax at rates of perhaps 50% or more. The high taxes in the war years put a premium on conservatism which none could ignore, and in the Act of 1918 the Congress gave legislative sanction to a reasonable conservatism in the accounting for profits as between the taxpayer and the taxing authority by the provision that net income should be computed in accordance with the method of accounting regularly employed in keeping the books of the taxpayer, unless that method did not clearly reflect income.

In this provision Congress went further than the English practice; there the law taxed annual gains and profits without defining them; and the courts had held that profits were to be determined in accordance with the usages of business men, and that estimates must be recognized where it was usual and practically necessary to make them.

For instance, the House of Lords approved * a method of computation of the income of a fire insurance company which involved the use of the customary 40% reserve for

* *Clark v. Sun Insurance Office*, A. C. (1912), 443.

unearned premiums, Lord Atkinson saying, in an opinion which will repay perusal:

It is obvious that the amount of the taxable profits and gains can only be ascertained by some system of averages or estimation, or by some other practical rule of thumb based upon experience and the facts of different cases.

Congress not only accepted the English view that profits are to be determined by the methods used by business men but provided in substance that where those methods vary, any reasonable and well-established variant employed regularly by a taxpayer should be accepted. Ever since the Act of 1918 was passed, however, minor administrative officials and some of the courts have whittled away from the importance of this provision, and have stopped short of the English precedent in recognizing common business usage, instead of going beyond it as the Congress did. They have, for instance, refused to approve the use of estimates in circumstances in which they are customarily employed in business and undoubtedly would have been sanctioned by the English House of Lords. They have attempted to establish rigid and uniform methods and to set up utterly impracticable standards of exactness in the attribution of income and expenses to particular periods of time. As a result, many of them (and many others) have come to believe that the amount of the profits of a given business for a given year is a fact almost as precise as the amount of gold in a twenty-dollar coin.

At first the effect was to increase the tax revenues by denying to taxpayers the benefit of methods of accounting, legitimately conservative, which they had employed for many years for good reasons quite unrelated to taxation. But any seeming advantage to the Government was short-lived and the position soon reversed, so that today there are many corporations computing their taxable income with the approval of the authorities on bases far more conservative than those they employ in their reports to their stockholders. Now it may be argued that stockholders who share losses as well as gains and who may cease to be stockholders any day should be furnished with reports which represent the management's best judgment of the profits fairly attributable to the year for which the report is made, without exaggeration and without conscious understatement, and that a more cautious view may quite properly be taken and should be permitted in returns to a government which takes a toll of all profits from year to year but bears no share of losses, except of course as such losses may reduce its share of future profits.

These considerations are certainly not those which determined the attitude of the authorities; and personally I am not convinced that the view is a sound one, but believe that in the long run the best interests of the stockholders will be served by making reports to them on a basis at least as conservative as tax returns. I should perhaps make it clear that I am here referring only to alternative bases of accounting, such as are applied for instance to installment sales, and that my remarks have no reference to deductions allowed by statute, such as discovery depletion, which have nothing to do with the determination of actual income.

I come now to a third influence on accounting practice which is of very great importance, namely, the change in the form and nature of ownership of business. In 1897 there were about thirty industrial stocks listed on the New York Stock Exchange; today there are about a thousand, and the listings on other Exchanges have increased similarly. The income tax statistics show that of the total net income reported by the 450,000 corporations which make returns, more than one-third is reported by about 200, and more than one-half by about 1,000 corporations.

These two sets of figures illustrate two pronounced tendencies of the last thirty years; one towards mergers and consolidations, and the other towards diffusion of the ownership of corporations. The first tendency has manifested itself in various ways. In the first part of the period combinations were mainly in the form of what is sometimes called vertical integration, that is, the combining of the ownership of enterprises engaged in the successive stages of the process of conversion of raw materials into final products; later horizontal integration came into favor and combinations were formed of businesses which were related to one another mainly by having similar markets and marketing problems. The chain system has also developed on a large scale in the last quarter of a century. In some cases chains have been created through the opening of new branches by an existing corporation, but in other cases the chains have been constituted largely by the combination of existing companies. Incidentally, as this development threatened the existence of the wholesalers, we have recently seen some important combinations of wholesalers in an effort to maintain their place in the economic life of the day.

Another influence which has greatly affected accounting practice has been the general rise in price levels brought about by the war. This change affected accounting practice directly in various ways, some of which are being discussed at this meeting. For instance, it raised the question of the wisdom of adjusting book values of capital assets to the new price levels, and also the question of the validity of costs and profits which were computed on the basis of charging exhaustion of plant only at cost. It also affected accounting practice indirectly through the change in the attitude of investors which it produced. Holders of fixed income securities who saw the capital value of their investments sink because of the increase in interest rates, and the purchasing power of the yield of their investments lessen because of higher price levels, began to wonder whether such investments afforded real safety or whether there was not ultimately greater safety to be secured by taking a certain commercial risk and investing in securities which possessed more capacity for adaptation to changed conditions. Common stocks which represented an interest in actual property obviously were more likely to maintain a constant real value in the face of a major change in the general standard of money values of property or in the yield from property than bonds or preferred stock the principal and yield of which were fixed in terms of money.

A realization of these truths brought common stocks into favor among investors and caused a marked enhancement in their market value. Furthermore, even those who were not prepared to make such a radical change in their investment policy as to buy common stock came to demand that fixed yield securities should carry with them some form of participation in excess earnings. This has led to the creation of an extraordinary variety of security issues carrying all sorts of combinations of preferential rights with participations in excess earnings, options and the like. There is little doubt that in many cases these securities have been created with only shadowy ideas in the minds of the creators as to the nature and extent of the rights conferred thereby. Present litigation indicates that this was true of issues of non-cumulative preferred stock in the past; and, while issues of that particular type of stock are not now common, stocks carrying a fixed dividend and an additional interest in the profits of any year in which more than a certain rate is earned on senior issues are common and present substantially the same question. It seems to me a fundamental objection to this type of security that it attaches an importance to the earnings of a particular year, which is undesirable in view of the extreme difficulty of the problem of subdivision of profit between years in a complex business.

I will defer discussing the effect on accounting of these developments until I shall have referred briefly to the last of the external influences which I propose to consider—my reason being that that influence operates, in general, in the same direction as the influences just mentioned.

The trend of modern legislation in regard to corporations, and particularly the developments following the authorization of stock without par value, seem to me to be of the utmost importance to accountants. The events to which I have already referred led to reincorporation of businesses on a very large scale and hence to keen competition among what have been described as the "charter-mongering States" for the business of the corporation lawyers—a competition in which the State of Delaware will, I think, be generally admitted to have outbid all its competitors. That state has, for instance, legalized the favorite device of promoters of get-rich-quick schemes of paying dividends to subscribers to capital stock out of the amounts paid in by them on their subscriptions; it has obliterated, so far as statutes can do so, the distinction between capital and income, and has enacted provisions which seem likely to destroy the significance of such terms as "dividend." Other states are not far behind.

In 1849, in one of the earliest of the English dividend cases, Lord Campbell said:

It is most nefarious conduct for the directors of a joint stock company, in order to raise the price of shares which they are to dispose of, to order a fictitious dividend to be paid out of the capital of the concern. Dividends are supposed to be paid out of profits only, and when directors order a dividend, to any given amount, without expressly saying so, they impliedly declare to the world that the company has made profits which justify such a dividend. If no such profits have been made, and the dividend is to be paid out of the capital of the concern, a gross fraud has been practised.

To the business man this is still sound sense, but anyone who indulges in any such inferences from the declaration of a dividend by a company incorporated in a state such as Delaware may find himself grossly mistaken and yet without any grounds for complaint in law. We are sometimes told that power to pay dividends, even though the paying corporation has not earned profits to the amount thereof, should be granted to meet the cases of successor corporations created by an exchange of stocks without any substantial change of interest and the like. It would seem that the ingenuity of lawyers should be equal to the task of devising provisions that would meet such cases (if that be really necessary) without providing such unlimited opportunities for abuse or destroying the significance of terms of established usage which the public believes it understands.

Our foreign visitors may not be aware that under some of our state laws stock which has no par value has a "stated value." It is common practice to fix this stated value at a low figure; companies commence business with a small stated value of capital stock and a relatively large excess of the value of net assets paid in over that stated value. In the general affairs of the company the stated value is ignored; it possesses only a technical legal significance.

It is not surprising that this lack of significance should tend to extend to the valuation at which capital assets are entered on the books—one curious result may be noted. If property acquired for stock having no par value is entered on the books at a nominal or low value, the annual charge for the exhaustion of this property is correspondingly reduced and the book profits to that extent increased. If then the value of a property or business is to be measured mainly by its earning capacity, the paradoxical result is reached that the lower the value at which the property of a business is recorded on the books the greater becomes the apparent value of the business.

It is true that numerous states have passed so-called blue sky laws designed for the protection of investors but, while some of these have had useful influence, they have not, as a whole, proved particularly effective. There is, I believe, more ground for hope in the activities of private organizations of which the most powerful is, no doubt, the New York Stock Exchange. Those who have followed the developments of the Exchange's policy in relation to the listing of securities in recent years will, I think, agree as to the value of its influence in promoting sound financial practices among corporations. That influence has been the greater because the Exchange has exercised its great powers with moderation and at the same time with courage. All accountants should lend their full support to such policies as that of the Exchange and other bodies which are aiming to bring about the adoption and maintenance of sound business standards through non-governmental regulation. If such efforts fail, we shall be likely to see rigid governmental regulation which, though it may curb undesirable practices, will also seriously hamper legitimate business.

Another phase of corporate development needing consideration at this time is the change in the relation of stockholders to the business, brought about by the development of non-voting stocks and the elimination of pre-emptive rights of stockholders to acquire new issues of stock. These two developments have done much to strengthen the position of the management of corporations. Once a group comes into control of a corporation it is a difficult task to dislodge it, and, if new capital is needed, the group can determine whether it shall be secured from old stockholders or from new sources. The stockholders' meetings which may be necessary will probably be formal affairs unless there is not only strong opposition but an opposition prepared to spend large sums of money to defeat the proposal to which it is opposed. So long as a management exercises its powers with discretion and shows even a moderate competence, it usually has little difficulty in maintaining its position.

It will be clear, I hope, that the tendencies I have mentioned affect accounting and accountants in an important way. The allocation of profits to particular years has become both more important and more difficult as a result thereof. The simple rule of conservatism, under which profits were never anticipated but probable or even potential losses were provided for, was satisfactory as long as the interests of only long-time stockholders had to be considered. It is not equally satisfactory to a management that feels that it may have occasion to trade with other companies on the basis of comparative earnings, and it is thought by some to be unfair to stockholders who may desire or be compelled to realize their holdings.

The task of those responsible for the financial reports of corporations has become more difficult and more delicate

and, since the accountants for the corporations should be
their most competent and disinterested advisers, the opportunity of the accountants, both corporation accountants and
practicing accountants, is enlarged. The service of the public accountant may take one of two forms; the first, and I
trust the most common form (in which he and the corporation accountant should be found in coöperation), should be
in giving sound advice to those responsible for the reporting
and financial policies of the corporations and in dissuading
them from any accounting policy which might be unjust
to any group of persons having a legitimate interest therein;
the second, where the first fails, lies in protecting the interests of those who may be adversely affected by action of the
management by insisting on a proper disclosure of what has
been done either in the accounts or in the auditors' certificate.

I would like, however, to emphasize that even when the
accountant has done his best to attain accuracy, investors
must still recognize the limitations on the significance of
even the best of accounts, and the shorter the period covered
the more pronounced usually are these limitations. Accounts
are essentially historical records and, as is true of history in
general, correct conclusions cannot be reached by a hurried
survey of temporary conditions, but only by a longer retrospect and a careful distinction between permanent tendencies
and transitory influences. I cannot help feeling that today
undue importance is frequently attached to the earnings of
a single year or even a single quarter.

Modern developments have tended also to reduce the importance of the balance sheet, and they seem to me to necessitate reconsideration of the methods of preparation of corporate reports.

As business grows more complex it becomes more and
more impracticable to present in a single picture a representation of the position of any important corporation which
will be accurate in detail and perspective in all its parts, and
will tell an intelligible story to the average investor. A series

of pictures, rather than a single one, is needed—and in such a series the balance sheet will perhaps be of least significance to any but the technical experts who will find in it a check on other parts of the series.

Corporations have generally forsaken the old debit and credit account form of income statement for the narrative form which is more intelligible to the layman though less elegant in the eyes of the technician. They need to do something of the same kind for the balance sheet which is, even more than the old income account, a creation of technique. It should be made clearer to the general public that only in part is a balance sheet in the nature of an instantaneous picture and that in part it is merely historical and in part purely conventional. It is beyond the scope of this paper to explain why this should be so, but even if it must remain so, the fact should be more generally known and the historical, conventional and photographic parts more clearly identified.

An annual report which contains a series of separate statements including: (1) a well-arranged income and surplus account; (2) a classified statement of quick assets and liabilities; (3) summaries of capital obligations and capital assets; and (4) a lucid statement of resources which have become available during the year, and the disposition thereof, will not gain greatly by the addition of a balance sheet in which all assets and liabilities are brought together, though custom and a sense of completeness may call for its inclusion.

Finally; the legal position has become so unsatisfactory that accountants guided by sound principles and the best opinion of the day must assume a large responsibility in approving or disapproving practices admittedly not illegal. Thus, as I see the position, the opportunity for us to render service of a highly professional and valuable character is greater today than ever before, and I trust we shall prove equal to the opportunity offered us.

VII

EFFECT OF INDUSTRIAL MERGERS ON ACCOUNTING PRACTICE *

(1929)

THERE is one tendency in modern corporation development that I would like to speak on especially—that is the tendency towards mergers and consolidations throughout the country. I suppose it is an economic development that can hardly be arrested, but it brings in its train a great many unfortunate consequences, as I suppose is true of all important economic changes.

I cannot view, without regret, the elimination of so many independent business men throughout the country or their being forced to choose between accepting the position of salaried employees and being forced out of business altogether, though this is an inevitable incident of this development.

Another thing that I view with regret is the displacement of local auditors of these smaller concerns and their replacement by firms which enjoy a national reputation. The relations between the national firms and the local firms have always seemed to me a question of very real importance to the profession. I have never regarded their positions as at all antagonistic. In the past, undoubtedly a certain amount of work of the local accountants has passed in the natural development of business to the national firms, but I have felt that that was far more than compensated for by the general development of accounting throughout the country, which could not have been accomplished without the national firms, and I still feel that the national firms ought to be an asset to the local firms.

* Excerpt from an address delivered at the New England regional meeting of the American Institute of Accountants held at Boston, May 6th, 1929.

I do not think that the national firms any more than the local firms can prevent the operation of an economic trend such as I have referred to. I know—speaking for my own firm—we have tried at times to do it but unsuccessfully. We have never wished to grow at the expense of the local accountants. We have encouraged our clients more than once to retain the local accountants where we felt there was reason to believe that the local accountant could render all the service that was required; but I know that, nevertheless, we and other national firms must have taken a very considerable business from local accounting firms and that the loss of that business to the local accounting firms has been far more important to them than its gain has been to us. Now, what can we do to compensate? The one thing above all that I think every national firm should do is to maintain standards commensurate with its position; I fear that there are some national firms that do not, either in the ethics of getting business or in the ethics of doing business. I think it is the duty of the big firms to fight the battles for the whole profession. They can do it at much less relative cost. In order to fight these battles of principle, one has to be prepared to lose connections which carry remunerative fees or prestige that is valuable in itself. If the small firm loses an important audit, it means a substantial share of its total business; a big firm can lose a number without really feeling it. And that is why I feel that the first and foremost duty of the national firms is to take the strongest possible stand on questions of ethics and on questions of principle, and in both these fields to fight the battle of the whole profession. Now, I don't think that we are all doing it, but I think we ought to do it, and I am glad of an opportunity to express myself very plainly on the subject.

I sympathize very heartily with the local firms, which are doing good work in a professional spirit but complain that the national firms are not always maintaining the standards of either accounting principles or ethics that they advocate and seek to impose on the profession as a whole.

There is no doubt that there is room in the profession for both national firms and local firms, and I don't think if the two work together properly that anything essentially antagonistic in their position can develop. That it is possible to make a great success without having a national organization is obvious.

VIII

THE ROYAL MAIL (KYLSANT) CASE *

A LETTER TO H. L. H. HILL, ESQ., PRESIDENT OF THE INSTITUTE
OF CHARTERED ACCOUNTANTS OF ENGLAND AND WALES

(1931)

My dear Mr. Hill:

As a result of the Royal Mail case the Institute is obviously
face to face with one of the greatest problems and, as I see it,
one of the greatest opportunities presented to it in the course
of its existence.

For many years I have taken an active interest in the question of disclosure of financial information to shareholders,
and at the moment I am chairman of a committee of the
American Institute, appointed to coöperate with the New
York and other stock exchanges in this field. This may serve
as my excuse for laying before you, as President of the Institute, the views herein expressed. If I put them forward
merely as my own views, it is because I have had no
opportunity to discuss them with others who might be interested and entitled to address you; but they are the result
of many discussions and of contributions from many and
varied sources.

I do not feel any embarrassment in discussing the question
by reason of the fact that one of my partners was involved in
the Royal Mail case, because the view taken here (and, as I
judge, in London) has, I think, generally been that upon the
accounts charges in that case it was a *system*, rather than individuals, that was on trial; and I think the general conclusion
has been that though the individuals were clearly entitled to
acquittal, the system must be condemned and must be
changed.

* *Rex* v. *Kylsant* (1931).

It has come as a surprise to many people here to find that the practice in respect to disclosure was so much better than in England. Many, both inside and outside the accounting profession, had thought that by long and laborious effort they were gradually raising the standard to a point which had been reached in London many years ago; and to find the case entirely otherwise has come as a distinct shock to them.

I think opinion here would generally agree with the view expressed in the evidence submitted on behalf of the Institute before the Greene Committee in 1925, that the form and content of commercial accounts are matters that cannot be satisfactorily dealt with by legislation. There are, however, it would seem, two corollaries to this proposition: the first, that neither directors nor auditors can properly regard legal requirements as setting the measure of their obligation to shareholders; the second, that it is incumbent on all the parties interested to work continuously to improve standards, and by precept and example to endeavor to secure a reasonable degree of publicity in corporate accounts.

If I might offer criticisms of the evidence to which I have referred, my first would be that it failed to emphasize these corollaries. For instance, the Institute, in my opinion, cannot properly take the position (which it took in its evidence) that the requirements for disclosure should not be enlarged by law, unless it is prepared to do everything it can to insure that auditors shall use their power and influence to secure a reasonable degree of disclosure; it cannot properly oppose enlargement of the rights of shareholders to inspect books unless it can say that it is improper practice for any of its members to certify accounts which do not constitute a reasonably adequate and fair disclosure; and it cannot properly oppose disclosure in regard to secret reserves unless the code of practice which it enforces, or at least enjoins on its members, calls for adequate disclosure when such reserves are established or drawn upon. The case is the stronger where the shares of a company are listed on the Stock Exchange and the public thus invited to buy and sell them.

I cannot help thinking that it is a reproach to all concerned in the City—the Stock Exchange, the banks, the accountants, the solicitors, and the directors of large commercial companies—that the standards of disclosure by public companies should have remained or become so low, while the distribution of shareholdings has been becoming so much wider. I recognize that such powerful bodies as the Stock Exchange and the big banks have been inert, and that this has made the task of improving standards more difficult. But it seems to me that this merely made the opportunity of the Institute the greater; and that with the stronger position given auditors under the Act of 1908, and with the enhanced prestige which accountants have enjoyed, especially since the war, the profession could have accomplished most of what was needed without other aid.

Undoubtedly the American point of view on these questions has been greatly influenced by the extent of the effort which has been made to convert shares of industrial and other companies into a more liquid form of asset. Obviously, if such shares are to be regarded as a liquid asset and freely traded in, there must be available at all times reliable information upon which estimates of value may be predicated. Whatever may be the cause, there is no doubt that in the last twenty years there has been an enormous improvement in the standards of disclosure here. That improvement has been brought about by the coöperation of a number of bodies; the banks through their credit departments and the Stock Exchange through its listing committee have played a very important part, but the accounting profession has, I believe, also contributed in a very substantial way to the results which have been achieved.

My second criticism of the Institute's evidence would be of the statement that to attempt to prescribe that there should be a profit and loss account published as well as a balance sheet "is considered likely to do more harm than good." It is, I think, generally recognized that earning capacity is the most important single test of value; and if any accounts are to be given to shareholders, it is difficult to see why the profit and loss account is not at least equally as important as the balance sheet.

Since this evidence was given, Parliament has, of course, reached a conclusion opposed to that reached by the Institute, and a profit and loss account is now required by statute. The question at present, therefore, is what is the object of the profit and loss account, and how can that object be best served without detriment to other interests of the shareholders.

The answer to the first part of the question is, I suggest, that the profit and loss account is valuable to shareholders principally for the light it throws on the efficiency of the management and on the earning capacity of the company under the conditions existing during the period to which it relates, and the form and content of the account should be determined with the purpose of making it as effective as possible for these uses. It is not to be expected that the account will afford complete illumination on either point; but present shareholders in respect of the first, and both present and potential shareholders in respect of the second point, are entitled to demand that it shall afford them all the light that can properly be given, and above all, that it shall not mislead them.

It is easy to cite difficulties which may be encountered in formulating accounts; but experience shows that in the great majority of cases the issues are simple, and the auditor has no real difficulty in determining whether accounts submitted to him for approval are adequate or inadequate, helpful to shareholders or misleading; and every auditor should as a matter of professional ethics, not of law, refuse to recognize law or custom as justification for signing them if he regards them as either inadequate or calculated to give rise to inferences which are not warranted by the facts. If a new management draws on secret reserves created by conservative predecessors, to eke out the meager results of its own inefficiency, without disclosing the fact to the shareholders, can there be any doubt that the auditor has a moral duty to reveal it?

In saying this, I am in no wise oblivious of the impossibility of establishing fixed standards of accounting, nor of the necessity of leaving the control of company matters generally in the hands of directors. Within the limits of a reasonable difference of opinion an auditor may properly subordinate his own judgment to that of directors, and unless the point is of crucial importance he can quite properly refrain from telling the stockholders of that difference of opinion. Nor have I any sympathy with the view that the so-called "man in the street," supposedly of subnormal intelligence, should set the standards of disclosure. If the accounts are clear enough to enlighten a normally competent analyst, that is sufficient; he can interpret to the less intelligent, if necessary.

It must be borne in mind that when a reputable company publishes and a reputable auditor accepts accounts which are lacking in fairness or frankness, the value of all accounts and of all audits is impaired. If some accounts bearing eminent names are known to be unreliable as indices of value or of the results of operations, the public has no means of knowing which are and which are not reliable.

Before concluding, I should like to say a word on the difficult question of wholly owned subsidiaries. The present English law on the subject seems scarcely worth the paper on which it is written. I suggest that the Institute should tackle seriously this vexed question. Accounts which ignore the operations of subsidiaries except the payment of dividends are inadequate. How the facts regarding such operations should be disclosed is a matter of judgment, and I should not advocate insistence by the Institute on any particular method. But at least it can and should insist that if the operations of the subsidiaries are not fairly reflected in the dividends received by the parent, some proper reflection must be given if the auditor is to certify that the accounts of the parent company show the true position of its affairs.

The Institute and the leading firms have an opportunity

at the present time by a display of courage and independence to effect a great reform and are assured of public support in doing so, and I hope they will make the most of the opportunity.

Yours very truly,

GEORGE O. MAY.

August 21, 1931.

IX

INFLUENCE OF THE DEPRESSION ON THE PRACTICE OF ACCOUNTANCY *

(1932)

I AM not one who believes that any benefit can be derived from the mere contemplation of misfortune, and I should not, therefore, undertake to address you today were it a question merely of dwelling on the unfortunate immediate effects on the profession of the unparalleled depression through which we have been passing. I deeply regret the loss of employment by many worthy members of our profession and the difficulties which some of our practitioners have experienced; but I should not feel that the depression would be worth our study unless we could derive either some légitimate satisfaction or some instruction, or both, from the process.

I think we can derive satisfaction from the abundant evidence of the importance of our profession which the depression has elicited. The numerous defalcations which have unfortunately but naturally resulted from it have brought home the importance of detailed audits by outside auditors in the case of those companies which are not of sufficient magnitude to justify the maintenance of an adequate system of internal check. Other incidents have demonstrated the importance of external audits in the case of companies at the other extreme of the range: namely, those companies which in their magnitude and importance have sometimes been deemed to be above the need of auditing. I think that in both fields we can look forward confidently to a permanent growth in the work of the profession as the result of

* An address delivered at the annual meeting of the American Institute of Accountants, Kansas City, Missouri, October 18, 1932. Cf. *The Journal of Accountancy* (November, 1932), Vol. LIV, pp. 336-50.

this temporary depression and that the outlook is favorable to those carrying on efficiently either large practices or small. It is, however, the lessons which we can learn from the depression that I propose particularly to consider.

It is in times of stress that defects and inadequacies of a structure become most readily apparent; and it has seemed to me that it would be worth while to consider what defects in the economic structure the present depression has revealed, and how far accountants have any responsibility therefor or any opportunity to bring about improvement in the future. Obviously, the depression is not the resultant of any single cause but of a multiplicity of causes. Of the many to which it has been partly attributed, most lie in fields with which the accountant as such is not concerned, and this group includes those in regard to which controversy has been the keenest—such as the relation to the depression of the development of intense post-war nationalism, tariffs, war debts, and the gold standard. Some, however, seem to me to relate to phases of our economic life with which the accountant has a very direct concern.

First of all, I propose to discuss a phase of the question with which, as Chairman of your Committee on Coöperation with Stock Exchanges, I have been much concerned in recent months. No one doubts that one of the major contributing causes to the depression was the enormous volume and extravagantly high prices which characterized the dealings in corporate stocks in the period prior to the collapse of 1929. An outstanding characteristic of that movement was the new emphasis laid on earning capacity as the measure of value of such securities; and, as frequently happens when new recognition is given to an old truth, we have seen during periods of inflation and deflation this truth applied in a most reckless and ill-advised manner, not only by investors, but by many who have undertaken to advise others. Such people were no doubt right when they argued that earning capacity was usually the main criterion of value. They may have been right in their second proposition, that the fair value of securities of a given type was a multiple—ten, or fifteen, or twenty—of the earning capacity attached to the security. They were, however, hopelessly wrong when they predicated their calculations on the assumption that the earning capacity was fairly measured by the past or prospective earnings for a comparatively short period, without any adequate knowledge of the way in which the figures of earnings employed in their calculations were derived.

Nothing has astonished me more in conversations with men fairly well versed in financial matters than their failure to appreciate the importance of methods of accounting in relation to corporate earnings and to capital values predicated on earnings. We accountants know how varied are the methods commonly and legitimately employed, how great the effect of a difference of methods on the earnings of a particular short period may be, and how erroneous may be conclusions as to capital value based on such earnings. An illustration may make clearer the point I have in mind.

Let me take a simple case of one of the unemployed who joined the apple-selling rush in the winter of 1931. He started on the first day believing that he could sell two crates of apples, which cost him $2.00 each, at a profit of more than one hundred per cent. At the end of the first day he found that he had sold the contents of one and collected $5.00. The wholesale price of apples remained unchanged and it was quite clear to him, and it must be to everyone else, that he had made a profit of $3.00.

The second day, however, complications arose. As a result of the rush, the wholesale price of apples had risen to $2.25 a crate, and at that price he bought one crate. He was also able to increase his price slightly, and the sale of one crate produced $5.50. Apples were still quoted wholesale at $2.25 when he ended his day's work, and the question arose in his mind whether his profit for the day was $3.25 or $3.50. Looking at the matter one way, he had $3.25 more cash than he had at the beginning of the day, and he had one crate of apples on hand just as he had at the beginning. Looking at it another way, the crate of apples that he had bought that day had cost him $2.25 and was still worth that sum, and what he had sold was the crate of apples bought the previous day at $2.00; and as he had realized $5.50, he had made a profit of $3.50.

The third day, the public demand for apples began to decline. He was able to buy another crate of apples for $2.00, and the sale of one crate produced only $4.50. To make matters worse, he found that by the end of the day the wholesale price of apples had fallen to $1.75. He was sorely puzzled to determine how much profit he had made that day. He still had a crate of apples, as he had had in the morning, and he had $2.50 more cash, so that from this standpoint his profit was $2.50. If, however, he took the view that what he had on hand was the crate he had bought that day, and that what he had sold was the crate which had cost $2.25 the previous day, his profit was only $2.25. Looking at it in a third way he perceived that at the close of the previous day he had had a crate of apples that had cost him and was worth $2.25; at the end of that day he had a crate of apples which was worth $1.75 and $2.50 in cash, a total of $4.25, so that from this standpoint his gain for the day was only $2.00.

He concluded that, anyhow, the business was an unsatisfactory one, and decided to buy no more apples; and on the fourth day he was able to sell the contents of the crate he had on hand for $4.00.

Looking back over the experience of the four days, it was clear that he had bought four crates of apples at a total cost of $8.25 and had sold the contents for a total of $19.00, and thus had made a total profit of $10.75. It was apparent, however, that the profit from day to day varied according to the way in which the stock he carried over from day to day was treated. The only day in which the amount of profit was clear was the first day. The following table shows the distribution of profits between days on the different theories, which I may now describe in the terms in which they are commonly described by accountants, to whom all three methods are familiar:

	First day	Second day	Third day	Fourth day	Total
On the basis of stating the inventory at latest cost, the profit was	$3.00	$3.50	$2.25	$2.00	$10.75
On the basis of inventorying at cost or market, whichever was lower	3.00	3.50	2.00	2.25	10.75
On the basic stock method (that is, valuing stock at a uniform price)	3.00	3.25	2.50	2.00	10.75

If next we assume three men, A, B, and C, having exactly the same experience but using the three different inventory methods, respectively, in the order above named and reporting their profits accordingly—then if we were to appraise the value of the respective businesses by multiplying the profits shown in, say, the second period, by a uniform multiple, we should reach the conclusion that the businesses of A and B were worth substantially more than that of C; while if we made the calculations a day later and used the third period as our basis, we should conclude that C's business was by far the most valuable of the three.

Of course, on the illustrative case assumed the conclusion is fantastically absurd; but enlarge the scale of the illustration in volume, time and complexity, so that it will deal with years and millions of dollars instead of days and dollars, and you have exactly the situation that has been presented in the period that has elapsed between the close of the last depression in 1921 and the present time.

Nor do the three methods of computing profits for the different periods exhaust the variations in commercial practices. Some corporations, for instance, would treat the reduction of inventory from cost to market value as a charge to surplus, and show:

Net income

First day............................. $ 3.00
Second day........................... 3.50
Third day............................ 2.25
Fourth day........................... 2.25

$11.00

Less—Charge to surplus

Third day............................ .25

$10.75*

Now investors, and even some who undertake to advise investors, are apt to give the same weight to profits of companies in the same business without knowing whether the profits to which their calculations are applied have been computed on the same basis or how great the effect of a difference in method might be. And as most of you probably know, such computations have frequently been made on the basis of profits for a single year if not for a shorter period. I remember, for instance, the case of a banking house acquiring the business of a large corporation for the purpose of resale to the public on an agreed basis measured by the earnings of a past year, without any specification of the way in which the earnings had been or were to be determined except that it was to be in accordance with good accounting practice; and as this paper was being written I happened to see a publication of a firm of investment advisors containing this language: "When the statement is made that the majority of common stocks are overvalued at current levels, it is meant that they are selling at higher values than are justified by a six to nine months' improvement in earning power at the best rate foreseeable."

By comparing the figures in the table I have already given,

* Those desiring to pursue the question further may be interested to compare the annual reports for 1931 of the National Lead Company, the Goodyear Tire & Rubber Company and the American Smelting and Refining Co. Such a comparison affords much food for thought, and I was very much interested, therefore, to see a question in a recent examination paper on accounting principles of the Harvard Graduate School of Business Administration, calling for a discussion of the difference of method between the Goodyear and National Lead companies.

you will notice that the method of valuation at cost or market, whichever is lower (which is by far the most commonly employed of all methods), results in showing larger profits in a period of rising wholesale and retail prices and lower profits in a period of declining prices than the basic stock method.   For this reason, it has been urged that the basic stock method is really a safer and saner way of measuring earnings than the cost or market basis.   I think it must be admitted that the cost or market basis is designed primarily to afford a sound balance sheet value, and that some change of method, or some change in the form of presentation of results, may be called for at this time, when the income account is becoming recognized as potentially, at least, more significant than the balance sheet.   But without passing on this minor question, I think we can agree on the major point that, particularly in times of changing prices, it is very important that those who undertake to appraise capital values on the basis of current earnings should know just how the earnings are computed.

I chose my illustration from the field of inventory valuation, but this is by no means the only part of corporate accounting in respect of which legitimate methods vary.   Methods of treatment of plant and equipment, for instance, vary even more widely.   I noticed recently a statement by an economist that the heavy investment in capital equipment characteristic of the present age tended to make the process of readjustment in a period of falling prices more painful and prolonged than it would otherwise be.*   Certainly, this characteristic of heavy capital investment gives rise to the most difficult problems of modern accounting—problems which cannot be solved by any precise mathematical or logical processes but require foresight and judgment in their handling if even measurably accurate solutions are to be reached.

The questions what expenditures ought to be capitalized

---

* Frederick C. Mills, *Economic Tendencies in the United States; Aspects of Pre-War and Post-War Changes* (1931).

and when expenditures so capitalized ought to be charged off are not easy to answer, and experience shows that corporations adopt an infinite variety of methods in dealing with them. At the one extreme are the methods prescribed by many public-service commissions, according to which all additions and improvements are capitalized and units of property are charged off only as they are actually retired or are about to be retired, when the charge may be made against either operating expenses or surplus. At the other extreme is the method formerly employed by the General Electric Company, by which all capital expenditures are charged off against income in the year in which they are incurred, no charge being made, naturally, for depreciation of previously existing plant. Between these extremes the accounts of corporations reflect every gradation from over-liberality to over-conservatism in attributing charges to capital and amortizing them through depreciation charges or otherwise. Here, again, anyone appraising the stock of a corporation on the basis of its earnings should know what methods of accounting have been followed.

It may be suggested that the accountant who audits the accounts of a corporation and satisfies himself that they are presented on a fair basis has no further responsibility to the individual investor or analyst who may draw unwarranted inferences from the accounts. That is, no doubt, quite true; but if the profession is to render the fullest possible service, surely it must keep in touch with the trend of economic developments and try to meet the legitimate demands that grow out of such developments.

Now, one of the major economic developments of recent years has been the change in the nature and status of corporate securities. This change has been brought about by two tendencies in the development of corporations: first, the tendency to consolidate businesses into large units and, secondly, the ever-widening diffusion of security holdings. The great social significance of these tendencies was recognized some years ago by the Social Science Research Council, and

that body instituted a study which resulted in the publication of a work bearing the title, *The Modern Corporation
and Private Property.** From this work it appears that
roughly 40% of the business wealth of the country (other
than banking) is controlled by the two hundred largest corporations. It also appears that the control of the two hundred corporations in turn is roughly as follows:

	By number	By wealth
Management control.....	44%	58%
Legal device............	21%	22%
Minority control.........	23%	14%
Majority ownership......	5%	2%
Private ownership.......	6%	4%
In hands of receiver......	1%	negligible
	100%	100%

It was impracticable to carry the study further to cover
smaller, but still large corporations, but the analysis shows
clearly how very far the separation between beneficial ownership and control of corporate property has already proceeded,
and doubtless the process will continue in the future.

Concurrently, there has been a constant attempt to make
corporate stocks, which in essence are capital assets, more and
more into a liquid security, readily marketable and suitable
as collateral for demand or short-time obligations. The
three tendencies combined seem to me to have created a legitimate basis for the demand for full and more enlighten-
ing information in regard to the operation of the larger
companies whose securities are widely distributed and subject to continuous market dealings. If market values are to
be fairly appraised, information throwing light on the earning capacity is of the first importance. The reports issued
by such corporations must not be regarded as having only
historical interest—it must be recognized that their principal
value lies in enabling thousands or tens of thousands of
stockholders to deal intelligently with their investments in

* A. A. Berle, Jr., and Gardiner C. Means, *The Modern Corporation and
Private Property.*

corporations and potential investors to form reasonably in-formed opinions on the attractiveness of the stocks of corpo-rations at the prices at which they are available. I think the accountant should take cognizance of this situation and do his part toward securing the fulfillment of the require-ments to which it gives rise, and I think his part can be made a very important one.

To my mind, the first essential is to bring about a better understanding by investors of what accounts are or should be, and what they are not and cannot be. Investors should be brought to realize that the value and significance of corporate accounts depena partly on the methods of accounting em-ployed by the corporation and partly on the degree of wis-dom and honesty displayed in applying those methods. And here it is important to note that the use of the most conserva-tive method may, for a short period, result in an overstate-ment of earnings. If, for instance, during a year of depres-sion, a corporation which capitalizes nothing and charges no depreciation, suspends all construction work, the results for that year will be presented in an unduly favorable light, al-though the accumulated surplus may still be conservatively stated.

In the second place, it seems to me highly desirable that the reports and accounts of corporations should be made more fully explanatory, so that investors and others inter-ested will know generally what methods of accounting have been followed and be in a position to appraise the value of the resulting figures accordingly. This development seems to me infinitely preferable to the alternative which at once suggests itself of uniform methods imposed by external au-thority. I think, also, that in the formulation of methods of accounting the preëminent importance of earning capac-ity should be recognized and the consequent importance of furnishing to stockholders and investors an income account which will give as fair an indication of the earning capacity of the business during the period to which it relates as can be given.

I think it only fair to add that, from a fairly wide international experience, I believe information is more fairly given in respect of corporate affairs in this country than in perhaps any other important commercial country. This, however, ought to be so, for the simple reason that the three tendencies to which I have referred (those towards concentration into larger units, diffusion of shareholdings, and the creation of a status of liquidity for corporate stocks) have proceeded much further in this country than elsewhere.

Your Committee on Coöperation with Stock Exchanges, of which I am chairman, has been much impressed with the determination of the New York Stock Exchange to exercise its influence more than in the past in the direction which I have indicated and with the possibilities of helpful coöperation on the part of accountants. This committee during the past year has given much consideration to the subject, and the views which I am expressing today are in a large measure the result of that consideration.

It is quite true that the public accountant has no power to initiate improvements in corporate methods of accounting or reporting, nor to exercise pressure to bring them about. The initiative lies theoretically with the shareholders; practically, with the directors or officers of corporations. The power to exercise pressure resides mainly in those bodies which afford a market in which dealings mainly take place. But the accountant who has earned the confidence of his clients can, by influencing them, contribute greatly to the success of the movement. Most corporation executives will, I believe, be found willing to afford reasonable information to their shareholders if the question is placed fairly before them.

I venture, therefore, to express the hope that accountants in their audit practice and in their conferences with corporate officers regarding the form and content of annual accounts will bear constantly in mind the desirability of indicating clearly on what bases assets and liabilities are stated and results computed; the growing relative importance of the income account as compared with the balance sheet; and the fact that the value of the income account depends on its being a fair indication of the earning capacity of the business under the conditions existing during the year to which it relates as determined by a fair and consistent application of acceptable methods of accounting.

There are one or two other problems in accounting which have assumed much greater importance as a result of the depression, and with which I should like to deal briefly. One is the acquisition by corporations of their own capital stock.

It would be out of place to discuss the broad question whether corporations should enjoy the unrestricted right to acquire their own capital stock, though accountants who have seen the unfortunate consequences that flowed from some such acquisitions in the latter part of 1929 and in 1930, and the abuses of the right in certain cases, cannot fail to recognize that there is a case for some restriction. I propose to deal only with the treatment in accounts of purchases actually made.

I have never been able to agree with the view that a corporation's own stock is ordinarily an asset of the corporation, though I have been willing to recognize the practical convenience of treating it as such where stock is acquired as a part of a related series of transactions which include its resale in the immediate future. Certainly, if it is to be classified as an asset it should be excluded from current assets (unless under contract for early realization) and should be separately disclosed. Even if such stock may be shown as an asset, it is incorrect, in my view, to include dividends thereon in the income of the corporation.

It is even more important that accountants should set their faces against the practice of treating a resale of the corporation's capital stock as producing a profit which can properly be credited to the income account. My objection to the practice is threefold:

In the first place, the view taken by the Bureau of Internal Revenue that a corporation cannot derive income from dealings in its own capital stock appears to me sound in theory.

A special case is presented where the corporation has agreed with the subscriber to preferred stock to repurchase that stock at a fixed price. There is some argument that when it purchases stock and thereby extinguishes such an obligation for less than its face value it makes a profit which is analogous to the profit on the retirement of a bond at less than par. But in the case of purchase and resale of a pure stock, I think the Bureau's rule is economically as well as legally correct.

In the second place, the case for permitting corporations to trade in their stocks is much weaker than the case for permitting mere acquisition. It is a plausible argument that the purchase of capital stock, when it is selling below its fair value and the corporation has available funds, is advantageous to all the shareholders: to those who sell or may want to sell, by tending to prevent the price from falling still further below its fair value; to other shareholders, by increasing their proportionate interest in the company on favorable terms. It is not easy to see in what circumstances a similar plea could be offered in relation to the resale. The acquisition of stock seems to me to be justifiable only for retirement or for use in some way other than in ordinary trading operations (*e.g.*, for issue to employees or in conjunction with a new acquisition of property); and such use should not be regarded as giving rise to income.

Thirdly, there is the important practical reason that recognition of such profits would open the way to a particularly vicious abuse in the case of corporations which have stock outstanding that is selling at a price substantially below the figure at which it is stated in the company's balance sheet. If the view were accepted that a profit which would be a legitimate credit to income might be derived from the purchase and sale of the capital stock of the corporation, the management would be able to buy the stock, and if the price should rise, to derive from resale a profit which could be credited to income; while if the price should decline, the company would be in a position to cancel the stock and thus to avoid any charge to income account, showing, instead, a credit to capital surplus arising from the cancellation of the stock acquired at less than book value.

Another practice is that of writing down the property accounts of a corporation and correspondingly reducing the depreciation charges against income. Whether such a procedure is proper seems to me to depend on the facts in relation to the property and on the way in which the transaction is effected and disclosed. Some would argue that the exhaustion of capital value (depreciation) during a year is a question of fact unrelated to the values at which the assets are carried; but this contention seems to me to be applicable where the object is to determine the profits of an enterprise (which is no doubt sometimes the proper objective of the investor or analyst), rather than in the ordinary case where we are trying to determine the profits of a continuing company which is carrying on the enterprise.

There must be continuity in corporate accounting, and the figures at which property legitimately stands on the books of a corporation cannot be ignored in calculating its depreciation charges. If a company has acquired assets at less than their fair present value, it is entitled to reap the benefit in its income account as the assets are gradually used up in service. The converse is in theory equally true; but, as a practical matter, if as a result of either purchases or revaluation at a time when price levels were higher a company is carrying depreciable assets at a figure clearly and substantially in excess of the fair value which such assets possess today and seem likely to possess in the near future, it seems to me desirable to permit it to deal with the excess book value as a capital loss and by formal action to reduce the book value of the assets to a fair figure and thereafter compute depreciation on the basis of the reduced value, unless such action would prejudice the position of a senior security which the corporation has a legal or moral obligation to preserve intact. If the company could legally accomplish the desired result by reorganization, it seems desirable to permit it to do so without that expense, provided that the same respect is shown for prior interests as would be enforceable in a reorganization, and that the action taken is fully disclosed and formally approved by the shareholders.

Such a course seems particularly justifiable where the market value of the stock of the corporation is far below the value at which it appears in the balance sheet. In such circumstances, it would be pedantic and foolish to insist that the company should by excessive depreciation charges make real a value for the capital stock which at present exists only on the books, especially as such a course would necessarily reduce reported earnings and tend to reduce the current market value of the stock so far as that value is predicated on earnings.

It is, however, always desirable to consider the collateral effects of any such action, as, for instance, in relation to taxes; and certainly no adjustment should be made unless the present value is carefully determined, the excess is substantial, and the management is satisfied that the level of values to which the properties are to be reduced is likely to persist for a period of years. Much embarrassment has been occasioned to companies which in the period of inflation wrote up their properties to values which have since proved to have been only temporary; and it is easy today to err in the opposite direction.

Moreover, the new value should be fair. It is obviously improper to reduce the book value to a value below the fair value, thus reducing the charge for depreciation to a figure which is less than the actual exhaustion of values that is taking place and overstating the earnings of the company. Experience shows this point to be one of very considerable importance; the attempt is sometimes made to pave the way for the future inflation of earnings by deliberate understatement of present assets.

As I have indicated, also, the rights of prior security holders should be respected. If, for instance, a corporation has issued prior securities on a representation as to the amount of assets available as security therefor, this would seem to imply at least a moral obligation to charge depreciation on a scale sufficient to maintain such values; and the reduction of book value, followed by a reduction of depreciation charges, might in such a case easily result in distributing, by way of dividends, sums that ought rightly to be retained for the protection of prior securities.

Action would seem to be permissible and desirable where the facts are such as those set out in the annual report for 1931 of the Union Carbide and Carbon Corporation, from which I quote:

During the past year a detailed survey of all plants, items of equipment and other fixed assets has been made to determine the changes which have taken place in their productiveness and replacement value. Since the formation of the corporation in 1917, there have been improvements in manufacturing methods and changes in location of plants to areas permitting more favorable manufacturing and distribution operations. Because of the decrease of approximately 21% in general construction costs during the past two years, the present book value of many items of property acquired, constructed or appraised during periods of high labor and material costs exceeds the present replacement value.

The constantly changing costs of labor and material make it impossible to maintain property records sufficiently flexible to show at all times the true replacement value of the fixed assets of the corporation.

However, when the change in values is as great as that which has occurred in the last few years, a restatement is desirable. To permit the records to continue to show the values of earlier years might easily become misleading, especially to those who lay great emphasis upon the 'book value' in evaluating the corporation's securities.

Accordingly, in the balance sheet submitted herewith the value of buildings, machinery and equipment has been written down to the extent of $39,794,031.11. A portion of this was charged directly to surplus and a portion to the reserve for depreciation. The amount charged to reserve has in turn been restored by a transfer from surplus as a provision for unidentified obsolescence, thus leaving the reserves for depreciation, etc., intact. It is true that many items of property, such as real estate, mining lands and water powers, have enhanced in value much beyond their cost and that this is nowhere reflected in the records. The enhancement of such items, not being structures, cannot be measured by the cost of labor and materials.

Aside from the consideration of a nearer approach to accuracy, the readjustment of the account will relieve the consolidated income from the burden of annual depreciation and amortization charges on property or values which do not contribute to earnings.

The percentage of reduction in capital value was less than the percentage of decrease in general construction costs, so that depreciation calculated on the reduced values would presumably be sufficient to provide for replacement of the property at current price levels; the revised value was carefully ascertained; the excess of book value to be dealt with was substantial; the amount of prior securities outstanding was small; the action taken was fully disclosed; and the amount written off was charged against a previously existing surplus.

There are other questions which have arisen or the importance of which has greatly increased as a result of the depression. On the other hand, the depression has both demonstrated the unsoundness and minimized the importance of the practices of treating stock dividends as income in the amount of the market value of the stock received, and regarding the proceeds of the sale of rights as wholly income, by means of which stocks of holding companies which formed the apices of pyramids were raised to heights from which they have since crashed, in some cases to complete ruin. This paper has, however, already reached its appointed length; and it has seemed to me better to concentrate our attention today on a small number of important issues, rather than to attempt to cover too wide a field.

In concluding, may I say that I recognize that the issues I have discussed are of particular importance to companies whose securities are listed on exchanges and to members whose practice brings them into contact with such companies. I should like, therefore, to explain that the choice is not due to any failure to recognize that such practice constitutes only a small percentage of the accounting work of the profession today, but to a desire to deal with questions in relation to which I could feel that my experience both in my practice and in my capacity as chairman of one of your special committees qualified me to express an informed opinion.

X

THE ADVANTAGES OF THE ELECTION OF AUDITORS BY THE SHAREHOLDERS *

(1932)

WHEN one finds people for whom one has respect expressing different views on a question, one is very apt to think that the real difference lies not in their opinions so much as in the subject with which they conceive themselves to be dealing. That is universally recognized in all sorts of affairs. Most of the plans for promoting peace between nations rest on the proposal that if people only agree thoroughly upon what they are talking about most of their differences will disappear.

So when I see people advocating different ways of appointing auditors, I think very possibly it is because they have different kinds of audits in mind and different purposes to be accomplished by auditors. Obviously there are at least as many different kinds of audits as there are different proposals before the meeting tonight. The officers of a company may desire an audit for a check on their employees. The directors may desire an audit as a check on their officers. The stockholders may desire an audit as a check on the directors. And possibly a large part of the difference that may develop tonight may turn on those differences in the purposes of an audit.

I have assumed, however, that we were talking about something such as your President just referred to, a proposal to require audits for the protection of investors; and if the audit is primarily for the protection of the investor, it seems

* From a discussion on "Election or Appointment of Auditors" at a meeting of the New York State Society of Certified Public Accountants, January 18, 1932.

to me entirely natural that the investor should be the person who chooses the auditors.

Now I think, by way of clearing the ground further, that we might as well be realistic and take it for granted that whatever form of election of auditors is provided for, the auditors will, in the first place, be chosen by the officers of the company in the great majority of cases.

I remember when the Canadian Bank Audit Act was under consideration I was talking to one of the most influential directors of one of the biggest banks, and I said to him, "I suppose that although the law calls for the election of auditors by the stockholders, they won't have anything to do with it; but do you, as directors, expect to have anything to do with it?"

He said, "Oh, good heavens, no! The general manager will pick the auditors." (Laughter.) But it is just because I think the officers will pick the auditors in the first place that I think they ought to be elected by the shareholders, although that may sound a bit paradoxical—but paradoxes are very often well founded.

In order to make my position entirely clear I would say that I do not think it is any use having auditors elected by the shareholders unless you take some further steps to safeguard the situation.

The real difficulty of the audit situation, viewed from the standpoint of the auditor as the protector of the investor, is that if the auditor and the management do not agree, it is the easiest thing in the world, as things now are, for the management, in saying good-bye to the auditors, to say, "We will get somebody else." That proved to be one of the great defects in England, where for many years they have had the system of election of auditors by the shareholders. So, to meet that situation, in a revision of the Companies Act some years ago in England, they put in a provision which has been very effective, or rather, two provisions:

First, that no auditors, other than the retiring auditors,

could be nominated unless notice were given to the shareholders at a certain time in advance of the meeting;

Secondly, that at any meeting of shareholders, up to the meeting at which the successors were elected, the auditors should have the right to appear and to address the shareholders. The result of that has been that if the auditors and the officers or directors fail to agree on a question, the auditors can say: "If you adhere to this position we shall have to qualify our certificate and appear at the annual meeting and state our reasons for doing so." It doesn't often happen that that comes about because the auditors won't take that position unless they are very sure of their ground. On the other hand, if the auditors are sure of the ground, the directors won't risk going to the meeting with a situation of that kind.

So that just gives the auditor the additional weight in the scales to enable him to stand up against the directors and management and insure what he regards as a proper presentation of the accounts, without being in such a strong position that he overrides the officers and directors. It brings about a very nice balance of power between them and, generally speaking, I think gives a very effective protection.

That is the scheme that I think ought to be employed if at any time the legislature in this State sees fit to prescribe an audit for the protection of investors. The audit as between directors and officers or as between officers and employees is a purely internal matter with which I think the State legislature should not concern itself, but I do think that the investor needs a great deal more protection today than he is getting.

The New York Stock Exchange is doing quite a little for him, but I don't think it ought to depend entirely on bodies of that kind, and I think it would be a great step forward if the legislature of New York, the great commercial State of the Union, would take the lead, as it took the lead in creating this profession as an organized profession, and adopt some measure requiring the election of auditors for the protection of investors.

I wouldn't by any means suggest that every corporation incorporated in the State should be required to have auditors— I think that would probably be premature at this time. But I do think that at least every corporation which offers its securities publicly for sale or causes its securities to be listed on any exchange might reasonably be subjected to that provision; and it might possibly also be wise to extend it to any corporation having an outstanding capital stock beyond a certain minimum and having more than a certain number of shareholders, although that is a secondary question on which I wouldn't pass at this time. But I do think that if they are going to do anything for the protection of investors they should let the investors who are the stockholders elect the persons who are to protect their own interest.

XI

KREUGER AND TOLL *

(1933)

From your experience in this entire Kreuger & Toll picture, what is your professional opinion of an arrangement wherein the auditor reports to shareholders rather than to the company, Mr. May?

Mr. May. Well, as the result of all my professional experience, I am heartily in favor of such an arrangement, and I have strongly advocated it; and I have had some part in bringing about the action of the New York State Chamber of Commerce recently favoring that action.

Mr. Marrinan. May I ask as a matter of helpfulness to the committee that you give us your professional opinion as to the relative development of accountancy in England and in the United States?

Mr. May. Well, that is rather a large order. It is by no means a one-sided question. In some respects English practice has gone ahead of American. In other respects I think American practice has gone distinctly ahead of English. I think it may surprise you, but American practice is distinctly ahead of English in the amount of information which is given to shareholders—unquestionably.

The Chairman. Do they seem to need more information over here?

Mr. May. Well, if you like I will tell you—I do not want to volunteer remarks, but if it will throw any light I will tell you how, in my judgment, that has come about. It happens to be a situation that I have studied rather intensively the last two or three years. I think there is a strong

* Testimony before Subcommittee of the Committee on Banking and Currency, United States Senate, "Stock Exchange Practices," 72nd Congress, Second Session, Part IV (1933). pp. 1265-66; 1273-74.

feeling to the same effect in England that information is inadequate in England. And the reason has largely been that the regulation in England is statutory. And, of course, statutes can lay down only what I call minimum standards, failure to comply with which subjects them to penalty. What we want is much higher standards than that. And the result of these standards laid down by law in England has been that company officials who were reluctant to give information have said, "Well, that is all the law requires, and you have got no right to ask us to give more." And some auditors have accepted that position. Whereas here I think the profession has taken the position that what is due to shareholders is a matter of good conscience and good business practice. And there are no legal limitations on it. So they must use their own judgments when they consider that the directors are giving a reasonable amount of information to the shareholders. That, I think, is the history of the development.

Mr. Marrinan. That does not, of course, prevent the possibility of regulation which would compel all necessary information?

Mr. May. Well, that is a difficult branch of legislation; and when you come to formulate it, I think you will find, for the reason that I have said, you can set down only a standard which everybody is bound to observe, and that must be a relatively low standard. You cannot put it so high as the best practice should be when you establish a practice by law.

.   .   .   .

Mr. Marrinan. We of course are searching the picture here, Mr. May, for any safeguards that may be discovered in this Kreuger & Toll secured debenture issue situation in behalf of the stockholders or investors. Would you say that in the field of accounting, and confining yourself wholly to the secured debenture issue, any adequate safeguards were set up in the matter of accounting?

Mr. May. I am not familiar with that particular issue.

I have seen the prospectus, but I have not carefully studied it. I do not know what kind of protection there was, if any.

Mr. Marrinan. There was no audit, Mr. May, of any kind, as nearly as we can ascertain. Would you think it possible to keep faith with investors without an audit?

Mr. May. In 1929; yes. Today, perhaps not. Then I would say, especially with a security issue, I would not have thought that an audit was a normal part of the protective machinery that was provided. That is one of the good things that I think has come out of this—that people have realized that, however trustworthy people may seem to be, some objective study is eminently desirable. In fact, the whole advance of accounting in this country is marked by a series of events like this. The Claflin incident gave tremendous impetus to accounting. Banks in those days used to say that they would not give that for an audit certificate when they had a name like Claflin on the papers. Now they have come to find that, even though it may be only one case out of a hundred, it may sometimes be a valuable additional protection. And I think it has developed fairly logically and fairly satisfactorily.

Of course, all these things are a question of balancing risks against costs. If you create a machinery of protection that is unduly expensive, you kill industry and you put a burden on new financing that is out of proportion to its value. It is a very nice question of adjusting the degree of precaution to the reasonable expense. And you will always find some outstanding cases where an exceptionally clever crook will beat the precautions that are, as a practical matter, advisable for the general run of business. It is no good legislating to surround every transaction with every precaution that seems necessary when you are dealing with a supercrook. And if you did so in ordinary banking, you would make ordinary banking out of the question. And if you take every precaution, you will realize that there will be a certain amount that will slip through in spite of the high degree of protection that you put forth.

Mr. Marrinan. By that statement you do not wish to be understood as minimizing the recommendations that you have made in your report?

Mr. May. Not at all. I think those are well within the limits, and I think if I should be erring I should err on the side of a little extra precaution. But at the same time it would be disastrous to attempt to weigh down business with precautions that would be very expensive and in ninety-nine cases out of a hundred would be supererogatory.

CONCLUSIONS OF FINAL REPORT OF
PRICE, WATERHOUSE & CO. ON THE KREUGER & TOLL
GROUP OF COMPANIES, 1932 *

In concluding this Report we propose to deal briefly with three questions of general interest, namely:

(1) Where has the money gone which the public has sub-scribed?
(2) To what extent were reported earnings real?
(3) How early did Kreuger's irregularities begin and what enabled them to be concealed?

To answer the first question it is necessary to deal with the combined position of five of the principal Companies taken collectively: *i.e.,* the three which sought money from the Public on a large scale, comprising:

(1) A. B. Kreuger & Toll
(2) International Match Corporation, and
(3) Svenska Tändsticks A.B. (The Swedish Match Company)

and the two underlying Finance Companies, *viz.:*

(4) N.V. Financieele Maatschappij Kreuger & Toll, and
(5) Continental Investment A.G.

The aggregate Funds made available to these Companies during the period of 14¼ years from January 1, 1918, to

---

* Printed in "Stock Exchange Practices," *op. cit.,* pp. 1262-4. Mr. May participated in the preparation of this final Report.

March 31, 1932, inclusive, and the eventual disposition thereof, as revealed by our Investigations, expressed in Swedish Kronor at par and in round numbers, is shown in the following statement:

Funds Provided

(1) Net Proceeds of Share and Debenture Issues, *i.e.*, including Premiums and deducting Discounts and Issue Expenses		2.104.569.000
(2) From Bank Loans and Bill Credits		613.892.000
(3) From Other Credits (Net)		5.320.000
(4) From Revenue Sources		
Net income before providing for shrinkage in value of Securities, Debenture Interest and Dividends paid		150.962.000
Total Funds Provided	S.Kr.	2.874.743.000

Disposition of Funds

(1) Debenture Interest and Dividends paid to Security holders outside the Group			668.280.000
(2) Withdrawn by Ivar Kreuger			
On Current Accounts	347.363.000		
Securities and other Assets appropriated	468.492.000	815.855.000	
Less:—Assets introduced		383.809.000	432.046.000
(3) Invested in Securities acquired and in Associated and Subsidiary Companies (Net)			
In Government and other Marketable Securities	1.127.405.000		
In Associated Companies	548.544.000		
Together	1.675.949.000		
Less:—Appropriated by Ivar Kreuger (included in appropriations shown above)	207.341.000	1.468.608.000	
In Subsidiary Manufacturing and Trading Companies		241.585.000	1.710.193.000
(4) Invested in Intangible Assets (Monopoly Concessions)			64.224.000
Total accounted for		S.Kr.	2.874.743.000

The approximate value of the Investments at March 31, 1932, as based on the best information available (*i.e.*, market quotations, carefully considered estimates and, as regards Investments in Subsidiary Manufacturing and Trading Companies, their provisional book values), is about S.Kr. 775.000.000, which, when compared with the aggregate

Book Value above shown of S.Kr. 1.710.193.000, reveals a shrinkage of about S.Kr. 935.000.000.

Turning to the second question, our examination has disclosed that during the same period of 14¼ years the apparent reported Earnings and Income of these Companies combined in the aggregate were grossly overstated. The extent of this overstatement is shown in the following comparison of the reported Earnings (adjusted to eliminate Inter-Company Dividends, Debenture Interest and other Items irrelevant to the present consideration) with the approximate aggregate Combined Earnings and Income as now ascertained:

Earnings and Income as based on Published or Book Figures adjusted to eliminate Inter-Company Dividends, Debenture Interest and other items irrelevant to the present consideration	1.179.357.000
Approximate Real Earnings and Income (both Normal and Extraordinary) on the same basis, which is before providing for shrinkage in value of Investments estimated at about S.Kr. 935.000.000	150.962.000
Excess of Reported Earnings as above over Real Earnings as above ....S.Kr.	1.028.395.000

This difference of S.Kr. 1.028.395.000 is made up of Fictitious Credits to Income Accounts, aggregating S.Kr. 1.043.693.000, less a sum of S.Kr. 15.298.000 representing the net adjustment of normal Profit and Loss Items.

The amount of Fictitious Earnings and Income includes some items which may have had an appearance of reality when considered solely from the standpoint of the individual Companies receiving the credits, in that they were supported by what purported to be Guarantees of another Company within the Group or by actual Cash Remittances.

There are a number of items, aggregating a fairly substantial sum, the genuineness of which is doubtful, and in regard to these the lenient view has been taken in that for the purpose of this analysis they have been classed as "Genuine."

The total Earnings of S.Kr. 150.962.000 shown above, which, it should be reiterated, are before providing for

Debenture Interest and shrinkage in Investment Values, are equivalent to about 1½% on the relative average Capital (Share and Debenture) invested in these Companies during the same period.

Neither these Earnings nor any other facts developed by our examination lend any support to the view that Kreuger possessed business ability so extraordinary as to warrant the grant to him of the freedom from control or disclosure of his actions which he enjoyed.

With regard to the third question, we have already indicated that the manipulation of accounts goes back at least as far as 1917. The fraudulent practices assumed large proportions in 1923 and 1924 and continued thereafter, culminating in the fabrication of £21.000.000 (nominal) of Italian Government Bonds.

The perpetration of frauds on so large a scale and over so long a period would have been impossible but for (1) the confidence which Kreuger succeeded in inspiring, (2) the acceptance of his claim that complete secrecy in relation to vitally important transactions was essential to the success of his projects, (3) the autocratic powers which were conferred upon him, and (4) the loyalty or unquestioning obedience of Officials, who were evidently selected with great care (some for their ability and honesty, others for their weaknesses), having regard to the parts which Kreuger intended them to take in the execution of his plans.

The absolute powers with which Kreuger was vested gave him complete domination of the entire Group and of all the Executive and Administrative Staffs. Indeed he conducted the entire business as though he was accountable to no one, as evidenced by his action in Inter-Company matters in respect of which the rights of third parties, such as the Security Holders and Creditors of each Unit, were completely ignored.

Closely related to the causes already mentioned are the complicated and confused bookkeeping in regard to many important transactions, and the gross inadequacy of the documentary evidence in support of accounting entries which our examination has disclosed.

The frauds could not have been consummated without assistance—witting or unwitting—of some of his associates, including some of the Officers of the Holding and Financial Companies; nor could they have been concealed if either the Audits of the Companies had been coördinated under a single control, or if the Audits, though not so coördinated, had been carried out in all cases with proper honesty, efficiency and independence. It is apparent that the employment of different Auditors for different closely associated Companies, restrictions in the scope of examinations, subserviency if not complicity on the part of some of the employees and some of the Auditors, and forgery of documents in order to meet demands for evidence confirmatory of book entries, all contributed to prevent such Audits as were made from resulting in exposure.

The history of this Group of Companies emphasizes anew the truth that enterprises in which a complete secrecy on the part of the chief executive officer as to the way in which important parts of the capital are employed is, or is alleged to be, essential to success are fundamentally unsuited for public investment, since such secrecy undermines all ordinary safeguards and affords to the dishonest executive unequalled opportunities for the perpetration and concealment of frauds.

Upon the conclusion of our investigation, which has now extended over seven months, we desire to place on record that in the course of our work we have received throughout the most sympathetic coöperation and support of the various Committees, Liquidators and Administrators, as well as the whole-hearted assistance of the present Officials and Staff. Our cordial thanks are due for this coöperation and for the unfailing patience and courtesy in difficult circumstances which have everywhere been accorded to us.

XII

AUDITS OF CORPORATE ACCOUNTS *

(Extracts from correspondence between the Special Committee on Coöperation with Stock Exchanges, G. O. May, Chairman, of the American Institute of Accountants and the Committee on Stock List of the New York Stock Exchange)

(1932-1934)

September 22, 1932.

The Committee on Stock List,
  New York Stock Exchange,
    New York, N. Y.

DEAR SIRS:

In accordance with suggestions made by your Executive Assistant, this Committee has given careful consideration to the subject of the general line of development of the activities of the Exchange in relation to annual reports of corporations.

It believes that there are two major tasks to be accomplished—one is to educate the public in regard to the significance of accounts, their value and their unavoidable limitations, and the other is to make the accounts published by corporations more informative and authoritative.

The nature of a balance sheet or an income account is quite generally misunderstood, even by writers on financial and accounting subjects. Professor William Z. Ripley has spoken of a balance sheet as an instantaneous photograph of the condition of a company on a given date. Such language is apt to prove doubly misleading to the average investor—

---

* "These letters constitute a history of an important development in the recognition of the place which accountancy occupies in modern finance and business." The first communication which follows was placed in evidence by the Chairman of the Committee on Stock List of the New York Stock Exchange in a hearing before the United States Senate Committee on Banking and Currency, January 12, 1933.

first, because of the implication that the balance sheet is wholly photographic in nature, whereas it is largely historical; and, secondly, because of the suggestion that it is possible to achieve something approaching photographic accuracy in a balance sheet which, in fact, is necessarily the reflection of opinions subject to a (possibly wide) margin of error.

Writers of textbooks on accounting speak of the purpose of the balance sheet as being to reflect the values of the assets and the liabilities on a particular date. They explain the fact that in many balance sheets certain assets are stated at figures which are obviously far above or far below true values by saying that the amounts at which such assets are stated represent "conventional" valuations. Such statements seem to involve a misconception of the nature of a balance sheet.

In an earlier age, when capital assets were inconsiderable and business units in general smaller and less complex than they are today, it was possible to value assets with comparative ease and accuracy and to measure the progress made from year to year by annual valuations. With the growing mechanization of industry, and with corporate organizations becoming constantly larger, more completely integrated and more complex, this has become increasingly impracticable. From an accounting standpoint, the distinguishing characteristic of business today is the extent to which expenditures are made in one period with the definite purpose and expectation that they shall be the means of producing profits in the future; and how such expenditures shall be dealt with in accounts is the central problem of financial accounting. How much of a given expenditure of the current or a past year shall be carried forward as an asset cannot possibly be determined by an exercise of judgment in the nature of a valuation. The task of appraisal would be too vast, and the variations in appraisal from year to year due to changes in price levels or changes in the mental attitude of the appraisers would in many cases be so great as to reduce all other elements in the computations of the results of operations to relative insignificance.

Carrying the thought one stage further, it is apparent that the real value of the assets of any large business is dependent mainly on the earning capacity of the enterprise. This fact is fairly generally recognized by intelligent investors as regards capital assets such as plant and machinery, but it is not equally generally recognized that it is true, though to a lesser extent, in respect of such assets as inventories and trade accounts receivable. Those, however, who have had experience in liquidations and reorganizations realize that in many industries it becomes impossible to realize inventories or accounts receivable at more than a fraction of their going-concern value, once the business has ceased to be a going concern. To attempt to arrive at the value of the assets of a business annually by an estimation of the earning capacity of the enterprise would be an impossible and unprofitable task. Any consideration of the accounts of a large business enterprise of today must start from the premise that an annual valuation of the assets is neither practical nor desirable.

Some method, however, has to be found by which the proportion of a given expenditure to be charged against the operations in a year, and the proportion to be carried forward, may be determined; otherwise, it would be wholly impossible to present an annual income account. Out of this necessity has grown up a body of conventions, based partly on theoretical and partly on practical considerations, which form the basis for the determination of income and the preparation of balance sheets today. And while there is a fairly general agreement on certain broad principles to be followed in the formulation of conventional methods of accounting, there remains room for differences in the application of those principles which affect the results reached in a very important degree.

This may be made clearer by one or two illustrations. It is a generally accepted principle that plant value should be charged against gross profits over the useful life of the plant. But there is no agreement on the method of distribution. The straight-line method of providing for depreciation which is most commonly employed by industrial companies, the retirement-reserve method used by utilities, the sinking-fund method, the combined maintenance-and-depreciation method, and others, are supported by respectable argument and by usage, and the charges against a particular year may vary a hundred per cent or more according as one or the other permissible method is employed.

Again, the most commonly accepted method of stating inventories is at cost or market, whichever is lower; but within this rule widely different results may be derived, according to the detailed methods of its application. For instance, at times like the present, cost of finished goods may be deemed to be the actual cost, as increased by subnormal operation, or a normal cost computed on the basis of a normal scale of operations. It may or may not include interest during the period of production or various kinds of overhead expenses. Market value may be either gross or net after deducting direct selling expenses. The choice between cost or market may be made in respect of each separate item or of classes of items or of the inventory as a whole. Frequently, whether a profit or a loss for the year is shown depends on the precise way in which the rule is applied. And since the conventions which are to be observed must, to possess value, be based on a combination of theoretical and practical considerations, there are few, if any, which can fairly be claimed to be so inherently superior in merit to possible alternatives that they alone should be regarded as acceptable.

Most investors realize today that balance sheets and income accounts are largely the reflection of individual judgments, and that their value is therefore to a large extent dependent on the competence and honesty of the persons exercising the necessary judgment. The importance of method, and particularly of consistency of method from year to year, is by no means equally understood.

In considering ways of improving the existing situation, two alternatives suggest themselves. The first is the selection by competent authority out of the body of acceptable methods in vogue today of detailed sets of rules which would become binding on all corporations of a given class. This procedure has been applied broadly to the railroads and other regulated utilities, though even such classifications as, for instance, that prescribed by the Interstate Commerce Commission allow some choice of method to corporations governed thereby. The arguments against any attempt to apply this alternative to industrial corporations generally are, however, overwhelming.

The more practicable alternative would be to leave every corporation free to choose its own methods of accounting within the very broad limits to which reference has been made, but require disclosure of the methods employed and consistency in their application from year to year. It is significant that Congress in the federal income-tax law has definitely adopted this alternative, every act since that of 1918 having contained a provision that the net income shall be computed "in accordance with the method of accounting regularly employed in keeping the books of such taxpayer" unless such method does not clearly reflect income. In its regulations the Bureau of Internal Revenue has said, "The law contemplates that each taxpayer shall adopt such forms and systems of accounting as are in his judgment best suited to his purpose." (Reg. 45, Art. 24.) The greatest value of classifications such as those imposed on regulated utilities lies in the disclosure of method and consistency of method which they tend to produce.

Within quite wide limits, it is relatively unimportant to the investor what precise rules or conventions are adopted by a corporation in reporting its earnings if he knows what method is being followed and is assured that it is followed consistently from year to year. Reverting to the illustrations already used, the investor would not need to be greatly concerned whether the straight-line or the sinking-fund method of providing for depreciation were being employed by a given corporation, provided he knew which method was being used and knew that it was being applied in the same way every year. But if depreciation is charged in one year on the straight-line basis applied to cost and in another is charged on a sinking-fund basis applied to a valuation less than cost, the investor may be grossly deceived unless the change is brought to his notice. For this reason, the requirement of the Exchange that the depreciation policy of a company applying for listing shall be stated in the application is valuable, and it might well be amplified to include an undertaking to report to the Exchange and to stockholders any change of policy or any material change in the manner of its application.

Again, it is not a matter of great importance to investors whether the cost-or-market rule for stating inventories is applied to individual items or to the inventory as a whole, but it is very important to the investor that he should be advised if the test is applied to individual items at the beginning of the year and to the inventory as a whole at the close thereof.

It is probably fairly well recognized by intelligent investors today that the earning capacity is the fact of crucial importance in the valuation of an industrial enterprise, and that therefore the income account is usually far more important than the balance sheet. In point of fact, the changes in the balance sheets from year to year are usually more significant than the balance sheets themselves.

The development of accounting conventions has, consciously or unconsciously, been in the main based on an acceptance of this proposition. As a rule, the first objective has been to secure a proper charge or credit to the income account for the year, and in general the presumption has been that once this is achieved the residual amount of the expenditure or the receipt could properly find its place in the balance sheet at the close of the period, the principal exception being the rule calling for reduction of inventories to market value if that is below cost. But if the income account is to be really valuable to the investor, it must be presented in such a way as to constitute to the fullest possible extent an indication of the earning capacity of the business during the period to which it relates. This Committee feels that the direction of the principal efforts of the Exchange to improve the accounting reports furnished by corporations to their stockholders should be towards making the income account more and more valuable as an indication of earning capacity.

The purpose of furnishing accounts to shareholders must be not only to afford them information in regard to the results being achieved by those to whom they have entrusted the management of the business, but to aid them in taking appropriate action to give effect to the conclusions which they reach regarding such accomplishments. In an earlier day, stockholders who were dissatisfied with the results secured by the management could perhaps move effectively to bring about a change of policy or, failing that, a change of management. With the growth in magnitude of corporations and the present wide diffusion of stock holdings, any such attempt is ordinarily impracticable because of the effort and expenditure that it would entail. The only practical way in which an investor can today give expression to his conclusions in regard to the management of a corporation in which he is interested is by retaining, increasing or disposing of his investment, and accounts are mainly valuable to him in so far as they afford guidance in determining which of these courses he shall pursue.

There is no need to revolutionize or even to change materially corporate accounting, but there is room for great improvement in the presentation of the conclusions to which accounts lead. The aim should be to satisfy (so far as is possible and prudent) the investor's need for knowledge, rather than the accountant's sense of form and respect for tradition, and to make very clear the basis on which accounts are prepared. But even when all has been done that can be done, the limitations on the significance of even the best of accounts must be recognized, and the shorter the period covered by them the more pronounced usually are these limitations. Accounts are essentially continuous historical records; and, as is true of history in general, correct interpretations and sound forecasts for the future cannot be reached upon a hurried survey of temporary conditions, but only by longer retrospect and a careful distinction between permanent tendencies and transitory influences. If the investor is unable or unwilling to make or secure an adequate survey, it will be best for him not to rely on the results of a superficial one.

To summarize, the principal objects which this Committee thinks the Exchange should keep constantly in mind and do its best gradually to achieve are:

1. To bring about a better recognition by the investing public of the fact that the balance sheet of a large modern corporation does not and should not be expected to represent an attempt to show present values of the assets and liabilities of the corporation.

2. To emphasize the fact that balance sheets are necessarily to a large extent historical and conventional in character, and to encourage the adoption of revised forms of balance sheets which will disclose more clearly than at present on what basis assets of various kinds are stated (*e.g.*, cost, reproduction cost less depreciation, estimated going-concern value, cost or market, whichever is lower, liquidating value, *et cetera*).

3. To emphasize the cardinal importance of the income account, such importance being explained by the fact that the value of a business is dependent mainly on its earning capacity; and to take the position that an annual income account is unsatisfactory unless it is so framed as to constitute the best reflection reasonably obtainable of the earning capacity of the business under the conditions existing during the year to which it relates.

4. To make universal the acceptance by listed corporations of certain broad principles of accounting which have won fairly general acceptance (see Exhibit I attached), and

within the limits of such broad principles to make no attempt to restrict the right of corporations to select detailed methods of accounting deemed by them to be best adapted to the requirements of their business; but—

(a) To ask each listed corporation to cause a statement of the methods of accounting and reporting employed by it to be formulated in sufficient detail to be a guide to its accounting department (see Exhibit II attached); to have such statement adopted by its board so as to be binding on its accounting officers; and to furnish such statement to the Exchange and make it available to any stockholder on request and upon payment, if desired, of a reasonable fee.

(b) To secure assurances that the methods so formulated will be followed consistently from year to year and that if any change is made in the principles or any material change in the manner of application, the stockholders and the Exchange shall be advised when the first accounts are presented in which effect is given to such change.

(c) To endeavor to bring about a change in the form of audit certificate so that the auditors would specifically report to the shareholders whether the accounts as presented were properly prepared in accordance with the methods of accounting regularly employed by the company, defined as already indicated.

This Committee would be glad to discuss these suggestions with you at any time, and to coöperate with the Exchange in any action it may see fit to take along the lines indicated.

Yours very truly,

GEORGE O. MAY,
Chairman.

EXHIBIT I

It is suggested that in the first instance the broad principles to be laid down as contemplated in paragraph 4 of the suggestions should be few in number. It might be desirable to formulate a statement thereof only after consultation with a small group of qualified persons, including corporate officials, lawyers and accountants. Presumably the list would include some if not all of the following:

1. Unrealized profit should not be credited to the income account of the corporation either directly or indirectly, through the medium of charging against such unrealized profits amounts which would ordinarily fall to be charged against income account. Profit is deemed to be realized when a sale in the ordinary course of business is effected, unless the circumstances are such that the collection of the sale price is not reasonably assured. An exception to the general rule may be made in respect of inventories in industries (such as the packing-house industry) in which owing to the impossibility of determining costs it is a trade custom to take inventories at net selling prices, which may exceed cost.

2. Capital surplus, however created, should not be used to relieve the income account of the current or future years of charges which would otherwise fall to be made thereagainst. This rule might be subject to the exception that where, upon reorganization, a reorganized company would be relieved of charges which would require to be made against income if the existing corporation were continued, it might be regarded as permissible to accomplish the same result without reorganization provided the facts were as fully revealed to, and the action as formally approved by, the shareholders as in reorganization.

3. Earned surplus of a subsidiary company created prior to acquisition does not form a part of the consolidated earned surplus of the parent company and subsidiaries; nor can any dividend declared out of such surplus properly be credited to the income account of the parent company.

4. While it is perhaps in some circumstances permissible to show stock of a corporation held in its own treasury as an asset, if adequately disclosed, the dividends on stock so held should not be treated as a credit to the income account of the company.

5. Notes or accounts receivable due from officers, employees, or affiliated companies must be shown separately and not included under a general heading such as Notes Receivable or Accounts Receivable.

The Exchange would probably desire to add a rule regarding stock dividends.

EXHIBIT II

The statement of the methods of accounting contemplated in paragraph 4a of the suggestion would not be in the nature of the ordinary detailed classification of accounts, nor would it deal with the machinery of bookkeeping. It should constitute a clear statement of the principles governing the classification of charges and credits as between (a) balance sheet accounts, (b) income account and (c) surplus account, together with sufficient details of the manner in which these principles are to be applied to enable an investor to judge of the degree of conformity to standard usage and of conservatism of the reporting corporation. Its content would vary according to the circumstances of individual companies, but some of the more important points which would be disclosed thereby would be as follows:

THE GENERAL BASIS OF THE ACCOUNTS:

Whether the accounts are consolidated, and if so, what rule governs the determination of the companies to be included in consolidation; also, a statement as to how profits and losses of subsidiary and controlled companies not consolidated are dealt with in the accounts of the parent company.

THE BALANCE SHEET:

(a) In respect of capital assets, the statement should show:

(1) What classes of items are charged to property account (whether only new property or also replacements and improvements);

(2) Whether any charges in addition to direct cost, either for overhead expense, interest or otherwise, are made to property accounts;

(3) Upon what classes of property, on what basis, and at what rates provision is made for, or in lieu of, depreciation;

(4) What classes of expenditures, if any, are charged against reserves for depreciation so created;

(5) How the difference between depreciated value and

realized or realizable value is dealt with on the sale or abandonment of units of property;

(6) On what basis property purchased from subsidiary companies is charged to property account (whether at cost to subsidiary or otherwise).

(b) In respect of inventories: The statement should show in fairly considerable detail the basis of valuation of the inventory. The statement under this head would be substantially a summary in general terms of the instructions issued by the company to those charged with the duty of preparing the actual inventories. It would not be sufficient to say that the inventory was taken on the basis of cost or market, whichever is lower. The precise significance attached to these terms should be disclosed, for the reasons set forth on page 3 of the letter.*

The statement should include a specific description of the way in which any intercompany profit on goods included in the inventory is dealt with. It should show under this head, or in relation to income or surplus account, exactly how reductions from cost to market value are treated in the accounts and how the inventories so reduced are treated in the succeeding period. It is, for instance, a matter of first importance to investors if inventories have been reduced to cost or market at the end of the year by a charge to surplus account, and the income for the succeeding year has been determined on the basis of the reduced valuation of the inventory thus arrived at. Obviously, under such a procedure the aggregate income shown for a series of years is not the true income for the period.

(c) In respect of securities: The statement should set forth what rules govern the classification of securities as marketable securities under the head of "current assets" and securities classified under some other head in the balance sheet. It should set forth in detail how any of its own securities held by the reporting corporation, or in the case of a consolidated statement any securities of any company in the group held by that or any other member of the group are dealt with in the balance sheet. (Stock of subsidiaries held by the parent will of course be eliminated in consolidation.) The disclosure of the basis of valuation of securities is covered in paragraph 2, page 6, of the recommendations contained in the letter.†

* Cf. above, p. 115.   † Cf. above, p. 119.

(d) Cash and receivables present few questions, though where sales are made on the instalment plan, or on any other deferred basis, their treatment should be fully set forth, including a statement of the way in which provision is made for future collection or other expenses relating to sales already made but not liquidated, and to what extent deferred accounts are included in current assets.

(e) Deferred charges: The statement should set forth what classes of expenditures are in the company's practice deferred, and what procedure is followed in regard to the gradual amortization thereof. (This question is of considerable importance, as substantial overstatements of income may occur through deferment in unprosperous periods of expenses ordinarily chargeable against current operations, possibly followed by writing off such charges in a later year against surplus account.)

(f) Liability accounts: There is normally less latitude in regard to the treatment of liability accounts than in respect of assets. The statement should clearly show how unliquidated liabilities, such as damage claims, unadjusted taxes, etc., are dealt with. The statement should disclose whether it is the practice of the company to make a provision for onerous commitments or to deal with such commitments in any way in the balance sheet.

(g) Reserves: A statement of the rules governing credits and charges to any reserve account (including both those shown on the liability side and those deducted from assets) should be given in detail. It is particularly important to know whether losses, shrinkages or expenses which would otherwise be chargeable against income accounts are in any circumstances charges against contingent or other reserves, and whether such reserves are built up partly or wholly otherwise than by charges to income account.

THE INCOME ACCOUNT:

An adequate statement in regard to the treatment of balance sheet items discloses by inference what charges and credits are made to income account or surplus. The additional points required to be disclosed are the principles followed in allocating charges and credits to income account and surplus account respectively, and the form of presentation of the income account. The form should be such as to show separately: (a) operating income; (b) depreciation and/or depletion if not deducted in arriving at (a), in which case the amount of the deduction should be shown; (c) income from companies controlled but not consolidated (indicating the nature thereof); (d) other recurring income; (e) any extraordinary credits; (f) charges for interest; (g) income taxes; and (h) any extraordinary charges.

The company's proportionate share of the undistributed earnings or losses for the year of companies controlled but not consolidated should be disclosed in a note or otherwise on the face of the income account. Stock dividends if credited to income should be shown separately with a statement of the basis upon which the credit is computed.

January 6, 1933.

An announcement by Richard Whitney, President of the New York Stock Exchange, in regard to the requirement adopted by the Exchange that listed companies have their annual accounts audited by independent public accountants.

Since April of 1932 all corporations applying for the listing of their securities upon the New York Stock Exchange have been asked to enter into an agreement to the effect that future annual financial statements published more than three months after the date of the agreement shall be audited by independent public accountants qualified under the laws of some state or country, and shall be accompanied by a certificate of such accountants showing the scope of the audit and the qualifications, if any, made by them in respect thereto. The Committee on Stock List has considered any reasons advanced why this procedure should not apply in particular cases, but has made exceptions only in the case of certain railroad companies.

During this period, the New York Stock Exchange has not required that audited statements be filed with applications for listing, because it was felt that applicants who had relied upon the former practice of the Exchange would have been subjected to undue delay if the Committee had pursued any other course.

The New York Stock Exchange now announces that its present policy in this respect will be continued until July 1, 1933, after which date all listing applications from corporations must contain the certificate of independent public accountants, qualified under the laws of some state or country, certifying to the correctness of the balance sheet, income statement and surplus statement for the most recent fiscal year. In general, the audit or audits must cover all subsidiaries, and the scope of the audit must be not less than that indicated in a pamphlet entitled "Verification of Financial Statements" issued by the Federal Reserve Board in May, 1929, and obtainable from that board at Washington, D. C. All applications must include an agreement to the effect that future annual reports published or sent to stockholders will be similarly audited and accompanied by a similar certificate.

The Committee on Stock List may make exceptions to these requirements in unusual or extraordinary cases where the enforcement of the requirements would, in its opinion, be manifestly unwise or impracticable. The Committee has concluded that for the present it will not require audited statements from railroad companies reporting to the Interstate Commerce Commission, except in the case of those railroads whose accounts have heretofore been currently audited by independent accountants.

Representative houses and banks of issue have been advised of the foregoing program, and have expressed themselves as in accord with the plan outlined above which they believe is sound and consistent with the importance of affording to the public the most complete and accurate information in regard to the financial condition of corporations whose securities are publicly dealt in.

Letter to presidents of corporations listed on New York Stock Exchange

NEW YORK STOCK EXCHANGE

OFFICE OF THE PRESIDENT

January 31, 1933.

DEAR SIR:

The New York Stock Exchange has recently announced its intention of requiring audited statements in connection with listing applications made after July 1, 1933. The public response to this announcement indicates clearly that independent audits are regarded by investors as a useful safeguard.

If, however, such a safeguard is to be really valuable and not illusory, it is essential that audits should be adequate in scope and that the responsibility assumed by the auditor should be defined. The Exchange is desirous of securing from companies whose securities are listed, and which now employ independent auditors, information which will enable it to judge to what extent these essentials are assured by such audits. In furtherance of this end, we should be greatly obliged if you will secure from your auditors, upon the completion of the audit for the year 1932, and furnish to the Commitee on Stock List, for its use and not for publication, a letter which will contain information on the following points:

1. Whether the scope of the audit conducted by them is as extensive as that contemplated in the Federal Reserve bulletin, "Verification of Financial Statements."

2. Whether all subsidiary companies controlled by your company have been audited by them. If not, it is desired that the letter should indicate the relative importance of subsidiaries not audited as measured by the amount of assets and earnings of such companies in comparison with the total consolidated assets and earnings, and should also indicate clearly on what evidence the auditors have relied in respect of such subsidiaries.

3. Whether all the information essential to an efficient audit has been furnished to them.

4. Whether in their opinion the form of the balance sheet and of the income, or profit-and-loss, account is such as fairly to present the financial position and the results of operation.

5. Whether the accounts are in their opinion fairly determined on the basis of consistent application of the system of accounting regularly employed by the company.

6. Whether such system in their opinion conforms to accepted accounting practices, and particularly whether it is in any respect inconsistent with any of the principles set forth in the statement attached hereto.

I shall personally appreciate very much your prompt consideration of this matter and any coöperation which you may extend to the Exchange in regard thereto.

Faithfully yours,

(Signed) RICHARD WHITNEY,

President.

NEW YORK STOCK EXCHANGE

COMMITTEE ON STOCK LIST

October 24, 1933.

To the Governing Committee,
    New York Stock Exchange.

GENTLEMEN:

On January 31, 1933, the President of the Stock Exchange addressed a general inquiry to all listed corporations, designed to secure information regarding the scope of audits and the responsibilities assumed by auditors which would put the Exchange in a better position to judge the value of audits to investors. In this letter, the request was made that companies whose accounts were audited should secure from their auditors and furnish to the Exchange, for its use and not for publication, answers to six questions. Of these questions, three dealt with the scope of the audit and three with the principles governing the accounting methods of the corporation and the form of presentation of accounts to shareholders.

The response to this request has been satisfactory, replies having been received from a large majority of the companies employing independent auditors regularly. A careful study of the replies received has brought to the attention of the Committee a number of points affecting particular companies which it has been deemed desirable to take up with those companies. In a few cases, the questions involved have been of very substantial importance, but the majority have been of relatively minor significance.

The replies have indicated very general acceptance of certain principles which the Exchange regarded as of primary importance and set forth in a statement attached to the letter of request [see above].

This Committee feels that all these principles should now be regarded by the Exchange as so generally accepted that they should be followed by all listed companies—certainly, that any departure therefrom should be brought expressly to the attention of shareholders and the Exchange.

In announcing on January 6, 1933, its intention of requiring after July 31, 1933, that there should be included in all listing applications, certificates of independent accountants in respect of the balance sheet, income statement and surplus statement for the most recent fiscal year, the Exchange indicated that in general the audit must cover all subsidiaries and the scope thereof be not less than that indicated in a pamphlet entitled "Verification of Financial Statements" issued by the Federal Reserve Board in May, 1929. The request of January 31 called for information as to whether these standards were currently being maintained in the audits of listed companies.

Upon the subject of the scope of audits, the existing position is outlined in a communication addressed by nine leading firms of accountants to the Exchange under date of February 24, 1933, a copy of which is attached hereto. In the interests of investors it seems desirable to make clear what is the scope of audits as currently conducted and to consider how far it is practicable to extend such scope and the responsibilities of auditors within the limits of a wise economy.

The bulletin issued by the Federal Reserve Board, to which reference has been made, indicated clearly that the scope of the examination therein provided for was not such as would lead naturally to detection of (1) defalcations on the part of employees or (2) any understatement of assets and profits resulting from charges to operations of items which might have been carried as assets. The nine firms of accountants in the letter above referred to pointed out that the former limitation is particularly applicable to examinations of the larger companies which, generally speaking, constitute the class whose securities are listed on the New York Stock Exchange.

Your committee is satisfied that the detailed scrutiny and verification of the cash transactions of large companies can most efficiently and economically be performed by permanent employees of the corporation, particularly today, when bookkeeping is to so large an extent done by mechanical means, and that it would involve unwarranted expense to transfer such work to independent auditors or to require them to duplicate the work of the internal organization. Your committee, however, feels that the auditors should assume a definite responsibility for satisfying themselves that the system of internal check provides adequate safeguards and should protect the company against any defalcation of major importance. Unless so satisfied, the auditors should make clear representations on this point—in the first place, to the management and, in default of action by the management, to the shareholders. Your committee also suggests that this limitation on the scope of the audit, though an entirely proper one, should be specifically mentioned in the common form of audit report.

The Committee feels that the auditors should recognize a responsibility to verify and, if necessary, to report to the shareholders upon any transactions affecting directors or officers of the corporation in respect of which there might be a conflict of interest between such directors and officers and the general body of shareholders.

Turning to the second limitation on the scope of audits as outlined in the Federal Reserve bulletin, the accountants indicated that, generally speaking, their examination of the income or profit-and-loss account was perhaps less extensive than the procedure contemplated in that bulletin. The classification of the income or profit-and-loss account is clearly a matter of great importance to investors. Whether income is of such a nature that it may reasonably be expected to recur or is of an exceptional character is often a vital consideration in the appraisal of an enterprise, and failure to make such distinctions clear in annual accounts is one of the defects to which the Exchange has had to call attention most frequently in the accounts of listed companies.

The Committee recognizes that it is neither necessary nor reasonable to hold auditors responsible for minor errors in classification, or to ask corporations to incur the expense of examinations such as would justify the acceptance of such a responsibility. Auditors should, however, in addition to satisfying themselves that the net income reported is not overstated, accept the burden of seeing that the income received and the expenditures made are properly classified in so far as the facts are known to them or are ascertainable by reasonable inquiry. For instance, when non-recurring income, shown separately on the books, is merged with recurring income in the annual accounts, or when items properly chargeable against current income are charged against surplus or reserve, the facts are bound to come to the attention of the accountant who makes even the most cursory examination, and he should not certify without a clear qualification accounts in which anything of this kind has been done.

The inquiry has again emphasized the importance and the difficulty of the problem of properly reflecting the operations of subsidiary and controlled companies. Consolidation of accounts of companies in which there are very substantial outstanding interests is not a satisfactory solution—indeed, the Committee is satisfied that no method can be prescribed which could be applied in every case. Operations of controlled companies may be as important an element in the value of the parent company as those of the parent company or its wholly-owned subsidiaries. Even where the operations of controlled companies are conducted at a negligible profit or loss, this fact cannot be ascertained if the result of such operations is nowhere reflected in the published financial statements. The Exchange has recognized that there must be an element of flexibility in the method of such presentation, so that corporations may choose, from among the several methods which will give the desired information, that one most suitable to its individual circumstances. For a considerable period of time past, the agreement covering this matter which the Exchange has requested from corporations applying for listing has read as follows:

To publish at least once in each year and submit to stockholders at least fifteen days in advance of the annual meeting of the corporation, but not later than . . . ., a Balance Sheet and Income Statement for the last fiscal year and a Surplus Statement of the applicant company as a separate corporate entity and of each corporation in which it holds directly or indirectly a majority of the equity stock; or, in lieu thereof, eliminating all intercompany transactions;

A similar set of consolidated financial statements. If any such consolidated statements exclude any companies a majority of whose equity stock is owned, (a) the caption will indicate the degree of consolidation; (b) the Income Account will reflect, either in a footnote or otherwise, the parent company's proportion of the sum of or difference between current earnings or losses and the dividends of such unconsolidated subsidiaries for the period of report; and (c) the Balance Sheet will reflect, in a footnote or otherwise, the extent to which the equity of the parent company in such subsidiaries has been increased or diminished since the date of acquisition as a result of profits, losses and distributions. Appropriate reserves, in accordance with good accounting practice, will be made against profits arising out of all transactions with unconsolidated subsidiaries, in either parent-company statements or consolidated statements.

Such statements will reflect the existence of any default in interest, cumulative dividend requirements, sinking-fund or redemption-fund requirements of any controlled corporation whether consolidated or unconsolidated.

The most costly, and the less satisfactory in some respects, of the suggested methods is the publication separately of the financial statements of each unconsolidated controlled corporation, for the reason that this imposes upon the stockholder, or analyst, the burden of determining for himself the equity of the parent company in the earnings of each such corporation, making it a burdensome matter for him thus to secure a true picture of the results of operation of the system as a whole.

With less information than is suggested by one of the methods in the foregoing agreement, the reports of any company having unconsolidated majority-owned companies are necessarily incomplete and may be positively misleading. The Committee believes that this is a subject which might well receive the consideration of corporate management and of organized bodies of accounting officers and independent accountants in order that adequate disclosure may become generally prevalent and not be confined merely to those companies which have executed the foregoing agreement with the Exchange.

At the same time, it might be desirable to attempt to develop a form of audit report or certificate which would be more informative to and more clearly understood by investors than the forms now currently in use. It would, in the opinion of the Committee, be advantageous if audit reports were so framed as to constitute specific answers to the last three questions embodied in the President's letter to listed companies of January 31, 1933, namely:

4. Whether in their opinion the form of the balance sheet and of the income, or profit-and-loss, account is such as fairly to present the financial position and the results of operation.

5. Whether the accounts are in their opinion fairly de-

termined on the basis of consistent application of the system of accounting regularly employed by the company.

6. Whether such system in their opinion conforms to accepted accounting practices, and particularly whether it is in any respect inconsistent with any of the principles set forth in the statement attached hereto.

As suggested earlier in this communication, also, it might contain a clear statement of the scope of the audit in relation to detection of defalcations by employees.

The matters herein discussed seem to the Committee those in respect of which clarification and improvement of accounting practice are most desirable in the interest of investors. It suggests to the Governing Committee that these matters should be brought to the attention of listed companies and organized bodies of accountants and accounting officers, with a view to definite action along the lines indicated herein.

By the direction of the Committee on Stock List,

J. M. B. HOXSEY,
Executive Assistant.

RESOLVED, That the Governing Committee of the New York Stock Exchange concurs in the suggestions herein contained and authorizes the Committee on Stock List to bring them to the attention of those concerned, as recommended.

ASHBEL GREEN, *Secretary.*

October 25, 1933.

Following is the text of the letter written by nine accounting firms and enclosed with Mr. Hoxsey's letter of October 24th:

New York, February 24, 1933.

RICHARD WHITNEY, ESQ., *President,*
New York Stock Exchange,
New York, N. Y.

DEAR SIR:

As auditors of a substantial number of corporations whose securities are listed on the New York Stock Exchange, we have received copies of the letter in relation to audits addressed by you to such companies under date of January 31. We are anxious to do everything in our power to assist the Exchange, and it has seemed to us that it will be helpful and more convenient to the Exchange for us to deal with some of the general phases of the subject under consideration collectively in a single letter, reference to which will make it unnecessary to discuss these points in the letters which we shall in due course furnish to our clients and which they in turn will presumably furnish to the Exchange for its confidential use.

We fully recognize the importance of defining the responsibility of auditors and of bringing about a proper understanding on the part of the investing public of the scope and significance of financial audits, to the end that their importance should not be underrated nor their protective value exaggerated in the minds of investors. This is the more necessary because the problem of delimiting the scope of audits or examinations is essentially one of appraising the risks against which safeguards are desirable in comparison with the costs of providing such safeguards. The cost of an audit so extensive as to safeguard against all risks would be prohibitive; and the problem is, therefore, to develop a general scheme of examination of accounts under which reasonably adequate safeguards may be secured at a cost that will be within the limits of a prudent economy. The position was clearly stated by a partner in one of the signatory firms in 1926 as follows:

In any such work we must be practical; it is no use laying down counsels of perfection or attempting to extend the scope of the audit unduly. An audit is a safeguard; the maintenance of this safeguard entails an expense; and this expense can be justified only if the value of the safeguard is found to be fully commensurate with its cost. The cost of an audit so extensive as to be a complete safeguard would be enormous and far beyond any value to be derived from it. A superficial audit is dangerous because of the sense of false security which it creates. Between the two extremes there lies a mean, at which the audit abundantly justifies its cost.

We are in accord with the general concept of the scope of an examination such as would justify the certification of a balance sheet and income account for submission to stockholders which is implied in the reference to the bulletin "Verification of Financial Statements" contained in the first question asked by the Exchange. That bulletin was designed primarily as a guide to procedure which would afford reasonable assurance that the financial position of the borrower was not less favorable than it was represented by him to be; and, as the bulletin explicitly states, it was not contemplated that such an examination would necessarily disclose under-statements of assets (and profits) resulting from charges to operations of items which might have been carried as assets or defalcations on the part of employees.

This latter point is particularly applicable to financial examinations of larger companies which, generally speaking, constitute the class whose securities are listed on the New York Stock Exchange. Such companies rely on an adequate system of internal check to prevent or disclose defalcations, and independent accountants making a financial examination do not attempt to duplicate the work of the internal auditors.

The bulletin "Verification of Financial Statements," to which reference has been made, was, as was clearly pointed out in the first edition, framed to fit the case of borrowers engaged in business on a relatively small or medium-sized scale. It was recognized in that bulletin (see paragraph 131 of the present edition) that an effective system of internal check would make some portions of the procedure outlined in the bulletin unnecessary. Naturally, the larger a corporation and the more extensive and effective its system of accounting and internal check, the less extensive is the detailed checking necessary to an adequate verification of the balance sheet. Since companies listed on your Exchange are among the larger corporations, it is in general true that the procedure in examinations of annual accounts is less detailed in the case of those companies than in the class of cases which the framers of the bulletin had particularly in mind. It is, however, true, we think, that the examinations made by independent auditors in such cases, coupled with the system of internal check, constitute at least as effective a safeguard as is secured in the case of smaller corporations having a less adequate system of internal check, in the examination of which the procedure outlined in the bulletin has been more closely followed.

The ordinary form of financial examination of listed companies, in so far as it relates to the verification in detail of the income account, is not, we believe, so extensive as that contemplated by the bulletin. To verify this detail would often be a task of a very considerable magnitude, particularly in the case of companies having complex accounting systems, and we question whether the expense of such a verification would be justified by the value to the investor of the results to be attained. The essential point is to guard against any substantial overstatement of income, and this can be reasonably assured by the auditor's satisfying himself of the correctness of the balance sheets at the beginning and end of the period covered by his examination and reviewing the important transactions during the year.

The second point on which information is requested in your letter to listed companies relates to subsidiary companies. This question is obviously pertinent, and presents no difficulty to the accountant called upon to reply to it.

The third question, calling for a statement whether all essential information has been furnished to the auditors contemplates, we take it, that the auditors shall indicate whether all the information which they have deemed essential and sought has been furnished to them. It is obviously conceivable that a management might be in possession of information which would have a material bearing on the accountant's view of the financial position if he knew of its existence, but that the auditor might have no way of discovering that such information existed.

Your fourth question relates to the form in which the accounts are submitted. We take it that you desire to be informed whether the accounts in the opinion of the auditor set forth the results fairly to the extent that they purport to do so, and that the inquiry does not go to the question whether regard for the interests of the stockholders calls for more detailed statements of the financial position and the operations of the company than those now given. The question how much information should be given to stockholders is one on which wide differences of opinion exist, and it is not our understanding that the Exchange is attempting to deal with this point in this inquiry.

Referring to the fifth question, we attach as great importance as the Exchange evidently does to consistency of method in the presentation of financial statements by corporations. The only further comment on this question which seems called for is to emphasize the part which judgment necessarily plays in the determination of results, even if principles are consistently adhered to. There would, we take it, be no objection to an accountant's answering the fifth question in the affirmative, even though in his opinion the judgment of the management had been somewhat more conservative at the close of a year than a year earlier, or vice versa. We think it well to mention this point and to emphasize the fact that accounts must necessarily be largely expressions of judgment, and that the primary responsibility for forming these judgments must rest on the management of the corporation. And though the auditor must assume the duty of expressing his dissent through a qualification in his report, or otherwise, if the conclusions reached by the management are in his opinion manifestly unsound, he does not undertake in practice, and should not, we think, be expected to substitute his judgment for that of the management when the difference is not of major importance, when the management's judgment is not unreasonable, and when he has no reason to question its good faith.

Your sixth question, apart from the specific reference to the principles enumerated, aims, we assume, to insure that companies are following accounting practices which have substantial authority back of them. Answers to this question of an affirmative character will not, of course, be understood as implying that all of the clients of a given firm observe similar or equally conservative practices, either in the case of companies engaged in the same industry or in the case of different industries, or even that the accounting principles adopted are precisely those which the accountant would have himself selected, had the sole choice been his.

We agree with the five general principles enumerated in the memorandum attached to your letter, but it may, we suppose, be understood that rigorous application of these principles is not essential where the amounts involved are relatively insignificant. We mention this point not by way of any substantial reservation, but to avoid possible later criticism based on narrow technicalities.

We shall be glad, if desired, to go further into any of the questions herein discussed, in such a way as may be most convenient to the Exchange.

AMERICAN INSTITUTE OF ACCOUNTANTS

SPECIAL COMMITTEE ON COÖPERATION
WITH STOCK EXCHANGES

135 CEDAR STREET, NEW YORK

December 21, 1933.

MR. J. M. B. HOXSEY, *Executive Assistant,*
  Committee on Stock List
  New York Stock Exchange
  New York, N. Y.

DEAR SIR:

The copy of the communication addressed by your committee to the governing committee of the Stock Exchange under date of October 24, 1933, regarding audits, which was sent to the President of the American Institute of Accountants, has been referred to this committee. We welcome the suggestion that the matters therein dealt with should be brought to the attention of listed companies and organized bodies of accountants and accounting officers, and shall be glad to coöperate with the Exchange in the manner contemplated.

We are glad to note that the replies received to the letter of the President of the Exchange dated January 31, 1933, indicate general acceptance of the principles set forth in the communication of this committee to the Exchange dated September 22, 1932, and we propose to recommend to the Institute that these rules, and such acceptance, should be brought to the attention of all members of the Institute.

We have noted with interest the views expressed by the committee on stock list with regard to the problem of safeguarding the transactions of corporations. While agreeing with your committee that in the case of large companies the safeguarding of transactions is primarily a matter of internal organization, we should like to make it clear that we fully appreciate the value of the detailed audit in appropriate cases. Where the internal check and control are necessarily limited or severely restricted, the detailed audit serves a most useful purpose, though no audit should be regarded as taking the place of sound measures of internal check and control, except in cases where the organization is so small as to make adequate internal check impracticable.

We believe that accountants, in cases where they do not make a detailed audit, now regard it as a part of their duty to inquire into the system of internal check—indeed, this duty is expressly recognized in the pamphlet "Verification of Financial Statements" as revised by the American Institute of Accountants in 1929, the first sentence of the general instructions contained in that pamphlet reading in part:

The scope of the work indicated in these instructions includes . . . an examination of the accounting system for the purpose of ascertaining the effectiveness of the internal check.

We would, however, point out that it is always a matter of judgment on the part of corporate management to weigh the risks against which safeguards are desirable in comparison with the cost of providing safeguards. The whole matter lies in the field of discretion, and if in any case a defalcation should occur and escape detection, the accountants cannot be expected to accept any financial responsibility, but only to accept such blame as may attach to a possible error of judgment on their part with respect to their review of the methods and extent of the internal check and control. The effect on the reputation of a public accountant, arising from such an error of judgment, is serious and quite sufficient to ensure care on his part.

We agree with your committee in the view that auditors cannot properly disclaim all responsibility for the correctness of the classification of an income or profit-and-loss account merely because they are not in a position to assume full responsibility therefor. Your suggestion that auditors should "accept the burden of seeing that the income received and the expenditures made are properly classified in so far as the facts are known to them or are ascertainable by reasonable inquiry" seems to us a reasonable one, and we believe it is calculated to afford investors in the great majority of cases the protection which your committee desires. Our only further comment on this portion of the communication is that where the facts are clearly disclosed on the face of the statement it may not be necessary for the accountants to embody a qualification in their report.

We agree that the problem of reflecting the operations of subsidiary and controlled companies is one of real difficulty. Experience here and abroad confirms the view that there is no single satisfactory solution. We believe, however, that if corporate managements and accounting officers approach the question with an honest desire to make the statements as fair and informative as possible, a solution appropriate to each individual case will always be found, and we propose to ask the Institute to bring the point to the attention of all its members and urge their fullest coöperation to this end.

We shall be very glad to join in any coöperative effort to develop a form of accountants' reports which will be more valuable to investors. We agree that such reports should be so framed as to constitute answers to the three questions contained in President Whitney's letter of January 31, 1933, mentioned by you; *viz.:*

Whether in their [*i.e.*, the auditors'] opinion the form of the balance sheet and of the income, or profit-and-loss, account is such as fairly to present the financial position and the results of operation.
Whether the accounts are in their opinion fairly determined on the basis of consistent application of the system of accounting regularly employed by the company.
Whether such system in their opinion conforms to accepted accounting practices, and particularly whether it is in any respect inconsistent with any of the principles set forth in the statement attached hereto.

We think it desirable, also, as suggested in our report of September 22, 1932, to emphasize the fact that accounts, and consequently any statements or reports based thereon, are necessarily in large measure expressions of opinion. To this end, we think it desirable that the document signed by the accountants should be in the form of a report, as in England, rather than a certificate, and that the words "in our (my) opinion" should always be embodied therein. It is impracticable to indicate in a standard form of report exactly the procedure followed, since it will vary in different cases, and it will be desirable to use language which may understate what has been done rather than to incur the risk of the extent of the examination being exaggerated by the reader.

With these considerations in mind, we have drafted as a

basis for discussion a form of report, a copy of which, with some explanatory notes, is attached hereto, and we should be glad to have an expression of opinion thereupon from your committee or others interested. As indicated in the first note, it would be our view that before issuing such a report as we have drafted the accountant should have at least made an examination of the character outlined in the bulletin, "Verification of Financial Statements" as interpreted in the communication of your committee to the governing committee of the Exchange dated October 24, 1933.

With renewed assurance of our willingness to coöperate, and awaiting your advice as to the way in which you think such coöperation can best be extended, we are

Yours very truly,

GEORGE O. MAY, *Chairman*.

REVISED SUGGESTION OF A FORM OF ACCOUNTANTS' REPORT

TO THE XYZ COMPANY:

We have made an examination of the balance sheet of the XYZ Company as at December 31, 1933, and of the statement of income and surplus for the year 1933. In connection therewith, we examined or tested accounting records of the Company and other supporting evidence and obtained information and explanations from officers and employees of the Company; we also made a general review of the accounting methods and of the operating and income accounts for the year, but we did not make a detailed audit of the transactions.

In our opinion, based upon such examination, the accompanying balance sheet and related statement of income and surplus fairly present, in accordance with accepted principles of accounting consistently maintained by the Company during the year under review, its position at December 31, 1933, and the results of its operations for the year.

NOTES

1. It is contemplated that before signing a report of the type suggested, the accountant should have at least made an examination of the character outlined in the bulletin, "Verification of Financial Statements," as interpreted in the communication of the Committee on Stock List to the Governing Committee dated October 24, 1933.

2. The report should be addressed to the directors of the company or to the stockholders, if the appointment is made by them.

3. The statement of what has been examined would, of course, conform to the titles of the accounts or statements reported upon.

4. In the second sentence, any special forms of confirmation could be mentioned: *e.g.,* "including confirmation of cash and securities by inspection or certificates from depositaries."

5. This certificate is appropriate only if the accounting for the year is consistent in basis with that for the preceding year. If there has been any material change either in accounting principles or in the manner of their application, the nature of the change should be indicated.

6. It is contemplated that the form of report would be modified when and as necessary to embody any qualifications, reservations or supplementary explanations.

XIII

THE IMPORTANCE OF INSISTING ON SOUND METHODS OF ACCOUNTING *

(1933)

THE recent action of the New York Stock Exchange and the similar action on the part of the Curb and the New York Produce Exchanges, which followed quickly, mark a very important step in the development of financial auditing. These developments are undoubtedly due largely to the experience in the Kreuger and other cases. That experience has also created a demand for legislation for the protection of investors which might or might not be of a character favorable to the profession. In our view, the profession stands today at a critical moment in its history, and on the way in which it discharges the responsibilities placed upon it within the next year or two will depend to a very large extent its future.

Holding these views, and realizing as we do the responsibilities which attach to the position our firm holds in the profession, we wish to impress on all offices the importance of insisting on sound methods of accounting and presentation of facts, however difficult the circumstances may be and however important may be the client with whom the questions are raised. We are perfectly prepared to sacrifice present business and profits to maintain the position of the firm and discharge our obligations to the profession, and have no doubt that such a policy will also prove ultimately the most profitable. Naturally, we do not wish to be too technical, nor to attempt to override ruthlessly the judgment of directors and officials; but we must not lay ourselves open to the criticism of being subservient to our clients.

* A letter to all United States and Canadian offices of Price, Waterhouse & Co., January 16, 1933.

145

We request that you bring to the notice of this office any proposals as to the form or substance of accounts with which you are not in entire agreement and upon which you are not able to induce your clients to accept your views.   In this way you can share with this office the responsibility of deciding whether to withdraw objections or to insist on a position whatever the consequences may be.

We must, of course, have proper regard for the views of directors, but we should be careful not to allow ourselves to be put in the position of accepting views with which we are not in full accord on the plea that the directors have determined the question, without satisfying ourselves that the views are really those of the directors and not merely those of the officers, and that the directors have reached their conclusions with the full knowledge of the considerations which have led us to disagree therewith.

This general question is likely to be under discussion in the Institute and with the exchanges in the near future, but we think it is well to write you promptly so that there may be no question of our failing to recognize our full duty to the profession at this time.   Obviously, unless the leading firms take a stand for proper principles when the necessity arises, it is not fairly to be expected that the smaller firms, which occupy a much less favorable position, will do so.

PART II
DEPRECIATION

I

THE PROBLEM OF DEPRECIATION *

(1915)

IN recent years the problem of depreciation has received steadily increasing attention as its importance has become more widely recognized. Its treatment even today is, however, not in general adequate or satisfactory, and undoubtedly this condition is in a large measure attributable to a failure to appreciate fully the many-sided character of the problem. In this article, therefore, an attempt will be made to analyze it and to point out its more important features, and at the same time some consideration will be given to the question as to how far the problem is one of accounting and how far it is one of physical inspection and valuation.

In the first place it is necessary to consider the causes which contribute to bring about depreciation and the influences which tend to modify or obscure its effects.

The most convenient subdivision of the natural causes of depreciation is threefold:

(1) Fall in new value due entirely to external conditions and not caused in any way by age or change in conditions of use of the property;
(2) Exhaustion through age or wear of the property;
(3) Obsolescence or supersession by superior types or methods.

.   .   .   .

The essential distinction between the three causes of depreciation is readily apparent. The first is an influence which is spasmodic and uncertain, and its effect today may

* The Journal of Accountancy, Vol. XIX (January, 1915), pp. 1-13.

be offset by an exactly opposite tendency tomorrow. The second is a relentless force operating continuously in one direction only. Its effects may be modified by skillful, or aggravated by unskillful, management, just as human life may be prolonged by care and shortened by neglect; but its ultimate effects are certain. The third cause is like the second in that it operates in one direction only, but differs in that its operation is not steady and persistent but extremely uncertain. In some industries at some stages it may almost cease to be felt; in other industries or at other stages it may be the most potent influence of the three.

In any consideration of the question of depreciation the corresponding question of appreciation cannot be ignored. The word "appreciation" is etymologically so precisely the converse of "depreciation" that the element is often regarded as an equally complete offset to the element of depreciation. It is important, however, to note that (except possibly as to the increase in efficiency up to the point that a plant has "found itself") appreciation is practically the converse only of the first class of depreciation above enumerated.

In addition to causes beyond human control, depreciation may arise from causes which are within human control, such as neglect, misuse or disuse; on the other hand, depreciation may be arrested or diminished by human effort either through renewals which restore usefulness or changes which arrest obsolescence.

Any adequate disposition of the question of depreciation must, therefore, deal with numerous influences which may be conveniently tabulated as follows:

Causes	*Countervailing Influences*
Beyond human control	*Beyond human control*
Fall in new value	Rise in new value
Exhaustion	
Obsolescence	

Causes	Countervailing Influences
Within human control	*Within human control*
Neglect	Renewals which prolong useful life
Misuse	Changes to retard obsolescence
Disuse	

The next step in any attempt to deal with the problem must be a consideration of the purposes for which depreciation is required to be measured. These purposes may be stated broadly as twofold:

(1) In order to determine the value of property; and
(2) To ascertain what provision is required to be made out of earnings before the true operating profit can be determined.

Considering these two purposes in relation to the foregoing analysis of the classes of depreciation, it is apparent that the depreciation due to fluctuations in new value and the corresponding appreciation have a very important bearing on the valuation of property, but have no proper place in the determination of the results of operations. Property employed in operation is not purchased with a view to sale but, with the exception of land, is intended to be used in production and distribution. Therefore, any increase or decrease in the new value thereof has little or no practical bearing on the question of operations. In an extreme case the fall in new values may be so great as to render a unit obsolete, but such cases are comparatively infrequent and form a part of the problem of obsolescence rather than a part of the question of fluctuations in new value. In measuring depreciation for operating purposes, therefore, fluctuations in new value may be and usually are disregarded, but in any attempt to maintain continuously a figure of capital investment based on valuation these fluctuations would be a most important and difficult factor to deal with.

In the case of obsolescence the difficulties are greater from the operating than from the valuation point of view. In dealing with this question for the purpose of valuation of any unit it is sufficient to determine whether changes in methods or types have already taken place to such an extent as to cause an impairment in its value beyond the impairment due to exhaustion. From an accounting standpoint it is necessary to go further and in fixing charges against operations to allow for the probability that in the future the life of the unit will be terminated by obsolescence rather than by exhaustion.

The uncertainty as to the precise effects of obsolescence is sometimes urged as an argument in favor of making no provision therefor; but though the effect of obsolescence on individual units is uncertain, it is usually possible to estimate its effects on the operations of a business as a whole—and depreciation schemes are almost necessarily based on averages. Moreover, unless some provision is made, it will be necessary to write off large sums against operations when units are abandoned on account of obsolescence before being exhausted by use. A failure to provide for obsolescence is therefore open to the objection that it tends towards wider fluctuation in results and is lacking in conservatism. If a provision is made on a larger scale than proves necessary the ultimate result will be merely to increase profits in the future. If, however, provision is omitted, it may result in inability to meet requirements for modernizing in the future which may be essential to the continued success or even to the existence of the business.

The proper course is, therefore, clearly to attempt to provide in advance for obsolescence, though on account of the uncertainty characterizing the element such an allowance cannot be calculated with the same degree of accuracy as that for exhaustion of life through use or wear. All that can be done is to make the provision as accurate as possible by the exercise of good judgment and by frequent revisions and reconsiderations of operating conditions.

The foregoing considerations suggest the reason for the difference between engineers and accountants in their attitude on the subject of depreciation. Engineers are more frequently required to consider the question from the standpoint of valuation; accountants are usually concerned to ascertain the proper charge against operations. As has been indicated, the problems have very different features; indeed, it is not going too far to say that periodical valuations may be a hindrance rather than an aid to an accountant in the determination of a proper charge for depreciation.

To illustrate this point:

Assume a plant unit of which copper is an important part, say, for simplicity, one containing 5,000 pounds of copper, and whose cost, apart from the copper, is $200. If bought when copper is at 16¢ it would cost $1,000 and naturally the new value would fluctuate $50 for every fluctuation of 1¢ in the price of copper.

Now assume that a valuer making periodical inspections and valuations finds the depreciated value to be 96% of new value at the end of the first year; 92% at the end of the second year; and 89% at the end of the third year; and that at the end of those years the price of copper is 18¢, 13¢ and 15¢.

From the standpoint of valuation—

at the end of the first year the new value of the unit
would be $1,100 and the depreciated value 96%
of $1,100, or $1,056, showing an appreciation of $ 56.00
at the end of the second year the new value would
be $850 and the depreciated value 92% of $850,
or $782, showing a depreciation for the year of.. 274.00
at the end of the third year the new value would be
$950 and the depreciated value 89% of $950, or
$845.50, showing an appreciation of........... 63.50

From an accounting standpoint the operations of the first year would be considered chargeable with 4% of $1,000, or $40, instead of being credited with $56; the second year would similarly be chargeable with $40 instead of $274; and the operations of the third year would be chargeable with $30 instead of being credited with $63.50.

The illustration is perhaps an extreme one, but it serves

to bring out the dangers involved in basing depreciation charges against operations on periodical valuations without further analysis.

The fairly common opinion that periodical valuations form the best, if not the only satisfactory, way of dealing with depreciation does not stand analysis. The object of a valuation is to determine the present depreciated value of property in use, and before the depreciated value can be ascertained it is necessary to establish the basis upon which the total ultimate loss from depreciation on any given unit shall be distributed as between the part of the term of use of the unit already expired and the part still lying in the future. Moreover, the final valuation is liable to be so largely affected by fluctuations in new value (which must be excluded from consideration in measuring depreciation from use and obsolescence) as to make it by itself quite inconclusive on this point. This is not to say that the work of the valuer may not be made extremely useful in considering the depreciation problem.

The work of inventorying and the observation of the present condition, which are a part of the valuation, are of course of the utmost value in the determination of a proper charge to operations. The work of the valuer can, however, be useful to the accountant only for the purpose of fixing charges against operations if the latter has an opportunity to analyze the valuation and ascertain how much of the change in value between two dates results from factors of which the accountant must take cognizance in order to arrive at correct operating results, and how far it is due to mere fluctuations in new value which for that purpose should be entirely excluded from consideration.

The fact is that while the phrase "depreciation" strictly covers a decline in value from any conceivable cause, its use in accounting practice is generally in a more narrow and restricted sense, and many of the difficulties which the accountant has to face in his efforts to secure a proper treatment of the subject arise from misapprehensions as to the precise meaning of the term. To those approaching the subject for the first time or looking at it superficially an entirely wrong line of thought is suggested by the word "depreciation"; it immediately suggests appreciation. A manufacturer who is urged to provide for depreciation of his plant replies that it is fully offset by appreciation in his real estate, or other assets, and the etymological correspondence between the two words is so complete that he regards the offset as being as natural and perfect as that between debit and credit. If he were carrying on his books 1,000 tons of material of which 50 tons had been consumed and he were asked to write off that 50 tons he would concede the propriety of the request at once and his thoughts would not in the same way turn to the appreciation of his real estate. A little consideration will show that the exhaustion in the course of manufacture of one year's useful life of a plant which can only be expected to last twenty years is practically identical in its nature with the use of 50 tons of material out of a total stock of 1,000 tons.

Many attempts have been made to meet the terminological difficulty, but it is not easy to bring a new phrase into general use or to devise one which will be both short and clear. "Expired outlay on productive plant" is a phrase suggested and used by one English authority, and whilst it is not everything that could be desired in simplicity and brevity, it does have the merit of suggesting the real nature of what is commonly termed "depreciation of plant" more clearly than does the latter phrase. It does emphasize the fact that it is not merely a decline in value but a permanent exhaustion that is taking place; and this is the fact which needs to be emphasized and reiterated until it is fully recognized and accepted.

If the necessity of distinguishing between fluctuations in new value and actual exhaustion of useful life of a plant be conceded, it still remains to consider whether both should find expression in a company's accounts. At first sight such a course may seem desirable, as it has the apparent merit of keeping the books in closer accord with existing conditions; but upon fuller consideration it is questionable whether it is wise to advocate such a course in the case of a going concern. In the present state of the law it seems clear that there is no obligation on a company to provide for a decline in new value of fixed assets, and the probable result of advocacy of the policy of adjusting fixed properties to valuations would be that such adjustments would be made where the valuations exceed the book figures but not where the tendency is in the opposite direction.

The idea of writing plant values up to valuation figures is usually attractive to the owner of the plant. Such a course results in a surplus which, however incapable it may be of being distributed, is still a surplus. Possibly also the suggestion of skill or good judgment in the original construction or acquisition of the plant implied in the adjustment appeals to him. The benefits are, however, largely illusory. Appraisals are so much a matter of individual opinion and temperament that men of wide business experience attach little weight to a surplus resulting from an appraisal; and, on the other hand, if the property is adjusted to higher values the depreciation charges to be made out of future operations must be correspondingly increased so that ultimately the amount added in a lump to plant values, other than real estate and surplus, has to be wrung in annual installments out of operations.

In cases where new value is less than original cost, operating officials may urge that the valuation should be recognized and that the plant be charged only with depreciation based on the new and lower values. They may argue that it is not fair that their operations should be burdened with a depreciation charge based on prices which were paid before they were responsible for the operations of the plant and which are in excess of the price at which replacements could now be effected. No year's operations of a plant are complete in themselves; in innumerable ways they derive the benefits or inherit the burdens resulting from transactions of the past, and the primary requirement is clearly to ascertain the results of operations under the conditions which do exist and not upon the basis of imaginary conditions which might have existed. In judging the efficiency of the management by comparisons with other plants it may be entirely proper to make allowance for higher capital costs and for every other operating advantage or disadvantage attaching to the plant; but before and beyond all these more speculative calculations the essential problem is clearly to ascertain the results of things as they are.

A further question may possibly arise as to whether obsolescence should be dealt with as a separate problem. There is much to be said for such a course or at least for dealing with the question of exhaustion of life in two parts: first, by a carefully calculated provision based on what can reasonably be foreseen; and secondly, by a more general provision for possible curtailment of life through unexpected developments. Thus a manufacturer may be satisfied to buy a machine with the expectation that apart from obsolescence it will do service for from twenty to thirty years and with a realization of the probability that apart altogether from wear it is to be expected that developments in the art will make it wise to abandon the unit in twenty years or so. There is, of course, always the possibility that some totally unexpected development may render it obsolete in three, or five, or ten years, and conservatism would call for some recognition of this possibility.

In these circumstances it would seem entirely reasonable to make provision for depreciation based on estimated life somewhat shorter than the maximum life apart from obsolescence (say, in the illustrative case mentioned, twenty years) and to supplement such provision by a general provision out of earnings against which could be charged losses resulting from unusually rapid obsolescence. On the other hand, all provisions for exhaustion of life are uncertain, and to many an attempt to deal separately with the different degrees of uncertainty may seem an unnecessary or useless refinement.

The question is one largely of temperament. A manufacturer who is willing to give the necessary time and attention to deal with the problem in detail may probably find the subdivision valuable; a manufacturer who is content to look at the matter more broadly and to aim at safely conservative rather than exact calculations may find it unnecessary. The question is not, like the distinction between exhaustion of life and fluctuations in value, fundamental, since all exhaustion of life, whether due to wear or obsolescence, must be provided for out of the operations before a profit can safely be said to have been earned.

The next subject for consideration is depreciation due to causes which are within human control. In establishing provisions for depreciation it is usually assumed that everything that is practical and economical in the way of current maintenance will be done to prolong the life and the cost thereof absorbed in operations quite apart from the depreciation provision. There is often some difficulty in discriminating between maintenance charges which should be so absorbed and renewals which fall within the classification next to be considered, and on this account the course of making one provision to cover maintenance and depreciation has been advocated and is sometimes adopted; but while in some cases such a method may give good results, it is scarcely suited for general adoption.

The cost of current maintenance varies largely with the efficiency of the management. The work if carried out economically at opportune times may cost far less than it would if less efficiently conducted. The old proverb that "a stitch in time saves nine" emphasizes the saving which is effected by making needed repairs promptly and the dangers of deferment. Repairs which are made with the plant's own facilities at slack times should cost less than repairs carried out by outside contractors at less favorable times.

To merge the question of maintenance with that of depreciation therefore involves adding considerably to the possibilities of error in the provision made. Another disadvantage of the method is that it affords an opportunity of unduly relieving operating expenses by charges against the fixed provision set aside. If the manager of a plant knows that his operations are charged with a fixed sum to cover both depreciation and current maintenance, he will realize that every dollar he can charge to maintenance rather than to operations will result in an increase in the amount of the apparent profits from his operation. Another disadvantage is that no incentive is given to the manager to be economical in his maintenance work. For these reasons it is usually desirable to deal with current maintenance entirely apart from depreciation. It should perhaps be noted that where depreciation has not been provided and an attempt is being made to restate accounts to include a proper provision therefor, maintenance expenditures must be considered, as in such cases usually amounts will have been charged to maintenance which if a depreciation reserve had existed would properly have been charged against the reserve.

Turning now to the countervailing influences of renewals and changes, a fundamental question arises which it is essential to decide when the formulation of any depreciation scheme is under consideration.

The problem of depreciation is often broadly stated to be that of distributing the cost of plant (less salvage) over its estimated life,* and it is not always realized that this is only true if the phrase "estimated life" is used in one of the two widely different senses in which it is used in different depreciation schemes. Estimated life may mean either maximum life of a unit extended to the uttermost by rebuilding and renewals or the minimum life ignoring any such possible extensions. If estimated life is used in the former sense renewals must clearly not be charged against the pro-

---

* An alternative theory is that business may be regarded as permanent and that the problem of depreciation is to provide the sums necessary to renew units as such renewal becomes necessary. The comparative merits of the two theories form an interesting question which is, however, beyond the scope of this article. The principal difference is that the sum to be provided on the renewal theory is based on probable cost of replacement rather than upon original cost of units.

visions thus created but must be absorbed as an additional charge to operations; and, moreover, the scheme will not distribute the loss from wear and tear equitably over the period of years but will result in heavy charges in those years in which renewal and rebuilding take place. If, however, estimated life is used in the alternative sense of a minimum life, then all renewals and rebuildings which substantially prolong life are properly chargeable against the fund and the burden of wear and tear is distributed equitably as between years. Probably the majority of depreciation schemes are based on the last-mentioned conception of estimated life, but a notable example of the alternative course is the scheme of depreciation on railroad equipment now in force.

Another problem offering some difficulty is that of distinguishing between renewals which may be charged against the depreciation fund and repairs which must be charged against operations. Whilst this difficulty undoubtedly exists, it is true of all classifications that they merge one into another, and in recent years marked progress has been made in the direction of an adequate and practicable distinction between repairs and renewals.

Summarizing the considerations affecting the various causes of depreciation and the relations of the accountant and other experts thereto, it may be said that the rise or fall in new values is entirely a question for the valuer and is of relatively little importance to the accountant, since its bearing is limited to the determination of present value for special purposes and since it should not enter into revenue accounts and is not necessarily (or perhaps even preferably) recorded in the books of account at all. The accountant's main concern with this element is to ensure that its operations are not allowed to obscure the effects of the other elements.

The question of the exhaustion of useful life is one of estimate based on experience and checked by observation, and enters into the problem to an equal extent whether depreciation is sought to be measured from the standpoint of valuation or of operating results. It is both difficult and important; and operating officials, valuers and accountants can usefully contribute towards securing the best possible treatment of it.

The question of obsolescence is one of observation so far as the present valuation is concerned, and one of judgment and conservatism from the standpoint of operating results. On this point the experience of the operator familiar with the industry and the conservatism of the accountant can usually be combined to reach a sound conclusion.

As to depreciation due to causes within human control, provisions for exhaustion are usually based on the assumption that the property will be as fully maintained as possible out of operations. Whether the assumption in a particular case is valid is clearly a question which cannot be completely answered from the books and records only. An examination of maintenance accounts may indicate that the expenditures made have not been sufficient for the proper current maintenance of the plant; but even if the amounts expended are such as would, if well spent, suffice for that purpose, it is still possible that the expenditures may have been injudiciously made and the property allowed to fall below the proper standard of maintenance. On the other hand, the plant may have been maintained to the satisfaction of an engineer but the books may show that the cost has in part been excluded from operations. Consequently, coöperation between engineer or valuer and accountant is required to deal with the question.

As to the countervailing influences of renewals and changes to restore usefulness or prolong life, their treatment depends on the general theory of depreciation adopted. This whole branch of the depreciation problem can most effectively be dealt with by a careful analysis of expenditures and reports of the precise nature of any work undertaken not obviously in the nature of current maintenance, and falls therefore to the accountant. It would, of course, be possible for a valuer making periodical inventories and valuations of the plant to ascertain the amount of such renewals by careful comparison of the inventories, but the accounting record will usually be the safer guide, though inventories may be useful as a check thereof.

From the foregoing brief analysis of the problem of depreciation, its complexities are apparent. It is also evident that the problem is not one with which the accountant can deal adequately single-handed, but that the services of skilled operators or engineers are required if the most accurate solution is to be reached. It is, however, equally clear that the accountant cannot be ignored in any attempt to deal to the best possible advantage with the problem. In many phases he is the primary authority, and while an engineer or other technically qualified person may be needed to pass upon other phases, the services of the accountant are again necessary to ensure a proper correspondence between the physical facts and book records.

It is recognized that the real difficulties arise after the problem of depreciation has been stated and when the attempt has been made to reach a solution thereof in practice. An adequate conception of the questions involved is, however, not only essential to the accountant to whom falls this difficult task but extremely desirable in all those called upon to decide whether his recommendations shall be carried out, many of whom today oppose proper treatment merely through lack of comprehension of the problem itself.

II

ON A PROPOSED DEFINITION OF DEPRECIATION *

(1922)

The basic idea conveyed by this word is indicated by its derivation—*de,* down, and *pretium,* price—that is, a reduction in price or value.

Depreciation is loss in physical or functional value of physical property other than wasting assets due primarily and chiefly to ordinary wear and tear which has occurred *theoretically* in the past and which is not offset by adequate repairs and/or replacements. Obsolescence and inadequacy are included by regulatory bodies and taxing authorities as contributory causes, but it is more in accordance with fact to treat these two elements as separate from ordinary wear and tear on the ground that the loss incident thereto does not usually accrue and cannot be foreseen with any degree of accuracy. Depreciation, however determined, is at best only an *estimate.* [Cf. *The Journal of Accountancy,* Vol. XXXIV (1922), p. 232.]

I think it is unfortunate to stress the derivation of the word "depreciation," because the basic idea of depreciation as used in accounting practice is not primarily one of values but one of exhaustion of useful life. The word "theoretically" used in the second paragraph of the definition seems to me wholly out of place; it is not a question of theory but of fair assignment of the total loss ultimately to be liquidated, as between the period already elapsed and the period remaining in the future. I agree that depreciation is necessarily an estimate but, as Lord Justice Buckley said: "The ascertainment of profit is in every case necessarily a matter of estimate and opinion." The provision for extraordinary storms, etc., referred to in the definition seems to me altogether unrelated to depreciation; moreover, to my mind it

* From a letter written in 1922.

is not only irrelevant but essentially different in character. Depreciation is something which must be provided before a profit can be said to have been made; a provision for a contingency which may or may not happen in the future is a reservation of profits.

I gather that some accountants do not agree with this view and that they regard a provision for depreciation as a reserve coming literally within the terms of the definition of a reserve as a segregation of profits. Such a reserve is often loosely spoken of as being provided out of profits, but strictly speaking the phrase should be "provided out of gross profits or earnings." And the reserve is sometimes regarded as remaining a part of the undivided profits or surplus. This view was frequently expressed twenty-five years ago when I first started practice, but so far as my experience qualifies me to express an opinion the vast majority of bankers, business men and accountants, both practical and theoretical, have by now completely discarded it. When the Interstate Commerce Commission and innumerable public service commissions have ruled that depreciation is an operating expense, and when Congress has provided that depreciation is a proper deduction from gross income in determining net income, it seems to me idle for any accountant to take the stand that depreciation is a segregation of profits. It reminds one of the ancient remark of the fond mother as the regiment passed by: "They are all out of step except our Jock."

Depreciation undoubtedly is an extremely difficult problem and I do not know whether the most satisfactory exposition of just what it is, is not that I heard given many years ago by a very brilliant lawyer; I am afraid, however, it would not be suitable for your purpose. He said that depreciation always seemed to him to be like the advertisement of Ivory Soap: you looked at it from one angle when you were going up before a public service commission and all you could read was "$99\frac{44}{100}$ pure"; you looked at it from another side when you were trying to sell securities and all you could read was "It Floats"; and the rest of the time you looked straight at it and it was just plain "Ivory Soap" and God knew what that was. I cannot help thinking that the drafter of your definition has looked at the advertisement too much from the first-mentioned side and that his views have been colored by his close association with one important industry to which it has seemed advantageous to get a higher capital value for rate purposes by ignoring all depreciation in excess of observed depreciation, even at the price of surrendering any claim for such depreciation as a part of its operating costs.

III

"A CONFUSION OF TERMS" *

(1927)

Editor, The Journal of Accountancy:

Sir: There are a number of points in Professor Cole's interesting article in your March number † which it would be interesting to discuss.

I am, for instance, less amazed at the difficulty which some business men find in interpreting financial statements to which he refers than the certitude with which others interpret them and the undue significance they attribute to their interpretations.

Again, while I agree with Professor Cole that the significance of a reserve for depreciation is frequently misapprehended, I believe that far more misapprehension arises in respect of the word "depreciation" than in respect of the word "reserve." Professor Cole seems at times to be himself a victim of this misapprehension. The reserve for depreciation of plant in common practice is not an attempt to measure "overvaluation of assets." The treatment of depreciation is based not on valuation, but on exhaustion. Depreciation is frequently provided where values are increasing.

My object in this letter is, however, merely to suggest a solution of the problem of ambiguity in the use of the word "reserve" different from that proposed by Professor Cole.

The use of the term "reserve" for profits withheld from distribution is, I think, becoming less and less frequent in the United States. The practice of allocating practically the whole of the profits of a year, which is usual in England, is not ordinarily followed here. Where they appropriate part

* *The Journal of Accountancy*, Vol. XLIII (1927), pp. 310-11.
† W. M. Cole, "A Confusion of Terms," *ibid.*, pp. 192-98.

of the profits for dividends and carry a further sum to "general reserve," leaving a small amount to be carried forward in undivided profits account, we should ordinarily declare the dividend and allow the balance automatically to fall into surplus. The fact that surplus is unavailable for distribution in dividends and not intended to be so used is sometimes emphasized by showing it as "appropriated surplus." It might be satisfactory and probably it would be easier to standardize the use of "appropriated surplus" in the sense to which Professor Cole would restrict the word "reserve" and limit the word "reserve" to those uses to which he would apply the terms "allowance" and "provision."

I cannot agree with Professor Cole that such a use of the word "reserve" is incorrect. It is quite true that what he would call an allowance for depreciation is not a reservation of profits, but it is a reservation nevertheless (if not of gross income at least of gross proceeds from sale), and there is no reason why a reserve should necessarily be a reserve of profits. One advantage of the course I have suggested is that a reservation of profits is a part of surplus, not something distinct from surplus, and is therefore most appropriately described by the use of the word "surplus" with a qualifying word or phrase which indicates in what respect it differs from the rest of the surplus.

This leaves the term "reserve" available for the use in the sense in which it is, I believe, most commonly used in this country—a reservation out of the gross proceeds of past business to meet charges which will or may arise in the future out of that business.

From the standpoint of history, convenience, practicability and psychology, I believe this line of distinction is preferable to the distinction suggested by Professor Cole.

Yours truly,

GEORGE O. MAY.

March 14, 1927.

IV

RAILROAD DEPRECIATION *

(I.C.C. NO. 15100)

(1927)

THE Transportation Act of 1920 requires the Interstate Commerce Commission to determine:

The classes of property for which depreciation charges may properly be included under operating expenses and the percentages of depreciation which shall be charged with respect to each of such classes of property. (Section 20, Paragraph 5.)

Depreciation charges into operating expenses may, I assume, properly be made if they tend to produce results which will be superior to those derived without such charges. The superiority may consist in greater theoretical accuracy, a more equitable or more convenient distribution of burdens as between the carriers and the public, or greater simplicity—or these various considerations may be in part conflicting and the propriety of the system of depreciation charges may depend on where the balance of advantage lies, which in turn may depend on the importance attached to the possibly conflicting considerations of theory, simplicity, equity and convenience.

It could scarcely be held that a system which was both theoretically sound and equitable must be rejected on the ground that it involved complexities and inconvenience, though where equity is not involved, convenience and simplicity might well outweigh purely theoretical considerations.

It may, therefore, be most convenient to consider the Com-

* Memorandum submitted November 1, 1927, in relation to the Report of the Interstate Commerce Commission in No. 151000, set for rehearing on November 9, 1927.

168

mission's scheme primarily from the standpoints of theory and equity. In such an approach to the problem three major questions arise:

The relation of the problem to that of valuation, involving consideration of the principles of valuation to be assumed for the purposes of considering this relationship.

The relation of the problem to that of maintenance in general, involving consideration of the principles governing the determination of charges against operating expenses in respect of all forms of property exhaustion.

The relation of the problems to the practice in the past, involving consideration of the proper treatment of any depreciation which would, upon the scheme proposed, be deemed to have accrued in the past.

I propose to discuss these three aspects of the problem in turn, dealing in connection with each phase with any major considerations of convenience or practicability which seem to me to have a bearing on the question.

RELATION OF THE PROBLEM TO VALUATION

Depreciation in its broadest sense is a lessening of worth from any cause whatsoever; it is, however, commonly used to signify the lessening of worth in service due to exhaustion of useful life, other factors in value being left out of account. Depreciation charges, moreover, are frequently made on still another basis which does not necessarily imply any very close relation to the rate of lessening of value—namely, such a basis as will in a systematic way distribute the original value of a property unit (less estimated salvage, if any) over the probable term of its useful life. The last is the sense in which the term is commonly used in industrial practice, the distribution of the charge for the unit over its useful life being based on a variety of considerations, and bearing little relation to the course of values during that life.

The language of the Act clearly excludes the possibility that Congress used the word "depreciation" in Section 20 in its broadest sense. Declines in the value of property due to purely external causes are not chargeable to operating ex-

penses nor are they capable of determination on any percentage basis. The language of the Section is not, however,
sufficient to determine what was intended as between the
second and third concepts of depreciation charges above
mentioned, and it would therefore seem that the decision
must be governed by consideration of the general purposes
of the Act and of other acts regulating relations between
the carriers and the public.

One of the main purposes of the Act was to provide for
the determination from time to time of the fair value of the
property of carriers, and to regulate rates and limit the returns to the carriers on the basis thereof. The question arises,
then, whether Congress contemplated that the depreciation
charges referred to in Paragraph 5 of Section 20 above quoted
should enter into the determination of the fair value of the
property as well as into the determination of operating expenses.

The Commission proceeds on the hypothesis that there is
necessarily a direct and immediate connection between the
charging of depreciation to operating expenses and the determination of the rate base value; it says (Report, page
310):

In our consideration, therefore, of the relative burdens
imposed by the depreciation and retirement methods of
accounting, *we must start with the premise that the former
presupposes full deduction of accrued depreciation in ascertaining the rate base value* . . .

If this premise be accepted it follows that the depreciation
system must be one that not only results in a fair charge
against operating expenses but also measures with substantial
accuracy the lessening of worth in service due to exhaustion
of useful life.

The approach to the question as a dual one, affecting both
operating expense and the rate base, presents serious difficulties.

While the Commission proceeds on the hypothesis that the

depreciation charged into operating expenses must be deducted from the rate base, the Supreme Court has made it clear that the rate base must represent the fair present value, and that in determining that fair value the lessening of worth as compared with new value must be not wholly theoretical or based on percentages of general application, but primarily founded on observation.

There is obvious difficulty in attempting to reconcile the two positions. In so far as it is possible to do so at all, the result can be achieved only by adopting a theory of depreciation which will measure with reasonable accuracy the lessening of worth for use in the service due to exhaustion of useful life, on the basis of cost, and of normal maintenance, leaving modifications in respect of variations in new value and of maintenance above or below normal to be dealt with separately. The straight line method which the Commission proposes to enforce wholly fails to meet this requirement.

THE STRAIGHT LINE METHOD OF WRITING OFF DEPRECIATION IS DEMONSTRABLY INAPPLICABLE TO THE COMPUTATION OF VALUES

If property be conceived, as the Commission conceives it, as representing a capacity for uniform service at a uniform yield over a definite period of years, the new value of such a property is (ignoring salvage) the present value of the annual yield to be expected from the employment of such capacity during its useful life, and the value at any later date is similarly the value of the yield to be anticipated in the years of life then unexpired. Clearly the rate of lessening of worth in service in such a case is to be found not by straight proportion but by reference to annuity tables. If, for instance, a unit of property is viewed as representing a capacity for uniform service at a uniform yield over a period of 50 years, its service value at the end of 25 years is that fraction of the original value, the numerator of which is the value of an annuity for 25 years, and the denominator the value of

a like annuity for 50 years. Assuming an interest rate of
6%, the numerator of the fraction would be 12.78336, and
the denomination 15.76186; in other words, the lessening of
worth due to the exhaustion of one-half of the life of the
property would be less than one-quarter instead of one-half,
and the true value on the Commission's own hypotheses actually nearer to cost than to the depreciated value as computed by the Commission's method.

The incorrect results produced by the straight line method
of depreciation may be illustrated in another way. Upon the
Commission's hypothesis that a given unit of property will
yield uniform service over a specified period of time, clearly
the charges against the traffic in respect thereof in each year
should be uniform. The Commission says, page 353:

The principle is fair, however, that the cost resulting
from the using up of property in service should be shared
equally by the years which have had the benefit of the use.

But the charges against the traffic are twofold: first, a charge
for exhaustion; second, a charge for use, computed as a return on investment, and the truly fair principle is that the
combined charges should be the same in each year. On the
Commission's method, assuming a 6% rate of return, and a
unit costing $1,000, there would be in the first year a charge
against the traffic of $60.00 for use of the property; and as-
suming a 50-year life, a charge of $20.00 for exhaustion of
the property—a total of $80.00. In the 50th year the charge
for return on investment would be only $1.20 (6% on
$20.00) and the charge for exhaustion $20.00, as before—a
total of $21.20, or not much more than one-quarter of the
charge in the first year.

THE ANNUITY METHOD OF COMPUTING DEPRECIATION IS THE
ONLY ONE CONSISTENT WITH THE COMMISSION'S HY-
POTHESES AND PURPOSES

The error in principle here disclosed would be corrected
by the adoption of the annuity method of provision for de-

preciation; and it seems to me a matter not of argument but of simple mathematical demonstration that the annuity method is the only one that is consistent with the Commission's own hypotheses and upon those hypotheses reflects the relation between the value of a new unit and that of a partly exhausted one.

This may be made clearer by assuming the case of a carrier offered the alternative of purchasing a new unit with a useful life of 50 years and a unit exactly similar one year old and with an unexhausted useful life of 49 years. All the carrier would gain by acquiring the new rather than older unit would be the service of the unit *in the fiftieth year in the future* and all it could prudently pay for this advantage would be the present value of the yield from that service to be received in fifty years. Assuming the annual yield (covering depreciation and return on investment) to be $1,000, and the rate of return to be 6% per annum, the present value of the yield in the fiftieth year is found from the tables to be $54.29.

The value of the new unit would be $15,761.86
and that of the unit one year old 15,707.57
the difference being, of course, ... $ 54.29

as compared with $314.15 depreciation computed on the straight line basis. The percentage of reduction of worth in service due to the exhaustion of one year's useful life out of a total of fifty years is thus not one-fiftieth or 2%, but just over one-third of one per cent; the straight line method overstates the lessening of worth sixfold.

In order to illustrate the importance of the point the following comparisons are made of the results by the annuity and straight line methods respectively in the case of property units, each costing $10,000 and having assumed annual lives of 30, 50 and 100 years, respectively:

	Straight line method	6% Annuity method
Thirty-year life:		
Charge for depreciation, 1st year.............	$ 333.33	$ 126.49
Return on investment, 1st year...............	600.00	600.00
Combined charge, 1st year................	$ 933.00	$ 726.49
Charge for depreciation, last year.............	$ 333.33	$ 685.37
Return on investment, last year..............	20.00	41.12
Combined charge, last year...............	$ 353.33	$ 726.49
Accrued depreciation at midlife.............	$5,000.00	$2,944.15
(End of 15th year)		
Fifty-year life:		
Charge for depreciation, 1st year.............	$ 200.00	$ 34.44
Return on investment, 1st year...............	600.00	600.00
Combined charge, 1st year................	$ 800.00	$ 634.44
Charge for depreciation, last year.............	$ 200.00	$ 598.53
Return on investment, last year..............	12.00	35.91
Combined charge, last year...............	$ 212.00	$ 634.44
Accrued depreciation at midlife.............	$5,000.00	$1,889.69
(End of 25th year)		
One-hundred-year life:		
Charge for depreciation, 1st year.............	$ 100.00	$ 1.77
Return on investment, 1st year...............	600.00	600.00
Combined charge, 1st year................	$ 700.00	$ 601.77
Charge for depreciation, last year.............	$ 100.00	$ 567.71
Return on investment, last year..............	6.00	34.06
Combined charge, last year...............	$ 106.00	$ 601.77
Accrued depreciation at midlife.............	$5,000.00	$ 514.99
(End of 50th year)		

It will be observed that at mid-life the loss in value measured on the annuity basis is 58.9% of the amount of "depreciation" computed by the straight line method in the case of a unit having a total estimated life of 30 years, 37.8% in the case of a unit with 50 years life and no more than 10.3% in the case of a unit having 100 years life.

I see no escape from the conclusion that either the annuity method must be substituted for the straight line method or all suggestion of close relationship between depreciated values and fair value in service abandoned.

THE ANNUITY METHOD DISCUSSED

It may be noted that using the same interest rates, the sinking fund and annuity methods give practically the same results. The sinking fund method, however, contemplates the return of the investment when the unit is retired and is adapted rather to retirement reserves than depreciation provisions. The annuity method is consistent with the Commission's theory that the investment is returned to the investor gradually and therefore seems to be the only logical method for the Commission to adopt on its own hypotheses, the validity of which I need not for the present discuss.

The Commission does not discuss the annuity method, but expresses the view that the premises that underlie the straight line method are in accord with the principles which have been enunciated by the Supreme Court of the United States, and that the method is simpler and easier to apply, and adds:

Nor are the practical results of the two methods very different . . .

The straight line method is simpler; but for the reasons I have given above it seems to me that the method produces results that are wholly at variance with the views enunciated by the Supreme Court, and the tables which have been given show conclusively that the results of the sinking fund (or the annuity) method are widely different from those produced by the straight line method. In the case of a property with a reasonably long average life the accrued depreciation on the sinking fund or annuity method at any given date would not for many years after the initiation of the enterprise be more than one-third of the amount computed by the straight line method.

It should be understood that the views expressed above are based on my understanding that under existing law present value is the measure of the rate base. I am not concerned with the question how the present value is to be determined; the material bearing of the law on the point here involved is that it seems to require that in determining the rate base the deduction for depreciation from year to year shall follow the course of value which the straight line method does not and is not intended to do.

I recognize that upon some different conception of the principles governing the determination of a rate base, upon which the rate base would be the result of a computation rather than a reflection of value, unexpended depreciation provisions created by charges against operating expenses might appropriately operate to reduce *pro tanto* the rate base. If such a concept of the rate base were adopted, however, the whole question of depreciation would require to be considered on a different footing. The majority of economists would, I believe, take the view that upon such theories the problem of depreciation does not arise.

I have not undertaken to discuss here the question why, in view of the objections to the straight line method which I have urged, that method is freely employed in industrial practice. That the governing considerations are materially different in the two cases is apparent, and whatever may be the merits of the straight line method as an empirical method of distributing the cost of property over its useful life, it is not properly applicable and is not applied in industrial practice to the valuation of property. A discussion of the industrial problem does not seem strictly relevant to the question under consideration, but in case the point is regarded as of interest I attach in a note to this report a brief statement of some of the major differences between the two problems.

RELATION TO OTHER MAINTENANCE CHARGES

In considering a scheme of depreciation charges, a second fundamental question is whether the charges against the traffic in respect of property exhaustion should in any given case be measured by the original cost of the unit exhausted or by the cost of the replacing unit.

Under the regulations of the Commission now in effect,

operating expenses are charged with the *cost* of equipment *retired* through depreciation charges, with *cost* of structures *retired,* when retirement takes place, and with the *cost of the renewal,* when renewal takes place, in the case of track material.

In such circumstances, and in view of this historical aspect of the question, it seems to me that the Commission begs a vital question when it accepts as axiomatic the proposition that the *cost* of property used up in service is the proper measure of the charge against the traffic in respect of such exhaustion. It says (page 303):

There also can be no doubt that the cost of such wornout or abandoned property units is a part of operating expense to be charged against the service. The basic question is whether such cost should be charged in bulk at the time when each unit is retired, or should be anticipated by periodical installments spread over its service life.

and again (page 306):

The cost of property consumed in operation is plainly a part of the cost of rendering service.

SHOULD THE COST OF ORIGINAL INSTALLATION OR THE COST
OF REPLACEMENT BE CHARGED AGAINST OPERATION?

The question whether original cost or cost of renewal should measure the operating charge is not of great importance so long as price levels are reasonably stable, but if price levels materially vary or, in other words, if there is a substantial change in the value of money, then the point becomes important and also, I think, the unsoundness of the axiom becomes apparent. This may be illustrated by considering the point in relation to the German railway system and the post-war currency depreciation in that country. At the lowest point of currency depreciation, the pre-war investment in the German railways expressed in marks would have had a value in stable currency of less than a dollar, and the annual exhaustion of property (or the retirements) in respect thereof computed in marks upon the cost in marks would

have been equivalent to less than a cent. This is, of course,
an extreme case, but the same question is presented in a less
acute form whenever there is a substantial change in the
value of money such as the fall that occurred in the United
States as a result of the war.

It is inherently fair that traffic that is paid for in currency
that has depreciated should be charged with the cost of
property used up in operation on the same scale of values.
Suppose that in a given year property is made good to an
extent exactly equalling the amount of property used up in
operation (measurement being made in physical units).
Justice to all concerned would seem to be achieved by charging the cost of making good property during the year against
the traffic of the year. When the value of money has fallen
there is no basic reason why the increased currency cost of
the new property over the cost of exactly similar property
used up in operation should be added to the capital account
of the railroad to constitute a burden on the patrons or the
public in later years.

The Commission dismisses as of little importance the question of the equities as between patrons at different periods of
time, but the question is not merely one between the patrons
at different times but ultimately one between the patrons
as a whole and the carriers. If a method be adopted which
wrongfully relieves the present patrons and throws an undue
burden upon the patrons of the future, there is a probability
that the patrons of the future will through their representatives take steps to relieve themselves of this unjust burden
and the railroads would not be able successfully to resist
such attempts on the ground that they constituted confiscation of railroad property. For it would be easy to prove that
any confiscation there might be was not the result of the revised regulations but the result of the action of the regulating
bodies in the past, and that the proper time for the railroads to have raised the question was at the earlier date.

If the principle be accepted that the sum on which the
carrier is entitled to a return as compensation for the *use* of

property in service is its fair present value, consistency would suggest that the measure of the compensation for property *used up* should also be its fair present value or, in other words, the current cost of replacement of what is exhausted.

I believe also the same result is reached on the assumption that the rate of return is to be computed upon the amount of the prudent investment in the property. This theory rests upon the proposition that when an investment is made in railroad property it is a permanent investment and the investor exchanges a present command of purchasing power for a right to receive a reasonable return thereon in the future, and that thereafter fluctuations in the value or cost of reproduction of the property represented by his investment are of no practical significance to him. It seems to me a necessary corollary of this proposition that the burden of maintaining the property should fall on the users of the property and that fluctuations in the cost of its maintenance should be treated as at their risk and charge.

The Commission takes a somewhat different view and proceeds upon the theory that on the replacement of any property the original investment should be regarded as having been returned to the investors and a fresh investment made by them in the replacing unit. This, however, seems to me not only contrary to the normal course of events but to be inconsistent with the basic idea of the prudent investment. It seems to me to be a necessary feature of the prudent investment theory that the investment should be voluntary, and it is only the original investment which can be said to be voluntary, replacement being a need which grows out of the voluntary act of creating the original property.

SUPPORT FOR THE REPLACEMENT BASIS IN PRACTICE

The economic arguments in favor of charging the cost of replacement rather than the cost of the original unit against operating expenses, find ample support in practice; it is the method that has consistently been followed in Great Britain, and, though methods of railroad accounting and reporting there have been the subject of numerous official inquiries, so far as I know no suggestion has ever been made that the practice should be modified. It was also, I believe, the common practice of the best-managed railroads in the United States prior to the regulation of accounting by the Interstate Commerce Commission; it is the practice which has been required by the Commission under the existing regulations for the last twenty years in respect to important classes of property, such as track material.

This being so, the Commission, carrying out its instructions to determine the classes of property to which depreciation charges should properly be supplied, is scarcely entitled to assume as established the proposition that cost is universally the proper basis for charges against operating expenses in respect of the maintenance or exhaustion of property.

TO WHAT EXTENT ARE DEPRECIATION CHARGES ECONOMICALLY WISE?

I might agree with the Commission that if the prudent investment theory of rate base were to be adopted, and if, moreover, depreciation charges were to be set aside, then the unexpended depreciation provisions should be deducted from the gross investment in arriving at the rate base. But I agree with those economic authorities who hold that upon this theory no provisions for depreciation are, upon consideration of the economic and practical aspects of the question, necessary or desirable.

In order to consider this question dispassionately it may be well to look at it from the standpoint of a community in which a new railroad enterprise is under contemplation. Let us assume that it is agreed between the promoters of the railroad and the community that the former shall be entitled to a reasonable opportunity to earn a fair return on their investment in the line, and that the community shall have the right to restrict closely the profits of the railroad to that fair return. Would competent economic advisers of the community advocate such a system of charging depreciation as the Commission now proposes? It has already been shown that the result of this method is to throw the heaviest burden in respect of use and exhaustion of each unit of property upon the earliest years of its life. In these earliest years the amount of service rendered would be less than might reasonably be expected in the later years; consequently the charge in respect of the property per unit of service would be still more burdensome in comparison with the charge for the service of later years. Such a condition would seem to be exactly the reverse of that which would be economically desirable from the standpoint of the community. Its interests would be served by keeping the charges in the early years down to the minimum consistent with maintaining the efficiency of the property, thus enlarging the volume of the commodities which could profitably be transported, and building up both the traffic and the community more rapidly than would otherwise be possible. The best interests of the community in such a situation would, it would seem, be served by a mutual agreement to ignore the depreciation on the property in so far as it could never be made good while the property was being operated—the owners of the railroad agreeing that this depreciation should not be treated as a part of cost of operation and the community agreeing on the other hand that in computing return no deduction should be made from the original investment in respect thereof.

THE REPLACEMENT PRINCIPLE SHOULD AT LEAST BE RETAINED IN CASES IN WHICH IT IS NOW APPLIED UNDER THE COMMISSION'S REGULATIONS

It cannot be denied that there is a very substantial case, economic, historical and practical, for the replacement principle in general; and it seems to me that the case for the retention of that principle in dealing with the classes of property, such as track material, to which it is now applied is convincing, unless real and substantial advantages from the change to the depreciation principle can be demonstrated. I can see no such advantage.

While the application of the depreciation scheme to rails and ties now treated on the replacement basis is simple so far as the material cost is concerned, the Commission itself is forced to the conclusion that it is impracticable in the case of the labor cost. The application of the scheme to miscellaneous track material contemplated by the Commission presents exceptional difficulties, which can be overcome only by the most arbitrary rules.

The depreciation section of the Commission recommended that the principle be not extended to track materials, but the Commission rejected this recommendation, apparently in an effort to achieve consistency; and apart from this one consideration the Commission's discussion of the subject constitutes a statement of arguments against its own conclusions which, though overruled, are not met.

DEPRECIATION CHARGES MIGHT WELL BE CONTINUED IN RESPECT OF EQUIPMENT

In the case of equipment, on the other hand, the historical argument runs the other way. Many who disapproved of the establishment of the depreciation charges in respect of equipment would concede that it would now be unwise to reverse that policy. In passing, it may be noted that the Commission is in error in assuming (page 304) that such a reversal would add the amount of the existing reserves to the surplus accounts of the carriers. The true alternative to the depreciation system is the charging of the cost of replacements to operating expenses. Under the existing system the excess of the cost of the replacements of equipment over that of the units replaced is capitalized, and reversion to the alternative method would require the charging of the excess which has been so capitalized to surplus as an offset to the credit arising from writing back the depreciation reserve. In view of the great increase in the cost of equipment in recent years the offset would clearly be very substantial.

THE PROBLEM OF EXTRAORDINARY REPAIRS

The Commission's order contemplates a substantial change in the treatment of equipment depreciation, the provision being revised to cover not only the cost of the unit but the cost of extraordinary repairs during its life. The annual depreciation charge is to be determined by adding to original cost the estimated cost of extraordinary repairs before final retirement and deducting estimated salvage, and dividing the net total by the number of years expected to elapse between installation and retirement.

The Commission admits the "great practical difficulties" presented by this method, but says that inclusion of extraordinary repairs is "absolutely essential to a properly comprehensive system of depreciation accounting."

The proposals of the Commission for solving these difficulties are put forward tentatively. The Commission admits that "somewhat arbitrary rules" have had to be made, but even so the provisions as they stand are clearly inadequate.

The question at once arises how the cost of extraordinary repairs is to be estimated; are the estimators to take into account the probable price levels at the time when the extraordinary repairs will be made, or are they to assume that the price levels at that time will be the same as those prevailing when the original unit is installed; and how are differences between the estimated cost of repairs and the actual costs to be dealt with? No answer to these questions is found in the report.

It is apparent also that the attempted distinction between ordinary and extraordinary repairs would offer great opportunities for the manipulation of operating expenses. The line between the two is proposed to be and must be arbitrary; and it would be easy for carriers desiring either to swell operating expenses or to minimize them to do so by splitting up major repairs into a series of minor repairs which would be chargeable to operating expenses, or allowing minor repairs to accumulate into a major repair, which would be chargeable to Depreciation Reserve.

A further consideration is that to base operating expenses on amounts reserved for future expenditures and to charge current expenditures against reserves created in past years, tends to lessen the sense of responsibility of those in all ranks who are charged with the control of maintenance expenditures. It may be doubted whether any system of charging expenditures in the first instance to operating accounts and adjusting these accounts to the depreciation basis by any subsequent transfer will be wholly effective in preventing this highly undesirable result.

I am prepared to agree with the Commission that extraordinary repairs have an essential relation to the problem of depreciation, but the Commission's attempt to deal with such repairs as a part of its depreciation scheme in the case of equipment, seems to me to introduce complexities and detract from the significance of the resulting figures without solving the problem or producing any compensating advantages. The difficulties in the measurement of the charges to operating expenses on the basis proposed are serious but perhaps not much more so than those presented in relation to other classes of property. The problem of insuring that only so much of subsequent maintenance expenditure as has been allowed for in the original provision for depreciation is charged against the depreciation fund, presents far greater difficulties, and the report of the Commission fails to indicate how these difficulties are to be met.

DEPRECIATION ON OTHER CLASSES OF PROPERTY

There remain for consideration the accounts which at present are treated on the basis that the charge to operating expenses is based on the cost of the unit retired, but the charge made only when retirement occurs, and those continuous structures which are seldom retired as units.

The class of property to which a depreciation or replacement scheme is most clearly applicable comprises those structures, such as important bridges, which will require to be replaced as units and the retirement of which would seriously distort operating expenses if the cost of the retired unit or the cost of replacing it were charged into operating expenses when the retirement occurs. The life of such structures may be difficult to estimate, but the application of such a scheme entails less practical difficulties and possesses more obvious advantages than in the case of almost any other class of property.

If the depreciation system is to be extended, application to this class of property would, probably, be the most generally approved extension. It is also to this class of property that the annuity or sinking fund methods can most conveniently be applied, and the life of such structures being usually fairly long, errors in the estimate thereof would be of little effect in the early years and could be corrected before over- or under-provision would have become serious.

I see, however, no practical advantage in attempting to depreciate property from its installation if its useful life is estimated at as much as 80 or 100 years. The value of a unit having 50 years of useful life unexhausted is on a 6% basis over 94% of the value of a like unit with 100 years life unexhausted.

Putting the matter another way, if money is assumed to be worth 6% (or even only 5%) and a unit with a useful life of 100 years could be purchased for $100,000 but its life made perpetual by the expenditure of an additional $1,000, it would not be economical to spend the additional $1,000, since the investment of this sum for 100 years would produce far more than $100,000. The distinction between permanence and an assumed life of 100 years is therefore too slight to justify depreciating one asset and not the other. It would be quite adequate to begin to charge depreciation when the unexpired life falls below, say, 35 years or, at the outside, 50 years.

In the case of continuous structures, a detailed depreciation scheme seems to possess very little value and to present almost insuperable difficulties. To determine what shall be charged against the reserve and to ensure that such charges shall correspond to those provided for by credits to the reserve seem to me problems almost impossible of solution within reasonable limits of expense. I do not desire to burden this memorandum with discussion of technical questions of secondary importance and therefore merely observe that these problems do not appear to me to be solved, even in theory in the Commission's plan.

PAST DEPRECIATION

The third important relationship involved in consideration of any depreciation scheme for the carriers is the relationship to the operations of the past. The Commission does not attempt to pass finally upon the question how depreciation, which under its scheme is deemed to have accrued in the past, should be dealt with. It proposes that for the present the amount should be set up on the books of the carriers in a suspense account; it does, however, indicate its views in the following language:

The theoretically correct way of meeting this situation would be to establish the amount of past accrued depreciation which has not been provided for, and concurrently credit this amount to the depreciation reserve and charge it to profit and loss. It is the latter account which has profited in the past from the failure or partial failure to accrue depreciation charges.

It seems to me that this statement of the position is inadequate and, as a result, unjust. The omission of depreciation provisions in the past is supported too strongly by theoretical, economic, historical, and practical considerations for such omission to be justly characterized as a failure on the part of the carriers. It seems to me humanly certain also that if a system of depreciation charges had been inaugurated at the commencement of railroad enterprise in the United States, the development of the railroads would have been made more difficult and the growth of the country greatly retarded.

Upon a broad view of the situation it seems to me quite impossible therefore to hold that it is the profit and loss accounts of the carriers alone which have profited by the omission of depreciation charges in the past. The above considerations apply with peculiar force to depreciation on the classes of property such as track material, which under the Commission's own regulations have been dealt with up to now on the basis of charging renewals into operating expenses. It would probably be reasonable to treat any past omission to provide adequately for depreciation of equipment as a failure on the part of the carriers, seeing that depreciation provisions have been in force now for twenty years. If, however, depreciation is to be set up in respect of other classes of property, the further question arises whether the amount of the depreciation deemed to have accrued at the date when the change becomes effective should be provided in the future through charges against operating expenses or net income before arriving at the income subject to recapture.

THE NECESSITY OF DEPRECIATION CHARGES FOR THE PROTECTION OF THE CARRIERS

Commissioner Woodlock in his concurring opinion expressed the view that a system of depreciation charges into operating expenses was necessary for the due protection of the carriers. If depreciation is to be deducted from valuation, it is reasonable that the carriers should be given an opportunity to recover depreciation computed on a like basis through operating expenses. The question, however, is not one of great urgency and might well await some further determination of the principles of valuation and the methods of computing depreciation in connection therewith. When this point is reached a system of depreciation in harmony with the principles of valuation established could be formulated. It seems likely to result in confusion and not advantage to adopt in the meantime a system of depreciation which is not in harmony with the existing decisions with regard to valuation and with the prospect of modifying it substantially when the principles of valuation are more fully established. When those principles are established better protection to the carriers and the public could probably be secured by a broad scheme for accumulating a depreciation reserve bearing roughly the same relation to the investment as the depreciation deducted in the net valuation might bear to the gross valuation, rather than by attempting to follow the history of units, often small, in meticulous detail.

It is quite clear, moreover, that no system of depreciation will adequately protect the investment or maintain the efficiency of the property, and if this is to be the objective of the Commission's efforts, then, even should its present depreciation scheme be adopted, it will require to be supplemented by some scheme for dealing with other forms of maintenance charges.

SUMMARY

Summarizing my views regarding the proposed scheme, I recognize that it is a logical complement to the Commission's theories of valuation, and if the validity of those theories were established, the broad outlines of the scheme would be established with them.

I am disposed further to agree with the Commission, that apart from question of law or constitutional right the principle of the prudent investment theory would probably be as satisfactory as any other method of arriving at a rate base. I feel, however:

(1) That until legal principles are more clearly established, the adoption of a general scheme of depreciation charges for all or nearly all property subject to exhaustion is unnecessary and inopportune.

(2) That the straight line method is wholly inapplicable to the measurement of the lessening of worth in service due to partial exhaustion of useful life.

(3) That the Commission's proposal fails to deal ade-

quately with changing price levels as a factor in the problem.

(4) That a plan for dealing with any depreciation attributed to the past which shall be equitable, having regard to the past history of railroad practice and regulation, is an essential of any satisfactory depreciation system. This the Commission's proposals do not provide.

(5) That the adoption of the scheme would produce no gain in accuracy, but would greatly complicate accounting, detract from the significance of the accounts, and increase rather than diminish the opportunities for manipulation.

(6) That the weight of argument against setting up on a straight line basis which does not measure the lessening of worth in service depreciation reserves which can in practice never be expended, is today overwhelming.

In the Commission's proposals there is an alternation of sacrifice of theory to practicability and of practicability to theory which produces a result neither reasonably practical nor substantially sound in theory.

The establishment of a system of depreciation charges is itself a sacrifice of practicability to theory; the distribution of the charge for property exhaustion on the basis of time without regard to use, and the acceptance of the straight line method are sacrifices of theory to practicability so sweeping as to destroy the prospects of any substantial gain in theoretical accuracy from such a system. Similarly, the inclusion of extraordinary repairs in the scope of depreciation charges is a major sacrifice of practicability to theory, but wholesale sacrifices of theory to practicability are, as the Commission's report indicates, necessary to make this part of the scheme workable.

The first suggestion which I would make is that the Commission should aim either at substantial theoretical accuracy or at greater simplicity.

If the former alternative is chosen, the annuity method should be substituted for the straight line method. If special tables were compiled, an easy task, the application of the method would not thereafter entail practical difficulties substantially greater than those involved in the straight line method.

The second problem involved in this alternative, that of including extraordinary repairs within the scope of the scheme, undeniably presents greater difficulties. There is need for elaboration and classification of the proposals of the Commission in regard to the charges against the reserve under this head and the treatment of the problem of extraordinary repairs made when the price level is materially different from that prevailing when the unit was originally installed.

If the second alternative is adopted the broad policy should, I think, be:

(1) To limit depreciation charges to equipment and major units with perhaps in addition a relatively small general reserve to meet extraordinary retirements of property not covered by specific reserves.

(2) To depreciate structures on an annuity basis.

(3) To initiate depreciation charges on long-lived property only when the unexpired life becomes less than forty years.

Undeniably there is much to be said for approaching the question from the entirely different standpoint of endeavoring to make the maintenance charge for any year reflect as accurately as possible the exhaustion of property during the year converted into money on the basis of the price level of the year. A plan might be devised under which prudent investment would be the foundation of the rate base, and any material deficiency or excess of maintenance in any year would be expressed in terms of money at current values and charged or credited to operating, the corresponding credit or charge being a maintenance equalization account which would enter into the computation of the rate base.

The practical difficulties of such a plan would be slight compared to those inherent in a scheme such as the Commission proposes, and such a plan would have obvious theoretical merits. It must be recognized, however, that at the present time there is no satisfactory basis in law for such a proposal and also that the principle involved is altogether different from that which the Commission has followed in the past, so that the Commission could not reasonably be expected to adopt such a plan unless it were as a part of a thorough revision of the principles of accounting of the carriers, which might well be undertaken, however, since the accounts are now in large measure an accounting between the carriers and the public.

NOTE

The problem of depreciation in industrial accounting differs from the problem of depreciation in the case of public utilities subject to rate regulation or recapture of earnings in the following, among other, respects:

(1) The value of property employed and of the property used up by a public utility in rendering service are essential and major factors in the determination of the charges for such service. It is mainly from this fact that the Commission's concern with depreciation arises.

The same factors have relatively far less bearing on prices in the industrial field. This is true for various reasons. Capital assets, to begin with, constitute a much smaller proportion of the investment in the case of industrial enterprises than in that of public utilities. More important is the fact that in the industrial field prices are determined to a far greater extent by considerations other than cost, such as value to the purchaser, competition, etc.

(2) The predominant consideration in industrial accounting is conservatism rather than theoretical accuracy. This is well illustrated in the rule for valuing inventories at "cost or market, whichever is lower"—a rule founded obviously not on logic or theory but on abundant caution. The Commission is not justified in requiring or permitting a method which errs demonstrably on the side of conservatism to a material

extent; the result almost inevitably would be injustice to the carrier or the patron.

(3) The accounting for capital assets in industrial practice does not aim at recording the course of value in service. This is well illustrated by the practice in charging depletion commonly followed and accepted by the Treasury. Mines are usually valued by taking the discounted present value of the estimated yield from unmined tonnage. Other things being equal, the value at the end of a year's operation would be found by making a similar calculation in respect of the reduced tonnage. Depletion charges are, however, almost universally computed by dividing the value of the mine originally determined by the estimated tonnage, and thus computing a rate per ton which is applied uniformly from year to year. No one would suggest that the deduction of the depletion so computed from the original cost or value of the mine would in any circumstances be a proper method of computing residual value of the mine.

(4) The distinguishing characteristic of American industry is the readiness with which property units are discarded when superior types become available. In such circumstances common prudence suggests, in the case of highly competitive industry, the desirability of writing off a large proportion of the investment over the early years of use, conditions during which can be forecast with some degree of confidence. Hence the straight line method is appropriate in industrial practice; indeed, the diminishing balance method which produces even greater charges in the early years is sometimes employed.

The Commission's hypotheses, if they do not exclude the application of these considerations to railroad property, reduce their weight to inconsiderable proportions. Upon its view, if a purchase of property is prudent when made, the carrier is assured of an opportunity to earn a return on its cost during its useful life. The incentive to retire the unit on account of obsolescence before its efficiency is seriously impaired is almost wholly lacking.

It may be added that the argument advanced by the Commission, that the depreciation charge in respect of a unit should be equal in each year of its useful life, has more validity in the case of an industrial enterprise than in that of a public utility.   It is not customary in industrial practice to include interest in cost, so that the depreciation charge is the only property charge, and the point made on page 4 of the memorandum that it is the combined charges for depreciation and return, rather than one separate charge that should be uniform, does not arise.

V

CARRIER PROPERTY CONSUMED IN OPERATION AND THE REGULATION OF PROFITS

A DISCUSSION OF THE I.C.C. REPORT ON DEPRECIATION *

(1929)

I

In determining whether a given rate structure of a carrier is compensatory or confiscatory, it is necessary to make two allowances on account of carrier property: first, an allowance for the use, and second, an allowance for the consumption of property in rendering service. Some property may be indestructible, so that no allowance under the second head is called for; other property may be consumed so rapidly that there is no charge under the first head on account of it. But in most classes of property both allowances are necessary.

It is generally agreed that the charge for use should be in the form of interest or return at a percentage rate upon a fair capital value for the property employed in rendering service, often called the rate base. Controversy arises over the questions how the capital value—the rate base—should be computed and upon what principles the rate of return thereon should be determined. In respect to the allowance for consumption of property the questions arise, upon what basis the allowance should be made in money and whether it should be made (in the case of property whose useful life extends over a considerable period) as the consumption proceeds, when it becomes complete, or when it is made good.

Now, while much has been written and conflicting views have been expressed by courts, commissions, economists and others on the questions how the rate base should be computed and how the rate of return to be applied to that rate

* *Quarterly Journal of Economics*, Vol. XLIII (February, 1929), pp. 193-220

base should be determined, and also upon the question whether the allowance for consumption should or should not be made as consumption proceeds (or, as it is commonly phrased, upon a depreciation basis), comparatively little consideration has been given to the question how the money value of property consumed should be computed. Some consideration of it might have been expected in connection with the determination of the extent to which depreciation charges should form a part of railroad accounting, which was required of the Interstate Commerce Commission under the Transportation Act of 1920. The Commission instituted an inquiry (Case 15,100) and held extensive hearings. But in the decision that the Commission rendered under date of November 2, 1926, the question how the money value of property consumed should be computed was scarcely discussed. The Commission passed it over in the following language:

There also can be *no doubt that the cost* of such worn-out or abandoned property units is a part of operating expense to be charged against the service. The basic question is whether such cost should be charged in bulk at the time when each unit is retired, or should be anticipated by periodical instalments spread over its service life.

But the proposition that cost is necessarily and universally the proper basis of the charge for property consumed is by no means axiomatic. On the contrary, it is far from being demonstrably sound in theory and equally far from being adopted in practice—even under the Commission's own regulations.

In the course of the decision the Commission said also:

In our consideration, therefore, of the relative burdens imposed by the depreciation and retirement methods of accounting, we must start with the premise that the former presupposes full deduction of accrued depreciation in ascertaining the rate base value.

Since the Commission had deducted depreciation on a straight line basis in its valuations, it naturally adopted the same basis in the decision in question. Furthermore, harmony with its valuation practice necessitated the application of depreciation to such property as miscellaneous track material, though the Commission's accounting section had advised against such an application on the score of impracticability. It also entailed a substantial change in the method of application of the straight line depreciation plan from that heretofore applied in the case of equipment.

Here again, however, the Commission seems to stand on insecure ground, for the conditions which it postulates regarding the deduction of depreciation in determining the rate base, coupled with its adherence to straight line depreciation, bring its position into direct opposition to Supreme Court decisions on the point. Thus the Commission's whole case rests heavily on an axiom and a postulate, both of which lack validity. The explanation is apparently that the Commission, or some members of it at least, still clings to the hope that the Supreme Court will reverse its past rulings regarding the rate base and accept the line of reasoning advanced in various minority opinions, notably in the dissenting opinion of Mr. Justice Brandeis in the Southwestern Bell Telephone Company case.*

The Commission's decision of November 2, 1926, gave rise to much criticism and to requests for rehearing. These requests were granted and the rehearing, which is now in progress, seems to be developing, as it rightly should, into a broad reconsideration of railroad accounting methods in general. In the circumstances a discussion of the depreciation problem seems opportune, particularly as the accountant's view may differ from that of either the lawyer or the economist.

II

The specific questions which it is proposed to discuss are:

1. Should charges for consumption of property in rendering service be based uniformly on cost: (a) for purposes

* 262 U. S., 276.

of rate and profit regulation; and (*b*) for current accounting purposes?

2. Should the charge for property consumed be made in bulk at the time when each unit is retired, or should it be anticipated by periodical instalments spread over its service life?

3. If consumption charges are to be made as consumption proceeds rather than when it becomes complete, on what basis should the accrual be deemed to take place and be computed?

The relation between the basis of exhaustion charges and the principles of computation of the rate base is, as the Commission points out, direct and vital. Some economists * hold that if the so-called prudent investment theory is to prevail, depreciation provisions cannot possibly have any proper place in the scheme of things. It therefore seems desirable as a preliminary step to discuss briefly the two principal conflicting theories of rate base determination.

The difference between the two theories, sometimes referred to as the "present value theory" and the "prudent investment theory" respectively, is understood by all students of the subject and is sufficiently indicated by two sentences—one from the majority opinion and the other from the dissenting opinion in the Southwestern Bell Telephone Company case. Mr. Justice Brandeis, advancing the prudent investment theory, says: "The thing devoted by the investor to the public use is not specific property, tangible and intangible, but capital embarked in the enterprise." Mr. Justice McReynolds, in the majority opinion, however, quotes from the decision in the Minnesota rate cases: "The property is held in private ownership and it is that property, and not the original cost of it, of which the owner may not be deprived without due process of law."

Mr. Justice Brandeis supported his contentions by a force-

---

* No attempt is made to cite authorities for this or other economic arguments herein advanced, since the writer's knowledge of the authorities is not wide enough to enable him to make just attribution. His acknowledgment of indebtedness to economic writers must be general, not specific.

ful presentation of the economic and practical advantages of prudent investment as the measure of the rate base. The refusal of the majority to accept his conclusion does not necessarily imply dissent from this part of his argument. Their view is perhaps rather that the Court is not free to apply whatever rule may seem economically wisest. Apparently in the majority view present value must, under the Constitution, be the measure of the rate base; cost is significant only in so far as it reflects fair present value. Economic considerations may, and indeed must, be taken into account in determining present value, but the Court is not free to adopt or approve a basis for regulation which, though perhaps economically wise, disregards present value. Mr. Justice Brandeis does suggest that cost is the only practical measure of present value, but in his main argument he attempts to support cost as a measure of the rate base without linking it to present value. To a layman his failure to carry the Court with him in this part of his argument seems inevitable; but the whole discussion illustrates very clearly how the difficulties of the problem have been accentuated by the way in which we have drifted into it.

The problem comes before the courts as a conflict of constitutional rights which are unequivocally recognized but not clearly defined. On the one side there is the right of the people through its representatives to regulate business affected by a public interest; on the other the right of the carriers to protection against complete or partial confiscation of property. The Supreme Court, in holding that it is the present value of the property employed that must, under the Constitution, form the basis for determining whether any regulation is confiscatory in its effects, does not imply that in its judgment present value is, from the standpoint of either carriers or the public, the most satisfactory basis for regulation of rates or profits.

Looking backwards, one might say that the acts under which carrier enterprises were originally undertaken should have recognized the constitutional rights of the carriers and the public, and have laid down principles for determining fair compensation which would have been binding on both parties on the acceptance of the acts by the carriers. It may well be, also, that prudent investment would, in such circumstances, have been the most appropriate measure of a proper return and its adoption desirable in the interests of all parties. No such action was, however, taken. The questions may not have been anticipated or, since the economic gains which would result from the construction of railroads were obvious, all parties may have been concerned to get them built and disinclined to raise questions likely to delay action and not of immediate importance. Apparently for years after the initiation of the great era of railroad construction, competition and similar natural economic forces were deemed an adequate safeguard against excessive rates. Conceivably those who foresaw that the question would arise may have been content to await the day without prior commitments, and so to be free then to urge whatever theory might seem most advantageous to the interests with which they were concerned. Certain it is that the way in which we have drifted into the problem, with no clear principles laid down, but with broad constitutional rights on each side, makes any present-day solution far more difficult.

The approach to the problem from the standpoint of prudent investment offers the practical advantages which Mr. Justice Brandeis pointed out: it recognizes the essential fact that, once money is invested in a railroad, the investment is valuable only for what it can produce; it has the merits of continuity and relative certainty. On the part of carriers, the main objections to prudent investment as a measure of the rate base are perhaps first and foremost that it denies the carrier any benefit from the increment in land values which railroad construction has created, and second, that it fails to produce a fair return when the currency has depreciated or there has been a marked rise in price levels. However, if the carriers are to be participators in the increment in values which they have created, it should be possible to find a fair and more practical measure of their just share than the hypothetical appreciation of land which they own but cannot sell, if at all, without sacrificing other values. And similarly, if the return to carriers is to vary with changes in the value of the currency or of price levels, an adjustment on the basis of the changes in the value of currency as measured by general internal purchasing power or international exchange value might be simpler and fairer than one measured by changes in the values of the particular units of property that go to make up a railroad.

The question is, largely, what form of assurance of return is calculated to secure capital most advantageously. It is all very well to say that security is the first requisite, but what constitutes security? Is it a stable income or a stable capital value, and in either case is the stability to be measured in terms of money or in terms of purchasing power? Prior to the war, fixed money income was perhaps mainly sought. But the course of security and commodity prices during and since the war has brought home to investors the possibilities of loss inherent in a fixed-income investment when interest rates and prices both rise; and in recent years the importance of stability of real income and of capital value has been more appreciated than formerly. One manifestation of this trend is the increased popularity of common stocks among investors.

The prudent investment theory is capable of adaptation so that it will tend to meet whatever form of assurance is deemed most desirable; but when interest rates and price levels fluctuate, only one form of stability can be obtained by any one method, and the choice of any one form implies definite relinquishment of the three other forms of stability.

The alternatives can be summarily stated thus:

1. If the return is restricted to a fixed rate on actual investment, it is the *fixed money income* that is stabilized, and the investor assumes the risk of fluctuations in the purchasing power of this income and in the capital value of his

investment. This is the position under the English Gas and Water Company Acts.

2. If the fair return is measured by the actual investment and current rates of interest, it is the *capital value of the investment in money* that is stabilized. This seems to be the principle favored by Mr. Justice Brandeis.

3. If a *stable real income* is desired, the result can be obtained by using a fixed rate of return but using as the rate base the actual investment adjusted for changes in the general price level.

4. Finally, the *capital investment measured in terms of purchasing power* can be stabilized by adjusting the prudent investment in respect to the change in the general price level, and applying to the rate base so ascertained a rate of return based on current rates of interest.

The method of applying a fair current rate to a fair present value of the property employed in rendering service, which has the support of the Supreme Court, differs from the principle last mentioned in that it takes account of changes in value not attributable to changes in price levels, and reflects variations in price of the particular commodities by which the investment is represented instead of changes in the general price level.

Theoretically there might be an alternative application of the present-value theory under which a fixed rate of return would be applied to the rate base determined on present values. It would, however, be illogical to determine the rate base with reference solely to existing conditions and to ignore existing conditions in fixing the rate of return. This being so, the alternative scarcely needs consideration. For the same reasons the variant (3) of the prudent investment theory, above mentioned, may be eliminated or left to come into existence as a part of a general scheme of stabilization of the purchasing power of money.

Of the other variants of the prudent-investment theory, the last mentioned, (4), which contemplates adjustments for changes in price level and interest rates, has received little consideration, though the acceptance of this modification would go far to reconcile the theory with the basic constitutional requirement that the ultimate rate base must be defensible as a reflection of present values. The prudent-investment advocates, as a rule, favor the actual money investment as the measure of the rate base.

The Supreme Court rejects this view and insists on present value. But what is present value? The Court has said that actual investment, present cost of reproduction, and other elements are all factors in determining it. The conclusion reached in any case will depend on the weight assigned to the various factors. At the moment, however, the legal standard of present value seems to tend to approximate cost of reproduction (with some adjustment for decline in value due to condition).

Notwithstanding the pronouncements of the Supreme Court, the Interstate Commerce Commission has continued to express its convictions in favor of prudent investment, and in some cases to attempt to give practical effect to those convictions. In the following discussion of the treatment of property consumed in rendering service, both the prudent investment and the present value theories of compensation for property use will therefore be kept in mind, the prudent investment theory being deemed to imply the use of actual investment, and the present value theory the use of substantially present cost of reproduction as the rate base. The question whether any deduction, and if so, what deduction, shall be made from the gross value for decline from new condition is reserved for consideration as the discussion proceeds.

III

We may now consider the specific questions raised above, and first the question, "Should charges for consumption of property in rendering service be based uniformly on cost (a) for purposes of rate and profit regulation; and (b) for current accounting purposes?"

The question is subdivided into these two parts in order to emphasize the point that the considerations affecting the two aspects of the question are not identical. Nevertheless, while it is not in theory essential that the treatment of charges for consumption of property in rate cases should be identical with that in the current accounting of the carrier, obviously serious inconvenience would result if different methods were employed for the two purposes; indeed, it is scarcely too much to say that practicability requires identical treatment. It follows that any method prescribed by the Commission should be reasonably appropriate for both purposes.

As has already been suggested, the assumption made by the Commission that the charge for property consumed should be based uniformly on its original cost does not find support either in theory or in past practice.

Where rates are being regulated there are at least two other bases for which theoretical arguments can be advanced: current cost of reproduction and probable cost of replacement. Prospective cost of replacement seems in principle the most appropriate basis if the prudent investment theory of rate base is accepted; if the present value theory of rate base is adopted, current cost of reproduction from year to year seems theoretically the correct basis for the computation of the exhaustion charge.

It is inherently fair that, if traffic is paid for in currency which has depreciated, the charge against the traffic for property used up in operation should be calculated upon the same scale of values. Suppose that in a given year property is made good to an extent exactly equaling the amount of property used up in operation (measurement being made in physical units): justice to all would seem to be achieved by charging the cost of making good property during the year against traffic of the year. When the value of money has fallen there is no valid reason why the increased currency cost of the replacing units over the original cost of exactly similar property used up in operation should be treated as capital expenditure so as to constitute a burden on the patrons of a later time.

Further: if the principle be accepted that the sum on which the carrier is entitled to a return as compensation for the *use* of property in service is its fair present value, consistency would suggest that the measure of the compensation for property *used up* should also be its fair present value, or, in other words, the current cost of replacement of what is exhausted. The point may be made clearer by an illustration.

Take the first year of the life of a locomotive: suppose its cost to be $25,000; suppose the fair rate of return for use (exclusive of exhaustion) to be six per cent; suppose it is agreed that three per cent of new value is a fair measure of the annual charge for exhaustion; then the charge against the traffic for the locomotive is nine per cent (six plus three) of $25,000, or $2,250. Now consider, say, the tenth year, when through currency depreciation the new value is $60,-000, and the condition of the property, as the result of exhaustion on the one hand and rebuilding on the other, is 80 per cent of new value—interest rates being unchanged. On the present value theory the rate base for the locomotive is 80 per cent of $60,000, or $48,000, and the use charge six per cent thereon, $2,880. Is it not clear that on the same theory the exhaustion charge should logically be three per cent on $60,000, rather than three per cent on $25,000?

The practical objections to the application of this principle are so great as perhaps to compel its rejection. If so, it may be argued that whichever of the other bases more closely approximates to the theoretically correct one should be chosen. But clearly actual reproduction cost would normally tend to be closer to original cost in the earlier years of the life of a unit, and to prospective replacement cost in the later years, so that there could be no preponderance in favor of either of these bases.

In these circumstances it may be said that the theoretical arguments are equally balanced, and that the choice between original cost and probable replacement cost should be determined by practical convenience. This would mean that if the charge is to be made for exhaustion as it proceeds, original cost would be the preferable basis, since original cost could be more easily ascertained or estimated than probable replacement cost. If, on the other hand, exhaustion is to be provided for in bulk when the unit is retired, the actual cost of replacement would be a more convenient basis for the charge than an actual or estimated original cost. On the whole it may be said that, if the present value theory of rate base is to govern, there is no balance of argument on the score of either theory or practical advantage in favor of either original cost or replacement cost as the basis of the charge to operations for property exhaustion.

Let us now consider the question on the assumption that the use charge is to be computed upon the prudent investment theory. This theory rests upon the proposition that when an investment is made in railroad property it is permanent, that the investor exchanges a present command of purchasing power for a right to receive a reasonable return thereon in the future, and that thereafter fluctuations in the value or cost of reproduction of the property represented by his investment are of no practical significance to him. It seems a legitimate corollary of this proposition that the burden of maintaining the property should fall on those who benefit from the use of the property, and that fluctuations in the cost of its maintenance should be treated as at their risk and charge. This would mean that, if the prudent investment theory is to control, prospective cost of replacement should be the basis of the exhaustion charge, whether such charge is to be made as the exhaustion proceeds or in bulk as units are retired.

The Interstate Commerce Commission in its report on Case 15,100 takes a somewhat different view, and proceeds upon the theory that on the replacement of any property the original investment should be regarded as having been returned to the investors and a fresh investment made by them in the replacing unit. This, however, seems not only contrary to the normal course of events but inconsistent with the basic idea of the prudent investment. It seems to be an essential feature of the prudent investment theory that the investment is voluntary; and it is only the original investment that can be said to be voluntary—replacement being a necessity that grows out of, first, the voluntary act of creating the original property, and second, the use of the property in rendering service.

This theoretical argument in favor of charging the cost of replacement rather than the cost of the original unit against operating expenses finds ample support in practice. It is the method that has consistently been followed in Great Britain; and though methods of railroad accounting and reporting there have been the subject of numerous official inquiries, apparently no suggestion has even been made that the practice should be modified. Railroad accounting in Great Britain has always proceeded on the principle that the original cost is a permanent investment and that the maintenance of a property, including the replacement of units, is to be effected out of revenue. This was also, it is believed, the common practice of the best-managed railroads in the United States prior to the regulation of accounting by the Interstate Commerce Commission; it is the practice that has been required by the Commission under the existing regulations during the last twenty years for important classes of property, such as rails, ties and other track material.

It must be remembered that the original construction of a railroad, particularly in a new country, often involves costs not entailed in the subsequent replacement of units. For instance, rails may have had to be hauled on mule-back over mountains at a cost exceeding the cost of the rails at the point of production, whereas when replacement becomes necessary they can be shipped over the railroad itself at a fraction of the original transportation cost. The extraordinary transportation cost of the original rail can rightfully be regarded as attaching to the railroad as a whole, rather than to the particular pieces of metal in the track, and every economic and financial requirement is met when the replacement of the rail is provided for through operating expenses on a basis including a normal current transportation charge.

The answer to our first question may then be stated as follows:

1. If the rate base is to be computed on the present value theory, then the balance of argument is slightly in favor of *original cost* as the basis of the exhaustion charge if provision is to be made as exhaustion proceeds, and slightly in favor of *replacement cost* if the charge is to be made when exhaustion is complete.

2. If the rate base is to be computed on the prudent investment theory, then the balance of argument is decidedly in favor of replacement cost as the basis of the exhaustion charge if exhaustion is provided for as it proceeds, and still more decidedly if the charge is to be made only in bulk when the exhaustion is complete.

IV

We may now consider the second question stated on page 197, which is in substance whether provision for consumption as it takes place—or what is commonly called a depreciation scheme—is or is not desirable for various classes of railroad property.

The reasons that have led the Commission to favor a complete depreciation scheme appear to be four:

1. That existing methods do not take out of capital or charge into operating expenses an exhaustion of value that has undoubtedly taken place;

2. That the existing methods facilitate manipulation of operating expenses through excessive or inadequate expenditure for maintenance;

3. That such a plan strengthens the financial position of the carrier and puts it in a position to render better service;

4. That it is necessary, as the Commission sees it, to bring accounting and valuation methods into harmony.

The theoretical correctness of the first point may be conceded and yet the wisdom of the suggested change, from the standpoint of the carrier and the public alike, still be seriously questioned.

If we consider the usual history of a railroad from its creation as a new property, we find that, for some years, while wear and tear will be taking place, it will not be practicable or economical to make good this wear and tear. Consequently the renewals will be light and the unexhausted service value of the property will diminish until a point is reached where any further deterioration would mean a loss of efficiency. At this point renewals will begin, and every such renewal will tend to restore or extend the original life of the unit to which it is applied. The point at which such renewals become necessary will vary with each unit, even of the same kind. Once the point is reached, the group cannot further depreciate if it is properly maintained; and hence, in practice, while single units may and frequently do run down to a point much below this average without becoming absolutely inefficient, a complete property, if properly maintained, arrives at a more or less stationary value and never reaches the theoretical scrap value. At this point proper maintenance will call for expenditures for renewals and replacements which will approximately equal the depreciation charge; renewals and replacements, due either to wear and tear or to obsolescence, all the time tending to postpone the date when final replacement occurs.*

This brief outline suggests a number of considerations. There is clearly in the case of a matured property a substantial exhaustion which will never be made good. In the accounting of a new company is it necessary or desirable to

* It may be of interest to mention that this paragraph is substantially a quotation from a communication addressed to the Interstate Commerce Commission by the writer's firm in 1908, questioning the soundness of a system of depreciation which merely distributed the original cost over estimated life as extended probably by important renewals without making any allowance for the cost of those renewals. The Commission in its decision in Case 15,100 has attempted to meet such criticisms by a modification of the scheme.

provide out of earnings for this exhaustion? If, in the case of a mature company, no such provision has in fact been made heretofore, should it now be made and, if so, how and by whom should the cost be borne? Precisely what purpose does such a provision serve? Is it to offset a loss of value? If so, what is the real loss of value? It is to provide for replacement? If so, is it not a fact that so long as operations continue there will always be substantially the same amount of exhaustion not made good, and that if operations cease no further replacements will be made?

In order to consider dispassionately the question whether any depreciation provision is economically desirable, it may be well to look at it from the standpoint of a community in which a new railroad enterprise is under contemplation. Let us assume that it is agreed between the promoters of the railroad and the community that the former shall be entitled to a reasonable opportunity to earn a fair return on their investment in the line, and that the community shall have the right to restrict closely to that fair return the profits of the railroad. Would competent economic advisers of the community advocate a system of depreciation charges, and, if so, of what type? The result of a depreciation plan is obviously to throw an added charge for use and exhaustion of property upon the earliest years of operation, years in which the traffic development would be in progress and in which consequently the charge would be more burdensome than in later years. Such a condition would seem to be exactly the reverse of that which would be economically desirable from the standpoint of the community. Its interests would be served by keeping the charges in the early years down to the minimum consistent with maintaining the efficiency of the property, thus enlarging the volume of the commodities that could profitably be transported, and building up both the traffic and the community more rapidly than would otherwise be possible. The best interests of the community in such a situation would be served, it would seem, by a mutual agreement to ignore the depreciation on the property in so far as it could never be made good while the property was being operated, the owners of the railroad agreeing that this depreciation should not be treated as a part of cost of operation, and the community agreeing on the other hand that in computing return no deduction should be made from the original investment therefor.

If a universal depreciation scheme was not desirable in the interests of the carrier or the public at the time when railroad enterprises were in their infancy (and none was ever put in force, if indeed ever seriously suggested), there is an even stronger case against imposing such a scheme today upon railroads which are now highly developed and have been built up under a system of accounting that contemplated no provision therefor. If a depreciation scheme is to be adopted, how is the amount of depreciation deemed to have arisen prior to the initiation of the scheme to be provided? If it is to be provided at the expense of the public, an unnecessary burden will be imposed on the traffic; it could hardly in common justice be established at the expense of the carriers. The Commission expresses no final opinion on this question; it does, however, indicate its views in the following language (page 384 of the Report):

The theoretically correct way of meeting this situation would be to establish the amount of past accrued depreciation which has not been provided for, and concurrently credit this amount to the depreciation reserve and charge it to profit and loss. It is the latter account which has profited in the past from the failure or partial failure to accrue depreciation charges.

This statement of the position is inadequate and, as a result, seriously unjust. The omission of depreciation provisions in the past is supported too strongly by economic, historical and practical considerations to be justly characterized as a "failure on the part of the carriers." It seems humanly certain also that if a system of depreciation charges had been inaugurated at the commencement of railroad enterprise the development of the railroads would have been made more difficult and the growth of the country greatly retarded.

Upon a broad view of the situation it is quite impossible, therefore, to hold that it is the profit and loss accounts of the carriers alone which have profited by the omission of depreciation charges in the past. As regards equipment, it might be reasonable to treat any past omission to provide adequately for depreciation as a failure on the part of the carriers, seeing that depreciation provisions therefor have been in force now for twenty years. But in the case of properties such as rails, where neither the Commission nor the practice in other jurisdictions has in the past called for depreciation provisions, the fact that they have not been made cannot reasonably be treated as a delinquency on the part of the carriers, nor could the surplus of the carriers justly be diminished by whatever amount of depreciation the Commission might, upon some new theory, decide to attribute to the past. The only alternative is that the provision in question, if made at all, should in some way be set aside out of future earnings. Possibly the most equitable way would be to accumulate it gradually out of earnings after the carriers have received a fair return and before any recapture provisions become effective. In any event, the adoption of such a scheme would impose an unnecessary burden on someone in the future.

The economic considerations thus seem to lead clearly to a conclusion adverse to the proposal.

Turning to the Commission's second point, there is the gravest doubt whether the opportunities for manipulation would be lessened by the adoption of a general depreciation scheme. This is a highly technical question, which cannot be fully dealt with here; anyone interested in it will find some aspects dealt with in a memorandum by the writer introduced in Case 15,100, and forming a part of the record in that case.*

It is suggested that the results sought by the Commission in this direction, and also the financial strengthening con-

---

* See above.

templated in the Commission's third point, could be secured at least as adequately in other ways under the Commission's powers of regulation and supervision, and that there is no real argument under either head for a depreciation scheme. Some system of reserves for the equalization of maintenance charges, such as have been employed in the past by sound railroad managements here and abroad, should under the Commission's supervision meet these requirements, as they have in the past met them without the safeguard afforded by that supervision. It may be added that no system of book charges for depreciation will by itself prove very valuable in maintaining the carriers' financial integrity. This is particularly true if the depreciation reserve is to be regarded as available for financing capital additions, as the Commission contemplates. If, on the other hand, the reserve is to be kept invested in liquid form, the investment of the huge sums which would accumulate would present another grave problem and afford opportunities for serious abuses.

We come, then, to the fourth consideration influencing the Commission, namely, the relation between maintenance charges and valuation. In reading the report one feels that it is this consideration which has weighed most heavily with the Commission and largely determined its conclusions.

In maintaining its position upon this point the Commission labors under the difficulty that its position is completely at variance with the Supreme Court's decisions. In the Indianapolis Water Company case * the Supreme Court made it clear that in valuing property for rate purposes the only permissible deduction for depreciation was the actual lessening of worth as compared with new value, and added that such lessening of worth must be not wholly theoretical nor based on percentages of general application, but primarily founded on observation. Now, not only is the Commission's proposed method theoretical and based on percentages of general application, but the particular theory of depreciation which it advocates is one that clearly does not

* 272 U. S., 400.

even approximately reflect the lessening of worth in service due to the partial exhaustion of useful life.

V

This brings us to a consideration of our third question: on what basis the accrual of depreciation or exhaustion shall be deemed to take place and be computed.

In practice there are perhaps four well-recognized methods of providing for depreciation:

1. *The straight line method.* This is by far the most common in industrial practice. It contemplates the distribution of the cost of property (less salvage value) over the useful life in equal instalments.

2. *The sinking fund method.* This aims to set aside annually such a sum as will, if invested, produce an amount equal to the cost of the property when the life thereof is exhausted.

3. *The annuity method.* This regards property as representing capacity for service over a period of years, and its service value therefore as that of an annuity for a gradually diminishing term of years, and adjusts the valuation from year to year accordingly.

4. *The diminishing balance method.* This involves the application of a uniform percentage of reduction to the balance of the property account from year to year, so that the property will stand at its salvage value, or a nominal figure, when its useful life is exhausted.

It will be observed that the second and third methods are substantially similar. Since the sinking fund method contemplates the return of the investment or provision for its replacement when the unit is retired, it is perhaps technically the better adapted to replacement reserves (based on estimated *cost of replacement*), while the annuity method is more strictly applicable to a depreciation scheme designed to provide gradually for writing off the *cost* of the original unit.

The diminishing balance method is of limited application: to cases in which the prospects of profitable use are assured for a brief period only, or to accounts representing a mass of small units of property which it is impossible to account for separately.

The straight line method has the virtues of comparative simplicity and conservatism, but since it ignores interest and the time element, its adoption necessarily implies renunciation of any attempt to reflect the course of unexpired values in service.

The annuity method reflects the course of value in service, and is the only logical method to be followed if the object is to provide for the return to the investor of the lessening of worth of a property unit due to the gradual exhaustion of its useful life as that exhaustion takes place.

Neither the fundamental character of the differences in principle and purpose between the straight line method and the annuity (or the sinking fund) method nor the wide difference in the results reached, according as one or the other is employed, appears to be adequately appreciated by the Commission.

It has expressed the opinion that the principles underlying the straight line method are in accord with the principles enunciated by the Supreme Court—a statement which it is difficult to accept—and says, "Nor are the practical results of the two methods [that is, the sinking-fund or annuity method and the straight line method] very different"—a statement which is clearly incorrect.*

It seems to the writer a matter not of argument but of mathematical demonstration, that the annuity method of computing depreciation is the only one which is consistent with the Commission's own hypotheses and which upon those hypotheses reflects the relation between the value of a new unit and that of a partly exhausted one. It follows

* A discussion of this point will be found in the memorandum by the writer of this article filed in Case 15,100. An illustration there given shows that in the case of property having an assumed life of 50 years, the value in service (taking money to be worth 6 per cent) at the end of 25 years is 81.11 per cent of new value, which is also the depreciated value on the annuity basis; as compared with 50 per cent on a straight line basis.

either that the annuity method must be substituted for the straight line method or that all suggestion of close relationship between depreciated values and fair value in service must be abandoned.

If the annuity method is properly applied the depreciated value will be the fair value in service, subject to fluctuations in new value and to the effecting of normal maintenance; this is as near the goal of reflecting true value as percentage depreciation schemes can come.

The Commission's arguments for the straight line method are as untenable as the argument of the carriers that there is no lessening of value as long as property is maintained in serviceable condition.

VI

Now the type of depreciation scheme that is applicable, if any is to be applied, has a most important bearing on the decision whether any should be adopted.

The difficulties of even the simplest system of depreciation —difficulties that lie less in establishing the amounts to be set aside than in determining what outlays shall be charged against the fund so created—are sufficiently indicated in the report on Case 15,100. It can scarcely be claimed that adequate solutions of such problems as the treatment of extraordinary repairs or depreciation of miscellaneous track material and continuous structure are formulated or even suggested in that report. But if to the inevitable complexities of even a straight line system of depreciation are added the further complications inherent in the application of the sinking fund or annuity principle, the resulting method would be, if not beyond the limits of practicability, at least so close to these limits that only a compelling need could justify its adoption. Dispassionate consideration leads to the conclusion that no such compelling need exists, even if it were granted that a general depreciation scheme is, in the abstract, desirable.

VII

The conclusions to which this discussion leads may be summarized as follows:

1. Unless a depreciation scheme is in force, cost of replacement rather than original cost is the proper basis for charges for property consumed in operation.

2. While depreciation schemes are an invaluable part of industrial accounting, a general system of depreciation charges for railroads is not today desirable.

3. The case for such a system would be weakened if the prudent investment theory of rate base were to be adopted as the Commission seems to think it should be.

4. The particular form of depreciation scheme put forward by the Commission—the straight line method—is demonstrably inappropriate for the purpose sought to be achieved.

5. The Commission's plan lacks one essential of any satisfactory scheme, namely, a practicable and equitable method of dealing with the depreciation deemed to have accrued prior to the initiation of the scheme.

What, it may be asked, are the alternatives? It is suggested that since a depreciation scheme for equipment has been in force for many years it might well be continued and extended to all classes of movable property, and also to any classes of property which are essentially in the nature of industrial plant. It might also be desirable to initiate depreciation provisions computed on the annuity, or sinking fund, basis for the replacement of exceptionally large units replaceable only as a whole.

The only further provision that seems to be called for is a reserve for the equalization of maintenance charges based on the reasonable expectations for a period of, say, five or ten years in the future. In the management of such a reserve the carriers should be given fairly wide discretion, though the Commission should retain power to deal effectively with any case in which the maintenance charges might be grossly inadequate or obviously excessive. Transfers to and from the reserve should appear as separate items in the accounts so that the actual maintenance expenditures would not be obscured. So long as the present rules governing the determination of the rate base prevail, this reserve should not in any event be allowed to exceed the percentage of the book value of the property to which it would relate, which would be deductible from the new value of similar property as "observed depreciation" in a valuation proceeding.

It is believed that a program such as is here outlined would accomplish all the desirable objects which the Commission aims to accomplish by a depreciation system, and would be free from the objections to the Commission's proposals which have been set forth herein.

Upon the larger question of fixing a rate base, the best interests of all parties would seem to call for a settlement by agreement between the carriers and the Commission. For the moment the carriers have the advantage in the courts. But few suppose that the carrier groups will in practice ever be allowed to earn a return on the full present undepreciated reproduction cost of their property, and the next turn of the wheel may leave them in a far less satisfactory position than they now occupy. They can afford to make considerable abatements of their claims to secure certainty. The Commission can scarcely hope to maintain its claim that straight line depreciation should be deducted from new value to arrive at present value in service, nor the carriers their claim that there is no loss of value where there is no observable loss of efficiency. If the parties could approach the question in a sincere effort to reach by agreement a reasonable settlement, instead of advancing extreme claims, a solution of a difficult and vital problem should be attainable that would be fair to carriers and the public alike. Probably new legislation would have to be enacted and accepted by the carriers to enable settlements to be made which would be permanently effective and binding, but the advantages to all parties of a fixed method of determining the rate base as compared with the ill-defined and uncertain methods which the Supreme Court has felt compelled by the Constitution to prescribe, are so apparent and substantial that it should not be an extremely difficult task to secure the passage and acceptance of the necessary laws.

VI

FURTHER THOUGHTS ON DEPRECIATION AND THE RATE BASE *

(1930)

The decision of the Supreme Court in the Baltimore Railways case (*The United Railways and Electric Company of Baltimore* v. *West et al.,* Public Service Commission of Maryland, decided on January 6, 1930) adds a new chapter to the legal history of the depreciation question in relation to rate regulation. While the decision of the question immediately at issue was one of great technical interest, the implications of the decision are perhaps of even greater importance, though that importance may not be so immediately apparent. It is proposed to deal briefly with both points.

Depreciation enters into rate cases in two ways. Depreciation attributable to a particular period is a charge against the earnings of that period, and the accumulated depreciation at any given date operates to reduce the rate base (that is, the value of the property employed in rendering service) at that date. In this instance it was the first only, the charge against earnings, that was in question; the rate base was practically agreed, and the treatment of depreciation in fixing that base was not before the Court.†

The problem of fixing a depreciation allowance to be recouped out of charges for service is, in part, one of deciding what exhaustion is to be provided for, and, in part, one of

---

* *Quarterly Journal of Economics,* Vol. XLIV (August, 1930), pp. 687-97.

† In the present note, only those parts (much the most important) of the majority and minority opinions are considered which discuss the matter of depreciation. There was also discussion (as well as dissent) as regards the fair rate or percentage of return, which should be allowed on the basic sum—the rate base. The majority held that a return of 7.44 per cent sought by the Company itself, was the least that could be· deemed non-confiscatory; whereas Justices Brandeis and Holmes maintained that "a net return of 6.26 per cent would seem to be compensatory."

expressing the exhaustion in terms of money. Under the first head come such questions as whether the allowance is to cover only wear and tear, or wear and tear and also obsolescence; and whether it is to be measured by observation, or in some other way. Under the second head comes the question whether the exhaustion is to be expressed in terms of money on the basis of original cost, present reproduction cost, or probable replacement cost.

Questions under both heads had been considered by the Maryland Commission and the Maryland Court of Appeals, but only the second phase was discussed by the Supreme Court. The Maryland Commission, in its decision of the rate case, had adopted two principles: first, that the annual allowance for depreciation should be determined on the basis of original cost; and second, that the allowance should be sufficient to "provide a fund out of which retirements may be met as they occur, and also to create a reserve out of which ordinary obsolescence may be cared for."

The Court of Appeals of Maryland had approved the Commission's decision on the second point, but had held that the allowance should be based on present value instead of original cost. The Commission had then recomputed the allowance on that basis, the result being an increase in the amount for the year under review from $883,544 to $1,658,650.

The Supreme Court, in concluding that the order of the Maryland Commission was confiscatory, deducted the larger sum of $1,658,650 from the earnings as the necessary provision for depreciation, thus in effect upholding the decision of the Maryland Court of Appeals on both points. It did not discuss the principle that a depreciation fund should provide for retirements and ordinary obsolescence, but its approval of this principle is clearly implied in, and necessary to, the conclusion reached.

In the majority opinion of the United States Supreme Court, the discussion of the depreciation question begins as follows: "The allowance for annual depreciation made by the Commission was based upon cost. The Court of Appeals held that this was erroneous and that it should have been based upon present value. The Court's view of the matter was plainly right." But in spite of this clear-cut declaration, the effect of the decision on the question of the basis on which the exhaustion is to be expressed in terms of money is not free from doubt.

The standard sum with which the probable yield of a rate structure is to be compared in order to determine whether that structure is compensatory or confiscatory may be conveniently regarded as composed of three parts:

1. An amount to cover a fair return on capital investment.
2. An amount to cover exhaustion of property.
3. An amount to cover all expenses of or incidental to operation, except those of making good exhaustion of property.

The first amount is, under a long series of decisions of the Supreme Court, in the nature of compensation based on value, not on cost. The third is merely a reimbursement of cost. The question remains whether the second amount should be determined like the first, as compensation based on value, or like the third, as a reimbursement of cost? If the latter, should the measure be the original cost of the property exhausted or the cost of making good the exhaustion?

The majority opinion decides categorically that the allowance for exhaustion must *not* be computed on the basis of original cost of the property exhausted. It seems to leave open, however, the question whether the allowance should be computed as a compensation based on value, or as a reimbursement of cost based on the actual or probable cost of replacing the property exhausted. For after upholding, in the language above cited, the use of present value in the case at bar, the Court entered upon a discussion which leaves a doubt as to whether present value was adopted as the basis because it was present value or because it was the most practical approximation to probable cost of replacement. After quoting the language of the Knoxville Water Company case to the effect that the utility "is entitled to see that from earnings the value of the property invested is kept unimpaired, so that at the end of any given term of years the original investment remains as it was at the beginning," * the Court adds: "This naturally calls for expenditures equal to the cost † of the worn-out equipment at the time of replacement; and this, for all practical purposes, means present value."

So far, the argument would appear to lead to the conclusion that in principle the allowance was to be based on actual or probable cost of replacement, and that for the purposes of the instant case, at least, present value was a reasonable guide to probable cost of replacement. But in the ensuing sentence the Court said: "It is the settled rule of this Court that the rate base is present value, and it would be wholly illogical to adopt a different rule for depreciation." Here, the Court seems to adopt present value upon its own merits and not as a guide to replacement cost.

Mr. Justice Stone, while concurring in a dissenting opinion of Mr. Justice Brandeis, added a vigorous attack of his own on the validity, either generally or in this particular case, of the assumption that replacement cost means, for all practical purposes, present value. His opinion concludes as follows:

To say that the present price level is necessarily the true measure of future replacement cost is to substitute for a relevant fact which I should have thought ought to be established as are other facts, a rule of law which seems not to follow from *Smyth* v. *Ames,* and to be founded neither upon experience nor expert opinion and to be unworkable in practice. In the present case it can be applied only by disregarding evidence which would seem persuasively to establish the very fact to be ascertained.

* In passing it may be remarked that this sounds like an echo of the prudent investment theory.

† Cost here evidently means cost of replacement, not original cost.

Mr. Justice Stone did not discuss the argument that it would be illogical to adopt a rule for depreciation different from that adopted in determining the rate base. Mr. Justice Brandeis rejected the argument, on the ground that the depreciation charge is designed to distribute the total net expense of plant replacement over the period of use. One is probably justified in concluding that the Court upheld the present value basis as being, for all practical purposes, equivalent to the cost of replacement, and that the argument by analogy from the method of determining the rate base was thrown in rather as a makeweight.

Whether a depreciation scheme for a regulated utility should be based on original cost or probable cost of replacement is, from a practical standpoint, a relatively minor consideration. But it is essential, and the point is important, that depreciation shall be recognized as a reimbursement of cost and treated accordingly. Certainly there is nothing in the decision to preclude the Court from so interpreting it in any future case, and the hope may be expressed that it will adopt this interpretation should the question arise, as it probably will.

Any depreciation scheme is necessarily based to a large extent on estimates and assumptions. In order that it may operate equitably, the original estimates and assumptions must be reasonable, the scheme must be continuously and consistently carried out from year to year, and proper provision must be made for the correction (without undue disturbance of the operating or financial situation) of estimates made in earlier years which in the light of later experience may prove to have been too high or too low. A further essential is that the theory of distribution of the cost of property over its useful life shall harmonize with the theory of valuation on which the rate base is to be determined. Finally it is highly desirable, if not essential, that the scheme shall be suitable for the current accounting of the utility, as well as applicable in the determination of rates.

All these requirements can be met so long as the allowance is treated as a reimbursement of costs, actual or prospective. If replacement cost is used rather than original cost, the basic problem is not changed, even though a new assumption becomes necessary, and continuity and provision for adjustment become the more necessary. If, however, the view were to be accepted that for rate purposes the allowance for any year should be determined as compensation for the exhaustion of life occurring within the year, measured by observation and expressed in money in terms of current reproduction prices, the whole computation being made without regard to the provision made in any other year or to the actual outlays for original purchase or replacement, then all the essentials above recited would be sacrificed and a method would be substituted which would be discontinuous, conjectural, and utterly unsuited for any other purpose, if not, indeed, for the purpose contemplated.

These considerations become even more important if the depreciation scheme aims to provide for obsolescence as well as mere physical exhaustion. In the Baltimore case, the Commission upon the original hearing stated its position as follows: "In making an allowance for depreciation the Commission will endeavor to provide a fund out of which retirements may be made as they occur, and also to create a reserve out of which ordinary obsolescence may be cared for." As already stated the Court of Appeals of Maryland upheld the Commission on this point.

Now, allowance for obsolescence is, to repeat, hardly practicable except under a scheme continuously and consistently applied, with provision for adjustment of estimates on the basis of experience. Accounting control and observation are both essential to the proper administration of such a depreciation plan. The courts, whose relation to the question is more remote and spasmodic, are apt to stress the importance of the second essential, observation; but commissions, whose relation is closer and more continuous, perhaps realize more fully the importance of accounting control.

With the modern development of accounting methods,

book records, supplemented by such engineering reports as a competent accounting officer will naturally call for, will prove the most effective and reliable basis for computing and adjusting depreciation allowances. To illustrate the point from another field: book inventories, properly maintained (as they now are by most important corporations), have proved to be more reliable in the case of any large and complex business than inventories based on physical examination, count, weight, and measurement. Much the same is true in the field of depreciation.

It has been mentioned above as an essential of a sound system of depreciation for regulated utilities that the methods and theories upon which the annual allowances are computed must harmonize with the methods and theories governing the determination of the rate base. It would seem inevitable that the courts must accept this principle when once it is clearly presented. If obsolescence is to be allowed for in determining the annual allowance, it must be allowed for in the fixing of the rate base—otherwise, the consumers will inevitably be subjected to a double charge. But the application of the principle obviously presents a problem of considerable difficulty.

In this problem, obsolescence may be considered in two parts: first, what may be called demonstrated obsolescence; second, potential obsolescence. At the earliest stage—say at the end of the first year of operation of a new plant—some reserve will have been set aside for obsolescence; but presumably there will be little if any demonstrable obsolescence to be provided for and the reserve will be applicable only to potential obsolescence. How is such potential obsolescence to be allowed for in the determination of the rate base?

If the rate base were being determined on the basis of original cost, it would be a simple and equitable solution to treat the excess of the reserve set aside for depreciation in the year, over and above the observed depreciation, as being a reserve for potential future obsolescence, and the desired consistency would be secured by deducting it, as well as the observed depreciation, from that cost, to arrive at the rate base.

Where the rate base is computed on present value, probably the only practical way of making the proposed adjustment would be by use of ratios. The cost value of the property subject to obsolescence and the reserve for obsolescence in respect thereof being known, the deduction for obsolescence from the reproduction value might be computed at the same percentage as the actual reserve for obsolescence might be found to bear to the cost value of the property subject to obsolescence.

In the case of the plant of a utility which had been operating for a long period of years, there would be both demonstrated or observable obsolescence, and potential obsolescence. It would certainly be desirable, and should be practicable, to express the demonstrable obsolescence in terms of money.

Let us suppose, for instance, the case of a unit which cost originally $1,000 but would now cost $1,200 to replace in kind. Assume that it has been in service ten years and that from the purely physical standpoint it would be good for another ten years' service. Suppose, however, that it is capable of being replaced with a unit of a new type which would cost $900, which would be estimated to have a life, allowing for physical exhaustion and ordinary obsolescence, of fifteen years, and would effect an economy in operation of $36.00 per annum. Let it be assumed that the fair return on investment in the utility is 7 per cent, and that depreciation allowances are being computed on a sinking fund basis, with interest at 4 per cent.

Upon the foregoing suppositions, would it not be fair to hold that the value of the existing unit, depreciated for obsolescence, is determined by consideration of the cost of the new and superior type? If so, it seems clear that allowance for demonstrated obsolescence (even without taking into account further potential obsolescence) brings a result that is very close to valuation on the basis of the current cost of the most effective unit that could be substituted for the existing unit, rather than upon the cost of reproducing the unit actually existing.*

The courts in the past have been reluctant to go into this question. In the Indianapolis Water Company case (272 U. S., 400) the Supreme Court said:

There is to be ascertained the value of the plant used to give the service and not the estimated cost of a different plant. Save under exceptional circumstances, the Court is not required to enter upon a comparison of the merits of different systems. Such an inquiry would lead to collateral issues and investigations having only remote bearing on the fact to be found, *viz.*, the value of the property devoted to the service of the public.

But with all respect, it would seem that the Court here begged the question. Why should the *value* of the plant actually used be measured by the *cost* of reproducing it, if a more efficient type of plant could be constructed at a materially lower cost? Even if the new value of an existing plant may properly be computed on the basis of reproduction cost, certainly its value as depreciated for use or obsolescence cannot be determined without consideration of the question of its relative efficiency and economy in construction and operation as compared with the most efficient and economical substitute that could be created.

This line of thought suggests that the implicit approval by the Supreme Court of the recognition by the Commission of obsolescence as an element of depreciation in rate cases may be quite as important as its explicit rejection of original cost as the basis of the calculation of the allowance. Indeed it may be that further consideration of the depreciation ques-

---

* The calculation in detail might be as follows:

The sinking fund required to write off $900 in fifteen years at 4 per cent would be $44.95; the annual return on $900 at 7 per cent would be $63.00—together, $107.95. Deducting $36.00 from this amount for the greater economy of the newer unit leaves a balance of $71.95, which would seem to represent fairly the annual value in service of the existing unit. The corresponding capital value of the unit on the basis of ten years' unexpired life, allowing a 7 per cent return and a 4 per cent sinking fund, would be $469.37.

tion may eventually shake the foundations of the current theory of present value. Even if it be granted that, in principle, present value is a more appropriate basis for calculation of the fair return than original cost, it is obvious that the current theory of computation of present value is highly artificial and the results often lacking in reality.

The validity of the conclusions reached under the current theory depends on the validity of the underlying assumptions which must be made if a computation is to be possible. It is necessary to make assumptions as to the conditions immediately prior to the theoretical reproduction, which, in the case of a really important property, such as a large railroad system, are highly speculative and unreal. Again, as already noted, in order to keep the inquiry within bounds the courts have felt compelled to indulge the presumption, frequently unwarranted, that the existing plant would be worth reproducing if it did not exist. For instance, the value of a building and the site on which it stands is assumed to be the aggregate of the value of the land and of the cost of reproduction, less depreciation, of the building; though the land may be taken at its value for an entirely different purpose, and the true aggregate value of the property may be the value of the land, less the probable cost of removing the building.

The resulting valuation is thus a conventional, not a real, figure. This may not be a fatal objection, but at least conventions should be applied with reasonable consistency. If it be accepted as a convention that properties properly maintained do not depreciate, then it should be accepted as a convention that earnings are determinable without any allowance for depreciation. If a convention closer to reality is to be adopted, that properties depreciate through age and obsolescence, even though well maintained, and that an allowance for such depreciation must be made in determining earnings, then allowance for depreciation from age and obsolescence, and not merely for observed depreciation, should be made in fixing present value.

How far afield and to what results the consistent application of the doctrines and conventions now current would lead is a question of vital importance to public utilities and to the public. At the least, it would seriously modify existing practice in rate regulation; it might result in the breakdown of the whole present system. Discontent with that system is rife, and much of the discontent well-founded. It is perhaps a question whether regulation on the basis of fair return is really practicable or effective. Constitutional limitations may prevent the substitution of other methods which have been suggested. But, if this be so, the result may be a drift toward something entirely different, public ownership.

Taking the long view, no problem perhaps possesses more importance for the utilities than that of presenting some constructive plan for securing justice to the consumers as well as reasonable opportunities for profit-making for themselves. At the moment, however, the utility managers seem, in general, content to do nothing, and to rely upon the decisions of the Supreme Court, and upon the fog with which the whole question is shrouded as a result of those decisions, for the maintenance of a situation which for the time is financially satisfactory. They are not likely to change their attitude until they are convinced that the protection on which they rely is not so complete nor so well assured as they have thought it to be. There is danger to them in a fuller recognition by the Court of the limited significance of cost of reproduction of existing plant and of the essential importance of coördination between the different parts of the problem of regulation and, more particularly, between the charges against earnings for depreciation and the deduction from the rate base on account thereof.

The Supreme Court is not committed to any rule of law which assures to cost of reproduction the importance which in practice has been given to it in some recent decisions. If the Court should accept—as in the end it may be compelled to do—the logic of cost of production of the most efficient substitute (less depreciation) as the basis of valuation, while the results would still be uncertain, the uncertainty would be fraught with grave danger to the utilities. They would be wise to recognize this danger, to admit the unsatisfactory state of regulation, and to devote their experience and their knowledge of the problem to finding a solution that would be just to the public as well as fair to themselves.

VII

THE UNITED RAILWAYS DECISION EXAMINED *

(1930)

THE Supreme Court, in its recent decision in the case of the United Railways & Electric Company † of Baltimore, handed down as we go to press, has accepted a logical corollary to its former decisions. It has long been clear that in determining whether or not a given rate structure is confiscatory the test is to compare the probable yield thereunder with the aggregate of three things:

(1) The amounts necessarily expended for supplies consumed, wages and salaries paid and expense incurred in rendering the service;
(2) Compensation for the partial exhaustion of the property used in rendering service;
(3) A return at a reasonable rate on the value of the property necessarily employed in rendering the service.

In previous cases the court had held consistently that the third element must be computed upon the present values of the property, and it is entirely logical that it should now apply the same ruling to the second element in the computation. Any doubts as to the soundness of this decision must be based on practical considerations. The difficulties inherent in such a method of determination are dwelt upon by Mr. Justice Brandeis in a long dissenting opinion. To the accountant, much of this opinion will probably seem persuasive, though it is lengthened and weakened by references to industrial practices which seem irrelevant to the present discussion. Industrial precedents are not valid, because cost is the foundation of industrial accounting just

---

* An editorial contributed to *The Journal of Accountancy*, Vol. XLIX (February, 1930), pp. 81-83.
† Cf. 278 U. S., 567.

as surely as present value has become the basis of rate regulation through the decisions of the Court.

Viewed from the professional standpoint, the decision unfortunately seems to imply a further enhancement of the importance of the engineer and a corresponding diminution of the part to be played by the accountant. The question whether rates are or are not confiscatory will become more and more an engineering question. Up to the present, the practical application of the test above-mentioned has been based mainly on cost of reproduction, which is comparatively easy of ascertainment; but the next logical step would seem to be to base the determination on a consideration of the cost and the rate of exhaustion of an ideal plant capable of rendering the same service. If the value of the property employed or exhausted is to be the test, that value is no greater because the plant rendering the service is expensive and subject to rapid depreciation than it would be if the same service were being rendered by a different type of plant, cheaper to construct and subject to less depreciation. If this view is correct, the determinations of the courts in future cases may become more and more speculative and the practical outcome depend largely on the skill of the professional advisors to the two sides of the controversy. Our engineering friends are to be congratulated on the prospect thus opening up, and we have no doubt the utilities, with their aid, will fare well in the courts. For the present, and until the price curve turns downward or new inventions render existing plants obsolete, the public may expect to bear not only the cost of higher compensation to the utilities but the higher cost of securing that compensation.

Of course, there is another side of the picture. The courts have always insisted that rates must be reasonable and may not be increased, even if they are not fully compensatory, if an increase would make them unreasonable. While this limitation is itself difficult of enforcement, the American public by and large gets its service from the utilities at reasonable prices. Perhaps, therefore, there will be no general complaint if a part of the skill and resourcefulness which is constantly being devoted to reducing the cost of operation is diverted to the task of increasing the limit of gross revenues. Furthermore, a meed of praise should be accorded to those who presented to the Court in the Baltimore case a record which forced the Court to the conclusion that a return of 6.26 per cent certainly was not, and a return of 7.44 might not be, sufficient to attract capital into the street railway field.

PART III
VALUATION

I

THE VALUATION OF GOODWILL *

(1912)

Question: Coming to the question of the value of the good-will, will you please tell us how you estimated that value? *Answer:* The value of the goodwill was a very difficult problem indeed. In the first place, I adopted the method that has been used in numerous cases which have come to my notice in the sale of goodwill, of determining the value solely on the basis of the earning capacity or of the past earnings. Some time before May 20, Mr. Ordway asked me a question on that subject, and I worked out the value of the goodwill for him on the basis of deducting from the earnings interest on the investment, tangible assets, and then capitalizing the excess on the basis of five years' profits. Now, taking the profits for the five and a half years ending January 31, 1910, I arrived at a value of eight hundred and fifty thousand dollars, allowing seven per cent interest on tangible assets, or a million dollars allowing six per cent. In considering the question on May 20, I used that calculation as a starting point, and considered what seemed to me to be the modifying factors. First of all, the profits for the year 1909 had amounted to only three hundred and ten thousand dollars, or seventy thousand dollars less than the average which I had used in the earlier calculations, so that if the last year's profits were taken as the basis I figured the result would be to reduce the value of the goodwill by a sum of three hundred and fifty thousand dollars. Then the other factors which I considered were first of all as regards the wholesale department. There had been considerable discussion of a proposed sale of the wholesale department

---

* Excerpt from testimony, *In the Matter of the Estate of E. P. Hatch, Deceased* (Lord & Taylor), (1912).

without any payment for goodwill, and in the course of discussion on that subject I learned that there was some doubt as to the permanency of that business, and furthermore that it was a question whether the goodwill of the wholesale department did not inhere to a large extent in the two managers who had direct charge of the business and who were in personal touch with the manufacturing houses and the trade. Then a further element that detracted from the value of the goodwill seemed to me to be the dissension amongst the management, which was undoubtedly operating adversely to the business. Then again, there was the fact that most leases of the premises expired in 1914, so that there was the prospect of having to move the business. Of course it is not possible to assign specific weights to each one of these considerations, but weighing all of them together—I do not know whether I should go any further—I think I have probably answered your question.

Q. Did you take into consideration the efficiency of management in the retail department?

A. Yes. Of course the retail department—the ratio of profit in that department had been so much reduced that at that actual time I should say the profits being earned in the retail department would not have justified any payment for goodwill of that business as it stood, although of course the established name does give the goodwill a value in strong hands.

Q. Did you also take into consideration the lack of working capital?

A. Well, that was a factor not so much in the valuation of the goodwill as in the desirability of the proposed sale as a whole, the lack of working capital; it was a very important element in that.

.   .   .   .

Q. Had you any immediate or direct knowledge with regard to the inefficiency of the management of the retail department?

A. Well, I had a number of criticisms of it, but the main

factor to my mind was the low ratio of profit. That, it seemed to me, must be evidence of inefficiency somewhere.

Q. Where did you get at the figures of the ratio of profit in the two departments?

A. Well, various statements were prepared.

Q. Were they the result of any researches which you made in the books of Lord & Taylor or were they based upon reports which came to you from others?

A. Do you mean that I made personally?

Q. Yes.

A. Or through my representatives?

Q. That you made personally.

A. Not on those that I made personally, except in part they were figures according to the books and in part they were figures made up by my subordinates.

Q. Not from the books?

A. Well, from the books with adjustments. Some of them were absolute book figures.

Q. When you speak of adjustments do you mean adjustments in this sense, that somebody took up the accounts as they stood on the books, and they from time to time made, so to speak *nunc pro tunc,* reservations and deductions as you would have made if you had been there at the time?

A. Yes, that is what I mean by adjusted figures.

Q. Take, for instance, in 1910, you assumed a certain adjustment made for the year 1906, which in point of fact had not been made in 1906, is that the idea?

A. Yes, that is what I referred to.

Q. And so on all through the years in succession?

A. Yes, but then I also considered the unadjusted figures. I have here a statement.

Q. As regards the working capital, should you say to us the same thing that you said in regard to all those other elements of your judgment, that you attributed to it no particular value in the deductions which were to be made?

A. I think "particular" is an unfortunate term to use,

because saying "no particular value" might be considered as meaning "no material value." I attached no specific value to it, although I did attach considerable importance to it.

Q. You think that "specific" in this relation might have a different meaning from "particular"?

A. Well, I do not think it would be so ambiguous.

Q. Have you now told us all that you are able to recollect with regard to the—if you do not object I shall use the same word again—particular value that you assigned to these different elements of diminution?

A. Yes.

Q. Now, lumping them all together as you have done, what was their aggregate value as a figure to be deducted from the figure at which you started?

A. Well, I did not feel it quite necessary to put an aggregate value.

Q. Did you simply guess at it?

A. No, I did not.

Q. Did you make an accurate computation?

A. No—

Q. You did not?

A. I took—

Q. One moment. Did you make an accurate computation?

A. No, I did not.

Q. And you did not guess at it?

A. No, I did not guess at it.

Q. And you did not average it?

A. No, I did not average it.

Q. Then will you tell us precisely what you did with it?

A. Well, I took the maximum value for the stock as determined by my starting point, and the value that I was asked to consider for the common stock, and asked myself the question: Is the difference between those two values, those two figures, sufficient, in the light of all those circumstances and of the whole proposed arrangement, to justify you in advising the executors not to make the proposed sale? That is substantially how I dealt with the question.

.   .   .   .

Q. Mr. May, in this question I do not mean to make any imputation at all upon your purposes, but should we not be quite right in understanding that when you certified the balance sheet as of January 31, 1910, you believed that balance sheet which you certified to be correct?

A. Yes, certainly. Perhaps I ought—if you will allow me, I will elaborate that.

Q. You say you did understand it to be correct?

A. Yes, it is correct.

Q. What you said was, "We certify that the above balance sheet correctly sets forth the financial condition of the company at January 31, 1910."

A. Yes.

Q. Did you believe that statement to be true?

A. I believed that to be true, yes.

Q. Do you now believe it to be true?

A. I still believe it to be true.

Q. When you signed that statement in those words were you making any mental or other reservations?

A. Well, I do not know quite what you mean by that. The way I would—

Q. Have you not heard the expression of saying a thing with a mental reservation?

A. Yes.

Q. Well, you know what the phrase means, don't you?

A. Well, it has a rather sinister sense, in which sense of course I had no mental reservations.

Q. You do not now wish to express any mental reservation, do you?

A. No, of course a balance sheet is always a question of opinion.

Q. It was your opinion, was it not, that this balance sheet correctly sets forth the financial condition of the business?

A. Yes, it was—

Q. Was it your opinion or not?

A. It was my opinion that—

Q. Can't you answer my question yes or no?

A. I think not without giving rise to misunderstanding.

Q. I understand you to say that you are not able to say categorically either yes or no to the question I put to you, whether in your opinion this balance sheet correctly sets forth the financial condition of the company; is that so?

A. Well, of course I can say it is a correct statement, but I do not know that that is the whole answer. At the same time I do not want to inject anything.

Q. Now, Mr. May, when you make that remark are you not really telling us that you made that certification with some mental reservation?

A. No, all I mean by that: for instance that balance sheet might have been made up to show a surplus of two hundred and fifty thousand dollars less, and I would still have said that it showed the correct position of the company.

Q. Now, how will you explain that discrepancy? You have certified that when you showed a surplus of four hundred and eighty-six thousand dollars that statement was correct; now you say that if you had certified to a surplus of two hundred and thirty-six thousand dollars, that also would have been correct.

A. Yes, that is—

Q. Now, they both would have been correct?

A. Well, I think they would have been both correct in that they would be both fair expressions of opinion; and that is all a balance sheet ever is.

Q. Oh, you do not regard a balance sheet then as representing a state of fact, but as representing a state of mind, is that the idea?

A. Well, I would state my position exactly as Lord Justice Buckley stated it, that it is necessarily a question of estimate and opinion, every balance sheet.

Q. Did he say that about your opinion?

A. He did not say that about my opinion, he said that

about every balance sheet; and the greater of course includes the less.

Q. We all recognize the influential value of expressions of opinion by Lord Justice Buckley, we do not at all mean to disparage that, but of course you know, Mr. May, that the opinion which we are now dealing with is Mr. May's opinion.

A. Exactly. But I did not feel that I could improve on the language of the Lord Justice nor did I care to plagiarize it without acknowledging the source.

Q. Now, then, you tell us that it would have been just as true to certify to a surplus of four hundred and eighty-six thousand dollars as it would have been to certify to a surplus of two hundred and thirty-six thousand dollars?

A. Both would have been certified and both would have been correct statements.

Q. So you might have cut off two hundred and thirty-six thousand dollars, might you not?

A. Yes.

Q. And leave no balance?

A. Oh, a further two hundred and thirty-six thousand?

Q. Yes.

A. Well, I do not know how far one could go, but I just took the figures of the two hundred and fifty thousand less as representing in my mind the reasonable limit of the opinions.

Q. Now, if you could with propriety certify to a surplus of two hundred and fifty thousand dollars less than you have certified to, might you not with propriety have certified to a surplus of two hundred and fifty thousand dollars more than you certified to?

A. No, I am quite satisfied as to that.

Q. Then your opinion would only be justified in the descending scale?

A. In the case of this particular balance sheet.

Q. Once again, if it would have been equally true to say that the surplus was two hundred and thirty-six thousand dollars as it was to say that the surplus was four hundred and

eighty-six thousand dollars—once again, would it not have
been equally true to say that the surplus was nothing at all?

A. Not necessarily. No, not in fact, I think.

Q. Where would you draw the line between two hundred
and thirty-six thousand dollars and nothing at all?

A. Well, I would not draw a hard and fast line anywhere;
but in that balance sheet there are at least—

Q. Wait a minute. I am not talking about that. I am
asking you to give us an answer to my question. You say
you would not draw a fast and hard line anywhere; now, give
us a wavy line somewhere.

A. Well, it is very hard to do.

Q. Is it too hard for you to do?

A. Well, it is too hard for me to do offhand without careful consideration.

Q. You mean that in order to do it you would have to
sit down with that large bundle of papers that you have be-
side you and work out some mathematical computations?

A. No, I would have to sit down and consider what I
considered the limits of value—of reasonable difference of
opinion as to value of certain assets in that balance sheet.

Q. If I follow you, that would not then be a mathematical
computation but it would be an evolution of opinion, is that
it?

A. That is it, purely an expression of opinion and judgment.

Q. So that when we are talking about this balance sheet
of January 31, 1910, when you certified that the correct
financial condition of the company shows a surplus of four
hundred and eighty-six thousand dollars, are we to understand that that figure merely represents the evolution of your
opinions up to that time?

A. No, I think that would be an erroneous impression.
But it is our opinion that it is correctly adjusted and it is correctly stated in respect, of course, to the majority of items, in
my opinion; but there are certain items, as I said before, that
are of doubtful value, and in those cases, as I said before,

we have accepted values placed upon the properties by the Finance Committee or officers of the Company; and in regard to those assets there is room for a certain latitude of opinion.

.   .   .   .

Q. Will you tell me once again what you mean by tangible assets of this concern?

A. The excess of all assets, excluding goodwill and trade-marks, over liabilities. Net tangible assets is the expression I would use.

Q. You have not used that word "net" heretofore when I asked you the questions.

A. Well, I used the same phrase, the investment in tangible assets.

Q. If you leave out net, and we are talking about tangible assets, you would regard, wouldn't you, the whole amount of merchandise as a tangible asset?

A. Yes.

Q. And all the horses and wagons as tangible assets?

A. Yes, certainly.

Q. And fixtures?

A. Yes.

Q. Would you regard accounts receivable as a tangible asset?

A. Yes, I would include everything on the assets' side of the balance sheet except the goodwill.

Q. Is it customary in your profession to call an account receivable a tangible asset?

A. Yes.

Q. What is the meaning of the word tangible as it is used in your profession?

A. Well, I think it is—unfortunately the whole terminology of my profession and of finance generally is pretty loose, but I think its significance is best reached by saying that it is everything that is not intangible, and intangible includes goodwill, trade-marks, patents, franchises, and that class of property.

Q. I infer, Mr. May, from your experience and from the degrees which you hold of which you have told us, that you know what in ordinary speech the word tangible means, don't you?

A. Yes.

Q. Well, what do you understand it to mean in ordinary speech?

A. Something that can be touched, I imagine.

Q. Like merchandise?

A. Yes.

Q. You can touch merchandise or horses?

A. Yes.

Q. Can you touch an account?

A. You can touch the debtor.

Q. Is that the basis on which you include the debtor's debt as tangible?

A. It had not occurred to me before, but possibly it is.

II

VALUATION OF MINES *

(1916)

It is apparent that the maximum value of the mine will be found by valuing it on one of two theories: the first, that the mine would be operated until the stock should accumulate to a point where further accumulation would be unprofitable (assuming that the mine would continue to yield for that period) and that then the mine would be closed down and the sulphur on hand liquidated; the second, that the current production of the mine would first be liquidated and that the accumulated stock would be sold only when the mine ceases to produce. Whichever method gives the higher capital value is properly applicable. Calculations show that on the basis of any probable volume of sales the first method gives the higher values (using the same basis, figures of sales, expenditures, and rate of profit) and this is true even if, for the purpose of the second method, the operations are assumed to continue indefinitely. The first method is therefore applied in the calculations which follow, in spite of the fact that it is more complicated in application.

The present value of a sum of money to be received at a future date varies according to (1) the interval that will elapse before its receipt, and (2) the rate which is taken as the proper rate of return upon the present investment.

If the interval and rate of return are known or assumed, the present value can readily be calculated or found in interest tables. In the same way if the rate of return and present value are known, the interval can be calculated. This is the form in which the problem occurs in the present case. This problem is: How long can the company afford to carry

* Excerpt from an affidavit in the matter of appraisal under the Transfer Tax Law—Estate of Herman Frasch (Union Sulphur Co.), April, 1916.

stock before selling it? If the selling price is, say, three times cost, the question is: How many years can the sale be deferred and still leave the present value of the proceeds (at whatever rate of return is decided upon) more than one-third of the face value?

The first requirement is, therefore, to ascertain certain basic factors for the calculations, *viz.*:

(a) Probable annual sales (tonnage)
(b) Probable net selling price
(c) Probable production cost
(d) Possible rate of production (assuming operations continue)
(e) Rate of profit which anyone engaged in the venture would reasonably expect it to yield.

I will next deal with the reasonable expectations in regard to the volume and prices of sales and the volume and cost of production.

In forming estimates in regard to future production or sales the natural starting point is the experience of the past. It is apparent, however, that past results are not in themselves conclusive; the operations of a patent-owning company for a period immediately preceding the expiration of its patents being, for instance, useless as an indication of its future prospects. It is necessary, therefore, in connection with the results of the past to consider what changes in conditions have occurred or can reasonably be foreseen which will be reflected in the future operations.

The accounts for the 5⅓ years ending April 30, 1914, which are in evidence, show that during that period the average sales amounted to 270,000 tons; and, in view of the large accumulation of stock, it is safe to assume that every effort was being made to press the sales as much as possible while maintaining prices. During the period, the company had practically no competitors in the United States, but it appears from the record that at April 30, 1914, serious competition was in sight from the Freeport Sulphur Company which had produced upwards of 100,000 tons. Bearing in

mind that within four or five years from the date of commencement of its own operations the Union Sulphur Company was producing more sulphur than the market could
absorb, the seriousness of this factor in the situation is apparent. A prospective purchaser looking at the situation at
the date of Mr. Frasch's death would naturally assume that
this competition would result in one or both of two things;
either a drastic reduction in selling prices, or allowing the
Freeport Company to take a fair proportion of the volume
of business to be done with a corresponding reduction in the
volume of business to be done by the Union Sulphur Company. If such reduction were calculated at one-third of the
average business of the preceding five years of the Union Sulphur Company, this would leave the prospective sales of the
Union Sulphur Company at 180,000 tons per annum. I
think, therefore, that an estimate of 200,000 tons annual sales
is as high as could reasonably be assumed for the future.

As to the price, it appears from the record that the net
price of sulphur at the mine was about $16.40 per ton.
This was arrived at by deducting from the gross price realized the cost of freight and all selling expenses. It is, however, necessary to consider also for the present purpose the
working capital required to be invested in carrying on the
operations, because any proceeds from the sale of sulphur
would have to yield a return on the working capital invested
as well as on the price paid for the stock of sulphur itself.
The net assets of the company, exclusive of the mine and
stock of sulphur and its investments in subsidiary companies,
have been computed at $4,317,205.54. Allowing 7% as the
rate of return on this working capital, the rate normally
paid on the preferred stock of industrial companies, would
give an annual charge of over $350,000, or more than $1 a
ton. Allowing for this item and for the fact that with a
smaller volume of business the selling expenses would probably be relatively higher, past experience would indicate $15
as the price per ton to be assumed for the purpose of calculating the present value of the stock of sulphur.

In view of the fact that the sulphur price had remained substantially unchanged during the 5⅓ years in which the company had a practical monopoly, it seems reasonably clear that no increase in this price could be expected, especially having regard to the prospective competition of the Freeport Sulphur Company and possibly other companies, to the large stocks which the company had accumulated, and to the wide margin between cost and selling prices (selling prices being at least three times cost). There would seem to be more reason to anticipate a reduction in selling prices, but in the absence of any measure of the probable reduction, I have adopted the figure of $15 and merged the hazard of reduced prices with the other hazards which are reflected in the rate of profit allowed in the computation of present values.

As to the volume of production and the costs, there are statements in evidence showing the production and cost by years. These figures are as follows:

		Production (tons)	Outlays
Year	1909	270,725	$1,273,850
"	1910	246,510	1,445,802
"	1911	204,220	1,727,200
"	1912	786,605	2,119,214
"	1913	478,565	1,795,768
4 months ending April 30, 1914		103,080	556,319

Inasmuch as the results for the year 1911 were doubtless seriously affected by the expense incidental to the violent physical disturbances which it has been testified took place in that year, I think these figures should be disregarded in forecasting the future (except in so far as they indicate the financial importance of some of the hazards attaching to the business). The figures for the period prior to 1911 are also of little value inasmuch as the change of methods necessitated by the disturbance in 1911 has permanently affected the cost of operation. Comparing the figures for 1913 with those for 1912 it will be observed that a decrease of 308,040 tons in output was accompanied by a decrease of only

$323,446 in outlays; and working out the annual equivalent for the figures for the four months ending April 30, 1914, a reduction of 169,325 tons a year in production is accompanied by a decrease of only $126,811 per annum in outlays. It is readily apparent therefore that the expenses of conducting operations are affected to only a very small extent by the tonnage of production; and the annual expenditures necessary may be analyzed into two component parts—a fixed expense of approximately $1,350,000, and expensès fluctuating with the output which may be taken at about $1 per ton. On this basis a scale of costs according to the volume of production can readily be computed as follows:

Annual Production (tons)	Fixed Cost	Cost varying with Production	Together	Per Ton
200,000	$1,350,000	$200,000	$1,550,000	$7.75
250,000	1,350,000	250,000	1,600,000	6.40
300,000	1,350,000	300,000	1,650,000	5.50
350,000	1,350,000	350,000	1,700,000	4.86
400,000	1,350,000	400,000	1,750,000	4.38
450,000	1,350,000	450,000	1,800,000	4.00
500,000	1,350,000	500,000	1,850,000	3.70
550,000	1,350,000	550,000	1,900,000	3.45
600,000	1,350,000	600,000	1,950,000	3.25
650,000	1,350,000	650,000	2,000,000	3.08
700,000	1,350,000	700,000	2,050,000	2.93
750,000	1,350,000	750,000	2,100,000	2.80

In passing, it may be noted that the expenses have increased appreciably, the fixed expenses being now greater than the total outlays for 1909. Such an increase is to be expected in view of the testimony as to the necessity of pumping out cold water from the property since 1911 and as to the increasing distance which material has to be moved to fill in on the surface of the property.

From an examination of the record it appears that the production averaged:

for the   5⅓ years   391,820 tons per annum
  "   last 3⅓   "   471,741   "
  "   " 1⅓   "   436,234   "

The production of 1912 must be regarded as abnormally high, just as that for 1911 is abnormally low. On the whole a production of 450,000 tons per annum would seem to be a fair assumption as to tonnage. This would mean total outlays of $1,800,000 and a cost of $4 per ton.

From the foregoing consideration we may use as reasonable estimates for the future the following data:

Annual sales.....................   200,000 tons
Probable selling value (net)........ $15 per ton
Probable production.............   450,000 tons
Cost of production............... $4.00 per ton

The period of operation is entirely uncertain and the question of how best to deal with the uncertainty will be considered later.

A further point remaining to be considered is the question of taxes, particularly taxes in Louisiana. It appears from the testimony that the mine taxes amounted to about $2\frac{1}{4}\%$ on the assessed value of the mine. The calculation of the value of the property will be based on a gradually declining stock of sulphur and mine value, and it is therefore proper to assume that the taxes will be correspondingly reduced. The most convenient way of allowing for this factor will be by adding $2\frac{1}{4}\%$ to the rate of profit determined in the following section in order to provide for these taxes. Thus if a rate of profit of 15% per annum is assumed, the calculations of present value must be based on a rate of 15% plus $2\frac{1}{4}\%$, or $17\frac{1}{4}\%$, and so on. Next to be considered is the rate of return that is proper to be applied.

In determining the rate of profit which an investor in this undertaking would reasonably expect it to yield, the first requirement is to consider in a general way what the investment would involve. Roughly it would mean an investment of $10,000,000 more or less in the acquisition of a stock of sulphur and a mine, as to the future production of which it would be impossible to make any forecast, and there would be a further investment of about $4,300,000 to provide the working capital needed in the business. In the previous section I have assumed a rate of return of 7% on this working capital, so that it is necessary now to consider the rate of return only as the more speculative investment. The amount to be invested is, of course, substantial, and the situation is not therefore comparable to one in which an investor may make a relatively small investment. The difference between the wholesale and retail prices of investments are as real and marked as the difference between the wholesale and retail prices of commodities, especially where it is an outright investment of capital and not a loan that is offered.

The business and the risks attending it are unusual in character, which fact would eliminate the conservative type of investor entirely. To attract the more speculative investor a relatively higher rate of return is essential. The opportunities for remunerative investment in business in this country are greater than the funds seeking investments in which a speculative risk is involved. Consequently, capital is reluctant to go outside well understood lines of activities unless special inducements are offered. There is always and everywhere a tendency to overrate risks which are unfamiliar and to demand greater margins of safety or larger returns to compensate therefor.

If the reasonable expectations above referred to were realized, the investment would be repaid, together with the return assumed by instalments over a period of 9½ years. Taking first the investment in the stock of sulphur, any rate of return assumed would be seriously diminished if either the volume of the sales or the selling price should fall short of such estimates. There is far more ground for expecting a reduction in price than an increase; and as to the volume of tonnage I think it would be fair to say that the prospects of the actual results' falling short of 200,000 tons sales are at least equal to the prospects of that volume's being exceeded. The profitableness of the business depends largely on the practical monopoly which the company has enjoyed; and whilst some allowance has been made for the effect on that monopoly of the operations of the Freeport Sulphur Company, it has been testified that still further competition is well within the bounds of possibility.

The investment would therefore clearly be one attended with substantial hazards, and the rate of profit should be determined with reference to the rate at which earning capacity is bought or sold rather than with reference to rates of interest on money borrowed or loaned. Having regard to my experience in purchases and sales of businesses and earning capacity, I am convinced that 15% is a moderate rate to apply to this part of the investment.

The mine and the sulphur must, however, be considered together for, as already pointed out, the restricted market for sulphur is one of the most essential features of the situation; and no one could afford to buy either the mine or the sulphur separately and be faced with the destructive competition which would begin immediately.

In any computations based on future tonnage, in view of the impossibility of foreseeing the future of the mine, a higher rate of profit than for the sulphur now on hand is clearly necessary. In the calculations which follow, the absolute uncertainty as to whether the mine will continue to yield is not taken into account, except in the rate of return assumed, these calculations being made on the basis of the mine's continuing to yield up to the point where further production would not be profitable. This method involves assumptions of future production of from 600,000 to 1,900,-000 tons (see above). To provide for the hazards involved in these assumptions (which include the hazards as to the maintenance of the volume of sales and selling prices during the period necessary for the realization of this stock), an addition of 5% to the 15% used for stock actually on hand is, I consider, undoubtedly a minimum. I do not feel that any extended discussion of this addition is needed as the justice of the assumption will, I think, be universally admitted.

The conditions of this particular mine are almost unique, and it is therefore almost impossible to find exactly analogous cases of purchase and sales. Comparisons with other mining properties are valueless unless all the facts as to ore reserves, etc., are fully known. Such instances are comparatively rare, but I recall one sale of a mining property for a sum amounting to several million dollars which fits the case closely. The transaction was between a buyer and a willing seller. From the standpoint of monopoly and breadth of market for its output, the company was at least as advantageously situated as this company, and there were no special hazards or uncertainties attending the operations. There was a substantial agreement between the parties as to the tonnage actually in sight and the rate at which it could be mined and marketed. The purchase price asked yielded, on the basis of what was regarded by both parties as the minimum annual tonnage and the minimum selling value, a return of over 17% on the investment. On the basis of tonnage and selling prices which both parties regarded as reasonable and which were in fact more than realized, the yield amounted to approximately 25%. In this case the undeveloped ore was believed and was proved to be very large, but at the time of the sale was incapable of estimation.

While stock exchange values are affected by such varied conditions that it is difficult to draw conclusions therefrom, it would be easy to cite many instances of companies engaged in staple industries earning profits equivalent to considerably more than 15% upon the average market value of their stock.

My firm has recently compiled from reports on examinations made by it, taken at random, a statement showing the average percentage of profit actually realized in a large number of companies large and small, and the result of this compilation, which included some companies operated at a loss, showed that the average return on the investment for the 158 companies was 13.67%. These are of course realizations, not anticipations.

I have frequently known of offers of businesses being rejected because the earning capacity on the investment was not sufficient, where such earning capacity would have amounted to over 15%. As indicating the commercial value of earning capacity when attended with any hazards, I might cite as one of many such instances coming under my personal observation in the course of my practice the issue of common stock of the Willys-Overland Company in 1912. This company was capitalized with a common stock of $20,000,000 and a preferred stock of $5,000,000. The earnings were rapidly increasing and for the last completed year were equivalent to just 17% on the common stock. The estimate for the then current year's earnings (which was more than realized) was about 22% on the common stock. Upon this showing the stock was offered to investors, or at retail, at a price of $67.50 per share, and the market value shortly fell and long remained below that figure. This is only one of many cases which I could cite.

Earning capacity of the most stable industrials is seldom valued at a higher cash value than five years' purchase, that is on the basis of a 20% return. A 15% rate is equivalent to six and two-third years' purchase.

It may be suggested that the stock of sulphur should be valued more from the standpoint of merchandise. I do not think this would affect the conclusion, though I do not think the standpoint is the correct one. A merchant buying at wholesale with a view to retail distribution may be satisfied with a profit, after deducting all expenses, of 5% on stock which he can turn over four or five times a year or oftener, but 15% would be a minimum profit on stock which could be turned over only once a year; and it clearly follows that if the stock will take more than a year to turn over, the rate must be 15% for each year the stock has to be held before sale, which is precisely in accord with the method I have adopted.

In this discussion I have mentioned some among the many considerations leading to the conclusion that a rate of 15%

per annum as to the stock on hand and a rate of 20% as to any tonnage assumed to be mined in the future constitutes a moderate basis for the determination of the present value of the sums expected to be received from the business in the future. It is important to note also that these rates can be applied only to assumptions as to the future such that the chances of failure to realize them are at least measurably offset by chances of more favorable realizations.

CALCULATION OF VALUE OF THE STOCK OF SULPHUR AT THE
MINE AND THE MINING PROPERTY

For the purpose of this calculation the following data has been arrived at:

Factors required	*My computations regarding same*
Probable volume of sales	200,000 tons per annum
Probable net selling price	$15 per ton
Probable production	450,000 tons per annum
Probable production cost	$4 per ton
Rate of profit which anyone engaging in the venture would reasonably expect it to yield	Not less than 15% as to tonnage actually on hand and 20% on any additional tonnage assumed to be mined in the future
Amount to be added to rate of return to allow for taxes	2¼%

The ratio of selling price to cost is $15:4 or 3¾:1. The first step is, therefore, to ascertain how long payment of $3.75 may be postponed without reducing its present value below $1. Since we are dealing here not with stock actually on hand but with sulphur to be mined, the rate of return to be used must be 20% or, adding 2¼% for taxes, 22¼%. From interest tables the period is found to be 6 years. If we go beyond this period, say to 6¼ years, we find the present value of $1 due in 6¼ years (at 5½% payable quarterly which for convenience I have used as the equivalent of 22¼ per annum) is 26.22¢, so that the present value of $3.75 is

98.32¢, or less than $1.   The limit of accumulation is therefore six years stock:

6 years sales at 200,000 tons = 1,200,000 tons
The stock on hand is   867,613 "
          Difference   332,387 tons

Now the quarterly output is 112,500 tons (¼ of 450,000) and the quarterly sales 50,000 (¼ of 200,000), so that the stock will increase 62,500 tons per quarter and will increase by 332,387 tons in somewhat over 5 quarters.   After that time further production would be unprofitable unless the volume of profitable sales could be increased.   Any further production would have to remain on hand more than 6 years, and the present value of the sales price would at 20% be less than the cost of production.

If the production were reduced, the cost per ton would be increased, and the time when the amount of stock that could be accumulated profitably would be lessened.   If the production could be kept at a higher figure, the period of profitable operations would be extended, though not very greatly, as will appear from later calculations.

The only hope of realizing greater values would lie in increasing the sales, without unduly reducing the sale price.

Returning to the calculations, the outlook on the assumed data is therefore:

	Tons	Tons
The stock on hand is............................	867,613	
which will be sold at the rate of 50,000 tons per quarter for 17 quarters and in the 18th quarter		850,000 17,613
There can be profitably mined at the rate of 112,500 tons per quarter for 5 quarters................	562,500	
and in the 6th quarter.........................	69,887	
Which will be sold..............................		32,387
in the 18th quarter and at the rate of 50,000 tons per quarter in the 19th to 30th quarters........		600,000
	1,500,000	1,500,000

The computation is then as follows:

AMOUNTS TO BE RECEIVED AND PRESENT VALUE THEREOF

Sales out of Stock:
850,000 tons at rate per quarter of 50,000 tons at $15 per ton = $750,000 per quarter for 17 quarters, or $12,750,000.
Present value of which per tables (15% return plus 2¼% taxes) is .... $ 8,775,412.50

17,613 tons in the 18th quarter at $15 per ton = $264,195.
Present value per tables (15% return plus 2¼%
taxes) $125,474.13

Sales out of Future Tonnage:

32,387 tons in 18th quarter at $15 per ton = $485,805.
Present value per tables (20% return plus 2¼%
taxes) 185,320.03
600,000 tons at rate per quarter year of 50,000 tons at $15
per ton = $750,000 per quarter for 12 quarters,
or $9,000,000.
Present value of which per tables (20% return
plus 2¼% taxes) is 2,465,760.00
Together............................. $11,551,966.66

From which must be deducted:

Present value of expenditures to be made, *viz.:*
Operating costs of producing 632,387 tons as
follows:
562,500 tons at rate per quarter year of 112,500 tons at $4
per ton = $450,000 per quarter for 5 quarters.
Present value per tables (20%)......$1,948,266.00
69,887 tons in 6th quarter at $4 per
ton = $279,548.
Present value per tables (20%)...... 208,604.31   2,156,870.31
Net present value of Stock of Sulphur and
Mining Property .... $ 9,395,096.35

A greater capital value would attach to the property if the
volume of sales could be increased, and to a lesser extent if
the volume of production could be increased, with a resulting decrease in cost per ton. As indicating the range of
values, I have computed the capital value based on sales as
high as 270,000 tons and production as high as 750,000 tons
at a cost of $2.80 per ton. These results may be tabulated
as follows:

| Assuming | | | Limit of Profitable Future | Capital Value of Stock |
Sales (tons)	Production (tons)		Production (tons)	of Sulphur and Mine
200,000 per annum	450,000 at	$4.00	632,387	9,395,000
200,000 "	750,000 at	2.80	882,387	10,042,000
270,000 "	450,000 at	4.00	1,832,387	11,847,000
270,000 "	750,000 at	2.80	1,899,887	12,800,000

It will be observed that the last two calculations involve
not only unduly optimistic hypotheses as to rate of production and sales, but also very large assumptions as to the tonnage which can be secured.

In considering these two calculations it is particularly important to note:

(1) That the sales during the 5⅓ years were evidently pressed to a maximum, and the sales for the last four months of the period were almost exactly the average of the entire period. Consequently, there was at April, 1914, practically no prospect of the tonnage of sales being increased, but there was almost a certainty of the sales being reduced through the competition of the Freeport Sulphur Company, which was then for the first time beginning to be felt.

(2) That the price of sulphur during the period had remained constant. Here again, therefore, there was no prospect of more favorable prices but serious danger of a reduction in prices, having regard to the wide margin between cost and selling prices, the impending competition, and the enormous accumulations of stock on hand.

(3) That these calculations assume a future production of nearly 2,000,000 tons. In this connection it is most important to observe that while any falling short from this assumed production would unfavorably affect the value of the property, there would be no favorable effect on the value if the mine should be capable of producing a larger tonnage, since the calculations assume the production of the maximum tonnage that could be profitably marketed on the assumed volume of sales.

(4) Finally as to the rate of profit assumed, the rate of 15% applied to the stock on hand is undoubtedly moderate in view of the hazards, and the rate of 20% would be entirely too low to be applicable to any calculation involving such optimistic assumptions. It is used here for the sake of uniformity and not on account of a belief in its applicability. In considering this question it must be remembered that the rates in question are applied only to the hazardous or speculative part of the investment and that for the assets other than the mine and stock of sulphur (amounting to over $4,300,000) a rate of only 7% has been allowed, this allowance being made in the form of a deduction from the gross selling value.

Combining the investment in sulphur stock capitalized at 15% and that in working capital at 7%, the average yield on the two parts would not exceed 12%.

On each of the four underlying assumptions, therefore, there is no reasonable prospect of changes which would tend to increase the value, but serious prospects, amounting in some cases to practical certainty, that less favorable results would be secured.

Taking all the considerations together, I am of the opinion that from the standpoint of scientific computation on the broad lines usually followed in valuing mining properties, with only such adaptions as are needed to meet the very unusual features of this case, the value of the stock of sulphur and the mine together could not be deemed to be more than $10,000,000.

The alternative method of valuation would be to regard the sulphur in stock as a reserve and to value the mine and the stock on the assumption that the current production of mine will be sold first and that the reserve stock will be realized only as and when the current production proves insufficient to meet the sales. Possibly, indeed, this is the more practical method. In mining operations it is customary to block out reserves of ore in advance of mining operations; and the stock of sulphur in this case seems in many respects analogous to such ore reserves, with the difference that the reserve is carried on the surface instead of in the mine, this difference being a necessary incident of the character of the mining operations.

This alternative method will, however, give lower values than the method I have adopted upon any reasonable assumptions as to sales and using the same rates of return, and so will any intermediate course. As already stated, demonstration of this fact led me to adopt the method which I have outlined, in spite of its complexity.

I realize that in practice, theories, and especially theories the application of which involves some complicated calculations, are often regarded with distrust and are not carried to their logical conclusion. But this merely means that the maximum theoretical value will not in practice be realized, some part thereof being sacrificed to a natural disposition to follow on more normal lines which will be regarded as safer, though it may be questioned whether they will prove so. It may well be that some deduction should be made from the results I have calculated to allow for these practical considerations, but for the purpose of taxation at any rate, no exception can be taken to the failure to make such a deduction.

CALCULATION OF VALUE OF CAPITAL STOCK OF THE UNION SULPHUR COMPANY

Value of sulphur at mine and other mining property, say.....	$10,000,000
Other property in Calcasieu Parish........................	379,350
Stock of sulphur other than at mine at $15 per ton...........	582,780
Miscellaneous assets as to which no question arises (less liabilities)	3,355,074
Investments in subsidiary companies	885,369
	$15,202,573
or say per share....................................	$7,600

III

THE MAXIMUM SELLING PRICE OF NEWSPRINT PAPER *

(1918)

THE annexed testimony was given before the Federal Trade Commission in a proceeding to determine the maximum selling price of newsprint paper, pursuant to an agreement which provided for the determination of the price by the Commission subject to a right of appeal to the Circuit Judges of the United States for the Second Circuit.

The Federal Trade Commission made no express findings on the questions covered by the testimony, and fixed a price on newsprint paper in carload lots of $3.10 per hundred pounds. Upon appeal the Circuit Court fixed the maximum selling price at $3.50 per hundred pounds and in doing so made the following specific findings:

In valuing the capital investment used in producing newsprint, prices before the present European War should be adopted.

In ascertaining capital investment, *i.e.*, the present value of property actually used in paper production, we exclude timber lands whether owned or leased, also undeveloped or potential water power, *i.e.*, water rights; but include mill and town sites, terminal facilities, and improvements on or development of natural water powers, together with any investment by way of actual payment for power rights. The foregoing allowed elements of capital value are the "tangibles."

A fair maximum return on said capital in a business of the hazards proven is 15% per annum.

The Court found the depreciated present value of "tangibles" at pre-war prices to be $25,000 per ton of daily capacity, and, adding 10% for going value and $12,000 per

* Testimony before the Federal Trade Commission (March 22, 1918).

ton for working capital, arrived at an investment of $39,500
per ton. They applied their findings to a plant having a
daily capacity of 100 tons as follows:

> The capital invested is 39,500 × 100 = $3,950,000
> The fair annual return, 15%   =   592,500
> To be obtained by selling all of an
> annual production of 30,000 tons,
> or a profit per ton of   19.75

.   .   .   .

Mr. Wise. In your work as accountants do you have occasion to be consulted on the question of value of properties?

Mr. May. Well, we do not go into the field of valuation of
properties, but we have a great deal to do with questions
of value as affected by earning capacity.

Q. Yes, and with earnings?

A. And with earnings.

Q. Upon the value of the property?

A. Yes. We have acted for a great many people contemplating purchasing a business or selling a business, and they
have frequently called on us for advice as to the wisdom of
buying or selling property.

Q. As a preliminary to that advice, I take it, you have to
make an examination of the books of the properties to determine what is shown on those books?

A. Yes.

Q. And in this work have you made a study of the question of the rate of return on invested capital?

A. The question of return on invested capital is a subject that I have given a great deal of consideration to for the
last fifteen years.

Q. As to industrial businesses?

A. Yes. Perhaps I may explain that I approached the
question from an entirely different angle from Mr. Erickson.
I do not claim to have made an exhaustive study of the
underlying theories that he has. My ideas are based on practical experience, and I came in from the standpoint, not

originally of rate cases of price fixing, but from an entirely different angle.

Up to about ten years ago I do not think my firm was ever engaged in a rate or price-fixing matter, and since then I do not think we have been engaged in more than one or, perhaps, two a year; and my interest in the matter has developed originally from the fact that there was a tendency to value assets, particularly mining properties, on the basis of estimating the future earnings and then discounting those values at a given rate of interest.

Now, we have always been advocates of conservatism in accounting and finance and were satisfied that people were using too low rates of return in those calculations, and, unfortunately, some of the States were supporting them—entirely for tax purposes—one of the most extreme cases being Minnesota, which valued on the basis of estimating the future return, and discounting it at 4 per cent. I was convinced you could never get people to put money into any business of that kind on a 4 per cent basis. I was originally interested in that subject largely for the purpose of convincing our clients it was not wise to establish any such theories, and later I became convinced that the same fallacy was being adopted in the regulation of rates, and I felt sure that the Commissions in fixing too low rates were flying in the face of an economic fact and going to do more harm in the long run to the public than to the railroads, and that is how I became interested in value—from this angle.

Q. Now, in the past you have had occasion, I take it, to audit the books of a good many of the newsprint manufacturing concerns in this country?

A. Yes, we have done quite a number of them. More of the other paper than of newsprint, as a matter of fact.

Q. In the recent past you have had occasion to make a special examination into the accounts of the companies involved in this particular proceeding, have you not?

A. Yes, we are doing that now.

Q. And as a result of your studies in the whole field of

accountancy and of your particular studies of the companies involved here, have you formed any opinion as to what is a proper rate of return upon the investment?

A. Well, to state what is a fair rate of return today is a little difficult question, and the immediate effect of war conditions is rather difficult to estimate accurately. Of course, the answer depends, in some measure, on how you value your property. If you in valuing your property take the highest point of the present costs, you do not have to give the same liberality in return as you have if you take a lower level as the basis of value. Naturally the two are always linked up together, but I would say, based on pre-war conditions, a prospect of a return of 15 to 20 per cent has always been necessary to attract capital into a business of moderate hazards. This, I would say, would certainly not be more than covered by those rates.

I think that property has to earn that in order to attract capital into the business. In saying that, I am basing it largely on my actual experience of cases where even that return has failed to attract purchasers. You would be surprised if you had seen as many cases as I have where earnings which showed approximately 15 per cent had been turned down by people contemplating buying. I was surprised myself, because I approached it purely from the professional standpoint, earlier in my experience. I have seen so many now that I am convinced of the fact that that is so, and in recent years I have given a good deal of thought to the reasons.

I imagine Mr. Wise will want me to state some of the reasons I have for saying it, entirely from the practical standpoint of experience.

COMMISSIONER MURDOCK. Let me follow that. Supposing I came to you and said, "Mr. May, I wish you would go out here to Podunk, Indiana, and look over a mill out there I want to buy." You go and look over the mill and come back and report to me and say, "They have got $100,000 in that mill supported by $10,000 earnings, but my advice is not to buy it."

Mr. May. I would say that, but I do not base so much on my advice as on the number of cases where I reported to people and they refused to buy.

Within the last sixty days I had a business in New York that was earning $100,000 a year which had between $600,-000 and $700,000 of assets. Those people could not get a buyer for the property. Finally it was sold for $500,000. That is an actual case within the last sixty days. People who have not been through it do not realize it. That is why I have been concerning myself with trying to explain the phenomenon.

COMMISSIONER FORT. Do you not consider that now that condition may be worse largely on account of the war?

Mr. May. As a matter of fact that particular plant had more opportunities during the war. During the war it will earn a great deal more than in normal conditions.

COMMISSIONER FORT. You do not think conditions as to the uncertainty of business, owing to the war, had anything to do with it?

A. No, I do not think so.

COMMISSIONER MURDOCK. As a matter of fact, the answer you would return to me in that case, Mr. May, would be this: If the facts were verified, showing it is a sure thing that there is $100,000 in that mill I have looked over, and I found this is the maximum earning for several years, but there seems to be an upward tendency in the mill and I think it is going to earn more in a few years. That is about the way you would report to me.

In other words, in surveying the property for me you would not take merely the present into your consideration, but you would take a survey of the past and just as near as you could form a survey of the future as you were able to in your report to me.

Mr. May. Of course, if I could put my finger on anything that was earning only 10 per cent and I felt satisfied that it would earn 25 per cent I would say go ahead and buy it, but, of course, that is a rather different question from the proposition of fixing a maximum rate of return you are going to allow them to earn in the future.

COMMISSIONER MURDOCK. I wanted to get it just as simply as possible.

Mr. May. The more questions you ask the better I will be pleased, because I do not want to leave any point that is not clear in your mind if I can help it.

Mr. Wise. You say that 15 per cent return is needed to attract capital into an industry of moderate hazards. What would you say of the paper industry? Does that come into the class of industrials where the hazards are moderate?

Mr. May. I would say it was an industry of moderate hazards although not one of the lowest of that group.

Q. What would you regard as the hazards of the business?

A. Well, first of all, the uninsurable risks; and the second, which I think has regard to a large part of the industry, is the fact that it is engaged in a business in one country and selling its product largely in another country, and is, therefore, subject to the operation of the fiscal policy of the two different countries and to the elements of government control by two different governments whose interests may not always be identical; that is a distinct hazard in the business.

Then there is another equally important hazard in it, and that is the fact that it takes such a large return in proportion to the sales. If you have a business with sales of four or five times the capital, you can always provide the return on capital by a reasonable percentage of the sales, and nobody would say that is an exorbitant return on your investment, but when you have to get a large percentage on your sales, people are always apt to say, "Why, half the selling price is profit, or 25 per cent is profit; that must be too much." Whereas it is not at all necessarily so in an industry like this where the capital is large in proportion to the sales, and 20 per cent or 25 per cent profit on sales would not be anything like as remunerative as 2 or 3 per cent profit is to John Wanamaker,

Sears, Roebuck, or Woolworth, or any of those people. Therefore, I always feel where they have to have a large investment in proportion to the sales it detracts from the attractiveness of the investment.

Q. Well, what is the basis of your calculation for your return?

A. The investment value of the property. I noticed Mr. Erickson discusses the question to some extent from the standpoint of bonds and stocks, and, therefore, I would like to say that in my view of the case the controlling factor is the investment value, that is, the total present value of the investment, and the question whether capitalized by bonds or stocks does not enter into it in my view of the case at all.

Mr. Wise. Does it make any difference to you how many times the turnover in that business occurs in a year?

Mr. May. How do you mean?

Q. Sales?

A. I think it does, in this way. The return must be based on the investment, but if the turnover is small, as I said, your percentage of profit to sales looks so high that there is always a tendency to cut it unduly; that is your hazard.

Q. Are you speaking with the idea of only one turnover of capital per annum in a business?

A. In this business I suppose you do not turn over your capital once a year. Comparing the agricultural implement industry and the packing industry, it is much more difficult for the agricultural implement industry to get a fair return on capital than the packers, because the same rate of return would constitute something like eight or nine times the percentage of sales in the case of the agricultural implement industry that it would in the case of the packers.

Commissioner Murdock. Mr. May is speaking of the gross sales as contrasted with the capital. He is talking about the turnover.

Mr. May. Yes, the turnover. The turnover is the relation of sales to capital investment.

Commissioner Murdock. That is, the more rapid the

turnover, the lower the rate of profit on the investment.

Mr. May. No, I do not say that. I say that theoretically they should be the same, but practically, because a given profit is a higher percentage of sales, you have more difficulty in getting it. That is one of the hazards of the business. That is the point I was trying to make.

COMMISSIONER FORT. Well then, in your idea, the profit should be the same on every sale of a concern that has but one turnover per annum as the concern that has five turnovers per annum.

Mr. May. Percentage of investment.

COMMISSIONER FORT. That may make quite a difference.

Mr. May. Of course the percentage of investment should be the same, although the percentage of sales would be much higher in the case of the company with a small turnover than the one with a big turnover.

Mr. Wise. Can you explain that any further?

Mr. May. No, I think that is all.

Q. Now you stated, Mr. May, that as a basis of the return you take the investment regardless of how that investment is placed, whether it is in stocks, in bonds, or part in stocks and part in bonds?

A. Yes, sir.

Q. In other words, it is no matter whether one company has a $50,000,000 and another a $5,000,000 outlay, they are entitled to the same rate of return?

A. That is my feeling.

Q. I wish you would go right ahead and explain your position here without my having to prompt you or question you at all, and testify as to your opinion for a rate of return on the basis that you have recited.

A. All right. I hope you will interrupt whenever you see fit.

In the first place, before I start to discuss reasons for the opinion I want to emphasize two points: first, I take it that what we are discussing is a maximum price and that there is no guarantee you are going to get that price, and that there is no guarantee of a minimum price. I think that is a point fairly agreed-upon. In the second place, I want to emphasize the distinction between the profits that a business must earn and the profits which can be distributed to the investors in that business.

A large part of the earnings of every successful company has to be reinvested in that business, or, as Mr. Schwab put it once, a dollar for dividends and a dollar for plant, and it is curious how nearly accurate that is.

In preparing a brief for the Senate Finance Committee on the excess profits tax payment dealing with that point, I took at random forty companies, railroads, public utilities and manufacturing companies and miscellaneous companies, and when we checked all the figures back that were drawn at random it showed over a five-year period they would actually distribute in dividends almost exactly 50 per cent, within 1 per cent of 50 per cent of the total earnings in the five years. So if you happen to earn your 15 per cent or 20 per cent you won't be able to distribute year in and year out more than half of it. That is the first point.

COMMISSIONER MURDOCK. Mr. May, I do not quite get that in my mind. What I would like to know is what you are feeding that 10 per cent to. If you allow 20 per cent to go in the business and give 10 per cent to the stockholders, where does that other 10 per cent go?

Mr. May. It goes to build up the business. Of course, it ultimately accrues directly or indirectly to the benefit of the stockholder. There is no doubt about that. As long as he gets only half distributed in cash he feels that the other half is going to build up the business. It may or may not. Some do get it.

COMMISSIONER MURDOCK. The ordinary method, as I have observed it, is to divert that 10 per cent which is not distributed as dividends into some reserve fund or surplus.

Mr. May. Yes, that is so, but my experience is that a man is attracted if he thinks he has a fair prospect of being able to get that 15 or 20 per cent out of the business, half in cash and half in equities piling up for the future. That is the way he sizes it up, as far as my experience goes.

COMMISSIONER FORT. That extra 10 per cent is not distributed in dividends and you do not care whether it is carried in surplus or a sinking fund or put into new machinery as long as it is carried.

Mr. May. Yes.

Mr. Wise. It is a fact that it is never as such handed back to the stockholder.

Mr. May. Yes, he has got to leave it in to insure he is still going to have a cash dividend in the future.

Q. He is simply switching his principal all the time to insure him of his return.

A. That is right. I have made some examination of the actual facts. Take the Report of the Commissioner of Corporations on the investigation of the Steel Industry. You will find that year in and year out he said that the price of $28 for steel rails was the fixed price and that it never varied for years, or that there were very slight fluctuations. That yielded a profit of 18 per cent on the investment to the steel corporation, including 18 per cent on the relative investment in ore properties and 18 per cent on the relative investment in transportation facilities, taking ore properties, transportation, blast furnaces, mills, working capital, all along the line invested in turning out a ton of steel rails, that the price of $28 yielded a return of 18 per cent on the entire capital, and yet, so far as my experience goes, nobody ever seriously questioned the fairness of the price of steel rails, and it remained for fifteen years, I suppose.

COMMISSIONER MURDOCK. Of course, it has been traditional in the United States for thirty years that they sold cheaper abroad than at home.

Mr. May. That, I think, is one of the things that has often been said but has never been proved.

Then there is another report, taking the smaller companies. If you will refer to the Report of the Commissioner of Corporations on the investigation of Independent Tobacco Industry at the time it was being oppressed by the Tobacco Trust, as the report puts it. It shows for 48 independent companies—let me see, I have the exact figures here, I think—an average profit of 15.9 per cent, and it is rather amazing to note that the Commissioner drew attention to that fact as evidence of oppression because the Tobacco Trust itself was earning 40 per cent.

Then there was another interesting thing that developed in the same connection some three or four years ago. In the course of a study of this question my firm took at random a series of records at our own offices. There were all kinds of businesses, largely small manufacturing companies, and we just took them as they came. We said to a man to go and pick out 200 reports, to take them straight out of the files, leaving out all public utilities and non-industrial concerns, pick them out and find out their capital, and we found the average of those 158 companies was 13.67 per cent. Those were accounts where we knew a proper provision had been made for salaries, depreciation and everything, so that we were dealing with reliable data, and they were just picked out at random.

. . . .

COMMISSIONER MURDOCK. That is 6½ per cent to the stockholders and 6½ per cent to the business?

Mr. May. Yes, sir.

Mr. Wise. Some of the companies made less than 6 per cent altogether and others made as much as 24 per cent?

Mr. May. Some of them made a loss as the actual facts show. Out of the 158 cases there were 70 that earned over 15 per cent. Now these companies, as stated, were selected in 1913; they were not picked out but just taken at random in 1913. I thought that for this purpose it would be interesting to take as many of those same companies as I could find and find out what their last report showed. I was able to find in our office files the corresponding records for 86 of those 158 companies.

COMMISSIONER MURDOCK. As of what year?

Mr. May. The year ending 1916 or 1917. Those 86 companies in the earlier period averaged 13.11 per cent, and the same companies in the later period averaged 20.37 per cent. I also have the percentage here of the individual companies showing the different ranges in the earlier period. There were 16 earning between 15 and 20 per cent and 24 earning over 20 per cent. There are 40 earning over 15 per cent today and there are 7 earning between 15 and 20 per cent, and 39 earning over 20, making 46 out of 86 that are earning from 15 per cent, and about 60 per cent of those companies, between 50 and 60, are companies with a capital investment of under a million dollars. They are not big trusts, they are small and medium-sized corporations.

This is another light on the question, and I have prepared some figures which seem to me particularly illuminating in view of the fact many of the parties to this proceeding are Canadian corporations. Now, Canada's normal source of supply of capital is Great Britain, and, therefore, it seems to me that figures showing the return in industry in Great Britain, and in countries capitalized in Great Britain, would be relevant. The London *Economist,* which is the best-known of the financial journals of London, gives each year a summary of the profits shown by corporations whose accounts are published in its columns during that year. I have prepared the figures from those summaries, by industries, leaving out the railways, public utilities, mines and financial companies like banks and trust companies. I have had them prepared under different groups and I have worked them out to show the percentage of profit to the total capital, whether borrowed capital or stock capital, during these years. The averages are as follows: at the end of the year June 30, 1914, the average of all companies is 11.25 per cent; 1915, 10.32 per cent. That is when they felt the adverse effect of the beginning of the war; 1916, 12.65 per cent; 1917, 13.27 per cent.

.   .   .   .

Mr. Wise. How many companies does that represent?

Mr. May. It represents about 650 companies with a total invested capital of about 550,000,000 pounds sterling.

Q. Good, bad and indifferent?

A. All that are published. I will draw attention to the breweries, which come at the top. English breweries are notoriously overcapitalized. They were a very, very successful industry. They were capitalized on the basis of their earning capacity during their palmy days. Undoubtedly they are overcapitalized. If you leave out the breweries in any year it raises the average of the rest about one per cent. In my view they are extremely interesting and I think relevant as regards this proceeding.

COMMISSIONER MURDOCK. That is on the aggregate of these industries, less the breweries, the rate would be for the year 1917, 14.37?

Mr. May. About that, 14.37, if you leave the breweries out. Breweries earned only 6.7.

Then there is another significant figure, that is, the earnings of our national banks. The reports of the Comptroller of the Currency show that the earnings of national banks in the last fifteen or sixteen years—it does not make much difference what period you take—they averaged 9.7 per cent on the total capital and surplus invested. Now there is a really attractive industry, the national bank. Your capital is in there and you can take it out and liquidate it if you do not like that kind of investment. It is entirely different from locking up property in bricks and mortar. They are not any good unless they be put to some such use as you build them for. That has always seemed to me a very good index and it seems to me is entirely in line with the general conclusion that you reach from studying the industrial businesses, because there cannot be any question as to the attractiveness of a national bank investment.

COMMISSIONER FORT. Except in one respect, double liability on stock.

Mr. May. That is true.

Mr. Wise. What is the percentage of loss in that case?

Mr. May. I think that is the key to the explanation of the condition that I have been discussing, and what is the actual reason for that is significant. The actual losses are less than five-hundredths of one per cent. Yet one of the first things a man thinks of when he thinks of a national bank investment is the liability of it and the risks he is running, and that influences his judgment as to the attractiveness of that investment far beyond the mathematical value of the risk, and that is the clue, I think. That is the clue to the whole thing.

Take fire insurance. Every man is considered lacking in all business prudence if he does not insure, yet he is paying double the mathematical value of the risk for the insurance. Not more than 50 per cent of the premiums paid go to pay losses. I happened to be talking last week to a Mr. Graham Harding, who is an assessor for Lloyd's in London. His firm have acted for Lloyd's for 120 years and he was talking about the business that Lloyd's do in insuring all sorts of extraordinary risks, and he said, of course, they make some spectacular losses, to be sure, but they are making all the time spectacular profits—because people are willing to pay many times the mathematical value of the risk.

I think that is the one factor more than any other that accounts for the high rate of return that you have got to give to attract capital into industry. I do not know of any single factor that is more potent. Now, of course, there is a suggestion that grows out of that, namely, that by our system of distributing securities you can spread your risks and therefore you do not sustain those losses. In our country there are two ways of financing industry, practically. One or two men or a group of men go in and put up all the capital and control the business or else shares are distributed to the public. Now if a few men put it in they are the men who control it; and if they go in, the way they look at it is somewhat like this: Well, we have looked to make a certain profit and if we make more than that profit it will give us a little more income, but as we come up the value of the income is relatively less. If you have an income of $25,000 a year and increase it to $30,000 you have added $5,000, but you have not added 20 per cent to the enjoyments you get out of life. It is just the same as building a steamer. When you get up to a twenty-knot steamer its costs a lot more money to add a little speed. The higher you get the less in the way of additional speed you get for your money. That is the way we live, the more income you get the less you really get out of it for the additional income. On the other hand, if they should lose the whole thing, that is a loss that is far more felt than any small addition to their income, if successful. Therefore, only a prospect of getting a liberal return attracts them. On the other hand, if you are trying to distribute to small holders you come up against another factor, that is, the factor in the high cost of everything in this country, the high cost of distribution and the high profits of distributors, and that applies to securities and the selling of securities. In other words, it applies to the raising of money just the same as it does to the problem of distribution of commodities. There is the same difference between the prices that the farmer gets and the price that the consumer pays, and between the cost of money to the industry and the return on the investment to the ultimate distributees of those securities. The discrepancy is almost as large in one case as in the other. And, of course, you have got to make things reasonably attractive to the individual small holder. In this case his risk is not quite so large. But there is another factor that operates far more with him than it does with the big investor. When a few men take hold of a business they do not worry much about the hazards of bad management. They are generally willing to admit that they can give good management, but the small investor has to take the risk of bad management as well as risks inherent in the business. He sees the possibility of losses from bad management. So that in the long run it does not make very much difference which way you go about getting capital into the industry, because to make it attractive you must give just about the same return in the one case as the other.

COMMISSIONER MURDOCK. There must be some point, however, in your reasoning upon this proposition at which you come to the conclusion that the rate of return is unreasonably high. Where does that point arise in your mind?

Mr. May. When you say rate of return unreasonably high, that is a somewhat difficult question to answer in connection with competitive business. My thought is that regulation and protection ought to go hand in hand. If you do not give any protection you are not in a position to insist on regulation. If you give a minimum of protection you cannot insist on a maximum of regulation. If you fix a minimum return you can fix a maximum return. If you do not give any sort of protection at all it is rather difficult for me to see on what you may base any regulation of return other than a paramount public interest or something of that kind, of course. All I can see is that in so far as a regulative body can control the situation they would not do anything that was calculated to promote extravagantly high returns, and in the interest of the consumer, ultimately, just as much as of the producer, you have got to fix that fairly high if you are going to make it a maximum. Commissions may be the primary regulators but capital is the ultimate regulator, because the necessity of attracting capital into enterprise and keeping capital in enterprise is, after all, the paramount consideration; and that, I think, is particularly true when you are dealing with an industry that is largely outside of your own jurisdiction, as you are in this case. You cannot compel capital to stay in newsprint in Canada by any proceeding in this case if you fix the return so low as to discourage them from staying in it.

Mr. Wise. You can compel them to stay in the United States?

Mr. May. By a gradual extension of the powers of the Government which might make the return in all industries unattractive. I mean by that that they would rather stay in the frying pan than jump into the fire.

COMMISSIONER FORT. There is another situation there. You say the voluntary bringing of them into another jurisdiction. They may of necessity, if they wish to carry on their business, be compelled to bring them into another jurisdiction because they have not enough demand at home.

Mr. May. If you drive him out of the industry, he can go out of the industry and, of course, a lot of these water power companies could turn their service to other uses. They may have to come in here if they want to stay in the newsprint business. If they come into the United States and it should regulate the return in this industry they would be no better off. If they should go out of the industry they would go into something else in Canada.

COMMISSIONER FORT. And make a profit?

Mr. May. Yes.

. . . .

COMMISSIONER FORT. Would you consider an allowance of 5 per cent profit on an industry with two turnovers a year a fair profit?

Mr. May. No, I do not. Nothing but compulsion or patriotism, I think, would keep capital in that industry very long on that basis.

Mr. Wise. Have you given any particular thought in your work on the question of whether or not in figuring the investment there should be any item included for what is known as the going value?

Mr. May. Going value or goodwill?

Q. I distinguish between goodwill and going value.

A. All right.

Q. In fixing a price do you think that the goodwill of a business is to be considered?

A. Goodwill, as I see it, rests primarily on earning capacity. In determining what the earning capacity shall be you cannot predicate your action on the capital value of that earning capacity. I do not think goodwill enters into it at all. As to going value in the sense of the value of the developed industry as compared with the position of an industry that is just completed—a plant that is nothing more than a plant I think, within reasonable limits—that should be recognized as part of the investment on which a return should be figured.

. . . .

COMMISSIONER MURDOCK. Mr. May, what is your definition of going value?

Mr. May. I think, as far as going value should be recognized in a case of this kind, it would simply represent the reasonable cost of additional value resulting from the act of building up the plant from the point where the plant is completed to the point where it has a successful business going. It is a difficult thing to measure, I admit. In an industry where there is a big investment like this, of course, there is the actual expense and loss of return during the preliminary period immediately following the completion of the plant. That is the best criterion of it that I think suggests itself.

Mr. Wise. Do you consider it to be a proper form of accounting for a manufacturer, in an industry such as this, to set up a charge for depreciation?

Mr. May. Why, yes.

Q. How long has it been the custom with accountants in this country?

A. Well, it is a development. It is pretty hard to say. I know in the early days of my experience here I lost a great deal of work because I refused to sign accounts as being correct unless they had provided for depreciation. But it is a development, more or less general, I should say, during the last ten or twelve years. I would say that the Federal Trade Commission itself has assisted the accountants a great deal in spreading the recognition of it, although, to be perfectly honest, I think perhaps the income tax has done even more to stimulate the practice.

COMMISSIONER MURDOCK. It is growing all the time?

Mr. May. As the tax rate grows, you can rely on its growing.

Commissioner Fort. I did not suppose there was any question about setting up depreciation.

Mr. May. No; I do not think there is.

Commissioner Fort. Nor is there any question either, in good bookkeeping, as to setting up depletion—

Mr. May. No.

Commissioner Fort. Where at the end of a specified period of time the industry may be depleted so that there is not any. Now, is there any other way to provide for the carrying of the repayment of the 10 per cent to the stockholders, if you keep on paying dividends?

Mr. May. That is the point.

Commissioner Fort. Take the coal industry. Here is a coal field, say ten acres square. There is a vein running through it. The coal company is incorporated for a hundred thousand dollars. I make that figure because it is small. The stockholders put their hundred thousand dollars in there, and at the end of a period of twenty years you have exhausted your coal, and you have paid out your money in dividends, and by methods of various kinds, taking care of your machinery, and so forth; and when you get through, your machinery is practically junk. Now, what are you going to pay your capital stock on, if you do not provide for depletion?

Mr. May. If you pay out all your current earnings, you are not, strictly speaking, paying dividends; you are paying out of capital, and it ought to be recognized as such.

Commissioner Fort. Then you would not get any interest on your capital.

Mr. May. You should get a fair return plus depletion.

Commissioner Fort. Six per cent does not take care of your principal?

Mr. May. Oh, no.

Commissioner Fort. If you get six per cent, and at the end of a period of twenty years your coal vein is exhausted, how are you going to pay your stockholders back their money?

Mr. May. Charge it into the cost, and set aside a fund for depletion.

COMMISSIONER FORT. Depletion; yes.

Mr. Wise. And they have not all done that?

Mr. May. No.

COMMISSIONER FORT. The result of the investigations we made here as to the coal industry was that 60 per cent of the coal mines of the United States charge neither depreciation nor depletion.

Mr. May. I can believe that is true.

Mr. Plante. They cannot eat the cake and have it, too.

COMMISSIONER FORT. There is a larger percentage on depletion, but I take the average as to both.

IV

CROSS EXAMINATION IN *Allied Chemical & Dye Corporation* v. *The Steel & Tube Company of America*

(1923)

THIS was a proceeding involving the adequacy of the price at which the defendant agreed to sell his assets to the Youngstown Sheet & Tube Company. Mr. May was a witness for the defendant.

The attack was based largely on the point that the price to be received was admittedly substantially below the valuation of the assets that would be reached on a replacement basis less depreciation for the capital assets and the ordinary going concern methods of valuation for the current assets. In previous discussions, Mr. May had suggested to Mr. Joseph P. Cotton, of counsel for the defense, that it was a very common practice to speak of the value of the assets of the United States Steel Corporation as $300 a share, but that the market value of the stock ranged around $100 a share, and inquired whether there was any way in which this point could be brought out in direct testimony. Mr. Cotton decided that it could not, but said that it would be all to the good if counsel for the plaintiff would be led to ask a question which would bring the point into discussion.

Leading counsel for the plaintiff very obviously declined to enter into this field when the opportunity offered; but after he had completed his cross examination, his associate intimated that he desired to conduct a short examination, and after a few preliminary questions, developed the following cross examination.

Q. Have you not observed in the work that you have done in your profession, that the market value of stocks is variant from the value of the assets of the Company?

A. Well, that involves determining what is the value of the assets of the Company, and "value" nowadays certainly is a term that it is almost impossible to define without some qualifying phrase. What is "value" is the starting place for a dissertation rather than something that calls for a definite answer.

Q. Stock values vary from day to day and sometimes within a very short time, they vary a very large percentage?

A. Yes, obviously at times the fluctuations are so extreme as to be—not representative of the permanent values.

Q. For instance, if you could imagine the stock of the Ford Motor Company upon the market, do you think that the market value of that stock would be any indication of the assets of the Company?

A. I think it would be bound to be some reflection of the assets of the Company.

Q. But it would be not very close to the—

A. I should think it would be fairly close to it. There would be particularly a case.

Q. How about the Durant Motor Company?

A. I do not know anything about the Durant Motor Company to hazard an opinion.

Q. How about the United States Steel?

A. Well, I think the United States Steel is fairly representative of the value of its assets.

Q. Is it not a common understanding—well, derived from their published reports—that the assets behind the common stock of the United States Steel Corporation is in the neighborhood of $300 a share?

A. Well, it depends on what you call value. I think the fair inference from the fact that over a long series of years the Steel stock has never approached those values, is an in-

dication that the market value of the Steel Company's assets
is not $300 a share of the common stock.

Q. Have you considered the earnings of the Steel Corporation, both those that had been distributed, and those
that had been retained and "plowed in," to use the expression, would the value of the assets of the Steel Company be
in the neighborhood of $200 and $300 a share?

A. On an earning capacity basis?

Q. Yes.

A. No, I should say decidedly not.

Q. During the existence of the United States Steel Corporation in the past twenty years, it has put away among
its assets, a great deal more than its original assets; is not that
true?

A. I do not know whether that is true, but it has put aside
a very large sum.

Q. Well, approximately so?

A. Yes.

Q. And yet that fact has not been reflected in the value
of the stock?

A. It is not reflected in the earnings of the stock today.

Q. You mean by the earnings, the dividends of the Company?

A. No, what the Company earns.

Q. Today?

A. The earnings of the Company today are not commensurate with the earning capacity at the formation of the
Company together with a fair return on the amounts that
have been put into the Company since.

Q. Do you mean literally today?

A. I do not mean for the month.

Q. 1923?

A. But I mean for a series of any—over any period long
enough to be representative.

Q. You do not mean 1923?

A. I do not mean at the moment, because I do not attach
much importance to the earnings of a moment.

Q. Well, the stock of the United States Steel Corporation is ruling in the neighborhood of par, because it pays only to the holder, and has paid for the last twenty years only to the holder, about $5 a year?

A. That is not the sole factor. That is one of the factors.

Q. Is not that the important factor?

A. I would not say that it is the important factor, because you find the same sort of relation if you take Bethlehem Steel, for instance, which has been criticized for paying out too much to its stockholders. On the one hand, there is the Steel Corporation, which is criticized as not having paid enough. On the other hand, there is the Bethlehem, which is criticized as having paid too much, and yet the market value of the common stock is, I believe, somewhere about the same fraction of value computed in the way that you have spoken of, that would give the United States Steel stock a value of $300 a share; so that I do not think the determining factor can be the dividend policy. In fact, it is true of all Steel Companies that I know of, whatever their dividend policy.

By Mr. Fawsett:

Q. What is true?

A. That the market value of their stocks is only a small fraction of the value computed in the same way that gives the United States Steel stock a value of $300 a share.

V

VALUATION AND THE BUREAU OF INTERNAL REVENUE *

(1924)

Doctor Adams. May I ask you a question right here?

Mr. May. Yes, sir.

Doctor Adams. I think you will agree that a large part of our difficulty comes from valuation, and that a large number of those valuations are concerned with capital assets, so called. Now, at the present time, we have a limited rate on gain derived from the sale of capital assets, and it is proposed in the House bill to limit the allowance for losses. In that connection, my question is this: Assuming that the action reported in the newspapers by the Senate Committee, namely, of limiting the rate to 12½ per cent of the gains, but allowing losses in value; assuming that that goes through, do you believe that the Government would gain or lose by eliminating the taxation on capital gains and losses altogether?

Mr. May. If they would cut out the limit on losses, they are bound to lose.

Senator King. Surely.

Doctor Adams. Therefore, do you think that if they maintain that attitude toward losses, we could simplify the law indefinitely by abolishing all reference to capital gains and losses?

Mr. May. Of course, as I think you know, that is a subject that I have been very much interested in. I wrote a paper on that subject, which you have read, undoubtedly. My mind has been working toward the solution of it, in spite of the *prima facie* arguments in favor of taxing capital

* From *Hearings, Senate Committee on Investigation of the Bureau of Internal Revenue,* 68th Congress (1924), pp. 267-270.

gains; but from the standpoint of revenue, it would be better to eliminate taxation of capital gains and allowance of capital losses.

Senator King. It may be interesting to know that I have an amendment, as one member of the Committee, to strike out all of those provisions of capital losses and gains. I reached that conclusion long ago.

Mr. May. Of course, in all of these changes, you usually exchange one set of troubles for another.

Senator King. Yes.

Mr. May. But you find the weak points in method largely by experience, and you do not want to reject a method, when you have found out its weak spots by experience, without very carefully canvassing the weak spots of any alternative that you are going to adopt. It is not difficult to sort of cast what is really income into the form of a capital gain.

Senator King. There is the danger.

Mr. May. Personally, I do not think that the drafting of provisions that would put a reasonable limit, that would stop a great deal of that kind of evasion, would be anything like as difficult as the drafting of the restrictions under the present law.

The Chairman. But, after all, that is a question of policy for the taxing committee, rather than improving the methods of the Internal Revenue Bureau.

Mr. May. Well, it is on the question of simplification. It will undoubtedly be a great simplification.

The Chairman. I know; but you cannot afford to change the whole taxing policy in order to simplify the method of calculation.

Mr. May. But I think, if well drafted, it would not involve any sacrifice of revenue. That is my general impression.

·   ·   ·   ·   ·   ·   ·

Doctor Adams. May I ask you, in general, about valuations? I ask that because I think that no one thing so conduces to delay and complexities of tax laws as the necessity for valuations. I would like to know, first, if you indorse that general view?

Mr. May. Oh, yes; that is, a large part of it.

Doctor Adams. It would follow from that, then, that valuations should be omitted and eliminated wherever possible?

Mr. May. Yes; the more you can do without valuations, the better.

Doctor Adams. I would like to ask you if you have any general notion about the reasonableness, the excess or defect of valuations, made for the purposes of depletion?

Mr. May. Well, speaking for myself personally, I have always felt that valuations for tax purposes, for mineral areas, were too high. I mean not only for income tax purposes, but for local tax purposes.

Senator King. Pardon me, but you know, of course, that in a great many States they do not tax the property, except the improvements. It is a tax upon the mineral output.

Mr. May. Yes; but in Minnesota—

Senator King. Oh, yes.

Mr. May. I think the Minnesota valuation of mines has cost the Federal Government a lot of money, because they value the mines, as I recall, on a 4 per cent basis.

Doctor Adams. The Michigan valuation?

Mr. May. Michigan was 5 per cent, as I recall, and Minnesota at one time was on a 4 per cent assessment basis. They got a very high valuation for the mines. When you were valuing those same mines for income-tax purposes, and those valuations were made long before March 1, 1913, in Minnesota, and you were predicting the calculations on the assumption that local taxes on those high valuations would continue, it was very difficult to resist the argument of the taxpayer that he is entitled to at least as high a valuation for depletion as he is for the purpose of tax on capital. That, to my mind, started off depletion valuations on a high level.

Then, again, there is another factor that is almost impossible to get out of your mind. It is almost impossible for a man, after a period of inflation has gone, when prices were high, to get his mind back in the state in which it would have been on the 1st of March, 1913, and make a retrospective valuation, which absolutely ignores everything that has happened since. It is almost impossible to do it, and I think the tendency, therefore, from that cause also has been rathe' upward, on the high side. That is my general theory.

Doctor Adams. In general, if any method fair to the in dustry can be devised to replace the present discovery depletion, which in the case of oil and gas calls for recurrent and continual valuation, would it not be most desirable to substitute a different method?

Mr. May. I should say decidedly so.

Doctor Adams. In other words, the valuation in itself is to be avoided if any satisfactory substitute can be secured?

Mr. May. Personally, I have always felt that it was un fortunate that that discovery provision got into the law.

VI

THE GOODYEAR TIRE & RUBBER REORGANIZATION OF 1920 IN RETROSPECT *

(1927)

Q. Something has been said here about reserves being set up there as being, as it proved to be, inadequate, because some nine or ten million dollars had to be taken out of operating profits or at least absorbed to pay for some of these unfortunate commitments for future delivery: will you elaborate that a little?

A. That, if I may say so, is rather a different question. That question arises on the balance sheet of February 28th before you attempt to give effect to the plan.

Q. Yes, that is true.

A. Giving effect to the plan merely substitutes for a commitment that will ultimately be payable in cash, an obligation on the part of the commitment creditor to take prior preference stock to a certain extent in lieu of cash: that all arises after—I think it will serve to make things clear if I make that distinction at the outset.

Q. Fine.

A. Before giving effect to the plan at all we had decided that .a reserve of approximately $24,000,000 was needed to provide for the excess cost of fabric under these commitment contracts over any fair market value as of that date, as at the date of the balance sheet.

We felt that that was a material factor in the financial position of the company which ought to be reflected in its balance sheet.

The amount of that reserve was a matter partly of knowledge and partly of judgment.

* From testimony in *S. C. Tomlinson, et al. v. Clarence Dillon, et al.,* #61,971 Court of Common Pleas, Summit County, Ohio (1927).

Mr. Thompson. Mr. May, I hope it is not discourteous to you to ask if in the October 31 statement you did not under your certificate estimate $19,000,000?

The Witness. $19,000,000 at that time.

Mr. Thompson. And by February 28 that had grown to $24,000,000; is that it?

The Witness. Yes.

Mr. Thompson. Thank you. I just wanted to connect the two events.

Q. But your October 31 statement was not giving effect at all to a big, comprehensive scheme of refinancing?

A. I do not think that really bears on it, Mr. Buckner.

Q. I mean Mr. Thompson is wondering if you are wishing to say that that item for instance was only $5,000,000 worse as a mere actual fact, quite apart from the prospects of the company?

A. In the balance sheet of October we merely referred to it in our certificate. The company was not prepared to recognize it on its books. Mr. Seiberling at that time, particularly, thought that it was merely an accountant's idea. I think he did not take it very seriously.

Q. I am anxious to get at the $24,000,000.

A. But the $24,000,000 is comparable to the $19,000,000.

Mr. Thompson. That is the point I wanted to get.

The Witness. Undoubtedly. But as I recall it the situation had in some respects become worse and the efforts to get consents and things like that had developed the existence of more commitments than we previously had knowledge of. That is what I think accounts for its being $24,000,000 instead of $19,000,000. Mr. Jackson could tell you more of that than I could. Shall I resume where I was?

Q. I wish you would.

A. That $24,000,000 was arrived at on a certain basis, which was the result of a conference amongst our people, a conference with officers of the company and some of the merchandise creditors themselves, I remember myself mentioning it to Mr. Myron Taylor: some views were expressed that that reserve ought to be larger and other views were expressed that we were going to ruin the company for a hypothetical adjustment, the prices might come right back and there was no need for so much reserve, and if that reserve were put in the balance sheet it would be impossible to finance the company at all; certainly if it were made any larger it would become increasingly difficult if not impossible to finance it.

My associates who were engaged on the work put that question up to me and said that I must make the decision and assume the responsibility for the firm.

As I say, I talked to Mr. Taylor and I talked to some other people and discussed it with our people, and it seemed to me that on the whole $24,000,000 was a pretty fair figure; it seemed to me that it was reasonably fair to the people who were being invited to come in to buy bonds on the basis of this balance sheet; and it seemed to me reasonably fair to the people who were trying to save their interest in the business.

If we had had a little more margin to play with I would have been glad to have seen it some millions larger, but it seemed to me a reasonable figure, and Mr. Jackson told me that, using it as a basis, it seemed to him that the company ought to be able to make some money in the subsequent operations.

After a fairly extended discussion of it I said I thought I would assume the responsibility of a balance sheet in which $24,000,000 was inserted to provide for that element of vital importance in the financial position of the company.

Q. Did you assume, in finally fixing that $24,000,000 as a deficit to take care of losses on delivery under contracts at higher prices, that the company would not have some grief and would be in 100 per cent condition, or did you have something else in mind?

A. I realized that probably if they were entirely footloose they could make new contracts on an even better basis than that; but that seemed to me to be a reasonably practical view

of the situation, which left something to be worked out but
did not leave an undue burden on the company.

Q. Do you recall, for instance, whether you included in
that reserve anything at all for carrying charges on deferred
deliveries of rubber and fabric when the company would
ask a man—

A. No, we left that to be cared for as it cropped up.

Q. That would be a very substantial item, of course,
would it not?

A. These general expressions like "substantially" are a
little dangerous, because the figures vary so much here; but
I mean it is a matter of perhaps three or four millions, possibly.

Q. Yes, of course.

A. Which in general one would say were substantial, but
in proportion to some of the figures here involved looks relatively small.

Q. For example, in proportion to the deficit as of February 28, 1921, if you had not given effect to the whole
plan of reorganization you say the deficit would have been
$75,000,000?

A. Yes; in proportion to that it is relatively small.

Q. It would be relatively small?

A. Yes.

Q. In fixing this reserve then you were not attempting to
put this company in a condition better than all the other
rubber companies, for instance, under the same conditions?

A. I did not know enough about the other rubber companies, but it was just what I say: a reasonable exercise of
business judgment is what I meant to accomplish.

Q. Then that is one item of what you might colloquially
call "grief" that the company out of its operating expenses
would have to take care of. Was there any other item that
might bring some grief to the company that they would have
to take care of as they went along on their way after reorganization that you now remember?

A. You mean in connection with those commitments?

Q. Yes.

A. I remember it was suggested that in addition to—we wrote down only the cotton element in the specified commitments; we did not attempt to write down the conversion cost.

Q. Although there were a lot of commitments for—

A. Those conversion costs were higher than the conversion costs that we agreed on about that same time in respect to the unspecified commitments.

Q. You knew that there would be some grief there that the company would have to absorb?

A. Yes, there was some grief; of course no rubber company was going to come into this situation without some hangovers of that kind.

Q. I understand.

A. And that seemed to us to put them on a reasonably competitive condition as far as that is concerned, and also it would be reasonable from the standpoint—provide reasonable protection for the new security holders who were invited to come in.

Q. But was that item of conversion something that might well run into a few million dollars, or do you remember?

A. Oh, yes. As a matter of fact the company, after paying those conversion costs for a time, as I remember effected some reductions and ultimately also paid some sums to cancel the contracts.

Q. In setting up reserves for inventory, what was the basis of fixing the reserves for the write-down on inventories, since the value of tires of course had dropped precipitately?

A. We wrote the inventories down; we wrote down rubber to a base of 20 cents, which as I recall was approximately the market at the time that we did it, although before the actual transaction was consummated it sagged off, the nominal market at least sagged off lower, I fancy it was about 17 cents; and the finished goods, the inventory, the cost was above the selling value; so that we merely reduced them to the net selling value, on which basis we assumed that the company would not make either any profit or a loss on liquidating those inventories.

Q. When you say they would not make a loss, suppose you took all the finished goods that were ready for delivery and you marked them down or you set up a reserve rather, to account for current market prices: did you allow anything at all for the large overhead, the administrative expenses, etc.?

A. Not the general administration, only the direct selling costs.

Q. So that whatever the general administration expenses were, chargeable to selling that inventory, which was then marked down, that would be another item at least which would have to be absorbed?

A. Yes, in that colloquial sense.

Mr. Hostetler. In writing a balance sheet like this of February 28, in April, take for instance on a material like crude rubber, that fluctuates rapidly, do you use the market price as of February 28 or as of the date that you make it?

The Witness. You ordinarily use it as of February 28.

Mr. Hostetler. In other words, while it is on the books—

The Witness. But in making a balance sheet for this purpose, in making a reserve for a future situation, if there were any substantial fall between the date of the balance and the date when you gave effect to a new transaction, you would have to reflect that in some way in the balance sheet.

Mr. Hostetler. In other words, in these values of inventories, raw material and completed, you gave the best of your judgment in April when you made the sheet, rather than as of February 28?

The Witness. Yes, that would be so. We did not attempt to— I mean the markets were to some extent nominal; you had to exercise some judgment all the way around.

Q. Do you remember what market you took for cotton? You told us you took about twenty cents for rubber, although it dropped a little.

A. As I remember it, they used a special grade of cotton, as I remember it was a thirty-cent base for a certain long staple cotton, which was their main grade that they used.

Q. In the petition in this case and during the taking of these depositions the statement has been very frequently made that the reorganization plan provided an excessive amount of cash for the company, at least that is my impression. Whether that is true or not, will you give us your views—it is stated in the petition that the amount of cash far exceeded the reasonable requirements of the business. From your connection with this matter, will you give us your view as to whether or not this plan provided an excessive amount of cash, that is, the proceeds of the bonds, the proceeds of all this money that the bankers had to put up, or any other available source of revenue; whether the amount of cash was excessive in view of the circumstances that confronted you in April, 1921: give us your view on that from your experience and from your special knowledge of this situation.

A. It did not seem to me so at the time and it does not seem to me so now.

I should think it would be improbable that it would be so, because there was a lot of work over this plan, with people having different interests, and some of them very shrewd men like Mr. Myron Taylor and Mr. Jenckes, to get out of the banking field; but the fact which has seemed to me to be most persuasive on that question, a fact which I think comparatively few people have recognized, that this plan did nothing more than replace the loss of working capital that had taken place since August 31, 1920.

Q. How much in round numbers was the—

A. I picked August 31, 1920—

Q. Give us the amount of cash?

A. —because that was the first balance sheet that we were invited to consider when we were called into the matter with a view to arranging the financing.

If you take a comparison of the situation then and the situation when the plan was issued, you will find that the plan, leaving out the funded debt altogether, the net working capital under this plan, after the issue of the bonds and the prior preference stock, is less than the net working capital shown by the balance sheet of August 31, 1920, after deducting the bank loans and everything else from that working capital, although at that time the company had no funded debt.

You can check up in various ways. The balance sheet of August 31—

> *Mr. Thompson.* Have you got that with you? We haven't heard of that.
>
> *The Witness.* I haven't got it with me. That is the company's balance sheet of that date.

I am mentioning this only because this is the way it occurred to me, because that was the starting point as far as we were concerned: it does not make a particle of difference whether you take October 31 or August 31, excepting the reserves for inventories are made first in the October balance sheet and none was in the balance sheet of August.

Q. Take it in your own way.

A. But the balance sheet of August 31 showed a surplus of some $9,000,000; there were certain liabilities like taxes that were never put on the books until paid, it ought to be taken off in order to make any kind of a fair comparison: that would have brought the surplus down to $5,000,000.

When we came to the balance sheet of February 28, the deficit after providing for inventory reserves and commitments had grown to somewhere around $75,000,000.

Now the new plan provided for the payment of debt or the provision of new capital to the extent of between $74,-000,000 and $75,000,000.

I can give you roughly the compensation of that deficit which will show how the events have happened. The books of the company before adjusting for inventories showed a loss for September and October of approximately $8,000,000 —I am including the subsidiaries.

Q. Yes.

A. Now some part of that possibly would on an accurate accounting be thrown back of August 31, but it would not be relatively very important. The books showed an operating loss including subsidiaries of roughly $13,000,000 for the four months ending February 28. The books showed a loss for March and April of $5,000,000. So that over the period of eight months there was a loss of between $25,000,000 and $26,000,000.

Q. You mean just an operating loss?

A. An operating loss, including the financing charges, of course: there was a loss of we will say twenty-five—it is between twenty-five and twenty-six million, without providing for write downs or inventories or commitments.

Mr. Thompson. That is from August 31 to May 1?

The Witness. To May 1, yes.

The inventory adjustments were $18,000,000, and the reserve for commitments was $24,000,000. Then in our calculations we took roughly $4,000,000, the officers' accounts which at any rate were frozen, out of working capital, without going any further than that, and approximately $2,600,-000 that was paid out in dividends in September and October, 1920.

If you add those up you get $75,000,000—I get it $75,-400,000, which is roughly the amount of new cash that was provided under the plan. When I say new cash—either in the form of cash or the extension of liability.

Now of course the position of a company that has a funded debt of $57,500,000—the position of such a company in regard to lack of capital is very different from that of a company which has no funded debt; and this company had to operate, as I see it, without any general credit until a new credit could be built up after the reorganization.

It has never been clear to me how it could seriously be argued that a reorganization which did nothing more than replace the working capital that had disappeared in the period of eight months could be regarded as grossly over-providing working capital.

Q. Just putting back the working capital of eight months before, is that right?

A. There is another factor that should be taken into account: you see, it was uncertain what capital would be needed to clean up the capital situation, plants and so on: during, as I recall, the period from October, 1919, to February, 1921, under the old management some $20,000,000 had been spent on capital account in the way of plants, extensions and so on, while there was no—of course there was no provision of working capital then to finance any further capital expenditures than the mere replacement of the working capital.

I want to be entirely fair of course in presenting this, and therefore I would point out that naturally with falling prices and the shooting to pieces of the volume of business which had occurred during the period of or between late in 1920 and early in 1921, the immediate requirements of working capital were reduced; but clearly the company could not go on, could not legitimately put out a scheme of this kind unless it looked forward to regaining something of the position in the rubber industry that it had occupied—not its whole position, but some position in the rubber industry for the new company—and whenever that happened they would need a greatly increased working capital over their immediate requirements at the time the plan was issued; and of course, although the prices were low then, if prices subsequently increased, there would again be a demand for further working capital.

Q. You mean that the facts here looked forward to an achievement of success rather than a conservation of failure?

A. Yes. I think they had to, if they were going to have any moral justification for putting forward the plan at all.

Q. Exactly. What was the feeling of all of these people, these merchandise creditors and bankers' creditors, Dillon, Read & Company, all the bankers, yourself, Price, Waterhouse, as to whether or not there would be an opportunity of an encore here if there was a second collapse?

A. I cannot speak for them, but it is perfectly obvious in a situation of this kind it is no good trying to make two bites of a cherry: you have to clean it up once for all. I think on that everybody will agree.

Q. You did not feel that a second collapse would meet with such applause that you would all be called upon to respond to an encore?

A. No, I did not think so.

.   .   .   .

By Mr. Buckner:

Q. Mr. May, before passing to a new topic I want to revert to the subject you were discussing just as we adjourned yesterday. You called our attention to the fact that the new capital, new money rather, provided by the reorganization plan either in cold cash or the cancellation of obligations, I believe, was something in round numbers like $75,000,000.

A. Yes.

Q. You pointed out that that $75,000,000 so provided was no more than the amount of working capital which had been lost by the company within, roughly speaking, the preceding eight or nine months. Remembering that none of us is an accountant, will you elaborate a little bit on what you mean by the phrase "working capital"?

A. By working capital I mean substantially the sum of money that is sometimes termed net current assets, that is the excess of current assets over current liabilities.

Q. Current assets?

A. By current assets I mean such items as inventories, accounts receivable, temporary investments, if any, and cash;

and by current liabilities I mean items as accounts payable and payrolls, current taxes and any bank debts or loans or any short term obligations of that character.

I distinguish between current assets on the one side and fixed assets, and between current liabilities and funded liabilities on the other.

Q. Take a brick building, would that be working capital?

A. A brick building used in the operation of the plant?

Q. Yes.

A. No.

Q. Take $1,000,000 in Liberty bonds held by the company, would that be working capital?

A. Yes, that would be part of the working capital.

Q. Take $10,000,000 cash in the bank, would that be working capital?

A. Yes.

Q. Take your finished product on hand ready to be sold, would that be working capital?

A. Yes.

Q. I suppose that capital would not work unless it could be sold?

A. Of course every balance sheet of a going concern is predicated upon the assumption that it is going to continue to go.

Q. Oh, I see. So that the assumption at least is, if you got some beautiful tires all ready to sell, especially if they were Goodyear tires, that they will be sold?

A. Yes.

Q. And accounts payable?

A. Accounts payable, yes.

Q. Predicated upon the theory that people will pay their debts within the customary time?

A. Yes; with of course due provision for any cases where that does not appear to be a reasonable presumption.

Q. The percentage of reluctant or discouraged debtors is usually taken care of by some arbitrary reserve set up, isn't it?

A. Some reserve more or less arbitrary, according to circumstances.

Q. So that as we would understand it, working capital is either cash or a very near relative?

A. Yes.

Q. Which could easily be put in the place of cash, is that it?

A. Less the things that have to be paid out of cash in the near future.

Q. Less the things that have to be paid out of it, of course. The evidence shows here that the first mortgage bonds, for example, bore an 8 per cent coupon and that every year for 20 years there would be a percentage of those bonds drawn by lot and redeemed at 120 over the 20 years; the evidence shows that the debentures I think carried a coupon of 8 per cent. The prior preference stock carried 8 per cent interest; that the debentures which were sold to the bankers in place of their debt carried with them stock warrants, the bankers being required to put up $100 of new money for every $100 that they were already in for; and, generally speaking, the plan has been said to be from time to time drastic or expensive. What was the alternative to a reorganization on these lines, under all the circumstances existing in the spring of 1921?

Mr. Thompson. Objected to as leading.

Mr. Buckner. What was the alternative? There is nothing leading about that.

The Witness. Do you want me to answer?

Mr. Buckner. Yes, what was the alternative?

A. My judgment is that if permanent financing had not been accomplished just about the time that this was accomplished, a receivership would have been practically inevitable.

Q. Have you any judgment—I do not know exactly how close you were to what might be called the banking situation: have you any judgment as to whether or not this reorganization could possibly have been put through on any other terms than this term, in a broad, general way?

A. I do not think I could say that I was close enough to answer that question in that specific form.

Q. We are getting that from the bankers but I do not know how you—

A. I was in general touch and I might have an opinion, but it would not be a sufficiently well-informed opinion based upon my own knowledge to justify me in answering that specific question.

Q. You will stick right to the Price, Waterhouse boundaries?

A. I want to talk about things that I know about.

Mr. Thompson. Some have not done that, Mr. May.

Mr. Hostetler. No; the lawyers have been very lax.

Mr. Thompson. We will accept it if you will. [Discussion off the record.]

Q. Let us look at the situation after the reorganization: whatever happened to the bank debts of Goodyear?

A. They were retired under the plan of reorganization through the operation of the debenture issue.

Q. What had happened to all the obligations that were owed to the merchandise creditors who had sold cotton and fabric and machinery and rubber, etc.?

A. In the main, they had been provided for by issues of prior preference stock.

Q. What was the result of that so far as cash or its equivalent now in the possession of Goodyear after reorganization with which to do business and as to its quick assets: that is, the net result of that reorganization in that way?

A. The company started off—I cannot give you the exact figure except on the footing of the balance sheet that we used and which I can say that it would have started off at January 28 if the plan had been consummated at that time, instead of actually at April, because it is impossible to get the actual financial position actually at the time the plan went into effect, so that I have to make any answers subject to that modification; the plan will show, but as I recall it started the company off with approximately $54,000,000 of net working capital and somewhere around ten or eleven million dollars in cash.

Q. That is a matter of record, of course.

A. Yes.

Q. Were the terms of this reorganization, the terms of the refinancing, due to Dillon, Read; Goldman, Sachs; National City Company; Chase Securities Company and three other names read by Mr. Thompson yesterday: was it due to these bankers or was it due to the financial condition of Goodyear?

A. Well, the major factor in determining the basis on which finance can be accomplished is clearly the financial situation of the company that is seeking it.

Q. You spent a lot of time studying, either at first hand or with your other partners, the conditions in the Goodyear Company, did you not, before Dillon, Read were in it at all?

A. Yes. I will not say before Dillon, Read were in it at all. I do not know when they went in. At any rate, when they went into any specific commitment.

Q. And so far as you know when they were in it at all?

A. Yes. I don't know when they went into it.

Q. Did you find any evidence out there in Akron that Dillon, Read had gotten this company in a condition where on February 28 their balance sheet would have shown a $75,000,000 deficit?

A. No, I do not say that.

Q. Whose party was that, I mean what had brought about conditions where a balance sheet without reorganization would have shown a deficit of $75,000,000: what had brought that about?

A. Fundamentally, of course, it was the general condition that supervened in 1920 when the general deflation took place; that is the primary cause. And I think the reason why it was so severe in the case of Goodyear was that, first of all

I think that industry was one of the industries that was relatively hard hit by the deflation and Goodyear was certainly the hardest hit so far as I could judge of any of the companies in the industry, because apparently it was overextended.

Q. That is just what I want to know, why was the Goodyear harder hit than the other tire companies?

A. Because it had such an extended commitment position, that is fundamental, that is the particular manifestation, and if you want to go back of that to more general causes I can do it, but I want to stick to—that is the important situation.

Q. You can use your own judgment in any way—

.   .   .   .

Q. —in any way that you feel is a proper way to answer the question.

A. Well, based on my examination of the situation at that time the real trouble seemed to me to be that Goodyear was well organized on the manufacturing side, the selling side and the general development of the business, and therefore it was able to take full advantage of favorable conditions; but it was weak as I see it on the side of control of purchases, control of finance and general control of accounts. Those are the weaknesses that become vital and fatal when you strike real adversity. They were unfortunate in being weak on that side when they struck a period of exceptional adversity which hit their particular industry particularly hard. To put it in a nut shell, I think probably in the organization, in addition to the manufacturing personnel, that if there had been a good hard-headed Scotchman that we would have—

Mr. Thompson. An Englishman would not have done?

The Witness. No, a Scotchman; a good hard-headed Scotchman to watch the finances, we none of us would have been here today.

Q. You have some Scotch partners, have you not?

A. Yes.

Q. We had one of them here, Jackson: I wanted to ask him if Price, Waterhouse selected him as treasurer because he was a Scotchman, but I was afraid he might not enjoy the comedy. What do you mean by being well equipped for everything except adversity: what do you mean, why is that important in a large industry? After all this thing had grown up into an enormous company, had it not?

A. Yes. But unless you are well equipped for success you will never make a big success and, on the other hand, if you are not equipped for adversity you may make a very big failure. That is really two sides of the picture as I see it.

Q. The Goodyear Company was a fair weather sailor, is that it, from your examination of the books and the situation: as long as everything went all right they went all right?

A. Yes. I do not think they would listen to the advice of Horace about taking half your canvas in when more than a propitious gale fills your sail. I think that is probably their real trouble.

Q. Was the canvas all out when you went out?

A. I think they were carrying on a bit longer than most of us would in a race.

Q. And the wind was then blowing, was it?

A. Very strong.

Q. I read you from paragraph 45 of the petition as follows [reading]:

Owing to the large earning power of the Company and the inherent soundness of its financial condition, within three months its former debts to banks were funded; its former obligations for merchandise paid in stock; its quick assets exceeded its current debts by more than ten to one; it possessed no banking indebtedness, and had over twenty-three million dollars ($23,000,000) in cash, bankers' acceptances and securities of the United States of America.

Without regard at the moment to the precise accuracy or otherwise of the amount of cash and ratio of quick assets to current debts, I want to ask you if the condition described in that paragraph, after three months from reorganization, was due to the large earning power of the company and the inherent soundness of its financial condition, or was it due to what the reorganization had brought about in the way you have described?

A. I should say that it was due to the substantial soundness of its financial position after the reorganization had been effected, and that the effecting of that reorganization was of course only rendered possible by the belief that the company had under fairly normal conditions an earning capacity; but apart from the reorganization, obviously the company had no inherent financial soundness.

Q. Exactly; of course it would not be reorganized if they did not believe that the company would pull out if reorganized, naturally.

.   .   .   .

Q. Now will you put your mind on the month of November, 1921, after the reorganization in May, 1921, and from your knowledge of the situation and from your experience will you tell me whether in November, 1921, the Goodyear Company could properly have retired all or any substantial part of its debentures which had been held by the Blair-Hallgarten syndicate and which were sold in November to a syndicate headed by Dillon, Read?

Mr. Thompson. Objected to as leading.

Mr. C. Crawford. I object to it on the ground that the witness is without jurisdiction to decide the issues of this case.

Mr. Thompson. I object to it as leading, too.

Mr. Buckner. Answer the question, Mr. May.

A. My judgment, not of course as a legal conclusion, but as a business man, is that they could not have done so from a business standpoint, nor do I see how they could have done so from a moral standpoint: I will exclude the legal standpoint altogether.

Q. Take up first the business standpoint and then take up the moral standpoint and tell us what you mean by that.

A. I would rather take them in the other order, if I may.

Q. The other order, all right.

A. These debentures had been issued as a part of a general plan and for the reorganization of the company which had been agreed to by a large number of persons in interest, and through the sale of first mortgage bonds new money had been brought into the company on the faith of that plan. Now between the date of the plan and September 30 nothing had happened of a favorable nature to the company, as I see it, that was not contemplated in the plan. The earnings had been no greater than those on which the plan had been predicated. In those circumstances it seems to me that the company could not well have applied any of the money that was raised under that plan to the retirement of securities which were junior to the first mortgage bonds which had recently been subscribed for on the faith of that plan and the representations made in pursuance of that plan.

Turning to the—

Mr. Thompson. Now that is the moral side.

The Witness. That is the broad moral side. From a business standpoint it seems to me that the company had just had an extremely narrow escape from a business failure due substantially to a lack of proper prudence in finance. Its general credit had been injured, and one of the first requisites to its future success was that its general credit should be rehabilitated, and for that reason more than customary financial prudence seemed to me to be called for at that time.

In the third place, while the company at that time had a large amount of cash and securities on hand, its business had been greatly injured by the unfortunate events of the previous year, and if it was to be a financial success it had to restore its volume of business, which would entail an increase in the amount of working capital in the form of accounts receivable and so on, even though there were a diminution of the amount of working capital in the form of cash and securities.

Furthermore, the company's business rests on raw materials, which are subject to very wide fluctuations. They had been through a serious situation caused by concurrent declines in the prices of rubber and fabric. If within one or two years they should have struck a situation where there were concurrent high prices for rubber and fabric, they might have needed very much more working capital to conduct their business, even than they had then had.

Then the company had a lot of troubles that were not entirely straightened out; that was in the nature of things; the major troubles were connected with the reorganization, but inevitably there were a lot of things still to be cleared up. The unspecified commitment situation was one of some difficulty and uncertainty. The industry had been going through something of a change; the type of common tire had altered; the future of the business—the industry as a whole was in a very interesting condition, and looking at it from that standpoint it seemed to me that at that time the position of the cash resources, the potential resource that could be drawn in at any point where there seemed to be an advantage to use it, was from the standpoint of all the security holders of the company far more important than any saving of interest charges that might result from the retirement of debts. I know that our people always felt that a concurrent serious movement in either direction of the basic raw materials of the industry at any time within two or three years after the reorganization might be a source of serious embarrassment to the company, and they were very fortunate in the fact that no such concurrent movement took place during 1921, 1922, and 1923. When the fabric situation was a bit unfavorable the rubber situation helped us out, and vice versa; but it seemed to me you always had to be prepared, particularly at that time, for a concurrent movement of the raw materials which might have been very embarrassing.

For all these reasons, in my mind it was perfectly clear that from any standpoint of either moral obligation or practical common sense it would not have been an appropriate thing for the company to apply its cash resources to the retirement of the debentures. Personally I think they were wise in keeping cash resources, but if they wanted to apply them to the retirement of debt it seems to me the only proper use would have been to retire first mortgage bonds.

Q. As a matter of fact did not the very thing that you are saying might be on the cards any year actually happen in 1925 when rubber jumped up like a thermometer, or do you know about that?

A. Yes, I know something about that, yes; it did happen, yes.

Q. The company actually had to issue still more securities in 1925, did it, or do you remember?

A. Yes, it had to issue $15,000,000 of notes, as I remember.

Q. Do you recall, too, whether or not the fall of the year is the time when anybody in the tire business accumulates more cash than it has in the spring of the year, let us say?

A. Yes.

Q. And is this cash a curve or wave, rather, in the tire business?

A. The fall of the year is the low point of the requirements for the working capital other than cash, and therefore you have to have more cash at that time if you are going to have adequate working capital for the spring season, when the other demands are greater.

Q. What is the justification, if any, for any industrial company to have bank deposits drawing banking interest at 3 per cent at a time when they may have outstanding bonds and debentures drawing 8 per cent?

A. Well, of course, every company must have some cash

resources at all times. But my experience has been that a substantial cash reserve over and above the bare requirements is a real source of strength to any company. You will find, of course, the Steel Corporation is one of the conspicuous illustrations of a company that has always carried very large cash balances, and the value of it is measured by the potential uses of the cash as well as the actual uses of the cash, just as in naval affairs, in Admiral Mahan's expression, a fleet in being has a great value quite apart from the existence of its influence on the immediate area in which it is located.

Q. Let us get down to the spring of 1923, the early part of 1923. I have in mind, say, the last week in January. I may say that at that time the company was offered by a syndicate headed by Dillon, Read & Company the privilege of buying all or any part of all of the outstanding prior preference stock which in round numbers was about $33,000,000 par value. They were offered the privilege of buying that at $85.60, which is just what it had cost the Dillon, Read syndicate. They actually did purchase $13,000,000 par value at that discount. I would like to have your views in the same way as you have given in the debentures as to the propriety of the company either from a business standpoint or a moral standpoint, if they are both involved, in purchasing any or all of that outstanding block of prior preference stock at that time when they were given the opportunity at that price. That is about the last week in January, 1923, a little less than two years after the reorganization.

A. Well, that is a little further away from the date when I was making a more intensive study of Goodyear, and therefore I do not feel so well equipped to discuss all the business aspects of the situation; but I did know about that incident at the time, and it seemed to me then a very grave question whether, having in mind the spirit of the plan of reorganization and not merely its letter, the company was justified in buying as much prior preference stock as it did. The first mortgage bonds and debentures were secured by agreements which contained various restrictive covenants. One of those, as I recall, was that no dividends should be paid on the prior preference stock or any stocks, in fact, to the extent of more than two-thirds of the surplus accumulated subsequent to May 1, 1921. The balance sheet of December 31, 1922, showed a surplus, as I recall, of very close to $8,000,000, and two-thirds of that would be somewhere under five and a half million, and I have always had difficulty in seeing how the directors felt justified in retiring more than could be purchased with five and a half million dollars from the standpoint of the spirit of the arrangement. Clearly, retiring prior preference stock, so far as any effect on the debentures was concerned, was precisely the same as paying the money out in dividends on the prior preference stock. I do not know anything about the legal aspects of the question, but if I had been a director I should have hesitated a great deal about going further than that in retiring the prior preference stock. As a matter of fact, I do not think it injured the debenture holder—

Q. The way it worked out?

A. [Continuing] —as it worked out, and it proved beneficial to the junior stockholders undoubtedly and to the rest of the prior preference stock, so that from that standpoint you may say that I should have to admit that the directors took a risk I would not have taken, but that it worked out very well for everybody concerned.

Q. That is, after the event?

A. After the event.

Q. When you said a while ago that the Seiberling management needed a Scotchman, did you have in mind a Scotchman that would look ahead or a Scotchman that would look back after the event?

A. Scotchmen are generally regarded as being good at looking forward.

Q. A forward-looking Scotchman, as we would say?

A. Yes.

Q. Well, from your thirty years' experience with apparently pretty large industries and institutions, do you attach any importance to the element of management of an industrial company?

A. Well, it seems to me obviously the vitally important element.

Q. Why?

A. Provided of course that you are in a business where there are some possibilities of success. Why?

Q. Yes. Why is it so important in an industrial concern or any concern?

A. Well, because when you really get down to essentials the value of a business depends ultimately on its earning capacity, and its earning capacity is largely determined by the character of the management.

. . . .

Q. [Reading]:

That the accounts of the Goodyear Company were in such a state of confusion as to require months of work by certified public accountants to arrive at even a reasonable approximation of the correct situation.

Was that statement true or not?

A. Well, my information is not very detailed about that, but the position that was reported to me was that the general detailed accounting of the company was good.

Q. Yes.

A. But there was not any adequate general control, and the records on some material—essentials perhaps I had better say—on some essential features, such as commitments, were quite inadequate. There was no place in the organization where you could go and either be given or directed to a source of information which would be comprehensive. That was our fundamental difficulty, as I see it. But I would like to make it quite clear that the general accounting, the detail accounting, was quite satisfactory.

Q. I understand that.

A. I did not want to reflect on anybody unjustly.

Q. I understand that. The point is that the ledger account as to how much the Main Street Garage owed for tires was accurate, but you seem to refer to something higher?

A. Yes; there was no one that was really on top of the whole situation from the financial side and had a picture of it all.

Q. Exactly.

A. This, as I think, was the fatal defect of the organization. If there had been, I think there would have been an entirely different result.

.   .   .   .

RE-CROSS EXAMINATION BY MR. THOMPSON:

Q. Mr. May, United States Rubber and Goodrich were much older companies than Goodyear, were they not?

A. I do not know the actual age of Goodyear, but as substantial competitors they certainly were.

Q. The growth of Goodyear in volume of business was very rapid up to 1920, was it not?

A. It was.

Q. And the real, serious trouble, as you have depicted it to us, was a failure to have the seer's vision and to prepare for the bad days that perhaps a Scotchman would have foreseen: that is one of the outstanding things, isn't it?

A. Well, I do not think you needed to be a seer, exactly. I think my statement would rather be that there had been undue concentration on development and inadequate consideration of the dangers of the business: too much realization of the opportunities and not enough realization of the pitfalls.

Q. In other words, the chief executive appears to you to have been a man with vision and energy in building up a business, but not possessed of those hard-headed qualities of a cold-blooded financier?

A. Yes, I think that is true, that he needed—it is very difficult to get that combination of qualities in one man.

Q. He had not equipped himself with the right type of treasurer: that is what you mean, do you not?

A. I should think that a strong financial vice-president would have been what was needed for that business.

Q. And what had happened was that, with too much optimism probably due at least in part to the rapidity of the growth of the business, they had committed themselves for rubber and fabric at prices that turned out to be very unwise: now that is the real situation, isn't it?

A. That is the vitally important element in the situation, undoubtedly.

Q. And as you have very accurately described, that really was the crux of the trouble that the company was confronted with in the fall of 1920?

A. Yes.

VII

THE BETHLEHEM-YOUNGSTOWN MERGER SUIT *

(1930)

Q. Why is it these physical valuations, physical appraisals, to your mind are of so little value regarding the real worth of properties, the real relative worth of properties, the real relative worth of two business institutions?

A. Well, in the case of steel industries, the big steel plants of the country have grown up in locations that were determined on the basis of conditions existing a number of years ago because once you have made your choice of location, you are more or less committed to it even if it appears years later the place you would have chosen is another spot. Now, discussing values, they come under two heads, one the physical valuation and the other the commercial valuation.

Q. Before you proceed suppose you define what you mean by physical valuation. Possibly we all mean the same thing, but let us make certain.

A. I think that will appear more clearly as I explain what seems to me involved.

Court. Involved in the place of the physical structure?

A. Yes, on the so-called physical question I have given a great deal of time in connection with the railroad rate regulation problem, on which I have studied and written. The physical valuation theory starts on the premise that if the property did not exist it would be economically wise to reproduce it where it is and as it is.

Q. In kind?

A. Yes. In regard to a very large part of the steel industry such a premise is totally unwarranted. I think everyone will agree there are large parts of the steel industry

* From testimony in *Wick & International Shares Inc.* v. *Youngstown Sheet & Tube Co. and Bethlehem Steel Corporation.*

which if they didn't exist would not be reproduced where they are located or as they are. Take an extreme illustration: the physical reproduction theory would assign greater value to a steel plant at the North Pole than one on Lake Michigan because it would cost more to build it there. But in a reasonable way there is no doubt that the value of a steel plant is very largely affected by its location and type of construction, and it is quite unsafe to assume as a measure of value that they would be reproduced as they are and where they are. In this particular case it certainly appears that the Coatesville plant, for instance, and some of the Mahoning Valley properties—

Court. Excuse me. You use the illustration of a hypothetical plant at the North Pole and one somewhere near here. Would there be such a disparity if they were both valued as to their purely physical valuation by one's advantageously comparing it with the other?

A. It depends upon what you mean by their purely physical valuation. If you assume physical cost of reproduction—

Court. I do not, I do not mean that at all.

A. Then your physical valuation is very much what I would call the commercial physical valuation. The physical valuation that takes into account the location and advantages and disadvantages—

Court. I merely mean that taking a plant, physical structure here and one at the North Pole, considering their condition of depreciation, that is, their obsolescence, etc., and their condition as productive physical properties designed to produce the product for which they were intended—comparing one with the other regardless of location—

Witness. Regardless of location? The value would be the same if the buildings were the same and depreciation conditions were the same?

Court. Yes.

Witness. That being so, that seems to me necessarily would be a very unsafe guide to property value.

Court. It is, however, one element that enters into an appraisal?

Witness. It is one element that may enter into it, it does enter into the ordinary physical appraisal.

Court. There are, however, other considerations I understand you classify under the heading of commercial?

A. Yes.

Q. So in the understanding of this question of equality of reproduction costs designed to illustrate there are two things, first the replacement values: it is higher at the North Pole than in the Mahoning Valley because it would cost more to get the material up there to build it. Secondly, built at the North Pole it would be susceptible of less use than in the Mahoning Valley and consequently would be worth less.

A. That is the second part of my view that I hadn't reached yet.

Q. Well now, proceed.

A. Now, coming to the question of commercial valuation. It is perfectly obvious that if you have two identical plants and one is better located than the other—

Q. Now, if I may interrupt—I don't want to seem to lead you—assuming these two plants you speak of having identical valuations, is that your assumption?

A. That is the assumption, that if they were identical and in the same state of observed depreciation, or whatever you would call it, they would still not be of the same commercial value if one were much more advantageously located than the other.

Court. To location of raw materials?

A. Yes. Therefore, those factors would have to be taken into account in what I call commercial valuation. As I see it there are two approaches to the commercial valuation, the one is to take the physical value of an ideally located and constructed plant and then measure the value of a less favorably constructed and located plant by deducting from the value of the ideal plant an estimate of the capital sum equivalent to the disadvantages of the less favorably located plant. Perhaps I can make it clear by the use of figures. If, for instance, the necessary investment in a steel plant of a given type would run to, say, ⸢ 100 per ton on the annual production, and let us say $12 would be the amount necessary to provide depreciation and a fair return on the cost, then if you have two plants and one is at a disadvantage to the other to the extent of more than $12 that second plant is practically worthless. It would be cheaper to scrap it and build somewhere else than to do anything with it. On the other hand, if the disadvantage of the second plant as compared with the first is, let us say, two or three dollars a ton, it is by no means worthless but is worth less than a more favorably located plant, one might say 75% of the more favorably located plant. In my mind that is one way of approaching a commercial value of some reality for the purposes of the business man.

Court. For the purposes of comparison?

A. Yes, sir, the disadvantage of that is that it involves a great many speculations, hypotheses and differences of opinion. The other method of approach, as I see it, is to take what the properties are actually earning if you can assume the present operation is fairly reflective of their relative normal earning ability, and capitalize that earning capacity in the two cases at the same rates, making allowances in that capitalization both for what would be needed for return on investment and for what would be needed to be set aside by the purchaser for depreciation on the price he paid for the property.

Court. But on that basis would you consider it better, would you consider these elements of physical valuation or commercial valuation that would be included in the term appraisal—do they have any bearing on it?

A. If I may use a homely expression, it seems to me most of these appraisals are like going around Robin Hood's barn to get to a place where you can get to directly with less uncertainty. I think the most outstanding development of the financial history of this country is the growing recognition of the truth which the economists have recognized—that commercial value depends upon the probable yield in the future. The cost of reproduction is only a limiting factor on value. I think the true definition of value, if I may go into theoretical and economical definitions, is that the value of industrial plant is determined by the prospective earning capacity, with the physical cost of reproduction as the upper limit. It can't be worth more than it would cost to reproduce it. Neither can it be worth less than its salvage value if it were destroyed. Its actual value is determined by its prospective earning capacity, and that prospective earning capacity can best be judged on its actual earning capacity. I think that truth has become more and more recognized in all financial practice in the United States in recent years. I think if you will follow the literature you will see that an increasing stress on earnings and a diminishing stress on physical values is by far the most conspicuous feature in recent development.

Court. Pardon me, yet regardless of its immediate past earning record the commercial valuation enters into the appraisal by reason of its probable obsolescence—I am not so good at these terms as you.

A. I get your point quite clearly.

Court. Or does immediate wiping out of the value by changes in the arts enter into it?

A. Unquestionably.

Court. Then how when you are making a comparison on the basis of earnings immediately past, how do you take that factor of commercial value, which may entirely remove any earning power for consideration? Am I clear to you?

A. Yes, entirely. I think that is one factor that has to be taken into account. In any approach I have made to commercial valuations along the lines I have indicated I have always left that to the parties concerned to be dealt with.

Court. Then that is not included in your advice?

A. It is not, it cannot be; that is a question for the people

who are thoroughly familiar with the industry, essentially.
The point is absolutely sound, there is no question about
that.

Q. And not to anticipate or to lead, but I think it has
already been testified that you called that factor to the attention of the parties at the time you made the oral recommendation on the thirteenth of February?

A. I did very pointedly.

Court. But did it enter into the basis of your suggested
relative values of trading of stock or whatever you might
call it?

A. No, what I said to these gentlemen was: This is the
recommendation I would make from the studies of the recent past and from what you may call the accounting and
statistical approach. There are certain things you will have
to pass on for consideration, and most important is your respective views of the future of the steel industry, and that
is particularly important in this case because you are engaged
in different branches of the industry and there may be a very
marked difference between the prospects in the different
branches of the industry; that is a question on which I would
not undertake to pass.

Court. One more question if you will pardon me? Mr.
Wood?

Mr. Wood. Yes.

Court. So that in your recommendation of 1.2—

A. I prefer to call it one and one-fifth because it was not
made with the decimal accuracy of 1.2.

Court. We will take the vulgar fraction. Your recommendation of one and one-fifth to one left for the consideration of those using your figures as a partial basis—it was understood it was only a partial basis in your recommendation.
This element or those elements of both physical and commercial valuation—

A. It left it to this extent, it left to them the question
how far the prospective developments they could see would

vitiate a conclusion that was based on the recent past. That was essentially the point I put up to them.

Court. From your experience in all these mergers you have detailed, was that wholly a matter for the determination of those in charge of the policies and general operation of the plants to determine or would it require experts in the determination of the physical and commercial values ordinarily known as appraisals?

A. I think that varied according to the number of companies concerned and their relative importance. If you have a group of 15 or 20 companies it is very often helpful to have somebody from the outside to reconcile the differences. In my experience where you have one or two or three large companies they have been able to reach a conclusion without outside assistance. That basic question arises in every merger of importance.

Court. Assuming, however, there were two companies, that each one had had some thorough examination of the physical properties and locations of the others—

A. I don't think really the physical examination of the properties is so important. A man who has lived in the industry and had to make his money in the industry, that is, the successful man, is much better able in my experience to forecast the future than a looker-on.

Court. And arrive at the obsolescence?

A. The prospective obsolescence.

Court. I mean that.

A. Of course, there is really a difference between a present obsolescence and a thing which is in danger of obsolescence. You were looking to the future, Your Honor?

Court. Yes, thank you.

. . . .

A. Yes, my whole method of approach to problems of this kind is to try to get someone to approach it from the standpoint of detail and someone else to approach it from the standpoint of a broad consideration, and it is a matter which as a senior partner I would rather reserve to myself because it involves more mental and less physical work than the details—

Court. Sometimes we who work mentally would like to trade with the other fellow.

A. At times, but broadly speaking I think we prefer the mental exercise, and I was considering the problem from that standpoint all the time, and by so doing I think I can fairly say with a fairly broad background in regard not only to these companies but as to the steel industry as a whole. Do you want me to—

Q. I would just like to have you go on and state in your own way.

A. It seemed to me that there were three or four major points. After all, steel company accounting is among the relatively simple of the industrial accounting problems. It is not complex like that of many other industries. There are only comparatively few problems in it.

Mr. Wood. I hope I don't have to go into another one.

Court. Everything certainly is relative.

A. I think that is true. You don't, broadly speaking, in the steel industry have many difficult inventory problems or bad debts or problems of that kind. They narrow down substantially to the general problem, the maintenance and depreciation problem. That is the only big problem in every steel comparison or steel audit. Apart from that the differences between the two companies were largely the differences in financial structure, which are not so difficult from a financial man's point of view.

. . . .

Q. In comparing the liquid assets of a corporation it might be important to know something about their current liabilities, might it not?

A. Yes.

Q. The fact that you had a lot of money in the bank oughtn't to make a firm rich if you have a lot of bills you haven't paid?

A. That is quite true.

Q. Now, isn't it a common thing in examining into the financial state of a company to regard the current assets as being more or less applicable to the current liabilities and the fixed assets to the capital liabilities?

A. That is a common practice.

Q. There may have to be adjustments in specific cases?

A. Yes.

Q. It is true, isn't it, that the ratio of Youngstown's current assets to its current liabilities is higher than Bethlehem's at the end of December 31, 1929, notwithstanding this $50,000,000 of cash?

A. I am not sure about that, but of course Youngstown is a business that involves a great deal of money locked up in inventories and consignments and stocks of that kind which are not in the same category as these Government securities so far as they are available to meet the debts.

Q. That is a factor to consider, is it not, Mr. May, in determining on the value to Youngstown of Bethlehem's liquid assets—its need of assets?

A. Youngstown's need for liquid assets makes this attractive, yes; Youngstown's need for liquid assets makes this merger attractive.

Q. Isn't it true that Youngstown's current asset position is and always has been in the last three years stronger than Bethlehem's?

A. I don't think so; it depends somewhat on what you mean by strength.

Q. The ratio of current assets to current liabilities is larger in the case of Youngstown?

A. That may have been so; to me that doesn't demonstrate strength. . . . The point is . . . the excess in the case of Youngstown is in the form of inventories, which to my mind is a weakness rather than an element of strength.

Q. And Youngstown has never been in the last six or eight years embarrassed for lack of cash?

A. No, I mean a comparison of the current assets which includes inventories is not an index of the relative cash position of the two companies because the nature of Youngstown's business, particularly through Continental Supply and the oil field business, involves a lockup of a great amount in inventories in the field; that is a source, as I see it, of weakness rather than strength in the case of Youngstown.

Q. You don't think Youngstown would have any difficulty in any circumstances that are now visible in getting any cash it might need?

A. No, I am addressing myself to the question of what constitutes strength and weakness in current assets.

Q. You don't think Youngstown in a merger ought to pay any premiums besides for liquid assets?

A. I think the excess liquid assets of Bethlehem are a factor which they are entitled to have considered.

Q. To the extent that Youngstown—how should they be considered?

A. If you take the value of a business, the earnings of a business are the earnings on the property that is necessary to the business, which include not only the plant which produces the goods but the inventories which it is necessary to have on hand and accounts receivable arising from the business less the accounts payable. When you get a big block of government securities like Bethlehem has, that is not necessary to the earnings of the business, the earnings upon that are not business earnings and are not capitalizable in the same way as business earnings. That is one of the elements, one which we took into account.

Q. Now, Mr. May, suppose you had a company that was embarrassed financially, that proposed to merge with Bethlehem, and that they had bond interest coming due and no way to meet it, and everybody was standing around waiting to see whether the sheriff was going to get them or not and they would like to have Bethlehem's cash position, that matter would be extremely valuable and an inducement, a strong inducement for them to merge, would it not?

A. Yes, sir.

Q. A company of that sort could afford to pay Bethlehem

a substantial premium for relief, for its cash assistance which would afford the merging company a financial position?

A. Yes, sir.

Q. Now the premium value of the cash naturally diminishes as applied to a company whose credit position is strong, does it not?

A. That is true.

Q. And when you get a company which has paid dividends for 25 years and which has largely built or rebuilt its plant out of earnings, whose credit is good and whose bonds are selling at five per cent, its cash is worth its face value, isn't it?

A. Exactly, and that is all the weight I wish to give to it, and that is all of the weight I have given it.

.   .   .   .

Q. Well, when you come to figure out the savings on bond interest that will be effected when the bonds are lifted in February, 1930, you are going into the future, are you not?

A. No, I think not; I think you are giving retrospective effect to something that has occurred.

Q. Well, giving retrospective effect to something that has occurred, is about the same thing as looking forward from the time of occurrence to the future events; it is the difference in the way you state it, isn't it?

A. I don't look at it quite that way.

Q. Very well. Now prior to the issue of the Bethlehem— the 800,000 shares of Bethlehem common stock in October, 1929, it had outstanding 2,400,000 shares of stock, did it not?

A. Yes.

Q. The number of shares outstanding were increased by this 800,000 issue just one-third?

A. Yes.

Q. The earnings were affected by that, as you give retrospective effect to it here by $4,565,702, were they not?

A. That is the effect that is given to it, here.

Q. Yes, well, whatever the proper figure is; now the effect of that issue of 800,000 shares of common stock so far as the earnings per share of the corporation were concerned was to reduce the earnings per share, was it not?

A. Yes.

Q. And so if you were computing the effect on Bethlehem—the value of Bethlehem common stock of that issue of 800,000 shares and the application of it to the retirement of funded debt upon a purely earnings basis—you would reach a conclusion, would you not, that the total value of the Bethlehem common stock had not been increased $86,000,-000 by the issue of the stock and the application made of the proceeds?

A. I don't think so; obviously, if you reach such a conclusion, there must be some fallacy in it.

Q. Well, the fallacy, if there is a fallacy, or the cause of the conclusion is, is it not, that we are now considering the value of the outstanding Bethlehem stock on a purely earnings basis?

A. Yes, but if you consider it on an earnings basis you must consider what the nature of the earnings is, as I said before; earnings that represent a prior charge can't be capitalized at the same rate as earnings that represent a small equity and the greater the equity the lower the rate of capitalization that is properly applicable.

Q. Of course, Mr. May, when the corporation issues 800,000 shares of stock and receives $86,000,000 for it and applies that to the retirement of funded debt, it is getting value wholly apart from any effect on earnings, is it not?

A. I don't understand the question.

Q. Well, when a corporation issues common stock and applies the proceeds to the reduction of its bonded debt, it is improving its financial structure in the direction of stability, is it not?

A. Yes.

Q. And that improvement in financial structure gives a value to the common stock wholly apart from the effect of the transaction on earnings per share, does it not?

A. Oh, I see, yes, you are right.

Q. Yes.

A. Your point is, as I understand it, that the value derived from the issue of the capital stock to retire bonds is not measured by the mere interest saving it produces.

Q. Exactly.

A. That is right.

Q. And it isn't reflected by the effect it has on the earnings per share of the common stock because it is giving the common stock value in other directions; that is correct, is it not?

A. That is true, yes.

Q. But if you take that transaction and consider it purely on the effect it has on earnings per share, that effect is materially to reduce the earnings per share of the entire 3,200,000 shares?

A. That is true.

Q. So that again confining our consideration to value as affected by earnings and not—dismissing for the moment value as reflected in other directions by greater stability and certainty of yield and so forth—the $86,000,000 added to the corporation by the sale of this stock is not reflected in the value of the total outstanding shares on a purely earnings basis, is it?

A. Well, when you say a purely earnings basis, I don't want to quibble with you, that is the last thing in the world I want to do, but as I say, when you limit it to an earnings basis, the earnings basis you have got to employ must vary according to the character of your earnings and by using a lower rate of capitalization on the new figure you should get substantially the same result as you got before, but if you add to your question "on the basis of capitalizing earning capacity at a fixed rate" your point is quite correct.

Q. And as long as you understand that you are limiting your consideration to the effect on earnings, there is no mathematical absurdity involved in that at all, is there?

A. Well, I don't think—you mean if you leave out an essential element of the proposition you say there is no mathematical absurdity; but the thing that is absurd to me is leaving out the essential element of the computation.

Q. All right, the essential element of Basis K is a comparison of earnings for the year 1929 as adjusted, is it not?

A. Yes.

Q. It is not a comparison of capital structure, is it?

A. The question of capital structure is implicit in it; obviously, you could not make a relative computation at the same rate of capitalization if in one case the stock represented a small equity, and in the other case the entire investment is subject to no prior charge; so that you must be satisfied that, broadly speaking, there is a relatively fair capital structure before you are justified in making any computation.

Q. Exactly, but there is a difference, a radical difference, in the capital structure of Bethlehem before the 800,000 shares were issued and its proceeds earmarked for debt retirement?

A. There is, yes.

Q. Now, the only interest we have in the effect upon Bethlehem of that financial operation is its effect on earnings per share, is it not, on this page?

A. Yes.

Q. That is correct?

A. Yes.

Q. On Basis K. Nobody is interested at the time of this merger in a comparison between the present Bethlehem and the Bethlehem prior to October?

A. Well, you have to take that into account if you are going to base it on earnings for a period which extends back of October.

Q. Yes, but you have to give effect to it as earnings?

A. You have to give effect to it as earnings in an intelligent way.

Q. And the effect of it on earnings is substantially to reduce earnings per share?

A. That is true.

Q. Now, as you have said in your direct examination, it would have been most unfair to have compared Bethlehem's earnings on the 1,800,000 share basis with those of Youngstown, that would have been unfair, would it not?

A. That would have been unfair.

Q. That is why you rejected one of these calculations?

A. That is true.

Q. And it would have been unfair until this new common stock was issued and the proceeds received to put Bethlehem's capital structure on a basis which would make a comparison of earnings relevant?

A. That I think is substantially what I said in my testimony.

Q. And that is of course perfectly true?

A. Yes.

Q. Now, you arrive in the first column of Basis K at the figure $39,948,031 as being the adjusted earnings for Bethlehem in the year 1929?

A. Yes.

Q. You then divide that $39,948,031 by the 2,500,000 shares and reach an earning per share on 2,500,000 shares—that is, after the elimination of 700,000 shares—of $15.98 per share?

A. Yes.

Q. Now, up to this date you are dealing with a purely hypothetical Bethlehem Steel Corporation of 2,500,000 shares of common stock, are you not?

A. Yes.

Q. There is not and never has been such a corporation?

A. That is true.

Court. It was the only corporation that would be comparable, however, for the basis of comparison with Youngstown?

A. This was, as Mr. Crawford says, this was sort of a hypothetical presentation of the situation, which I adopted to arrive at the result that seemed to be fair.

Q. Now the actual Bethlehem that was going into this merger was a Bethlehem with 3,200,000 shares?

A. That is true.

Q. 700,000 shares more?

A. Yes.

Q. Now for the actual Bethlehem to have earnings of $15.98 a share it would have to earn some $51,000,000, would it not?

A. Yes, I think that seems about right.

Q. It would have to earn $11,186,000 more than $39,-948,031?

A. Yes.

Q. Now, to arrive at a figure, a ratio of 1 to 1.203 for the actual Bethlehem and the actual Youngstown on an earnings basis, you would have to assume earnings of $11,186,000, if that is the correct figure, on 700,000 shares, would you not?

A. On an earnings basis, yes.

Q. Did you arrive at the ratio of one and a fifth to one on an earnings basis?

A. I did up to the point of the 2,500,000 shares and then I dealt with the 700,000 shares as I stated in my direct testimony.

Q. You arrived at a ratio on the basis of earnings?

A. I mean in Basis K, you are still talking about Basis K?

Q. Yes, you arrived at the ratio on a basis of earnings so far as 2,500,000 shares were concerned, and upon some other basis or bases for the other 700,000 shares?

A. Yes.

Q. And as I understand you the basis which you used with reference to the 700,000 shares was not even an estimate of future earnings on the amount of capital that you allocated to the 700,000 shares?

A. That is true.

Q. Now, would you tell me, Mr. May, just what was the basis that you used with reference to the 700,000 shares?

A. ·Well, the way I dealt with the 700,000 shares was to put the question whether Bethlehem stock would have been worth materially more or materially less if it had had 2,500,000 shares outstanding and $70,000,000 less cash than it was worth having 3,200,000 shares outstanding and $70,000,000 additional cash—and the conclusion that I reached was that the actual intrinsic value of Bethlehem was not far away from $100 a share and therefore the value would neither be greatly increased nor greatly diminished by the change in the situation which I have just recited. Now, that is the way I approached it in my own mind and that is the way in which I presented the question to the principals at the meeting of February 13.

Q. What I perhaps did not ask for is what I want to get at and intended to ask for: What were the considerations that led your mind to the conclusion that the value was not substantially affected by either the presence or absence of the 700,000 shares and the $70,000,000?

A. Because I did not think Bethlehem was worth intrinsically or statistically or by comparison with other similar stocks materially more or less than $100 a share.

Q. Well, now you are saying you did not think it worth materially or intrinsically—you mean by that, Mr. May, do you mean worth from an asset basis or an earnings basis or what sort of a basis?

A. Whether you take the elements of value either statistically or marketwise or in comparison with other stocks like the United States Steel Corporation, for instance, or any of them.

Q. Well, one way of determining the worth of a corporate stock, or one factor in determining the worth of corporate stock, I take it, is security of the investment, the judgment or estimate of security?

A. Yes.

Q. Another is the rate of return?

A. Yes.

Q. And you give, in considering the rate of return you give the effect of past earnings, and from the past earnings try to arrive at an estimate of future earnings?

A. Yes.

Q. The condition of the industry in which the company is engaged is another factor?

A. Yes.

Q. Its competitive position?

A. Yes.

Q. And the character of its management?

A. Yes.

Q. It is often materially affected by the position and standing and connection of the people that have invested heavily in its stock, those things may affect the value?

A. May affect, yes.

Q. There are a great many considerations. Now from which of these considerations did you arrive at the conclusion?

A. Well, I arrived at them as a matter of judgment from the basis of some statistical comparison with other companies in the same industry and the market prices and so on; it was a personal judgment, and I so expressed it to the principals and suggested that they should also form their personal judgments.

Q. Well, now the problem that you had as to the $70,000,-000 was one of determining what its value to Youngstown was in this merger?

A. I do not think so.

Q. The fact there was $70,000,000 excess cash as you considered it?

A. I do not think that is the viewpoint at all. I was not acting for Youngstown; I was acting for Youngstown and Bethlehem.

Q. I mean the point of view as to what was the weight to be given in this merger to the fact that there was $70,000,000 excess cash there that you regarded as uninvested?

A. Yes.

Q. Now it is a common financial problem, is it not, Mr. May, to deal with the effect upon the value of a corporation's security of the presence of uninvested cash resulting from the sale of stock or securities?

A. It is a question that arises in various negotiations in financial matters.

Q. For instance, suppose a corporation that has been running along for a number of years wants to raise additional capital and issues some preferred stock—the people who buy that preferred stock are interested in the security of the dividend, are they not?

A. Yes.

Q. And for that purpose they look at the past earnings of the corporation, do they not?

A. Among other things, yes, very largely.

Q. And then they give effect in earnings to the presence of this uninvested capital cash by adding interest at a conventional, or earnings at a conventional, rate for that new capital?

A. Well, without identifying them I don't know whether I can say what they do.

Q. It is a common thing for banking houses?

A. Oh, yes.

Q. Ordinarily to do?

A. Yes.

Q. That is, for instance—

A. But you would not suggest that was analogous to this case.

Q. Well, let us see what they do: first they are interested for the purpose of determining the security of their dividends, in determining what the future earnings of that company will be, are they not?

A. Yes.

Q. So they take its past earnings—

A. Yes.

Q. —and figure what the past earnings will yield on the new security, the new stock that is going out?

A. Yes.

Q. And then they take the proceeds of the sale and perhaps use six per cent, add that to the annual earnings, so that the earnings, on this basis—the company's earnings as adjusted for the new capital—are three times the dividend, or something of that sort?

A. That is a common form of bankers' representation to potential investors.

Q. And that is the same thing—the Youngstown stockholders are being asked to invest in Bethlehem common stock, to the extent of all the assets, the net assets of the Youngstown Sheet and Tube, are they not?

A. Yes.

Q. And wouldn't you think that a reasonable basis for determining the value to them on this $70,000,000 of uninvested cash that are the proceeds of a recent stock issue would be to add to Bethlehem's past earnings some reasonable conventional figure—I am not trying to commit you to any particular figure—as a return on that cash?

A. I do not think so at all.

Q. You do not think so?

A. No, I think that would be quite a mistaken point of view.

Q. You think the way to do it is simply by resorting to statistical information about steel companies generally and coming to the conclusion that on the whole, taking one thing with another and this and that together, a Bethlehem Steel Corporation with 2,500,000 shares of common stock and some $39,000,000 of earnings is worth about as much as one with 3,200,000 shares of stock and $51,000,000, is that right?

A. That is not involved at all, Mr. Crawford.

Q. Well, the fact is that you were commissioned to recommend a basis for this merger, or a ratio for this merger, on the basis of 1929 earnings, were you not?

A. No, I was commissioned to recommend a basis that would be fair in my judgment and I was instructed—it was agreed—that 1929 earnings were a fair measure of the relative earning capacity of the two companies.

·   ·   ·   ·   ·   ·   ·

VIII

FAIR MARKET VALUE OF STOCK ON JULY 10, 1929 *

(1933)

Q. What in your opinion was the fair market value of Continental stock and Fidelity-Phenix stock on July 10, 1929?

A. I would say that the fair market value of Continental stock was in the neighborhood of $55 a share, and I would take that as the figure that I would regard as most representative of the fair market value. In the case of Fidelity-Phenix I would say $65 a share.

Q. Now, will you, in your own words, state the reasons which lead you to assign these two figures as the fair market values of the two stocks?

A. The first stage is to consider what method one should adopt in arriving at a fair market value. I have taken the view that in doing so you should give weight to both the word "fair" and the word "market," and the most practical way of doing so seemed to me to deal with the matter in two stages: first to consider what would be a fair value computed by methods usually employed, if there were no market; secondly, to consider the quoted market prices, and from those two deduce a figure which may be regarded as a fair market value. In the final stage, one would have to determine how much weight to apply to the two elements in the calculation, which in turn involves considering what margins of difference or error there might be in computing value, and also what is the character of the market by which one has to be guided as to quoted market values. The quoted market value being readily ascertainable, I think it is useful and

* Testimony in *Strong* v. *Rogers,* United States District Court for the District of New Jersey (November 8, 1933).

simplest to present the other elements of value first and then compare them with the market value.

Q. May I interrupt by a suggestion, that you state to the Court the current market prices on the New York Stock Exchange on July 10, 1929?

A. The current market price, as I recall, was approximately $90 for the Continental and $106 for the Fidelity-Phenix. That was merely a matter of taking it off the record. In arriving at a fair value, if there is no market, you have to consider what a share of stock represents, what elements of value it possesses. I think it is generally recognized that those elements of value are the assets back of it and the earning capacity which it possesses or may be expected to possess in the future. Of the two, undoubtedly the earning capacity is theoretically, and practically, the more important. You will find, for instance, in the present market [1933] a number of cases in which securities are selling below the asset value or liquidating value, as it is sometimes called, based on current quotations of the assets owned by the company, the reason being in part that there is no way in which this liquidating value can be realized by the shareholders; they are merely stockholders in the company, and unless and until dissolution proceedings take place they don't themselves realize the liquidating value.

Now, the question of earning capacity of the stock may be looked at again from two standpoints: first, there is the current yield, the current dividend. In this case, both Continental and Fidelity-Phenix were paying dividends at the rate of $2 a year. If you assume that a stock of that kind should yield 5 per cent, that would represent a capital value of $40, and therefore if you said 4½ per cent it would be $44 a share; if you said 4 per cent it would be $50 a share. So that on the basis of yield there is nothing to suggest that the value is as high as the figure at which I arrived for the fair market value, and of course it is very much less than the quoted market value. However, in all financial companies it is well recognized that the accumulation of earnings within the company are perhaps as important to stockholders as the distributions. Financial stocks are very largely held by people who are not dependent on them for current necessities, and they are largely people who are content to have the companies reinvest a part of the earnings instead of receiving them as dividends, paying a tax on them and reinvesting them themselves. So that one has to look behind the dividends and see what the earning capacity of the business is. . . . Now, when you come to the earning capacity, the value of the stock based on its earning capacity, you have to be guided by the past, but you have to bear in mind that the past is relevant only in so far as it affords a fair indication of what may reasonably be expected in the future. Past figures have not an absolute significance. Their significance is wholly dependent upon their being a reasonable indication of the probable future.

Now, in the case of an insurance company, its income is of two fundamentally different kinds, although the two sources of income are naturally very closely related. There is the underwriting income and the investment income.

Q. What do you mean by the underwriting income and the investment income?

A. The underwriting income is the profit that is made from the actual profit or loss as it may be that is made from writing insurance, paying expenses, paying issues out of the premiums, and there is either an underwriting profit or loss when the business is concluded.

Q. And an investment income?

A. An investment income is really the major item in the insurance companies, because the main source of profit in an insurance company is the fact that it collects its premiums in advance and pays its losses after the event. So that from the underwriting business, as from its own capital, it derives a substantial sum which it can invest and derive income during the period that it holds it.

Now, the two classes of income stand on different footing. I think for the purpose of estimating the future from the

past, so far as investment income is concerned, if the income
is steady or steadily received, latest figures are probably the
best index of what may be expected in the immediate future, unless you anticipate and provide in advance for some
revulsion such as actually occurred in the fall of 1929, which
for this purpose I do not propose to do.

On the other hand, the underwriting business, the insurance business, is essentially a business of averages, and in
order to estimate the reasonable expectation for the future,
you must take an experience over a period of years. Now,
proceeding on that basis, I find from the experience of the
Continental Insurance Company over a period . . . of ten
years including 1929 (1929 carries past the critical date and
therefore perhaps should be left out for this purpose), the
profits of the underwriting department are, including '29,
which was a good year, a little over about 3½ per cent on
the gross premium income; over a five-year period ending
with 1928 the figure is about 3.8; over a nine-year period
it will be less than 3.8. I have thought it fair to estimate
the underwriting profit capacity of this company year in and
year out at roughly 4 per cent on the current premium income—on the premium income of '28—or, say, a million dollars a year.

By the Court:
Q. Why did you think 4 per cent fair?
A. The experience over ten years is 3½; the experience
over five years is 3.8; 1928 and 1929 were both good years.
So I thought it was fair to take the little higher figure than
either the five-year or ten-year experience.
Q. Why?
A. Give a little extra weight to the later years when the
experience was high.
Q. It never had reached four?
A. Oh, yes. In '28 it was considerably more than four
for that single year.
Q. It was? How much was it?

A. In 1928 it was 10 per cent. It is a very fluctuating business.

Q. But the average is 3.8?

A. The average is 3.8 over a period of five years, and slightly less for a period of ten years including '29. I thought four was a reasonable figure to take under all the circumstances, and on that basis I got a million dollars as the earning capacity represented by the underwriting business. Then the second element—

Q. That is the net?

A. That is the net after losses and expenses.

Q. Expenses are deducted?

A. Yes. The net investment income for 1928, the last year prior to the merger, prior to the critical date, I think was about $3,100,000; it was on a rising scale, and I think it would be fair to take three and a quarter millions for this purpose as the investment income, which would make four and a quarter millions for the direct earning capacity of these companies. However, these companies own interests in the other companies here, the Fire Buildings and the American Eagle Insurance. Those companies were not paying out to the parent companies the full amount of their earnings by any means. I think it is a somewhat liberal view to take as the measure of the earnings of those companies, not reflected in the figures I have already used, the actual figures shown by this last exhibit which you handed me. . . . That would be approximately $750,000 a year. I say that is liberal because it gives the full weight to the exceptionally good underwriting experience of the American Eagle Fire Insurance Company in 1928, but I think that is fair and certainly not understating a reasonable estimate of the earning capacity represented by this stock at July, 1929.

Now, adding the three items together, a million for the direct underwriting, three and a quarter millions for investment income and seven hundred and fifty thousand for earnings of subsidiary companies not distributed to the parent, I get the figure of, say, five million dollars, somewhere between four million eight to five million dollars is about the right figure, I should say. On a million and a half shares of stock, that is equivalent to—five million dollars would be equivalent to $3.33⅓—three dollars thirty-three cents a share.

BY MR. ANGELL:

Q. You are discussing the Continental now?

A. I am still talking of the Continental. Then the question is: What is a fair capital value to assign to such an earning capacity? There may be room for some difference of opinion on that. If you say that such a stock should earn, whether distributed or not, 8 per cent, you would get a value of about $48 a share. If you say 6 per cent you would get a value of about $55 a share, which is figured at—I wouldn't say it was my final index of the value of the stock—I think 6 per cent by itself would be too low a rate and therefore $55 on this criterion alone would be too high a figure.

But I pass on next to the consideration of the assets. The assets of this company consist mainly of its portfolio, its buildings, and its business. I have had calculated what may be called a "breakdown value" of the assets of the Continental Company. By "breakdown" I mean valuing the assets behind the stock, on the basis of the current market quotations for those assets which, as I will point out, brings in the market at that point in another phase.

Q. I show you a document, Mr. May, captioned "The Continental Insurance Company, Fidelity-Phenix Fire Insurance Company, Computation of Valuation of the Capital Stocks of the Companies Based on Market Prices of Underlying Securities as at July 10, 1929," and ask you whether this is the computation to which you have referred?

A. Yes.

Q. Will you explain this document briefly, Mr. May?

A. This document starts from the capital and surplus of the company at July 1, as shown by its published statements. Its capital and surplus together with the reserve for market fluctuations, which is only another form of surplus, are added together, those being what is sometimes called the book value of the stock. Then, in the next section of it, there is an adjustment made for changes in the value of the portfolio directly owned during the period from July 1 to July 10. That is merely to bring it up to date, from July 1 to July 10. Then there are adjustments resulting from substituting the values of June 10 for the book values—

Q. July 10?

A. July 10, I mean to say, for the portfolio. Then there are adjustments of the values of the subsidiary companies, and some adjustments for proportions of earnings applying to the ten days; and finally there is brought into account— there is an amount described which is 40 per cent of the company's reserve for unearned premiums on July 1, 1929, and their proportionate share of the unearned premiums of the underlying companies. That is the figure which I put in to represent what may be called the "intangible values" of the company, in addition to its portfolio, buildings, and so on. That I would like to amplify a little later.

For the convenience of the Court I have prepared a further statement which, instead of merely showing the procedure by which this figure is built up, shows the result of the figure, how much of the value is represented by portfolio, how much by buildings, and so on.

> .   .   .   .

Q. What are the ultimate figures, valuation figures, a share, Continental and Fidelity-Phenix, as disclosed by these statements?

A. Well, this figure gives $55.92 for the Continental and $69.06 for the Fidelity-Phenix. . . . I brought in items which aggregate ultimately twelve and a half millions in the case of Continental and ten million eight hundred thousand in the case of Fidelity-Phenix, under the title of 40 per cent of underlying premiums to represent the intangible assets of the company. . . . The question of those intangible values may be considered from various angles. One way is to take a percentage of the unearned premiums. That is a method that is common to insurance companies, according to my experience, because it is peculiar to that business. The more common way is to take the earnings of the business and capitalize them, or else to take the earnings and deduct a fair return on the tangible assets, and capitalize the excess as representing intangible values. I think that the Bureau of Internal Revenue has approved of both the second and third methods.

As a result of tests which I have made, and on the basis of the figures of earning capacity which I have already outlined in the case of Continental, I do not think any reasonable method of appraising the intangible values would give a figure substantially in excess of the figure that I have taken up as unearned premium. So that in my judgment, the statement of the $56 represents a full valuation of the assets and liabilities of the Continental Company, both tangible and intangible.

I might mention two or three technical points, just so that it may not be thought they have been overlooked. Theoretically, in the Continental there is a large portfolio; it has a large excess value over its original cost, so that if the company attempted to realize that value, it would incur very considerable income taxes as well as other expenses in realizing those values. I have thrown off that figure. I have not brought it into account, although it wouldn't be inconsiderable; it might be two or three million dollars.

Another factor is that the calculations which I have given are based on the situation immediately before the acquisition of the Niagara and the Fidelity-Casualty. It will perhaps be more logical to take the figure mentioned after those acquisitions.

Q. Have you those figures, Mr. May?

A. Calculations which I have made show that the effect would be to reduce both the breakdown value and the earning capacity a share; so that if there were any error in taking the figures prior to the merger, it would tend to produce a higher valuation than would be produced if the figures after the merger were used. The differences are not very substantial, and it would make the matter much more complicated to take the post-merger figures.

I would like now to turn to the Fidelity-Phenix. The statement of underwriting income for that company shows that its underwriting experience had been much less favorable than that of the Continental; for the whole ten years including 1929 its underwriting profits had averaged only $350,000 a year, and if the exceptionally good year of 1929 were left out the average would be reduced to about $160,-000 a year. So that I think the fair estimate of the earning capacity of Fidelity in respect of its underwriting could not be put higher than $250,000 or $300,000 a year—$350,000 perhaps at the outside. Its underwriting income—put it at $350,000 a year. Then its investment income, net investment income, for 1928 is $2,475,000, and allowing for some increase for the future it might be reasonable to take $2,750,-000 for that. Then we have $750,000 from the subsidiary companies, the same figure as in the case of Continental, each company having the same interest in the subsidiary companies, and that gives us a figure of $3,950,000 or, say, $4,000,-000 as roughly the earning capacity represented by the stock of the Fidelity-Phenix Company, or we will say $4 a share on the million shares of stock outstanding before the merger. That, again, on an 8 per cent basis would represent a value of $50 a share; on a 7 per cent basis it would represent a value of $57 a share; on a 6 per cent basis it would give a value of $66 a share. I have already said that the breakdown value of the Fidelity-Phenix before the merger works out at $69 on those figures—I regard $65 as a fair value to attach to that stock in round figures.

In that case I may say, if you use the post-merger figures, the effect on the Fidelity-Phenix would be rather more adverse than in the case of the Continental.

Q. That is, it would tend to reduce them?

A. Tend to reduce the figures more in the case of Fidelity-Phenix than in the case of Continental.

The Court. You have fixed it in this analysis at how much?

The Witness. My final figure is $55 for the one and $65 for the other. The breakdown value is $56 and $69.

The Court. Not $65?

The Witness. No, $65 is what I used; taking into account all the factors, I think $65 is a fair figure. I haven't changed that figure—that is a computation based on assets; but I was taking into account assets and earning power and everything.

The Court. You have not now reduced that by the other elements that you have taken into account?

The Witness. I would say on an asset basis $69, before the merger; $63¼ would be the asset value after the merger.

The Court. Well, then, where does the figure $65 come in?

The Witness. That is the composite figure that I finally arrived at after taking into account assets, earning capacity and other elements of value.

. . . .

Q. I handed you and asked that you assume as correct tabulations which were entitled "Investment Profits and Rents, Dividends, Interest." How much weight do the figures set forth in that statement have with you in reaching your conclusions of the fair market value of the stocks?

. . . .

A. They play this, they have just this weight: that if computations were based on the published figures of the Continental and the Fidelity, without taking into account the hidden equities of the subsidiary companies, you would get an undervaluation of the securities; and by placing in those figures, I have avoided that undervaluation which would otherwise result.

Q. In other words, a consideration of these figures would tend to increase rather than decrease your value?

A. Oh, yes, it would increase it, legitimately, undoubtedly. If you took the quoted figures without regard to them, you might underestimate the value of the stock.

Q. But you wouldn't overestimate it?

A. No, it couldn't have that effect.

Q. You have testified, Mr. May, that in your opinion the fair market value on July 10, 1929, of the Continental stock was $55 and the fair market value of Fidelity-Phenix $65. I think you also referred to the fact that the current market quotations on the New York Stock Exchange on that date were approximately $90 a share for the Continental and $106 a share for the Fidelity-Phenix. Why do you feel justified in departing from the market prices to this extent in fixing the fair market value of the stock?

.   .   .   .

A. Well, that opinion that the difference is appropriate in determining a fair market value is based mainly on a consideration of the character of the market in 1929. In considering the character of the market we have first of all to consider its breadth. I would hardly say that the market in these stocks was broad enough to form an entirely satisfactory basis for determining the sale value of a block of stock of the size involved in these transactions. It is, however, only fair to say that these stocks being listed on the New York Stock Exchange had a broader market than insurance stocks in general. So that I don't lay so much stress on the question of the breadth of the market as I do on the character of the market. Now, I was told that I might assume that in certain circumstances it might be appropriate to go beyond the current market quotations to determine a fair market value. Now, that has been done so far as I know on a number of occasions in other connections. In the insurance field it has been done at least three times in the last thirty years: in the depression of 1907, during the war, and in the current depression. The Insurance Commissioners expressly authorized insurance companies to take as the fair market value of their securities prices in excess of the quoted market prices in the periods of depression. Now, it would seem to me that that rule might fairly be deemed to work in both directions, and if ever there was an occasion in which the market might be said to be not fairly representative, because it was too high, I should say it was the market that immediately preceded the events in the early fall of 1929. Now, I don't by that mean to say that you can entirely ignore the market of that period.

Q. You mean in July, 1929?

A. 1929. And carrying the matter a little further, I think that in the period that culminated in the summer of 1929 there was a steady and, in my judgment then, and I think events have since proved, probably an excessive appreciation in the values of securities based on earning capacity. That I think was true, generally speaking, of companies of almost every kind. It was, however, much more pronounced in the case of the group of finance and holding companies than it was in the case of what you may call primary companies which were producing income. The extreme examples are found in some of the investment trusts and in some of the utility holding companies, such as the Insull group, where the appreciation in the market value of the holding companies far exceeded the appreciation in the values of the properties which those stocks represented. That, I think, was true of holding companies; it was true of practically all kinds of financial companies in some degree, and you can see it, for instance, in some of the banks, like the Chase and National City Bank and other big New York banks; and you can see it, I think, in the insurance companies, particularly in the insurance companies whose investments consisted to a substantial extent of common stocks. Now, in my approach to the question I have felt that when I gave pretty full weight to the market appreciation of the underlying assets owned by these companies, I had given reasonable weight to the current market, and that the excess of the market value of these stocks over what I conceived to be the fair market value of the underlying assets is not in any economic sense certainly a fair value, and once you go beyond quotations I don't see what you can have as a test of a fair market value except whether it is within the reasonable range of economic valuation. It may be a high economic valuation and still be reasonable. But if it gets beyond any reasonable limits, I think that would be a test that a market was not fair, because it was too high, just as when securities fell to values that were only a fraction of the intrinsic values behind them, the Insurance Commissioners and the Comptroller of the Currency and people in offices of that kind felt warranted in authorizing institutions under their charge to treat as the fair market value of their securities figures based on something other than market quotations, on the ground that those market quotations were too low to constitute a fair market value. I have had considerable experience in dealing with questions of this kind with the Bureau of Internal Revenue in connection with income and inheritance tax cases, and on more than one occasion the Bureau has gone behind market quotations, even where they were in fair volume, to arrive at a fair market value. That was true certainly in regard to transactions in the early part of 1921 when we had a sudden fall in prices.

Mr. Hanson. Of course, we object to this, Your Honor, as not binding on the Government or on the defendant in this case.

The Court. As I understand it, this testimony of the witness is being produced—he is an expert—as disclosing the manner and method by which he has arrived at the conclusions which he has heretofore testified to. Am I correct?

Mr. Angell. That is correct, Your Honor.

The Court. You, of course, will have a full opportunity to cross examine.

Defendant's counsel prays an exception, which is hereby allowed and sealed accordingly.

A. [Continuing.] And that, I may say, was before the Act of 1924 was passed which expressly required the Commissioner to have regard to the assets of the company as well as the market quotations for its securities in determining the March 1, 1913 value, which in any such transaction as this is the other end of the yardstick. As a matter of fact, as consultant for the Treasury and also a member of the Advisory Committee of the Joint Congressional Committee, I participated in a great many discussions on this question at different times, and I know the changes of feeling that have been adduced by different cases on this question of fair market value. Of course, it is easy to say that the recipient of this stock could have gone out and sold it. In all such cases where there is a large block handed out to a number of stockholders, a certain number of shareholders could have done that successfully without affecting the market, but probably not the whole or a substantial part of the whole could have done so without affecting the market. . . . I can't conceive of any economic theory on which the market values of these securities could reasonably have been given a fair value so large as the market quotations of July, 1929; and in my own mind, I feel that the situation is largely accounted for by this new enthusiasm for investment trusts, and corporations of that kind, which resulted in attributing to holding companies, security holding companies, values on the market for the time being greatly in excess of the value of the properties on which those stocks in fact rested. So that I feel no difficulty, if I am allowed to exercise any judgment, in saying that in my judgment the market quotations of July, 1929, for these securities were not a fair market value, because I can't in my own mind discover any process of reasoning which on a fair analysis of the facts would reach figures approximating the market values.

Now, in my Exhibit, I have taken forty per cent of the unearned premiums. Well, now, if you went to an extreme and took a hundred per cent of the unearned premiums, you would still be twenty points below the market; and that being so, as I say, if I have any right to go behind the market, I have no difficulty in reaching the conclusion in my own mind that that market was not a fair reflection of the values represented by these stocks.

Q. In your opinion, Mr. May, why was it that market quotations in July, 1929, went up so substantially above what you, having considered the underlying facts of the case, consider the fair market value of the two stocks?

. . . .

A. Well, that is a fairly large question. Do you want me to limit it to this particular class of stock or do you want me to discuss the market in general?

Q. No, limit it to this particular class of stock.

A. Well, I think the outstanding factor, as I see it—

Mr. Hanson. What class of stock is he talking about?

The Witness. Well, I will define the class of stocks to which I think this belongs.

A. [Continuing.] The class of stocks whose assets consists largely of securities of other companies. That falls mainly in that group, although it isn't the outstanding example. The outstanding examples are the investment trusts and the purely holding companies.

Q. You are referring to the Continental and the Fidelity-Phenix?

A. The Continental and Fidelity-Phenix. To my mind one of the main features was a failure to distinguish between real income and capital changes in determining earnings, the capital value of which represents or is a measure of the security value.

Perhaps I can best illustrate it by taking a simple illustration. If you had a company, we will say, that in 1924 was earning $10,000 a year, in some ordinary business, and from 1924 to 1929 its business steadily improved so that in 1929, instead of earning $10,000 it was earning $15,000—well, quite apart from anything else, if that seemed to be a permanent trend, and, of course, that is a question of opinion on which the market must decide, it would be reasonable to say that the value of that stock had appreciated, let us say, from ten times ten thousand, that would be a hundred thousand, at the beginning, to a hundred and fifty thousand in 1929. Now, during that period there was an influence at work which tended steadily to reduce the yields on securities of that kind; or, in other words, to increase the capital value relative to earnings.

In examining the portfolio of this company, I noticed cases of large blocks of stocks on which the yield had diminished from about five and a half per cent to three and a half per cent. Now, in those circumstances, take our company A, whose earnings have increased from ten thousand to fifteen thousand; the value of its stock would increase because of its increased earnings. It would also increase because of the higher rate of capitalization applied to earnings in 1929 as compared with 1924. So that that stock might appreciate from—not from a hundred to a hundred and fifty thousand, but from a hundred thousand to two hundred thousand, or a hundred per cent.

Now, let's take a company that owns twenty per cent of the stock of that company. Its holding was worth $20,000 in 1924, and in 1929 its holding was worth at market value, let us say, $40,000. There was a tendency to treat that increase of $20,000 as an income of that company which itself could be capitalized in order to arrive at the capital value of that company. So that you were getting a sort of a squaring of the appreciation, instead of an appreciation in direct relation to the earnings; it tended to vary, you may say, as the square of the increase of earnings. And that is why I think the general range of stock values of that class of company was particularly out of line. I want to be entirely fair and say I don't regard the insurance companies as an extreme example of that kind. Of course, if you take some of these extreme cases, like, well, some of the Insull companies and companies like the American & Foreign Power, you get a much more exaggerated rise, but still I think that such a condition did affect to a very marked extent securities of the kind of Continental and Fidelity-Phenix stocks.

Q. Now, in Exhibit P-22, which is the analysis of shares

and so-called "breakdown value" in the case of Continental, the portfolio taken at market is $66.79 a share, and the market prices on the Stock Exchange were around 90?

A. Yes.

Q. Does that divergence between the value of the portfolio and the market quotations indicate in your opinion the situation which you have just outlined as existing in the case of the market quotation of the stock of the Continental and the Fidelity-Phenix?

A. That fact in conjunction with the facts as to earnings, which I have already recited, led me to that conclusion.

CROSS EXAMINATION BY MR. HANSON:

Q. And in round figures I believe you used an earning capacity for the Continental of $5,000,000?

A. $5,000,000.

Q. As representing the average earnings which you sought to capitalize?

A. Yes.

Q. And those were capitalized by you, I believe, at various rates?

A. Various rates.

Q. The final rate being used was 6 per cent, was it not?

A. That was the lowest rate, that wasn't the final rate.

Q. What was your final rate?

A. The way one does things of that kind is to assemble figures on different bases and then reach a conclusion on the picture as a whole; that was the method that I proceeded on.

Q. That is, you didn't select your rate until you knew what the answer was?

A. If you care to put it that way. I think that is merely an attack on my intellectual honesty, that's all.

Q. No, indeed. I am inquiring as to your method of procedure.

A. I have explained my method of procedure.

.   .   .   .

Q. Notwithstanding the fact that this company made $3,-000,000, in excess of $3,000,000, on the sale of securities in 1928 and notwithstanding the fact that they had made gains on the sales of securities in practically all other years since their organization, you did not include in the earning capacity of this company for the year 1928 any amount because of similar gains?

A. No.

. . . .

Q. You did not include in the earning capacity of the Continental any gain carried on the books of account and records of the Continental or gain reported during the year 1928 to the Insurance Commissioner of the State of New York because of the appreciation in the value of the assets which had been purchased in prior years and which were held throughout the year 1928?

A. That is true.

. . . .

Q. I invite your attention here in Exhibit M over the five-year period from, or over the period commencing in 1922 and ending with 1928; I invite your attention to the sales of securities made during that period of time.

A. Yes.

Q. During that period of time the volume of sales was almost equal to the entire portfolio of the company, isn't that a fact—to the entire portfolio of the company as of 1928?

A. I haven't checked it—that is broadly true, I should say; if you take in '29 it would be true.

Q. During that period of time the profits actually were realized?

A. Yes—well, substantial profits were realized.

. . . .

Q. Now, assuming, Mr. May, that the item of $3,220,000, which you say is the profit which was realized in the year 1928 upon the sale of securities, should be actually included in the earning capacity of the Continental for the year 1928. Can you then compute at the rates previously employed by you the valuation of the stocks through capitalization of earnings?

A. No.

Q. You cannot do it?

A. No.

Q. Why not?

A. I can make a mathematical calculation, of course, a mere matter of arithmetic.

Q. That is all I ask you to do.

A. But I couldn't say the definite result in a value, I mean, if you take one assumption and apply to it figures based on an entirely different assumption, the combination of the two won't produce a homogeneous result; it will be a meaningless figure.

Q. You can make the computation, however?

A. Obviously, as a matter of arithmetic.

Q. Will you do so before the court, please?

The Court. How would you establish the rate which he is going to capitalize this sum at?

Mr. Hanson. I am asking him to use his own rate, Your Honor.

The Court. Let's find out what his rate will be.

The Witness. If I used the method at all, I should use an entirely different rate, but I should not use the method at all.

The Court. It is a mere mathematical calculation; you consider the capitalization of appreciation of securities is unsound?

The Witness. Capitalizing appreciation in valuation of securities even if realized as earnings is unsound in principle, in my mind, so I wouldn't be prepared to say what rate I should adopt if I were forced to adopt a principle that I regarded as unsound.

By Mr. Hanson:

Q. Now, would you say that that method of procedure would be unsound with reference to a company engaged solely in buying and selling securities?

A. Yes, I would think that you would have to value its stock on an entirely different basis.

Q. Under your computation you gave no effect whatsoever to the earning capacity obtained through or realized by the sale of securities—isn't that right?

A. I don't regard that as earning capacity that should be capitalized.

Q. It was a gain, however?

A. It was a gain, yes; a capital gain, to my mind.

Q. A capital gain?

A. A capital gain, economically.

The Court. And what do you mean by that, Doctor?

The Witness. Well, I am trying to restrict myself to answering the question.

The Court. Yes, yes.

The Witness. So that I may make my position entirely clear. If you would like me to—

The Court. But what do you mean by the expression "economically"?

The Witness. Well, that is the point that I made just now, that what was going on during these periods was a steady lowering of the rate of yield on securities. Now, if you take advantage of that by selling out securities, it doesn't represent any permanent earning capacity for the future. On the contrary, the fact that securities are steadily going up during that period creates a probability that there will be a fall in the later period, and, as a matter of fact, the insurance companies in 1929—I think these and others probably—were carrying reserves to provide for that contingency which they foresaw. The underlying assumption in this method which Mr. Hanson puts to me is that the rise in securities that was going on from 1924 to 1929 was going on continuously up and up. To my mind that is economically—well, I would say, impossible; certainly, highly improbable. And therefore, in forming a reasonable estimate of the future, I wouldn't predicate any calculation on the assumption that that would continue indefinitely.

By Mr. Hanson:

Q. Might it not maintain an even level?

A. But you—

Q. Will you answer that question, please?

Mr. Angell: Let him answer in his own fashion.

A. It might not—you say, it might not what—maintain an even level?

Q. The earnings resulting from or through a sale of securities.

A. Not unless there was a continuous fall in the rate of yield on securities.

Q. Well, there had been a fall for some time, had there not?

A. Yes, and I think that created the presumption that the longer it lasted, the more likely it was to come to an end. I mean if you get a barometer rising steadily, for a time, it is evident that you are going to have good weather, but when you get it up, right up to set fair, you are pretty sure that the next change is going to be a fall in the barometer, not a further rise.

Q. This factor, which you have given no consideration in your computation, what part did it play in the growth of the company?

A. It played some part, a substantial part, in increasing the assets value of the portfolio.

Q. Well, isn't it a fact that with only a paid-in capital of $2,000,000 in 1928, there was a surplus of something over $30,000,000, just because of this very factor which you have eliminated in your computation?

A. Well, I have given them credit for the increase in the assets that they produced, but I say that it doesn't represent a permanent earning capacity, in my judgment. In 1929, no one making a forecast for the future would—

Q. Notwithstanding the fact that there had been earnings each year since the organization of the company, because of that very fact?

A. The earnings had increased so rapidly from that source in recent years that I think there was every reason to expect a reversal of the trend rather than a continuation of it.

Q. But over a long period of time, the experience of the company indicated that substantial earnings were to be realized from that source?

A. That is true. I mean I don't want to accept—I take exception to the word "earnings": I don't want to accept that.

Q. Substantial gains?

A. Gains, yes.

Q. And that was actual realized profit?

A. It was an actual realized profit, yes.

Q. Notwithstanding the fact that you are of the opinion that the gains realized from sales of securities are not properly includable in the earnings of the Continental, such gains are a really important element in computing the value of that stock, are they not?

A. I think that if I were attaching any weight—if I were trying to measure the weight to attach to them—I would, I think, in 1929, endeavoring to put myself back in that position, have said that there was more reason to anticipate a reversal of the trend in the subsequent years, and that therefore I was giving a full valuation by ignoring the question altogether.

.   .   .   .

The Court. In your study of these figures, Mr. May, would or would it not be proper and logical to take into account any item based upon fluctuation in the value of money itself?

The Witness. Well, that is really what underlies this question of gain, Your Honor.

The Court. Well, now, will you clear that up for me? I think you can do that, so that I will understand these conclusions of yours better—if you will explain how the fluctuation in the value of the dollar has affected this problem we are dealing with.

The Witness. I don't think the fluctuation in the value

of the dollar had very much to do with it at this time. As I remember, the value of the dollar measured by the cost of living indices or anything of that kind did not change very much between, say, 1925 or 1926 and 1928 or 1929. It was a rather different phenomenon, which, however, operated in very much the same way; let me discuss fluctuation in value due to an absolute change in the value of the dollar. It seems to me that as regards earning capacity, you would have to leave out, in arriving at the value based on earning capacity in a period when the value of the dollar was violently changing, you would have to exclude gains or losses in dollars that were due merely to the realization of securities on the basis, we will say, of a depreciated dollar as compared with the purchase price before the dollar had begun to depreciate. If the dollar had depreciated, however, it might be reasonable to assume that over a period of years the real earning capacity measured by current actual production of income would increase because all units of value would rise and therefore sales would increase in price—in this case premiums would increase in amount, losses would increase in amount, and it would all be stepped up; so that if we had an earning capacity of $5,000,000, to take these figures, and realized gains due to depreciation of the dollar of three and a half million dollars, it would not, in my judgment, be correct to add those two together and make a calculation. The right thing would be to say, well, the three million and a half has got nothing to do with the question, but the five million dollars, now that the dollar is worth, we will say, sixty cents, will probably increase in the ratio of one hundred to sixty, because over a term the value of property will increase in terms of the depreciated dollar, the insurance written on it will increase, the losses will increase, the expense will increase, and no necessity of earning $5,000,000 in future, we will have earned a larger sum than five, and it will have to be a conversion of the regular current income and have nothing whatever to do with the purely incidental profits derived in the

particular period from the conversion of assets which have
been bought on one level of the dollar compared with the
period when the dollar had an entirely different value. I
don't know as that helps Your Honor.

The Court. Yes, it has.

IX

FAIR MARKET VALUE OF STOCK IN 1930 *

(1934)

Mr. Green. Mr. May, I am going to ask your opinion as to the fair market value on June 12, 1930, of a block of 1,825,-000 shares of common stock of Pacific Gas and Electric. You have seen the two stipulations that are in this case?

Mr. May. Yes.

Q. And also the additional data read into the record at the beginning of the trial, namely, the statement of P. G. & E. stock outstanding at various dates, a New York Stock Exchange Bulletin and Chart showing the price range of P. G. & E. common on the New York and San Francisco Exchanges, and a schedule bringing down through 1933 the figures contained in paragraph 25 of the main stipulation.

In addition to that, assume that the P. G. & E. took its depreciation on the sinking fund basis, and not the straight line basis; and that if it had taken depreciation on the straight line basis with the same factors, the amount of its depreciation would have exceeded that actually taken by approximately $3,681,000 for 1927; $4,484,000 for 1928; and $3,838,000 for 1929.

Also assume that P. G. & E. charged to construction the following amounts for general and administrative expense, and had the following amounts of gross construction:

* Excerpt from testimony in *Western Power Corporation* v. *Commissioner of Internal Revenue* (1934). Determination of the fair value in June, 1930, of a block of 1,825,000 shares of Pacific Gas & Electric Company, being approximately 32% of the outstanding stock.

Year	Gross construction	General and administrative expense charged to construction
1927	$25,824,923	$1,627,633
1928	20,942,156	1,512,864
1929	41,888,366	1,593,105
1930	44,894,383	1,928,329
1931	23,513,945	1,617,257
1932	9,007,406	1,188,559
1933	4,431,783	778,783

And that in 1929 about 40 per cent of the general and administrative expense charged to construction existed and would have been incurred regardless of construction; and that this percentage of the total would tend to rise as the amount of construction decreased.

Assume further that the plants and properties carried on the consolidated balance sheet of P. G. & E. at December 31, 1929, in the gross sum of approximately $407,000,000 had a rate base value, in accordance with the practices of the California Railroad Commission, of about $372,000,000; that in computing the company's rate base, there would also have been included its materials and supplies, and other net current assets only to the extent of two months' operating expense.

Also assume that in January and February, 1930, the California Railroad Commission entered orders decreasing the rates for electricity, effective as of March 1, 1930, which reduction in rates would amount to an annual reduction of $3,000,000 for P. G. & E. and Great Western together.

Also assume that Pacific Gas and Electric Company during the years 1929 and 1930 went into the natural gas business.

I now ask what, in your opinion, was the fair market value on June 12, 1930, of a block of 1,825,000 shares of common stock of the Pacific Gas and Electric Company?

Mr. May. In my judgment, the fair market value of such a block of stock on the facts cited here and assumed, and the evidence contained in the stipulations, would be in the neighborhood of $35 a share, and perhaps somewhat less. [Quota-

tion on New York Stock Exchange, June 12, 1930, was
61¼-63½.]

Q. Can you give a minimum and a maximum?

A. I should say a fair range would be between, say, $30
and $40 a share.

Q. Will you give us the reasons that lead you to that
result?

A. The way that I approach a question of that kind is that
if you are trying to determine the fair market value, the first
requirement is to determine the market which is available.
The New York Stock Exchange, which is perhaps the first to
suggest itself, is a market in which stocks such as this are
dealt in at retail, and in regard to this particular stock, it
was clearly not broad enough to constitute a market for a
block of anything like this magnitude.

Therefore, I should say that tne New York Stock Exchange
quotations have no direct bearing on the fair market value
of a block of this size.

The markets that would be available in normal times
would be what may be called the wholesale distributing
markets, of the large corporate investment markets; corporations which buy large blocks of stocks of public utilities or
other classes of companies, with the idea of holding them as
long term investments.

The wholesale distributing market is, of course, based indirectly on the retail market, allowing for the costs of distribution and the compensation and the risks assumed in
undertaking such an operation; and therefore must bear
some relation to the New York Stock Exchange prices or
to San Francisco Stock Exchange prices.

In June, 1930, the demand by wholesale distributors for
securities for distribution was very limited. They were not
undertaking the hazard of such distribution at all freely.

Our business in that field was almost at a standstill. I
question very much whether the stock could have been sold
advantageously in that particular market. My own judgment would be that the large corporate investor would be

more likely to give a price for a block this size at that time. Such purchaser is not, I think, in my experience, greatly influenced by current market quotations. The price that he is willing to pay is determined, rather, by the basic elements of value, and the inherent merits of the security, so that he would look at it from the standpoint mainly of prospective earning capacity.

In the case of a public utility, that involves a number of questions: There is the question of the rate base. I should say that the relation between the rate base and the book values of the property were such that that would not be a major element in the determination of the price.

Then there is the question of prior charges. They, of course, tend to increase the earnings in periods of prosperity on the equity stock to the extent that the earnings on the money invested exceed the rate of return that has to be paid to the holders of private securities. In time of adversity, they operate in the opposite direction.

The Pacific Gas and Electric was, of course, a strong financial company at that date. Then we come to the question of earnings, which is the critical consideration.

After the purchase of the Western Power Company properties, the earnings of the properties included in the P. G. & E. System for the three years ending 1927, 1928 and 1929, would be equivalent to about $2.80 a share on the amount of the stock that would have been outstanding if the purchase of the Western Power properties had taken effect at the beginning of that three-year period.

Those earnings are computed on the basis of the California Railroad Commission classification, and all who are experienced in these matters know that such classifications tend to give higher earnings than the ordinary reasonably conservative, industrial accounting, largely by reason of the two points mentioned in your hypothetical question, that the depreciation is calculated on the sinking fund basis, or on a relatively low basis—in this case, on the sinking fund basis which tends to give a low charge during the early years of the life of the property and the higher charge as the property approaches maturity. That is a very important factor, particularly in property that is expanding, and particularly if the expansion is likely to be checked; because during the period of expansion, the depreciation charge is bound to be relatively low, and it is bound to be relatively high as the new property in the total becomes smaller. The depreciation charge of Pacific Gas & Electric was to my mind distinctly low.

In the second place, the public utility accounting calls for capitalizing large amounts of administrative expense which will be equally incurred, whether there are capital expenditures in progress or not; but the general rule in industrial accounting is to capitalize only such administrative expense as would not have been incurred had the capital expenditure not been undertaken.

Taking those elements into consideration, I think one may say that the excess of earnings of $2.80 over a dividend rate of $2.00 a share, was mainly traceable to those two causes; and if the accounts were restated on what you may call an industrial basis, there would be little, if any, margin during those three years over the $2.00 dividend rate.

In 1930, the reductions of rate had been put into effect, and quite apart from that, a person of the type managing the large investing corporation would assume that conditions in the near future were not likely to be so satisfactory as during the three years 1927, 1928, and 1929. That was a period of marked prosperity, which had been definitely broken in June, 1930.

I do not think that anybody in June, 1930, would have apprehended the depth of the depression which has since developed; but I think reasonably prudent men would have foreseen a substantial recession and would have counted upon reduction in earnings and probably in dividends.

In such circumstances, it seems to me that a vendor trying to sell a block of this stock would have to be forced to accept a price of $35 a share on which the dividend would be slightly less than 6 per cent, and might well have had to take a lower figure.

That, in a broad line, is the basis of my opinion.

Q. I take it, then, that when you give a range of 30 to 35, you are allowing for various factors here, are you not?

A. Yes. It is a little difficult to explain exactly. I would like to make my exact position clear. I am trying as best I can to judge what a person of that type would have been willing to pay. In doing so, frankly I have taken into account the fact that public utility securities had, I find at that time, generally, a value higher than, I think, pure reasoning would have attributed to them; and that is reflected in the range of prices I have given. It is not an attempt to estimate what I would consider the fair market value ought to be, but what I think the fair market value would have been.

Q. I take it that your own opinion as to what the fair market value ought to have been would be the lower?

A. Somewhat on the lower side.

.   .   .   .

On cross examination, a great deal of emphasis was placed by the opposing attorney on the Stock Exchange quotation, in an attempt to get Mr. May to admit that these quotations had some value. However, Mr. May insisted that the quotations would be a fair index for small blocks of stock, which could readily be marketed in ordinary course on the Exchange, and that the difference was essentially one of the retail market as distinct from what might be termed the wholesale market; and that in a block of the size involved the quoted market price has no appreciable bearing on the actual fair value. Moreover, he made the point that "the fair market value is the value that one could expect to realize in the market in which the sale would have to be effected."

After certain other witnesses had testified, quoting a Supreme Court decision in which a definition of fair value is given as that which a willing buyer would give to a willing seller, and both parties being equally informed as to the merits of the property, Mr. May was again put on the stand

and asked whether in view of this definition the quotations on the Stock Exchange would have significance, and Mr. May answered, "Most emphatically not," and went on to say:

I think that they represented the fair market value for small blocks of stock, on the basis of my definition of fair market value as being the price which might reasonably be expected to be realized in the market in which the property would naturally be sold.

On that basis, I think, for small blocks of stock, and except in very unusual circumstances, the New York Stock Exchange prices could be regarded as fair market value; and that is obviously a rule of practical convenience; but if you once import into the definition of fair market value the assumption that the parties to the transaction are both reasonably informed, adequately informed as to the value of the property, then I would say that the New York Stock Exchange market quotations do not represent a fair market value under such a definition, but merely a market value, eliminating the word "fair"; and for this reason: In the first place, the amount of information available is quite inadequate to form the basis for a determination of the true value of securities; the value of a security depends on the future.

Now, some isolated facts in regard to the past are available, and what inferences may be drawn from those facts as to the future, is purely a question of judgment; and only those so intimately associated with the operations or with the business are in a position to form such judgments.

In the second place, a very large percentage of the operators on the New York Stock Exchange do not take advantage of the information that is available, so that in the large percentage of the transactions, one, at least, of the parties in the transaction is not in possession of even such information as is available.

In the third place, the large amount of operations on the Stock Exchange are based on market hunches and tips, and beliefs in what they are going to do—"they" being a mysterious group of supposed market leaders which may or may not exist, but whose actual or supposed transactions has a very large effect on market quotations.

I, of course, in my business, see a great deal of the inside of large corporations, and it is a very common experience with me to find corporation executives concerned with the prices at which their stocks are selling, knowing that they cannot be worth those prices; so that on the basis of the definition of fair market value, which assumes adequate information on the part of both parties to the transaction, I would say that the New York Stock Exchange transactions do not conform to that requirement, and are not therefore indicative of fair market value.

On cross examination the opposing attorney tried to show that there was inconsistency in this view with the treatment given in balance sheets which were certified. The market value might be different for balance sheet purposes from that used for income tax purposes, but as regards Stock Exchange houses they were dealing on the Stock Exchange and that would logically be their market.

TWENTY-FIVE YEARS OF ACCOUNTING RESPONSIBILITY

1911-1936

VOLUME TWO

GEORGE OLIVER MAY

TWENTY-FIVE YEARS OF ACCOUNTING RESPONSIBILITY
1911-1936

ESSAYS AND DISCUSSIONS

Edited by

BISHOP CARLETON HUNT

SCHOLARS BOOK CO.
Box 3344
Lawrence, Kansas 66044

CONTENTS

Volume Two

PART IV

Regulation of Securities

PART V

Taxation

A. General

v

PART VII

Reviews and Criticisms

PART III (Continued)
VALUATION

X

TESTIMONY IN *State of Minnesota* v. *Republic Steel Corporation*

(1934)

Q. Are you familiar with the terms on which businesses of various kinds are bought and sold?

A. I have seen different plans, arrangements, and various bases on which businesses have been attempted to be sold, and I have sat in on the negotiations in a great many cases.

Q. I will ask you to say whether or not you are familiar with the method of valuation employed by the Minnesota Tax Commission? *

A. Yes, I have read that several times.

Q. You have been familiar with that method ever since its adoption?

A. Yes, sir.

Q. Now, Mr. May, from your experience would you say that the method of valuation so employed by the Minnesota Tax Commission is such as to produce a figure which fairly may be regarded as indicative of a price at which an iron property of Minnesota would sell at a voluntary sale, for cash, on any particular valuation date?

A. I don't want to go into detail—but the general method is one which is quite familiar in the valuation of any particular property, and I think it does afford a guide to what a buyer would expect or could afford to pay, or a seller could expect to get for a property. Of course the factors would have to be determined carefully.

Q. Are there any exceptions to the method to which you would like to call attention?

A. You mean to this precise method?

* See *Report of the Minnesota Tax Commission* (1932), pp. 46-7.

3

Q. Yes.

A. Well, as to the precise method, I would like to make some criticisms and some reservations.

Q. Yes.

A. I think the method is open to criticism in that it attributes the whole profit of mining that is anticipated to the ore, whereas some part of that profit will be required to provide a return on the working capital employed in operating and some part will be required to provide a return on the future expenditures necessary for plant and property, from the time the expenditures are made until the time when, under the plan, they are to be recovered from operations. That is, I think, a criticism which is proper. I think, also, it is probably a little defective in the treatment of taxes, and it won't, I think, allow adequately for the taxes which will have to be paid in the future if the same general method of assessment and the same general methods of taxation procure into the future. I am speaking now of the taxes for the later period. That might not be such an important factor because the amount of taxes which will accrue thirty years hence will be not of such great present value. As regards the method in general, I think it can only be used with the reservation that it does not indicate value unless conditions—the general conditions—as of the time at which a valuation is being made are substantially similar to the conditions existing during the basic period on which the valuation is predicated. That is true of all valuations, of course. Take an extreme example: It would obviously have been improper to value—let us say the brewery industry, immediately after the prohibition amendment became effective, at the figure which might be shown to be the valuation based on a five-year period immediately prior to the coming of prohibition. That is an extreme case, but I think this same point has a bearing on this particular case because I do not think that anyone would say that conditions generally, either on May 1, 1932—which I understand is the basic date here—or at any time since then have been substantially similar to those in the period from 1927 to 1931, the five years immediately prior to May, 1932. Those are, generally, the questionable things involved, in my view.

Q. Have you, in connection with the work you have mentioned, given any special attention to the rate required in order to attract capital into an industry or make the purchase of any particular business attractive?

A. Yes, my firm and I have given particular study to that kind of business for very many years.

Q. What in your opinion is the proper method of determination of value and rate of return for an investment in an iron property in Minnesota on May 1, 1932?

A. Well, as I have indicated, if you narrow it to May 1, 1932, I think any sales made on that date would be made only on a sacrifice basis, so you cannot approach that on the line you have in mind; but if, as I take it, what you have in mind is the appropriate rate, assuming restoration of fairly normal conditions?

Q. Yes.

A. So I can assume a normal and not a sacrificial basis?

Q. Yes, that is true, I used the date of May 1, 1932, because that is the valuation date involved here.

A. Yes, I just wanted to make myself clear on the basis of my opinion. I would say, in my opinion, that ten per cent was a minimum rate.

Q. You think that ten per cent would be necessary in order to attract capital into the industry?

A. That would be my judgment.

Q. Now, Mr. May, will you tell us upon what you base that conclusion?

A. Well, it is really based upon my whole experience of the last thirty-five or forty years. I am not familiar with a very large number of cases in which sales of iron ore properties have been made, particularly since the depression, which to my mind has substantially changed our whole industrial situation—so I cannot speak specifically of iron ore properties from recent experience—but my view, and my experience also, is that generally speaking, business men regard ten per cent as practically the minimum rate for an investment which involves the hazards of business. One would have to make an exception to that statement in respect to the period from 1927 to 1929, when, as the Senate Committee on the investigation of stock exchanges stated in its recent report, "the whole country was swept by a fever of speculation from which not even the financial leaders were immune." Leaving out of consideration a situation like that, I think that business men would generally regard ten per cent as the minimum rate of return subject to business hazards. Prior to the depression, I think steel men and engineers in the steel profession, and many others were disposed to attach higher values to ore property than would be arrived at on that basis, and in our negotiations which have involved doing business with the steel business and the banks, I frequently observed a tendency on the part of steel men to attach greatly exaggerated value to iron property, and, generally, the bankers have discounted considerably the values attached to the properties. I think the position as to over-rating of ore properties was in part due to over-stressing the consideration that mining on the Lake Superior Ranges is comparatively free from what you may call mining hazards, as compared with other types of mining industry, but hazards are of at least three general kinds. There are the hazards incident to production, which in this case are relatively small.

Q. You refer to those as mining hazards?

A. Yes, that refers to mining hazards. Then hazards incidental to the sale and disposition of the product, and then there are what you might call the general economic and social hazards, the hazards of changes in social policy involving such questions as regulation, taxation, tariff policies, and monetary policies. Different businesses are affected to different degrees by different classes of hazards, but the second and third classes are always present.

In my experience, business men generally discount valuations made by engineers—almost invariably. I think that is true because engineers are apt to consider only the hazards that they think they can reasonably foresee, and business men realize that the hazards which they cannot account for and readily foresee constitute important factors for their consideration. Perhaps I could make a little clearer what I am trying to say by illustrating from specific cases that have come under my notice.

Mr. Blu. That is perfectly proper.

A. One striking case that I had in mind is that a few years ago I had to go down to Chile on business and visit nitrate plants down there. Now, the nitrate rock lies close to the surface and the available supply can be estimated accurately just as I understand you can estimate, with reasonable accuracy, the available ore on the Mesabi Range. Formerly in England the shares of nitrate companies were quite a popular investment, and in some other countries also. When I was down in Chile, which was just before the depression had started, they were trying to do something to save the nitrate industry in Chile. Today it is, I should say, almost ruined. I noticed the other day the bonds of one of the companies, six per cent bonds of the Lautaro Nitrate Company, were selling on the New York Stock Exchange at 10. Now, that ruin was brought about by two things, broadly. The first thing that affected the industry seriously was the steady increase in the export taxes levied by the Chilean government, which, ultimately, became larger than all the costs of operation put together. But the more important thing was that during the war, Germany was unable to get a supply of nitrate which was essential in the production of explosives, and was forced to turn its attention to some way of supplying or getting nitrogen out of the air; and the nitrates produced in that way are practically ruining the natural Chilean industry.

Q. Have you other similar examples that you can cover briefly?

A. Take the radio, that completely ruined the makers of pianos, pianolas and victrolas, and seriously affected the whole music industry. The discovery of a process for making a substitute for silk out of wood pulp had a very serious effect upon the silk industry. The copper industry has been very seriously affected, and it is now in a serious condition as the result of the development of new low-cost supplies partly in Chile but more particularly in Africa. It is much easier to conceive of changes in either metallurgical methods, or monetary conditions, or tariff policies, or things of that kind, which might seriously affect the steel industry than it was to conceive that the nitrate industry would be ruined by the discovery of methods of getting nitrates out of the air, or the piano industry would be ruined by the discovery of inventions such as the radio.

I remember some years ago, in a railroad case, the claim of some allowance for risk in the return to railroads was met by the statement that the railroads were a basic industry, or a basic enterprise, the prosperity of which was essential to the country; it could never be dispensed with. Certainly, at that time, no one foresaw the effect of automobiles and aviation on the condition of the railroads. Those are the sort of things that I have in mind that every business man knows are inherent in any business .investment. He cannot say precisely what form they are going to take, but he needs some compensation for that risk in the rate of return which he uses to compute the value that he can afford to pay for a property.

Q. And it is considerations of the kind you mentioned upon which you base your opinion that a ten per cent rate of return is appropriate in the case of iron ore property?

A. Strictly speaking, I have gone only so far up to now— I have covered only the point as to why some considerable excess over what you may call the safe rate on money is necessary to induce people to assume business hazards. How much that excess should be is the next question, which is a part of the problem that you have to solve before you can fix any particular rate. On that point there are some considerations that I think are very important. I have given a lot of thought to the philosophy of the problems of the risk, the compensation for risk, and that leads me to the conclusion, which observation confirms, that the allowance you have to make for risk is bound to be substantially greater than what you may call the purely mathematical value of the risk.

If you take insurance—we all know that for every dollar we pay for fire insurance, roughly 50 cents is absorbed in expenses and the profit of the insurance companies, and only 50 cents is necessary to compensate for the purely mathematical value of the risk. Now, that sort of consideration applies when you ask an investor to take a risk. He wants something more than the mathematical value of the risk. How much more is something that depends upon a whole lot of circumstances; but I should say that he usually expects, like the insurance companies, something like twice the mathematical value of the risk, and that, I think, has always been so; and I think as our country becomes more settled and less of a pioneer country, that consideration will rather grow in importance. I think it was Mr. Morgan who said, "The growth of the country corrects all but the worst mistakes." It was true in the earlier years, and there were prospects of results far exceeding a reasonable estimate which went a long way to offset the prospects of losses. But as you get further and further from the earlier stages of development of the country, that consideration tends to lose force. I think also the whole system of graduated income tax, for instance, and taxation of capital gains, and things of that kind have operated in the same direction. I don't mean I disapprove of the policies. On the whole, I approve of them, but they do have that effect; so that I think today you have got to give substantially more than the mathematical value of the risk to an investor to assume a hazard. As I say, those considerations were rather lost sight of, perhaps, in the days of 1927 and 1928 and 1929. But the depression has brought them back to mind with a vengeance, and I don't think people are going to ignore them for a good many years to come. To my mind, the really important effect of the depression on industry—I mean upon the value of investments generally—is not the current operating losses—those have been very considerable in a number of cases—but I have a feeling that people have now come to realize that values, prior to 1929, were exaggerated, and they are going to take a very much more conservative view as to what they can afford to pay for property, and be more conservative in the return that they ask, if they are going to assume new risks.

Q. Is that all you care to say on that subject?

A. I could talk for a long time, and I have tried to give the general idea.

Q. Can you tell us, in a general way, how you consider the percentage should be determined which must be added to the rate on reasonably secured loans to cover the extra hazards involved in outside investment, say, in a mine in Minnesota?

A. Well, perhaps I have pretty well covered that in my answer to the last question. It comes, ultimately, to a question of judgment and the position we have. But my own opinion is that in present-day conditions ten per cent is certainly not a high rate. I should hesitate a great deal to advise any person to buy an iron ore mine on a prospect of ten per cent return. But I realize an iron ore mine is not an individual investment in an ordinary way. I would not advise any client to figure less than ten per cent in determining the price they can afford to pay for iron ore properties.

Q. Mr. May, can you recall any specific cases of mine valuations which you think are fairly comparable to the purchase of an iron ore property on the Mesabi Range?

A. I don't remember very many actual sales of mines in my experience that I consider comparable. Curiously enough, the only two I can think of as reasonably pertinent happen to be the first I ever had experience with, and the last. The first one in which I was actively concerned was the sale of the copper mine at Copper Cliff, Ontario, to the International Nickel Company in 1902. That was a cash purchase. I worked out the yield on the assumed factors myself and I remember it worked out just about ten per cent, on the basis of the proven ore, the current price for nickel and copper, and current cost of production, and, I think, at the time there were reasonable grounds to expect that the price could be increased, the cost probably reduced and a large additional tonnage would be developed. That was an important consideration in the case, because the life assumed was not very many years, so that if additional tonnage were developed and brought in it would have a considerable present value.

Q. How did those matters turn out in that immediate case, Mr. May?

A. All three were realized—the International Nickel got a very handsome thing out of the investment, although, incidentally, I remember that the vendors thought they had gotten an extremely good price for their property. That was a case where everybody was satisfied.

The other one is the experience I had in connection with the Kreuger interests. One of the estates of the Kreuger group had a large interest in the Boliden gold mine in Sweden. Our committee made an effort to get the Swedish government to buy that mine at a generous price as a sort of relief to the foreign investors who suffered so badly. The government undertook to give the matter consideration and appointed a commission. The liquidators appointed experts to examine the mine. They made a report and gave a valuation based, as I recall, on the current price of gold, the estimation that costs in the future would tend to increase by about ten per cent which they allowed, and that the proven ore could be mined out over a period of fifteen years; applying a discount factor of six per cent, they arrived at certain figures, and the liquidators offered an option on the mine at that price to the government commission. The chairman of the commission took the view that the offer indicated that the liquidators had no real desire to sell. The matter came before our committee and I found that the two bankers who were associated with me—Mr. Hugh Kindersley of London and Mr. Wallenberg, a Swedish banker—both agreed that if we could get a purchaser who would accept the experts' conclusion, except for the substitution of ten per cent for six per cent, it would be a very advantageous arrangement for everybody to effect the sale; and since I returned from Sweden I have learned that a sale has been effected on substantially that basis.

Q. How recently is that?

A. Within the last month.

Q. Mr. May, is ten per cent higher or lower than the rate you would normally use in the case of an industrial property?

A. Lower, unquestionably. As a matter of fact, in this same Kreuger matter, I was asked to value a large number of manufacturing properties of the group in various countries including the United States and countries like Sweden, Norway, and Denmark, where conditions as to investment are fairly comparable to the United States, as well as other countries where conditions may be different, like Czecho-Slovakia and Hungary, where values are definitely more speculative. But in the valuations which I am making I am not using any rate lower than twelve and a half per cent, and after consultation with the other members of the committee I find that they share my views.

Q. You are familiar, I take it, with what is generally known as the analytical appraisal method in arriving at the valuation of iron ore and other properties?

A. Yes. That is the method that is in general outlined in the commission's report.

Q. Would you consider this ten per cent rate that you mentioned appropriate to use in the computation of the present worth of profits estimated to be derived from an iron mine in Minnesota?

A. That would depend to some extent on the way in which the factors in the calculation were determined. If the factors were chosen allowing for all reasonably probable contingencies but not making any special discounts for unforeseen hazards and that sort of thing, I should say that ten per cent would generally be, perhaps, about the sort of rate, the minimum rate, but before I expressed a conclusion on a specific problem I would want to examine the factors in some detail myself.

Q. Now, you have not heard the testimony that has been given here or all the assumptions that have been made by expert engineers. I might tell you that in computing present worth in this case an exhaustion period of forty years from May 1, 1932, has been used for iron ore properties on the Mesabi Range.

A. That is an engineering question on which I would have no opinion.

Q. Another assumption that has been made is an assumed selling price for iron ore based upon the average Lower Lakes price of iron ore for a statistical period from 1927 to 1931, both years inclusive; what would you say as to that assumption?

A. That seems to me to raise perhaps two points; the first is whether the five-year average is a fair basis; it is not an unfair method in general and would be applicable, I should say, and be as good a guide as you could get if you are basing your assumption on the resumption of normal conditions, as I said before. The other question is as to whether the Lake Erie price is a proper figure to take, and no doubt there may be a question raised on that on the ground that a large, the larger part, by far, of the tonnage is what you may call consumer-owned, and therefore the Lake Erie price is not exactly the same as a price in a market in which the consumer and the vendor are unrelated; that question might arise—I am not an expert on the steel industry—that is, the tonnage and sales of the steel industry; all I can say on that is that Lake Erie prices have always been used as the basis of valuations that has been employed in merger negotiations and that kind of thing, and I think in the past they were accepted by all the parties concerned even though the different parties had unbalanced ore positions. But, of course, few of those mergers went through in their original form, and in no case were any final prices determined on the basis of specific valuations of the ore property. Where anything went through it was the result of a horse trade so that the only bearing, I suppose, that it has is that they had chosen that basis, and that they used that as a suitable starting point even though they had unbalanced positions.

Q. Another assumption that was made here was mining costs based on this same statistical period.

A. Well, if you assume the sales price within that period, it is almost inevitable that you assume the costs unless you have some definite reason for assuming or foreseeing some change in the costs, because the spread is probably as good a guide as your sales of ores, that is, as to cost.

Q. If the factors I have mentioned are assumed, would you consider the rate of discount or rate of return you mentioned appropriate to apply to the computation of present worth of the future income from these iron ore properties in Minnesota?

A. I should think it was appropriate, yes, an appropriate rate to use for such a purpose.

Q. Mr. May, you are familiar with the so-called Hoskold formula?

A. Yes.

Q. In applying that formula to the computation of the present worth of income from iron ore properties here, what have you to say about the rate of discount to cover the risk and the rate the sinking fund accumulation should bear?

A. Well, I think engineers generally have used a somewhat lower rate of return; in fact, sometimes a considerably lower rate of return than the ten per cent that I have mentioned, and have included with it a sinking fund at a rate assumed for a safe reinvestment of, say, four per cent. I would say that certainly if you used a return rate of less than ten per cent you would have to couple it with a reinvestment sinking fund rate at a substantially lower figure in order to get at a basis that would be at all attractive to the average investor, or to a likely purchaser.

Q. If a ten per cent risk rate or an eight per cent risk rate were used, what would you consider the appropriate rate for the sinking fund?

A. Well, if an eight per cent rate be used, the common thing, I think, and the one being very frequently used by the treasury, I think, is eight and four. In fact, I think four per cent is almost invariably used as a sinking fund rate by the Bureau of Internal Revenue, according to my experience.

Q. Would you think, then, that a ten–four combination or an eight–four combination would be appropriate to use in discounting the present worth of profits on these iron ore properties?

A. Well, if I were making a recommendation I might not insist on the four per cent if the return rate were as high as ten, but if it were less than ten I should certainly expect the sinking fund rate to be coupled with it. As a matter of fact, I think in theory the sinking fund method is perfectly sound; but—well, in a tax case in which I was interested one of the Circuit Courts of Appeals, in deciding that a method of computing of tax including the result of algebra was not intended by Congress, said that algebra is not lightly to be imputed to legislators, and I think in the same way higher mathematics is not lightly to be imputed to business men. They take calculations from the engineers and experts in whom they have confidence on the basis that those men consider sound in principle, and then they apply to them pragmatic tests to see how it is going to work out to them, and that is what they base their final conclusions on. I think that is the actual machinery of it. As a rule, they reach a lower valuation by that method almost invariably.

Q. I did not understand the last part of your statement; what did you say?

A. As a rule they reach a lower valuation as the result on that.

Q. Who reach lower values?

A. The investors.

Q. That is all, Mr. May; you may cross examine, Mr. Ryan.

CROSS EXAMINATION

By Mr. Ryan:

Q. Mr. May, do these hazard factors which you speak of always work one way?

A. No, they don't.

Q. Do you make any allowance for the possibility that conditions, general economic and social conditions, may improve?

A. Well, I think that carries one off into another somewhat philosophic angle of the question. If you want me to discuss it I will be glad to. That is, the benefit that an investor derives if results are better than his expectation are not so valuable to him as the injury to him if the results fall short of his expectation. That is a phase of the question of the diminishing value of wealth. At every stage, as you grow more prosperous, each accretion to your prosperity is of comparatively less value than the amount you had before, so the accretions, the prospect of accretions from the investment standpoint, are not an offset to the prospects of decrease or falling off. That, of course, is accentuated very much by the system of graduated income taxes and taxation of capital gains, particularly from the standpoint of the large investor. You take the large investor, which is the one question—you really have two problems in this question, as I see it. You can consider the large investment, that is one problem, the large investor. If results are more favorable than he anticipates, the excess profits, the higher profits are taxed at a continually growing rate and capital gains are taxed without corresponding relief in the case that he has capital losses, so that he does not consider that a prospect of the return being more favorable offsets with him the prospect of the results never being attained by an equal amount.

Of course, if you take the small investor and assume a distribution of your investment so that the risk is spread, you have a somewhat different problem. There the risk element is not quite the same, is not so pronounced as it is in the case of the large investor, but then you come to the high cost of distribution, which applies not only to commodities but to securities, so if you try to finance a purchase by distribution among small investors what you save in the risk element you lose on the higher cost of distribution. That is the philosophy of it, as I see it.

Q. Your answer has had a relationship to the risk factor as between gain and loss; as applied to an individual, stated in dollars, would the same answer be true?

A. No. I would say that the social hazards are distinctly in the direction of reduced profits, and the social hazards are more likely—changes in social conditions, broadly speaking— are more likely to reduce profits than to increase them. I think that is true.

Q. Well, the answer is that in your judgment social and economic changes are likely, more likely to reduce profits over those you assume than they are to increase profits over those that you estimate?

A. I think that is particularly true, particularly in what you may call basic industries.

Q. And why is that?

A. Well, because the tendency is almost constantly toward increasing taxation; the public spends, and the burden of taxation is increasing, and also when you get into the basic industries you are faced with problems of regulation and additional taxation the moment you begin to show increase of profit, without any corresponding expectation of relief if your profits fall off. The more essential an industry is to the life of the nation the less chance there is of substantial increase of profit as a cyclical trend, I would say.

Q. In other words, in the broad, general proposition, it is your belief that the tendency in the future is that profits of large industries will be reduced rather than increased?

A. I think that is the general trend one must expect. Especially in basic industries, I would add to that.

Q. Doesn't that lead to the view that the expected return on invested capital will also tend to decrease?

A. Not necessarily, I think. It may to some extent, but I think that newer enterprises will be more profitable, and that is where the opportunities for investment will be. And you are indulging in rather general speculation, but I look for the movement of capital, of intelligent capital out of the more basic, what would be regarded as the more basic, industries into the newer industries. That is the trend of investment, I would say.

Q. Capital will go looking for these hazards, will it?

A. What?

Q. Capital will go looking for these hazards, will it?

A. No. It will rather choose to go where the prospects of gain will offset the hazards that attach to all business.

Q. To what?

A. To all business.

Q. Would you not say that, generally speaking, the new business, as you describe it, was more speculative and more hazardous than an established, settled business or a business with extensive operations behind it?

A. Well, the course of the value of business is something like the life of man, I think. In the early days it is hazardous, and then it comes to the prime of life, and then it passes out into an older age, and what investment seeks are industries in the prime of life.

Q. Is that true of basic industries?

A. Well, I think in industries there is nothing that is permanently basic, but we come to regard them as basic.

Q. Well, you say that there is no basic industry. You spoke of the hazards which should be taken up in your ten per cent return as a hazard incident to sale of the commodity in which your capital is embarked. May not that hazard work as well in favor of the owner as against him?

A. You mean in the case of the steel industry?

Q. No, generally, I am speaking now, and ask for your answer in dollars, not the relative value of a dollar to a man who has a million and the man who is out on the street begging—the dollar?

A. Well, that is a thing that you could not generalize on. I mean, you would have to consider each industry on its merits, I would say, in that case.

Q. Well, I understood that generally you calculate these hazards, and generally in dealing with all business, and that generally you regard one of those elements of hazards that is incident to the sale of your product; isn't that right?

A. Yes, that you may lose your market.

Q. What?

A. The hazard that you may lose your market through one cause or another.

Q. Yes. Is not a hazard incident to sale, isn't it likewise true that there is some likelihood, at least, of an unexpected gain through increase of prices?

A. Theoretically it exists, but certainly in the steel industry I should think that the probabilities are rather the other way.

Q. I am talking generally now without reference to the steel industry.

A. That is a fairly large question. Of course, you cannot say that any particular rate is generally appropriate without stating the facts of the particular situation, but if I might put it in sort of legal terms, I think the average business man thinks that the burden of proof is heavily on anybody that undertakes to convince him that he should make an investment on less than a ten per cent return.

Q. Oh, no, no. We are examining into that ten per cent return; we want to find what it is made up of. It is made up, as I understood you to say, of these hazards, and the hazards are all, in the implication at least, against the investor; now, is that true?

A. That is not the point. I do not think that to be accurate. What influences the decision is not the actual probability as to the hazards, but what the contemplating investor thinks the hazards are going to be. Value is largely a matter of psychology of the purchaser.

Q. There you are taking one end of the problem exactly as you do on these hazards. Doesn't what the seller thinks have something to do with the transaction?

A. Maybe.

Q. So that the psychology has to include the psychology of both buyer and seller?

A. Yes, that is true.

Q. And the seller does not think of any of these factors, does he, of hazard?

A. I think he does, yes. He probably thinks of them somewhat differently.

Q. He thinks of them from quite an opposite viewpoint?

A. Yes, maybe; to some extent undoubtedly, yes.

Q. If we go off this method of determining values and steel in psychology we have got to get in to the seller as well as the buyer?

A. Well, the real problem in industry is to find a buyer.

Q. Is that true with the enormous amount of money seeking investment as there is today?

A. Yes, it is true today, distinctly true, today.

Q. It is true?

A. I think capital is less disposed to assume hazards at this precise moment than it has been for a long time. When I say "a long time" I mean the period from 1929 down to date. Business is very reluctant to assume hazards.

Q. Well, business is reluctant to assume hazards?

A. What?

Q. Business is reluctant to assume hazards?

A. Capital. Capital is the word. I say, capital seeking investment. Capital is reluctant to assume hazards; that is why there is so much surplus capital in the country that is not being employed.

Q. That is due to the existing depression when people figure there is nothing in sight; isn't that correct?

A. Yes, they think the future holds more hazards in sight than it did, we will say, ten years ago.

Q. Will not the state be reached, just how soon nobody knows, at which this capital now idle in enormous quantities will seek investment?

A. Yes, it is bound to find some sort of investment ultimately.

Q. And isn't this broad proposition true, that doesn't the condition of depression and the large amount of idle capital tend to reduce the returns which an investor can get on his capital?

A. That may be true on safe investments.

Q. Well, broadly, over any investment?

A. It is curious, but if you take the period of depression you will find that the spread between the safe return and the speculative return widens.

Q. Yes, but the safe investment, the absolutely safe investment—

A. Of course, there is no absolutely safe investment.

Q. But between that and the speculative investment there is competition in some degree?

A. Not always.

Q. In some degree?

A. In some degree.

Q. Not always, but you say there is an increasing spread due to various factors?

A. Yes.

Q. But they are all dollars, and all dollars are in competition so far as investment goes?

A. Well, they are not necessarily in dollars.

Q. What?

A. You mean in the United States?

Q. **Yes.**

A. This money that is seeking it is all dollars, yes.

Q. Now, does the relationship of consumer-ownership have any effect upon the hazards incident to the sale of the product involved in the particular transaction?

A. I think that takes us off. You can see each one of these questions would form the starting point for a half hour's talk, I think, really, and I do not want to carry the point too far.

Q. I would suggest that we are talking in generalities all the way through here, and may we not have a general answer as to this tendency?

A. Well, I think myself that that brings in another question to which I have given very considerable thought. I think the result of this depression is going to be a reversal of the trend toward integration. I think that this consumer-ownership idea is pretty well demonstrated—I won't say "demonstrated," but I think there is a strong feeling coming that it has been proved to be fallacious and an unwise policy. As a matter of fact, I think the length and severity of the depression is partly due to integration of industry. On this question,—I do not know whether you want me to follow it any further or not. I want to answer your question, but I do not want to start a philosophical discussion,—well, what is your question?

Q. The question was: Does the relationship of consumer-ownership tend to decrease the risk factor involved in making sales of the product involved?

A. I don't think so. To state the thing broadly, I think the steel companies would be better off if they did not own the ore properties, and had relatively less investment.

Q. Would a separate corporate ownership, the ones owning the mines, be better off if they were divorced from the consuming steel company?

A. I do not think so.

Q. Then I take it that the summary is that there is an element of risk as to price calculated by you as a hazard which is not reduced when the buyer of the product has a fixed, complete market for his product?

A. May I hear that question again?

[Question read.]

A. I didn't make any specific calculation of hazards, and I assumed that the whole problem was one of valuation of property without relationship to its ownership. I didn't attempt to go into the effect on the value of property of its being owned by "A" rather than "B."

Q. That is the way we want it gone into.

A. What?

Q. Since we mixed theory with condition, I would suggest that we mix them at that point, too.

A. Would you like me to discuss that?

Q. Yes, as to whether or not, generally speaking, where the relationship of consumer-ownership exists, does not that fact broadly and generally tend to reduce or limit, reduce the price hazard in respect to that property?

A. Well, in that case the price hazard is transferred to his ultimate product. I think the basic thing about the iron ore industry today is that it is the raw material of a relatively unprosperous industry.

Q. Mr. May, you say that the steel industry is a relatively unprosperous industry; do you know about what the rate of return on capital in the industry is?

A. Well, I base that statement partly on general knowledge and partly on some figures that came to my attention recently as a director of the National Bureau of Economic Research. Some years ago we induced the Department of Commerce to accept the view that it was very desirable to get some figures on profits of industry, and the Department of Commerce took on its staff Professor Epstein and arranged for him to have access to the income tax returns and he got out a lot of figures for a fairly representative sample which were published as what he called a source book, and from that material he is preparing a book, and the manuscript was submitted to the directors of the National Bureau of Eco-

nomic Research in accordance with the requirements of
that Bureau that every manuscript shall be submitted to the
directors before publication, and, as I recall, his figures cover
a period of 1924 to 1928. During that period the average
earnings of, I think it was 2,046 companies, manufacturing
companies, which represented, as he said, nearly 50 per
cent of the total business of the country in manufacturing,
and those figures showed an average for the five years, 1924
to 1928, on capitalization, including bonded capitalization
and the profits earned before interest, of approximately 10.2
per cent. For the same five years, by way of comparison,
I think the United States Steel Corporation, for instance,
showed an average of somewhere about 7 per cent.

Q. Do you know whether or not those averages would
depart from that appreciably if they were for the period
1920 to 1931, inclusive?

A. I have not got any figures covering the later period,
but my impression is from such figures as were available—
for instance, the National City Bank gets out some figures
which are not strictly comparable to these, for, I think, about
1,300 companies, something of that sort, and their profits,
after interest charges (which makes it not comparable to the
earlier ones); and as I recall it those figures were for 1929,
1930, and 1931, and the relation of the Steel Corporation to
the total of the group was less favorable than for the period
from 1924 to 1928.

Q. Was that true of the other groups?

A. I said the relation. Of course, 1929 was no doubt
better than 1928, and 1930 and 1931 were less favorable than
the average of the five years, but the point I was making is
that the Steel Corporation figures fell off in comparison with
the previous period to a greater extent than the other industries.

Q. I see. Did that change of relationship, in your judgment, make such difference? Did that change which you say
for the years 1929, 1930, and 1931 make enough difference
to discredit this figure which I quote from the magazine *Steel*

to the effect that, "The weighted average 1920 to 1931 net profit on invested capital of the United States Steel Corporation was 5.16 per cent."

Mr. Blu. 5.16?

Mr. Ryan. 5.16.

Mr. Hartley. What years?

Mr. Ryan. 1920 to 1931, inclusive.

A. Well, that comparison is a little bit difficult to make. I may not understand a part of the difference. I know a good deal about the Steel Corporation naturally, being the auditor, and in the calculation which I made the Steel Corporation gradually and some time in 1928 wrote off excessive capitalization, or whatever you may care to call it, in an amount of $508,000,000. Now, I should imagine that the *Steel* magazine figures are before making an adjustment for that $508,000,000, whereas that capitalization of the Steel Corporation now being reduced by that $508,000,000, I am making my calculations on the reduced capitalization.

The Court. Will you read the question, Mr. Reporter?

The Witness. Perhaps I could restate it, if Your Honor would like, a little clearer. It is probably not so clear as it should be.

[Answer read.]

Q. What, in your judgment,—

Mr. Hartley. Has the witness finished his answer? He seems to be looking at some paper.

The Witness. If Your Honor would like to see the figure I am referring to, it shows up in the annual report.

The Court. If it is important it will probably be in-troduced in evidence.

Q. What I wanted to get at, Mr. May, was—in answer to this question you stated that the steel industry was an industry, as a whole, with a relatively low rate of return and I asked what figure you were using to express its rate of return.

A. Well, you asked me to explain the difference between the two figures.

Q. Yes, this is another question.

Mr. Blu. Just read it to him, Mr. La Baw, please. [Question read.]

A. The first figure I had in mind was that 7 per cent for the steel industry, as illustrated by the Steel Corporation, was relatively low.

Q. The figure that you have mentioned as being relatively low is 7 per cent?

A. Yes, under normal conditions.

Q. Yes.

A. I don't mean under depression conditions. We have always got to be clear, I think, whether we are talking about today's conditions or normal conditions.

Mr. Blu. Is that for the period you stated, Mr. May?

The Witness. The 7 per cent is what you might call fairly normal, perhaps a little high, for the period from 1924 to 1928. It leaves out the recent peak of 1929 and leaves out the depression years.

Q. And the rate to be arrived at varies with whether or not you let the statement of capitalization stand at one figure or whether you write it off and use another figure?

A. Yes. Oh, of course it does.

Q. On what theory or basis was this $508,000,000, if that is the figure,—

The Court. That is right, Mr. Ryan.

Q. $508,000,000 written off?

A. Well, the report describes it in these words: "From this surplus there has been appropriated to amortize costs to the United States Steel Corporation of stocks of subsidiary companies in excess of their investment in tangible property."

Mr. Blu. What report, Mr. May?

The Witness. Well, this is in any report. I have before me the report for December, 1931, page 20.

Mr. Blu. Of the United States Steel Corporation?

The Witness. Of the United States Steel Corporation.

Q. What does that mean in language that is understandable to a person like me, for instance?

A. Well, I think probably it is intelligible to you as it stands, but what it really means is that the Steel Corporation paid more for the subsidiaries than the value of the tangible property those subsidiaries had, and until these entries had been made, that excess was a part of the capitalization of the Steel Corporation. They have now eliminated that amount from their capitalization so that their capitalization now is based on tangible assets of the corporation without any addition for the excess price paid by the Steel Corporation for the stocks of the subsidiary companies, shares of the subsidiary companies which represent those assets.

Q. Does that report indicate that they have now written off all those excess values?

A. The language implies that.

The Court. What did it leave the capitalization of the United States Steel Corporation at the present time, Mr. May?

The Witness. You mean the total invested capital?

The Court. What they carry.

The Witness. When I say "invested capital," it is, of course, the capital stock, the bonds and the surplus. That amounts now, I think, to,—I can tell you, something over two billion dollars.

The Court. What is the capital stock?

The Witness. The capital stock is $868,000,000 of common and $360,000,000 of preferred, as I recall.

Mr. Ryan. I want to say I have not had an opportunity to look at this but I have no doubt counsel will be willing to have the report in evidence.

Mr. Blu. Yes.

Mr. Ryan. Then we will offer that in evidence.

Mr. Blu. You mean the whole report in evidence?

Mr. Ryan. Yes.

Mr. Blu. I thought you meant that statement that he was testifying about. I do not think that whole report of the United States Steel Corporation for any year, Your Honor, bears on the value of iron ore property in Minnesota on May 1, 1932.

Mr. Ryan. Of course, I would not want to make it a part of the record that subsequently would have to be printed, but I would like to offer it in evidence, with the view and privilege of referring to any part of it that might be material and having the Court, in a sense, take judicial notice of it.

Mr. Blu. Well, I don't believe that is something the Court would take judicial notice of.

Mr. Ryan. It will not take judicial notice of it, but I suggest, to avoid encumbering the record, that it be admitted in evidence for counsel on either side to refer to any part of it which they may deem relevant to the issues in this case.

Mr. Blu. We want to object to that, Your Honor. We have no objection to cross examination of this witness on the part of the report that is brought out here on cross examination. Counsel can develop anything further along the line he is talking about without having that whole report in evidence.

The Court. The evidence of the witness, and other witnesses have been produced for the same purpose, has gone along the line of profit to be made on investment. I suppose in cross examination anything in the report that bears on that question may be put in evidence.

Mr. Blu. Well, what part of the report do you think is material?

Mr. Ryan. I don't know.

Mr. Blu. I think it should be developed by cross examination.

Mr. Ryan. I am offering it with a view that we may refer to any part of it which may seem to us to be material, with the like privilege on your part.

The Court. Well, of course, without knowing what is in the document, if the whole exhibit were received some of it might not be pertinent to any point in the case.

Mr. Blu. That is my point.

The Court. I take it you may go through it later, Mr. Ryan, when you have time, and re-offer the part that you wish to have introduced.

Mr. Ryan. That is perfectly satisfactory. The point is we cannot stop now and go through this report.

The Court. No; the offer may be made later when you are advised as to what part you want to offer.

Q. Do you know at what rate of interest the steel industry, as represented by the companies of the steel industry, can borrow money in normal times?

A. No, I could not answer that question. I do not think, generally speaking, that steel companies are current borrowers. They make bond issues from time to time. They are not currently in the borrowing market.

Q. Do you regard selling and issuing bonds as borrowing money?

A. Yes, but those are special transactions; we should assemble the transactions and try to get an average on it. I could not offhand give an answer to the question.

Q. Could you give us a percentage rate which would fairly indicate the rate at which the United States Steel Company can borrow money through the sale of bonds?

A. I don't think the United States Steel Corporation has sold any bonds for a long, long time.

Q. Have they paid off bonds recently?

A. They have paid off bonds, yes.

Q. Do you know what rate of interest those bonds bore?

A. I think most of them were 5 per cent bonds, but I don't think most of them were sold. They were issued originally as a part of the consideration, a great part of them, I believe.

Q. Do you know whether or not any of the steel companies have recently issued bonds or paid off bonds?

A. I do not recall any specific figures at the moment.

Q. Is it your impression that all of the bonds which have been paid for by the steel companies represent bonds issued in purchase of property?

A. Not all of them, perhaps. I think, as I remember, there was an issue of bonds by the Steel Corporation early in its career, about 1903 or '04, something of that sort, but I don't recall. I would not undertake to say, without refreshing my memory, what happened.

Q. How long have you been auditor for the United States Steel Corporation?

A. Ever since it was formed.

Q. From your knowledge of the affairs of that company can you express an opinion at what rate the company can borrow money?

A. I would not undertake to express an opinion without giving serious thought to it. It depends to some extent on the amount of money. I mean, if they wanted to borrow, say, up to half their investment in the property, that would be one rate; if they wanted to borrow up to 25 per cent that would be another rate; if they wanted to borrow up to 75 per cent that would be another, if they could do it at all.

Q. You haven't an opinion as to what any of those rates would be?

A. I would not offhand say.

Mr. Blu. Do you mean at the present time, Mr. Ryan, or what period?

Mr. Ryan. Any time.

Mr. Blu. Any time back to 1902?

Mr. Ryan. Any time in normal conditions.

The Witness. That involves too many uncertainties for me to express an opinion.

Q. I have assumed that a problem of that kind involved a great many uncertainties. Any values you might put on an ore body would involve a great many uncertainties.

A. You asked me how much,—at what rate the corporation could borrow, without any indication as to time or amount or terms, the length of the loan or anything. That is entirely a speculative proposition.

Q. I suggest you supply your own qualifications and give us figures with any qualifications you choose to add to them.

A. For instance, if I say that the Steel Corporation might have borrowed money in 1924, we will say, you get a different factor in '24; and '29 and '34, you get quite different factors.

Q. Let us say normal?

A. What is normal?

Q. What forms the basis for the calculation which you have in mind, just individual judgment?

A. No; my judgment as to how investors feel about these things, and what they know. It isn't an attempt to determine what investors ought to think; but what I think is the practical problem of inducing an investor to invest.

.   .   .   .

Q. You assume, I take it, you expect an investor will want a rate of return,—the investor in an iron mine will want a rate of return reflected in a 10 and 4 combination of interest, meaning a 10 per cent return on his investment after the payment of all forms of taxes, including his income tax; is that right?

A. I didn't say a 10 and 4, if I remember rightly. I said if you used a rate lower than 10 you would put a sinking fund, you would combine a sinking fund method with it. I am just correcting the statement of my position, in your question, in that answer. I said, if you went below 10, for instance to 8 per cent—if an investor considered 8 per cent he would want a sinking fund tacked onto it. But I said if you got 10 or over you might get him to take it on a straight basis.

Q. A straight rate of 10 per cent?

A. Yes, without the sinking fund, which you get up to **that.**

Q. Isn't it a fact that your sinking fund—don't you in that calculation increase your rate of return as compared with any rate lower than the one you used for a sinking fund?

A. I did not contemplate a sinking fund in connection with the 10 per cent at all.

Q. You just took it straight 10 per cent return?

A. Straight 10 per cent return; but if you went below 10, then I would say at least you would have to give the investor the benefit of the sinking fund accompanied with any lower rate; for instance, I said 8 and 4; that is the rate that the Bureau of Internal Revenue uses.

Q. Which would give you the higher rate of return on your investment, a straight 10 or a 10 and 4?

The Court (Judge Freeman). Eight and four?

Mr. Ryan. No; a straight 10 or a 10 and 4.

A. If all your expectations worked out, 10 and 4 would give you the higher rate. You would get more money out of it in the end that way.

Q. The sinking fund factor is a charge against the investor, isn't it?

A. What?

Q. The sinking fund factor is a charge against the investor, isn't it?

A. Yes, but the straight 10 per cent method implies a charge against the investor, 10 per cent on what he is getting back.

Q. You mean 10 and 10?

A. Ten and ten.

Q. Using the same term?

A. Yes.

Q. In that computation there?

A. Yes.

Q. You say reduced; you would not reduce correspondingly the two rates if you want, say, an 8 per cent investment return; you would not think an 8 per cent sinking fund rate would be proper?

A. As I say, I think the investor takes a more pragmatic

and simple view of the situation than that. Let me illustrate that. Perhaps this will illustrate it. This is the way
I visualize the investor looking at it. Let's suppose a simple
case that is fairly analogous to this case, reduced to simpler
terms rather than complicated figures. Suppose the investor
were asked to buy a mine that was supposed to contain 40
million tons that could be mined a million tons a year, with
a dollar a ton profit; that makes it a nice simple calculation.
Now an engineer recommends that, we will say, as a good
purchase, on a straight 8 per cent basis, 8 and 8 as you call it.
That means he would ask him to pay $11,921,000 for that
property. The way the business man looks at it is, "Well,
how am I going to get that investment back? On an 8 per
cent basis, if the mine were to last forever it would be worth
only $12,500,000. So all you are going to give me towards
getting back my capital at that amount in addition to the 8
per cent return is 8 per cent on $579,000 a year." Now, that
isn't good enough. That is really the way they do things.
That is the way the Internal Revenue Bureau figures it. I
got this wrong, I think, perhaps. I have got some tables
here that I worked out that will show it. Here is one
worked on the 7½ per cent basis, which is what I understand usually the State Tax Commission has used on the
40-year life. That gives a cost of roughly $12,450,000. Now,
if that is going to be mined with equal tonnage, the 40
millions, that represents 31 cents a ton. So that the first
year the man gets a million dollars. He gets a million
dollars; he sets aside $328,000. The way it is computed
for depletion on the straight loan basis he carries $671,000
to his income account; that gives him an immediate profit
of 5.57 per cent. That is the way it works out in practice.
The way the investor looks at it is that it isn't until 20 years
have elapsed that he has got an average rate of 8 per cent
on the money that he has had invested in the property.
Now, investors take a view of investments something like
that the insurance companies take of lives. You can foresee
something for the future, but the farther ahead you attempt

to see, the less clearly can you anticipate what is going to happen. Therefore, what sways the investor largely is the amount he is going to get in the first few years. Certainly in the case of a 40-year life what he is going to get in the first 20 years of the life is the thing that is vitally important to him.

Q. That would be the dominating thought of the ordinary investor, the mythical investor?

A. I just take that because that is the way the Internal Revenue Bureau figures his income, and through that that has become a very customary way of looking at it.

Q. Suppose this mythical investor, bringing it down somewhat nearer to earth—supposing the mythical investor has an enormous investment in steel plant, the value of which would wholly disappear if his mines were exhausted: Would the factor of extended future realization of his return weigh against his disposition to acquire a property with long life?

A. Well, I should say that is perhaps the most important result of the depression, that the delusion which lies at the basis of your question has been shattered. This idea of the necessity of manufacturing companies' owning their own reserves of raw materials for indefinite periods in the future is what has made a great many industries unprosperous and they are now, I think—I don't refer solely to the steel industry—recognizing the folly of it and trying to get themselves out of a position where they are what we used to call "land poor."

Q. Am I right in saying that that conjecture is based upon the theory that reserves which carry longer than approximately 40 years in the future are of no value and should not be bought?

A. Well, I think corporations largely are coming to realize that the attempt to supply their needs even for 40 years in the future is a mistaken policy, that they would be better off to have reasonably short reserves and rely on the general market, because what they save on carrying the investment in those properties would compensate them for any likely rises in prices.

Q. But your answer in that respect is influenced by your judgment that the past policies of the steel owners has been a mistaken one?

A. Oh, no, I wouldn't assume that far. It is based on my reading of the trend of opinion, not only in the steel industry but in other industries. I think there is no doubt—I don't mean only business men—but we have discussed this in purely academic discussions with the National Bureau of Economic Research, and there is a very interesting publication by Dr. Mills of the staff of that organization in which he expressed the opinion that one of the main contributing factors, or one of the important contributing factors, I should say, to the severity and the length of the present depression was that through this system of integration and labor-saving machinery so large a part of the cost of goods had come to be represented by money that was already spent anyhow. So that people were willing to sell at uneconomic prices if they could get back their new costs plus something towards the money they had already spent; and that, I think, as a result of all the discussions with the economists and others that I had, is one of the central facts of the present situation; and I think it has brought about a general reconsideration of this whole policy of large reserve for indefinite periods in the future and the attempt to keep anybody else from owning potential sources of raw material and all that sort of thing, and it is not limited to the steel industry.

Q. In part, at any rate, your views as they bear upon this case are influenced by your belief that the practice in the future, at least, will be different from what it has been in the past as respects the acquisition of ore reserves?

A. Yes, with the addition that my belief is based, not just on a process of reasoning, but based on knowledge of the trend of thought which I get in my business and other contacts.

Q. It is true, is it not, that considering what the buyer

would pay and the seller would sell for—mythical people—
that there is more or less of a problem to find buyers—that
the pressure is to sell rather than to buy—is that right?

A. Yes. Selling is regarded as the difficult end of the
job, usually.

Q. Doesn't that relative position between buyer and seller
change from time to time?

A. You mean in regard to the ::sual property investments? Of course, it changes to some extent, but a buyer's
market, broadly speaking, in commodities, is more common.
The selling problem is harder more of the time, you see.
That is why salesmen get more than purchasing agents.

Q. That is true as to the specific transactions, but generally speaking doesn't that relative position of buyer and
seller change with the general economic changes?

A. Yes, undoubtedly.

Q. So that in one year you will have a buyer's market
and another year you will have a seller's market?

A. Yes.

Q. Pressure to buy will operate in one year and pressure
to sell in another?

A. Yes. It would, I think, be more accurately stated that
the pressure to buy will operate in one year and the pressure
to sell will operate in n years, n being greater than unity.

Q. The depression indicates that. Aren't our views
somewhat darkly colored by the recent few years?

A. No; I think that merely leads us to attribute a higher
value to n, if I may put it that way.

Q. You say that a buyer will not acquire—normally—ore
properties unless he can get a rate of return of 10 per cent
after all his taxes connected with the investment, his income
in all respects, are paid. Would you say that it is also true
that a seller would be willing to dispose of his property at
a price which would give the buyer a 10 per cent return on
his investment after paying all taxes?

A. I don't recall that I said that a buyer expected a return
of 10 per cent after all his taxes.

Q. What is your statement?

A. I said that the existence of taxes led him to expect a return of 10. I am not deducting his personal income taxes—oh, no.

Q. What?

A. I am not contemplating deducting his personal income taxes in arriving at the sum to be capitalized at 10 per cent.

Q. Your calculation does not involve the payment of the Federal income tax in addition to that return?

A. Not to the individual, no, if you are still talking of an individual.

Q. May I state the question this way: Is it true that the vendor, the seller, will be willing to sell to a buyer at such a price as will enable the buyer to make 10 per cent net return on his investment after paying all the taxes assessed upon the property in which the investment is made?

A. All the taxes?

Q. Assessed upon the property in which the investment is made.

A. All those taxes and any other taxes that are incidental to carrying on the business, differentiating from the taxes which apply to the individual purchaser.

Q. Then, as opposed to excluding income taxes, you include all other taxes?

A. Yes, I would include among the deductions from the gross income all other taxes.

Q. And you would think that ordinarily a seller would be willing to dispose of his property at such a price as would give to the buyer a net return of 10 per cent on this class of property over and above the taxes on that property?

A. An expectation of 10 per cent; not an assurance of 10 per cent. That is the whole question, the difference between expectation and realization.

Take the steel industry: An addition to a steel plant is contemplated. No executive, as a rule, will authorize the expenditure unless an engineers' report shows that it may be expected to produce a saving or a gain equal to 15 to 20 or more per cent on the expenditure. That is because expectation and realization are two different things, and generally speaking, from the variety of circumstances, realization falls short of expectation.

Q. In other words, these engineers employed by the steel company guess that badly?

A. Not only by the steel corporation but all industry, because conditions change in the situation from day to day. You take an illustration: People spent money in 1929, expecting it to produce a certain return. They ran into a period of depression, during which their sales were small, which has lasted for five years. During those five years important new inventions in the field are developed so that if they were making the expenditure today they would buy something entirely different from what they bought in 1929; yet, because of the depression, they have got little or no return out of that expenditure between 1929 and today. Those are the things that bring about a difference between expectation and realization.

Q. And have the engineers so badly miscalculated those factors that when they suggest that a property can be purchased at a 10 per cent return the ordinary business man says that they are normally wrong, so that they won't purchase unless the engineers' estimate runs up to what—30 per cent?

A. In plant extensions, I think 15 to 20 per cent is what they figure on. Of course, that is more hazardous than an investment in iron mines because you may not make, as I say and as I showed in my illustration, your expenditure at the right time.

Q. Of course, in plant extension or any other expansion your engineer will at least attempt to calculate obsolescence, depreciation, and the like, will he not?

A. Yes, but this return would be over and above that.

Q. But I take it that your opinion is based upon knowledge of the facts that the ordinary level-headed person dealing with that problem, whether he will make that expenditure or not, will act upon the opinion that the engineer is so far wrong that he won't act upon an estimate of the engineer but will change his calculation to the extent of doubling their return factor?

A. Well, he expects more than 10 per cent net, of course, so it is not a question of doubling but of business men discounting engineers' estimates. There is no doubt about that, and it is not only in business. I remember when I was in Washington during the war—perhaps this is not relevant—the Vice-Chairman of the War Industries Board attributed the failure to make proper progress in one of the important departments to the fact that it was run by engineers who didn't figure on the difficulties which every business man allowed for after he got his engineering estimates.

.   .   .   .

Q. Do you know whether in the books of the Steel Corporation or in any of their reports there is set up the value of their ore reserves?

A. I don't think it has ever been set up in the reports and I couldn't answer as to the books. I imagine naturally the books of the iron mines must show some investment figure, but I don't imagine it represents the present value. It is probably some historical figure.

Q. Is there nowhere in their books a showing as to what their ore reserves consist of?

A. There must be in their records somewhere.

Q. Their records show what they consist of but you believe they do not set up any valuation upon them?

A. Ordinary accounting does not call for valuation of assets on the books of a corporation. They are carried at what they cost less amortization to write them off. That is the normal way. There may be adjustments from time to time but there is no attempt to reflect the value from year to year by changes in the figures which they carry on the books in any business.

.   .   .   .

By Mr. Blu:

Q. Mr. May, in answer to some question by Mr. Ryan, you stated that social hazards were tending or tended to increase. Can you give an illustration of what you meant by that?

A. Well, I would say that a good illustration is the tax hazard in Minnesota. For instance, if we put ourselves back in the position of anyone making an analytical appraisal in—say, 1905—he would figure taxes on the basis of the amount then being paid in the State of Minnesota. He would not look for the fact that in 1907 a new system of taxation would be initiated under which assessments of mineral property would be substantially increased. Again, if he were doing it in 1911 or 1912—and I had occasion to look into it at that time—he would have made his calculations on the basis of the taxes being paid in the period of, say, 1907 to 1911, during which substantial increase over the earlier periods had arisen, but he would not have allowed for the enormous increase in public expenditures that would occur in the next ten or twelve years and the enormous increase in taxes. As I recall the figures, roughly, local taxes from 1907 to 1911—about that period—absorbed from about 12 to 15 per cent of the earnings of ore mines, as I remember the figures which I then used; and in the last five years I think, judging from the Commission's report, they must have averaged nearer 40 per cent of the earnings for local taxes. That was one of the things I had in mind in talking of social hazards, because that is one of the results of social changes.

And it has always seemed to me that the ore industry is in an adverse position by reason of the fact that it is necessary to send the ore out of the State in order to convert it, so that the operations and the ultimate conversion are carried out in different tax jurisdictions. If nature had only been kind enough to do for Minnesota what it did for Alabama, and had deposited coal and limestone so that the iron could have been manufactured within the State of

Minnesota, I think that the tax hazard would have been reduced as the interest of the State would have been in the whole steel industry, whereas, as it is, the State's interest is limited to the ore end of the business.

Q. I was not quite sure as to what your answers were to some other questions relative to deduction of Federal income taxes; is it your opinion, Mr. May, that Federal income taxes should not be deducted at all in computing costs?

A. Well, that is a question over which there is a good deal of discussion. I have discussed that, very often, with Professor Adams.

Q. Who is Professor Adams?

A. He was formerly of the Wisconsin State Tax Commission, and, subsequently, professor at Yale, and principal advisor of Congress on taxation for a great many years. Discussions of the effect of income taxes and the proper treatment of them—that question came up many times. I think there is a variation of opinion among the tax experts; but I think my views and Professor Adams' are the same. To the extent that any tax is a true income tax you should not treat it as a cost in calculation. That would cover the English income tax which, if it is imposed on the corporation in the first instance, is deducted by the corporation from anything that is paid out—rents, dividends, or anything of that kind. But, as I look at the question, the corporation income tax is not a true income tax. It is something of a hybrid; to the extent of the amount of normal tax of individuals it is a true income tax, because if a corporation pays that tax and then pays the dividend, the taxpayer gets corresponding relief; and, personally, I would not treat that part of the income tax as a cost, although some people might.

As regards the balance, it is not a true income tax. It is merely an excise tax for the privilege of carrying on business as a corporation, and as such it is a part of the cost of doing business.

Q. Mr. Ryan attempted to show that if the property account of the United States Steel Corporation was overstated, that the rate of return would or should have been lower. Have you any reason to believe that the property account of the Steel Corporation is overstated, or is in excess of the true valuation?

A. No, I don't think there is any—I should say what general test you can apply rather indicates the contrary.

Q. Now, it seemed to me by reason of some of Mr. Ryan's questions that there was some confusion over the rate of return of bonds issued against a Mesabi Range iron ore property, and the rate of return that would be expected on the iron mining business. What is the distinction between those two things, Mr. May?

A. The distinction is that obviously the hazard of the person who takes a charge on the business is less substantial —less than that of a man who takes the whole risk of the business. In rate cases, for instance, there is a very substantial spread between the rate that is regarded by the regulating body as appropriate to the investment as a whole, or the business as a whole, and the rate at which the utility can sell its bonds. For instance, as I recall, your Commission here in Minnesota has fixed 7½ per cent as a rate for some utilities. That is not based on the assumption that utilities can sell their bonds only at 7½ per cent.

Q. Now, you mentioned public utilities; are you familiar with the rate of return of public utilities, generally?

A. No, I would not say that; I have studied the decisions as to reasonable rate of return.

Q. Having made such study, what do you consider a reasonable rate of return for a public utility company?

A. I don't think you can say on public utilities. They vary to some extent—the location and the nature of the business, and so on. For instance, in Minnesota I think 7½ per cent is allowed, and I suppose that is representative of conditions in public utilities in Minnesota.

Q. Well, what, generally, are the conditions as far as the public utility is concerned, compared with the conditions surrounding the mining of an iron ore property in Minnesota?

A. Regulation and a certain measure of protection go hand in hand, and it is the modern theory of regulation of utility corporations that they are protected against unreasonable competition, and on that basis the return that they can receive is restricted so that the rate should tend to be lower than in an industry that is not similarly protected from competition.

Q. Then, as I understand it from your last statement, you would consider the rate of return should be higher for iron ore property than for a utility company?

A. Certainly.

Q. For the reasons you have just stated?

A. Yes.

Q. This morning, I think you were attempting to make some comparison between a return of capital on a straight rate and a combination risk rate and sinking fund rate when you were interrupted with some question: I would like to have you go into that a little further and explain just what you were trying to show at that time?

A. Well, what I was starting out to discuss was the point of view of the ordinary business man toward the engineering calculations and other methods of approach to the question, and I was starting to take the illustrative case of an investment in a mine that is going to produce 1,000,000 tons a year, for 40 years. If an investor bought the mine on a 7½ per cent basis, that is 7½ and 7½, he would pay $12,594,000 for it. Now, the first year his receipts would be $1,000,000. The business man says: "Well, now, if I am expecting a 7½ per cent return, 7½ per cent on what I invested, it will absorb $944,550. That really leaves me $55,000 to set aside towards replacing my capital." The engineer replies: "That is true; but if you invest the $55,000 at 7½ per cent you will get your money back at the end of 40 years."

Q. Seven and one-half per cent or four per cent?

A. It is the 7½ and 7½. So the business man says: "I am not going to take the chance. I am not going to take the chance that I am going to be able to invest money at 7½ per cent, compound interest, continuously, for the next 40 years; I can see a few years into the future, I think, but I cannot see 40 years and I am not going to make a purchase that is dependent almost entirely, for the return of my money, on my being able to get 7½ per cent compound interest 30 or 40 years hence." Now, let me look at it my way: that is the income tax way—what I would have to pay income tax on—if I pay $12,594,000 for that mine, my depletion charge for the first year will be ¼₀ of that amount, which is $314,000. If I deduct that from my million dollars, all I have got left for interest is $685,000, which is less than 5½ per cent on my money. And the engineer says, "Oh, yes, but you will make that up through compound interest between 30 and 40 years hence." And he says, "Nothing doing." That is the position in regard to the method, as I see it. Now, I have made some calculations comparing different methods, and they show this: that if you assume 4 per cent sinking fund at the end of, say, 32 years, 80 per cent of the ore will have been mined, assuming equal proportions over 40 years; if you deduct your sinking fund from your investment, you will still have a net investment of 34 per cent on your original investment, as against 20 per cent on the ore still to be mined. If you buy on the 7½ per cent and 7½ per cent basis at the same date, you will still have 20 per cent of your ore to mine, but you will have 46 per cent of your investment still to get back. Now, business men are not going to take chances on what is going to happen 30 or 40 years hence, to that extent, and that is why, when you get down below a rate of 10 to a rate of 8 or 7 or 6 per cent, you have got to attach to it a sinking fund provision that won't make the investor depend upon getting a return of 7½ per cent or 8 per cent or whatever it is on the reinvestment of what money is returned on his capital. And, of course, when he says, "I expect a rate; I won't buy, unless I can see an expectation of a certain rate," what is in his mind if he does not say it in so many words is what I said this morning—if I buy a more or less hazardous investment on the reasonable chance of getting more than the safe rate, I know that I shall not get that excess in every case; but if I am reasonably clever in making my selection, and reasonably prudent in changing my investments from time to time, I may be able on an average to get 6 per cent instead of getting 4 per cent, on a safe investment, assuming that I start out with something that seems to hold a fair prospect of producing 8 per cent. That is what is really in the mind of the investor, so if you say that because he expects a prospect of 8 per cent it is reasonable to assume that he can reinvest his return of capital so as to produce 8 per cent, you are going contrary to the whole basic assumption upon which the action is based. I think what I have said would be made clearer by some tables which could easily be prepared.

Q. You have not prepared any such tables?

A. I have not got them. I am sure it is difficult for anyone to follow the argument without tables.

Q. You stated this morning that profits, in your opinion, were likely to be reduced in the basic industries in the future. Now, if that is true, what effect would that have upon the rate of return which capital would and should demand to cover the risks involved?

A. It won't mean that the rate of return sought by an investor will be reduced. It means that the capital value of the industry will diminish.

PART IV
REGULATION OF SECURITIES

I

MEMORANDUM REGARDING SECURITIES BiLL—
H R 4314

(1933)

I AM in favor of a substantial extension through the medium
of a Federal statute of the protection afforded to investors
in securities. I, however, recognize great practical difficulties
and I am not disposed to rate too highly the results that will
be immediately attained.

It is in the general social interest that new enterprises
should be undertaken and it is not, therefore, in the public
interest to make the provision of capital for such new enterprises unduly difficult.

It is an inevitable result of competition and the progress
of invention that many enterprises new and old should become unsuccessful. Indeed, if an attempt were made to
preserve the values of enterprises whose products have been
superseded and at the same time the new and superseding
enterprises were earning a fair return, the result would be
that the burden on the fruits of industry of the contribution paid to those whose claims rest on past savings and investment would become greater than the community would
be willing to bear. For either the total burden on consumers would become too great or the share of the fruits
left for those making a current contribution to production
in the form of labor, etc., would become inadequate.

The Congress must face the fact that a substantial percentage of industrial investment will in any event be lost.
This seems to me (1) to make it the more incumbent on
the Congress to see that investors have the opportunity to
make their investments on the basis of reasonable information, but at the same time (2) to make it in the highest
degree undesirable for the Congress to assume the responsi-

bility of requiring any governmental agency to decide either what is the true value of any investment security or even that the information available to the investor is all that is necessary to enable him to make a wise decision.

Indeed, while it is desirable that such protection as is practicable shall be given to those who invest in securities whose value is dependent on the profits earned by the maker thereof, it is in my judgment even more important to facilitate and encourage investment of small savings in government securities and other forms of holdings fraught with less risks and requiring less financial knowledge and less constant watchfulness than are necessary to even moderately successful commercial investments.

As I have indicated, I do not think the immediate practical results of the proposed legislation will be very considerable. A large proportion of the buyers of industrial securities are not investors, though they may think they are. They are not greatly swayed by the information given them, but are, I think, more generally influenced either by salesmanship or by general reputation either of the maker of the security or of the banking house issuing it. I am, however, hopeful that gradually the dissemination of better information will bring about an improvement in investment practice.

The problems to be solved in formulating legislation seem to me to be:

First, to determine the scope of the legislation;

Second, so to define the liability of directors and others as to impose penalties for fraud or culpable negligence without making the burdens so heavy that responsible persons will refuse to assume them and the business will pass into the hands of less responsible persons;

Third, to formulate requirements for proper disclosure by distributors of securities in respect of their compensation for and interests in the issue;

Fourth, to devise adequate but not unduly burdensome

provisions for the disclosure of information relative to enterprises upon which securities are based.

With regard to the scope of legislation, I strongly favor limiting it, at least in the first instance, to original offerings of securities, though I see no objection to including in the provisions regarding such new securities requirements for proper periodical reports subsequent to the issue. I believe that the Act should contain exemptions so as to exclude from it transactions which are not offerings to the public. Such exemptions require very careful study and I do not feel that I have any special competence for recommending what they should be.

The formulation of provisions which will impose proper penalties on directors and others responsible for an issue without deterring responsible persons from accepting directorships is a delicate one. It seems to me to be clear that provisions such as those contained in the original House Bill under which directors would be responsible for errors in statements of fact of which they had no knowledge nor any reasonable means of knowledge would defeat the ultimate purpose of the law.

The problem of proper disclosure of interest does not seem to offer very great difficulty, but this, again, is a feature in regard to which I do not feel competent to make specific suggestions.

The disclosure of information is a problem, however, which presents very great practical difficulties. Among the most important information is that which is of an accounting nature, and it is particularly with this branch of the question that I feel my experience gives me some qualification to express opinions as to what is essential and practicable and what is not.

The first difficulty that I see in the problem of formulating requirements for information is the impossibility of determining what facts are most essential in each case. The second is, that much which is loosely regarded as matters of fact is in reality matters of opinion. The third is, that the inferences drawn from facts and the opinions based on them are usually more important than the bare facts themselves.

In so far as accounting information is concerned, it seems to me fundamentally important to recognize that the accounts of a modern business are not entirely statements of fact, but are, to a large extent, expressions of opinion based partly on accounting conventions, partly on assumptions, explicit or implicit, and partly on judgment. As an English judge said many years ago when business was far less complex than it is today, "The ascertainment of profit is in every case necessarily a matter of estimate and opinion."

The most vitally important single factor in the value of a business enterprise is usually its future earning capacity. Such earning capacity may be estimated if someone is willing to prophesy, but usually the experience of the past is accepted as the best guide. What income is to be attributed to an accounting period of the past depends partly on accounting methods and partly on estimates. There is no escape from the use of conventions, because the income attributed to any period is not the fruit solely of actions and transactions within that period, but is affected by actions and transactions of the period prior thereto and the probabilities in respect of transactions in later periods. It is equally clear that estimates must be made and that they may prove incorrect even though made in the best of faith by the most competent persons. For instance, in order to arrive at the income for a given year it is necessary to estimate how long machinery in use will last and to place a value on unsold merchandise. But machinery capable of use for years may be rendered obsolete by new inventions perfected by others, the sale price of merchandise may be suddenly and vitally affected by, for example, a change in fashion, a revision of tariffs, development of cheaper methods of production, excessive production, distress selling by others.

I would, therefore, stress the paramount importance of

avoiding in the law anything likely to perpetuate the common misunderstanding that balance sheets and income accounts are statements of fact, and of doing whatever is possible to bring home to the investor that in formulating all such accounts conventions and opinions necessarily play an important part, and that their value depends on the competence and integrity of those exercising the necessary judgment. To this end, I should like to see either in the report accompanying the Bill or in the Bill itself a declaration of the purpose of the Bill in so far as accounts are concerned which should be to insure: (1) that, in balance sheets, the assets and liabilities shall be fairly classified; that the bases * on which the values are determined at which the assets are carried shall be fairly disclosed, and that a responsible person or persons shall have expressed an informed opinion that the balance sheet is fairly presented on the bases indicated and in accordance with acceptable accounting practice; and (2) that any statement of income shall be so framed, as in the opinion of competent and responsible persons, to constitute the best reflection reasonably obtainable of the earning capacity of the business under the conditions existing during the period to which it relates.

Since past earnings are significant to the investor only in so far as they are a guide to the future, it is desirable to do what can be done to safeguard the investor against statements of past earnings being put forward as evidence of the value of a security, unless those putting them forward disclose all knowledge which they may have of changes of conditions which have already taken place that would make such past earnings wholly unreliable as a guide to the prospective future earnings. It is perhaps impossible to provide complete safeguards on this point, but I believe that something can be done in this direction.

The accounting information which should be required by the statute should, I suggest, include:

---

* *E.g.*, cost, reproduction cost less depreciation, estimated going concern value, cost or market, whichever is lower, or liquidating value as of a specified date.

(1) A brief description of the general principles or methods of accounting regularly employed by the issuer in keeping its books and accounts and determining its income and financial position.

(2) A balance sheet or statement of assets and liabilities and capital of the issuer of the securities.

(3) A statement of income covering not less than three years, if the issuer has been so long in business.

(4) A declaration by the chief accounting officer of the issuer, or by an independent public accountant, that the balance· sheet and statement of income are, in his opinion, properly prepared on the basis of a fair and consistent application of the methods of accounting regularly employed by the company as described under subdivision (1).

(5) Special provisions to cover the case of companies operating through subsidiary corporations.

Such requirements would be substantially in accord with the recommendations of a committee of the American Institute of Accountants to the New York Stock Exchange which was favorably regarded by the Exchange and put in evidence by the Chairman of the Committee on Stock List in the course of his testimony before the Senate Committee on Banking and Currency on January 12, 1933. They would constitute a distinct advance in practice.

Specific suggestions for provisions to be inserted in the Bill in order to meet these requirements, which I had prepared, came to the attention of the Investment Bankers Association of America and have, I am advised, been embodied, substantially as proposed, in amendments which have already been suggested to the Committees of Congress considering the Bill, as follows (the notes are mine):

SUGGESTED SUBDIVISION OF SECTION 5 COVERING ACCOUNTING
REQUIREMENTS

(5) A brief statement of the general principles or methods of accounting regularly employed by the issuer in keeping its books and determining its financial position and income.

This requirement contemplates not a detailed explanation of the technical accounting methods, such as is embodied in what is commonly known as a "classification" or "card of accounts," but a statement of the broad accounting principles followed by the issuer.

In the absence of some such statement of principles there is nothing to which a declaration such as is contemplated in the fourth suggestion regarding the correctness of the accounts submitted can be related.

The Revenue Acts since 1918 have uniformly laid down as the general basis for determining income that it shall be computed "in accordance with the method of accounting regularly employed in keeping the books of such taxpayer."

The general nature of the information to be given under this head is indicated in Exhibit II of the report of the committee of the American Institute of Accountants to the New York Stock Exchange previously mentioned. Some of the more important points to be covered are the following:

(a) Upon what classes of property, on what basis and at what rates provision is made for, or in lieu of, depreciation;

(b) Upon what basis inventories are valued—whether at cost or market, whichever is lower, or on some other basis;

(c) What classes of expenditures are deferred instead of being charged directly to income account, and what procedure is followed in regard to the gradual amortization thereof; etc.

(6) A balance sheet showing a classified statement of the assets, liabilities and capital of the issuer at the latest practicable date prior to the filing of the registration statement, showing on what basis of valuation the several classes of assets are stated. If the balance sheet is not in accordance with the general books of the issuer, or with any previously published balance sheet of the issuer, as of the same date, information shall be given showing in what respects it differs from said books or such previously published balance sheet.

NOTE

While the basis of valuation of assets will be ascertainable from the statement of accounting methods, it seems desirable that the basis of valuation should be indicated on the face of the balance sheet so that the information will be as readily available to investors as possible.

No reference is made in this subdivision to contingent liabilities and obligations which may in effect constitute a liability which seriously affects the financial position. I have not found it possible to draw a specific provision which would meet all the possible situations satisfactorily, and I think it preferable to leave the point to be covered by the declaration that the balance sheet fairly presents the financial position, which declaration could not properly be given unless items of this kind were adequately disclosed in the balance sheet.

(7) A statement with respect to the income of the issuer for the latest fiscal year for which such statement shall be available and for the two preceding fiscal years, or, if the issuer has been in business for a lesser number of fiscal years, then for the longest practicable period during which the issuer has been in business; and, if the date of filing of the registration statement shall be more than six months after the close of the last fiscal year for which such statement shall be available, a statement of the income from such closing date to the latest practicable date.

Such statement with respect to the income of the issuer shall show the income fairly attributable to each fiscal period covered thereby. The following items shall be shown separately: operating income; non-operating income; interest charges; income taxes, and other fixed charges. Items of income or expense which are of an exceptional character and are not likely to recur shall, if they affect to a material extent the net income reported, be shown separately.

If the statement of income has not been prepared in accordance with the general books of accounts of the issuer, or with any previously published statement of income of the issuer for the same period or periods, information shall be given showing in what respects the statement of income differs from such books of accounts or such previously published statement of income.

NOTE

This subdivision and the succeeding one require, I think, to be amplified to cover the case in which the business to be carried on by the issuer was, during a part of the preceding three years, carried on by a predecessor organization or organizations. In such cases, statements of income and changes of surplus of the predecessor organization or organizations should be required.

(8) A statement showing the changes in the surplus of the issuer during the period covered by the statement of income required under subdivision (7).

(9) A declaration by the Treasurer or one of the principal accounting officers of the issuer, or by an independent public accountant or by independent public accountants that the balance sheet and the statement of income are, in his or their opinion, correctly prepared on the basis of a fair and consistent application of the methods of accounting regularly employed by the issuer in keeping its books, and fairly reflect its financial position as of the date of said balance sheet and its income for the respective periods covered by said statements of income, except as may be stated in said declaration; and a declaration similarly signed, dated not more than ten days before the date of the filing of the registration statement that, as of such date, the signer had no knowledge of any change since the date of said balance sheet, except in the ordinary and regular course of business, in the character of the assets or the financial condition of the issuer, which might adversely affect the securities proposed to be issued, except as may be stated in said declaration.

(10) Whenever the value of the security is dependent to a material extent upon the financial position or income of a corporation or corporations in which the issuer has a controlling interest, through stock ownership or otherwise, the registration statement shall include the same information regarding the assets, liabilities, capital and income of such

controlled corporation or corporations (either separately or collectively) as is required in respect of the issuer by this subsection, or in lieu of or in addition to such information in respect of the issuer, consolidated statements (containing like information) of the assets, liabilities, capital and income of the issuer and of any or all such controlled corporations as may be proper in the circumstances of the case.

NOTE

This provision is made flexible so as to meet all the varied conditions that are encountered, including the cases not only of controlled companies that are substantially wholly owned, but also of controlled companies in which there are substantial outside minority interests.

As I have already indicated, I think the Bill might well contain provisions for periodical accounting reports subsequent to the issue. I suggest the following:

1. Whenever, while an issue of securities to which this Act applies shall be outstanding, the issuer shall change the general principles of accounting employed by it or shall change in any material way the manner in which practical application is given to such principles, a full statement of the change shall be filed with the Commission within sixty days of the date on which such change becomes effective.

2. Any issuer of securities to which this Act applies shall, so long as the securities shall be outstanding, file annually with the Commission within ninety days from the close of its fiscal year statements in respect of its financial position at the close of such fiscal year and its income for the year, in such detail and form as the Commission shall prescribe, provided that the Commission may in its discretion extend the time for filing such statements in any case in which it shall be satisfied that it is not reasonably practicable for the issuer to file the required statements within the time prescribed by this Act; and provided, also, that the Commission shall not be empowered to require under this section any information which it would not be empowered to require

in respect of a new offering of securities under Section 5 of this Act.

The adoption of provisions such as I have suggested would, I believe, bring the requirements into accord with the best current practice, and all that would be necessary to meet the varied conditions that will arise would be to provide for the making of such detailed rules and regulations as might be necessary to give full effect to these provisions.

II

THE PROSPECTUS AND THE INVESTOR *

(1933)

THE Securities Act and such discussion of it as is contained in Professor Frankfurter's article in *Fortune* seem to me quite unrealistic. Professor Frankfurter's article, by the way, if regarded as a prospectus under the Act, could readily be shown to be characterized by misstatements and omissions such as would make the author of the prospectus liable to the full penalties of the Act.

The investor who actually relies on specific statements in a prospectus is a comparatively rare bird. Subscriptions to new securities from such sources would not supply a fraction of the needs of the country. The great bulk of the subscriptions come from persons who rely on more general considerations, such as their belief in the issuer or in the underwriter. The underlying assumptions of the Act, however, are that every investor relies on the specific statements made to him, and that if any material statement proves to be incorrect and he sustains loss, the doctrine of *post hoc, ergo propter hoc,* shall be applied and his loss shall be conclusively presumed to be due to the misstatement even though the contrary could readily be demonstrated.

It seems to me that we are embarking on an extremely dangerous course when we deliberately predicate legislation on assumptions which we know to be contrary to fact. However, in the present temper it is unlikely that this principle will be revised in any new legislation, though I am convinced that it will have to be revised sooner or later—either by new laws or by the courts. At present, we must content ourselves with seeking the closest approximation to

* From a letter to the late Colonel M. C. Rorty, October 28, 1933.

justice which is obtainable without complete abandonment of this underlying theory.

The form which this theory takes is that the Act is based on the principle of rescission, and it should not, therefore, be too much to hope that the Act can be amended so that liability will not extend beyond the point that can be reached by a reasonable application of the doctrine of rescission. Obviously, the doctrine of rescission cannot fairly be applied to sub-underwriters and dealers except to the extent of the securities distributed by them. Nor has it any conceivable application to experts. It seems to me that the most important amendment to the Act, therefore, is to limit the application of the principle of rescission so that: (a) only the issuer and any issuing house which has put its name on the prospectus shall be liable in respect of the full issue; (b) sub-underwriters shall be liable only in respect of securities sold by them, either directly or through agents; (c) make these persons liable only to those who purchase directly from them or to others who purchased within a limited time after the prospectus was issued; (d) limit the liability of directors and experts to damages shown to have been due to acts or default on their part.

III

THE SECURITIES ACT OF 1933: ITS PEDIGREE *

(1934)

In bringing about a recovery from the depression, the British nation, so far as I can judge, has not followed methods in all respects identical with those which we have adopted in an effort to achieve the same result. While the old economic order has received a rude shock there, it is not entirely discredited. They have not felt that a method of recovery was outmoded because it has been successfully employed before; they have not even reached the point of recognizing that only the young are wise.

Sir George may be interested and possibly gratified to know that in spite of the general discarding of precedents and experience, the exponents of the New Deal in their advocacy of the Securities Act have clung tenaciously to their argument that it was substantially the British law. This has seemed to me a strange thing—strange that they should regard that as a recommendation, stranger still that they should think its substantial inaccuracy could escape detection. I have been reminded of a song that was popular about the turn of the century, when the Anglo-maniac was a favorite butt for ridicule, which ran somewhat as follows:

> If they saw it on the Strand,
> They wouldn't understand,
> But it's English as you see it on Broadway.

Now, I am quite sure that if in the law courts which dominate the Strand, counsel should be so venturesome as to cite the Securities Act, or a decision thereunder, as relevant on the ground that that Act was substantially the English

---

* Excerpt from introductory remarks at a dinner given by the Council on Foreign Relations for Sir George Paish on April 4, 1934.

law, the court would fail to recognize the identity. I believe, also, that the English bar and the English legislature would be quick to disclaim paternity. I entertain the hope that the enlightenment on this point may reach in Oxford the distinguished professor who was so largely responsible for the Securities Act, and may modify the views which he entertained at the time when he discussed that law in *Fortune* last August.

IV

LETTER TO THE HON. JAMES M. LANDIS

(1933)

My dear Mr. Landis:

I read your address before the New York Society of Certified Public Accountants with great interest.

I was particularly pleased to note your recognition of the undoubted fact that accounts are expressions of opinion. This seems to me to be the only sound starting point for any regulations relating to accounts or accountants. I agree with you that, in the past, efforts have frequently been made to represent accounts as being statements of fact to a greater extent than they can possibly be, and no doubt accountants must assume a part of the responsibility. However, some accountants, including myself, have for years been very insistent on the opposite view, and I think that academic authorities have had more influence than accountants. Professor Ripley, with whom I joined issue on the question in 1926, Professor Rorem, and others all have some responsibility for the tendency to regard accounts as statements of fact. However, the main cause no doubt is what Newton D. Baker once in conversation with me referred to as "the human craving for certainty."

I do not know if you are familiar with the report which the Committee on Coöperation with Stock Exchanges of the American Institute of Accountants made to the New York Stock Exchange in September, 1932, but I enclose a copy, from which you will see that the limitations on the significance of accounts was the first point to be emphasized therein.

Incidentally, while comparisons with the British system are frequently made, to the disadvantage of our system here,

I think that so far as the disclosure of accounting information in prospectuses is concerned, the practice on this side has for many years been superior to the British practice. Undoubtedly the gravest abuse here has been in connection with the employment of high-pressure salesmen, some of whom made representations not warranted either by the prospectus or by the facts.

I have myself been asked to make an address upon the Act before an accounting body; and though I am so convinced of the desirability of Federal legislation on the subject that I am reluctant to appear in a position adverse to any provisions of the law, I confess that I have had a difficulty, which your address does not remove, in reconciling the provisions relating to the liability of experts with any of the general concepts of law I have had, or in convincing myself that we, as a firm, can afford to accept the possibility of ruinous liability involved. It does not seem to me that the liability can fairly be said to be founded in either the law of negligence or the doctrine of rescission.

I realize that it is the function of the Commission to administer the law rather than to change it, but I realize, also, that by wise regulation the Commission can do much to reduce the risks, and I should very much like at some time to have an opportunity to discuss with you the general principle.

Looking at the matter quite objectively, my own feeling is that the provision is not in the public interest. In discussions of the debt situation, one meets the argument that, after all, as long as the debt is internal, what is a liability to one person is an asset to another, so that the net effect of the existence of the debt cannot be seriously adverse to the country as a whole. This, however, overlooks the fact that a bad debt remains a liability of the debtor after it has ceased to be an asset of the creditor. In the same way, the seriousness of an indefinite liability to a responsible obligor is far greater than its value to the obligee or obligees.

I expect to be in Washington shortly and hope then to have the pleasure of meeting you and discussing some of these matters with you.

Yours very truly,

GEORGE O. MAY

November 2, 1933.

V

THE POSITION OF ACCOUNTANTS UNDER THE SECURITIES ACT *

(1933)

BEFORE I pass to the subject set for discussion tonight, may I say a word about a great citizen who belonged to your city and who was laid away this afternoon. During the War I was privileged to work closely with him and came to know him well. He was not an accountant, but his qualities were those which make men great in any sphere. He had that devotion to the interests he was called upon to represent without regard to self that marks the truly professional man. He had the insight and judgment which enabled him to penetrate to the heart of a problem, however beclouded it might be by sophistries or confused by side issues, and to recognize the worth of men of the most varied types, in the most diverse walks of life. He had the courage, force and character that enabled him to follow the course dictated by his convictions without being greatly elated by praise or affected by abuse. And above all, he had a great simplicity, a broad humanity and a generous sympathy which inspired loyalty and affection and enabled him to elicit from those associated with him the very best of which they were capable. We may differ in our ideas about future existence; but there is a kind of immortality which great men must enjoy through the influence which they exercise on the lives of those around them and they, in turn, on others. As one who has benefited from his influence, I am glad of the opportunity to pay here and today a tribute to Alexander Legge.

I have been asked to discuss tonight the Securities Act of

* An address before the Illinois Society of Certified Public Accountants at Chicago, Illinois, on December 6, 1933. Cf. *The Journal of Accountancy,* Vol. XLVII (January, 1934). The initial paragraph being extemporaneous does not appear in the prepared manuscript as heretofore published.

1933 from the point of view of the accountant. Few, if any, measures have ever been passed possessing so much importance to the profession, and it is not possible within the limits of a single address to consider all the questions of interest to us which it raises. I propose to limit my discussion mainly to two points: the liability arising under Section 11 of the Act, and the powers to define accounting terms and make regulations granted to the Federal Trade Commission by Section 19 of the Act. As I shall point out later, Section 19 may afford a means of mitigating to some extent the harshness of Section 11.

No one who has watched closely the developments of the past ten years can wonder that a securities law should be enacted, or even be greatly surprised at the form which it has taken. Nor would it occasion surprise if more recent revelations should prove to have made it difficult to bring about modifications in the Act, or perhaps have created a demand for still more drastic measures. But to say that legislation was natural, and perhaps inevitable, is not to approve all its provisions; and while the Act possesses many merits, the wisdom of some of its provisions (notably those provisions relating to the liability of underwriters, directors, officers and experts) is open to serious question in the minds of those genuinely interested in the protection of investors.

It is a commonplace that extreme measures defeat their own purpose; but people are seldom willing to give practical effect to this commonplace. Fifteen years ago, we adopted a constitutional amendment designed to put an end to admittedly great evils. When legislation enacted in pursuance of that amendment proved ineffective, we passed more severe measures; but as the law became more drastic, its enforcement became more and more impossible. Yesterday, we took the final step to reverse the well-intentioned but unwise action of fifteen years ago. We all realize, however, that it will take years to eradicate the evils which that unwise action brought into existence. Surely there is a lesson here for those who seek to regulate the issue of securities.

Many who originally supported the prohibition movement, including, as I particularly recall, a bishop of the church, finally became convinced that it should be repealed on the simple ground that it placed the distribution of liquor in the worst possible hands. In the same way, a too drastic securities law will place the distribution of securities in the worst possible hands.

I cannot believe that a law is just, or can long be maintained in effect, which deliberately contemplates the possibility that a purchaser may recover from a person from whom he has not bought, in respect of a statement which at the time of his purchase he had not read, contained in a document which he did not then know to exist, a sum which is not to be measured by injury resulting from falsity in such statement. Yet, under the Securities Act as it stands, once a material misstatement or omission is proved, it is no defense to show that the plaintiff had no knowledge of the statement in question or of the document in which it was contained, or that the fall in the value of the security which he has purchased is due, not to the misstatement or omission complained of, but to quite different causes, such as the natural progress of invention, or even fire or earthquake. The Securities Act not only abandons the old rule that the burden of proof is on the plaintiff, but the doctrine of contributory negligence and the seemingly sound theory that there should be some relation between the injury caused and the sum to be recovered.

It is frequently suggested that the Act follows closely the English law; but as one who has followed the development of the English law for nearly forty years I am bound to say that whether this statement be regarded as praise or censure, it is unfounded. None of the departures from ordinary legal principles to which I have referred finds its counterpart in the English law. The right of rescission is enforceable only against the issuer, and before the purchaser can recover from a director or other person concerned in the issue he must show that he relied on the prospectus, and then can recover only for injury due to the untrue statement which he proves.

Finally, as indicating the difference in temper of the English law, let me read a section which deals not with this specific question, but with the liability of directors and officers to the corporation for negligence or breach of trust:

If in any proceeding for negligence, default, breach of duty, or breach of trust against a person to whom this section applies it appears to the court hearing the case that that person is or may be liable in respect of the negligence, default, breach of duty or breach of trust, but that he has acted honestly and reasonably, and that, having regard to all the circumstances of the case, including those connected with his appointment, he ought fairly to be excused for the negligence, default, breach of duty or breach of trust, that court may relieve him, either wholly or partly, from his liability on such terms as the court may think fit.*

The answer of Congress to those who urged that the English law should not be followed because it was too severe and tended to check the flow of capital into industry, was that of the son of Solomon, who, refusing to listen to the elders, and following the advice of the young men, said: "My father hath chastised you with whips, but I will chastise you with scorpions." And you will remember that the answer was, "What portion have we in David? . . . to your tents, O Israel," and the biblical narrative concludes with the statement, "So Israel rebelled from the house of David unto this day." So, too, there is reason to fear that responsible people will refuse to accept the unfair liability imposed on them by Congress under this Act, and will continue to refuse until juster provisions are enacted. If they do so, their action can be regarded only as the course dictated by common prudence, and not as indicating factious opposition to the main purpose of the Act.

If we limit our consideration of the liability provisions of the Act to their effect on accountants, their punitive character becomes even more apparent. As between an innocent

* Companies Act, Sec. 372 (1).

but negligent vendor and an innocent but negligent purchaser, there may be some consideration of public policy in favor of requiring the vendor to return what he has received if his representations are proved to be false in fact although he believed them to be true. This consideration may be particularly applicable where the purchaser is a small investor who has neither the ability nor the resources for determining the truth which are at the command of the vendor. It is difficult to see, however, upon what principle of justice the accountant or other expert whose good faith is not challenged, but who is held to have failed to live up to the high standard of care required of him, can fairly be called upon to do more than make good the injury attributable to such failure for the benefit of a purchaser who perhaps did not even know of his existence at the time of the purchase, and took no pains whatever to investigate the security he purchased.

But even though we feel the provisions to be unjust, we cannot expect them to be modified merely because they are unacceptable to accountants. The hope of securing amendment lies in demonstrating that they are not in the interest of the general public, or of the investing public in particular; and this seems to me to be so clearly the case that there should not be any great difficulty in demonstrating it to open-minded people possessing some general familiarity with business. I believe anyone who will take the trouble to consider carefully the work of the accountant in connection with new issues, and the practical consequences of these new provisions, will be forced to the conclusion that in the public interest these provisions should be substantially modified.

The services of the accountant in connection with a new issue, are, broadly, to report upon statements relating to the financial position and operations of the issuer. The first important point to be noted is, that while the statements in question rest on a basis of fact, the facts in the case of any considerable business enterprise are both complex and incomplete, so that any report upon them is predominantly an expression of judgment and opinion. To illustrate—the most important single figure will usually be the profits for a particular year. Only the slightest consideration is necessary to bring realization of the fact that the transactions of the year are inextricably interrelated with those of earlier and subsequent years, and that how much profit is fairly attributable to a particular year is ultimately a matter of convention and judgment.

The function of the accountant, therefore, is to express an honest and informed judgment regarding the financial position and operating results of the issuer according to some acceptable standard of accounting conventions. It is not merely a fact-finding function.

We may now consider how this function is in practice discharged. While the work of accountants today involves the use of a large staff, it is obviously impracticable for the accountant even with a large staff to examine all the transactions of even a moderate-sized corporation. His procedure is, therefore, a varied one—in some cases, he will make a fairly complete independent check; in other cases, he will make tests; in still other cases, he must rely on the records of the corporation, satisfying himself that they are so kept and checked as to justify such reliance as a reasonable business procedure.

In considering, therefore, what degree of responsibility may wisely and rightfully be imposed on the accountant, one must start from the premises that: (a) his work is in part in the nature of confirmation of facts, and in part an expression of judgment; (b) his procedure is necessarily to a large extent one of testing—he cannot scrutinize every transaction; (c) his work is necessarily carried on largely through subordinates.

It is clear that the accountant may incur liability under the Act without being guilty of either moral culpability or recklessness, if a court holds that either: (a) facts within his knowledge were presented in such a way as to mislead; or (b) the tests which he made were not sufficiently extensive to justify him in forming a belief; or (c) he was not justified in forming a belief on the evidence which he examined without probing deeper. Furthermore, he will presumably be liable for any misstatement which may be attributable to the failure of his assistants to take steps which they should have taken, even though he instructed them to take such steps and believed, and had a right to believe, that they had done so.

Surely, if any liability is to be so founded, it should at least be restricted to the damage shown to have been caused by the default proved against him or his assistants.

It is unnecessary for me to spend much time in pointing out how far beyond such a standard of liability the Act goes. The point has already been fully discussed in the pamphlet entitled "Accountants and the Securities Act," which has been circulated to its members by the American Institute of Accountants, and in addresses to accounting bodies made by the Chief of the Securities Division of the Federal Trade Commission, the Honorable Baldwin B. Bane, on September 19, and on October 30, by Commissioner James M. Landis. The discussion of the question by the former concluded with the statement:

Thus both theoretically and practically there is no probability of one's liability exceeding the aggregate amount at which the securities were offered to the public.

Commissioner Landis, taking what he seemed to regard as a more hopeful view, said:

It should be observed that each person whose liability on the registration statement has been established is responsible in damages to any purchaser of the security, whether such person shall have purchased from him or from some other person. Theoretically this means that each person so liable can be held to a liability equivalent to that of the total offering price of the issue. Practically, of course, no such large liability exists. Several factors will operate to keep the liability within much smaller bounds. For one thing, the value of a carefully floated issue can hardly be assumed to reach zero. For another, every purchaser would hardly be likely to bring suit. Again, the issue of liability—generally, a complicated question of fact—would be retriable in every suit, and it beggars the imagination to assume that every jury faced with such an issue would come to the same conclusion. Furthermore, each person liable has a right of contribution against every other person liable, unless the one suing is guilty of fraud and the other is not. So that even eliminating the other practical factors that I have mentioned, it would be necessary for every other person liable on the registration statement to be insolvent, in order that one of them would be affixed with the large theoretical responsibility.

These being the views entertained by persons who sought to reassure us so far as they honestly could, it is quite unnecessary to consider what has been said by those who sought to excite our fears. The liability is obviously one that no prudent business man would be justified in assuming. And certainly accountants have no right to be guiding investors if they are not practical business men as well as technically qualified accountants.

Let me emphasize again that in order to be subjected to such a liability it is not necessary that the accountant should have been fraudulent, or even reckless or incompetent. He may be held liable merely because of an error of judgment regarding the extent of the examination which he ought to make, or through honest error or oversight on the part of a competent and ordinarily reliable subordinate. And if he is held liable in an important case, the cost to him may easily equal the savings of his whole professional career.

I believe that in the case of most accountants—certainly it is true in that of my own firm—the amount of fees received from work connected with new financing is a relatively small percentage of their total annual fees. Why should they jeopardize not only the earnings from their entire business, but their savings, in order to undertake work which brings in perhaps five or ten per cent of their total income?

Every reputable accountant should be perfectly willing to assume a reasonable liability in respect of injury which can be shown to be attributable to acts or default on his part, and no one would quarrel with the imposition of a liability of a punitive character in cases of fraud; but only the clearest and most urgent requirements of public policy could justify making accountants or other experts liable for damages which bear no relation either to the injuries they have caused or the compensation they have received. I am convinced that no such requirement exists—on the contrary, I believe that a wise regard for the public interest would rather limit the financial responsibility of professional men for errors of professional judgment. This, incidentally, is the policy embodied in the new legislation on the question of auditors in Germany,* under which the liability of the accountant cannot exceed a fixed sum unless fraud is shown.

It is not easy to see upon what theory of law the provision of the Act is based. Clearly, it is not founded in the ordinary law of negligence; nor can it be brought within the doctrine of rescission. It seems to me to be justifiable only on the theory that any issue of securities in connection with which a material misstatement is found to exist is a conspiracy, even though the misstatement is due to oversight or even honest error. There is nothing in the history of accounting in recent years to warrant such an attitude towards the profession or that provision which puts on the accountant the burden of proving his innocence whenever a disgruntled purchaser of securities or striker makes charges against him.

In my judgment, it is always wise to use restraint in imposing financial liabilities upon professional men for errors of professional judgment. Such errors, particularly where they become publicly known, result in serious injury to the professional reputation of the persons making them, and it is quite unnecessary to add a personal liability in order to impress the professional man with the necessity of care and thoroughness in forming his professional judgments. The effect of imposing a pecuniary liability out of all proportion to the compensation paid for the opinion will inevitably be

---

* Cf. *Handelsgesetzbuch* (Commercial Code), (1931).

that those best qualified to express opinions will refuse to assume the risks involved in doing so.

In the present instance, the risks are multiplied by the vagueness and uncertainties of the obligations imposed. The Act makes the accountant liable if the part of the registration statement for which he is responsible "contained an untrue statement of a material fact or omitted to state a material fact required to be stated therein or necessary to make the statements therein not misleading, . . ." and in providing that it shall be a valid defense that the accountant "had reasonable ground to believe and did believe, . . . that the statements therein were true and that there was no omission to state a material fact required to be stated therein or necessary to make the statements therein not misleading, . . ." it prescribes that the standard of reasonableness "shall be that required of a person occupying a fiduciary relationship."

What explanations are going to be necessary in order to comply with these requirements? Let me take a simple case. The insurance commissioners have on several occasions prescribed valuations for securities which were far in excess of current quoted prices therefor. If one were consulted by someone to whom one had a fiduciary relationship regarding a proposed investment in an insurance company, certainly he would not be content to explain that the securities were valued in accordance with the schedules of the Insurance Commissioners without pointing out that these valuations were substantially higher than those currently realizable on the market. Suppose, however, that in a balance sheet forming part of a registration statement securities were taken on the basis of the Commissioner's valuations—would it be sufficient to state that fact, or would the accountant be guilty of omission of a material fact if he failed to make any statement regarding the relation between such valuation and the quoted market prices? Again, many public utilities provide for depreciation on bases approved by state commissions, which many accountants regard as quite inadequate. Is the accountant safe if he states on what basis the depreciation provision has been made, without expressing his own convictions regarding the inadequacy of the provision?

In each of these cases it would seem that the accountant must be safe on the ground that he is entitled to rely on legal authority whether his own judgment coincides with the view of the authorities or not. In many instances, however, the authority for the practice followed will be accepted custom, rather than specific authorization from a governmental body; and what is to be the position when the accountant disagrees with the custom?

Here let me draw attention to a point which perhaps has escaped your attention—that the position of the accountant under the Act differs from that of any other expert. Others may "report" and be liable only for the truth of the statements contained in their report; the accountant is called upon to certify, and is liable for the truth of the statements certified, not merely for the truth of the statements contained in his certificate. Under a strict interpretation of the law, the accountant would seem to be liable if part of a statement covered by his certificate is held to be untrue or misleading, even though he, in his certificate, disclaimed responsibility for that particular part of the statement. It may be said that such an interpretation would be unreasonable; but it is certainly no more unreasonable than the explicit provision that his liability is not to be measured by the injury caused by his act or default. Further, it may be merely the reflection of the not infrequent view that an auditor should give no certificate whatever unless he can vouch for the complete truthfulness of the statement certified.

The fallacious view is quite widely held that the work of the accountant is purely a fact-finding function, and that when his work is completed he is in a position (if it has been properly performed) to make findings of definite and incontrovertible facts. The Special Committee on Coöperation with Stock Exchanges of the American Institute of Accountants, whose membership has included partners in several of the largest firms in the country, became convinced of the extreme importance of correcting this too common misapprehension, and in a report which it made to the New York Stock Exchange in September, 1932, it stressed this point as the first on which the Stock Exchange should concentrate in its effort to bring about more enlightened investment. It began its report with the following statements:

It [the Committee] believes that there are two major tasks to be accomplished—one is to educate the public in regard to the significance of accounts, their value and their unavoidable limitations, and the other is to make the accounts published by corporations more informative and authoritative.

The nature of a balance sheet or of an income account is quite generally misunderstood, even by writers on financial and accounting subjects. Professor William Z. Ripley has spoken of a balance sheet as an instantaneous photograph of the condition of a company on a given date. Such language is apt to prove doubly misleading to the average investor—first, because of the implication that the balance sheet is wholly photographic in nature, whereas it is largely historical; and, secondly, because of the suggestion that it is possible to achieve something approaching photographic accuracy in a balance sheet which, in fact, is necessarily the reflection of opinions subject to a (possibly wide) margin of error.

It then proceeded to discuss the problem in some detail; and in concluding the report and making certain recommendations, it offered this comment:

. . . But even when all has been done that can be done, the limitations on the significance of even the best of accounts must be recognized, and the shorter the period covered by them the more pronounced usually are these limitations. Accounts are essentially continuous historical records; and as is true of history in general, correct interpretations and sound forecasts for the future cannot be reached upon a hurried survey of temporary conditions, but only by longer retrospect and a careful distinction between permanent tendencies and transitory influences.

I was extremely glad to note that Commissioner Landis, in his address to which I have referred, recognized the point which I have been trying to emphasize, in the following paragraph:

Much also depends upon the method of expression, for what should appropriately be expressed as inferences or deductions from facts and hence as opinions, are too often expressed as facts themselves and hence for the purposes of legal liability, whether at common law or under the Act, become facts. It has been said, and very rightly in my humble opinion, that most of accounting is after all a matter of opinion. But though this may be true, I have still to see the case of a prospective investor being offered a balance sheet and having it carefully explained to him that this or that item is merely an opinion or deduction from a series of other opinions mixed in with a few acknowledged facts. Accounting, as distinguished from law, has generally been portrayed as an exact science, and its representations have been proffered to the unlearned as representations of fact and not of opinion. If it insists upon such fact representations, it is, of course, fair that it should be burdened with the responsibility attendant upon such a portrayal of its results.

I have read the entire paragraph because it seems to me to have a double importance. In the first place, it indicates an appreciation on the part of a member of the Commission of the point that accounts are not statements of fact; and such recognition is fundamental to the development of any sound regulations relating to accounts and accountants. In the second place, it emphasizes the danger which accountants run in putting forward as facts what are really expressions of opinion.

That the danger is not exaggerated by the Commissioner is apparent from a consideration of the Ultramares case. That case would apparently have been finally decided in favor of the accountants by the Court of Appeals of New York if the accountants concerned had not stated as a fact that the balance sheet which they certified was in accord with the books of the Company. Doubtless they thought this was a fact, and doubtless it was a fact in the sense in which they meant the language to be interpreted, that the balance sheet was in accord with the general books. But Chief Justice

Cardozo decided that a court might properly regard the language as implying an agreement between the balance sheet and the books as a whole, and there were books which contradicted the general books. Obviously, upon such an interpretation, whether a balance sheet agreed with the books must always be in reality a matter of opinion (if for no other reason because no accountant can be sure that he has seen all the books that exist), and obviously even if the statement were made as one of fact, no one was injured by it, for no one would lend a nickel on the faith of a statement that a balance sheet agrees with the books. Nevertheless, such is the mysterious nature of the law, this point was sufficient to result in an order for retrial.

In the last sentence which I quoted from Commissioner Landis, he seemed to imply, although he did not specifically say, that the portrayal of accounts as statements of fact had been made by accountants. I am not sure that this is so. Accountants may be subject to some blame for not having done so much as they might have done to resist the tendency of other people to regard accounts as exact statements of fact, but I think that they themselves have almost invariably put forth their reports as expressions of opinion. Both here and in England, the words "in our opinion" have for years been a standard phrase in accountants' certificates. As long ago as 1913, Dickinson, in his *Accounting Practice and Procedure,* commented on the phrase at length. His comment began with the statement: "Every balance sheet must be largely a matter of opinion," and ended with the sentence:

> So far from weakening the certificate, they [*i.e.,* the words "in our opinion"] may rather be considered as strengthening it, in that they imply that the signer has given his certificate, not with foolhardy assurance, but with a realization of the inherent impossibility of saying, absolutely, that one balance sheet is correct and any other incorrect.*

And while very little testimony was given on behalf of accountants before the committees which considered the Securi-

* Arthur Lowes Dickinson, *op. cit.,* pp. 236-37.

ties Act, the little which was given included this colloquy between the members of the Senate Committee on Banking and Currency and Colonel A. H. Carter, who was, I·believe, the only accounting witness:

Mr. Carter. I mean that that statement itself should have been the subject of an examination and audit by an independent accountant.

Senator Gore. Before filing?

Mr. Carter. Before filing.

Senator Gore. Is that patterned after the English system?

Mr. Carter. Yes, sir.

Senator Reynolds. Together with an opinion.

Mr. Carter. That is all they can give; that is all they can give. That is all anyone can give as to a balance sheet.

Senator Wagner. Well, basically, are not these facts that have got to be alleged rather than an opinion?

Mr. Carter. Under the terms of the bill it has to be given under oath. I do not see that anyone can certify under oath that a balance sheet giving many millions of dollars of assets is as a matter of fact correct. He can state his opinion based upon a thorough investigation.

But whatever they have been represented or supposed to be, accounts are not mere statements of fact, but represent the application to facts of judgment and accounting principles. Truth in accounts is not, therefore, a simple matter of correspondence between fact and statement—accounts are true if they result from the application to the relevant facts of honest judgment and reasonable accounting principles. The question that should really be put to the accountant is not whether the balance sheet is true, but whether it is fair —fair in the accounting principles on which it is based; fair in the way in which those principles are applied to the facts; and fair in the way in which the results are presented. These are matters of opinion.

The Act stresses the obligation to state every material fact necessary to make the registration statement not misleading, and among the material facts in relation to any accounts none is more material than the fact that the accounts themselves and the certificate required from the accountant in relation to those accounts are, and must of necessity be, expressions of opinion. Indeed, the Act, in speaking of truth in accounts without some such qualification is itself apt to mislead investors, in the same way as was Professor Ripley's reference to a balance sheet as an "instantaneous photograph."

At this point, I should like to suggest that Section 19 can be used to clarify and modify the provisions of Section 11. Clearly, only action by Congress can remove the fundamental and, as I feel, insuperable obstacles to the free acceptance by accountants of appointments under the Act; obstacles which have been created by the imposition of a liability bearing no relation either to the injury caused by the accountant or the compensation received by him. If, however, this major difficulty could be removed, the remaining problem could probably be solved by judicious use by the Commission of the powers conferred on it under Section 19.

Under that Section, the Commission has power for the purposes of the Act to define accounting terms used therein and to prescribe the method to be followed in the preparation of accounts. It seems to me highly desirable that under the provisions of this section the Commission should define what constitutes a "true" balance sheet or a "true" profit and loss statement. Such definition would, I think, necessarily follow the general line that I have indicated. Accounts would be held to be true if they represented the application of honest judgment and acceptable methods of accounting to all the relevant facts which were known or ought to have been known to the person preparing or certifying them at the time of preparation or certification. I suggest, also, that the Commission should supplement the definition by indicating that accounting principles would be deemed acceptable which are either (a) prescribed or approved by governmental authorities to which the issuer is subject; or (b) sanctioned by common practice, it being recognized that in many instances alternative methods are sanctioned; or

(c) are inherently fair and appropriate. It should be emphasized that principles will not be regarded as reasonable unless they are mutually consistent and are consistently applied.

The point may be urged that what must be shown in order to avert liability is not that the balance sheet or profit and loss account as a whole is true, but that the statements of fact contained in it are true. Balance sheets and profit and loss accounts are not, of course, couched in the form of statements of fact; but a description with an amount set opposite it is fairly capable of being judged as a statement of fact. The common heading: "Land, buildings, plant and machinery, at cost," with a figure set opposite, seems at first blush to be a simple statement of fact; but in practice, what is fairly to be regarded as cost will often be a difficult matter of opinion, and always the question remains whether any, and if so, what amplification of the heading is necessary to make the statement not misleading.

You may think that I am being technical; but may I remind you that our own accumulated savings may be at stake in this matter, and also that the highest court of Massachusetts held not many years ago that a statement was false, and that its falsity gave rise to liability on the part of those signing it, on the sole ground that a reserve for depreciation had been shown under the heading "Reserves" on one side of the balance sheet instead of being deducted from the assets on the other. It was only after this decision that the law of Massachusetts was amended by the insertion of this proviso: ". . . provided, that if a report of condition as a whole states the condition of the corporation with substantial accuracy, in accordance with usual methods of keeping accounts, it shall not be deemed to be false."

I am convinced that to make the Act practicable in its working it is essential that some general ruling, of the tenor I have suggested, as to what constitutes truth in accounts shall be put forward by the Commission. As I have indicated, such a statement would serve the double purpose: first, of tending to prevent the investing public from attaching undue significance to accounts; and, secondly, of preventing accountants from being harassed or penalized through unduly technical interpretations of the provisions of the law.

I would not have you think that in this discussion I have exhausted the points in the Act which are of interest and importance to the profession. I should have liked to discuss at length the provision by which the burden of proof is thrown upon the defendant; the opportunities that the Act offers to blackmailers; the absence of any provision by which those unwarrantably attacked can recover the costs of their defense; and other features which seem to me to require amendment if a just balance is to be struck.

In conclusion, I desire to say that I am in full sympathy with the general purposes of the Act, and that the criticisms which I have offered of some of its provisions are not merely inspired by a narrow self-interest, but rest upon the profound conviction which I expressed at the beginning of this address, that unduly drastic measures defeat their own purpose and are not in the ultimate interest of those whom it is sought to protect. I should be extremely sorry if the effect of the Securities Act should be to place the distribution of securities and all the work attendant on such distribution in the least responsible hands.

I think, also, that in any discussion of the Act, we as accountants owe a duty to small investors to point out that the ordinary vicissitudes of business make commercial securities necessarily hazardous and unsuitable for the investment of small savings, and that even if a securities act diminishes the hazards in some respects, it cannot change their essential character. A realistic view would recognize the necessity for some governmentally fostered system for the safe investment of small savings; a broad market, subject to requirements for frank disclosure with penalties not unduly drastic attaching thereto, for what may be termed "business investments"; and some medium, entirely divorced from the idea of investment, for the gratification of the seemingly ineradicable instinct for gambling.

VI

THE OPPOSITION TO ANY AMENDMENT OF THE SECURITIES ACT *

(1934)

It is, surely, as important that legislation should be based on adequate and reliable information as that investment should be so based; and those who undertake to present information in support of legislation are chargeable with a fiduciary standard of care as justly as those who present information in order to sell securities. A survey of articles in support of the Securities Act and against any change therein reveals more than one which fails to live up to this standard—indeed, one might say that if such articles were prospectuses coming within the provisions of the Act, many of the authors would incur serious liabilities. No doubt all these authors are perfectly honest in their purpose (though this is a more charitable view than they appear to take of those who are opposed to them), and the question that I raise is, whether their articles are free from misstatements or omissions of material facts which by the exercise of a fiduciary standard of care they could have avoided.

I distinguish between those parts of such articles as are frankly argumentative and those which purport to be statements of fact. Partial statements in argument indicate only that the writer is an advocate and not a disinterested witness.

In discussing the provision which relieves the purchaser from proving reliance on the prospectus, it is not unreasonable to argue that the purchaser relies indirectly, if not directly, on the prospectus or registration statement if his purchase takes place shortly after the issue is made. But surely it is a material fact that the Act will indulge the same

* A letter to the New York *Times* (January 28, 1934).

85

presumption even though the transaction takes place long afterwards when the presumption has become wholly unreasonable. Again, in discussing the provision of the Act which permits recovery of the purchase price of the security and absolves the plaintiff from the burden of distinguishing between injury due to material misstatement and injury due to quite unrelated causes, it is true to say that the burden of separation would often be difficult for the plaintiff to sustain. But here again it would seem to be a material fact that under the Act the defendant's liability remains even if he is willing to assume the burden and is able to prove conclusively that the injury sustained had nothing whatever to do with the material misstatement complained of. However, incomplete statements on such points merely indicate how difficult it is for a partisan to avoid omissions of material facts which tell against the cause in which he wholeheartedly believes.

The points with which I am principally concerned are those which relate to the English Companies Act. No argument in favor of the Securities Act has been more stressed, or probably carried more weight, than the argument that the Act is substantially the English Companies Act modified to suit American conditions. To the impartial student the differences between the two Acts must, I believe, seem more significant than the points of resemblance; and when those opposed to any revision of the Securities Act talk about differences in conditions which justify its greater harshness, they seldom mention the very material difference in conditions that in England the successful defendant can recover compensatory costs and, where necessary, obtain security therefor, before the suit against him is proceeded with. While recommending innovations alleged to be based on English practice, and imposing burdens and liabilities hitherto unknown to the law of any country, the framers of the Act might well have introduced this measure of protection.

Most of all do the two laws differ in spirit. The difference in spirit is implicitly admitted in an article which was read into the Congressional Record of January 12 in the statement, "In substance, the Securities Act *is* the English Companies Act, modified to come within the constitutional power of the federal legislature to regulate interstate commerce, and to recognize the fact that in England, except for a very unusual Hatry or Kylsant, the distribution of securities is a decorous, traditional business, offering its wares only to institutions and wary family solicitors, while in the United States it has been a high-pressure racket that jangled every housewife's doorbell." Is this really so?

The limitations on the federal legislative power are no doubt sufficient to account for some of the differences between the two laws, but perhaps the most striking instance of the kind is that the English law does, and the American law does not, attempt to deal with the evil of *"jangling the housewife's doorbell."* Section 356 of the Companies Act of 1929, which begins: *"It shall not be lawful for any person to go from house to house offering shares for subscription or purchase"* completely negatives any suggestion that the English law was designed to meet a situation in which securities were bought only by institutions and family solicitors—a suggestion, incidentally, which no one who had read the Greene or the Macmillan report, or even had been present in an average English household when the morning mail arrived, would have dreamed of putting forward. The whole argument of the writer quoted and of others who have advanced the same contentions rests upon a statement as fact which a mere perusal of the English Act would have proved to be incorrect. In England, as here, the major evil has been this "jangling of the housewife's doorbell"—not the inadequate or misleading prospectus.

Indeed, it is the undue concentration on the prospectus, and the fact that Congress whether through inability or by design did not deal with the evil of high-pressure salesmanship or make any provision for publicity in respect of the affairs of the issuer subsequent to the issue, that form the broadest ground for criticism of the existing law. Of course, if provision had been made for subsequent publicity, it would have been impossible to maintain the legal fiction that the purchaser of a security relies on the prospectus even though he buys long after the prospectus has ceased to have any real bearing on the current value of the security; and this fiction is an essential part of the scheme whereby the liability of those concerned in an issue is continued for ten full years.

Among the principal provisions of the Securities Act which are criticized are those which deal with the burden of proof; those which permit rescission on account of misstatement or omission in the registration statement in cases in which the assumption that the purchaser relied either directly or indirectly on the prospectus or registration statement is obviously contrary to fact, and also in cases in which his loss is due to circumstances in no way related to any such misstatement or omission; and those provisions which make experts and others liable for sums entirely out of all proportion to any injury caused by acts or omissions on their part. None of these provisions can be justified either by English precedents or by any difference in conditions between England and the United States.

One of the most noteworthy differences between conditions in the two countries is that the strike action which disfigures our system is comparatively rare in England. This is due to a variety of causes, of which the fact already mentioned that in England a successful litigant recovers compensatory costs from the unsuccessful party is one. To protect honest issuers so far as practicable against such suits is as much a part of the problem of just legislation as is the protection of the investor against the dishonest or negligent issuer. But the framers of the Securities Act seem to have ignored this phase of the problem. The inordinate expansion of the content of the registration statement, any material misstatement in which gives rise to a cause of action; the vagueness of some of the vitally important provisions; the conferring of concurrent jurisdiction on federal and state courts; the absence of any provision for the recovery of compensatory costs by the successful defendant; the creation of conclusive presumptions in favor of the purchaser, which will often be contrary to demonstrable fact; and the imposition of liabilities bearing no relation to injury caused, combine to constitute an invitation to those who bring suits in the hope of being bought off, which no one who is invited to assume responsibilities under the Act can afford to ignore.

The appeal to British experience inevitably includes references to Hatry and Lord Kylsant, but it is seldom explained that neither was charged under the Companies Act. The writer to whom I have referred speaks of the interpretation of the British Act "in the celebrated Lord Kylsant case." The facts are that Hatry pleaded guilty to forgery and conspiracy to defraud, and the charges against Lord Kylsant were brought under the Larceny Act of 1861, which antedated not only all the laws for the protection of investors, but even the first effective general limited liability company law—that of 1862. The Royal Mail Company was not formed under the Companies Act. In the interests of historical accuracy it may be added that the basis of Lord Kylsant's conviction is incorrectly stated in the same article.

It is interesting to note that an article (anonymous) appeared in the London *Economist* of January 6, much of the argument in which is identical with that of the article read into the Congressional Record. Needless to say, however, it did not contain the incorrect statements regarding things English to which I have drawn attention.

Now, these are errors and omissions which, it would seem, could have been avoided by a fiduciary—or even a reasonable —standard of care, and they are made by experts in dealing with a relatively simple matter. Is it unreasonable, then, that other experts, conscious that they might unwittingly be betrayed into error in dealing with the far more complex affairs of large corporations, should be reluctant to accept the liabilities, bearing no relation to any injury attributable to their errors, which the Act would impose upon them? The contention sometimes advanced that such reluctance is inspired by unworthy motives, or is part of a conspiracy, has a familiar, unconvincing ring.

Are we likely in the long run to do better by continuing the extreme measure enacted under great provocation and even more certain to produce hardship and injustice than to accomplish its beneficent purposes, than by limiting the law in the first instance to provisions which are clearly just and endeavoring to cope with further problems which arise in ways that will be consonant with justice? The answers to this question will differ according to the views taken of the Act. Those who see in it a medium for the punishment of bankers, or a step towards the goal of financing industry by Government, will answer "Yes." Those who regard the purpose of the Act as purely remedial and constructive will be bound to answer "No."

Amendment of the Act is opposed by some on the ground that to admit publicly any defect in a part of the Administration's program would invite attack on the whole of it. This attitude is strangely at variance with that of the President himself in the announcement that he was going to try new measures and would be ready to retrace his steps or change his course whenever he might be convinced that he had gone too far or was heading in the wrong direction. It is to be hoped that this more courageous policy will prevail, and that modifications of the Securities Act may be effected which, without weakening of the provisions relating to fraud or wilful misstatement, will afford some protection against blackmail and will at least limit the liability for honest error to the damage fairly attributable thereto.

VII

TESTIMONY ON THE NATIONAL SECURITIES
EXCHANGE BILL *

(1934)

Mr. May. I do not wish to deal with the strictly stock-exchange regulation features of the Bill. That is outside my province. I wish to limit myself to a subsidiary but still important part of the Bill, the provisions regarding accounts and reports. That is principally Sections 12, 17 and 18 (b). Practically my whole point of view is based on the fact that accounts are necessarily the result of the application of accounting conventions and judgments to facts and are not pure statements of fact, and I think any sound legislation on these points must give more weight to those considerations.

The Chairman. Do you favor the idea of providing for a uniform system of accounting?

Mr. May. I do not, Senator, as I will come to later. Not at the present time, certainly.

. . . .

The point that I wanted to bring home to the Committee, or emphasize to the Committee, is that accounts for a short period, while they are useful to people who deal in securities, may easily be given an exaggerated importance and thereby result in more harm than good to the small man, with whom I imagine you are particularly concerned.

My feeling on this question, I think, must be very much that which the Committee feels in regard to the larger subject. You want to do everything that you can to make buying and selling securities, particularly by the small man, safer and surrounded with more information. But you must realize that all you can do will not reduce the risks that he

* "Stock Exchange Practices," *Hearings, Senate Committee on Banking and Currency,* 73rd Congress, Part 15, pp. 7175-83.

is bound to run very greatly, and there is always the danger that by legislating you create a feeling of confidence in the securities that are offered which legislation cannot possibly impart to them.

Now, that is the thought that is in my mind. I attach great importance to accounts, but I think there is always a danger that people will attach too much importance to them, and I think undoubtedly a large part of the stock markets of 1929, the outrageous prices that were reached then, was attributable to the basing of values on large earnings for short periods of time, which were not representative of the permanent earning capacity of the business. Whilst I think, therefore, that you should do what you can to give investors ample information, you should not do it in a way that can possibly encourage them to attach more importance to accounts than they properly deserve.

The specific suggestions that grow out of that, first of all, are in Section 12, which provides for audited quarterly statements. Personally I have never favored the suggestion that has been made that the Stock Exchange should uniformly require quarterly statements. In a great many cases they are helpful. In some cases they are more apt to be misleading than helpful. That is particularly true in the case of companies where inventories play a very large part in a determination of their results. The difference in the inventory valuation at the beginning or the end of a quarter may make all the difference between a profit and a loss. That is true, for instance, of packing houses and leather companies and the like.

So that I would suggest that a provision should be left in the bill so that the regulating body could dispense with the quarterly statements in any case where they thought that the publication would not be in the public interest.

Senator Townsend. Would you suggest semi-annual statements or yearly statements?

Mr. May. Personally, I was going to suggest the second point, Senator; if I may go on—I would strongly oppose audited quarterly statements, although it may seem to be against my interest as an accountant to take that position. But my opposition is not because of the expense, although that would be considerable. It is not because it would delay the publication of the quarterly statements—and if they are to be published at all they ought to be published promptly. It is because of the thing that I have just been emphasizing, that if you certify them people will think that they are something absolute and accurate, that they can rely on implicitly; whereas, being for a short period, they must necessarily be arbitrary and estimates.

Therefore, my suggestions on that would be to eliminate the provisions for quarterly audits and to provide a power in the regulating body to dispense with quarterly statements, particularly in any case in which they might think it was expedient.

Now, I think myself, as far as audits are concerned, that an audited statement once a year ought to be sufficient. But there is one very practical consideration which I would like to bring to your attention. I think the Committee has an opportunity to do a very useful thing by a very simple measure, quite apart from the general purposes of the Bill.

If the amount of auditing required were expanded as this Bill would necessitate, it would tax the resources of the accounting profession. The great difficulty of the present position is that nearly all companies end their year at December 31, and if the amount of work to be done at December 31 were so enormously increased as this Bill would increase it, then I do not think it would be within the capacity of the accounting profession, by any reasonable expansion, to take care of that work within a reasonable period after the end of the year.

And to meet that situation, I would like to suggest that there should be a discretionary power so that not all auditing statements would have to be at the end of the calendar year. I suppose convenience for tax purposes and so on has led a lot of companies that used to close their year at other periods to turn to the calendar year. A few still stick to some other period. The large packing houses close their accounts at the end of October. Well, September and October would be a much more natural time for the automobile companies and the tire companies to close than December 31. The railroads all used to close at June 30. Now they have all shifted to December 31; June 30 is a much more natural time.

I would like to see introduced into the Bill a provision which would help to distribute the work of auditing over the year. I think it would enormously increase the value of the audit to the investor. It would increase the efficiency of the audit. It would reduce the cost, and it would be infinitely more convenient to all the regulating bodies and statistical people who have to study audited accounts when they come in, and under present conditions get them all in a bunch at the end of the first two or three months of the calendar year.

That is a very small and noncontentious suggestion, which I think would have very great practical consequences for good.

Senator Kean. Would not it be just as well to have them all come in on the first of July as June 30?

Mr. May. If you could get them distributed. Of course, the ideal thing would be to have a quarter on the 31st of March, a quarter on the 30th of June, but you never could get that. But I think if you left some flexible provision in so that the regulating body could work it out as might seem to the general interest, that would be a very helpful measure which would have a general advantage quite apart from the provisions of this particular Bill.

Mr. Saperstein. As the Section now stands, Mr. May, there is no date fixed for the filing of those statements, and that matter is left to the discretion of the Commission.

Mr. May. I understood that it was fixed as far as quarterly audited statements were concerned.

Mr. Saperstein. It does not indicate upon what day. It

says simply that they shall file with the Exchange or the Commission in accordance with rules and regulations to be prescribed by the Commission and in such form and in such degree as the Commission may by rules and regulations prescribe in the public interest. That more or less leaves it for the Commission to indicate upon what dates these shall be filed, does it not?

Mr. May. Of course, if you require quarterly statements subject to the reservation that I have suggested before, and provided that once in each year, under regulations of the Commission, quarterly statements should be audited, that would satisfy us. I want only to suggest the idea. The exact form you take is a matter that is a simple matter of draftsmanship. That is the point I had on Section 12.

My point on Section 17 is on exactly the same ground. Quarterly statements, particularly, are very largely matters of judgment. If the investor is to get the benefit of that at all, he should get the reports promptly; and, that being so, I think it is not right or wise to impose a penalty for errors, either of judgment or of fact, in statements prepared under those conditions.

I would like to see the provisions of Section 17 limited to misrepresentation in statements. I think, as a broad question of public policy, it is not wise to impose liabilities on the basis of errors of judgment or of fact, where the facts are not definitely known and where judgment necessarily has to be exercised in order to reach a conclusion. That is the suggestion that I have on Section 17.

The Chairman. Most of these corporations make at least annual reports for their own benefit, do they not?

Mr. May. There should be an annual report, of course, sir. But I think, as a matter of fact, if I am not going too far afield, that a quarterly statement really is a part of what I may call the "paraphernalia of speculation" rather than the machinery of investment. It is a very striking thing. I do not think that there is any doubt that in Europe there are relatively more investors in securities and fewer speculators.

The speculators do their speculating on the race track, and they have lotteries to a greater extent. It is a very significant thing that statements more frequent than annual are practically unknown in Europe.

When this question came up I cabled to my associates in London on this question and asked them how far quarterly statements were known in London. They said they did not know of any company that ever published a quarterly statement. One or two published half-yearly statements, but the great majority published them only annually.

I cabled to my associates on the continent of Europe and they said, "Neither we nor any of our friends whom we have consulted know of any corporations on the continent that publish statements more often than annually."

I do not think that is a mere coincidence. I think, as a matter of fact, a quarterly statement serves a useful purpose to the intelligent investors, and it is useful to the person who is stirring up speculation. I think, particularly, if you had audited quarterly statements you would be imposing a very heavy financial burden. The cost would be quite considerable. It would be practically on the investors in corporations for the benefit of speculators in securities, if it benefited anybody at all—which I do not imagine is quite the line that you are endeavoring to follow.

. . . .

Mr. Saperstein. It was suggested by the previous witness that one of the dangers inherent in Section 12 was that the information contained in these statements might be appropriated by competitors in this country or in foreign countries. Is there anything in your experience that would lend color to that suggestion?

Mr. May. Of course there is a certain weight in that always, but I think, generally speaking, that a little too much weight is attached to that. That has been a ground of opposition in England to the publication of *any* results. I think business men are naturally secretive. Of course the point has merit. I do not think you should require information in too great detail. I would not attach very great importance to it, and I do think that when a corporation tries to get the benefit of greater liquidity for its securities by creating a market for them, it has got to pay some price for it; and reasonable publicity is part of the price.

The Chairman. What are your objections to a uniform system of accounting?

Mr. May. That is a subject that I have given a great deal of thought to. The fact of the matter is that accounting, especially industrial accounting, is essentially a matter of judgment, and you cannot put judgment in strait-jackets.

In the second place, uniformity, if I may say so, is illusory; it does not exist. Take the railroads and regulated corporations generally, and you will see a manual an inch thick, containing detailed specifications as to where everything from a toothpick to a locomotive shall be charged; but then you will find that the large maintenance accounts and the large loss and damage accounts, and so on, are distributed over the year or more than a year on the basis of a budget estimate, and they do not represent actual expenditures at all. So that you do not get the uniformity and you do not get the detailed accuracy that you think you do.

Take a large matter like depreciation. The variation in practice under a uniform classification is notoriously wide. The only safe thing is this: You have got to rely on judgment, and judgment ought to be attended by responsibility for the consequences that ensue. If you have uniform accounting it has got to be prescribed by somebody on the basis of general principles, and without any knowledge of the specific cases to which it will be applied. Rules are laid down by people who have no responsibility for the consequences that ensue, either legal or moral. That is one of my great objections to it. My other objection is that uniformity means a uniformly low standard. That is necessarily so. You cannot compel anybody to be conservative. Laws can lay down only minimum standards. It requires recognition of moral and ethical responsibilities to get anything higher than that; and I have no doubt in the world that the result of the regulation of railroads and public utilities has been to make their accounting less conservative than that of business corporations generally. I think any accountant who has studied the subject would agree with that view. Certainly that is true in my own experience with railroad accounts and business corporations which I audit. I think it is bound to be so. You would get a superficial uniformity which is not real. People are misled; the general public are misled into thinking that accounts are uniform and that the accounts of different companies are in fact strictly comparable when, as a matter of fact, they are not.

The Chairman. I would like to have you illustrate that. I can get your general view, but if you will illustrate it, it will make it a little clearer. I do not think I quite understand it unless you can illustrate it.

Mr. May. When I first started in the practice of accounting in New York, nearly 40 years ago, nearly all the railroads, when they laid down heavier rails in the place of lighter ones, charged the whole cost of the rails into operating expenses. Now they are required to show the excess weight of the old rails over the previous rails in capital. That is theoretically defensible, but it is practically unwise, in my judgment. All the way through the distinction of what shall be charged to capital and what shall be charged to expenses, which is the fundamental question of all accounting, the whole tendency of regulated accounting has been to throw things into capital instead of throwing them into expenses.

Senator Kean. Would you not think that charging the difference between a light rail and a heavy rail to capital, since the rates of the railroads are based on their capital, is against the public interest?

Mr. May. You touch the point. In the case of regulating bodies, of course, it ties into the whole question of regulation, and I agree with you, Senator, that it is an indispensable adjunct of the system of regulation, but nevertheless that particular effect of it I think is unfortunate, even if it is inevitable. When you get into general business you do not have the same considerations of rates based on capital structure, and I think only the unfortunate consequences would persist and the benefits would not be derived. That is my view of it. I have given the subject a great many years of thought.

Senator Kean. In other words, the piling up of capital in public utilities and in the railroads makes the capital so high that they can go to the commissions and demand higher rates than they otherwise would be able to charge?

Mr. May. That is one phase of it, Senator. But of course the elements on which the rates are based are: (1) return on capital, and (2) the actual expenses incurred. At the same time it increases the amount they get by way of return on capital, it decreases the amount they get as operating expenses.

I think it is getting rather far afield, but I would be glad to pursue it, if it would be of interest.

Senator Kean. I think it would be interesting.

The Chairman. Very well.

Mr. May. The system of regulation has inevitably tended to bring about that result, coupled with the theory of valuation which has practically prevailed in the Supreme Court decisions. The position has been like this. When a public utility or a railroad, or whatever it might be, put in its claim for its rate base, it added a whole lot of expenses like overhead expenses, which in ordinary practice are charged off into expenses, and it took off only what was called "observed depreciation." Now, regulating bodies were in the position of being forced to accept that by the Supreme Court decisions; if they at the same time allowed these companies to charge the same kind of expense into operating expenses and to charge off larger depreciation, they would be making the public pay twice, and therefore, as they could not prevent them from going into capital, because of the Supreme

Court's decisions, they said, "All right, you must take it out of expenses"—which was the only alternative left to them, and the result has been, as I say quite confidently, that the accounting of public utilities and regulated corporations generally is less conservative than that of business corporations; and it is because I am not convinced of the benefit of regulation. Uniform accounting would bring everybody down to the standard of the lowest, which is the standard which can be logically established to be the minimum—the fear of that is why I am opposed to uniform accounting. Of course it would make things much simpler for us.

Senator Kean. If they charge it off in operating expenses, that is one charge-off for that year.˙ When they put it into capital account it goes on forever?

Mr. May. That is true.

Senator Kean. Therefore it is a continual charge against the public?

Mr. May. That is true.

The Chairman. Are you discussing Section 18?

Mr. May. That is the section that gives the power to prescribe uniform accounting. That is what I was coming to next.

I think those are the points that I wished to deal with, and I wanted to come down rather than to make a prepared statement, because this is a subject that is much better developed by questions, and I thought if there were any questions that you wished to ask I would like to answer them, because my only object is to be helpful. I am not here in the interest of anybody. So far as the accounting profession is concerned, your Bill would apparently create a lot of additional work, so I would not be popular in the profession if I came down here and opposed it too strongly, perhaps. But I have tried to look at the public interest.

Mr. Saperstein. Is it your suggestion that Section 18 (b) be eliminated altogether?

Mr. May. I think so. As I understand, the Department of Commerce is at this time, through a very able committee, studying the whole question of uniform accounting. It is a very large subject, and it does not seem to me to be directly relevant to the main purpose of this Bill. I think it is a subject that would be better studied on its merits and dealt with, if at all, in that way, on the basis of the results of a study such as the Department of Commerce is now making. That would be my view of the matter.

The Chairman. If we had a uniform system, it would be much simpler for the accountants, would it not?

Mr. May. Yes; but the real value of accounting is a matter of informed and independent objective judgment. If you are going to just follow mechanical rules you can get into very, very disastrous situations by doing so. I think anybody who has had any practical experience will say that.

Senator Kean. It would be physically impossible, almost, would it not, with many of these large companies dealing all over the world, to make inventories every quarter?

Mr. May. In the case of some of these companies it would be absolutely prohibitive.

Senator Kean. For instance, take the Bell Telephone Co. I think you audit them, do you not?

Mr. May. No; we do not.

Senator Kean. Do you audit the Steel Company?

Mr. May. That is not so difficult. We happen to be discussing the question with the Standard Oil Co. of New Jersey just now in regard to what an annual audit might cost.

Senator Kean. What kind of a figure did you give them, if I may ask?

Mr. May. I told them it was so enormous that we could not make any commitment. But I should say an annual audit of the Standard Oil of New Jersey would probably cost, with all its several hundred companies included, certainly a quarter of a million, possibly more.

Senator Kean. A quarter of a million each time?

Mr. May. Yes. That would be doing it the quickest possible way. It would be doing it at the end of the year and not working on it all the way through. I should say the cost of quarterly audits would probably be at least three times that of an annual audit. I think $750,000 for the Standard of New Jersey would be a very low figure for quarterly audits. The consequence would be that of course the interval required after the statements are prepared by the company, for the completion of the audit, would make the quarterly statements almost out of date. They would be merely able to get the June statement out unaudited by the time they could get the March statement out audited.

Senator Kean. That is one of the things I wanted to get at, that with many of these companies a public audit would probably not be finished much before the next audit began.

Mr. May. There is an old Latin statement which applies very well to quarterly statements. A quarterly statement that comes out promptly is valuable, but if they come out too late—

The Chairman. If it is convenient to you, the Committee would be very glad to have you submit a memorandum on this subject.

Mr. May. I would be very glad to do so, Mr. Chairman.

The Chairman. We will put it into the record.

VIII

THE NATIONAL SECURITIES EXCHANGE BILL *

SENATE 2693

MEMORANDUM SUBMITTED TO THE SENATE COMMITTEE
ON BANKING AND CURRENCY

(1934)

In response to the request of the Chairman made at the conclusion of my testimony before the Committee on March 8, I submit a memorandum regarding the suggestions which I then respectfully offered. These suggestions were briefly as follows:

SECTION 12:

(a) Insert a provision enabling the regulating body to dispense with the filing of quarterly statements in any case or class of cases in which it might deem such statement likely to be misleading or the filing thereof undesirable for any other cause.

(b) Limit the requirement of certified statements to the filing annually of one balance sheet and one statement of income and profit and loss for a full year.

(c) Make the provision regarding certified statements sufficiently flexible to permit of the distribution of the auditing required so far as possible over the year in such way as may be most desirable in the general interest.

SECTION 17:

Limit the liability under this section to cases in which the issue of false or misleading statements is shown to have been wilful.

NOTE: The provisions in this section regarding the measure of damage seem open to criticism, but if the liability is limited to wilful misstatement this point becomes of minor importance.

* Cf. Testimony, *Hearings*, "Stock Exchange Practices," *op. cit.*, pp. 7183-88.

SECTION 18:

Strike out Section 18 (b), or amend it so as to limit the authority of the Commission to the power to prescribe what information shall be set forth in balance sheets and earnings statements.

Of these suggestions, that looking to the distribution of audit work more evenly over the year is put forward because on the basis of a long and wide experience I am convinced that the adoption of this simple proposal would add very greatly to the efficiency of audits and enable them to be conducted at lower cost and prove generally convenient to all those who are concerned with the study of audited accounts after they have been issued. All the other suggestions are inspired by a profound conviction of the importance of recognizing in any such legislation that accounts are not statements of fact, but necessarily represent the results of the application of accounting principles and judgment to facts.

The misconceptions on this point have been so widespread that it may be worth while to present an illustration which will emphasize the point I have made. I take one from the field of motion pictures, which has now become an important branch of industry. The income of a motion picture producer is, of course, derived mainly from rentals, and is largely dependent on the cost of the picture and the length of its run. In connection with the production of the picture many stage properties are required which may or may not be useful in other productions, so that the cost may or may not be chargeable in total against the picture for use in which they are purchased in the first instance. The studio will naturally have large overhead expenses which must be apportioned between the pictures which have been or are expected to be produced during the year. Some principles have to be adopted for apportioning this overhead expense, and there is need for the exercise of a considerable amount of judgment in applying the principles and dealing with such expenditures as those for stage properties. Supposing the cost of the picture to be satisfactorily determined—what proportion of this cost is to be charged against each dollar of rental received?

In the early days, the simple rule was adopted that all rentals were applied against the cost until the cost was recovered, and thereafter all rentals were profits. Obviously, such a result was conservative but quite unscientific. If the picture as a whole produced a profit, some part of each dollar of rental received should be deemed to be profit. After careful research it was discovered that the earnings of the ordinary picture followed a more or less well-defined curve, being naturally greatest in the early days of presentation and gradually tapering off to zero at the end of, perhaps, two years. Consequently the practice became general (and has been recognized by the Bureau of Internal Revenue) of computing the income on the basis of writing off the cost of the picture against the rentals on the basis of such curves. Clearly, however, there is even greater need for the exercise of judgment in determining the precise shape of the curves to be used, and naturally when this has been done the experience of every picture will not conform to any such curve, so that constant watchfulness and the exercise of constant judgment is necessary to insure proper statements of income.

The need for judgment in selecting and applying accounting principles or conventions which I have shown to be necessary in this case is necessary in greater or less degree in almost every business—certainly in every case in which either the exhaustion of fixed property or the carrying of inventories is an incident of the business. It is not true of only complex businesses. I chose for illustration on another occasion the case of one of the unemployed who engaged in the business of selling apples on the street corner and continued in it for only four days, and showed that the same situation (of course, on a small scale) existed in that case.

There is no dispensing with judgment in the preparation of accounts. Obviously, those most intimately associated with the business possess in the highest degree the knowledge which is necessary for the exercise of judgment. But they are not disinterested. The method of audited accounts which involves in the first instance the preparation of accounts by the officers of the company who are most familiar with its operations, and the examination thereof by qualified independent accountants possessing a wide general knowledge of business and able to take a disinterested and objective view of the position is, I believe, now generally recognized as the best combination that has been evolved for producing satisfactory accounts.

In so far as principles of accounting are necessary for the purpose, I think corporations should be allowed to exercise judgment provided that they recognize certain fundamental principles which are so well established that they may fairly be given general application, and provided, also, that these principles are definitely laid down and consistently followed. This method of dealing with the problem, I note, has recently been recommended by the Twentieth Century Fund as a result of its survey of the Stock Market (*Stock Market Control* by Evans Clark and others, page 174). Care must, however, be taken to limit the requirements of auditing so as to avoid making them unduly burdensome on the corporations and the investors therein.

With these general observations, I will proceed to a discussion of the specific suggestions which I have made.

SECTION 12:

It follows from what I have said that there is room for error or difference of opinion in regard to the earnings of a business corporation for any period, and, broadly speaking, *the shorter the period the greater relatively becomes the possible margin of error.* The extent thereof will vary with different businesses; it will be wide in any case in which inventories are large in proportion to profits, particularly if the inventory consists mainly of commodities which fluctuate in value. Thus monthly or quarterly statements of earnings of a packing house or a leather company are of little value and probably as likely as not to be misleading unless accompanied by very full explanations.

It is sometimes urged that such statements are at least valuable because comparison with the corresponding period of a preceding year can usefully be made. But unless much more than the bare results are published, this will not necessarily be true. Innumerable illustrations could be cited to demonstrate this point. I will take only one—a comparison of the earnings of a corporation engaged in the sale at retail of winter clothing for quarters ending in December and March, respectively, with the corresponding figures for the preceding year may be quite misleading if in one year winter has come early and in the other, late, so that in one case business was delayed until after January 1 which in the other case matured in December.

I have always been opposed to the suggestion that the New York Stock Exchange should make the publication of quarterly statements a uniform requirement for listing, and therefore I urge that power at least should be given to the regulating body to waive such a requirement in any case in which it believes that to do so would best serve the public interest.

If quarterly statements are to be published, I feel strongly that it is the duty of those who are seeking to help the public to emphasize the fact that while such statements may have value, that value is distinctly limited. This, for two reasons —first, that as I have already pointed out, allocations of profits to short periods of time can only be approximate and arbitrary; and, secondly, that the value of securities depends on the future, and that statements of past results are valuable mainly as they afford an indication of the reasonable expectations for the future, and profits for a quarter or other short period are an entirely unsafe basis on which to rest an estimate for the future.

The Committee is naturally anxious to do what it can to put those possessing inside information and the members of the general public as nearly as possible on an equality in dealing in securities, but it is faced with the insuperable obstacle that the advantage of the insider rests upon the fact that he has knowledge and qualifications for estimating the future which are not possessed by and cannot possibly be extended to the general public. His advantage is not that he knows what the past earnings have been, but that he can judge what future earnings are likely to be—and no one would suggest that corporation executives should be compelled by statute to prophesy.

To require that quarterly statements should be certified by accountants would be to ascribe to them an importance which they cannot possibly merit. This is the principal reason which leads me to suggest the elimination of this requirement from Section 12. Other reasons are, that to require that quarterly statements should be audited before being published would involve a substantial delay in the presentation of figures which owe a large part of any value they possess to their timeliness, and that it would involve a very heavy burden of expense. I have no means of estimating how great this burden of expense would be, but it would certainly run to very large figures. I should not regard this as a fatal objection, but I should regard the expenditure as not merely wasted, but as actually being devoted to an undesirable end.

I believe, however, that in this matter the Congress has an opportunity to take a very simple but very effective step to improve present audit practice. The most serious problem which the auditors of the accounts of listed corporations have to face is that audits are required at the close of the fiscal year, and that the great majority of corporations end their fiscal year with the calendar year, with the result that there is an enormous congestion of work in a few months. The existence of this condition adds to the cost and detracts from the efficiency of audits, and it could easily be avoided by a simple provision such as I have proposed.

In many industries, December 31 is a most unnatural time for closing the accounts. In a few instances, this fact has been recognized and another closing date has been selected—thus the packing houses generally close their accounts at the end of October. But assumed convenience in income tax affairs and similar considerations have led many corporations to adopt the calendar year as their fiscal year, although accounts for a period ending at some other date would be more informative. The natural closing date for automobile and tire companies would be September 30 or October 31. Formerly all the railroads closed their accounts at June 30. A discretionary provision such as I have suggested would admit of distribution of the work of auditing more equally over the entire year, thus not only reducing the cost and increasing the efficiency of audits, but contributing to the convenience of the exchanges and regulating bodies and others who are called upon to scrutinize audited accounts when issued. I recognize that in the past audits of corporations other than financial institutions have usually been made at the close of the calendar year, but any inconvenience that might result from a change in this respect would be trivial in comparison with the advantages to be derived from a better distribution of the work of auditing over the entire year. Of course, the requirement of quarterly audits as proposed in the bill would itself result in the equal distribution of work over the year which I regard as so desirable, but only at an undue expense to the corporation and the investors therein.

SECTION 17:

I urge that the liabilities imposed by Section 17 should be limited to cases in which the issue of false or misleading statements is shown to be wilful, because I am convinced that it is contrary to the public interest to impose such liabilities for honest error, either of fact or of judgment. Particularly is this true in respect of statements which are so largely matters of judgment as quarterly statements of profits. It is notorious that sometimes the most truthful statement may be the most misleading because of the unwarranted inferences to which it gives rise.

In the long run, the main part of the financial burden imposed by this Section will fall upon the corporation—that is, upon the investors—whereas the benefits thereof would accrue mainly to speculators, and I do not believe it is wise to place burdens on investors for the benefit of speculators.

The provisions of the Section relating to the measure of damages seem to me to be open to serious objection because, as has already been pointed out to your Committee, they would enable damages to be recovered which would bear no relation to the damage actually suffered, and this seems to me to be a vicious principle, particularly if it is to be applied to cases of honest error, either of fact or of judgment. If the Section is limited to cases of wilful misrepresentation, I do not suppose anyone would be concerned over a possible undue liberality in the measure of damages.

SECTION 18:

I now turn to Section 18 (b), which confers on the regulating body not only the power to prescribe the form in which accounts shall be presented, but how profits shall be computed.

I have said, and it cannot be too often repeated, that accounts necessarily represent the result of the application of appropriate accounting principles and judgment to facts. Upon the soundness of the judgment employed first in choosing and then in applying the guiding principles depends the value of the resulting accounts. Sound judgment can be based only on intimate knowledge and ample experience, and its exercise should be attended with responsibility. I believe the provision is unwise in so far as the Sub-section would vest the right to exercise this judgment in a commission which would have no responsibility, legal or moral, for the consequences that might ensue, and would necessarily lay down general rules which might or might not fit the specific cases to which they would have to be applied. I recognize that similar powers have been vested in the Interstate Commerce Commission and other bodies; but while our theories of rate regulation probably necessitated some such procedure in the case of railroads and other public utilities, the results are to my mind none the less unfortunate because they may have been inevitable.

In the first place, the idea that uniformity can be attained and the exercise of discretion rendered unnecessary by rules, however detailed, is entirely illusory. Today, after more than a quarter of a century of intensive development of the accounting classifications of the Interstate Commerce Commission, it is still possible to produce widely different accounting results from a slight difference in the form of treatment of substantially identical transactions. Moreover, under those classifications, while manuals running to hundreds of pages exist in which the treatment of innumerable items large and small is prescribed in meticulous detail, it is still necessary to allow the railroads to determine the monthly charges to many important operating accounts on the basis of budget estimates of future expenditures. In respect of other important elements, such as depreciation, the practice of regulated companies still varies widely. Meantime, the uninformed public assumes a uniformity and a comparability between accounts of different railroads and utilities which does not exist and can never be attained.

In the second place, uniformity necessarily means a uniformly low standard—indeed, laws can do no more than lay down minimum standards; higher standards can come only as the result of the recognition of ethical and moral obligations. The accounting standards of the majority of industrial corporations with which I am acquainted are distinctly more conservative than those of regulated corporations.

In 1932, a committee of the American Institute of Accountants, as a result of a study of the general question, rendered a report, a copy of which was put in evidence before the Senate Committee by the Chairman of the Committee on Stock List of the New York Stock Exchange on January 12, 1933. In that report, the Committee recommended to the Exchange, *inter alia,* to use its influence:

To make universal the acceptance by listed corporations of certain broad principles of accounting which have won fairly general acceptance, and within the limits of such broad principles to make no attempt to restrict the right of corporations to select detailed methods of accounting deemed by them to be best adapted to the requirements of their business; but:

(a) To ask each listed corporation to cause a statement of the methods of accounting and reporting employed by it to be formulated in sufficient detail to be a guide to its accounting department; to have such statement adopted by its board so as to be binding on its accounting officers; and to furnish such statement to the Exchange and make it available to any stockholder on request and upon payment, if desired, of a reasonable fee.

(b) To secure assurances that the methods so formulated will be followed consistently from year to year and that if any change is made in the principles or any material change in the manner of application, the stockholders and the Exchange shall be advised when the first accounts are presented in which effect is given to such change.

(c) To endeavor to bring about a change in the form of audit certificate so that the auditors would specifically report to the shareholders whether the accounts as presented were properly prepared in accordance with the methods of accounting regularly employed by the company, defined as already indicated.

I believe that this method of approach to the problem would prove more practically effective than an attempt to institute uniform accounting. I understand, however that the Department of Commerce is at the present time conducting a study into the whole question of uniform accounting and uniform statistics. Legislation on the subject does not seem to me to form an essential part of a law the primary purpose of which is the regulation of stock exchanges and stock exchange practices, and I would urge that Sub-section 18 (b) should be eliminated and the whole question dealt with on its merits in the light of full information such as I trust will be developed through the inquiry to which I have referred.

Respectfully submitted,

March 10, 1934.   GEORGE O. MAY

IX

INFORMATION FOR INVESTORS

THE TASK OF THE NEW SECURITIES AND EXCHANGE COMMISSION *

(1934)

AMONG the encouraging signs of the times are the first official actions of the Securities and Exchange Commission and the public statements of its Chairman, which indicate a disposition to deal with the problems entrusted to the Commission in a practical manner and with a desire to be helpful to the investor rather than to stress the punitive and restrictive possibilities of the law.

The importance of the Commission's attitude is obvious. Admittedly, the possibilities of more substantial recovery turn largely on the extent to which the demand for capital goods can be stimulated. There is no question as to the magnitude of the potential demand for such goods. In conversation recently, an executive indicated that in his own industry, three or four hundred million dollars could advantageously be spent in modernizing its equipment. However, the easy days in which new construction could be financed from undivided profits have come to an end. In the main, new construction waits on new financing; new financing, in turn, awaits the revival of confidence, and nothing is so essential to a revival of confidence as an administration of the new laws relating to security issues which will not subject corporations to excessive burdens nor the honest and well-informed executive or director to unreasonable hazards.

The new Commission would seem to be tactically in an extremely favorable position to give the needed impulse to business. It is an entirely new body and is therefore un-

* An unpublished memorandum written in 1934.

fettered by precedents—at the same time, it includes in its membership two former members of the Federal Trade Commission, who must be thoroughly familiar with the problem and with the impracticalities of the procedure required under the Securities Act of 1933. The Commission has been granted by Congress power to make rules which will not only bind but protect—indeed, the provision whereby persons acting in good faith in accordance with any regulations of the Commission are protected even though the regulations shall subsequently be revoked or held contrary to law, is potentially at least the most important amendment contained in the Act of 1934.

The difficulties of the task of the Commission must not, however, be underestimated. The greatest of all difficulties is to disabuse the public mind of the idea that regulation can secure safety of investment, and to protect it from the promoters of corporations which have no past and very little future, and who found it much easier to comply with the Securities Act of 1933 than did the established business corporations. Another is to make the public realize what accounts can and do mean, and what they do not and cannot possibly signify.

In the matter of earnings, for instance, what the investor would really like to know is what the business is going to earn in the future; but all that it is possible to tell him is what the business has earned in the recent past, according to a method of computation which is necessarily based largely on estimates and conventions.

Ideally, the proponents of an issue, who should have made a sufficient investigation to enable them to judge for themselves how far results of the past are likely to be reproduced in the future, should give to the potential investor the benefit of their judgment on this point. When an issuer voluntarily gives information regarding the past he, unless he indicates otherwise, impliedly represents to the public that he regards the experience of the past as a reasonable indication of the probabilities for the future. When, however, such information is given under the compulsion of a statute, obviously there is not the same implication. The Act, by way of alternative, contemplates that the issuer shall give a mass of supplementary information which would supposedly aid an intelligent investor in forming an opinion of his own on this vital point. The defect of this procedure is that the potential investor, who has not the ability to make an exhaustive study nor a financial interest that would justify him in doing so, may be left in a position of attempting to discover a needle in a haystack.

The Commission must expect that any regulations which it may put forward will be met with criticism from two sides: issuers of securities will complain that the regulations call for useless information; while potential investors will complain that the resulting statements afford no clear or simple guide to the merits of the investment. Experience has, it is believed, already demonstrated the desirability of curtailing the volume of the historical information to be embodied in the registration statement; but what is even more needed is a procedure under which it would be possible for issuers to select that part of the information still required, which they might regard as most vital, and furnish it to potential investors, without incurring penalties for doing so. The fact that further information would be on file with the Commission, and the existence of organizations created for the purpose of analyzing such information, should form an adequate protection against any gross abuse of such a procedure in connection with reputable issues. In the long run, whatever statutes may do, the investor will have to depend very largely upon the character of the management of the enterprise in which he proposes to invest, and the character of those upon whose recommendations he makes the investment. The whole purpose of securing information in regard to enterprises in which investment is contemplated is to form a basis for inferences and judgment. Unless the inferences and judgment are wisely formed, the mass of underlying information is valueless, if not misleading. It is the quality and the emphasis rather than the quantity of information that is important.

It is to be hoped that the Commission will receive the hearty coöperation of those best qualified to be helpful in the performance of its task, and that its rulings will be received sympathetically. We have made great progress from the early days of 1933, when it seemed as if justified indignation at then recent revelations had created a determination to punish bankers and to produce a law which not even the most ingenious lawyer could evade, which somewhat obscured the interests of investors and the needs of the country's industries.

It is to be hoped and expected that the Commission will not be led astray by the deceptive promise of uniform accounting, especially in view of the thoughtful and convincing discussion of this question contained in the report of the Committee on Statistical Reporting and Uniform Accounting for Industry to the Business Advisory and Planning Council for the Department of Commerce. It will no doubt use all its great influence to bring about by voluntary action as great a degree of uniformity in different industries as is obtainable, and will insist on consistency from year to year in the accounting of each corporation subject to its regulation. Here again, however, we have the position that if an issuer voluntarily uses a method of accounting, he implies to the investor that it is a fair way of determining profits as a guide to the future; but if he uses a method under compulsion, he makes no such implied representation.

There is little doubt that the fantastically high prices of utility securities during the boom were partly the result of a belief that public utility accounting, being under regulation, must be more reliable as a guide to investors than other accounting. The fact, as students of the question are aware, is that public utility accounting was and is far less conservative than that of the responsible industrial concerns which offered their securities to the public. It is today possible for a regulated utility to use in the sale of securities statements of account which conform to the regulations of the body to which they are subject and are therefore acceptable under the statute, but which would and should be rejected if proffered to the Securities and Exchange Commission by an industrial corporation.

The utterances of the Chairman of the Commission suggest that it will face in a realistic spirit each of its three major tasks, *viz.*:

(1) To frame regulations which will give investors reasonable information about respectable issues without placing undue burdens on the issuers;

(2) To make harder the work of those who seek to exploit cupidity by worthless issues;

(3) To educate investors to discriminate between securities and to appreciate both the value and the limitations of investment information.

It should not be forgotten that the evils of the pre-depression period were mainly connected with high-pressure salesmanship, and that except in the important respect of disclosure of the interests of those concerned in the issue, standard prospectus practice here was probably better than in any other important financial center. The Investment Bankers' Code has done much to curb the evils connected with high-pressure salesmanship and has helped to bring about a favorable situation for the creation of a sound system of distribution of securities.

X

DISCUSSION OF COMMISSIONER LANDIS' PAPER BY GEORGE O. MAY

AT THE MEETING OF THE AMERICAN MANAGEMENT ASSOCIATION ON OCTOBER 9, 1935

I DID not have the opportunity of knowing what Mr. Landis was going to say until I came here this morning, so that what I say may probably be very disjointed.

The last note that Mr. Landis struck impressed me as much as any. Many of us differ as to the wisdom of the scheme of the Securities Act, but I think all those who have been in touch with the administration of it have been immensely impressed with the understanding, the coöperative spirit and the efficiency with which it has been administered by the Commission of which Mr. Landis is now the head.

That, to my mind, is the great hope, because we accountants all know that a system is usually less important than the way in which it is administered. A good comptroller can make a success of a bad system and a bad comptroller can make a mess of the best system that can be devised.

I have seen, with regret, Mr. Kennedy leave the Commission, and my great fear is that we may not continue to have the benefit of the services of men like Mr. Landis as long as we should like. There is always a call for such men, and how long they will resist the call is hard to know, but certainly I think I speak for all those who have to do with the Commission in saying that I hope Mr. Landis will stay as long as possible, because he has that great quality which is essential in his work: that if he reaches a conclusion on purely intellectual premises, he is quite willing to modify it in the light of actual experience, and has no hesitation in changing his mind. We have had to change our minds, and it has been very nice to find the Commission was also willing to change its mind.

Those who came in at the beginning and realize the problems are the ones who can do the most efficient work in developing the administration of this task along the lines that are essential if it is to be a success.

I particularly welcome what Mr. Landis said about a shortened prospectus. In one of my discussions with the Commission I suggested that the first thing to be determined was the maximum useful length of a prospectus, and as much material as could be fitted in that should be chosen, with the rest eliminated. I think there is something in the thought. If we can find some way of permitting a short prospectus I think that would meet a lot of the criticism today because one criticism today is, I think, on the lack of emphasis in a prospectus.

Mr. Landis spoke of the importance of facts. I would slightly modify his statement and suggest that the implications that are drawn from the facts are the really important things. The fact that a company earned $1,000,000 last year is of very little importance to the future investor unless it implies there is a prospect of its earning $1,000,000 in another year. That is where the prospectuses of today are deficient as I see it; they do not place any emphasis on the essential points. There is a great deal of good information in the prospectus; there is no doubt about that. There is even more that is good in the registration statement. There is more brandy in a plum pudding than you could put in a liqueur glass, but if you want to get a stimulant you would be wiser to drink a glass of brandy than to attempt to digest a plum pudding; and if Mr. Landis can develop a procedure in which those who want a glass of brandy can get it, and those who want a plum pudding can take it and pull out their own plums, I think that would be a great step forward.

Mr. Landis spoke about accounting, and I think he was a little optimistic in suggesting that it was only the ignorant or small investor that was still under the belief that book values of assets could be realized without question. I think the belief is much more widely spread than his remarks suggested. I welcome one thing the Commission did particularly, and that was its emphasis on such points as that, and on the fact that accounting cannot be a rigid and inflexible thing but requires the exercise of judgment, and must change as conditions change.

In connection with another matter which I am dealing with, I came across two decisions of the Supreme Court which emphasize how even in law, opinions change. In the famous Knoxville Water case the Supreme Court talked about the necessity of providing for depreciation of property as it occurs. That was in 1909, but if you go back to 1878—or 1876—you will find the Supreme Court saying that it is a matter of common knowledge that people seldom set aside any provision for depreciation, and in a case in which a railroad sought to deduct depreciation in an accounting with the Government, it flatly denied the right to do so and said that only the actual amount expended could with any propriety be deducted or charged against earnings.

Personally, I have always regretted that in the presentation to Congress and to the country of the questions involved in the Securities Act more emphasis was not placed on the inherent dangers of what we are pleased to call investment, and the fact that the degree of hazard in seasoned enterprises is not going to be very materially affected by the difference between the kind of requirements that we have now and the requirements that used to exist. I wish more had been done to discourage speculation, and I am rather afraid that the tendency of the Securities Exchange Act is to encourage speculation, and I think that is a bad thing. We are always in a hurry. We want radical solutions and we want quick results. Those characteristics, and the habit of issuing questionnaires (which I think is one of the most pernicious practices that has developed), are some of our national habits that seem to me to be reflected to a large extent in the present Securities Act.

The Securities Act is defective, as I see it, in that it combines two inconsistent theories: (1) enacting numerous specific requirements, and (2) adding a general requirement that all material facts shall be stated. The moment you require a whole lot of information to be stated, you take the emphasis and implications off those statements. In the old days no respectable accountant was willing to certify to the statement of earnings for a prospectus for the past three years, let us say, unless he believed that those three years were a reasonable indication of what might be expected in the future, and I think that an issue that put forth a statement of that kind implied that was a reasonable indication of what might be expected in the future. When you are required by law to give the three years' figures, that implication no longer exists, and I think what you are giving to the investor in the way of additional information you are largely taking away in the form of depriving him of the benefit of judgment as to the implications of figures which are often far more important than the figures themselves.

I would like in concluding, if I may, to mention one more point. It relates to the Securities Exchange Act. I fear that the attempt to tie together the Securities Exchange Act and the Securities Act—the annual report and the prospectus —is going to have many very unfortunate effects. It is again emphasizing the point of view of the speculator rather than the investor. The annual report is essentially historical, and the prospectus is a statement put forward deliberately to induce people to buy. The annual report is not so intended. It is a report of stewardship by the stewards of a business. The attempt to convert it into a new edition of a prospectus is, to my mind, fraught with very serious dangers, and I think ought to be given a great deal of consideration. Prospectuses, I think, will become less informative if that policy is pursued, because already one finds a disposition on the part of executives to be unwilling to present figures in a prospectus in any different form from that presented in an annual report. In the old days the standard practice was to make such adjustments as were necessary to convert figures in an annual report which were part of a historical statement into figures that were appropriate in a document designed to sell securities. I would like to emphasize very strongly the difference between an annual report and a prospectus in that respect, and urge it should be kept constantly in mind in any regulations under the Act.

I will conclude my remarks as I began them, if I may, by asking you to believe that nothing that I have said is intended to be in the nature of hostile criticism of the acts of the Commission. I think I can speak for all of the experts with whom I have been in touch in saying that we regard its administration as highly efficient and sympathetic. My only fears are: First, that we may not be able to retain the services of those who are now giving us such excellent service; and, secondly, that there is always a danger that the efficiency of administration may blind us to defects of the law or the system that is being administered. I stress those two notes because I had a good deal of opportunity to see the working of the Revenue Act of 1917, which, as it left Congress, was about as unworkable a piece of legislation as was ever presented to an administrative group. A very able group of volunteers, called together by the present Secretary of Commerce, and headed by Dr. Adams, whose services in the field of taxation we can never too highly praise, undertook that administration and did a perfectly remarkable piece of work. Then the emergency passed and those men went out of office. The administration fell into less competent hands—into the hands of people with less interest in accomplishing something really worth while, with the result that much of the work of that early group was reversed or destroyed. The damage was mitigated in that case because it was a tax bill for only a single year, but it brought home to me very strongly the dangers that are inherent in allowing an unsound system to continue because it is being well administered.

While I think there is much that is good in the Act, there is much yet to my mind that needs to be eliminated, and I trust that Mr. Landis and his colleagues will remain in office at least long enough to make the changes which I am sure they, better than most people, must realize to be necessary.

PART V
TAXATION

A. GENERAL

I

THE TAX MAZE *

(1925)

I

MAZE.—A structure consisting of a network of winding and intercommunicating paths and passages arranged in bewildering complexity, so that without guidance it is difficult to find one's way in it.—*Oxford Dictionary*.

THE erection of the statue of Alexander Hamilton in front of the main Treasury Building in Washington raises the question who is to occupy the corresponding position in relation to the new Treasury Annex, devoted to the uses of the Bureau of Internal Revenue. The action of Congress on the Mellon tax plan last year suggests that the claims of the present Secretary would not—at this time, at least—be favorably considered. It may be that, rather than undertake the invidious task of passing on the relative claims of present-day statesmen, such as Representative Volstead and Secretary McAdoo, it would be safer to resort to classical mythology. A dethroned Bacchus is the first idea that suggests itself, but for a Bureau that includes the Income Tax unit as well as the Prohibition unit is there not at least as strong a claim to be made for Dædalus? And it was the same Congress which by the Volstead Act dethroned Bacchus that in its tax law outbuilt Dædalus. In maintaining its supremacy Congress has been at this disadvantage: that the labyrinth of Dædalus was designed only to entoil new victims, none of whom escaped to return and make a second attempt to solve its intricacies, whereas Congress had to prepare for adven-

* *The Atlantic Monthly* (April, 1925).

turers who would return year after year. It must be admitted that hitherto Congress has been extraordinarly successful in introducing new complexities with sufficient frequency to preclude any possibility of victims' acquiring familiarity with its maze; but is it right to ask or even to permit Congress to continue this effort indefinitely? Should not Congress now attempt to achieve something of the breadth and simplicity of the architecture of Athens, instead of continuing to emulate the complexities of Crete?

Those who are compelled to study the tax maze find in it an extraordinary series of contradictions. One of the most striking is seen in the lengths to which Congress goes on some points to define its purposes and to avoid leaving any discretion to the administrators of the law, and in the enormous range of discretion left to the administration on other points, with utterly inadequate provision made to ensure that such discretion shall be exercised on adequate information and competent advice. Pages of an Act are devoted to explanations on such points as when an organization is a reorganization and when a dividend is not a dividend, and most specific rules are laid down for the guidance of the Commissioner on such matters, yet a brief clause in the Act may be the sole authority of and the sole limitation on the Commissioner in dealing with subjects of vast importance.

That the impossibility of dispensing with discretion in administration is realized by some in Congress, but not by others, is indicated by the following colloquy between members of the Senate Committee investigating the Bureau of Internal Revenue:

Senator Couzens. But we want to know what the questions are at issue so we can pass a law to cover such cases, instead of leaving it discretionary.

Senator Ernst. I tell you, Senator, you will not be able to pass a law or laws that will cover all the questions that will arise in these cases, even though you pass laws from now until the end of time.

II

In the Act of 1918, in which the rates of tax ran as high as 82.4 per cent on corporations, deductions were authorized for a reasonable allowance for depreciation, based on the value of property at March 1, 1913. This simple clause implied the making or approving by the Commissioner of valuations of practically all the depreciable business property in the United States that was in existence at March 1, 1913: a problem in valuation far greater and of far more immediate and practical effect than the valuation of the railroads, on which the Interstate Commerce Commission and the railroads have spent upwards of ten years and upwards of $100,000,000 without completing the task. A provision for the amortization of the cost of war facilities entailed the even more difficult task of deciding what these facilities would be worth at some time in the future, and under conditions not easily capable of anticipation.

A clause allowing a deduction for depletion of natural resources implied a similar task of valuation as at March 1, 1913, in relation to the entire natural resources of the country; and in the Act of 1921 this task was complicated by the allowance of a further deduction in determining the taxable income from operations of oil and mining properties, in respect of the appreciation in value resulting from the discovery of minerals in hitherto unproven areas. This allowance not only ran counter to the whole general theory of the law and placed the industries concerned in a specially favored position, but it also created an administrative task of the utmost difficulty.

The discretion given to the Commissioner in regard to methods of valuing inventories involved the decision whether millions of dollars should be accounted for as income in years in which they would be subject to a tax of 50 per cent or more, or in years in which they would be subject to little or no tax.

The burden of dealing with these problems was imposed

on a Bureau that had been formed only a few years earlier
and had been administering a tax so low—1 or 2 per cent—
as to be a matter of comparative indifference to taxpayers.
Yet Congress created no new machinery to enable the Bureau
to cope with its enormously increased burdens and responsibilities.

Not only do these and similar problems in taxation involve in the aggregate billions of dollars, but there are a
large number of individual cases in which millions or tens
of millions are involved. In such cases the taxpayer can
afford to lavish money and skill on the study of every phase
of the case, and on the development of a form of presentation that will bring out the strong and minimize or conceal
the weak points. Consider for a moment the way in which
these cases are finally decided: on the one side the taxpayer
with millions at stake, familiar with every strength and
weakness of his position, advised possibly by an expert whose
compensation is contingent on results and who is therefore
personally interested in the outcome to the extent of tens or
hundreds of thousands of dollars; on the other side, the
Government representatives without the skill, the time, or
the organization to develop the case adequately, serving for
a low salary, with little prospect in the way of promotion,
with no interest in the result of the controversy except to
avoid prejudicing their position in the Bureau—unless, per-
chance, there be hope of appearing some day on the other
side of the table for other taxpayers—and possessing no element of strength except the power of decision. It is inevitable that, in a large number of cases, either the Government's representatives will be overborne by the weight of
the taxpayer's case, which they are unable to answer, or that,
realizing this inability but feeling that it may be due less to
the validity of the taxpayer's contentions than to the inadequacy of the Government's means of refuting them, they will
fall back on their power of decision and take an arbitrary
position without attempting to justify it. In either case it

is unlikely that even approximate justice will have been done.

It would be idle to suggest that the blame rightly attaches to Congress in all the many cases in which the Bureau of Internal Revenue has been subjected to legitimate criticism, just as it would be unfair to ignore the large amount of earnest, intelligent, and often really admirable work that has been performed in that Bureau.

In the circumstances outlined, however, a Senatorial investigation was hardly needed to show that the administration of the law has been far from perfect, or to prove that the administration has resulted in gross inequalities between taxpayers. It was obvious from the first that this must be so, but no more obvious than that the high tax laws were bound to operate with gross inequality, even if they could be perfectly administered. For instance: capital is a factor in producing income in almost every business activity, its influence varying in degrees by infinitely small gradations from practical insignificance to paramount importance. Yet in the Excess Profits Tax Law (1917) Congress attempted to draw an arbitrary line and to divide businesses into two classes, those in which capital is a material income-producing factor, and those in which it is not. Not only so, but it actually enacted the law in such a way that the minimum tax—8 per cent—fell on income derived from every business falling on one side of the arbitrary line of cleavage, and the highest rate of all—perhaps 60 per cent—fell on those businesses which happened to lie just on the other side of the line. In doing so it enacted a provision which was bound to create the grossest inequalities.

All this, however, while regrettable, was largely inevitable and, viewed in its proper perspective, constitutes only one of the minor injustices of war. Why one taxpayer should retain 40 per cent and another 80 per cent of the profit he made out of the war is a trivial question compared with the question why either should retain any profit when the soldier in the line suffered hardship, injury, and possibly loss of life, for a mere pittance. The only possible answer is, in both cases, that those measures had to be adopted which seemed at the time most likely to expedite the winning of the war and the termination of the whole series of injustices that were its inevitable accompaniment. What is both regrettable and preventable is that six years after the Armistice so many of the important tax-controversies should be still unsettled, and that, in regard to personal income taxation at least, our law should still operate in the same hit-or-miss fashion, and with inequalities almost as great as any that existed at the height of war taxation.

In liquidating the assets of a business the course most commonly followed is to realize in the ordinary way as much of the assets as can be disposed of within a reasonable time, and then to get rid of the remnants by some unusual and sweeping procedure. This analogy might well have been followed in the settlement of war taxes; and there is little doubt that even now the disposition of the outstanding tax-cases of the war years on broad lines would prove far more beneficial, both to the Government and to the taxpayers, than the continuance of the present weary process, and would be likely to come just as near a theoretically correct solution. Competent and disinterested advisers have repeatedly suggested in the past the constitution of a commission of high quality and large powers to dispose of all pending tax-questions relating to the war years, and the suggestion still holds the field, as presenting the best prospect of a satisfactory solution of this problem which the war has left us.

The settlement of large tax-cases calls, not for fine distinctions and meticulous accuracy, but for breadth and soundness of judgment based on wide experience, and for courage; and it would have been advantageous to taxpayers and the Government alike if the major cases could have been dealt with promptly and finally by a body possessing those qualifications. The number of cases in which taxpayers have paid substantially more in taxes for the war years than they were

prepared five years ago to pay is undoubtedly small compared with the number of cases in which they have paid, or
will pay, far less than they would then gladly have paid in
final settlement. Taxpayers in the aggregate have probably
lost as much in expense and in diversion of thought and
effort to tax matters as they have saved in taxes, and the
country as a whole is the poorer, not only for this wasted
effort, but for the demoralizing effects of tax controversies
as they are now too often conducted.

III

As regards current taxation: while the problems of valuation which have been referred to still remain, their importance in the case of corporations has become much reduced
since the tax on corporations has been stabilized at the relatively low level of 12.5 per cent. In the field of personal
income taxation, however, the rates of tax are still high
enough to make the inequalities in its incidence a serious
matter for those affected.

Here again is contradiction. One observes how wide the
net is cast to catch even the smallest of fish, and next one
observes how large are the holes through which even the
big fish may escape.

The chief executive of a foreign company who passes
through the United States on his way around the world is
held up at his port of embarkation and, because during his
stay in the country he has devoted a few days to calling on
agents or customers of his firm and discussing business with
them, is told that he must pay income tax on a corresponding proportion of his annual salary, as being income derived
from sources within the United States. He might be par-
doned for characterizing our system as closely approaching
conformity to the first two definitions of Euclid, and consisting of a law having length without breadth, administered
by persons having position but not magnitude.

A nurse, not yet naturalized, who upon going abroad with
her employer finds that in case she might not come back she

must pay fourteen dollars income tax, which she is assured will be refunded to her if she returns, and who is told on her return that there is no appropriation out of which her payment can be refunded, may not unnaturally feel that the United States is engaged in a rather petty business.

Nor, surely, could any doubts regarding the meticulous care with which the law is administered survive a reading of the recently published decision which, first holding that a cash allowance to an officer for uniforms was income to the recipient and the cost of the uniforms not an allowable deduction, went on to specify that epaulets and campaign bars were business expense, but cap devices and chin-straps were not.

Such cases indicate how wide is the net and how small the mesh. On the other hand, the recent publication of tax returns is in itself a sufficient demonstration of the size of the holes.

No one familiar with American business or social life, who has given even the most casual perusal to the published lists, can entertain any longer the belief that our present income-tax law possesses the basic justification of an income-tax system, that it levies taxation substantially in accordance with ability to pay. Any inferences that might be drawn from the published lists regarding an individual taxpayer might be wholly unfair, because under our system an individual of large regular income may have been liable for only a very small tax, by reason of capital losses or other factors determining his tax liability. But when name after name has set opposite it a tax figure which is ridiculously small in proportion to the obvious income and ability to pay of the taxpayer, even the most ardent advocates of the policy that has inspired our laws must admit that those laws have not up to now been effective in taxing large incomes with anything like the degree of universality and equality that is necessary to justify their existence and continuance.

Though the recent publication of tax returns has led to a clearer and more general realization of the inequalities of personal income taxation, it was not needed to demonstrate their existence. As Secretary Houston said in his annual report for 1920:

Tax returns and statistics are demonstrating what it should require no statistical evidence to prove . . . the fact remains that to retain such rates in the tax law is to cling to a shadow while relinquishing the substance.

While the rates when he spoke were higher than those of today, his comment is still largely applicable. But though Secretary Glass and Secretary Mellon have taken the same stand, Congress has refused to heed their advice and has continued to impose high rates of tax which in fact are, broadly speaking, not paid as contemplated by Congress, except by those whose income is earned and those possessors of investment income who are unwilling to adopt ordinary methods of avoidance.

It may be worth while briefly to consider some of these methods.

IV

Apart from the creation of trusts, the three principal methods of avoidance are, perhaps: investments in tax-exempt securities; losses, real or artificial; and the transfer of property to corporations that pay few or no dividends. The creation of trusts seems to stand on a somewhat different footing from the others, since it does involve the taxpayer's divesting himself of property, or at least of the income from property, though it may be in favor of a near relative.

Of the three remaining methods of avoidance, investment in tax-exempt securities is the surest, in that the protection it affords is based on the Constitution, and therefore the taxpayer resorting to it is not under the necessity of keeping a weather eye constantly lifting for any action of Congress that might affect his status. On the other hand, though the cost is small in proportion to the tax saved in the case of a wealthy man, it is nevertheless substantial.

Hence, while many prefer the freedom from both anxiety

and tax which tax-exempt securities afford, and are willing to pay the price, others prefer to risk hazards of the tax in an effort to secure immunity at low cost. And those who determine thus to venture into the labyrinth readily find daughters of Minos who know something of its secret and are willing to aid them; though, warned perhaps by the fate of Ariadne, they may insist that their reward be ample and well assured before that aid is given.

The success which has attended such efforts in the case of owners of investment income is notorious, and seems to have aroused the envy of some who have paid a higher price for immunity from tax by going into the tax-exempt field. Thus we have the spectacle of occupants of the invulnerable shelter of the tax-exempt stimulating and endeavoring to direct the attack on those who have found other and more precarious shelter.

In the law of 1924 Congress largely deprived the second method, that of taking losses, of its efficiency by limiting the saving in tax in respect of losses to 12.5 per cent of the loss; before doing so, however, it limited the tax on capital gains to 12.5 per cent, thus abandoning the attempt to levy high surtaxes on this form of income.

The third method, of transferring property to corporations which pay few or no dividends, continues to flourish, notwithstanding that it has been the special objective of the attack of a large section of Congress. Each new Revenue Act has contained a new provision for taxing undistributed profits, but there is little reason to think that even the latest effort will prove generally effective.

It will be observed that these various methods of avoidance, as well as the limitation of tax on capital gains to 12.5 per cent, ease the burden on the capitalist, but afford no means of escape to those who derive their incomes from their own efforts or the products of their own brains, and not from accumulated capital. Indeed, among the many contradictions found in the law, perhaps the most striking of all is that under legislation admittedly framed, not with an eye single to fiscal requirements, but with the avowed purpose of striking at the rich, the burden of the tax should in actual operation fall most heavily on earners who have little or nothing in the way of accumulated savings; and that special relief should be granted, not to those who are adding to the wealth of the country by their researches, their inventions, and their toil, but to the beneficiaries of unearned increment and to those whose profits are derived from the exhaustion of the natural wealth of the country. True, Congress in the Act of 1924 pretended to give relief to earners, as urged by Secretary Mellon, but the relief was so paltry as to be a mockery.

Some optimists may think that patient revision of the tax laws would in the course of time suffice to make the present high rates generally effective and equal in their incidence; they can, however, have little conception of the actual working of this laborious process of trial and error. A hole in the law is detected and a provision is enacted for the purpose of stopping that hole. To the extent that the provision is retroactive the action taken may prove immediately effective, and as our tax laws from 1913 to date have been retroactive to the extent of a minimum period of six months in the case of the law of 1924, and a maximum period of fourteen months in the case of the law of 1913, the extent of this effectiveness may be considerable, though its justice may be open to question.

The first effect of such a provision—aside from possible retroactivity—is a temporary suspension of the class of activities aimed at, while the tax lawyers, who include in their numbers some of the keenest minds in the country, decide on a modified course of procedure that will avoid the letter of the provision. Once such a procedure is developed, it quickly becomes common property among the class affected. The Government, however, remains in ignorance of its adoption, perhaps, until it comes to light two or three years later, in the course of the review of the returns in which the effects of the new provisions of the law were expected to be made manifest. When this happens the dreary round begins again, and it will continue so long as Congress refuses to recognize what successive Secretaries of the Treasury of both parties have pointed out—that it is attempting the impossible.

The various revisions of Section 220 imposing a tax on undistributed profits have caused stockholders much anxiety but little or no taxes, and there are large groups of rich men on whom the high surtax rates have been not a direct but an indirect burden. Undoubtedly the indirect burdens have been substantial. One form of the burden is the loss of income resulting from substituting tax-exempt securities for other forms of investment yielding higher returns, another the cost of advice on methods of avoidance. Another form occurs where the taxpayer transfers his property to a corporation; in such cases the difference between the normal tax on individuals of 6 per cent and the corporation rate of 12.5 per cent together with the capital-stock tax, which has been estimated to be equivalent to a tax of 1.5 per cent on income, may be regarded as in some measure a commutation of the surtax rates, and the amount, say 8 per cent, is not inconsiderable.

In this case the corresponding benefit does accrue to the Government, and the taxation of corporations at a rate substantially higher than that on individuals is perhaps the most practically effective measure for higher taxation of the rich that Congress has adopted, though not primarily designed for that purpose.

Undoubtedly, also, the reduction of the tax on capital gains to 12.5 per cent has resulted in large sums being taxed at that rate which had avoided, and would have continued to avoid, taxation at the regular surtax rates. Taxpayers controlling sources of income who were unwilling to take steps that would subject them to high surtaxes have consummated transactions that have resulted in their receiving as capital gains substantially what they were unwilling to receive as regular income. The capital gains reported in returns of over $1,000,000 in 1922 were greater than the entire net income reported in such returns in 1921.

Apart from their indirect effects and regarded solely as surtaxes, however, it is not putting the case too strongly to say that the higher rates have been as capricious and generally ineffective in their incidence as personal property taxes ordinarily are. So far as they have been effective they have fallen —and still fall—most heavily on earned income. Indeed, as advisers such as Dr. T. S. Adams pointed out to the committees in charge of the 1924 Bill, the reduction of 25 per cent in respect of earned income, which was urged by Mr. Mellon, would not have put its beneficiaries in a preferred position, but would merely have helped to redress the discrimination against them which in practice resulted from the law of 1921 and continues today.

V

The question has been and will be asked, why the high surtaxes should not be made more generally effective. It is impossible to deal fully with this question in a short article, but the basic reason is the elusive and Protean character of income. When and in what amounts income arises from a series of transactions are largely questions of opinion and business practice—questions, moreover, which cannot be satisfactorily answered unless the substance rather than the form is allowed to control the decision.

Great Britain attains a certain measure of success by restricting its taxation to recurring income, and laying down only very broad principles, which are administered by a highly trained and relatively well-paid civil service, vested with a very wide discretion. We, in reaching out for more, aiming perhaps at a higher ideal have only too often, in Secretary Houston's language, "grasped the shadow and missed the substance."

Further, the attempts to set forth in legislation what precise transactions of a non-recurring character give rise to taxable income result mainly in the great bulk of essentially similar transactions taking a slightly different form, not covered by the letter of the law.

If the maximum tax on individuals were reduced to a rate reasonably close to the corporation income-tax rate, wholesale avoidance would cease, simplicity would become possible, and the law would acquire that substantial equality of incidence and that universality which it now so completely lacks. Such a policy, it is believed, would be entirely compatible with the fiscal requirements of the United States and, like the reduction in tax on capital gains to 12.5 per cent, would bring under the surtaxes large amounts of income which up to now have escaped them.

Even, however, if surtaxes be substantially reduced, we should recognize that in some future emergency high taxes on income may become a national necessity, and should endeavor to put our income-tax system on a basis which would enable high tax-rates to be levied more simply, more equitably, and more effectively than has been accomplished under recent and existing laws.

Prohibition of future issues of tax-exempt securities is clearly one of the first and most important requirements to this end. No part of the nation's wealth should be in the position in which tax-exempt securities now are, that of being immune from taxation in any national emergency, however great.

A marked advance would also be made if a clearer conception and a closer agreement could be reached on just what is income and when it emerges. At present commercial and accounting ideas on these questions are at variance with the judicial decisions, with some economists holding still different views. Much of the inconsistency and vacillation in the income-tax administration may be attributed to differences between the legal and the accounting schools of thought, and to fluctuations in the degree of influence exercised by members of the two schools.

Our general theory of income taxation differs very materially from that of the much older British system, with which comparisons are most commonly made; but there is little reason to suppose that the differences are the result of careful consideration leading to the conviction that our methods are sounder, more practicable, or better adapted to our conditions. If our legislators found their inspiration in England, the home of the income tax, it must have been in the maze of Hampton Court, not at Somerset House.

Great Britain, it must be realized, possesses a number of natural advantages in imposing income taxation, such as the single Parliament, the absence of any constitutional limitations, the compactness and homogeneity of its territory; it also has the advantages of experience and a long-established civil service of high quality and traditions. Further, its income-tax system antedates the modern industrial development, which, therefore, in its growth has adapted itself to an existing income-tax scheme, whereas we are imposing an income-tax law on an already highly developed industrial and commercial organization. Those who have studied the proceedings of the last British Commission to report on income tax will appreciate how important a factor this is considered to be by British income-tax authorities. In these circumstances, the fact that British taxation has been restricted as it has possesses a special significance. It is only fair to point out that our freedom from tradition perhaps makes us more ready to deal with new issues in novel ways; and that our tax law, for instance, seems to be a distinct advance over the British on such matters as relief from double taxation, reciprocal exemption from taxation of international transportation, and taxation of income from international trade in general.

At present our law is being developed by court decisions dealing with single aspects of the question, the taxpayers' views on which are usually presented fully and skillfully with a view to securing the decision and without regard to the effect on the law as a whole. The Government's counsel have neither the time nor the technical advisers to enable them to present such cases in their proper relation to the whole subject of income tax, if indeed they are able to present the particular aspect involved in any given case with a skill or thoroughness approaching that of their opponents.

Court decisions, moreover, are governed largely by earlier decisions, rendered in a comparatively early stage of our commercial development and under conditions wholly unlike those now existing.

If the income-tax law could be taken out of politics and a body created in which the legislature, the administration, the interested professions—law, engineering, and accounting —the business world, the economist, and the individual taxpayers could all be represented, a new and sounder understanding of the problem might be attained, which would be of permanent value to the country.

If we cannot revise our income-tax system on its present lines so as to make it reasonably equitable and simple, and so as to rid us of methods of avoidance that are demoralizing to taxpayers and that make a mockery of the law, let us seek some new approach to the whole question. No better time could be selected for such a search than the present, when the country is prosperous and the Treasury overflowing, and yet the memories of the problems of war taxation are fresh in our minds.

VI

Summing up these reflections, the chief evils of our income-tax situation are, perhaps: the unsettled taxes for the war period, an unsound surtax system, and a law that attempts to be too specific on some points while leaving far more important decisions on other points to the administration—these last two leading to bewildering complexity, to wholesale and successful avoidance, and hence to gross discrimination.

The suggestions to which they lead are neither novel nor revolutionary; they are, first: that even now a commission to clear up the old war taxes would be desirable; second: that, unless and until surtaxes at the present rates can be administered with a reasonable degree of equality and generality of application, they should be reduced to a level at which those essentials of a sound tax system can be attained; and third: that the issue should be taken out of politics and a highly competent, nonpartisan body should be created—quite distinct from any body created to deal with the war taxes— in which the various elements of our community interested or able to make valuable contributions would be represented, to study the whole subject and to suggest revisions of our general scheme to make it simpler and more effective, and particularly to fit it for the strains that may require to be imposed on it in some great emergency in the future.

To accomplish this end we must impart breadth to the law instead of making it an ever longer and more intricate maze. If, further, we could revise our civil service, so as to make it appeal to men of greater magnitude than we can possibly hope to attract and hold—except in a small number of cases—under our present system, we should have laid the foundations of a sound income-tax system, which would be the mainstay of the Federal fiscal policy in normal times and would be invaluable in times of emergency. The only losers would be those "taxperts" who look forward to a long run of the present tragi-comedy, in which they may profitably play the rôle of Ariadne to the Dædalus of Congress.

II

THE TAXATION OF CAPITAL GAINS *

(1922)

THE treatment of capital gains under a steeply graduated income-tax law constitutes one of the most difficult problems in fiscal legislation, as is sufficiently evidenced by the changes contained in successive revenue acts. Impartial students of the subject will, it is believed, agree that the present state of the law is not satisfactory, and among the remedies which are receiving consideration is the abandonment of the taxation of capital gains and of the allowance of capital losses as a deduction from taxable income. In Great Britain, where capital gains have not heretofore been taxed or capital losses allowed as deductions, the question is being debated whether some change in the law is not necessary on account of the avoidance of taxation of what is essentially income by clothing it in the garb of capital. The time, therefore, seems opportune for a discussion of the problem.

1. THE NATURE OF CAPITAL GAINS

By capital gain is meant the profit upon the realization of assets otherwise than in the ordinary course of business, this profit being the excess of the proceeds of realization over the cost of the property realized.

In considering the proper treatment of capital gains under an income-tax law, it is desirable to keep in mind three different causes which may make a capital gain possible. These are:

(1) Change in absolute value due to natural growth or similar causes.
(2) Change in relative value of property in comparison with other property, due to external causes.

* *Harvard Business Review*, Vol. I (October, 1922). Cf. below, pp. 319-335.

(3) Change in the money value of property due to depreciation or appreciation of currency.

In most cases, of course, a capital gain is due to a combination of these influences, some perhaps operating in a favorable, others in an unfavorable, direction. All three, for instance, operating favorably might be found on the sale in the spring of 1919 of a privately owned barrel of whisky bought as new whisky in 1913. There would be first the increase in absolute value due to aging, second the increase in relative value due to the legislation enacted in January, 1919, and third the increase in money value, common to nearly all property, resulting from the expansion of currency and credit during the war.

Looking at the problem from the standpoint of principle, the gain due to the first cause is clearly only a special form of investment income and therefore naturally comes within the purview of an income tax. Gains due to the second cause are real gains, and therefore fairly taxable, even if not ordinary income. Indeed, if discrimination in favor of earned income as against investment income is well founded, it may well be argued that these gains from unearned increment should be regarded as less entitled to consideration than ordinary recurring investment income.

Gains from the third cause are more apparent than real. There would seem to be no true income or gain from selling property at double its cost, if everything which can be bought with the proceeds is also selling at double its former price. This has been a common situation in recent years and has been complicated by the factor of involuntary sale or realization. In recent tax laws attempts have been made to meet it: first, by replacement fund provisions under which no taxable profit is deemed to be derived from an involuntary sale if the proceeds are put aside to be employed in replacing the property; and, secondly, by the provisions in the 1921 law permitting exchanges of property without any liability to taxes as a result thereof.

II. RELATION OF CAPITAL LOSSES TO TAXATION OF CAPITAL GAINS

As a practical proposition it would be impossible to analyze every capital gain into its component elements and apply different rules to different elements. In particular it would be a hopeless task to convince the average taxpayer who had completed a transaction showing a loss, that he should pay a tax on the transaction because the loss was found upon analysis to be made up of an increase of value due to the first or second of the three causes above mentioned and therefore taxable, offset by a larger loss arising from the third cause and therefore outside the scope of the tax law.

The alternatives, therefore, are to tax all gains or to exclude all gains, except such as can be covered by simple rules. In considering the question whether capital gains should be taxed, the successive points which arise are:

(1) Is it in principle desirable to tax capital gains?
(2) If so, should capital losses be allowed as a deduction from taxable income?
(3) If both the first and second questions are answered in the affirmative, how serious are the dangers of evasion and how far is it practicable to guard against them?

It must be understood that the danger of avoidance is not disposed of by excluding capital gains and losses from the scope of the income tax, as is evidenced by the movement in England already referred to. A majority of economists would probably take the view that capital gains are not a proper subject for taxation under the guise of an income tax. Apart from this technical point, however, it would seem that in principle capital gains would form a most appropriate subject of taxation, and the Supreme Court has held that they can be taxed as income. Some theoretical considerations have already been briefly recited. Among other reasons which would have weight with a statesman as well as with a politician is the fact that the great accumulations of wealth by individuals in the country have largely been the result of capital gains, and the salary- or wage-earning classes might quite naturally feel that they were being unjustly discriminated against if they were taxed on their salaries or wages and the large capital gains of the very wealthy should escape taxation. Moreover, even if the taxation of capital gains be regarded as necessarily involving the allowance of capital losses, it would seem that treating both on the footing of income would ordinarily be expedient in a developing country in which naturally the capital gains would far exceed the capital losses. This proposition is, however, subject to the important qualification that it holds only so long as the form and degree of taxation are not such as to discourage the realization of gains and encourage the taking of losses, and thus to cause a serious disturbance of the normal balance between gains and losses.

Turning to the second point, while it may seem that in justice the rules regarding gains and losses in a tax law should be as nearly as possible similar, it may be recalled that this principle has not usually been applied in our income-tax laws. Even in the case of ordinary business, until the enactment of the present law, a taxpayer who made a profit on trading in one year and an exactly similar loss in another paid tax on the profit and obtained no relief in respect of the loss. As regards losses not incurred in the taxpayer's trade or business, the Act of 1913 allowed no deduction and the Act of 1916 allowed a deduction only to the amount of the gains of a similar character included in the same return. The tax rates under these Acts were, however, small as we now reckon tax rates, and the problem becomes difficult only when taxes are large. In 1917 when the maximum rate of tax was increased from 15 to 67 per cent, the limitation on the deduction of losses contained in the Act of 1916 was continued; but in 1918 when the maximum tax was still further increased to 77 per cent, all limitations on deductions of capital losses were removed.

Even under this law if a taxpayer pursued the even tenor of his way undisturbed, taking capital gains or capital losses as his judgment of present and prospective values dictated, and entirely uninfluenced by tax considerations, he was not in the position that tax relief resulting from a loss was exactly equivalent to the tax burden resulting from an equal gain. Such a taxpayer, if he incurred losses, was thereby relieved from surtax at the rates he would have paid on his regular income; if on the other hand he made a profit, he paid surtaxes at the higher rates applying to income in excess of his regular income.

Thus, to take the case of a man who had a regular income in each of the years 1919 and 1920 of $50,000 and sold one investment at a capital loss of $20,000 on December 31, 1919, and another at a capital gain of $20,000 on January 1, 1920; in 1919 he paid on an income of $30,000 a total tax of $3,890, in 1920 on an income of $70,000 a total tax of $16,490, together $20,380. If, however, both transactions had fallen in the same year he would have paid on an income of $50,-000 in each year a tax of $9,190; a total for the two years of $18,380, and his capital gain, therefore, cost him in taxation $2,000 more than he saved on his capital loss though the tax rates were the same in both years.

However, this discrimination against the taxpayer was of relatively minor consequence compared with the wholesale loss to the Government resulting from the fact that taxpayers liable to heavy rates of surtax very generally refrained from taking profits, but not from taking losses. It is impossible now to estimate the loss of taxes which resulted from this disturbance of the normal policy of investors, but it must have been enormous. At the same time transfers which were desirable from the broad standpoint of public welfare were retarded or prevented. Men of advanced years, who were anxious to turn over their business affairs to younger and more vigorous men, were deterred from doing so by the tax which would have fallen upon them in the event of a sale, and in innumerable ways the ordinary course of business was affected by the artificial restraint on sales at a profit and the encouragement of sales at a loss.

To meet some phases of the problem, extensive new provisions were introduced in the Act of 1921, mainly in two forms: (1) the limitation of the tax on capital gains in the case of investments carried more than two years to 12½ per cent, and (2) provisions under which capital assets could be exchanged rather than sold without any tax being incurred. Under this law the rule that what is sauce for the goose is sauce for the gander invoked by taxpayers in support of the removal of the limitation on deductible losses in 1918 was waived in favor of the taxpayer. Logically, the converse of the first provision just referred to would have been that a taxpayer sustaining a capital loss should pay the ordinary tax on his regular income and deduct therefrom 12½ per cent of the amount of his capital loss. The Act, however, permits him to save the maximum surtax he would otherwise have paid. Thus to use the same illustration as before, under the existing law a taxpayer with a regular income of $50,000, a capital gain of $20,000 in one year, and a capital loss of $20,-000 in the next, pays over the two years $2,800 less than if both transactions had occurred in the same year.

In the case of the very wealthy, therefore, the present law makes it distinctly advantageous to take capital gains one year and pay a maximum tax of 12 per cent thereon and take capital losses in another year, saving the maximum surtax to which the taxpayer would otherwise have been liable.

The position in regard to the exchanges is even more unfavorable to the Government. A taxpayer holding stock of the A. B. Company desires to dispose of it and reinvest in the stock of the C. D. Company. If the present market value of the stock of the A. B. Company is less than its cost to him he sells this stock and buys the stock of the C. D. Company and is entitled to a deduction from his taxable income of the loss on sale. If, however, the market value of the stock of the A. B. Company is above cost, he arranges an exchange of this stock for stock of the C. D. Company with a cash adjustment and under the law he derives no taxable gain and therefore pays no additional tax.

From this brief summary it will be seen that in less than 10 years the relation between the provisions regarding capital gains and those regarding capital losses has been changed from one of marked disparity in favor of the revenue to an even greater disparity in favor of the taxpayer. Probably, every change has operated to the detriment of the revenue except to the extent that legislation has been retroactive and heavy taxes have been levied on transactions which would never have been consummated if a change in the law had been anticipated. Retroactive legislation, however, is not a desirable practise; and while it was doubtless justified in a time of world warfare, it should be banned for the future, like many other practises developed during the war.

The above history of legislation since income taxes became possible on March 1, 1913, suggests that though the disparity in favor of the taxpayers may be lessened, it would not be practicable, even if desirable, to restore the old disparity in favor of the Government. It will be assumed, therefore, that if capital gains are to be taxed, capital losses must be allowed as deductions on at least an equal basis. Though specific provisions may facilitate tax avoidance or make it more difficult, the Treasury in dealing with all such problems suffers from the fundamental disadvantage that it is the taxpayer who not only decides the time and the form of transactions giving rise to capital gains or losses, but exercises the option whether they shall take place or not. To use a military analogy, the initiative, whose value in warfare is universally recognized, is always with the taxpayer. The Treasury has its fixed defences; the taxpayer moves only after careful study of these defences, and it is not surprising that the Treasury, with a defence impregnable against a frontal attack, often finds itself helpless against an enveloping movement which attacks it in the flank or rear. This disadvantage is increased by the fact that the distinction between ordinary income and capital gain is often a fine one, and a slight change in the form of the transaction may throw it into one class or the other. If, therefore, the Government decides to tax capital gains and allow capital losses as deductions, the taxpayer can refrain from taking gains but may take losses. If on the other hand the Government should exclude capital gains and capital losses from the scope of the income tax altogether, there is danger of transactions which essentially give rise to income being cast into such a form that the gain would technically be held to be a capital gain. How fine the distinctions are, and incidentally how unexpected may be the results to the Government and to the taxpayer of any action outside the ordinary course of business in a time when tax laws are rapidly changing both in form and in degree of severity, is very well illustrated in the case of the Phellis or du Pont case. This case and the Rockefeller-Prairie Oil and Gas case decided by the Supreme Court at the same time, constitute two of the most complete, and in amounts involved the most considerable, of the Pyrrhic victories of the Treasury in tax litigation. The point at issue was not, of course, whether the transaction involved resulted in a capital profit or in a profit in the nature of ordinary income, but what might seem a much simpler question, whether it resulted in any profit at all.

III. THE PHELLIS CASE

The amounts involved in the Phellis case are so large and its features so striking as to make it worthy of detailed consideration.

The facts are briefly that the E. I. du Pont de Nemours Powder Company of New Jersey in 1915 transferred all its assets to a Delaware company in consideration of debentures and stocks of that company, and retaining debentures of the Delaware company equal to the par of its common stock (approximately $30,000,000) distributed to its common stockholders two shares of Delaware company stock for each share of New Jersey company (or an aggregate of $60,000,-000). The market value of the Delaware company's stock at the date of distribution was $347.50 per share. The Supreme Court has now found that this distribution was a dividend taxable to the stockholders of the New Jersey company, and by this decision has added to the taxable income of 1915 an amount of approximately $210,000,000, or nearly 5% of the total taxable income disclosed by all the individual tax returns of that year.

The five judges of the Court of Claims agreed in the view that in substance there was no income to the stockholders of the New Jersey company because the stock of the Delaware company represented the same property and business as the stock of the New Jersey company had previously represented. This view was supported, however, by only a minority of the Supreme Court, the majority finding that both in substance and form the stock of the Delaware company constituted real income to the stockholders of the New Jersey company.

In passing, it may be remarked that while each of the courts looked beyond the form and discussed the substance of the transaction—one finding that in substance there was no dividend, and the other that the whole of the stock of the new company at its market value constituted a dividend—in neither Court was a third alternative discussed which seems most accurately to reflect the substance of the transaction. This alternative is that the stock of the new company represented substantially what the old stock had previously represented, and that the old stock, which after the transaction represented only an equal amount of debentures of the new company, was the real dividend. In substance the position of the stockholder after the transaction was almost identically the position in which he would have been placed had the New Jersey company created $30,000,000 of debentures and issued them to the common stockholders by way of dividend, or even if it had sold $30,000,000 of debentures at par and paid the cash to its stockholders. After the transaction, the stock of the old company represented to the stockholder of the old or New Jersey company something severed from the du Pont property and business which he could realize without reducing in any degree his proportionate interest in the general du Pont assets.

The controversy extended over six years, during which anyone who was a stockholder at the time of the reorganization and who subsequently sold a part or the whole of his stock in the Delaware company was unable to determine whether under the income tax law he had made a profit or loss by doing so. If, for instance, such a stockholder sold 10 shares of the Delaware company's stock for $2,000, the transaction would on the Government's theory result in a deductible loss of $1,475. If, however, the Government's contentions were overthrown, the result would be a taxable profit of a rather greater sum. The Government having won, it is interesting to consider what this victory has gained for it and what has been, or will be, the cost.

The keynote of the decision by which the Supreme Court held that stock dividends were not taxable was perhaps the statement that a stock dividend provided nothing out of which the stockholder could pay a tax without parting with some portion of his interest in the corporation. Assuming that the taxpayers who were called upon in 1921 to pay surtaxes on the profits which they are deemed to have made in the transaction of 1915, should have had recourse to the sale of their stock to provide funds with which to pay their tax, what will their position be?

The market value of the stock of the Delaware company was at the time of the decision roughly par. Any holder who received his stock as a dividend in 1915 pays tax in that year on the basis of a value of $347.50 a share, and if he sold in 1921 he is entitled to claim a loss on sale in 1921 of $247.50 a share. In 1915 the normal tax was 1 per cent and surtaxes beginning at incomes of $20,000 ranged from 1 to 6 per cent; in 1921 the normal tax was 8 per cent and surtaxes beginning at incomes of $5,000 ranged from 1 to 65 per cent. It will be apparent, therefore, at once how great the advantages of the decision to a taxpayer may be. Taking by way of illustration the case of a married man without dependents whose income apart from the dividend in 1915 or sale of stock in 1921 was $7,500 in each year, and assuming that he held 10 shares of the New Jersey company's stock and received 20 shares of the Delaware company's stock as dividend in 1915, and that he sold this stock in 1921 at $100 a share, it will be found that the dividend does not bring him into the surtax class for 1915, so that he has no additional tax to pay for that year, but the loss of sale in 1921 reduces his taxes for that year from $320 to $2.

Multiplying the figures twenty-fold and taking a man whose income was $150,000 in each year and whose original holdings of the New Jersey company's stock was 200 shares, it will be found that the addition of the dividend to his income for 1915 increases his taxes for that year by $5,950, and the loss on sale in 1921 decreases his taxes for that year by $51,650.

The full effects of the decision are not reflected even in these figures, as had the opposite decision been reached there would have been a taxable profit instead of a loss on any sale of stock in the Delaware company. Presumably the decision will also involve considerable saving of tax to the Delaware company.

No doubt some stockholders had sold a part or all of their stock prior to 1921 and in other cases the stock is held by persons who would not, and perhaps could not, without difficulty, sell any great proportion of their holdings. The cost of the victory to the Government will therefore probably not come near its potential limits.

It is, however, reasonably certain that the cost to the Government in the form of taxes lost will enormously exceed the additional taxes recovered as a result of the decision. One is tempted to ask questions like those of the children in Southey's poem "After Blenheim," and one finds no answer except Kaspar's:

'But what they fought each other for
I could not well make out.
But everybody said,' quoth he,
'That 'twas a famous victory.'

A similar analysis of the Rockefeller and Harkness cases
would lead to a similar conclusion.

The claim of the Government was at best largely technical,
since it could not be said that the du Pont stockholders realized true income from the transaction in an amount approaching the two hundred millions which the Court held
must in law be deemed to be derived therefrom. The case
turned on the special facts of a very unusual transaction and
established no new principle, and the net result of upholding
the Government's contentions was bound to be a loss of
revenue. It is surprising, therefore, that the Government
did not accept the verdict of the Court of Claims.

The position after this decision and the stock dividend
decision (*Macomber* v. *Eisner*) would have been most unsatisfactory if Congress had not in the Act of 1921 provided in
substance that no income should be deemed to be derived
from corporate reorganizations.

The interest of the case, in relation to the subject of this
discussion, lies in the evidence it affords of the room for wide
difference of opinion concerning the income-producing effect
of a transaction, even if the question is considered with regard to its substance and not merely to its form. The room
for difference of opinion on the question whether some of
the complicated transactions of modern corporate finance
produce income in the narrower sense, capital gains, or no
gain or income at all, is obviously even greater.

IV. CONCLUSIONS

Study of the subject over a period of many years has
led the writer to the conclusion that while either course is
fraught with danger and tax avoidance on a large scale is
bound to continue as long as high rates of surtaxes are maintained, the losses of revenue involved in the taxation of capi-

tal gains and the allowance of capital losses as deductions from taxable income are on the whole greater than those involved in the opposite course; and further, that the margin is so great as to outweigh the consideration that in principle it is preferable to tax capital gains. Neither the war period, with its extravagant gains and unmerited losses, nor the period of readjustment immediately after the war was an opportune time for a change of policy in this regard. As, however, we get back to more normal conditions, such a change seems worthy of the most serious consideration, more especially as the existing law in remedying defects of the old law has created new opportunities for tax avoidance from which the Government is bound to suffer very heavily.

If capital gains and losses are in general to be excluded from the scope of the income tax, safeguards will be necessary to prevent a wholesale escape from taxation of income by conversion into capital form. It is believed, however, that three provisions would be sufficient to prevent the great bulk of such evasion, namely:

(1) That where a capital gain or a capital loss arises in respect of an asset, which from its nature is subject to a natural increment or decrement in value, any gain shall be deemed to be income to the extent of a reasonable return on the investment for the period during which it has been held. Conversely, the natural decrement should be allowed as a deduction from taxable income.

(2) That where property is disposed of within, say, two years of its acquisition, the transaction shall be deemed to be a trading transaction and not a capital investment.

(3) A provision under which the tax would be levied on the sale of stock of corporations, particularly private corporations, where it might appear that there was a profit which was attributable to the accumulation of undivided profits by the corporation and that the sale was made to avoid the imposition of the tax which would be assessed on such profits if distributed as dividends.

Of the three provisions it is believed that only the third would offer serious difficulty in its formulation, and it should readily be possible to surmount these difficulties with the assistance of a group of persons familiar with business practise and with tax procedure.

Doubtless the adoption of this suggestion would involve the definite abandonment of a large amount of revenue which the Government ought some day to receive, but it is not believed that the sacrifice of revenue which the Government would otherwise be likely to receive would approach in amount the increase in revenue that would result from the elimination of deductions for losses.

Tax avoidance on a substantial scale would doubtless continue even if the suggestion were adopted, but this is bound to be true under any law so long as the extreme surtaxes now in force are continued. Most students of the subject are in agreement with the views expressed by the Secretary of the Treasury in his letter to the Chairman of the House Committee on Ways and Means of April, 1921, that the immediate loss of revenue that would result from the repeal of the higher surtax brackets would be relatively small, and the ultimate effect should be an increase in the revenue. Congress apparently clung to the outworn idea that such a repeal would result in a loss to the Treasury for the sole benefit of the rich. It will, however, ultimately be forced to recognize the shortsightedness of its policy, especially having regard to the existence of the huge volume of tax-exempt securities.

In justice to the present Congress one must recognize that not only is the problem an extremely difficult one, but it is made more difficult by the sacrifice of sound principles to political expediency in the original adjustment of income taxation to war necessities. Given a business world organized largely in the form of private companies which are practically incorporated partnerships, a world in which business transactions may readily be cast into different forms so as to produce ordinary income or capital gains as may be the more advantageous and given also a huge volume of tax-free securities; under such conditions the combination of a low normal tax on income of individuals and corporations with very high surtaxes is neither equitable nor effective. This is equally true whether capital gains and losses are treated as entering into the determination of income or not. The form of tax avoidance changes to meet either rule. The only real solution is to reduce the disparity between normal taxes and surtaxes.

Had the Congress recognized these facts in war time and raised the normal tax and the lower range of surtaxes to higher levels as urged by the Treasury, it would have been possible later to make reductions all along the line. It is not surprising however that the present Congress should look askance at a proposal to increase the normal tax and the lower surtaxes and reduce the higher surtaxes. Though in reality such a scheme would be sound finance and benefit the entire community, it seems on the surface too much like a scheme to relieve the rich at the expense of the relatively poor to be expedient from the standpoint of party politics. It is certain, however, that the high surtaxes will prove increasingly ineffective and injurious the longer the present system is continued.

In the meantime, it is believed that the revenues can be increased, tax avoidance greatly diminished, and greater equity secured by the abandonment of the rule of taxing of capital gains and, conversely, of allowing capital losses as a deduction from taxable income.

III

TAX-EXEMPT SECURITIES

(1923)

(1) TAX EXEMPTION AND THE CHAMBER OF COMMERCE *

THE report on tax-exempt securities which has been prepared by the committee on taxation of the Chamber of Commerce of the State of New York and which is to be considered
at the meeting of the Chamber tomorrow is a singularly unconvincing document. That the committee should report
adversely upon the Constitutional amendment prohibiting
the further issue of tax-exempt securities was not wholly unexpected, but it is to be hoped that the Chamber will not
adopt the resolutions suggested unless stronger arguments
can be adduced than are to be found in this report.

The Chamber certainly owes it to itself to insure that
whatever action it takes shall be based upon broad and
statesmanlike grounds, and not upon such narrow considerations as are embodied in the committee's report. That document deals with the question of tax exemption as if it were a
minor problem in arithmetic, and both its statement of the
problem and its arithmetic contain egregious errors. For
example, it compares the position of the holder of $1,500,000
of 4 per cent tax-free bonds with that of a man whose income
of $60,000 is wholly taxable, and reaches the conclusion that
the former, by foregoing 1 per cent interest on his investment in return for the tax-exemption privilege, incurs a
sacrifice of $15,000, while the latter's sacrifice is only $11,940.
Clearly, however, the comparison of the bondholder should
be made with a man whose income *after taxes* amounts to
$60,000; that is, with a man whose income is roughly $80,000.

* An editorial contributed to the New York *Evening Post* (January 31,
1923).

In that case his taxes would amount to $19,940, compared with the sacrifice of $15,000 by the bondholder. The correction of the committee's arithmetic completely destroys its conclusions and makes the case cited really an argument against tax exemption.

This case, however, is not a common one. Ordinarily the taxpayer will invest in taxable securities up to the point where tax exemption becomes really profitable, and in tax-exempt securities for the rest of his capital. A comparison of such a case with that of a savings bank investing the savings of the poor in State and municipal securities brings out clearly the way in which tax exemption operates to relieve the large taxpayers at the expense of the less fortunate. The question, however, involves much more than the elimination of minor inequalities in taxation. Perhaps that defect alone would hardly be sufficient to justify invoking the complex machinery for amending the Constitution. Nor does the case rest mainly on the argument that it encourages municipal waste and unwise extension of municipal enterprise, though this argument should appeal to members of the Chamber who "know the blighting influences of Government ownership," as another report to be considered at tomorrow's meeting states that they do. It is indeed disturbing to note that issues of municipal securities have increased over 300 per cent in ten years, while the issues of railway, industrial, and public utility bonds have increased only about 70 per cent.

The strongest argument for the abolition of tax exemption is to be found in the principle that in a democratic state it is altogether wrong that any substantial part of the country's wealth should be immune from taxation. A body which indorsed conscription of men in war time should hesitate to take the stand that billions of the nation's wealth should be free not merely from conscription but from taxation in time of war.

If the Chamber finally decides to come out for tax exemption it should make it clear that in reaching its conclusions it has had due regard for these and many other broad considerations in favor of the amendment which have been brought forward by such of its advocates as R. C. Leffingwell, former Assistant Secretary of the Treasury, and the Davenport committee. It should certainly not base its action upon any such narrow, and incidentally inaccurate, statement of the case as is contained in the present committee's report.

(2) TAX-EXEMPT BONDS AS ISLE OF SAFETY *

I regret that the Chamber of Commerce, in view of the clearly expressed doubts of its committee on finance and of the Secretary of the Treasury regarding the correctness of the premises on which the committee on taxation based its report on the tax-exemption amendment, did not yield to the request of a large percentage of the members in attendance for an opportunity for fuller and more adequate discussion of this important question. Had I secured the floor, as I endeavored to do, I should have given specific illustrations to show that these doubts were well founded. I should, however, have urged that the question be decided on broader grounds.

With the "States rights" phase of the question eliminated by the form of the amendment now proposed, views on the question of preventing future exemption should depend on the view one holds regarding the general principle of taxation on the basis of ability to pay, particularly as embodied in a graduated income-tax law and on the degree of faith one retains in American democracy in its attitude towards the institution of private wealth.

If you regard private wealth in the United States today as being in the position, as it were, of Holland; if you believe that it is constantly threatened with inundation by the waves of radical legislation and is protected only by the dikes built by the founders of the Constitution, you naturally regard the income-tax amendment adopted in 1913 as having swept away one of the main dike systems. It follows that you re-

* A letter to the New York *Evening Post* (February 6, 1923).

gard tax exemption as an inner dike system which, when the surrounding fields of commercial wealth are inundated, will preserve an island of refuge in which so much of private wealth as is represented by public securities may still find safety. You may have doubts whether as the tide rises the dike will be of more avail in resisting it than Mrs. Partington's mop, but you are determined to fight grimly to maintain the dike to the last moment. It would seem, however, that those members of the Chamber who belong to this school of thought should have opposed the second of the resolutions offered by the committee on taxation, which condemns the extension of tax exemption to farm loan bonds and similar securities; surely their aim should be to enlarge the borders of their island wherever possible, and there is the added consideration that by throwing a sop to the farm bloc they might secure some support from it in maintaining the dike.

The income tax is comparatively new to us but is an old institution in England, and in earlier days a similar school of thought existed there and included many eminent men such as Pitt and Brougham, the latter of whom characterized graduation as "a gross and revolting absurdity." The historian of the English income tax who cites this expression and others offers the comment: "As time went on it became increasingly evident that the old unreasoning position could not be maintained in the face of modern and more scientific doctrines of taxation." And however the Chamber of Commerce may be divided on the question, opinion in the country at large seems to be overwhelmingly in favor of the graduated income tax; indeed, it is difficult to see how the necessary taxation during the war could have been levied had the income-tax amendment not been adopted.

This is not to say that the manner in which the income tax was availed of was wholly satisfactory. I share the view that the high surtaxes are unwise from every standpoint. It is not, however, surprising that Congress should have used the new medium, which had become available only shortly before the war, with more zeal than discretion during that emergency, and the wisdom of a more moderate use of the principle of graduation is likely to receive increasing recognition. However that may be, if we are to have a graduated income tax at all, exemption of any particular form of investment of private wealth from its operation is contrary to the underlying principle of the system, constitutes discrimination in favor of unearned as against earned income, and (the report of the committee to the contrary notwithstanding) is financially unprofitable to government.

It is impracticable within the limits of this letter to analyze the committee's report in detail, but such analysis would show that the report utterly fails to meet the point made by the Secretary of the Treasury in his letter to the chairman of the committee, as follows: "To one purchaser the exemption may be worth little or nothing and to another purchaser who pays the same price the exemption may be worth the equivalent of 10 or 11 per cent on the taxable security." If, as Mr. Mellon and Mr. Kelsey both suggest, the maximum surtax should be reduced to 25 per cent, this disparity would be reduced, but it would still be substantial. In that case the true yield of a 4 per cent tax-exempt security would range from 4 per cent to a savings bank or exempt investor up to 6 per cent to investors subject to the maximum surtax. I do not think, however, we could afford to regard with equanimity the prospect of the wealthy investor receiving from the State an effective rate of interest half as high again as that paid to the less fortunate citizen. Secretary Mellon does not overstate the case in saying that "graduated additional income taxes cannot be effective when there exists side by side with them practically unlimited quantities of fully tax-exempt securities available to defeat them."

In considering this question too much regard should not be had to the conditions of the moment. The outstanding lesson we learned from the last war was the necessity and the practicability of conscription of man power on a large scale; we also learned that a great war imposes a strain on the material resources of the combatants far beyond that which it

had been supposed any nation could bear. If we should become involved in another great war, conscription of man
power would undoubtedly take place on an even larger scale
than in the recent war, and certainly every dollar of the
national wealth should be as available for the national defence as every man will have to be. This, however, cannot
be accomplished unless steps are taken to insure that as the
special privileges now existing in the form of tax exemption
expire they shall not be renewed, and that no new exemptions shall be created.

(3) TAX-EXEMPT BONDS AS BURDEN ON PUBLIC *

In view of the first paragraph of my recent letter to you,
I feel bound to accept the invitation extended by Mr.
Kelsey in his letter appearing in the same issue to criticize
the figures appearing in his committee's report and the inferences drawn from them.

The committee's whole report is vitiated by an assumption
which is contrary to all experience and probability. It assumes that the rich man who buys tax exempts buys them
blindly, whether it is profitable or unprofitable for him to do
so. The fact is that most rich men have investments with
which they are identified and which they could not and
would not convert into tax-exempt investments, and the
taxable income from these sources is more than enough to
bring their incomes up to the level where the purchase of
tax exempts becomes highly profitable.

The investor who has no business interests and an absolute
freedom of choice in investments studies each investment
carefully and buys taxable securities or exempt securities, as
expediency dictates. It is only natural that he should do
so, particularly as there is a wide range of gilt edge securities,
including Government bonds, outside the class of exempt
securities. The case on which the committee bases its computations—that of a man whose income is wholly derived
from tax-exempt securities—is therefore so uncommon that

* A letter to the New York *Evening Post* (February 9, 1923).

any general conclusions drawn from it are valueless. In the days of slavery there were, I believe, slaves who refused freedom when it was offered to them, and such cases go quite as far towards proving that slavery was a desirable institution as the committee's illustration does towards showing that tax exemption does not operate to relieve the rich from taxation.

Space will not permit of my discussing every point upon which I believe the committee has fallen into errors of fact or inference. I will therefore take a single case and will choose the point which the committee evidently regards as the most important—that which deals with the argument for the constitutional amendments, stated by it as follows: "It is said, though, that there is a great social reason why the issue of tax-exempt securities should be abandoned, that they are the means by which the rich unload the burdens of taxation on the poor. In fact, the whole agitation seems to be founded on this false premise. . . ."

The committee's counter-argument is in two parts: first, "the opposite is true until you get to incomes exceeding $60,000 a year . . ."; and secondly, "when it comes to equalizing the burdens between the two classes of incomes above the $60,000 mark, if it is important to do it, it can be accomplished by a reduction in the surtaxes, and that could be done and still leave the maximum surtax at *not more* than 25."

Upon the first point, it is difficult to see how the poor are in a position to unload burdens on the rich through the medium of tax exemption so long as there is no compulsion on any individual to buy tax-exempt securities. The committee's concern is unnecessary, and they may rest assured that the rich who buy tax exempts do it because they find it to be profitable.

Upon the second point, the committee assumes that the holder of 4 per cent tax-exempts forgoes from $\frac{1}{2}$ per cent to 1 per cent in interest in consideration of the exemption. If this is so, the exemption costs him from 11 per cent to 20 per cent of the income he would receive if the security were not exempt. The Federal tax rate is more than 11 per cent upon all income in excess of $14,000 a year, and more than 20 per cent upon all income in excess of $30,000 a year. Upon the committee's own assumption, therefore, exemption of income in excess of these levels clearly constitutes relief to the holders at the expense of someone else. The exceptional case used as an illustration by the committee is, as already stated, so uncommon as to be negligible.

Finally, how far can the burden on the possessor of earned income and the holder of tax exempts be equalized by the reduction of the surtax to 25 per cent? With 8 per cent normal tax this would make the burden on the earned income subject thereto 33 per cent, and the burden on the income from tax exempts is, by the committee's own assumptions, not more than from 11 per cent to 20 per cent. It is apparent that earned income would still be subject to a burden from 65 per cent to 200 per cent greater than that on tax-exempt income. The committee, however, says "not more than 25 per cent." There is much virtue in the "not more," for to effect equalization the maximum surtax would have to be reduced to 12 per cent or 3 per cent, according to the spread assumed between taxables and tax exempts.

At this point the committee's position stands revealed as the common position of opponents of the amendment: "Abolish the surtaxes or leave us tax-exemption as an avenue of escape from them."

IV

SCIENTIFIC TAX RELIEF *

(1923)

ADVOCATES of some relief from taxation for earned income should recognize that it is hopeless to secure the reduction of surtaxes by any clear, uniform, and universal measure of revision. The possessors of earned income should therefore try to devise indirect forms of relief similar to those which have robbed the surtaxes of their terrors to possessors of investment income and yet have enabled them to escape from the monotony of tax-exempt investments.

For instance, a provision entitling the possessor of earned income to make a deduction from his gross income in respect of the exhaustion of his natural life would with a sympathetic Natural Abilities Division afford a large measure of relief. If it is objected that the value and the term of life of an individual are incapable of determination, it is sufficient to answer that the difficulties are no greater than those in the determination of the quantities and values of the natural resources of the country, which the taxing officials have met and solved so nonchalantly and without hardship to the taxpayers. As the development of the natural abilities of its citizens is even more important to the country than the opening of new oil wells, Congress should recognize the justice of a "discovery" clause which would permit of the exhaustion allowance being increased if the taxpayer should develop hitherto unsuspected ability to make money. A raise of salary received by a man who has held his position more than two years might be subject to a maximum tax of 12½ per cent in the same way as gains on investments held for that length of time.

* An editorial contributed to the New York *Evening Post* (November 8, 1923).

Doubtless the opportunities now accorded to the owner of investments to reduce his taxes by incorporating himself could, even under the present law, be made available to some extent to the worker. It would not seem unreasonable, however, in view of the difficulties in his case, to request Congress to enact a provision that every individual earning an income which would subject him to an average tax of 12 per cent or more should be deemed to be incorporated and be assessed under the provisions relating to corporations. Many possessors of earned income have poor relations or have intimate friends who have suffered losses, and in such cases permission to make a consolidated return would prove helpful.

These are only a few of the methods that suggest themselves, but they are presented to the possessors of earned income with the suggestion that there is far greater hope of relief in provisions such as these, the exact consequences of which Congress cannot readily perceive, than in any clear and unequivocal reduction of taxes.

V

THE INCOME TAX: SECRETARY MELLON'S PROGRAM *

(1923)

Hon. William R. Green, *Acting Chairman,*
Committee on Ways and Means,
House of Representatives,
Washington, D. C.

My dear Mr. Green:

Having been a student of taxation for many years and having had the opportunity in various capacities to acquire some familiarity with the actual working of the income-tax laws, I venture to write you in advocacy of the program recently outlined by Secretary Mellon. Many of the suggestions contained in the Secretary's letter will, I imagine, be immediately understood and approved. The reasons underlying the suggested rearrangement of surtaxes on the higher incomes are, however, probably less generally appreciated, and I would like to submit some considerations bearing particularly on that recommendation.

The argument that the high surtaxes divert capital from productive industry and encourage municipal extravagance by unduly stimulating the market for tax-exempt securities is unquestionably sound. It is, however, becoming of less relative importance for the reason that tax avoidance is growing more rapidly and is less limited in scope than tax exemption. I believe the time has come when justice to the earners who cannot resort to tax avoidance, and to those possessors of investment income who do not resort to it, requires either that the present extreme surtaxes shall be made generally effective, or, if that be impossible, as it has proved to be up

* Cf. *The Journal of Accountancy*, Vol. XXXVII (January, 1924).

to the present, that the rates shall be reduced to a point where substantial enforcement becomes practicable.

.　　　.　　　.　　　.　　　.　　　.　　　.

I believe the conclusion is fully warranted that the taxable income reported today in the highest surtax groups is not more than between 10 and 20 per cent of what it would be but for tax exemption and deliberate tax avoidance. If earned income could be excluded from the computation, the percentage on the remainder would fall to still lower figures. . . .

Surely the continuance of the present high surtaxes is indefensible. . . . The present situation is not due mainly to defects in the form of the present law, although some defects exist which could be remedied with benefit to the revenue. The difficulty lies far deeper. The distinction between capital and income is at best difficult to draw, and the complexities of modern business have greatly enhanced this difficulty. Tax laws must be specific and according to well-settled rules of construction must be interpreted strictly—any ambiguities being resolved in favor of the taxpayer. The form of every business transaction, and indeed whether the transaction shall or shall not take place, is determined by the taxpayer, and his decision is reached with a knowledge of the tax law and is usually framed so as to produce the greatest possible profit after taking taxes into consideration.

The difference in taxation between corporations and individuals alone creates an almost insoluble difficulty. The ease with which incorporation and disincorporation are effected; the difficulty of making laws and regulations governing corporations which will apply with equal justice to the large public corporation and the small private corporation, which practically represents an individual fortune, and the further fact that between these two extremes there are innumerable gradations, so that it is impossible to draw hard-and-fast lines and to treat corporations on one side of the line in one way and corporations on the other side of the line in another— these and other such conditions make it impossible for legislation ever to do more than temporarily check the increase of tax avoidance, so long as the inducements to tax avoidance are so compelling as they are today in the case of all those possessing more than a very moderate income.

If it were possible to lay down a few broad principles and leave the administration of the surtax to the discretion of a highly competent taxing authority which could be governed by the substance rather than the form of the transaction, it might conceivably be possible to administer the surtaxes on the present scale with some measure of efficiency. This is, however, impossible and under any other conditions the form rather than the substance inevitably determines the tax, and the form is selected by the taxpayer so as to defeat the tax.

The continuance of the high surtaxes, therefore, means an unedifying contest of wits between the tax avoider and his advisers on the one side and Congress and the Treasury on the other—with all the advantages on the side of the tax avoider, and with those who are unwilling, or, like most earners, unable to avoid taxes, caught between the two and bearing the brunt of the conflict. Congress must legislate in advance and on broad lines to meet all conditions. The tax avoider acts after Congress has taken its position and deals with specific proposed transactions, capable of infinite variation in form and time to meet the rules laid down by the legislature. Naturally the result of the conflict is as disappointing to the Treasury as it is demoralizing to the taxpayer.

Whatever may be possible in time of war, all experience shows that it is impossible in times of peace to levy surtaxes on any such scale as is now in force with any degree of efficiency or with any approach to equity. I am convinced that readjustment of the surtaxes will ultimately benefit the revenue as well as the business of the country and will make taxation far more equitable. I hope, therefore, that your Committee will favorably regard the Secretary's proposals on this as well as on other points.

November 26, 1923. Respectfully, GEORGE O. MAY.

VI

SOME ASPECTS OF TAX AVOIDANCE *

(1924)

RECOGNITION of the truth of Secretary Mellon's statement that the high surtaxes are steadily becoming unproductive appears to be gradually dawning on Congress. In some quarters this recognition is evidenced mainly in a display of indignation that men or even natural laws should fail to conform to the ideas of Congress.

Recently a senator characterized as "little short of actual disloyalty to this republic" the truism repeated by a wealthy man, that wealth always seeks to avoid what it regards as excessive taxation.

Now we can all agree that in an ideal republic every man would conduct his affairs and pay his taxes according to the intent of the law-making body, and no one would change his business conduct as so to reduce his taxes in ways not contemplated by the legislature.

In this ideal republic, of course, the tax would be administered not upon technicalities and nice interpretations of the letter of the law, but upon broad considerations of equity and regard for its spirit. And above all the legislature would frame the tax law with an eye single to the apportionment of the inevitable burden among the citizens of the republic in the most equitable way that could be conceived.

So long, however, as the guiding principle in the allocation of the tax burden is political advantage and the assignment (in the first instance, at any rate) of the maximum burden to the minimum number of voters; so long, too, as the rule governing court decisions is that quoted by the Supreme Court recently from an English decision:

* An editorial contributed to *The Journal of Accountancy*, Vol. XXXVII (March, 1924).

If the person sought to be taxed comes within the letter of the law, he must be taxed, however great the hardship may appear to the judicial mind to be. On the other hand, if the crown, seeking to recover the tax, cannot bring the subject within the letter of the law, the subject is free, however apparently within the spirit of the law the case might otherwise appear to be.

So long as these conditions continue, is it not a little naïve for anyone to expect those at whom the measures are aimed to make no move either to defend themselves or to escape from the impost?

The more serious aspect of the situation is that the next phase is apt to be an ill-considered attempt to assert the dignity and power of Congress.

If one law fails to produce the result the legislator desires, let another more drastic be enacted. Its practical efficiency will probably be no greater and it will almost assuredly do much harm to many at whom it is not directed, but for the moment it will satisfy the outraged dignity and serve the political fortunes of the legislator who has pledged himself to the policy of making the rich pay without passing the tax on to others, natural laws and all other opposition to the contrary notwithstanding.

The professional man whose means of protection or escape are meager views the situation with deep concern, realizing that measures which the capitalist would probably be able gracefully to avoid would be likely to fall in their full weight upon him.

The ostensible beneficiary of such measures, too, would, if he appreciated the situation, be equally concerned because unsound schemes of taxation are sure in one way or another ultimately to prove injurious to the general community.

Much of the tax is passed directly on to the community; the demand for tax exempts stimulates improvident state and municipal expenditures, which in turn increase local taxes falling on everyone; the interest rate on issues not exempt is increased and the increase ultimately reflected in costs and prices. Thus and in innumerable other ways do men and economic forces "conspire" to defeat the efforts of Congress to run counter to natural laws.

In this connection the following extract from the examination of a witness by the English House of Commons is of interest:

Q. How is the assembly composed? What kind of people are the members; landholders or traders?
A. It is composed of landholders, merchants and artificers.
Q. Are not the majority landholders?
A. I believe they are.
Q. Do not they, as much as possible, shift the tax off from the land, to ease that, and lay the burden heavier on trade?
A. I have never understood it so. I never heard such a thing suggested. And indeed an attempt of that kind could answer no purpose. The merchant or trader is always skilled in figures, and ready with his pen and ink. If unequal burdens are laid on his trade, he puts an additional price on his goods; and the consumers, who are chiefly landholders, finally pay the greatest part, if not the whole.

The examination took place in 1766, and the witness was Benjamin Franklin.

The Ways and Means Committee, though retaining the 25 per cent deduction of tax on earned income, proposes to treat all income under $5,000 as earned, and all over $20,-000 as unearned; in other words, the Committee has concluded that anybody can earn $5,000 and that nobody is worth more than $20,000 a year.

As a recognition of the economic fact that the earner has to set aside out of his income capital to provide for himself in his old age, whereas the possessor of investment income is under no such necessity, the Committee's action hardly merits consideration, however interesting it may be as indicating the result of introspection and personal experience of its members. Its maximum effect would be to save the earner about $400 a year under the present scale of taxes, and $300 a year under the suggested Mellon scale. Such sums set aside annually for twenty years at 5 per cent would provide capital sums which would yield perhaps $500 or $600 a year thereafter.

The relief is in substance insignificant but being nominally large (25 per cent) may deprive taxpayers of real relief in some other form.

The salaried, professional, and artist classes whose hopes were raised by the Secretary's letter may well say with Macbeth:

> And be these juggling fiends no more believ'd
>   That palter with us in a double sense:
> That keep the word of promise to our ear,
>   And break it to our hope.

Many will regard this language as equally applicable to those members of the House who voted to continue tax exemption as a refuge for the rich, while vigorously demanding high surtaxes.

The opponents of the constitutional amendment differed on the question of how much the exemption feature saves in interest to the issuers of tax-exempt bonds. Clearly, however, this saving is trivial compared to the saving of tax to the rich buyers. Whether it is a little more or a little less than the Treasury estimated is of slight consequence. The greater it is, the more savings bank investors are being mulcted for a privilege that is valueless to them; the smaller it is, the less the wealthy are paying for a privilege that is most valuable to them.

The vital point is that it is entirely contrary to the principles of a democratic state that an amount of wealth increasing, it is estimated, at the rate of something like a billion dollars a year, should be completely beyond the reach of the taxing power, however great a national emergency may arise.

VII

METHODS OF TAXING WAR PROFITS COMPARED *

DIFFERENCES IN SPIRIT OF LEGISLATION WHICH CAUSE ENGLISH INDUSTRY TO ACCEPT A HIGHER RATE THAN IS PROPOSED HERE

(1917)

In the discussion of the pending finance bill reference is frequently made to the taxation of war profits in England. In general the position is stated to be that in England 80 per cent of the excess profits are taken by the government, and there is, broadly speaking, no complaint, whereas here it is claimed that substantially lower rates of taxation will work incalculable harm to industry.

The statement as to England is, I believe, true, and the question, Why should there be such a wide difference in the attitude of business men toward taxation on the two sides of the Atlantic? is a fair and pertinent one. I do not think the answer is to be found in any difference of degree in willingness to make sacrifices, but that it is to be found wholly in the difference in the methods and spirit governing the determination of taxable profits in the two cases.

The English law proceeds on the theory of giving the taxpayer a liberal pre-war standard and dealing equitably with special cases, and with this basis assured the manufacturer has no valid ground for objection to taxation of his excess profits, however high it may be.

A comparison of the pre-war standards allowed shows that in England the manufacturer is given a choice of two years out of three, each of which was a prosperous year in England. To protect the manufacturer in any special cases where the three years in question were not prosperous ones,

* A letter to the New York *Times* (August 28, 1917).

two alternatives are provided—either a choice may be made of four years out of six (if during the three years' period the profits of the business were 25 per cent below normal) or a reasonable rate of return on capital may be claimed as the pre-war standard. The rate is fixed by the law at a minimum of 6 per cent in the case of corporations, but a specially constituted board of referees has power to increase this rate in any given industry, and in practice the board has increased the rates allowed to 9, 10, 12, and in some cases $22\frac{1}{2}$ per cent.

The finance bill now pending in Congress, on the other hand, fixes arbitrarily as the pre-war standard the average of the three years of 1911, 1912 and 1913, an average which is undeniably subnormal in many industries, including such important industries as steel and leather, and without allowance for the fact that standards of values have completely changed since that period. The only alternative allowed is the average rate of earnings in the industry in which the corporation is engaged, which may give relief in a few cases, but does not meet at all the cases of whole industries which suffered from depression during the three years in question.

As to the determination of taxable profits, the pending finance bill bases the taxation on the returns for income tax, subject only to adjustments in respect of dividends received from other taxable companies. The result is that in many cases taxpayers are denied the full deduction for interest which they have paid, they are required to pay tax on profits outside the regular course of business, and in other respects are taxed on a sum exceeding their true income. No provision is made for dealing with special cases where the law operates harshly.

On the other hand, the British excess-profits tax law provides for modifications of the methods employed in ascertaining income for ordinary income tax purposes. It sets up special rules for determining the profits, but gives power to the Commissioners of Inland Revenue or the Board of Referees to modify these provisions in any case where it seems to them proper to do so by reason either of specific conditions recited in the act, such as the postponement by reason of the war, of repairs; exceptional depreciation or obsolescence of assets employed in connection with the war; or the necessity in connection with the war of providing plant which will not be wanted for business after the war; or by reason of "any other special circumstances specified in regulations made by the Treasury."

Whenever a case of hardship is established the Treasury shows a willingness to provide for it in such regulations. For instance, it was recently represented to the Treasury that the method of valuing inventories, having regard to the rise in prices during the war and probable fall thereof on the conclusion of the war, would result in injustice, and the Treasury, after conferring with leading accountants, issued regulations to cover the case. These regulations provide that after the termination of the last excess-profits period every corporation shall be given time to liquidate its inventories and shall have the right to adjust its returns for the last taxable year so as to take up in that year any loss that may subsequently have been sustained on such liquidation of inventories.

Another important feature of the British law which is entirely absent from the pending finance bill is its treatment of fluctuating business. If a corporation's profits largely exceed the pre-war standard in one year and fall short of that standard in the succeeding year, the corporation receives a corresponding refund of excess profits tax paid on account of the first year.

Another vital difference between the two bills is the provision as to the payment of the tax. Under the pending finance bill the tax is payable at the same time as the income tax. Many corporations which are making large profits have those profits in the form of increased inventories, accounts receivable, and even plants, and not in cash, and such corporations will be seriously embarrassed to meet the large tax payments required.

Under the British law taxes are payable two months after assessment, but the commissioners have power to allow payment to be made by instalments in such sums and at such times as they may fix, and in practice the commissioners have dealt liberally with the taxpayers under these provisions where they were satisfied that hardship would result from demand for immediate payment.

These are only some of the more important differences between the provisions of the two measures, but they are sufficient to indicate the difference in the underlying principles, and this difference is an essential factor in any comparison of the attitude of our manufacturers with that of the British taxpayers.

VIII

THE ADMINISTRATION OF THE BRITISH INCOME TAX LAW *

(1924)

IT is impossible in the brief space available to discuss the whole subject assigned to me in any detail. I have therefore thought it might be useful to try to answer a question recently asked by the Chairman of the House Ways and Means Committee, in the hope that the answer might incidentally be suggestive of ways in which our own tax administration might be improved. Early in 1924 Chairman Green addressed an open letter to Dr. Adams in which he asked the question, Why Great Britain could collect surtaxes on the scale on which the United States is attempting to collect them, and do it successfully, and yet the United States could not do it.

I shall attempt to answer that question. I would say that the answer is twofold. First, there are many reasons, political, legislative and administrative, why Great Britain should be able to do it; and second, it has not done it.

I will not attempt to discuss all the advantages they possess and I do not mean to say that they have nothing but advantages, but they have some striking advantages. Some of them are so universally recognized that I shall not do more than mention them, but others not so well recognized I would like to discuss very briefly.

First among the political advantages possessed by Great Britain I should place the executive responsibility for tax legislation instead of the separation of the executive and legislative responsibility that we have here. In the second place, I should mention something that perhaps is not so

* Proceedings, Academy of Political Science, Vol. XI (May, 1924).

fully recognized, the advantage that they possess in dealing with all legislation in one parliament. Take, for instance, the question of corporations. I should say that the greatest opportunity for avoidance of taxes here is by artificial transactions between individuals and corporations. In England, the control of corporation legislation rests with the same body that levies the taxes, and they have dealt with the corporation law so as to coördinate it with the tax law. If we could do that here, the stopping of the holes would be a much easier task than it is at present. The third political advantage is that the British have no constitutional limitation and no basic date such as March 1, 1913, which is a constant bugbear to anybody who has to frame tax laws here. Fourth, they have no tax-exempt securities. I do not think it is necessary to discuss that advantage; it has been so freely discussed heretofore.

Turning to their legislative advantages, I would place first their unwillingness to enact legislation until they are satisfied that the administrative problems involved can be successfully met. The English excess-profits tax in 1915, which was a brand-new experiment, was held up for a considerable time awaiting assurances of that kind, and the Chancellor of the Exchequer, in introducing it, pointed out that the machinery was as important as anything else in increasing taxation, and he went on to say that unless their whole tax proposals were to be a fiasco, they must see that the burdens which they were laying on the body charged with the administration of the tax were not greater than that body could successfully bear. I say without the slightest hesitation that this point was not considered at all in the law of 1917 in the United States and not adequately in the later laws, and that the burden that has been placed on the Bureau of Internal Revenue in this country has been far beyond the ability of any administrative body to perform. That, I think, is one of the main reasons why Great Britain has had relatively better success with high taxation during the war than we have had. Another factor that has contributed to their success, I think, has been their willingness to risk unpopularity, to recognize that the bulk of the taxes must fall ultimately on the bulk of the people and to place the burden on the many directly instead of trying to place it in the first instance on the few. Great Britain during the war went as high as a thirty per cent normal tax and never made the surtax more than one hundred per cent of the normal tax, whereas here we have been attempting to work with an eight per cent normal tax against a sixty-five per cent surtax, and we are coming down now to proposals of four per cent normal tax, twelve and one-half per cent corporation tax and fifty per cent surtax, a scale of relations that in my judgment makes satisfactory administration absolutely impossible.

The third advantage they have is in simplicity. The British excess profits tax law, with its appendix, occupied about fifteen pages and remained substantially unchanged during the war. They have accomplished that largely by the different way in which they have dealt with the hard case and evasion. We have attempted to do it by rigid rules which have made our laws complicated and yet have not succeeded in making them effective or equitable. They have been able to do it by leaving discretion to meet hard cases to apply the law so as to prevent avoidance.

That brings me to the final legislative advantage which they have and which has made use of this discretion possible; that is the creation of appeal bodies, independent both of the tax-collecting organization and the taxpayer. They have the local commissioners, and during the war they had also a board of referees, men of very high standing, serving without compensation, whose decisions, generally speaking, were accepted, if not gracefully, at least without open complaint by taxpayers.

I had the opportunity of discussing this subject with one of the important officials of the English system quite recently, and he told me how much they as administrative officers valued the services of the local commissioners and ιow freely they used them in dealing with the hard cases. The commissioners, more swayed by sympathy than officials would be, may decide a case on what they think are the equities. The surveyor of taxes, who is the man directly dealing with the case, says, "Well, I will not accept the principle, but I am not prepared to appeal," so the case is decided without establishing a precedent. By such procedure Great Britain has been able to ease the burden of the tax so as to make the collection substantial and yet not impose undue hardship, and so as to reduce the inequity between taxpayers.

First of the administrative advantages of the British income tax law is, naturally, that they had had an income tax for seventy years in England before the war broke out, whereas our income tax system was only four years old when we suddenly ran into the period of very high taxes. That advantage, with all that it means in the way of a civil service that has been built up with high traditions and a splendid morale, coupled with the Government's concern that the administrative problems should be solved before any tax law should be enacted, has been a tremendous one.

The second advantage—it may be a question of opinion but I think it is an advantage—is in their system of decentralization to some six hundred surveyors' districts, in a small country like England, where we centralize everything in a large country like ours. Then again, the system of appeals to an independent body to which I have referred is a very useful administrative aid. Finally, under that head, I would mention the fact that their laws have been so drawn that there is very little valuation necessary and there are no highly artificial and speculative concepts to be administered such as our so-called discovery value.

The problems of valuation that have been put on the Bureau of Internal Revenue in connection with discovery value, depletion, depreciation, capital gains, amortization and other items constitute a burden of valuation far greater than the task of the Interstate Commerce Commission in valuing the railroads of the United States. The Interstate Commerce Commission and the carriers have spent some hundred millions and ten years in the task of valuing the railroads, and still the task is by no means finished. The Bureau of Internal Revenue has been struggling with a greater problem of valuation with no such organization and without any general recognition of the enormous task that they were trying to perform.

I have given some of the reasons why I think Great Britain should be able to collect very large surtaxes relatively more effectively than we can. And now I come to my second point —that it has not done it. I have already explained that at no time has the surtax more than doubled the normal tax, whereas here we have had and talk of having surtaxes eight or ten or twelve times the normal tax. In five years they raised nearly as much by income and profits taxes as we did, but the percentage of the total represented by surtaxes was only about two-fifths of the percentage represented by surtaxes in our case,* this in spite of the notorious fact that surtaxes here have largely been avoided. Instead of citing Great Britain as an example, Chairman Green might have cited it as a contrast. For two policies could hardly differ more than their policy of a high normal tax (twenty-five to thirty per cent) combined with a surtax of about the same rate and our policy of a small rate of normal tax and surtaxes running up to many times that rate.

In my judgment any attempt to combine such rates as a small normal tax of say four per cent, a tax of twelve and one-half per cent on corporations and a fifty per cent surtax, with all the facility for incorporation and dissolution of corporations, and with the control of corporations vested in states entirely independent of the federal government that

* In the five years ending March 31, 1922, Great Britain collected £2,728,-000,000 in income and profits taxes of which £218,000,000, or rather under eight per cent, consisted of surtaxes. The returns in the United States for the five calendar years 1917-1921 showed total income and profits taxes of $14,774,000,000 of which $2,894,000,000, or about 19.6 per cent, were surtaxes.

is levying the income tax, creates an administrative problem that cannot be solved with any great degree of equity or efficiency. I do not think the administration of our Bureau of Internal Revenue has been by any means perfect, but I must say that to me the sight of Congress investigating the administration of the tax law is the very height of irony, for whatever the responsibility of the administration may be, it is insignificant compared to the responsibility of Congress for unsound tax legislation and for imposing burdens on the Bureau without any recognition of the administrative problem involved and without any attempt to provide the machinery or to pay the men necessary to carry it out with a reasonable degree of efficiency.

The main responsibility is, and I think always has been since the war taxes started, on Congress. Look back at the law of 1917, an ill-conceived compromise between the House Bill and the Senate Bill, which was handed to the Bureau of Internal Revenue to administer. It was three months or more after the Bill was passed before even the chairmen of the committees responsible for the Bill in Congress could feel any assurance that it was possible to administer it, and, as everybody knows, it was administered by strong-arm methods, by the adoption of regulations which were in many cases of very doubtful correspondence with the language of the law. Until Congress faces the problem of administration, which it has never seriously considered, and provides some tax legislation which is devised scientifically and with due regard to the administrative problems entailed, it is quite impossible to get efficient tax administration.

Just one more point, there is hardly a provision that has seemed more clearly necessary to justice than the application of the same rule to capital losses as has been applied to capital gains. Yet that was rejected in the Senate last year, and the Senate Finance Committee has thrown it out of the bill again. Such a policy seems to be a policy of high taxes, so that the people at large may think that Congress is putting the burden on the rich, with holes by which the rich may in fact escape. "High taxes and plenty of holes" is a system that is inefficient, inequitable and demoralizing, and makes tax-paying not a function of the ability to pay, as it should be, but a function of the conscience of the taxpayer.

IX

DOUBLE TAXATION *

(1926)

DOUBLE taxation is one of many subjects which have assumed much increased importance as a result of the war. Nor is the increased importance due solely to higher rates of taxation, though the imposition of taxes running up to more than 50 per cent has created situations in which double taxation of income amounts to practical expropriation. Another serious factor is the change in the fiscal situation of the leading countries which the war has brought about. Countries which before the war were in position to supply their own requirements of capital or even had a surplus for investment abroad, have become borrowers; other countries have found themselves not only in a position to invest abroad but almost compelled to do so. Our own country could hardly maintain its policies of restriction of imports through high tariffs, exportation of surplus food products, collection of foreign government debts and the building up of a merchant marine, without making foreign investments to balance the international account.

Again, lack of confidence in domestic finance and depreciation of currencies have created a demand for foreign investments even in countries whose capital resources are inadequate for their own requirements; and in the most stable European countries anxious investors having seen the disastrous consequences of war on the strongest of states, have felt it was unwise to put all their eggs in a single basket, and have invested part of their capital abroad.

The setting up as separate nations of what were formerly parts of a single kingdom, which remain more or less eco-

* *Foreign Affairs,* Vol. V (October, 1926).

nomically interdependent, as in the case of the succession states of Austria, is still another of the many contributing influences as a result of which the subject has assumed very real and general significance.

I

The problem arises mainly in relation to income and inheritance taxes. In its international aspects double taxation of income is by far the most important phase of the question, but in our own country double taxation of inheritances by the States has created a particularly unsatisfactory situation. Attempts to deal with the problem have been made in domestic legislation in our own and foreign countries, and through international conferences—notably those conducted under the auspices of the League of Nations—which have resulted in a number of international conventions for the mitigation of the burden.

Dealing first with the activities of the League of Nations, since these have included authoritative studies of the theoretical and practical aspects of the problem, the question was discussed at the Brussels conference (1920) and referred to the Provincial Economic and Financial Committee. In accordance with the request of this Committee, Sir Basil Blackett, of the British Treasury, submitted two interesting memoranda—one dealing historically with British income tax practice, and the other with the purely economic question of the effects of double taxation on foreign investments. In September, 1921, the Financial Section of the League invited a group of economists consisting of Professors Bruins of Rotterdam, Einaudi of Turin, and Seligman of New York, and Sir Josiah Stamp of London, to prepare a report on the subject. The group made in April, 1923, a full report dealing first with the economic consequences of double taxation on the equitable distribution of burdens and on the flow of capital, and second with the possibility of relieving or mitigating its evil effects either by domestic legislation of states or by international agreements.

The Committee next brought together a group of technical experts, requesting them to examine both this problem and the collateral problem of tax evasion from an administrative point of view. These experts used as a basis the report of the economists, which they characterized as a masterly report of inestimable value to them, and adopted resolutions that embodied the principles which in their judgment should govern the formulation of conventions for relief from double taxation. These resolutions were set forth with extended comments in a report published by the League under date of February 7, 1925. This report was brought to the attention of the International Chamber of Commerce, which had been continuously interested in the subject, and that body, after extended examination through a Committee headed by Prof. T. S. Adams, expressed its substantial agreement with the experts.

The next step was to ask the same group, enlarged to include representatives of other countries, to draft types of conventions of either a general or a bilateral character for the purpose of giving effect to the principles agreed on. The enlarged group met in Geneva in May last, but the session then held was occupied largely in securing agreement on principles on the part of the many new members, and it was not found possible at that time to do more than prepare preliminary drafts of conventions which are to be considered at an adjourned session to be held in October.

II

Double taxation of income arises from the fact that a tax may logically, and can effectively, be levied either where the income arises or where the recipient resides. In our own legislation both these principles are applied, and in addition a tax is levied on our own citizens even if they reside abroad and their income is derived from foreign sources.* The English income tax, the oldest of those in existence, though

* In the 1926 law exemption was granted to non-resident citizens in respect of earned income from foreign sources.

it is in the main a personal tax, nevertheless taxes the income of non-residents derived from English sources. As a practical matter, it is hardly conceivable that any state which levies an income tax would wholly relinquish this source of revenue.

The question of the ultimate disposition of the burden of a tax on income from domestic sources, levied upon non-residents, was considered at length by the economists selected by the League. In the case of a country seeking to borrow capital from abroad, a tax levied on the interest from the loan secured is likely to be thrown back either directly or indirectly on the borrowing country. Where, however, foreign capital is seeking to exploit the natural resources or commercial opportunities of a state, the tax on the income which that capital earns is not likely to be passed on.

As a logical consequence, countries whose natural resources are relatively large in proportion to the foreign interests of their residents are apt to stress the principle of taxation according to the source of income (especially as there would be strong political objection to the exemption of foreigners from a tax to which citizens engaged in similar enterprises would be subject); while the great capitalist countries are equally insistent on the principle of taxation according to residence.

The technical experts in their resolutions drew a distinction between taxes which are independent of the status of the taxpayer and those which are determined by such status; between impersonal taxes and personal taxes, or, using the French terms, between *impôts réels* and *impôts globals*. They suggested that the former should be levied only in the country in which is found the source of the income, and the latter only in the country of residence (domicile) of the recipient of the income. The practical value of the distinction has been questioned, and it must be admitted that the modern income tax is usually in some respects a personal and in other respects an impersonal tax.

In applying the distinction the experts laid down the general principle that taxes at progressive rates should be regarded as personal taxes, and should be levied only by the state of domicile. Acceptance of this principle would mean that no state would levy surtaxes on non-resident individuals on income derived from sources within the state, either with reference to their total income from all sources or with reference to their total income from sources within the state.

Both the United States and Great Britain at present attempt to levy surtaxes on non-resident aliens on the basis of their total income from sources within the taxing country. There is, however, reason to believe that such attempts are not very productive, and on practical as well as on theoretical grounds the two countries might well, under reciprocal agreements, forgo such surtaxes. The administrative difficulties of effecting collection are great, and in any case in which the sums involved are sufficient to warrant the expense the taxpayer can make these difficulties practically insuperable by measures such as the interposition of a foreign corporation under his ownership and control between the source of the income and himself.

Apparently also, though this is not perhaps absolutely clear from the report, the experts considered that no state should levy on the profits of an enterprise owned by non-residents taxes computed at progressive rates, even if the scale were established entirely without regard to the status of the owners. This question is one on which American and British practice have differed sharply.

The British laws have proceeded on the principle that the ability to pay, which is the broad justification of the progressive income tax system, is a purely individual matter; and while income taxes are collected in Great Britain from corporations as a matter of administrative convenience, the system of relief is so arranged that if the income of a corporation were wholly distributed and the income of every individual shareholder were nevertheless still below the exemption limit, the shareholders would in the aggregate be entitled to recover an amount of tax equal to the tax payable in the first instance by the corporation. We have adopted the view that not only may corporations properly be sub-jected to an income tax as separate entities, but the prin-ciple of ability to pay may properly be applied to them through a scale of graduated taxes without regard to the status of their shareholders. This was the vital difference between our excess-profits tax and the British. Whatever may be said on the question of principle, it is highly improb-able that states in which the most important enterprises are being exploited by non-residents will in practice forgo the right to levy graduated taxes on such enterprises.

It should be added that the experts clearly recognized that the principles laid down by them were not likely to be immediately and universally adopted, and made suggestions for procedure in cases where the states could not see their way to accept these principles in their entirety.

III

The experts next proceeded to lay down rules for deter-mining the sources of income. These rules have been ap-proved by the International Chamber of Commerce and are substantially similar to those embodied in our own Federal legislation. Income from real estate (or mortgages thereon) and income from agricultural enterprises are attributed to the country in which the property is situated; earned income to the country in which the services are rendered; income from business to the country where the business is conducted —an apportionment to be made if the business is carried on in more than one country, provided that in each there is a real establishment and not a mere agency. Incidentally, the experts recommended as a concession to practicability that maritime navigation undertakings should be taxed in only one country, namely, that in which the effective control was exercised—a provision similar to that in our own statutes exempting on a basis of reciprocity the earnings from ship-ping registered under a foreign flag. Some shipping inter-ests have urged that this rule should be accepted as based on principle rather than on expediency. It is difficult to see how such a contention could be situated, though the fact that shipping income is earned mainly on the high seas and the extreme difficulty of making any satisfactory apportionment thereof between states seem amply to justify the experts' recommendation.

In regard to interest on bonds, deposits and current accounts the experts suggested that:

The state in which the debtor is domiciled shall, as a rule, be entitled to levy the schedular tax, but the experts recommend the conclusion of agreements whereby (particularly by means of affidavits and subject to proper precautions against fraud) reimbursement of, or exemption from, this tax would be allowed in the case of securities, deposits or current accounts of persons domiciled abroad, or whereby the tax would be levied either wholly or in part by the state in which the creditors are domiciled.

They thus recognized the right of the debtor country to impose the tax and the practical consideration that the tax is likely to be passed back directly or indirectly to the debtor country.

The resolutions of the experts did not deal with inheritance taxes at length, but merely indicated that the rules for income taxes were applicable *mutatis mutandis* to them.

While the theoretical discussion was proceeding, substantial progress was being made in negotiation of treaties for the mitigation of double taxation. In June, 1921, a convention was signed at Rome between Austria, Hungary, Poland, Italy, Jugoslavia and Rumania. A large number of bilateral conventions have been entered into, Germany, Italy, Austria, Switzerland and Sweden being among the parties to them.

The bilateral conventions which have been negotiated· have followed generally the lines of the experts' resolutions. An interesting exception, however, is the convention between Great Britain and the Irish Free State, which adopts the principle of residence and ignores the source of income.

IV

Turning now to the consideration of internal legislation, the question of double taxation within the Empire appears to have been raised in the British Parliament as early as 1860, but it was not until the heavy war taxes came into effect that an attempt was made, in 1916, to alleviate the hardship. The question was discussed at an Imperial war conference in 1917 and was exhaustively considered by a Royal Commission in 1919, and that Commission laid down the principles which in its opinion should be the basis of any sound solution of the problem. The Commission also considered the question of double income taxes in relation to foreign countries but did not see its way in the existing circumstances to recommend any change in the British practice. British measures for relief have therefore, with minor exceptions, been limited to double taxation within the Empire.

In our Federal practice the question of double taxation was dealt with as soon as it became at all serious. The specific provisions enacted have exhibited much the same characteristics as our income tax laws in general. In many cases the spirit of the provisions has been broad, and, indeed, liberality has at times become prodigality. On the other hand, specific provisions have frequently been arbitrary and impracticable, and too often the administration has been productive of irritation and expense to taxpayers, rather than of revenue to the Treasury.

Since 1918 the law has contained provisions under which taxpayers might make a deduction from their United States income taxes in respect of income taxes paid in other countries. Such provisions were the more necessary because of our practice of imposing the tax on citizens irrespective of residence or the source of the income. We could hardly tax our citizens representing American business abroad on their income earned where they were residing, without substantial relief in respect of taxes paid in that country.

The allowances made have not always been based on well-established principles of taxation; at times they have been obviously excessive. For instance, under the 1918 law a citizen resident in the United States could deduct from his United States tax all taxes paid to foreign countries on his income from sources therein, even though such taxes exceeded the domestic tax on the foreign income in question. Thus, if his American rate were 20 per cent and one-third of his income were from foreign sources and subject to a foreign tax of 60 per cent, he would pay no American tax at all. A rule involving such sacrifice by our Treasury of taxes on income which was derived from American sources was quite uncalled for, and it was changed in 1921.

By a curious oversight an even more anomalous situation existed under the 1918 law, as a result of which a domestic corporation might in effect exclude from its gross income dividends received from a foreign corporation and yet deduct from its American taxes any taxes levied on those dividends by the foreign country. This error was also corrected in 1921.

The principle of allowing a credit against the American tax for foreign taxes paid has from the first been extended to taxes paid by foreign subsidiaries of a domestic corporation. The rules laid down in the statutes for computing the credit in such cases have however been, and still are, unsatisfactory and impracticable.

Ever since 1918 any allowance for foreign taxes to a resident alien has been conditional on his own country's granting a similar credit to citizens of the United States residing in that country. The general theory of reciprocal exemption is entirely sound, but our form of procedure is open to the objection that it requires foreign countries to conform to a method of exemption which we have devised, instead of to a method mutually agreed upon. This objection has particular force in a case such as that under our 1918 law, where our scheme was theoretically unsound and extravagant. It was not reasonable that a resident alien should be denied all relief under that statute because his own country did not grant relief to the same unreasonable extent as ourselves. The law surely might have provided for relief either to the same extent as our citizens were relieved in his country or to the extent of the relief granted by us to residents who were citizens, whichever might be the lower.

In 1921, as already noted, exemption from United States income taxes was granted to foreign shipping on a basis of reciprocity. This broad-minded provision, which undoubtedly involved a sacrifice by our Treasury greater than the immediate gain to our shipping interest, has been availed of by the principal maritime countries.

It is probable that any further steps in the direction of relief from double taxation which we may take will be in the same form. With our growing interests in foreign countries it would seem wise to adopt a liberal policy. There are activities other than shipping to which similar treatment might be given, and we might be well advised to offer exemption of non-residents from surtaxes on a reciprocal basis.

Incidentally, we should assuredly be wise to modify our attitude towards non-residents in the matter of returns, penalties and other matters of procedure. At present we proceed on the theory that it is the duty of everyone the wide world over to be familiar with our law and to file a return under it if he has income from an American source as defined by us, whether he has an agent or office here or not. Our laws levy the taxes on "every individual" and require a return from every individual having net or gross income from American sources in excess of specified limits, and our regulations interpret the language literally. Penalties are provided by law, and the regulations apply these provisions to residents and non-residents alike. The penalties collected from non-resident aliens must have been trivial, but the trouble, annoyance and expense occasioned by these provisions has been considerable. The English courts, construing provisions which required "every person" chargeable with supertax to make a return and made "every person" failing to make such a return liable to a penalty, held that a non-resident alien was not required to make a return nor liable to the penalty. The Lord Chancellor, Viscount Cave, said (*Whitney* v. *Commissioners of Inland Revenue*) it was not easy to understand "by what right such a penalty could even in express terms be imposed" and concluded that the provision could not have been intended to apply to such a person. Lord Phillimore said he was sure it was not the duty of a non-resident and undomiciled alien to know English tax law, and Lord Dunedin said:

The next step lay with the appellant, and he made no return, and I agree that the penalty section is inapplicable. For the appellant is not subject to the jurisdiction of the English Court, nor has the British Parliament power to enjoin him personally to do anything.

These views seem eminently reasonable, and it is much to be desired that the Treasury or the courts should interpret our law similarly or that Congress should modify it to the same effect. At present we are merely creating precedents to no profit, which may be followed by other countries to the detriment of our citizens.

V

Our State income tax laws are not—with few exceptions—unduly burdensome, though the methods of apportionment of income are in some cases intricate and unsatisfactory. It is in the field of inheritance taxes that our States have acquired unenviable fame.

The situation cannot be better stated than in the language of the President's address to the conference called at his suggestion, which met at Washington on February 19, 1925:

There is competition between States to reach in inheritance taxes not only the property of its own citizens, but the property of the citizens of other States which by any construction can be brought within the grasp of the tax-gatherer. A share of stock represents a most conspicuous

example of multiple inheritance taxation. It is possible
that the same share of stock, upon the death of its owner,
may be subject to taxation, first, by the Federal Government;
then by the State where its owner was domiciled; then by
some other State which may also claim him as a citizen; again
in the State where the certificate of stock was kept; in the
State where the certificate of stock must be transferred on
the corporation's books; in the State or States where is organized the corporation whose capital stock is involved; and,
finally, in the State or States where this corporation owns
property. All this means not only an actual amount of tax
which may under particular circumstances exceed 100 per
cent of the value of the stock, but the expense, delay and
inconvenience of getting clearances of the States who claim
a right to tax the property is a serious burden to the heir who
is to receive the stock. Particularly is this expense disproportionate to a tax paid by a small estate which has but a
few shares of stock. In many cases the expense alone must
exceed the total value of the shares which it is sought to
transfer. Looking at it from the standpoint of State revenue,
I am told it is probable that the full cost to executors of
ascertaining the tax and obtaining the necessary transfers
is in the aggregate nearly as much as the tax received by the
States upon this property of non-resident decedents. Here,
indeed, is extravagance in taxation.

As the President emphasized, the burden of expense and
trouble was in many cases more serious than the tax. By
the transfer of personal holdings to a corporation formed for
that purpose, and by other means, large taxes outside the
State of the residence of the decedent could usually be
avoided. The amount of tax thus became dependent on
the foresight and ingenuity displayed by the decedent rather
than on any ability to pay. Calculations made showing possibilities of taxes amounting to 100, 200 or even 300 per
cent of the estate were merely mental exercises of the expert.

Since the President's speech was delivered, various events
have improved the situation. By the Federal Tax Law of
1926 the credit for State taxes against the Federal tax was
increased from 25 per cent to 80 per cent of the latter. Next
came the decision of the Supreme Court in the Frick case

which declared invalid a tax on tangible personal property without the State, and held that the State of residence must allow the tax on corporate stocks owned by the decedent levied by the State of incorporation as a deduction from the value of the gross estate in computing its tax. This was followed by another Supreme Court decision which held invalid a tax on the transfer of stock of a foreign corporation owned by a non-resident, based on the ground that the property of the corporation was mainly within the State.

Important States such as New York, Connecticut, Pennsylvania, and Massachusetts, have enacted laws containing reciprocal exemption clauses, and conferences of the taxing authorities of these States have been held in an effort to make such provisions effective. What the League has been seeking to bring about in the international sphere has thus been happening in our own interstate field.

VI

In any review of the measures relating to double taxation which have been taken since the war, it must be constantly kept in mind that the period has been one of unexampled difficulties in the field of government finance. Allowing for this fact, the progress made cannot be regarded as unsatisfactory. The efforts of the League of Nations have borne and are bearing fruit.

The United States by reason of its prosperity and its increasing foreign investments should be the leader in the adoption of broad and liberal policies in this field. Notwithstanding the amelioration of the situation in the recent past, much remains to be done to put our State taxation on a fair and sound basis. There is room for improvement in our Federal law though even more in our methods of Federal tax administration. A Federal inheritance tax, for instance, is still levied on stock of a corporation owned by a non-resident decedent if either the corporation is organized under the laws of one of our States or the stock certificate is physically in the United States at the time of the death.

Surely we might, on a basis of reciprocity, grant exemption in such cases; at least we might adopt a single test of liability. The President's criticisms of the States in this respect are justly applicable to the Federal Law.

The United States has hitherto declined to join in the work of the League of Nations, but if our apprehensions preclude us from following the same precise path, we have at least taken some steps along parallel lines. We have the opportunity and it is to our interest to keep pace with, or even move ahead of, other nations and to offer reciprocal relief to any that are prepared to advance with us. The fact that some of the best informed students of the subject are among those whose judgment on tax questions is most highly valued by Congress gives some grounds for hope that we shall not neglect our opportunities and duties.

X

FEDERAL TAX LEGISLATION IN 1935 AND IN 1936 *

In June, the country was surprised by a Presidential message recommending heavy additional taxes on large incomes and inheritances and new taxes on corporations. The proposals came late in an exhausting session; the amount of revenue they were expected to realize was admittedly trivial in comparison with current deficits; the importance asserted for them was purely social. They were supported by a Treasury memorandum which was freely quoted by the President and which contained highly questionable economic doctrines, obvious misinterpretations of statistics, and disturbing administrative proposals. Hurried legislation resulted, the form of which was determined mainly by reluctance to repudiate the President and a desire to escape from the heat of Washington. The new provisions were not to take effect immediately, and it is intimated that the new Congress will be asked to repair some of the more obvious defects of the hasty enactment. It is opportune, therefore, now to reexamine the recommendations and the memorandum by which they were supported.

The proposals were put forward as calculated to improve the distribution of wealth. Everyone who feels any social consciousness would like to add to the well-being of the mass of our people. Those in political life have no monopoly of this praiseworthy desire, though they are sometimes more concerned with creating the impression that they are doing something to bring about an improvement than with the actual results of the measures which they advocate. Even the best-intentioned reformers, also, are apt, in the language of the great English economist, Alfred Marshall, "in

* Reprinted with Addenda, from "The Voice of Business" number of the New York *Sun* (January 4, 1936).

their anxiety to improve the distribution of wealth to be reckless as to the effects of their proposals on the production of wealth." And it is noteworthy that neither in the President's message, nor in the Treasury memorandum, nor in any other official presentation of the question to Congress, is the effect of the proposals on the production of wealth so much as alluded to.

This points to the real criticism of the proposals. That criticism is, not that the proposed taxes, particularly those on inheritance, were incapable of strict enforcement and therefore bound to result in inequality in their application; nor that the amount of revenue they would raise was relatively unimportant and that in the long run they would probably affect the revenue adversely. These are minor, though probably just, criticisms. The real criticism is that the proposals were calculated to destroy to a large extent the source from which the capital which is the life-blood of our industrial system has in the past been drawn, and that they failed to meet this objection or to indicate any alternative source of capital.

The importance to the great mass of our people of the continuance of a flow of capital into industry can scarcely be exaggerated. Perhaps I may quote what I said upon the question before the Senate Finance Committee: *

It is generally recognized that one of the most vital needs of an industrial community is an adequate supply of capital to be invested in new enterprises.

A little thought will convince that to keep our people busy, development of new industries must be on a constantly increasing scale. In the next generation, we must create new industries exceeding in magnitude the motor, radio, and other industries created during the last thirty years. Now, in the course of such development large losses of capital will be incurred. Professor Allyn Young, one of our greatest economists, used to say that he doubted whether, taking all enterprises together, there was such a thing as profit; that losses equaled profit over a reasonable rate of interest. The important consideration for our people is what effect the

* See below.

proposed taxes will have on the supply of capital for these purposes.

In England, Sir Josiah Stamp has estimated that roughly twenty per cent of the national income is required to be reinvested in industry in order to maintain a healthy progress, and has pointed out that the maintenance of this flow of capital into industry is vastly more important to the people at large than the question in whom the nominal ownership of the capital shall be vested. Mr. Justice Holmes has emphasized the same truth.

Statisticians of the right wing and those of the left wing may argue whether the amount which could be added to the weekly income of the less wealthy by a distribution of the excess income of the wealthy would be more or less by a dollar a week. They will agree that the amount would be small, and trifling in comparison with the improvement in well-being of the people at large that has in the past been produced and can again be produced in a generation or less from the employment of capital in the development of new inventions and new large scale industries, which in the President's own words bring "many things within the reach of the average man which in an earlier age were available to few" or, one might add, in many cases to none.

The omission to deal with these aspects of the question cannot be attributed to their novelty or to a dearth of evidence. Economists like Taussig, Carver and Adams have repeatedly emphasized the point that, while progressive taxation can be applied up to a certain point, once legislators "pass beyond this limit—apply progression so sharply or limit inheritance so narrowly that accumulation is seriously affected—and you must supply ways of filling the gap." President Wilson, in 1919, said:

There is a point at which, in peace times, high rates of income and profits taxes discourage energy, remove the incentive to new enterprise, encourage extravagant expenditures and produce industrial stagnation with consequent unemployment and other attendant evils.

In England, the question has been the subject of extended study by a committee of high quality, which in 1926 made a report known as the Colwyn report, which is regarded as perhaps the most authoritative pronouncement on the broad question. This report is of particular significance because for years proponents of higher income and inheritance taxes have pointed to England as the country where the very rich really paid high taxes compared to which ours were moderate. In its report, the Committee, after indicating its full acceptance of the principle of ability to pay as a guide in taxation, said:

But there is a complementary aspect which imposes a check on the application of the ability to pay principle. . . . The larger the income, the more room is there for savings; and the State, when putting a heavy tax on incomes with the greater margin, has to consider the risk of doing too much damage to savings. . . . The graduation now existing in this country, whether or not it has proceeded too far in the ultimate interests of society, has certainly been checked by the fear of entrenching too heavily upon the essential supply of capital. . . . We conclude with regard to the supply of capital from individual and corporate savings, that industry has suffered materially from the effect of high Income Tax and Super-Tax. This remains true, when full allowance has been made for the proportionate application of revenue to the large payments on account of the National Debt which accrue directly or indirectly to the benefit of trade (§§ 333, 373, and 444).

When this report was written, the maximum combined rate of income and super-tax was 50% and the maximum rate of estate tax was 40%, and it is pertinent to point out that not even the minority of that Committee recommended rates approaching those proposed in the bill which the House passed to give effect to the President's proposals.

The considerations which led the Committee to reject higher graduated taxes are strengthened in our country by two considerations which do not apply in England—first, that they do not tax capital gains and therefore the man who risks his capital has the opportunity of making non-taxable gains as well as a taxable income, whereas here we tax both incomes and gains, though we make no corresponding allowances in respect of losses; and secondly, that there is no isle of refuge for wealth in England corresponding to our tax-exempt securities.

The three commonly recognized main sources of capital for the creation of new and the expansion of old enterprises are private savings, corporate savings, and the State. In his discussion of the proposed additional taxes on corporations, the President said: "We should likewise discourage unwieldy and unnecessary corporate surpluses," which indicates that he did not propose that the main reliance for the supply of capital should be put on corporate savings. In any event the depression has made great inroads on corporate savings. A recent bulletin (No. 55) of the National Bureau of Economic Research states that "The situation revealed is a dark one. In the aggregate, the drain in the form of losses and dividends for the period 1930-1933 exceeded the corporate savings of the entire post-war decade."

The proposal that the State should supply capital for industry was therefore implicit in the Presidential message; and it is surely a just criticism that the real issue which should have been presented to our people was not whether they desired slightly to improve the distribution of wealth, but whether they desired to substitute a system of industry initiated, financed and controlled by the State for the system of privately financed industry under which we have lived and progressed for generations. If such an issue is once squarely raised, it is hardly conceivable that the common sense of our people will not lead them to recognize that a system of private enterprise, subject to the checks and controls of government, is preferable to conduct of industry by government—or, to speak realistically, by politicians.

Apart from the power which the control of capital gives, the benefits flowing from accumulated wealth which the nominal owners thereof can retain for themselves are obviously limited, and from a national point of view insignifi-

cant. Hence it is that the selfish creator of wealth unwittingly benefits his fellow men, while the well-meaning re-
former urging a redistribution of wealth is likely to do his
fellow men only an injury.

Anyone who will read carefully the sympathetic discussion
of *The Christian Ethic as an Economic Factor* contained in
Sir Josiah Stamp's social service lecture in 1926 will be
forced to agree with his conclusion that "In centering our
teaching and our hopes upon the point of redistribution to
produce greater well-being we are 'barking up the wrong
tree' and diverting attention from the more real and powerful remedies."

The attack on great wealth was, it may be noted, based
on the very fact that it was turned back into production. It
was not that wealth ministered to private extravagance and
waste—the complaint was that large estates were not being
squandered; that the old saying that wealth was dissipated
in three generations was being falsified.

The Treasury memorandum quoted by the President furnished statistics purporting to support this view, saying that
"even informed observers were startled at the tendency to
concentration, and the rate of concentration indicated by
the 1933 returns . . . in the face of generally declining incomes, and in spite of the bank holiday and other events
of that year, the number who reported net taxable incomes
of $1,000,000 or over more than doubled, having increased
from twenty in 1932 to fifty such persons in 1933."

The charitable view of this statement is that it was penned
by someone in the legal department of the Treasury un-
versed in the interpretation of statistics. Statisticians know
that the significance of our statistics of large incomes is practically destroyed by the inclusion in income of capital gains
and the frequent changes in the law relating thereto. A
man retires from active life and sells at a profit of a million
dollars a business which represents a lifetime of creative
effort. Thereupon, he makes his appearance (for one year
only) among the possessors of an income of a million dollars,

alongside the man who draws an income of a million dollars a year from industrial bonds.

Changes in the law are constantly occurring. Thus, 1932 was the last year in which capital net losses were allowed as a deduction, and 1933 the last in which capital gains could be taken on the basis of a relatively moderate flat tax—hence there were special incentives to take losses in 1932 and gains in 1933; devaluation, and the inflation market in the latter year added to those gains as measured in devalued dollars. Thus it is found, as was to be expected, that the incomes of over a million dollars in 1933 were made up largely (actually to the extent of almost exactly one-half) of net capital gains, whereas the same groups in 1932 had reported net capital losses of about a million dollars.

It was obvious that the Treasury's interpretation of the 1933 statistics could not survive the publication of the statistics for 1934. Nevertheless, it was a little surprising to find the Bureau of Internal Revenue interpreting the *Statistics of Income* for 1934, recently published (which showed a large increase in aggregate income and a marked decrease in the number of million dollar incomes) as evidence that a great redistribution of wealth had taken place since 1929. The statistics form no basis for such a wide generalization, but the indications are that the conclusion drawn from a study of the national income from 1914-1926, published by the National Bureau of Economic Research in 1930, is still true, and that "there is practically no tendency towards the putting of more income into the hands of the extremely opulent sections of the community."

Whenever the rate of tax on the transfer of property is made so high that the margin left to the taxpayer becomes small in proportion to the margin of possible error in the valuation of the property, the practical result is, inevitably, taxation at the discretion of the taxing authority. When the Treasury, in its memorandum, admitted that cases would arise which "will require sympathetic administration on the part of the Bureau if hardship is to be avoided," it merely stated in blander language the truth that the adoption of the President's proposals as embodied in the House Bill would have put large estates at the mercy of the Treasury.

As an example, the supposition that Mr. Henry Ford would leave his interest in the Ford Motor Company to Mr. Edsel Ford was taken in the discussions before the Senate Finance Committee. Under the House Bill, and upon the assumptions made by the Treasury representative, the tax that would have been payable by the estate and the beneficiary on such a transfer as is assumed would have approximated 90% of the value of the stock. Now, of three equally competent valuers, one would be quite likely to place the value of the stock at a figure 20% above and another 20% below that reached by the third. A tax of 90% levied upon 120% of the fair value would, of course, amount to 108% of that value. On the other hand, a tax of 80% of the true value would be 72%. Assuming, however, that the tax was levied on the true value, and that ten years were allowed for payment, the annual instalment (ignoring interest) would be, roughly, 9% of the value of the stock bequeathed. Now, assuming that the stock paid dividends equaling 10% on the assessed value, surtaxes under the House Bill would have absorbed 75% of such dividends, leaving an amount equal to only 2.5% on the original valuation available to pay the annual instalment of tax which, as already stated, would be 9% of the original value. Obviously, such a tax could not be collected, and the only question would be at what point could a figure be reached which the beneficiary would be willing to pay and the Treasury to accept.

It would be a gross mistake to suppose that such problems would arise in only a very few large cases. Even if the amounts involved were reduced to only two or three per cent of those assumed in the case of Mr. Ford, the annual dividends from the stock bequeathed would, after deduction of surtaxes, still fall far short of the amount required under the House Bill to pay one-tenth of the taxes annually; and it may be added that in these computations all questions of interest, state taxes, etc., are ignored, though in the aggregate they constitute a substantial additional burden.

That differences in legitimate opinion as to value would probably be far greater than has been supposed in the foregoing illustration is apparent from innumerable contested cases. To mention only one, which involved the value of the stock of the Ford Motor Company itself: Some years ago the Treasury fixed the fair value of this stock at March 1, 1913, at somewhat less than $3,600 a share, and held that all the proceeds of sale in excess of that basic value were taxable. After protracted hearings, the Board of Tax Appeals fixed the value at $10,000 a share, and the Treasury accepted its decision.

Now, we must assume that both of these valuations were made in good faith; indeed, on the basis of some personal knowledge of the case, it may be said that at least some of the officials of the Bureau of Internal Revenue believe that the value fixed by it was too high, though it proved to be barely one-third of the value fixed by the Board. If such legitimate differences of opinion as to value exist, can a system which levies taxes of 60% or 70%, or even more, upon such valuations, be wise or sound?

Fortunately in the Senate the proposed new inheritance taxes were eliminated and the law regarding valuation was liberalized so as to mitigate somewhat the extreme effects of the excessive estate taxes, but the law as passed was nevertheless economically and socially unjustifiable.

Before leaving the question of inheritance taxes, reference may be made to the regret which many will feel that Federal taxation should have made this further advance into a field which they believe should be left to the States. However, so long as the Federal Government continues to bear large burdens which seem to belong more properly to the

States, it can hardly be criticized for invading also their revenue preserves.

It cannot be said that the President's proposals in regard to corporations were supported either by evidence or by any sound principle of taxation. The statement that "The drain of a depression upon the reserves of business put a disproportionate strain upon the moderately capitalized small enterprise" is neither inherently reasonable nor in accord with experience—on the contrary, there is much more reason to think that the large corporations are so constantly in the public eye as to make it impossible for them to resort to economies which could be effected by smaller companies without difficulty. The conclusions drawn by the Treasury from unanalyzed statistics are at variance with the results of more thorough studies, such as those of Epstein. But schemes of capitalization, and fiscal policies, have doubtless had more influence than size upon ability to withstand the depression.

The statement, "We have established the principle of graduated taxation in respect of personal incomes, gifts and estates; we should apply the same principle to corporations," completely ignores distinctions which have been pointed out so frequently and insistently that it cannot be supposed that the President's advisers were unaware of them. However, it would be unfair to judge the proposals on their fiscal merits, for they are avowedly a part of a larger campaign against bigness.

The recommendation of an amendment which would permit the Federal Government to tax the income of subsequently issued state and local securities, and the taxation by state and local governments of future issues of Federal securities, is no doubt entirely sound from a purely tax standpoint; but even this recommendation would carry more conviction if it were made at a time when Government expenditures were being prudently limited and the budget balanced. The administrative proposals of the Treasury met with no favorable response from the Congress and need not be discussed here.

Our tax structure today includes an unsound income and inheritance tax scheme resting on an absurdly narrow base (less than seven per cent of the national income paid out to individuals paid even a normal tax in 1933) and imposing rates that are unwise and in some cases unenforceable. Among minor schemes, we have the linked capital stock and excess-profits taxes, which, though described as "rather clever," are certainly neither wise nor fair—for there is no justice in the assumption, which underlies them, that profits are excessive if they represent more than a moderate return upon the current value, at the bottom of a depression, of the capital invested in a business; and we have taxes levied on corporations, partly because of hostility to corporations and partly because this method disguises the burdens that ultimately fall on the individuals who constitute the electorate. No such structure can sustain the burdens which balancing the budget will entail.

The defects of our tax system are not chargeable to any one administration nor to any one Congress. The period of prosperity was the appropriate time for creating a system with a broad base and low rates of taxation which could be adapted readily to the needs of more difficult times. When the depression came upon us, new taxation, which would have balanced the budget, was rejected as politically impracticable. The proposals of last June, by carrying to lengths never before contemplated the false doctrine that the rich can be made to pay without burdening the less wealthy, made infinitely more difficult the task of creating a sound basis for a balanced budget, which must be faced before long if we are to be spared from the bitter awakening that follows the first pleasant dreams produced by Government spending and inflation.

Sound finance today obviously calls for the lowering of rates of taxation in the higher brackets and a real stiffening of the rates in the lower brackets, accompanied by a reduction of the exemptions. But a combination more unattractive politically can scarcely be conceived. There is danger that if the task is faced at all, some device which throws the added burden of taxation less obviously on those with small means will be preferred, though economists may urge the critical importance of bringing home directly to the people the cost to them of Government expenditures.

Measures designed to create a greater degree of social security will make a broader basis of taxation even more imperatively necessary. And surely the people at large, who are to benefit from such measures, would prefer to pay their fair share of the cost during their earning years. They would not be willing to accept private charity, and, logically, they should not be willing to accept public charity, but only benefits during sickness, unemployment or old age out of funds to which they have themselves made their just contribution. The idea that such schemes should be financed by levies on the rich is demoralizing as well as impracticable.

England, with less natural resources, has been able to balance its budget during the depression, though it has gone further than we have in social legislation, because of the broad basis of its tax system and its repudiation of the false notion that the rich can be made to pay the bulk of the taxes. Statistics show that in 1928 England raised a far smaller proportion of its revenue from taxes on income and property, including inheritances, than we did, and that since that time it has made only small increases in the scale of taxation, a large part of which has already been remitted. Today the highest income tax rate is 60% compared with our 75% and the highest estate tax rate 50% compared with our 70%. In 1930, the last year for which satisfactory comparisons can now be made, less than 6% of our total Federal income taxes were collected from persons with incomes of under $10,000; while England collected about 40% of its total from persons with incomes below £2,000. The report made last year by Treasury representatives on the English system shows that an income of $100,000 concentrated in one individual there paid 2½ times as much as the same income distributed equally between ten individuals; here, it paid seven times as much even before the 1935 law was passed. Much the same thing is true of inheritance taxes.

There is no hope of a balanced budget until a drastic curtailment of expenditures has taken place and we have an Administration and a Congress willing to face the fact that the bulk of the taxes must be paid by the mass of the people. It is too much to hope for either in an election year. In the meantime, some minor but important improvements might be effected.

First among these I would put the abolition of the tax on capital gains; or, if that is deemed too much of a sacrifice to sound principle, the substitution of a flat tax not large enough to act as a deterrent to sales of capital assets. I believe this alternative could be adopted without causing any serious loss of revenue, and with wholesome effects on the general situation through the encouragement of sales, otherwise likely to be withheld from the market for tax reasons.

In the second place, the principle admirably stated by the Democratic Chairman of the Senate Finance Committee in 1918, that what is, in fact, a single economic unit ought to be taxed as a unit, should be restored and the consolidated return again permitted; the tax on intercompany dividends should also be eliminated. If these two steps are not to be taken, at least the provisions relating to non-taxable reorganizations should be amended so as to permit corporate readjustments between affiliated companies to be effected without tax. Unless this is done, duplication of taxation as a result merely of the change of a long-established policy in the tax laws will result.

The indefensible linked capital stock and excess-profits taxes should be eliminated; a straightforward tax, designed to raise an equivalent amount would be more statesmanlike and infinitely less harmful in its direct and indirect effects than this exhibition of tax-craft.

Such changes as these would do something to arrest the decline in respect for Federal taxation, which today is too generally regarded as having reached a stage where justice and fairness to the large body of taxpayers have been lost to sight in reprisals against practices which, whatever their merits or demerits, are being followed by only a small number of those on whom the burden of such reprisals falls.

Administrative Proposals of the Treasury

In the foregoing article, considerations of space made it necessary to omit discussion of the administrative proposals of the Treasury; but, although these proposals met with no favorable response from the Congress, they were of such a disquieting character that it seems worth while to append a brief comment upon them. They related to the Board of Tax Appeals and to the Courts.

In regard to the Board of Tax Appeals, the Treasury memorandum said:

The device of permitting a litigation of tax first and payment afterwards, with no security, or penalty or disadvantage whatever for the delay is proving so costly as to present a challenge to effective enforcement.

It is stated by a retiring member of the Board of Tax Appeals that since 1926 the Government had lost two-thirds in amount of its cases before the Board of Tax Appeals, the average tax case involving a deficiency of $28,000.

This brief description of the existing system is inaccurate. The Treasury has and uses the power to require payment or bond for payment in any case in which it has reason to feel that the eventual collection of the tax in any case pending before the Board might be jeopardized. And since any judgments in favor of the Government carry interest, it is incorrect to say that there is no penalty or disadvantage whatever to the taxpayer for the delay. To an impartial observer, the fact that the taxpayers had succeeded in two-thirds of the cases before the Board might seem to be evidence of the need for continuance of the present system, in order to protect tax-payers from oppression by the Treasury. Only a belief in its fitness to exercise autocratic power can explain the contrary view expressed by the Treasury.

In respect of the Courts generally, the memorandum stated:

When the time comes to consider more fully administrative provisions, consideration should be given to settling valuation questions wherever they arise in tax administration in some manner other than by litigation. The litigation method of determining values is too technical, slow and uncertain.

If we could interpret this comment as looking to the creation of a body of some such character as the English Tax Commissioners, independent of both the taxing authority and the taxpayer, we might perhaps derive encouragement from it. But the Board of Tax Appeals, itself, was the outgrowth of such a suggestion; and the fact that the Treasury now regards the procedure before that Board as a challenge to effective enforcement makes such an interpretation quite improbable. The only alternative would seem to be a grant of final power in the matter of valuation to the Treasury, to be exercised by it "sympathetically" whenever sympathetic treatment seems to be called for. Admitting the defects of the legal apparatus for determining values, the Courts possess one advantage which more than offsets any which the Treasury may be presumed to have, namely, that their attitude is purely objective. In theory, the Treasury may recognize that it has a duty to be just to taxpayers as well as to collect revenue, but in practice it takes the position that its mission is to collect revenue, and that it is for the taxpayer to protect himself.

ADDENDUM II

Some Considerations Relating to the Taxation of Capital Gains

I. The present system of taxing capital gains without allowing equivalent relief in respect of capital losses is plainly inequitable. It therefore inspires disrespect for the law and affords a plausible moral justification for tax evasion. As between the alternative of allowing deductions for losses or abolishing the tax on gains, the latter alternative is sounder in principle and is steadily becoming more and more expedient from the fiscal standpoint.

II. At an earlier stage of our development, the argument that capital gains would normally greatly exceed capital losses went a long way to offset the consideration that whether a gain or loss should be taken lies with the taxpayer, so that the normal relation between capital gains and losses is liable to be violently disturbed whenever it is made advantageous for the taxpayer to take or to refrain from taking one or the other. Today, with the exploitation of the natural resources of the country as far advanced as it is, and with the prospect of growing social demands adversely affecting capital values, there is no reason to anticipate that the normal tendency, even if unaffected by tax considerations, would be to produce an excess of gains over losses.

III. The enactment of heavy inheritance and gift taxes has largely destroyed the argument in favor of taxation of capital gains that, in the absence of such taxes, unearned increment escaped all taxation. Capital gains are in the main either lost or added to capital. If they are lost, it is entirely unjust that the gains should be taxed but no relief given in respect to the losses; while, if relief is given, the fact that the taxpayer can choose the time of taking gains and losses will result in a reduction in taxes in respect of losses which will exceed the increase in taxes as a result of gains. To the extent that capital gains are added to capital, the Government now collects a substantial tax when that capital passes by gift or bequest—consequently, there is not the same argument as there would be for taxing gains as gains.

IV. The taxation of gains with equivalent relief in respect of losses produces additional revenue when it is least needed and impairs revenue when the need is greatest.

V. Taxation of capital gains also creates highly artificial

markets, through causing sales which would otherwise take place to be withheld from the market. Unquestionably, this factor is operating to a very considerable extent at the present time.

VI. The abolition of the taxation of capital gains would make possible the elimination of the extremely complex provisions for non-taxable exchanges and reorganizations, which constitute one of the most difficult branches of income tax practice and administration. It would greatly facilitate the corporate readjustments necessary to bring about the reduction in the number of holding companies which the Administration and the Congress seem to regard as highly desirable.

TESTIMONY BEFORE SENATE FINANCE COMMITTEE, AUGUST 7, 1935 *

Senator King. Will you state the capacity in which you appear, Mr. May?

Mr. May. I appear as an individual, primarily because of my interest in tax matters. I was connected with the Treasury during the war and later was a member of the Advisory Committee to the Joint Congressional Committee on Taxation. I am senior partner in the firm of Price, Waterhouse & Co.

I wish to speak very briefly on the question of the effect of the proposed taxes added to the existing taxes upon those not directly subject thereto. I do not propose to touch on the effect on the persons subjected to the tax except insofar as that is necessary to indicate the probable effect on the great majority of our population who will not be directly subject thereto.

It is generally recognized that one of the most vital needs of an industrial community is an adequate supply of capital to be invested in new enterprises. A little thought will convince that to keep our people busy, development of new industries must be on a constantly increasing scale. In the next generation, we must create new industries exceeding in mag-

* *Hearings on the Revenue Act of 1935,* pp. 303-10.

nitude the motor, radio, and other industries created during the last thirty years. Now, in the course of such development large losses of capital will be incurred. Professor Allyn Young, one of our greatest economists, used to say that he doubted whether, taking all enterprises together, there was such a thing as profit; that losses equaled profit over a reasonable rate of interest. The important consideration for our people is what effect the proposed taxes will have on the supply of capital for these purposes. Obviously, this phase of the case is far more important than the amount of revenue which is expected to be derived therefrom.

In a generation, according to the Treasury's estimates, that yield would not be greatly in excess of the deficit for the last year. Economists, even those who favor practically confiscatory taxes on wealth, recognize that such taxation will destroy the principal source of capital for new enterprises, and that if the community is to continue to exist in anything like the present scale of living, a new source for such capital must be found.

So far as I am aware, no study of the effects of such legislation on the supply of capital has been submitted to the Congress or any of its committees. The subject was very exhaustively studied over a period of 2 years by an English committee on national debt and taxation headed by Lord Colwyn, which made a report dated November 15, 1926, which is rated, I believe, as perhaps the most authoritative pronouncement on the subject available.

Senator King. Do you know whether our committee, of which Mr. Parker is a member, and who made a rather extensive study of the taxation system in Great Britain, took cognizance of Lord Colwyn's report?

Mr. May. I have not had the pleasure of seeing Mr. Parker since that report was made; I could not tell. I have a copy of it here if you would like me to leave it.

Senator King. I wish you would leave it with the secretary. I would like to examine it.

Senator Gore. How large is it? Could it go in the record?

Mr. May. It is a very big document [handing volume to Senator King].

Senator King. Is that the only copy you have?

Mr. May. I have another one in my office.

Senator King. Have you any objection to leaving that with the Committee?

Mr. May. I would be very pleased to leave it.

Senator King. Thank you.

Mr. May. This report is regarded as perhaps the most authoritative pronouncement on the subject available.

They started, as I do, with the assumption that graduated income taxes and inheritance or estate taxes were necessary and proper, and that the limits on such taxes should be either the limit of ability to collect them or the limit at which the injury to the community would be greater than could be compensated by the collections. In the course of the report they said:

Money in the free disposition of the citizen has a utility to the State as well as to himself. Saved and invested, it supplies the financial and industrial needs of the community. The special utility to the community only begins when the greatest utility to the individual has ceased. The larger the income, the more room is there for savings; and the State, when putting a heavy tax on incomes with the greater margin, has to consider the risk of doing too much damage to savings.

And elsewhere they said that the effect of an estate tax was substantially the same.

Again they said:

Any taxation which unduly diminishes the reward of entrepreneurs for taking pioneer risks is in that respect a source of harm to the community.

At the time when the report was written, the maximum rate of income and super-tax was 50 per cent and the maximum rate of estate tax was 40 per cent to which was added an inheritance tax which, in the case of direct descendants, was only 1 per cent and in no case exceeded 10 per cent. That is the same as today.

In their conclusion, the committee stated:

We conclude, with regard to the supply of capital from individual and corporate savings, that industry has suffered materially from the effect of high income tax and super-tax. This remains true, when full allowance has been made for the proportionate application of revenue to the large payments on account of the national debt which accrue directly or indirectly to the benefit of trade.

Of course, under the present proposals, there would be no compensating benefit from the reduction of the national debt. Everyone realizes what a problem the proposed taxes would create in a case such as that of Henry Ford, but it is a gross mistake to assume that the difficulties would arise in only a few extreme cases like his.

I notice that Mr. Jackson, in his testimony yesterday, estimated the value of Mr. Ford's holding in Ford Motor stock at $354,000,000. He said, quite fairly, that that was an exceptional case, but I think that in fairness he should have added that substantially similar results would ensue if the figures were only a tenth of those assumed by him.

In fact, they would be almost confiscatory if the figures were reduced to a bare 1 per cent of the figures in the Ford case. Since reading his testimony in the press, I have made a comparative table showing the results of the application of the proposed taxes to a case similar to that of Mr. Ford, using first, values of $350,000,000; second, values of $35,000,-000; and third, values of $3,500,000, the last being 1 per cent of the Ford figures, roughly. They show that if Mr. Ford left stock in the Ford Motor Co. having a value of $350,000,000 to his son, and the estate and inheritance taxes were payable over 10 years, without interest, and the stock received by Mr. Edsel Ford paid 10 per cent dividends annually, the net yield of those dividends, after deducting the proposed surtaxes, would amount to only 28 per cent of the annual installment of one-tenth payable on the taxes.

I think that is a point that was not clearly made in Mr. Osgood's presentation. He overlooked the fact that the tax would fall on the beneficiary and not on the Ford Motor Car Co., and you could raise money only on the stock, and you could get money to pay the tax only by dividends on the stock, and those dividends would be subject to these heavy surtaxes.

I have the table here; you might be interested to see the figures.

(The table referred to is as follows:)

Statement showing effect of existing estate state tax and proposed inheritance tax on an estate consisting of stock of a corporation left to a single beneficiary (son), assuming the value of the estate to be (A) $350,000,000, (B) $35,000,000, and (C) $3,500,000, and assuming (1) that the taxes could be paid in 10 annual installments and (2) that dividends on the stock may be expected at the rate of 10 per cent per annum on the valuation, and that the proposed surtax rates will be payable thereon (State taxes and interest on deferred payments of estate and inheritance taxes ignored).

(A) Valuation of estate.....................	$350,000,000
Estate and inheritance taxes thereon.....	312,970,750
Annual installment of tax, $\frac{1}{10}$..........	31,297,075
Annual dividends.....................	35,000,000
Surtax thereon.......................	26,091,000
Balance for payment of estate and inheritance taxes...............	8,909,000
Per cent of estate and inheritance taxes that could be paid out of dividends and inheritance taxes that could be paid out of dividends annually...............	2.8
(B) Valuation of estate....................	35,000,000
Estate and inheritance taxes thereon.....	29,470,750
Annual installment of tax, $\frac{1}{10}$..........	2,947,075
Annual dividends.....................	3,500,000
Surtax thereon.......................	2,481,000
Balance for payment of estate and inheritance taxes.................	1,019,000

Per cent of estate and inheritance taxes that could be paid out of dividends annually.............................. 3.5

(C) Valuation of estate................... $3,500,000
Estate and inheritance taxes thereon.... 2,031,168
Annual installment of tax, ⅒.......... 203,116

Annual dividends.................... 350,000
Surtax thereon..................... 185,000

Balance for payment of estate and inheritance taxes................ 165,000
Per cent of estate and inheritance taxes that could be paid out of dividends annually.............................. 8.1

Mr. May. Briefly summarizing this statement, the valuation of the estate is $350,000,000; estate and inheritance tax thereon, $312,900,000; the annual installment of the tax, one-tenth, $31,297,000; annual dividends, $35,000,000; surtaxes thereon, $26,000,000; leaves a balance for the estate and inheritance taxes of $8,900,000, which is 2.8 per cent of the total charges, or 28 per cent of the annual installment of the tax.

Senator King. Did you take into consideration the taxes that might be imposed in the various States?

Mr. May. I have left out the State taxes, interest on deferred tax, and everything of that kind.

Senator King. If they paid all of those, there would be nothing left.

Mr. May. When you get to 2.8 per cent, it does not make very much difference about the rest. It amounts to practical confiscation.

Senator Gerry. Was there not a suggestion made in the House in the hearings, if I recollect, that it can be worked out of income?

Mr. May. I believe Mr. Jackson did make that statement. But you see what that involves. You work it backward. You have, roughly, $31,000,000 of an annual installment to pay, and if you are going to pay that out of dividends, you have to have enough dividends to pay 75 per cent surtax and still have $31,000,000 left, and that means you have to have four times $31,000,000 in dividends, and that is $124,000,000 in dividends on the stock valued at $350,000,000, or, roughly, 35 per cent.

If a stock was going to pay 35 per cent, you would not get the Treasury to value it at par. I think you would have difficulty in getting them to value it at 10 times the annual earnings, which is the figure I have used in my calculations.

But as I say, that is a quite exceptional case, and that might be dealt with as a special situation; but when you divide the figures by 10 and come down to $35,000,000, you find that after the dividends have been paid and the surtaxes deducted, what is left is no more than 3.5 per cent on the amount of the tax. So that if the tax was paid over 10 years, it would be only 35 per cent of the annual installment of the tax.

And finally, if you get down to an estate which is 1 per cent of the size of Mr. Ford's—

Senator King (interposing). That is, three and a half million?

Mr. May. Yes. The annual installment of tax would be $203,000, and the balance that would remain out of the dividends after paying the surtaxes would be $165,000. So you would be able to pay 80 per cent of your annual installment, or 8 per cent of the total taxes. Those are the figures in the case of a $3,500,000 corporation.

Senator King. Supposing you had no dividends?

Mr. May. Then you would be out of luck.

Mr. Jackson also said that he thought this could be financed by a bond issue, and people would be glad to finance a bond issue. On $350,000,000, the taxes would be 89.5 per cent.

Mr. Jackson's experience with underwriters may be more favorable, although I think it is probably less extensive than mine; but I have never found a bond house that was able to underwrite a bond issue for 90 per cent of the value of the property, and I doubt if his hopes are well founded, and I doubt if anybody is going to try the experiment with a $350,000,000 issue.

Senator Gore. Could we not tax these underwriters if they did not do it? [Laughter.]

Mr. May. If the figures were reduced, as I say, to one-tenth of the figures used in the Ford case, the percentage borne by the net income on the stock bequeathed to the annual installment of taxes would not rise to more than 35 per cent; and even if the figures assumed are only 1 per cent of those in the supposed Ford case, the income from the stock bequeathed would fall substantially short of paying the annual instalment of the taxes. In either case of the first two assumed, the beneficiary would be better advised to let the Government take the property for the taxes and buy it from the Government on the best terms he could get, rather than pay taxes amounting, as they would, to from 84 per cent to 89.5 per cent of the Treasury's valuation.

In the first two cases, the beneficiary would be in little better position to pay the tax if he owned large amounts of other property in addition, for 90 per cent of all such additional property would be taken in taxes.

Further, in each of these cases a 10 per cent overvaluation would make the tax practically 100 per cent of the real value.

Another point I would like to make is that I do not believe that anybody could value the Ford estate holdings within a margin of 15 per cent one way or other from a given figure, or a total spread of 30 per cent.

If they put the valuation of that stock 10 per cent too high and taxed it at 90 per cent, that is 100 per cent of the true valuation.

That I think is one of the great points that has perhaps not been so fully stressed before your Committee as I would like to see it stressed—the importance of valuation in connection with this matter, and the wide range of difference of opinion that exists in respect to valuation.

At this point I would like to quote some illustrations to show the difficulties of the problem of valuation. I would recall, first, a case in which I was personally concerned, in which the District Court found as a fact and was upheld by the Circuit Court of Appeals in doing so, that the fair market value of an insurance stock was $55 a share on the day on which it sold on the New York Stock Exchange at $90, on the basis of which figure the Treasury proposed to tax the transaction.

In the case of the Tex-Penn Oil Co., the Board of Tax Appeals said:

Our problem, then, at this point is to determine the "fair market value, if any" of the 1,007,834 share block of Transcontinental stock. In determining the deficiencies in these cases, the respondent used a fair market value of $47.55. He has now abandoned that figure and asserts that the stock had a fair market value of $12 per share . . . we have determined that the fair market value of this stock of Transcontinental Oil Co. received by petitioners in the transaction before us was $7 per share.

Now, ignoring the Commissioner's first valuation in this case, it is obvious that a tax of 60 per cent, let alone 90 per cent, would amount to more than the total value found by the Board of Tax Appeals.

Another case which is perhaps pertinent is the case which involved the valuation of the Ford Motor Co. stock itself, the valuation of that stock as of March 1, 1913. In that case it was to the interest of the Government to put the value low. The Commissioner claimed that the value of the stock was $3,547.84—marvelous accuracy—a share. Eventually the Board of Tax Appeals found that the tax value was $10,000 a share or very nearly three times the figure fixed by the Commissioner.

The competent and honest estimates of the value of a business may vary 15 per cent to 20 per cent from a prior figure. To levy taxes which leaves a residuum less than the reasonable margin of error is unsound taxation.

The report of the House hearings contains a copy of a letter written by the Chief of Staff of the Joint Committee on Internal Revenue Taxation suggesting extraordinary measures to meet the hardships imposed on the estates of decedents who died in 1929, because of changing values. That was under a statute levying a maximum tax of 20 per cent. Even under that statute, it was frequently found to be impossible to collect the full tax so that valuation had to be arbitrarily reduced or a compromise worked out. Under the proposed bill that would be the normal case in respect of any considerable estate. The rates in the bill would in such cases be only nominally enforced. Taxation would, in fact, be at the discretion of the Treasury, as possibly limited by litigation.

I would like to draw attention to another consequence that would flow from such taxation, that is, that capitalists would be forced to spread their capital over numerous enterprises so as to avoid the effects that come if their capital is locked up in a single enterprise, with the result that our system of businesses owned by small private groups would disappear. The separation of beneficial ownership from control would be accelerated instead of being checked.

Senator Gore. That is the worst defect in our whole structure, as I see it now.

Mr. May. But the really vital objection to the measure is the effect it would have on savings and enterprise and, ultimately, upon employment and taxable income of the future.

It is difficult to see why capitalists should undertake new enterprises if the proposed burdens were added to the burdens of the existing laws, so long as any alternative might be open to them. Here there is the alternative of tax-exempt securities, which would at least avert surtaxes, and provide liquid funds to meet estate and inheritance taxes.

The disastrous effect of the general result now and on future enterprises is incalculable. To adopt the policy reflected in the bill without having first reviewed this alternative is rather like drawing water from a tested reservoir into

a cistern known to be leaking, and to do so without providing some other source of capital seems to me with all respect
to be improvident. I am reminded of the words of a great
English economist, Alfred Marshall, referring to the social
reformers who, as he put it, "in their desire to improve the
distribution of wealth are reckless as to the effect of their
schemes on the production of wealth."

Senator King. Mr. May, please state for the record your
experience in connection with taxation and revenue measures generally, and particularly measures relating to inheritance and estate taxes.

Mr. May. My experience has not been so much with inheritance and estate taxes, because they were not so active at
the time that I was engaged; but I was in the Treasury during the war and I made a trip to England on one occasion
at the request of the administration to study the English system while I was there; and later I was a member of the Joint
Congressional Committee, and I have been in consultation
with the Treasury Department very freely during the last
20 years; in fact, the first contact I had was with the present
Secretary of State when he drew the first income tax bill, and
I sat down with him and discussed the problems that presented.

Of course, in my business work I have a very close contact
with taxation, although I do not specialize in it personally.
That is handled by one of my partners, but I see it and its
effects on business in a very decided way.

Senator King. Price, Waterhouse & Co. has to do with
estates and with business generally, and their accounts and
investigations?

Mr. May. Oh, yes; we do a very large amount of accounting business in such fields.

Senator Gore. Mr. May, we have heard a good deal said
about the sharing of the wealth. In all of what you and
Mr. Osgood have said, don't you think that is rather conservative?

Mr. May. "Sharing" is not the word that I would have selected.

Senator Gore. That is the point.

Mr. May. I think it is an entire fallacy to believe that this would be a revenue producer, if you take account of the taxes that would be destroyed as well as the taxes that would be received. If you do that, I think it would be a net loser. The taxes that are received will show, they will show up in the return, and those that are lost will not be computed.

XI

THE PROPOSED GRADUATED TAXES ON UNDIS-
TRIBUTED CORPORATE PROFITS *

I AM going to discuss today the proposals made by the President and now before the Congress for graduated taxes on
the undistributed profits of corporations. I am not going
to discuss the details of the pending measure because they
are likely to be changed. I intend to discuss only the principles, and I want to talk about them from various standpoints such as those of practicability and justice; the administrative problems presented; and above all, the economic
consequences their adoption would be likely to produce.
In view of the fact that comparisons between our system and
the British are very frequent, and that some years ago I
made a study of the British system at the request of the
then Administration, I shall try from time to time to illustrate some of the points I make by comparison between our
methods and those employed in Great Britain.

My approach to the question is entirely non-political—in
fact, I have never been affiliated with any of the political
parties. My interest in the subject is a part of my general
interest in the whole question of taxation, which developed
when I was in the Treasury during the war and had something to do with the difficult problems of taxation which
were then presented. Even prior to that time, I had taken
some part in the formulation of the income tax law of 1913.
Since the war, through service on the Advisory Committee
to the Joint Congressional Committee, and in other ways,
my interest in the subject has been kept alive and active.

The new proposals may be divided into two distinct parts:
the first contemplates determining the tax on corporate
profits in so far as they are distributed according to the tax

* A lecture before the School of Business Administration of the University
of Buffalo, April 7, 1936 (slightly revised).

status of the individual who receives the dividend. This is the same principle as is followed in England, and there is much argument in its favor, although I am not prepared to say that I should be willing to accept the principle in its entirety, and I think that from an administrative standpoint the method of giving effect to it now proposed is open to very serious objection.

The second half of the proposal is a steeply graduated tax on profits of corporations which are not distributed. This, I believe, is a principle new to the tax systems of the world.

Before I discuss the present proposals I should perhaps give you a little of the background against which they have to be considered. At the present time, our tax system includes a small normal tax (4 per cent) and graduated surtaxes rising to 75 per cent on individual incomes; a tax on corporate incomes, into which last year a very limited application of the idea of graduation was introduced so that it now runs from 12½ per cent to 15 per cent; we have also a combined capital stock and excess profits tax which was introduced in 1933. Under the latter scheme, each corporation chooses its own valuation for its capital stock and pays an excess-profits tax based on the relation between its profits and the capital stock valuation it has itself fixed. The idea is that if a corporation tries to save money on one tax it will get caught on the other. The merit of ingenuity has been claimed for this tax, but I think that is its only possible merit; and one of the sound features of the present proposal is that it contemplates the abolition of this undesirable excrescence on our tax system.

In order to bring the new proposals into a clearer light it may be useful to compare the rate of tax paid on a given amount of income, the beneficial interest in which belongs to a taxpayer who already is in the highest bracket, under three different conditions. First, every hundred dollars of additional income earned by him directly pays a tax of $79.00; second, each hundred dollars of income earned on stock of a corporation which he owns pays a tax of $15.00;

third, if a hundred dollars of income is earned on a stock which he owns and the balance remaining after payment of the corporation income tax is distributed to him, the total tax paid on it is $78.75. The disparity between the tax in the second and third cases obviously creates an incentive for persons in the high income brackets to allow income earned on stock which they own to remain undistributed. It is this fact which underlies the present proposal. The vital question is whether the remedy proposed is a sound one and, frankly, I do not think it is.

You will readily perceive that the problem grows out of the wide disparities between the normal rate of tax on individuals, the rates of tax on corporations, and the surtaxes on individuals; and at this point I might refer to British practice, because there the problem is less acute, for the simple reason that the disparities between the different rates of tax are less. In England, the normal rate of tax on corporation profits and the normal rate of tax on individual incomes are identical—at the present time, 22½ per cent, which is five and one-half times our normal tax on individuals and half as much again as our maximum corporation income tax. The maximum surtax there is 41¼ per cent, which is not much more than one-half of our maximum of 75 per cent.

England makes no attempt to interfere with or influence the freedom of public companies in the distribution of dividends. The advantage to the national economy of the reinvestment of profits in industry is apparently deemed sufficient to outweigh any loss of surtaxes. A solution of our problem which would take the form of a closer approximation to the English rates would, I believe, be sounder from every point of view than the proposal now before Congress.

You are all no doubt familiar with the graduated tax on individual incomes, and I should like, therefore, to point out that there is no analogy whatsoever between the graduated tax on individual incomes and the proposed graduated tax on undistributed profits of corporations. I am entirely in sympathy with the principle of graduated taxes on individual incomes, though I believe we have carried the idea in practice further than is desirable in the economic interest of the country, or is advantageous to the revenue. This graduation is based on the theory of "ability to pay" or, perhaps, rather on that of "equality of sacrifice." The thought is that a rich man can well afford to pay not only more tax, but a larger proportion of his income in taxes than the poor man, most of whose income is required to meet the necessities of life.

The proposed graduated tax on undistributed corporate income rests on no similar principle. It is what may be called a "pressure tax," designed to compel a course of action which the Administration or the Legislature thinks desirable. It operates by imposing a very heavy penalty or tax upon those who do not follow the course of action desired by the Legislature. I shall develop this point more fully later. For the present, I merely wish to emphasize that any supposed analogy between a graduated tax on undistributed profits and a graduated tax on individual incomes is entirely specious and false.

I have already said that our existing system undoubtedly creates an incentive to withhold profits from distribution, and in such circumstances it is inevitable that profits should in some cases be withheld from distribution which ought to be distributed. This fact has long been recognized by the Congress, and for many years our laws have contained provisions for special taxation in cases in which it appeared that profits were being withheld for the purpose of avoiding the surtaxes. These provisions have been gradually made more drastic, and certainly today they provide the Bureau of Internal Revenue with a far more powerful machinery for dealing with abuses than, for instance, does the English law.

It is, I think, a common mistake to assume that our corporations generally distribute a smaller proportion of their profits than those of other countries. The only country with which it is readily possible to make any sort of comparison is Great Britain, and I think the evidence shows clearly that our companies, even in times of prosperity, distribute in the aggregate a larger percentage of their profits than do English companies. Not only so, but it is an unquestioned fact that during the depression American corporations have distributed dividends in excess of their current earnings to an amount exceeding the profits withheld from distribution in the preceding ten years. It therefore cannot justly be said that in the aggregate our corporations withhold more than they should. As I have said, there are unquestionably some corporations which could properly distribute far more than they do, but I believe the present law provides adequate machinery for dealing with those cases—if not, let the machinery be strengthened. If there will be some cases which it will not be possible to reach, we should not allow resentment over this fact to lead us to adopt measures that are economically unwise and unjust to the great body of corporate taxpayers.

While abuses undoubtedly exist, there is no room for doubt about the fact that the amount of profits withheld from distribution in order to save taxes is a relatively small proportion of the amount of profits that normally remain undistributed. The present proposal, however, contemplates treating all withholding of profits from distribution alike, whether they are actuated by a desire to avoid taxation, by statutory requirement, by contractual obligations, or by honest belief that such withholding is essential to the continued existence of the enterprise.

Since the proposals have been before the Congress, amendments have been suggested in the House Committee to modify the application of the principle in cases where it would be manifestly improper for the profits to be distributed; but in their latest appearances before the Committee the representatives of the Treasury have insisted that there should be no exception whatever from the scheme of taxation which they have put forward.

It cannot be denied that a universal application would

produce serious injustice and do great harm to important parts of our economic system, and it is a fair question to ask what are the arguments that can be advanced in favor of proposals which are bound to have such an effect. Though the measure was proposed originally as a means of meeting the so-called ordinary deficit in the budget for the fiscal year ending June 30, 1937, it is apparent that it would not serve this purpose—indeed, it is a practical certainty that it would lead to reduction of tax collections for that particular year. The loss of taxes on corporations would be felt immediately —the gain from additional taxes on individuals would, in the main, not be realized until 1938, if then.

Incidentally, I may say that I believe the estimates of probable revenues are excessive. I am convinced that they do not make adequate allowance for the changes affecting tax liability which such a measure inevitably brings about. For instance, reclassifications of capital stock or transfers of property from taxable individuals to charitable institutions might vitally affect the calculations. If I were convinced that the measure would produce a large increase of taxes I might be willing to support it even though I regarded it, as I do, as a bad tax. I think we are today in the position not that half a loaf is better than no bread, but that almost any taxes are better than none, because the alternative is inflation, which will do more injury to our people than even the worst of taxes.

If the purpose of the measure is not primarily an immediate increase of revenue, what motives have led to its being advanced at this particular time? Obviously, an election year is a most inopportune time for reforms in our general system of taxation. Sound tax proposals are seldom palatable to the great majority of the people, and an election year is apt to produce proposals which are popular in their appeal rather than sound in their principles, and which disguise rather than minimize the burden which really falls on the people at large.

It would be quite easy to make out a case that these proposals are deliberately socialistic in intent. Last year's high taxes on inheritance, as proposed by the President, might fairly be said to have been designed to strike a heavy blow at private savings as a source of supply for the capital of industry. This, it might be said, is an equally heavy blow at corporate savings as a source for such capital. Now, there are only three important sources for the supply of capital, which is the life-blood of industry; namely, private savings, corporate savings, and the State. If you eliminate private savings and corporate savings, the only recourse for a supply of capital is to the State, with the inevitable sequel that the State will control industry. In the present unprecedented depression, the State has had to come to the aid of industry to a substantial extent. If corporations are compelled by taxation to distribute all their surpluses in times of prosperity, it is inevitable that in any subsequent period of depression when they suffer losses they will be compelled to resort to State aid to a far greater extent.

But while the motive which actuates some of those who are supporting the present proposals may be socialistic, others, particularly in the Treasury, are, I think, supporting them for a somewhat different reason. I have spoken of the cases in which the present laws were abused, and I think some persons in the Treasury have their eyes glued on those cases, and in their attempt to penalize the small group of gross abusers of the law are willing to adopt measures which, they believe, would add to the burdens on that group; and lose sight of the injurious effects which such measures would have on the large body of taxpayers. The welfare of the many is lost to sight in the attempt to punish or thwart the few whose actions have doubtless in a substantial, but still relatively small, number of cases been anti-social.

Others are actuated, I believe, by a still different motive —concern about the power that is exercised by corporate wealth—and believe that the measures proposed, by decreasing or arresting the growth of corporate wealth, will lessen this power.

There is no doubt that the power of corporate wealth has at times been abused; but in the world as it is constituted today, great power must be entrusted to some individuals, and it may be questioned whether the situation would be improved by transferring the power now vested in those who administer large corporations to persons in the political world. If our present industrial system is judged by its abuses, no doubt it stands condemned; but, equally, if our political system were judged by its abuses, it could not survive a single day.

I turn now to consideration of the practical aspects of the measures proposed. This problem lies in the field of income taxation. It is a very common mistake to think of income as something very definite, simple and easily ascertained. Of course, when a man is living on a salary his income is well defined; but the income of a complex business is an extremely difficult thing to calculate. In practice, all calculations of it are provisional, and based on conventions, judgments and assumptions. What we call income today is income only on the assumption that certain things will happen in the future. Take a simple case: Suppose you are offered $25 for performing a task that will take three days, you to get nothing unless you complete the task. Well, you work hard and satisfactorily and do one-third of it the first day. In one sense, you have earned one-third of $25. But suppose something happens on the second day to prevent your completing the task. You have earned nothing. What is the true view of the situation—did you earn $8.33 the first day and lose $8.33 the second day, or did you earn nothing on either day?

That is a simple illustration of what runs through the whole determination of income. There is great room for legitimate difference of opinion whether a certain amount is income of one year or of another. Even under the existing tax law a great deal of injustice and hardship results from the fact that the taxpayer really thinks an amount is income or a deduction from income in one year, and the Bureau of

Internal Revenue decides that it belongs in another. The taxpayer, let us say, claims a deduction in 1933. Later, the Bureau says: "No; that should have been taken in 1932." You cannot take that deduction in 1933, and you cannot get any relief in respect of 1932 because that year is statute barred.

One must recognize that there is bound to be a certain amount of injustice under any tax law; but the object of the taxing authority should always be to try to frame tax measures so as to minimize that injustice. One of the simplest ways of doing that in the case of income taxation is by uniformity. If you have substantially the same scheme of taxation and substantially the same rates year after year, it does not make very much difference whether an item is taxed in one year or another. But if you have a constantly changing system of taxation, or if you have the rates of tax going up and down or steeply graduated, then the allocation of profits between years becomes a matter of great importance and great unfairness may result—either to the benefit of the taxpayer, or, more often, to his detriment.

Here, again, I should like to refer to English experience. Their system of taxation has remained substantially unchanged for many years except during the war. The war naturally led to a general rise in the rate of taxation, but I believe it is true that for the last dozen years, which cover the whole period of the depression, the English tax system, in principle, has remained unchanged and the rates of tax have varied very little. The income tax on corporations, which is the general normal income tax, has varied from a low of 20 per cent to a high of 25 per cent. That is a relatively small change, and in England it has not made a great deal of difference whether items were put in one year or another. During the same period our rates have varied greatly and, as I have explained, our system of taxation, itself, has been changed, and now we are contemplating another radical alteration in the system.

In the case of individual income taxes, steep graduation

does exist in England. The amount of the tax payment may vary considerably according as a particular item is added to the income of a year in which the taxpayer was in a low bracket, or to that of a year in which he was in a much higher bracket; but in relation to individual incomes the principle of graduation is, broadly, a just one, resting as it does on the principle of "equality of sacrifice," and in England graduation, though steep, is restricted within far narrower limits than with us.

In the present proposals, however, the graduation rests on no sound principle and is extremely steep, and the argument based on the fact that it will inevitably create gross injustice gains strength accordingly. The virtual certainty of injustice is strengthened by certain technical facts.

The first is that the tax is to be levied on the basis of profits as determined under the income tax law. Now, in business practice, there are many reservations which no prudent man can fail to make before arriving at the amount properly available for distribution, but which are not deductions for tax purposes until the loss in respect of which they are created is actually sustained and measured. In the second place, under our system we have what I regard as a most unfortunate practice of treating as income capital gains —gains on the sale of property not in the ordinary course of business. That practice produced a large amount of tax in the boom years, but the corresponding deductions for losses caused a great loss of revenue after the break of 1929, with the result that we now have in the law the very unjust provision that gains are taxable but losses are not deductible except to a very limited extent. So you have this possibility —a company might make a large capital gain in one year and a large capital loss in the next, but under the proposed law it would be liable for a heavy tax unless it distributed more than its actual income, whether or not you include capital gains and losses in the computation of income.

Another unfortunate phase of our system which makes this question of allocation to years vitally important is an administrative problem. The Bureau of Internal Revenue has to employ a number of agents to check tax returns. It has to find some way of judging whether the men are efficient, and unfortunately the most obvious test is how much additional taxation the agent has caused to be assessed. That being so, an agent who is charged with the task of examining returns for a particular year has an incentive to make the income for that particular year as large as he can—whether the increase is achieved at the expense of a corresponding reduction of the income of another year is immaterial from his standpoint. I know from actual experience that this system has resulted in reallocations between years that have often been quite unreasonable—sometimes unjust to the taxpayer, and sometimes unprofitable to the revenue. The possibilities of injustice inherent in this system of judging efficiency will become greatly enhanced if a steeply graduated tax is applied to the undistributed portion of corporate profits.

I come, now, to the vital question of the probable economic effects of these proposals. First, if I may, I will read to you by way of preface, a few words from testimony which I gave before the Senate in the Hearings on last year's tax bill:

A little thought will convince that to keep our people busy, development of new industries must be on a constantly increasing scale. In the next generation, we must create new industries exceeding in magnitude the motor, radio, and other industries created during the last thirty years. Now, in the course of such development large losses of capital will be incurred. Professor Allyn Young, one of our greatest economists, used to say that he doubted whether, taking all enterprises together, there was such a thing as profit; that losses equaled profit over a reasonable rate of interest. The important consideration for our people is what effect the proposed taxes will have on the supply of capital for these purposes. Obviously, this phase of the case is far more important than the amount of revenue which is expected to be derived therefrom.

It seems to me that this bill, if it operates in at all the way in which the Treasury expects it to operate, will have a most harmful effect on the supply of capital for industry, and particularly on the development of new industries. Businesses differ radically in their character. I will not try to classify them, but will take two extremes. There are companies which are in a stage of development—they are engaged in creating a new industry or in developing a new idea. At the other end of the scale are businesses in what may be called a liquidating stage—either because the nature of the business is liquidation in itself, or because they have seen their best days and are gradually passing out of existence. The outstanding case of companies that are liquidating in their nature is that of the mining companies. The mines are being worked out and the owners are gradually getting their capital returned to them in cash, as well as their profits. Such companies can well afford to pay out all of their profits in dividends—as a matter of fact, statistics compiled by the National Bureau of Economic Research show that in the last sixteen years the mining companies of the country as a whole have paid out in dividends more than their earnings, according to income tax standards, in every year except two, and in one of those years the two amounts were practically identical. That means substantially that mining companies would be free of taxation under this law.

On the other hand, take any company that is developing a business. It does not have cash on hand equal to its profits because the proceeds of sales are spent largely on development of new facilities, experimental work, additional inventories, etc. Such companies, if they paid out all the cash they had at the end of the year in excess of what they had at the beginning, would still be liable to a very heavy tax.

Does that seem to be the sort of thing that is economically desirable? Granting that any laws we frame are bound to operate with some inequality, is it economically desirable to frame laws so that those who are exhausting the natural resources of the country for private gain will be free from tax, while those people who are developing new industries which, if successful, will benefit them primarily but will also strengthen our industrial system, should bear the full brunt of the taxation?

To my mind, that is the vital economic question, and I cannot conceive of the possibility of anyone's reaching a conclusion other than that this sort of taxation is calculated to benefit the wrong class of companies—those that are liquidating in nature and those that are going down-hill, instead of those that are trying to build up additions to our economic structure.

The proposal seems also to constitute an unwise and unsound attempt to fetter judgment and substitute fixed rules and regulations for the wise discretion which must be exercised if an enterprise is to succeed. What proportion of its profits a corporation can wisely distribute is a matter of judgment dependent on the circumstances of the particular company and the particular time when the decision has to be made. To impose a rule of thumb, as this proposal contemplates, is bound to produce both unjust and economically undesirable results.

I have already mentioned the dilemma in which the Committee on Ways and Means finds itself. On the one hand is the Treasury, demanding that a rule shall be laid down to which there shall be no exception. On the other hand, are witnesses showing conclusively that such a rule would impose heavy penalties on corporations for withholding from distribution profits which they are debarred either by statute or other compelling considerations from distributing. The Treasury says that once you make exceptions there is no logical place at which you can stop doing so and this is true. The choice is between arbitrary and unjust rules and the exercise of judgment, with protection to the Treasury against abuse of that privilege. Only those with a myopic vision concentrated on a few exaggerated cases of abuse can question that if the choice has to be made, the rule which permits distribution to be made according to the ability and necessities of the individual corporation is the only one that is either just or economically wise.

The proposed law seems to me to be another manifestation of a tendency altogether too general in our country today to make fixed rules and regulations to govern everything, and to attempt to eliminate judgment from the whole scheme of things. Such measures are bound to operate unjustly, and tend in the direction of a narrow, bureaucratic control of our life, which means a very large sacrifice of individual freedom.

No doubt there are those who would differ from the views I have expressed, but no one, I think, can fairly claim either that the merits of the proposal are clear or that they have been examined sufficiently to enable an informed opinion to be reached that the merits outweigh the demerits. I suggest that no major change should be undertaken until it has been exhaustively studied and opinions upon it secured—not only from those who have a theoretical knowledge of the subject, or who are familiar with the problem only from the administrative side, but from those who are familiar with the practical aspects of taxation and are in a position to express an informed opinion on the question of the probable indirect effects of the measure proposed. We need something analogous to an exhaustive study by a Royal Commission, which in England invariably precedes any substantial change in the fiscal system or, indeed, almost any major modification of domestic policy. Those commissions consist of members of both houses of the legislature and men chosen from the worlds of finance, science, economics, and the professions. They seek testimony from competent witnesses on specific points. They cross-examine the witnesses, politely, but searchingly. They make a report (or majority and minority reports, if irreconcilable differences develop between the views of the different members). These reports are state papers of the highest value, and those who are called upon to vote on proposals can find in them an adequate and fair statement of the arguments for and against the proposals.

In conclusion, I would say this: on my way here I spent yesterday in Rochester, and I had a very interesting afternoon going over the Kodak plant—or rather, a small fraction of that plant. With this talk in mind, and thinking, also, of the first time I went over that plant thirty-nine years ago with Mr. Eastman, the founder of the business, I could not help thinking that there were object lessons which one could draw from the case of that Company. I recalled that on my first visit, in rather less than half the time we spent yesterday going over a fraction of the plant, Mr. Eastman and I went through every building and every department. The Eastman Kodak Company was then a developing business; it is now fully established and highly successful. I do not suppose this tax law would impose any additional burden upon it or its stockholders. On the other hand, anyone attempting to rival the business of the Company with a new company would be greatly hampered by this law. Further, if we can imagine this law having been passed back in the nineties, when that business was being built up, we may question whether in those circumstances that industry, and all the enterprises that have grown out of it, would have progressed at anything like the rate at which they did progress; and we must realize that the continued growth of new enterprises, and the continued development of new inventions, are essential to continued successful life as an industrial community.

Then, there is another thought which I brought very strongly impressed upon me away from Rochester. I looked at many huge machines that do the most complicated things in the most ingenious ways, and I thought that a new tax law was a very important new piece of Governmental machinery. And I contrasted the way in which the machinery of industry and the machinery of Government were being developed in our country today. I thought how before one of those industrial machines had been built the best theoretical and technical advice had been secured as to how a de-

TAXATION

sired result could, in theory, be attained; how the idea had then been subjected to the criticism of those familiar with the practical working of machinery; how working models had first been developed and subjected to all kinds of strains and stresses and experimental operations before the actual machines were put into operation. Not only that, but I observed the many ingenious devices to prevent those machines from doing injury to other property or people working in the plant, and reflected how those safety devices had been given as much consideration as the principles of the machines themselves.

Further, I thought how lightheartedly legislative proposals which may conceivably serve a given purpose, are put forward without much thought of all the indirect consequences —the injury, the unfairness, and the injustice—that might be caused by them. Does it not seem that since the power of Government machinery to influence the lives of our people is so much greater than the power of any industrial machine, we should give more care and thought to trying to make any new machine work with at least some part of the efficiency and safety which we demand and secure in the industrial field?

TESTIMONY BEFORE SENATE FINANCE COMMITTEE, MAY 6, 1936 *

The Chairman. Mr. May, you represent the firm of Price, Waterhouse & Co.?

Mr. May. Yes; I am senior partner of the firm, sir. I appear here as an individual interested in the subject of taxation, upon which I have worked from the time of the passage of the first income-tax law.

I was in the Treasury during the war and subsequently I served on the advisory committee of the Joint Congressional Committee on Taxation, and my interest in the subject has been active and continuous.

I represent no private interests of any kind, nor any clients

* *Hearings on the Revenue Act, 1936,* pp. 538-48.

or institutions in the country. I would like to state broadly the reasons why I am here today.

I am intensely sympathetic with the view of the Treasury regarding the avoidance of taxes by withholding of dividends. Nevertheless, I am convinced that a graduated tax on corporations' undistributed earnings is not a satisfactory solution, is unsound in principle, will cause great injustice, and the evidence that I have seen in the record does not lead me to believe that this bill will produce any substantial increase in revenue.

I would like to say in regard to that that my reason is not so much that I think the estimates of the revenue that will be produced are excessive—I am in no position to pass on that—but I think the Treasury underestimates the yield under the existing law if business picks up. I think the Treasury underestimates the effect of the recovery of earning capacity of the country under the existing law.

I would like in the first instance to address myself to the paragraph in the statement of the Secretary of the Treasury to this Committee which reads as follows:

What are the dimensions of tax avoidance with which we are dealing? A few simple figures tell the story. It has been estimated by the Treasury Department that under the present tax law the income-tax liability of corporations on the basis of 1936 earnings would approximate 964 millions. The Department has also estimated that under the present law more than 4½ billion dollars of corporation income in the calendar year 1936 will be withheld from stockholders and that if this income were fully distributed to the individual owners of the stock represented in those corporations, the resultant yield in additional individual income taxes would be about $1,300,000,000.

It is, I think, most unfortunate that the Secretary should have been permitted by his advisers to make, as he does make in this paragraph, an obvious and serious misstatement of fact upon such an important question. The misstatement is apparent on a comparison of his language with that of the Commissioner of Internal Revenue, who said:

The Treasury estimates that, if the present corporation income, capital-stock, and excess-profits taxes were repealed, and all corporation earnings during the calendar year 1936 were currently distributed, the income of individuals would be increased by more than 4½ billions of which approximately $4,000,000,000 would be taxable.

The Secretary says that the 4½ billion represents the sum available for distribution to stockholders under the existing law; the Commissioner makes it clear that the repeal of the existing law is prerequisite to the existence of the 4½ billion. Under the existing law, according to the Treasury tables, approximately $1,100,000,000 of the 4½ billion mentioned by the Secretary as being withheld from stockholders would go to the Federal Government in taxes.

In the second place, it is unjust to describe the figure, even when it has been reduced by a billion or more, as "tax avoidance." A very large part of this income accrues to public companies whose dividend action is not in the least influenced by thoughts of tax avoidance but is dictated either by legal or contractual requirements or practical necessities, or an honest regard for the best interests of the stockholders.

Senator King. There were considerable dividends from those corporations, I assume?

Mr. May. Yes; but some withheld profits for perfectly good reasons that have nothing to do with tax avoidance.

In the third place, I think the figure of 4½ billion dollars, even when interpreted as the Commissioner interprets it, is greatly overstated. This figure appears on the sixth line of the main statement submitted to the Treasury in support of the proposal which appears at page 36 of the House hearings. A careful study of that table leads me to the definite conclusion that the figure is excessive even as applied to the special circumstances of the year 1936. If it be regarded—as we are entitled to regard it—as an indication of the permanent increase in revenue which the proposed law is expected to produce, the overstatement becomes larger and even more apparent.

If the Treasury estimate of statutory net income for 1936 of $7,200,000,000 is correct, then the increase of yield which may be expected from this law if all net income is distributed thereunder, turns on the estimate of the dividend distribution which would take place under the law as it now exists. To secure a fair comparison this estimate should be an estimate of the dividends which will be paid out of 1936 earnings either in 1936 or in the first months of 1937. The Treasury, however, makes the comparison with the dividends which it estimates will be paid in 1936 partly out of 1935 earnings and partly out of those for 1936. Since dividends naturally rise as income rises, and since the Treasury estimates that 1936 income will exceed that of 1935 by $1,700,-000,000, or 30 per cent, this method of comparison artificially inflates the estimate of increase of yield from the new law by a sum which must run into the hundreds of millions. It is like comparing the rainfall in two places, A and B, taking the rainfall at A for the calendar year and that of B for the year ending on the 15th of March in the following year, with the knowledge that the first 75 days of the earlier years were in both places a period of relatively small rainfall.

Further, the estimate of distribution within the year 1936 seems to me to be low. The Treasury estimates that the increase of dividends in 1936 over 1935 will be from $3,600,-000,000 to $3,900,000,000, or 8⅓ per cent. Statistics for the first quarter, covering rather less than 3,000 corporations, show an increase from $659,000,000 to $781,000,000, or an increase of $122,000,000, equivalent to more than 18 per cent. If earnings continue to rise, as the Treasury estimates they will, then the rate of increase in dividends should grow. Only on Monday the General Motors Corporation declared a dividend on its common stock for this quarter which was greater by 43½ million dollars than the dividend which it paid to the corresponding quarter of last year. This is one-seventh of the total increase for all corporations for the entire year as estimated by the Treasury.

Approaching the question in a somewhat different way,

I find from a table submitted by the Treasury showing the statutory net income and dividends for corporations having net income that during the 12 years for which actual or approximate figures are given dividends have averaged about 66 per cent for statutory net income. The Treasury's estimate of $3,540,000,000 as the dividends which would, under the existing law, be paid by such corporations in 1936 is equivalent to about 49 per cent of the estimated statutory net income. The difference of 17 per cent amounts to about $1,200,000,000.

Apparently, also, the Treasury, while making its main calculation on the basis that all net income would be distributed within the year, assumes that the amount of dividends paid by corporations having no net income will not be affected by the change of law. This seems to me to result in an overstatement of the increased distribution to be expected by some two or three hundred million dollars.

Finally, the amount estimated as the increase in yield due to the change in law includes taxes which will or might be recovered under the existing law in respect of dividends unreasonably withheld by corporations, and I am not convinced that the Treasury has made adequate allowance for the changes in taxable status that such laws inevitably produce, such as charitable gifts, reclassifications of capital stocks, and so forth.

Taking all these considerations together, I do not find in the statistics presented any ground for believing that this law, if adopted, will increase the revenue. It is, of course, possible that it will do so, but the Treasury has not, to my mind, made out any case that it will. The position is such that immediate enactment of the law is certainly not necessary from a fiscal standpoint.

No doubt there is a large amount of tax avoidance through the device of withholding profits from distribution, and all taxpayers—especially, I might say, those professional men whose income is almost wholly taxable—are sufferers from it. It should be curbed, and I am entirely sympathetic with the desire of the Treasury to curb it. But measures which affect equally those who are and those who are not avoiding taxes are unnecessary and unjust, and too often, like Herod's massacre, they cause great suffering but fail to reach the particular cases which inspire them.

The figure of profits withheld should be revised and analyzed. Corporations may be divided into three groups— (1) a very large number of small corporations which in the aggregate contribute and should contribute only a small fraction of the revenue from taxation of corporate income; (2) a relatively small number of public corporations most of which are owned by large bodies of stockholders and follow dividend policies practically uninfluenced by consideration of taxability of their stockholders; (3) a relatively small number of privately owned companies, some engaged in business, others substantially private holding companies, the dividend policies of most of these being governed largely by tax considerations. If we knew how much of the profits withheld were retained by these different classes of companies, the formulation of sound legislation would be facilitated greatly.

After all, the problem is not one of stupendous magnitude. In 1933, for instance, about 10,000 corporations paid 90 per cent of the corporation income tax. An analytical study of those 10,000 cases would not be a burdensome task, and I think the Congress and the people are entitled to have some information of this kind furnished them and legislation framed in the light thereof, instead of being asked to support a hit-or-miss measure of the kind now before the Senate.

I would emphasize the fact that continuity in taxation is a consideration of great importance. It inspires confidence and it minimizes the injustice which inevitably results from heavy and changeable taxation applied to income on the basis of a necessarily very imperfect allocation of income to particular years. Hasty experiments are wholly undesirable.

I would point out, further, that income taxation, and the business to which it is applied, constitutes an intricate net-

work, and that any important change in the frame of this
network produces all sorts of strains and stresses which can
be guarded against only by very careful and prolonged study.
The Treasury, when proposing this measure, contemplated
its universal application. Some of the most striking injustices that this would produce have been brought to the
notice of Congress, and in the House provisions were im-
provised to guard against, or at least alleviate, these injustices. It cannot be supposed that all the important injustices have been developed. Obviously, the Treasury made
no exhaustive study of them, because it contemplated a rigid
rule, free from any exceptions.

I should like, purely by way of illustration, to mention
one or two injustices which immediately occur to me. Take,
first, the law which taxes capital gains but substantially
denies relief in respect of capital losses. Suppose a corporation to have an ordinary income of $100,000 in each of 2
years, and to make a capital gain of $100,000 in 1 year and
a capital loss of $100,000 in the other. Its true income over
the 2 years is clearly $200,000, whether capital gains and
losses are or are not considered as entering into the determination of income. This is the amount that it should be
required to distribute in order to get the maximum benefit
of the proposed law. Actually, it would have to distribute
practically $300,000 in order to get such a benefit.

Again, in this same field we have recognized that capital
gains should not be taxed in the year in which they are
realized in the same way as if they were ordinary income
of that year. We have provided that individuals making
capital gains shall pay a tax which decreases according to
the length of time for which the investment has been held.
An individual who sells property which he has held for more
than 10 years pays tax on only 30 per cent of the profit.
Under the proposed law, if a corporation in which he is interested makes such a profit, and in order to avoid taxes dis-
tributes all its statutory income, the individual would pay
tax on his share of the full amount of this profit—yet the

whole basis of the present proposal is that individuals should pay neither more nor less on profits which come to them through the medium of a corporation than on profits which come to them directly.

Section 27 (i) also violates this same principle, not only in respect of the holding companies at which it is aimed, but also in respect of minority stockholders in corporations in which such holding companies own a majority. Their tax is determined not by their own status but largely by the status of the other stockholders. This provision should be eliminated.

Many other instances of the same kind could be cited. I do not think it is possible to anticipate all the serious injustices. I am inclined to agree with the Treasury that once you begin to make exceptions there is no logical place at which you can stop. This, however, merely means that the real choice is between a rigid rule and the abandonment of the principle, and I have no hesitation in saying that the wise choice is to discard the principle.

I should like to point out, also, that all the injustices which result from the taxation of corporate income under the existing law will be magnified by the substitution of a steeply graduated tax on undistributed earnings for a practically uniform tax on the whole amount of earnings.

For instance, the injustice which even under the present law results from the discontinuance of consolidated returns will be aggravated. Certainly opportunities ought to be given to readjust corporate structures so as to prevent double taxation resulting from the discontinuance of such returns, and Section 112B (6) is quite inadequate for the purpose.

To sum the matter up, I think the bill is as likely to produce less revenue as it is to produce more, and to produce more injustice than it remedies.

When we consider the measure from the standpoint of social policy as distinct from fiscal policy, we of course enter the realm in which wide differences of opinion are possible. On this point I should first of all like to point out that this law does not constitute an application of the principle of "ability to pay" which underlies the graduated tax on individual incomes and has no analogy to that scheme of taxation. The closest analogy in the field of individual taxation would be a steeply graduated tax on income saved under which all individual income would be exempted from taxation if spent. It is a surprising thing to me that Dr. T. S. Adams—who regarded the opposite concept of a tax on spending which would leave saved income free as ideally preferable to the individual income tax—should be claimed as a supporter of a measure of this kind.

Senator King. What was your view when you were in the Treasury advising them?

Mr. May. As a matter of fact, I had extended discussions with Dr. Adams and Treasury officials on the question of a substitute spending tax. We agreed it was ideally preferable, but there were some objections on the ground of excessive accumulation of fortunes by individuals, and of practical advantage, and on the whole we advised against it. But certainly, in all the long and intimate talks I had with Dr. Adams I had never heard a word that would lead me to suppose he would support this measure.

Senator Barkley. A tax on spending is a sales tax.

Mr. May. A graduated tax on spending is paid by the individual.

Senator Barkley. That is a sales tax.

Mr. May. An ordinary sales tax is a regressive tax because it falls equally on all products.

Senator Barkley. Any sort of a tax based on spending is a tax on sales.

Mr. May. It is in one sense, but not when it is ordinarily thought of as a sales tax.

Senator Barkley. You have got to buy something when you spend anything, and you are taxed on that.

Mr. May. That is the same thing. The sales tax is usually levied on the sale.

Senator Barkley. Regardless of that, it is levied on the

price, whether you levy it on the sale or on the expenditure.

Mr. May. There is a great deal of argument that under an ordinary income tax there should be an exemption of saved income. I think the argument is against it.

Senator Walsh. Is a graduated spending tax a spending tax?

Mr. May. That is what we contemplate, a graduated spending tax. It would reach the man who spent his capital.

Senator Walsh. A man who spent $50,000 would pay a higher tax than a man who spent $5,000?

Mr. May. That is right.

Senator Hastings. Would the spending tax apply to the wages of a chauffeur, for instance?

Mr. May. Yes.

Senator Hastings. In that instance it is different from a sales tax.

Mr. May. Yes; it covers all expenditures for goods and services.

Upon the social aspects of the bill generally all I propose to do is to indicate some effect that it seems to me to be likely to have, leaving the Committee to decide whether those consequences are socially desirable.

I do not want to go over ground already covered by other witnesses. I agree with Mr. Ballantine that the adoption of these proposals will have a serious adverse effect on the development of industry and the ability of industrial corporations to withstand depression. Not only was the policy of withholding profits in periods of prosperity followed and approved before our income tax was initiated; it is common in all countries and was followed in England before the principle of graduation was introduced here. I believe that in recent years the proportion of profits retained by English companies has been as great as here even in the years of prosperity. To regard such retention by publicly owned corporations as tax avoidance or even as prejudicial to the interest of the revenue, is, I think, an error.

Clearly, if corporations are compelled by taxation to distribute all their surplus in times of prosperity, it is inevitable that in any subsequent period of depression when they suffer losses they will be forced into bankruptcy or compelled to resort to State aid to a greater extent than heretofore. The idea that they should sell additional stocks to finance future losses seems to me academic and unrealistic.

I think it is a great mistake in formulating measures such as this to attach much importance to averages. Taxes are not levied on averages, but on individual cases. Businesses differ radically in their character. Some companies are what may be called developing companies, creating a new industry or exploiting a new idea. At the other extreme are corporations of a liquidating character, either because the nature of the business is in itself liquidation, or because the businesses are declining. Mining companies, for instance, are essentially liquidating in their nature. Such companies can well afford to pay out all of their profits in dividends. As a matter of fact, statistics show that they do in almost every year in the aggregate pay out more than they earn.

Senator King. Now, in regard to profits, most of the mining companies have had no profits for many years.

Mr. May. That is true.

Senator King. Where one succeeds there will be two or three hundred who fail.

Mr. May. That is quite true; but as a matter of fact, the statistics show that in almost every year the mining companies, in the aggregate, pay out more dividends than they earn, so they would be practically free of tax under this law.

On the other hand, developing companies, if they paid out in dividends the net cash they received from operations during the year, would as a rule be liable under the law to a heavy tax. It seems to me a pertinent question whether it is desirable to frame laws which favor those who are exhausting the natural resources of the country for private gain, and handicap those who are developing new industries which they expect, no doubt, to be profitable to themselves but which, if successful, would also strengthen our industrial system.

I think it is unquestionable that the law will operate in favor of the large, established companies as against those of their aspiring rivals. This no doubt accounts for the fact that comparatively little opposition to the bill has come from the large corporations.

Senator Gerry. Mr. May, I notice in going over the House hearings that there were certain large copartnerships, 23 of them, if I recollect correctly, that had incomes of over a million. What sort of businesses would they be in?

Mr. May. Senator, I saw those figures myself. I thought that 23 must be on the low side, to be quite frank, because I thought I could have named 23 firms within a gunshot of the corner of Broad and Wall in New York that had incomes of a million, the large stockbroking firms which, under the New York Stock Exchange regulations, cannot incorporate, and the large Wall Street law firms, and other service firms of that kind, I should think would have numbered more than 23 alone.

Senator Gerry. How would the partnership compare with a corporation? Of course, the corporation has the advantage of a limited liability.

Mr. May. Yes. I think, broadly speaking, when you get into large partnerships they represent, in the main, different classes of business from corporations; comparatively few of your partnerships carry on an industrial business. They are mostly what I might call service businesses. Their income is derived in cash. They would make their returns on the cash basis. So they have cash equal to the profits that they return.

On the other hand, business corporations, as we all know, have either got to develop or else die, generally speaking. That means that they are constantly making new investments in plant and capital assets, and the reality of their profit today is dependent on the usefulness of their plant in the future. Their income is determined, as I see it, on a less favorable basis to the corporation than the average partnership's income is determined to it.

So I think the disparity between the two is somewhat exaggerated, and, incidentally, in relation to those figures that you mentioned, I think you will find that while the Commissioner took as an illustrative case a partnership with an income of $1,000,000 and four partners, the more typical company in that number of 23, or whatever the proper number may be, would be a firm with far more partners than that. Big law firms have, perhaps, 15 or 20 partners, which rather modifies the conclusion.

Senator Barkley. Mr. May, is your firm a corporation or a partnership?

Mr. May. It is a partnership, sir.

Senator Barkley. It is a partnership of certified accountants, economists, experts, or which?

Mr. May. Certified public accountants.

Senator Barkley. You appear here just as an *amicus curiæ,* a friend of the court, you do not represent anybody?

Mr. May. No; not at all, sir.

Senator Walsh. Mr. May, you stated that corporations could be placed in three classifications. One which you have stated was few in number. Are those the corporations that did not distribute their earnings because they wanted to avoid their taxes?

Mr. May. When I say "few," I mean relatively few, of course.

Senator Walsh. Have you any information as to their number?

Mr. May. No, sir; I have no knowledge at all. It must be a considerable number. You know, under the English law there is a distinction in taxation between the publicly owned corporation and privately owned corporation, and I always thought we ought to pursue the question in that way if we are to arrive at really satisfactory legislation.

Senator Walsh. You think that there are a considerable

number of corporations that withhold distributing their earnings for the purpose of taxation avoidance?

Mr. May. I have no doubt that that is a substantial element, undoubtedly.

Senator Barkley. What do you mean by the distinction between publicly owned and privately owned corporations? You do not mean that in the sense that we use the term "public ownership"?

Mr. May. No; owned by the general public. In England, of course, the legislature has a very great advantage. We have always got to recognize, in comparing our procedure with the English, that all their legislation is confined to the one body. They control corporations as well as taxation and they can classify corporations for their own purposes, which you cannot do, because the States have jurisdiction in one field and you are legislating in another. I do think that that whole problem could be intensively studied to great advantage.

Senator Barkley. Where is the line of distinction in the number of owners of stock in order to make it public or private?

Mr. May. You mean in England?

Senator Barkley. Yes.

Mr. May. In England there is a limit on the number of stockholders, and as a penalty for being a public corporation you have to disclose a lot of information which private corporations do not have to, and they offer advantages that counterbalance. On the other hand, the private companies stand in a different relationship for tax purposes from those that are called public companies, and they are a larger number.

Senator Barkley. What is the line of distinction?

Mr. May. Any line is bound to be more or less arbitrary.

Senator Barkley. Under the British law, how many stockholders form a private corporation and how many does it take to make it public?

Mr. May. I do not know at the moment. If I should

make a guess, I would say 20 was the figure; something of that sort.*

Senator Walsh. You do not mean that private corporations are personal holding companies?

Mr. May. No.

Senator Walsh. For your information, in connection with the question I asked you, the expert informs me that there are 4,000 personal holding companies who make filings under the existing law and who, in all probability, do so for the purpose of the tax.

Senator Barkley. Do you know whether the British law makes any distinction as to whether the shares of stock are listed on an exchange where they may publicly inspect and purchase them?

Mr. May. I do not think it turns on the listing on an exchange, but it does require disclosure of information to the Registrar of Companies. They have to give more information to the public than the private companies do.

Senator Bailey. You began by making a statement which indicated a contradiction of fact as between the Secretary of the Treasury and the Commissioner of Internal Revenue. I would like for you to make a statement about that. Just give me the facts over again.

The Chairman. May I ask you, was the Commissioner's statement from which you quoted made before the House Ways and Means Committee?

Mr. May. No; I think they were both made before this body.

The Chairman. You read the statement which was made before this Committee?

Mr. May. Yes; I think I am right about that.

---

* Under the existing English law a private company is one whose regulations limit the number of its members to fifty, restrict the right to transfer its shares, and prohibit any invitation to the public to subscribe for any of its shares or debentures. (Cf. Companies Act of 1929, Sec. 26.) The distinction between companies for purposes of the surtax no longer follows the distinction between public and private companies. In order to be liable to surtax on undistributed income, a company must *inter alia* be under the control of not more than five persons, as defined in the Act. (Cf. Finance Act of 1927, Sec. 31.)—Author's note.

Senator Bailey. Just what is the difference between them?

Mr. May. The Commissioner states that if the existing taxes were repealed, there would be four and a half billion dollars. The Secretary says—

Senator Bailey (interposing). Four and a half billion dollars of what?

Mr. May. Of income available for distribution, which the Treasury estimates would not be distributed. I think that is a fair way of saying it. The Secretary said there would be that same amount of money available under the existing law. The difference between the two statements is that the amount of the taxes under the existing law, which is a billion one hundred million dollars, roughly—

Senator Bailey (interposing). Is it possible that both statements could be reconciled?

Mr. May. I do not see how. It seems to me that the Secretary misunderstood the figure, and I believe the wording of the figure was a little unfortunate and may have given rise to that misunderstanding.

Senator Bailey. Did he adopt that figure for this statement from the Commissioner's statement without getting the facts upon which the Commissioner's statement was predicated?

Mr. May. I am not in the confidence of the Treasury.

Senator Bailey. Can you explain that?

Mr. May. I think there is no other explanation.

Senator Hastings. As I understand your position, you figure that there ought to be a billion one hundred million taken from the figures given by the Secretary of the Treasury?

Mr. May. I think one billion one hundred million should be deducted from his figure.

Senator Hastings. So that instead of his figure being four billion one hundred, it ought to have been three billion?

Mr. May. If he wanted to state it on that basis.

The Chairman. Thank you, Mr. May.

Senator Bailey. Your other statement is that, in your

opinion, the proposed legislation if adopted is not likely to raise much more money, if any, than the existing law? Is that your opinion about it?

Mr. May. And the reason is I think the Treasury underestimates the yield of the present law on the conditions.

Senator Bailey. We have been predicating legislation on the basis of fifty-five billions this year. I read in the New York *Times* this morning an article in which the President was quoted as saying that the annual income this year would be about sixty-five billion. Can you give me some information or view about that?

Mr. May. I am afraid I am not currently up to date on the statistics sufficiently for that, Senator. I am taking the same estimates that the Treasury assumes; they take as their basic year on which these calculations are predicated, an estimate of seven billion of statutory net income. I think the yield under the existing law would be larger than they have assumed on that basis. It is not that I think they are exaggerating the yield under the new law, but that they are underestimating the yield under the existing law.

Senator Bailey. Your theory is that the bill is wrong in principle and that we cannot get rid of injustices in it?

Mr. May. Yes. And I do not feel that we have adequate bases to formulate legislation in which we could reasonably limit the injustices.

Senator Bailey. Are you prepared to suggest to us legislation that would surely add $800,000,000 revenue as compared with the last bill?

Mr. May. I do not think that I can say that on the Treasury figures it is necessary to increase the yield of the taxation under the present law by $800,000,000 in order to reach the total taxation that is contemplated. I think you will get pretty close to it under the existing law, if all of the other estimates are realized; that is what I got from an analysis of these figures of the Treasury. Certainly my strong feeling is that there is not sufficient fiscal advantage in passing this law to justify precipitate action, and I would like to see a very careful study made and more considered legislation based on it.

Senator Connally. Would you rather raise the flat corporation tax, rather than this plan?

Mr. May. I would; I would rather see any rational levy raised, frankly. I would be willing to see my own taxes raised, because I think it is much better for us to pay more taxes than to leave the budget unbalanced.

Senator Connally. I congratulate you.

The Chairman. All right, Mr. May.

Senator Gerry. I would like to ask Mr. May a question, and see if I get it clear, on this last statement. What you feel is that the revenue raised by the present bill will be greater than the Treasury estimates?

Mr. May. Yes.

Senator Gerry. Under the present law?

Mr. May. Under the present law.

Senator Gerry. Than the Treasury estimates?

Mr. May. That is my feeling.

Senator Bailey. How much greater?

Mr. May. Very considerably, sir.

Senator Bailey. Six or seven hundred millions?

Mr. May. Of course, I have not got the detail, but I should say pretty nearly the amount that this increase was expected to raise. Five or six hundred million.

Senator Bailey. Could you prepare the data in a short time?

Mr. May. I could make a summary, as I have done here of the causes which lead to it; but I should have to have some information from the Treasury to convert increases in individual incomes into taxes on individual incomes, because they have figured it out on the distribution to be expected, which I have not.

Senator Bailey. I would like very much to have it.

Mr. May. I would have to have certain data from the Treasury in order to do it.

The Chairman. You believe the increase would come

under the present law because of the general increase in business?

Mr. May. Yes, sir.

Senator Connally. Disregard the income. Could you estimate how much the corporation income in 1936 would be over 1935 if we make no change in the rates? Can you give a rough estimate?

Mr. May. I do not carry those figures clearly enough in my head to make the estimate. I am cautious of making estimates except from actual figures.

Senator Connally. I am not calling for an opinion that I will pay you for as an expert.

Mr. May. My services are always at the disposal of the Committee.

Senator Connally. You figure the business in 1936 is going to be better than in 1935?

Mr. May. The Treasury estimates it, and I believe there is ground to believe it.

Senator Connally. But you do not know how much?

Mr. May. The Treasury estimates that there will be one billion seven hundred million increase in taxable statutory income, which, on a 15 per cent basis, would be $255,000,000.

Senator Barkley. You think that the present law, unchanged, would raise this eight hundred million in addition to the amount raised in 1935, or in addition to the Treasury estimates for 1936?

Mr. May. I think for the graduated tax end of it, it would raise the larger part of the six hundred million that it was supposed to raise over the Treasury's estimates for 1936; yes.

Senator Barkley. You think we are liable to be more prosperous than the Treasury does?

Mr. May. I think more money is going to be distributed than the Treasury estimated, and that will mean large increases to the individual income tax.

The Chairman. All right, Mr. May; thank you.

B. TAXATION AND ACCOUNTING

I

CLASSIFICATION OF PROFITS ON INVESTMENTS *

(1921)

THE question involved in the case of *Brewster* v. *Walsh* in which a decision was recently handed down by the Connecticut district court is one of far-reaching and great interest to accountants. That question is whether profits realized on investments are capital or income.

We shall not attempt to deal with the legal aspect of the question, but in the business and accounting world such profits would, we think, ordinarily be regarded as income. The average man also doubtless thinks that he can properly spend such profits without laying himself open to the charge of dissipating his capital: indeed he is likely to regard them as a peculiarly appropriate basis for expenditures on luxuries as being what is sometimes called "velvet."

There is a group of economists whose views are in accord with those of the District Court that such profits are not income. This group includes those economists who solve the problem of living within one's income for everyone by holding that whatever is spent is *ipso facto* income. We are very far from saying that this concept is useless or uninteresting, but we feel that it is so far at variance with the commercial concept of income that the economists in question would be well advised to adopt for it some name other than income. Fortunately there is a larger body of economists whose concept of income does include such profits as were involved in this case and is more closely in harmony

* An editorial contributed to *The Journal of Accountancy*, Vol. XXI (January, 1921).

with the accounting and commercial interpretation of the phrase.

We should be sorry to see the meaning of the word "income" restricted by the courts either on legalistic grounds or on the basis of an interesting but unpractical economic concept in such a way as to limit the ability of Congress to tax anything that is ordinarily regarded by the average citizen as being income. If a taxpayer by choosing investments, the fruits of which are to be expected in the form of the return of a larger sum at the end of a period of years rather than in actual income, can thereby escape the income tax altogether in respect of such investments, the opportunities to the rich taxpayer now offered by tax-exempt securities will be immensely enlarged, and dissatisfaction with the tax will correspondingly increase.

In our view it is desirable that the broadest possible interpretation should be given to the term "income," leaving the determination of the forms of income to be taxed to be considered by the legislative bodies.

II

THE SOURCE OF PROFITS *

(1922)

A PROVISION of the new tax law which has a general accounting interest apart from the tax feature, is the rule that profits
from the sale of personal property produced within and sold
without the United States, or produced without and sold
within the United States, shall be treated as derived partly
from sources within and partly from sources without the
United States, the Commissioner being authorized to prescribe processes, formulas and general apportionment for determining the portion of such net income attributable to
sources within the United States.

The previous act did not deal specifically with this question and the Attorney-General, when the question was referred to him, ruled that in such cases all the income was derived from sources within the country in which the goods
were sold. In the course of his opinion he said: "No income
is derived from the mere manufacture of goods; before there
can be income there must be sale; and there is no income
from sources within the United States from goods manufactured here unless there is in the language of Section 223 both
manufacture and disposition of goods within the United
States."

Many qualified persons felt that the Attorney-General had
been betrayed into an incorrect application of a sound accounting rule and that the argument just quoted was a clear
case of *non sequitur*. The completion of the sale determines the time of the making of the profit, but it does not in
the least follow that it determines the source. The real
source of profit in a manufacturing business is the employ-

* An editorial contributed to *The Journal of Accountancy*, Vol. XXXIII
(March, 1922).

ment of capital and labor in the conversion of goods; selling
is the realization of the profit rather than the source. The
amount of profit is affected by the degree of efficiency of
the methods of realization, just as it is affected by the degree
of efficiency of the capital assets and the labor employed in
production, and it is entirely equitable that there should be
attributed to sale some part (but certainly not the whole) of
the profit.

The new provision is therefore sound in principle. It
should be understood, however, that it does not lend any
sanction to the practice of taking interdepartmental profit
when goods are transferred from the manufacturing to the
selling department. This practice, thanks largely to its condemnation by accountants, is now comparatively seldom
adopted, and the new law should not be allowed to form an
excuse for its revival. The essential fact on which the accountants' opposition has always been based still remains.
There is no profit until the goods have been both manufactured and sold

III

TAXABLE INCOME AND ACCOUNTING BASES FOR DETERMINING IT *

INTRODUCTION

On various occasions when the question has arisen, I have been impressed by the uncertainties and misconceptions shown to exist concerning accounting bases for determining income for tax purposes and in regard to the significance of such terms as "the cash basis" and "the accrual basis" commonly employed in tax practice. It has therefore seemed to me to be worth while to devote some time to a consideration of this subject and in so doing to go back over the developments affecting it since the passage of the corporation excise-tax law in 1909.

As a preliminary to such consideration it seems necessary to inquire to some extent into the nature of taxable income, but I do not propose to go into this very large subject except in so far as may be necessary to an intelligent discussion of the accounting bases for determining income. To allay still further any anxiety created by the comprehensiveness of the title of this paper, I will add that I shall confine myself to commercial income, which constitutes the major part of the taxable income of the country and presents the more difficult problems, and I shall not discuss personal, professional or investment income.

In income taxation, the first problem is to define income and the second to allocate income in respect of time. The question of allocation to sources geographically arises in some cases and presents some difficulties, but this question affects only a restricted field.

The problem of definition resolves itself mainly into a

* A paper presented at the annual meeting of the American Institute of Accountants at Washington, D. C., September 15, 1925. Published in *The Journal of Accountancy*, Vol. XL (October, 1925).
267

choice between several different concepts of the nature of the income and, though important, is relatively simple. The more serious difficulties are encountered in determining when income emerges from the complicated business transactions of modern commerce so as to be properly taxable.

The accounting bases employed in determining income affect the time when income becomes taxable rather than the amount of income ultimately taxable, and this paper therefore has to do mainly with the time element in taxation. This is conspicuously a case where "time is of the essence." Whether an amount is to be deemed taxable in a year of high war taxes or in some remote future year may be of far more practical importance than whether the whole or only a part is to be finally taxed.

WHAT IS TAXABLE INCOME?

Since 1913 our income tax laws have been enacted under the authority of the sixteenth amendment to the Constitution, which authorized Congress to tax without apportionment among the several states "incomes from whatever source derived."

Now there are numerous theories as to what is income. In one case (*Doyle* v. *Mitchell*) the government argued that the gross proceeds of sale were income. Economists sometimes argue that earnings that are saved are not income, so that what is income is determined by how what comes in is subsequently expended. Apart, however, from any such extreme views, there are two materially different theories of income which are supported by considerable authority: One holds that income is necessarily gain, the other that it may be in part a conversion of capital.

The difference may be illustrated by the case of a man purchasing an annuity. The general public regards the whole of the annuity as his income and this view is shared, I think, by many economists and reflected in the English and probably other tax laws. The actuary and the accountant would, however, insist that only in part is the annuity rightfully called income, a part being a realization of capital. Congress in 1913 might, I suppose, have adopted either of these theories, and if its intent had been clearly manifested the Supreme Court would hardly have rejected that theory.

This, however, Congress did not do. The clauses of the 1913 and 1916 acts purporting to define income or gross income, as definitions, left much to be desired. What are we to infer from the definition of income as including "gains, profits and income" from certain specified sources "or from any source whatever"? Is income something different from gains and profits, and if so, what is the distinction? In Section 4 of the act of 1916 Congress provided that annuities in so far as they represented returns of premiums were not *taxable income*, but in doing so it in plain language characterized them as income; the law of 1918 retained the exemption but avoided the characterization [Sec. 213 (a)].

It might fairly be argued that Congress, taking the acts as a whole, indicated an intention to tax only gains. This view is supported by the provisions above mentioned and by those allowing depreciation and depletion. On the other hand, the fact that these items were allowed by way of deductions from income or gross income in arriving at taxable income, the limitation of the deductions in purely arbitrary ways, and the language of Section 4 of the Act of 1916 above alluded to, might be claimed to support the view that Congress intended to assert the right to tax as income what might be in part a conversion of capital, but not to exercise its rights to that extent.

However this may be, the Supreme Court presumably settled the matter when in the case of *Eisner* v. *Macomber* it defined income as the gain derived from capital, from labor, or from both combined.

This decision, for the reason that it contained the definition I have referred to and held that Congress had attempted to tax as income what was not income, is of great importance, and it may be worth while to discuss it briefly. Many passages from the opinion are of interest to accountants, but I will quote only one paragraph:

After examining dictionaries in common use (Bouv. L. D.; Standard Dict.; Webster's Internat. Dict.; Century Dict.), we find little to add to the succinct definition adopted in two cases arising under the corporation tax act of 1909 (*Stratton's Independence* v. *Howbert*, 231 U. S. 399, 415; *Doyle* v. *Mitchell Bros. Co.*, 247 U. S. 179, 185)—"Income may be defined as the gain derived from capital, from labor, or from both combined," provided it be understood to include profit gained through a sale or conversion of capital assets, to which it was applied in the Doyle case (pp. 183, 185).

In the dictionaries cited, both of the views of income above mentioned are set forth; the definition coming closest to that adopted by the Court is found in Bouvier's *Law Dictionary*.

Reference to the decision in *Stratton's Independence* v. *Howbert,* in which the definition was first used, discloses that in that case the Court was at pains to point out that, as at the time of the passage of the 1909 law Congress had no power to levy a general income tax without apportionment, the theoretical distinctions between capital and income were of little value to the Court in interpreting that statute. Curiously enough also, the case was one in which the court sustained the taxation as income of the proceeds of gold mining without any provision for the exhaustion of the capital represented by the mine. In *Doyle* v. *Mitchell,* arising under the same act, the Court adopted the same definition in a decision in which it ruled that the proceeds of lumbering could not be taxed as income without a deduction for the capital value of the timber exhausted. However, these decisions, being rendered under the excise-tax law, have no necessary bearing on the present question; and in *Eisner* v. *Macomber* which was decided under an income tax law, none of these special features was present.

Just how far-reaching the effect of that decision is in law is a question for lawyers. The Supreme Court decisions under the excise-tax law of 1909 rather suggest that Congress can levy an excise tax *measured by income* without availing of the sixteenth amendment, and in so doing can define income as it pleases without regard to the views of the Supreme Court or anyone else. So long, however, as it levies a tax *on income* it apparently cannot tax as income what the Supreme Court does not consider to be income.

The point is largely academic, and Congress has not shown any disposition to disagree with the general interpretation of income adopted by the court. The two bodies have, it is true, differed on the question whether stock dividends are income; but dividends constitute a special problem and are, both under the acts and under court decisions, an exception to the rule that there is no income unless there is gain. If an investor buys $100 shares of a company which has a surplus equal to its capital stock for $200 a share and if the next day the company pays a dividend of $100 a share and its shares fall to par, the dividend is not gain to the investor whether the dividend is paid in stock or cash. Dividends are however, in general, income; and it is so manifestly impossible to provide for treatment thereof varying according to the circumstances surrounding the holders' acquisition of the stock on which the dividend is paid, that purchasers of stocks of companies having large earned surpluses may reasonably be expected to realize that in making such purchases they not only acquire the prospects of dividends out of profits earned prior to their purchase but also assume the burden of any tax on the dividends they may receive. It was for this reason that Mr. Justice Pitney in the *Phellis* case said the hardship in the case of such purchasers was more apparent than real. It is on similar grounds that supporters of the English system justify its treatment of the proceeds of an annuity or of mining and similar operations as taxable income without any deduction for exhaustion of capital. In this connection it is pertinent to point out that the English income tax has been levied continuously since 1842 and that therefore the great expansion of industry and corporate enterprise has taken place mainly with notice of the burdens in the form of income tax to which it might be subject.

Other similar cases may arise where something which is not gain is taxed as income. It would probably be a fairly accurate statement to say that the general test of the existence of income is whether there is gain, but that items which ordinarily constitute gain and are commonly regarded as income may be taxed as such even though in exceptional cases they may not result in a gain to the recipient.

As regards commercial operations there are probably few exceptions to the rule that income must be in the nature of gain. Gain in commercial business is, however, usually not a separate item but a difference between items on opposite sides of the account. On the one side are the proceeds of sale, on the other the costs involved in producing the sales. Frequently also the gain is the result of a series of transactions or a gradual process extending over two or more distinct tax periods. If a taxpayer buys raw materials in one year, manufactures finished goods therefrom in another, sells those goods in a third and collects the proceeds in a fourth year, the ultimate gain is obviously not attributable wholly to any one of these four years nor is there any way of allocating portions of the gain to the operations of the several years, which can be said to be the scientific and only proper way. In one such series of transactions the main factor contributing to the gain may be cheapness of buying, in another low cost of manufacture, in another advantageous selling and so on. Further, the transactions of a taxpayer are frequently so interrelated that we cannot ascertain the profits of any given series separately. Commercial profit is in fact, as an eminent English judge puts it, necessarily a matter of estimate and opinion.

In the determination of income for commercial purposes the best practice is to be governed by considerations of conservatism. Profits are not taken except when and to the extent that they are received or at least reasonably assured. Losses that are foreseen are provided for even though not actually sustained or measured. The legislature naturally approaches the question from a rather different point of view. On the first point it may be questioned whether Congress has power to tax profits not actually received. On the second, if it allows actual losses as deductions it can hardly be expected to allow deductions for potential future losses to be made at the discretion of the taxpayer.

It should be said at once that Congress has shown no disposition either to tax income not received or to deny losses actually sustained. Indeed in at least one important instance it has deliberately allowed the anticipation of potential losses. The provision in the Act of 1918 that inventories shall be taken on the basis conforming to the best trade practice was enacted with the knowledge that one of the best trade practices was to value inventories at cost where cost was less than market, and at market where that was less than cost, thus anticipating a loss wherever market might be below cost. This recognition of one of the best established of those trade practices which find their justification not in logic or scientific considerations, but in conservatism and practical wisdom, is very significant. In 1921 also the law was amended to permit deduction of a reasonable reserve for bad debts instead of only debts ascertained to be worthless, thus recognizing another well-established trade practice.

Whether the deductions permitted for depreciation and depletion are properly regarded as provisions for anticipated losses is difficult to say. From the accounting standpoint the provisions for depletion and depreciation of manufacturing plant are elements of cost, which must be provided for before there can be said to be any gain. The decisions of the Supreme Court on this branch of the subject are not altogether easy to reconcile either with one another or with the Court's general definition of income. Quite apart from the decision in the *Stratton's Independence* case, under the Act of 1909, the significance of which may be lessened by the fact that the claimants were asserting that all the proceeds of mining were capital, the court has approved under an income tax law a purely arbitrary limitation on the depletion allowance which it would seem could hardly have been sustained except on grounds which would have applied equally to the total denial of any deduction. This, in turn, would seem to mean that depletion is not a factor necessarily taken into account in determining the gain.

One other point may be noted. In general our laws have taxed the income of the taxpayer from his business, which may be less than the total gain from the business to the extent of the portion of the economic gain which the taxpayer may be required to pay over to others in the form of interest, rentals and other participations. In this respect ours has differed from the English system, which assesses against the taxpayer carrying on the business the entire gain from that business without regard to any such distributions, leaving the equitable adjustment between taxpayers to be effected by a system of deductions by the taxpayer when making the distributions, and refunds by the revenue to the distributees if they should be exempt from tax. In the Act of 1909 and the income tax acts up to that of 1918, however, the interest deduction allowed to corporations was arbitrarily limited and the limitation was sustained by the courts. Here again the power to impose purely arbitrary limitations on the deduction would seem necessarily to imply power to deny any deductions whatever. In the cases which came before the court the objection urged was apparently that the limitation was discriminatory and the decisions may, therefore, not be authority for the proposition that Congress has the power to tax all that is economically income in the hands of the person who realizes the income, even though it is not all income to that person. The point might become important, for a tax so levied without some provision for the proper adjustment of the burden between the ultimate beneficiaries of the gain might easily result in a tax on a person receiving the income greater than the portion thereof which he might be entitled to retain. In the year 1917 the limitation on interest deductions undoubtedly worked some hardship, and would have caused gross injustice but for the action of the Commissioner in allowing, without any very obvious warrant in the law, the capital sum corresponding to the interest disallowed to be treated as invested capital.

While the arbitrary limitations to which I have referred, and which are now fortunately removed, were blemishes on the earlier acts, criticism of the methods of determining taxable income established by those acts must be directed mainly at their lack of precision and clarity and their failure to recognize business methods and considerations of practical convenience.

BASES OF ACCOUNTING FOR INCOME HISTORICALLY CONSIDERED

It is perhaps not surprising that at the outset receipt or payment in cash should have been adopted as the general basis for inclusion of items in income tax returns. Legislation is framed and interpreted largely by lawyers, and lawyers apparently seek to atone for the bewildering complexities they have introduced into their own sphere of activity by insisting on the utmost simplicity in other spheres. The legal mind that distrusts simple interest and regards compound interest as wholly pernicious is naturally suspicious of any account more complex than a cash account. In Great Britain, the home of the income tax, this tendency has been manifest, but in regard to commercial income it has been counteracted by another principle of judicial action, the principle that in commercial affairs the established practices of business men are a better guide than rules framed by theorists. Consequently, the courts there have always held that the determination of income from business was a business problem and that in the absence of express statutory provision to the contrary, established trade practices must be followed even though to the revenue authorities or even the court those practices might seem theoretically unsound or illogical. An excellent illustration is found in the methods of valuing inventories, the English courts having sustained both the "cost or market" basis and the "basic stock" method where a practice in the trade was shown to exist and there was no statutory prohibition.

In our case, however, the tendency towards the cash basis was perhaps strengthened by the accident that our first income tax was enacted in the guise of an excise tax. The law of 1909 was framed so as to provide that corporations should return income actually received and expenses actually paid. As soon as this became known the accountants vigorously protested to the Attorney-General that such a basis ignored the nature and practices of modern business and would entail inconvenience that would be more burdensome than the tax. The Attorney-General, however, remained unmoved by their protest, said that the straight cash basis was adopted advisedly, and retorted that he had too much confidence in the ability of the accountants to think that they would find the difficulties of complying with the law unsurmountable. His confidence was apparently justified, for with the assistance of accountants the Secretary of the Treasury issued regulations which certainly presented no special difficulties to taxpayers.

Some have thought that the authors of those regulations found their inspiration, where so many others have found inspiration, in the works of W. S. Gilbert. Certainly when one reads the provisions to the effect that the term "actually paid" does not necessarily contemplate that there shall have been an actual disbursement of cash or even its equivalent, and that an item is paid as soon as a taxpayer recognizes that it has to be paid, one is irresistibly reminded of Koko's explanation to the Mikado of his statement that Nanki Poo had been executed when in fact he was still alive.

When your Majesty says, 'Let a thing be done,' it's as good as done,—practically it is done,—because your Majesty's will is law. Your Majesty says, 'Kill a gentleman,' and a gentleman is told off to be killed. Consequently, that gentleman is as good as dead, practically, he *is* dead, and if he is dead, why not say so?

It is, however, quite possible to find a more logical justification for the method of determining net income established by the regulations at least in the main, though this justification, I admit, does not extend to the language in which the method is prescribed and ostensibly justified.

The Act of 1909 provided that the "net income" which was subjected to tax should be determined by deducting "from the gross amount of the income . . . received within the year from all sources:"

First. All the ordinary and necessary expenses paid within the year out of income in the maintenance and operation of its business and properties including all charges such as rentals or franchise payments required to be made as a condition to the continued use or possession of property.

Second. All losses actually sustained within the year and not compensated by insurance or otherwise, including a reasonable allowance for depreciation of property if any.

Third. Interest actually paid within the year subject to specified limits.

Fourth. All sums paid within the year for taxes.

Fifth. Dividends from other companies subject to the tax.

The regulations regarding commercial income apparently ignored the word "received" just as fully as the word "paid." It was not necessary that proceeds of sale should have been received in order that there should be taxable income therefrom. The regulation treated income from sales as received when the goods were exchanged for an account or note receivable or cash. This was, in ordinary cases, an obviously convenient rule (and in considering the almost complete acquiescence these regulations secured, it must always be borne in mind that the tax was so small as to make it not worth while to fight a reasonably convenient rule), but whether if challenged it would have been sustained is open to question. The courts have pointed out that the expectation of gain in the future is not present income and have been reluctant to sustain a tax where nothing had been received out of which the tax could be paid. The justification of the regulation would have had to be found in the argument that something equivalent to cash had been received, and in many classes of transactions the recognition of the principle of cash equivalence must be conceded to be practically essential to an effective income tax administration. Once this principle is adopted, however, it has to be admitted that in measuring the gain the proceeds must be reduced to a true cash equivalent. This would mean bringing provisions for the cost of collection, for discounts and for credit risks into account at the same time as the sale itself, which it may be noted the regulations did not permit.

The next point to be observed is that the proceeds of sale are not income (*Doyle* v. *Mitchell*); only so much as is gain is income. Assuming, therefore, that the gain is received when the proceeds of sale are received (not necessarily in cash), it follows that all costs attributable to the sale must be brought into account at the same time as the sale itself, whether such costs have or have not been paid. Otherwise, on balance, something which is not gain will inevitably have been brought into account and taxed as income. It is generally recognized that this is true of the direct cost of the goods sold, but it is not so universally understood that it is equally true of the cost of making the sale and the cost of collecting the proceeds. A commission paid in order to effect a sale is as much an element in determining the gain therefrom as the cost of the property sold. This point seems to me to have a most important bearing on the determination of taxable income whether the question be approached from the theoretical, historical, or practical standpoint.

In considering the proper treatment of any item in relation to taxable income, the first essential is to decide whether it properly relates to the determination of gross income or to a deduction from gross income. If the former, its treatment is not in any way affected by any limitations of deductions to amounts paid, accrued or incurred, as the case may be, since these limitations apply only to items which are *in fact* charges against gross income after gross income has been determined. As the Court indicated in *Doyle* v. *Mitchell* it is immaterial whether there is any express provision allowing elements in the production of gross income as deductions from gross proceeds, for until they are deducted there is nothing ascertained which Congress can properly tax as income.

This principle would have warranted a regulation that all costs of effecting sales, as well as the costs of producing the goods sold and provisions for the costs of collection, were allowable in the period in which the sales were returned, as a part of the computation of gross income. Only expenses not falling under any of these three heads would have been left to be taken as deductions under the head of "ordinary and necessary expenses actually paid within the year out of income."

Looking back on the problem of 1909 in the flood of light which the developments of the last sixteen years have thrown on the subject, one feels that along such lines a solution might have been found that would have been almost as convenient as the one adopted and would have avoided interpreting the words "actually paid" in the Gilbertian manner of the regulation then promulgated. It may be suggested that the language of the provision for deduction for business expenses stood in the way, but this does not seem to be necessarily so. That provision authorized the "deducting from the gross amount of the income all the ordinary and necessary expenses actually paid within the year *out of income.*" Expenditures necessarily made to produce income surely did not fall in any such category. In point of fact, expenses of maintenance of the property of the taxpayer were specifically enumerated in the Act among the "ordinary and necessary expenses," yet the regulations provided that expenditures for maintenance of manufacturing plant should be included in cost of goods sold in computing gross income and not under the deduction.

The regulations of 1909 did not follow the course I have suggested, but treated only cost of goods as a deduction from sales in determining gross income and dealt with cost of selling and collection as "ordinary or necessary expenses" to be deducted from gross income when "actually paid" providing, however, that when such items were duly set up on the books they were "actually paid" within the meaning of the law.

The convenience of the solution is undeniable, and it may be that the framers were governed by this consideration. They may well have felt that the solution was so convenient that no one would be likely to challenge it, and that if it were challenged they could readily show that it produced erroneous results only as regards expenses which were not a part of the cost of effecting and collecting the sales returned, the amount of which was in ordinary cases relatively insignificant.

In substance these regulations were sound, convenient and did little real violence to the language of the law. Their form, however, must be admitted to have been defective, particularly in its apparent disregard of the language of the law. No doubt if continued interest in the work of administering the law by men of the quality of those who framed the regulations could have been secured, the defects in form would have been corrected, while the advantages of the substance would have been retained. This, however, was not possible, and in the event just the opposite result followed. The influence of the defective form has continued long after the advantages derived from the substance have ceased to be felt.

One result of the defective form was that a widespread feeling was created both within and without the department that the regulations were at variance with the law and that any day dissatisfaction with their operation in a particular case might bring the issue into court and cause the whole house of cards to collapse. Another result was that the average taxpayer who was told that when used in connection with expenses the word "paid" did not necessarily mean a disbursement in cash, but that when used in relation to interest or taxes it did contemplate such a disbursement, felt that the law was unreasonable and so far as he was concerned incomprehensible. Still another result, certainly of a most unexpected character, which I shall discuss later in this paper, grew out of the establishment by the regulations of the making of book entries as a criterion of deductibility, a criterion not warranted, either in theory or in the language of the law.

Further, while the solution by the Secretary of the Treasury of the problem presented in the Act of 1909 produced immediate benefits in the form of convenience, it stood in the way of efforts to secure a more satisfactory wording when in 1913 the first income tax law was enacted. Efforts to secure an improvement were made by, among others, the American Association of Public Accountants. The suggestion of a change was met with the argument that the existing law had in practice worked quite satisfactorily and that if such a law could be applied to corporations there was even greater justification for applying it to individuals, most of whom would keep no books and would make returns on a purely cash basis. The law of 1913 thus followed closely the language of the law of 1909. The efforts were, however, continued, and in 1916 a modification was effected and taxpayers were given the option of making returns either on the statutory basis or on the basis on which their books were kept, provided the method of keeping the books was such as in the opinion of the Commissioner correctly reflected income. For various reasons which it is hardly necessary at this time to discuss, this provision did not work very well, and the regulations under the Act of 1916 continued to follow very closely those made under the Acts of 1909 and 1913.

In passing it may be pointed out that Article 126 of Regulations No. 33 issued January 2, 1918, strongly suggests that at the time those regulations were issued the line of reasoning which I have put forward above as an alternative to that indicated by the language of 1909 regulations had developed in the Bureau. It begins by apparently flouting the language of the statute in the most open and flagrant manner. The first sentence reads " 'paid' or 'actually paid'

within the meaning of this title, does not necessarily contemplate that there shall be an actual disbursement in cash
or its equivalent." The next sentence, however, states very
succinctly the underlying justification of the results of the
regulation which I have suggested. "If the amount involved
represents an actual *expense or element of cost in the production of the income* of the year, it will be properly deductible even though not actually disbursed in cash, provided it is so entered upon the books of the company as to
constitute a liability against its assets, and provided further
that the income is also returned upon an accrued basis."

It will be observed that this regulation does not in terms
permit the deduction of any expense which has not actually
been paid unless it is "an expense or element of cost in the
production of the income." To support such a position it
was not necessary to give a forced construction to the words
"actually paid" used in the statute. In practice, however,
the regulation was applied to all business expenses, and the
Bureau no doubt preferred to retain substantially the language of the regulations under the Acts of 1909 and 1913
and to be in a position to invoke the rule that re-enactment
of the provisions of an act by Congress with a knowledge of
the way in which it has been interpreted sanctions that interpretation.

When in 1917 the excess-profits tax law was passed levying
high taxes on the income determined under the 1916 law
and regulations, the whole question assumed new importance
and the need for revision of the law became apparent.

In the 1918 law, therefore, it was provided (in Section 212)
that returns should be made on the basis on which the taxpayer's books were kept unless that basis did not clearly reflect income, in which case returns were to be made on such
basis as the Commissioner might prescribe as clearly reflecting income.

In considering this section it is important to bear in mind
the provisions of the Act that the terms paid or incurred
(used in relation to deductions for expenses) and paid or

accrued (used in relation to deductions for interest and taxes) should be construed according to the method of accounting used in computing net income.

Even more important, however, is the provision that items of gross income were to be included in returns for the taxable year in which received, unless under methods of accounting permitted under Section 212 they were properly accounted for as of a different period.

The intent seems clear to give the fullest effect to sound accounting practice in the determination of gross income. It may be conceded that the law gave no authority to the Commissioner to prescribe or permit bases of accounting which would result in deductions from the gross income of expenses in periods other than those in which they were paid or incurred, or of interest and taxes in periods other than that of payment or accrual. "Incurred," however, is a sufficiently broad term and no serious criticism of the rules thus established could be offered by the most ardent advocate of the policy of allowing commercial practice to govern the determination of commercial income. The law certainly authorized the acceptance of well-established practices for determining gross income on the basis of the fair present value of the sales price, instead of its face value—in other words, the exclusion from the computation of gross income of so much of the nominal sale price as might be necessary to provide for discounts, for the credit risk assumed and the cost of collecting that sale price. It did not permit deduction from gross income of reserves for potential future losses nor for expenditures not yet incurred and not involved in the production of the gross sales reported. From the legislative standpoint such deductions could not reasonably be allowed, however legitimate or even praiseworthy purely precautionary reserves may be from the standpoints of sound finance and business prudence.

To most accountants the Act of 1918 seemed to dispose of the vitally important question of accounting bases for determining taxable income in a sound and satisfactory way.

It can hardly be said that the expectations entertained have been fully realized. The regulations (Reg. 45) seemed to observe the spirit as well as the letter of the law. Article 23, for instance, provided that "approved standard methods of accounting will ordinarily be regarded as clearly reflecting income" and Article 24 said "the law contemplates that each taxpayer shall adopt such forms and systems of accounting as are in his judgment best suited to his purpose." In such articles as 151 the propriety of computing gross income upon the basis of the cash equivalent rather than the face value of credit sales was recognized. Other articles explicitly recognized approved alternative methods of treating expenditures in the twilight zone between obviously capital expenditure and ordinary operating expense. In administration the law has frequently been construed with less breadth and with less regard for its spirit. In part this is perhaps attributable to failure to realize the nature of the problem of determining the income of a single year.

Accountants realize that income cannot with even approximate accuracy be allocated to a particular year, especially in the case of taxpayers carrying on an extensive and complex business. No year is sufficient unto itself—each year's operations are bound up with and dependent on the operations of earlier and later years. Consequently, any attribution of income to a single year in such cases must at best be no more than a very rough approximation based on accepted conventions. Many, however, who have not had much experience in such matters look on the income of a year as a very definite, significant and even a precise thing. They are reluctant to accept the proposition that there can be two ways of determining the income of a given year, which will give substantially different results and be equally admissible and correct. Experience suggests that such reluctance was very general among those in the Bureau of Internal Revenue, and when the 1918 act compelled recognition of the principle that there might be more than one legally correct way of computing income for a given year, they apparently resolved at least to limit the number of alternatives. Since the passage of the 1918 act the correspondence and briefs of the Bureau have contained constant references to the *two* bases of accounting permitted under the act, these two being described respectively as "the cash basis" and "the accrual basis." Of course, the more experienced members of the Bureau realized that there were far more than two bases of accounting possible and recognized under the Act, and doubtless many of those who spoke of *the* cash basis and *the* accrual basis used the latter term generically to describe anything other than a cash basis. But to a large number of the employees of the Bureau *the accrual basis* has become not merely a significant phrase, but an article of faith. Indeed, one can almost imagine such employees of the Bureau scattered over the land turning their faces towards the Treasury daily at the appointed hour and reciting their creed, "There is but one accrual basis and the Bureau is its prophet."

"THE ACCRUAL BASIS"

It may be worth while to inquire just what is meant by "the accrual basis." This is by no means clear, nor is it even clear precisely how it differs from the so-called cash basis as applied to commercial income since 1909.

It will be evident from what I have already said that both in theory and in practice cash has very little to do (in the case of commercial enterprises) with the determination of income on the "cash" basis, and very little reflection is necessary to a realization of the fact that accruals (in any proper sense of the word) have still less to do with the determination of income on the so-called accrual basis. This fact has been obscured by the practice, which has grown up, of using the word "accrue" in senses hardly dreamed of before the Revenue Act of 1916 was passed. The Bureau, having adopted "the accrual basis" as the only alternative to "the cash basis," has proceeded to term "an accrual" almost everything that is not a cash item. Thus, we find the Bureau speaking of taking up an inventory as an accrual and of "accruing accounts receivable from sales" and quite generally using the word "accrue" in a transitive sense as being equivalent to the "setting up on the books" which, as I have pointed out, was, under the regulations of 1909, established as being for tax purposes equivalent to actual payment. Applying Euclidean methods, we may deduce that since setting up on the books is equivalent to actual payment or receipt and is also equivalent to accrual, and since things which are equal to the same thing are equal to one another, accrual is equivalent to actual payment or receipt and the cash basis and the accrual basis are identical. Such use of the word "accrual" could not have been justified from the dictionary nor from common accounting or business practice. Indeed, the latest citation in any standard dictionary of the use of the word "accrue" in any transitive sense whatever, that I have been able to discover, is from a work published in 1594.

The fact is, that the word "accrue" is a singularly unhappy choice for use in income tax practice. One of the great difficulties of income taxation is that income earning is a gradual process, and yet the necessities of taxation require that particular portions of income shall be attributed to particular moments in time. It is not feasible to tax income during the period of growth, but only when it becomes definite and measurable. Now in its basic meanings, the word "accrual" is ambiguous when applied to such a situation, because one of its meanings is to "grow up" and the other is to "spring up" or "fall in," so that it is equally capable of application either to the period of growth or to the moment of falling in of income when it takes a definite form. There is a similar ambiguity in the legal and commercial uses of the word. When the term "accrue" is used in regard to interest, the reference is usually intended to be to the gradual accumulation of interest between one maturity date and another. In regard to taxes, it has repeatedly been held to mean "become due." The use of the word in the recent acts has been sufficiently confusing in that the two deductions in respect of which it has been used in the acts are interest and taxes, two items in relation to which it has quite different meanings. When to such ambiguities is added the further confusion arising from the use of the word by the Bureau in the transitive sense as equivalent to "set up," its last shred of descriptive value disappears.

One may wonder why of all the terms used in the acts this term, which is the least illuminating, should have attained the widest use in the Bureau. Partly, no doubt, it is due to the fact that of the various terms used such as "paid," "received" and "incurred," "accrued" is the only one from which an adjective is easily formed that is applicable to both sides of the account. Its use therefore achieved brevity, though at a complete sacrifice of significance. However this may be, I venture to suggest that the misuse of the word "accrue" has contributed to the confusion of the income tax administration in the later stages as much as the artificial solution of the problem presented by the words "paid" and "received" in the Act of 1909 occasioned in the earlier stages.

Before leaving the subject, I would like to admit that the accountants are not wholly without responsibility for the confusion that has existed. Our own use of terminology is lamentably inconsistent and reflects too often the idiosyncrasies of the individual rather than the established practice of the profession. I recall a statement put forward over the signature of a well-known accounting firm which began with a figure described as "gross income" from which allowances and refunds were deducted to arrive at a figure described as "net gross income." Operating expenses were next deducted and the result described as "net operating income"; the addition to which of net income from other sources produced a so-called "gross net income" which it must be observed meant something quite different from "net gross income." Our treatment of cost of goods, cost of selling and cost of collecting in relation to gross income has too often been determined by habit rather than by logic. Many of us have acquiesced in or even adopted the Bureau's unwarranted usage of "the accrual basis." Burdened with so much responsibility, we must be restrained in our criticisms of the Bureau which, facing a heavier task and equipped with less experience, has fallen into errors similar to our own.

CONCLUSION

We may now, I hope, look forward to rates that will be lower and more stable than in recent years with a resulting reduction of the temptation to taxpayers to allow their accounting methods to be influenced by tax considerations. If so, there will be even more reason than in the past why the Bureau should carry out the obvious intent of the law and adopt a broad policy towards taxpayers' accounting methods, which will make the law less burdensome in procedure as well as in amount.

In order to accomplish this result some old misconceptions need to be removed and some old truths emphasized anew. It would greatly improve the administration of the income tax if the Bureau generally—not merely those who frame regulations but all charged with the administration of the law—would realize that "the accrual basis" is a meaningless phrase; that the choice today is not between a so-called "cash basis" and a so-called "accrual basis" but between the basis on which the taxpayers' books are kept and the basis prescribed by the Commissioner as clearly reflecting income; and that as stated in Regulations 45, Article 24, the law contemplates that "each taxpayer shall adopt such forms and systems of accounting as are in his judgment best suited to his purpose."

They should keep constantly in mind the fundamental difference between the considerations governing the determination of gross income and those governing the treatment of authorized deductions from such gross income. In this connection they should realize that the mention of any class of items among the authorized deductions from gross income does not stand in the way of the deduction of similar items from gross proceeds in the determination of gross income where they are a part of the cost of producing that income.

For instance, the provision that taxes may be deducted either when paid or when accrued does not stand in the way of customs duties accrued and paid last year entering into the determination of the income of this year if the goods imported are sold this year. Similarly, the provision that debts actually ascertained to be worthless may be claimed as deductions does not stand in the way of valuing sales accounts receivable at their fair market value at the time when they are created, in determining the gross income from such sales, but merely limits the deduction which may subsequently be claimed for bad debts if the account receivable proves uncollectible.

They should never forget that income is at best a matter of estimate and opinion, and that in its allocation in respect of time, business practice and the treatment adopted in good faith by the taxpayer are entitled to great weight; also that the injustice of taxation of income which has not been received may not be adequately remedied by allowing the amount as a so-called loss against the income from other transactions in a later year. Both the law and business practice warrant conservatism in determining when income is received and is taxable.

These are the practical conclusions which seem to me to emerge from consideration of our subject. I hope you will feel that they give some present value to this paper, which otherwise might seem to have at best only historical interest.

IV

ACCRUAL ACCOUNTING AND RESERVES IN TAX PRACTICE *

(1925)

MAY I ask the privilege of your columns to discuss briefly two points arising, one directly and the other indirectly, out of my paper † which was published in your October issue? Of these points the first relates to the origin of the expression "the accrual basis of accounting"; the other to the treatment of reserves in tax practice.

In my paper I implied that the expression "accrual" accounting" had little if any currency among accountants prior to the development of the expression in tax practice. It has, however, been suggested to me that the phrase had been used for many years by economists, and it is I think due to your readers that the fact should be brought to their notice.

Professor H. C. Adams, in his *Public Finance,* published in 1898, uses the phrase and discusses the relative advantages of cash and accrual accounting for governmental purposes. Professor Adams does not seem to me to deal altogether satisfactorily with the question when items accrue, and the difficulty suggested in my paper as arising from the fact that to accrue may mean either "to grow up" or "to fall in," is indicated but not solved in his book. Thus, he regards taxes as accruing as assets to a government when they are assessed; interest he regards as accruing from day to day. Supposing then that a special annual tax be levied to meet interest on government debt, the income to the government (taxes) would be deemed to accrue on the day or days of assessment, but the expense to accrue from day to day. For the purposes of annual budgets the inconsistency would be of no

* A letter to *The Journal of Accountancy*, Vol. XL (December, 1925).
† *Taxable Income and Accounting Bases for Determining It.* (See above.)

great importance, but as soon as accounts are made up for a shorter period, or a balance sheet is prepared, the inconsistent uses of the term "accrued" give rise to serious difficulties.

That the phrase "accrual accounting," even though used by economists in regard to government accounting, was not generally employed by accountants even in that limited sense is indicated by the proceedings at the first congress of accountants held in St. Louis in 1904. A series of papers on municipal accounting formed an important part of the program at that congress, and the need for something more than "cash accounting" was one of the main points stressed in these papers; yet the alternative was nowhere, I think, described as a system of "accrual accounting." In the first paper Harvey S. Chase said:

The fundamental basis of correct municipal accounting is now being thoroughly discussed from a true accounting standpoint as witnessed in the other papers presented at this meeting. This true accounting standpoint is of course revenue and expense in contradistinction to cash receipts and disbursements.

Indeed, the title of one of the papers, which was presented by Professor F. A. Cleveland, was "Revenues and Expenses as Distinguished from Receipts and Disbursements in Municipal Accounting."

It is interesting to note that speaking of commercial accounting Professor Adams said, "Should we turn our attention from public [i.e., governmental] accounting to the best corporation accounting one will discover that 'earnings and expenses' have almost universally supplanted the older bookkeeping phrases of 'receipts and expenditures.' " Further evidence on this point is afforded by the correspondence between a number of accounting firms and the Attorney-General immediately prior to the enactment of the corporation excise-tax law of 1909. As opposed to the cash basis they advocated the basis of earnings and expenses, and throughout the correspondence used the word "accrue" only in regard to interest. They spoke of income *earned,* expenses *incurred* and losses *sustained, and written off* and when they came to taxes they used no qualifying adjective at all, from which it might, perhaps, be inferred that they were not prepared to suggest any alternative to taxes paid.

A discussion of English authorities would, I am sure, lead to precisely the same result, and the economists must therefore be left to share with the Bureau of Internal Revenue the credit or responsibility for giving currency to the phrase "accrual accounting." Incidentally, it is consoling to accountants, who are frequently criticized for adopting terminology for their own purposes without regard to practice in other fields of activity involving the same subject matter, to find that the economists apparently coined the phrase "accrual accounting" to meet a need without regard to the fact that accountants commonly used another term which if not quite so brief was at least clearer and more accurate.

It would, I believe, be an advantage if we should revert to the practice indicated by the correspondence with the Attorney-General, and restrict the use of the word "accrue" to interest and similar items which grow with the mere lapse of time, in which relation its sense is universally understood and agreed. In recent years its use has been extending in the same sense to items to which it is not properly applicable, and in other and ill-defined senses to still other items. This is particularly true, as pointed out in my paper, of tax practice, and even the tax law has for many years provided for the deduction of taxes *accrued* as well as interest *accrued.*

Now, undoubtedly the legal and accounting usages of the phrase "taxes accrued" differ, even if lawyers do not differ as to its legal, and accountants as to its accounting, meaning. Much controversy has arisen on the question whether the term is used in the tax laws in its general legal sense or in an accounting sense. It would be a distinct gain if accountants would cease to use the term "taxes accrued" in a sense altogether different from its legal meaning.

Consideration of possible alternatives brings me immediately to the second point on which I would like to comment in this letter. Probably the first alternative which would occur to most accountants would be "reserve for taxes," but the use of the word "reserve" in accounting practice must be admitted to be even more vague and inconsistent than any use of the word "accrue" to which I have referred. A reserve may be anything from segregated surplus to a mere accounting device for adjusting to a proper net value, assets which it is convenient to carry on the books at more than their actual value.

Accountants have recognized this unsatisfactory situation for many·years, but it must be conceded that they have done little or nothing to correct it. A perusal of the decisions of the Board of Tax Appeals, however, suggests that the Board does not sufficiently appreciate that the proper treatment of reserves cannot be determined without enquiry into their nature and their effect on the accounts.

The point may be illustrated by a decision in the case of M. I. Stewart & Co., Docket 473, decided September 30, 1925, on the question of reserves for discount. The Board disposes of the question in effect by saying, "Reserves are not allowable deductions from gross income unless specifically provided for by statute." True, but irrelevant. A reserve for discount is a step in the computation of gross income, not a deduction therefrom. If a trader sells on December 31, 1924, goods which cost $80 for a nominal price of $100 less 2% ten days, his gross income in that year from the transaction is but $18. The impossibility of maintaining any other view becomes apparent if we assume the debt to be paid on January 1, 1925. How can it be argued in such a case that the trader made a profit of $20 in 1924 and a loss of $2 in 1925 (as the Board's treatment implies) when he received exactly what he had a right to receive.

Correct accounting calls for determining income in such cases on the basis of taking accounts receivable at the sum, which if paid on December 31 would completely discharge the indebtedness. If through failure to pay promptly the debtors become obligated to pay more in the subsequent year, the forfeited discounts are income of that year. Whether such correct accounting is secured by taking the accounts receivable at their present value when created and taking up the discount as an asset, as, when and if, forfeited, or by setting up the accounts receivable immediately at their nominal sum on the one side and carrying a reserve on the other is immaterial. The so-called reserve is not a reserve but a mere accounting device the convenience of which is obvious. The Board in such decisions as above quoted is misled by terminology into taxing as gross income something which has not and may never become income.

The first essential to a correct disposition of so-called reserves in computing taxable income is to determine into which of various categories the reserves in question fall. If they are reservations made out of profits, the dictum of the Board above quoted from the Stewart case applies to them. If, however, they are merely a part of the accounting mechanism for determining either the gross income earned or the expenses incurred, then the sole question is whether the method of accounting is such as correctly reflects income.

V

OBSOLESCENCE OF GOODWILL

Haberle Crystal Springs Brewing Co. v. Clarke *

(1930)

IT is to be hoped that we shall not be suspected of introducing a highly controversial question of national importance into the columns of a technical journal if we discuss a recent decision of the Supreme Court of the United States in the case of the Haberle Crystal Springs Brewing Company; †️ nor, we trust, shall we be charged with a refusal to accept the decisions of the Court or with a lack of respect for its members if, in the course of discussion, we question the validity of the arguments by which the decision is supported in the opinion handed down. The case is interesting to accountants in more ways than one. The point at issue— whether under the tax law an allowance should be made for obsolescence of goodwill—is itself an interesting technical question. The decisions in the courts below turned largely on the legislative history of tax provisions, which accountants played an important part in formulating, and the whole history of the case indicates the strange turns of fortune to which taxpayers may be subject. We propose, therefore, to consider it in some detail.

Let us deal first with the proceedings in the Supreme Court. As has been said, the question at issue was whether or not under the Revenue Act of 1918 an allowance could be made for the obsolescence of goodwill. No question of fact was in dispute. In the language of the opinion, "The goodwill was that of a brewery and is found to have been destroyed by prohibition legislation. The deduction claimed

* An editorial contributed to *The Journal of Accountancy,* Vol. XLIX (March, 1930).
† 280 U. S., 384.

is for the fiscal year ending May 31, 1919, it having been apparent early in 1918 that prohibition was imminent, and the officers having taken steps to prepare for the total or partial liquidation of the company. The amount of the deduction to be made is agreed upon if any deduction is to be allowed." The sole contention of the Government, which brought the appeal, was that in the provisions of the Revenue Act of 1918 relating to exhaustion, wear and tear and obsolescence, "the statute only intended to embrace property of such a nature that it was decreased, consumed or disposed of by use in the trade or business, and goodwill is not such property."

As between the parties, nothing turned on the nature of the event which destroyed the goodwill. The Government's position would have been precisely the same had the case been one of a business brought to an end by an unexpected exhaustion of the world's supply of its raw material. The Court, however, decided against the taxpayer, on the ground that neither of the words "exhaustion" and "obsolescence" was apt to describe termination by law as an evil of a business otherwise flourishing; and that to make such an allowance would be to grant part compensation to the taxpayer for the extinguishment of his business by law, in the form of "an abatement of taxes otherwise due," and that it was incredible that Congress should have intended such a result. But it is difficult to perceive how any question arises of abatement of taxes otherwise due. The profits for the last years of the Company's operation had to be determined and taxed. The fact, conceded on the record, that the useful life of the capital assets of the business was to be cut short, was claimed to be under general provisions a factor which would reduce the taxable income and the tax. The Revenue Act did not exclude breweries from the benefit of these provisions. The taxpayer had been guilty of nothing illegal. Upon what theory, then, can the taxpayer be denied the benefit of the provisions and its tax increased by such denial? If the general provisions would not give the relief sought, if the premature termination of the useful life of an asset employed in a business which is brought to an unexpected end is not covered by the terms used in the act, the taxpayer has no right to succeed. But if they would afford that relief, there is nothing in the Revenue Act, nor surely in considerations of public policy, to deprive the taxpayer of the benefit on account of the nature of the event which brought the business to a premature end. Congress, acting within its powers, saw fit to enact prohibition without compensation; but there is nothing to suggest that it intended to impose an added burden on the industries affected by requiring that their taxable income, during the short period of legal operation left them, should, by an exception to a general rule, be determined as if that period had been unlimited. The opinion, we think, does an injustice to Congress when it imputes to Congress such an intention.

Mr. Justice McReynolds and Mr. Justice Stone concurred in the result, but wrote no opinion. Their decision probably turned on the question of the applicability of the clause relied upon to goodwill in general, rather than on the interpretation of the attitude of Congress toward a business which had become noxious to the constitution, which led to the rather summary dismissal of the taxpayers' contentions by Mr. Justice Holmes. The only words in his opinion which seem to bear directly on this question are contained in the sentence: "Neither word is apt to describe termination by law as an evil of a business otherwise flourishing, and neither becomes more applicable because the death is lingering rather than instantaneous." It may be that if the effect of the decision as an authority comes to be considered in a future case, the declaration that neither word (exhaustion or obsolescence) is apt to describe the termination of a business otherwise flourishing will be held to have been the basis of the decision, and the references to the prohibition law to have been merely *obiter dicta*. Accurately speaking, the question is perhaps whether either "exhaustion" or "obsolescence" is or is not an apt term to describe the effect on capital assets of an event which is about to bring a prosperous business in which they are employed to an unexpected end, rather than whether the words are apt to describe the event itself or not. In considering such a question, an examination of the history of the legislation and of the practice of the Treasury would seem, under the decisions of the Court, to be pertinent if not essential.

In the Bureau of Internal Revenue and in the court below, the question had turned on the interpretation of the provision of Section 234 (a) of the Revenue Act of 1918, allowing as a deduction from gross income, *inter alia*, "a reasonable allowance for the exhaustion, wear and tear of property used in the trade or business, including a reasonable allowance for obsolescence." Acting under this authority, the Treasury in 1919 issued a regulation providing for an allowance for obsolescence of goodwill of breweries as a result of prohibition. This ruling remained in effect from 1919 until 1927. In 1927, a case having come into the courts on the question whether or not the goodwill had, in fact, been destroyed in that case, a district court held that the provision relied on did not authorize a deduction in any case for obsolescence of goodwill. This decision being affirmed by the Circuit Court of Appeals, the Commissioner amended the regulations so as to deny the deduction. It is to be presumed that the great majority of the cases had been decided under the regulations in force from 1919 to 1927, so that only a small residue of taxpayers was affected by the change of position. The Circuit Court of Appeals, in deciding the case referred to (the Red Wing Malting Company case), held that the language, "including a reasonable allowance for obsolescence," did not add a new kind of deduction, and that the allowance for "exhaustion, wear and tear of property *used* in the trade or business" covered no more than the provision of the Act of 1916, which allowed a deduction for the "exhaustion, wear and tear of property *arising out of its use* or employment in the business or trade," and that therefore exhaustion was not allowable unless caused by use. This conclusion was based largely on the Court's reading of the legislative history of the provision, a history which is of particular interest to accountants.

The corporation excise-tax law of 1909 allowed the deduction of "a reasonable allowance for depreciation of property, if any." This act is memorable because it led to the first occasion on which the accountants of the country as a body presented the views of the profession on what they conceived to be unsound legislation, and also the first occasion on which members of the profession were called in to assist in framing regulations to give effect to an apparently unworkable act. Since the tax was in terms based on receipts and payments, any allowance for depreciation might seem incongruous if it were not well understood that the law was conceived and was to be administered as an income or profits tax, and that the words "received" and "paid" were used as what has since come to be known as camouflage, which was expected to protect the law from attack on constitutional grounds. In the regulations, the term "depreciation" was interpreted in the accounting rather than the etymological sense, and it was provided that the deduction should be "the loss which arises from exhaustion, wear and tear or obsolescence out of the use to which the property is put." There was, however, a disposition in the Treasury to make the determination of the allowance at least in part a question of value rather than of exhaustion.

When the Revenue Act of 1913 was being prepared, a committee of the American Association of Public Accountants, predecessor of the American Institute of Accountants, conferred with those who were drafting the bill and recommended, among other things, that the sense of the regulation under the Act of 1909 should be embodied in the text of the Act of 1913. That Act, when passed, provided for "a reasonable allowance for depreciation by use, wear and tear of property, if any." It was, however, apparent that depreciation of property used, which ought to be allowed, might arise while the property was in use, but not by or from use.

Such allowances were commonly made by the Treasury under the Act of 1913 and also under the Act of 1916. In 1918, income taxation had assumed a new importance, and, the 1917 law having proved almost unworkable, the Treasury, for the first time, was allowed to draft a law. The bill, as it passed the house, provided for "a reasonable allowance for exhaustion, wear and tear of property used in the trade or business." The Senate amended the provision to read, "a reasonable allowance for depreciation of property used in the trade or business." The conference committee changed the provision to read as it now stands, "a reasonable allowance for exhaustion, wear and tear of property used in the trade or business, including a reasonable allowance for obsolescence." The reasonable interpretation of the intent of Congress would seem to be that in 1918 it sanctioned the previous practice of allowing deductions for exhaustion of property used, even though that exhaustion resulted not from use but from other causes such as lapse of time, and that it specifically provided for consideration of the element of obsolescence in determining the allowance. It was upon this construction that the Treasury regulation, above referred to, specifically allowing obsolescence of goodwill in the case of breweries, was formulated. The Circuit Court of Appeals in the eighth circuit appears from the record to have based its decision adverse to this regulation in the Red Wing Malting Company case on a reading of this history which was not entirely accurate. The Circuit Court of the second circuit, in a careful opinion in the Haberle Crystal Springs Brewing Company case, sustained the regulation. It was on this narrow point of statutory construction that the latter case went to the Supreme Court, there to be decided, as we have said, on a point which apparently had not been considered by anyone in the ten years' history of the question.

This history strikingly illustrates the hazards involved in taking a tax case to court. The Red Wing Malting Company, presumably convinced of the soundness of its position on the question of fact which was at issue in the Treasury (*i.e.,* whether its goodwill had been destroyed or not), went to the courts only to have its contention on the question of fact sustained but the allowance denied as a matter of law on the basis of a new meaning read into the statute in the light of the previous legislative history of the question. The Haberle Crystal Springs Brewing Company, having succeeded in convincing one circuit court of appeals that the other circuit court had erred in its reading of legislative history and its legislative construction, was taken to the Supreme Court on this narrow question, only to have its case decided on a point which had never been urged or argued.

PART VI

THE INFLUENCE OF ACCOUNTING ON THE
DEVELOPMENT OF AN ECONOMY

THE INFLUENCE OF ACCOUNTING ON THE DEVELOPMENT OF AN ECONOMY

THE following three chapters constitute an expansion of a paper under the above title read before the annual meeting of the American Institute of Accountants in October, 1935. The first deals with the question of how accounting can influence the development of an economy, which involves some consideration of the nature and purposes of accounting. The second discusses accounting practice in the treatment of gain or loss on the sale of capital assets, and some of the economic effects of such accounting and of the habit of thought which it reflects. The third is devoted to a historical consideration of the accounting treatment of the exhaustion of property in the course of operation, in the case of railroads, and a discussion of the effect of the accounting theories adopted upon the growth of the capital equipment of the United States.

I

THE NATURE OF ACCOUNTING *

GROWING recognition of the importance of accounting is bound to result in closer examination of the relation between accounting and economics, a subject that has not as yet received very extended consideration. Professor John B. Canning, in his *The Economics of Accountancy*,† suggests that the accountant's approach to problems is similar to that of the economist, but there is little to suggest that the course of accounting has been consciously influenced to any considerable extent by economic thought. The fact is, rather, I think, that accounting is a tool of business, and that the development of accounting, like the development of business law, has been determined by the practices of business men.‡ Where accounting and economic thought are found to run along parallel lines, it is probable that both will be found to be running parallel to good business practice. Where accounting treatment diverges from economic theory, a similar divergence is likely to be found between economic theory and business practice.

To many persons, even in the business and financial world, the first question which our title would suggest is: How can accounting have any effect upon the development of a national economy? "Is not accounting," they would ask, "the application to particular facts of certain definite rules which can produce only one result?" Such a misconception of the nature of accounting is, I believe, less general today than it was a few years ago. During the last five years much has been done to secure recognition of the fact that accounting

* *The Journal of Accountancy*, Vol. LXI (January, 1936).
† Cf. below, pp. 371-73.
‡ This being so, the subject of this paper is, I recognize, merely one phase of the broader question of the effect of business practice on economic development.

is not exact and rigid but is based very largely on convention and judgment. To the necessary work of education on this point the New York Stock Exchange and the Securities and Exchange Commission have made important contributions. The regulations of the Commission have followed the policy adopted by the Exchange in allowing registrants to follow their own methods of accounting, provided that those methods were not obviously unacceptable and were clearly disclosed. I have understood that objection was offered to this proposal on the ground of its novelty, and it was, therefore, with particular interest that I read an editorial brought to my notice, in which this principle was referred to many years ago almost as a truism. The editorial appeared in the *Morning Chronicle* of London in 1849, when the question of railway accounts was being widely agitated and was under consideration by a select committee of the House of Lords:

What are the precise criteria which distinguish revenue from construction charges it is no easy matter to determine. . . . At present there is great room for controversy, but this, at least, will be generally agreed to, that the principle adopted by any company in the distribution of its expenditure between the two accounts is of comparatively minor importance, provided that the system pursued be distinctly avowed and understood by the shareholders.

The English courts, in decisions under the income-tax law, have repeatedly taken the view that what is profit is to be determined by the practices of business men. Moreover, as I have pointed out on other occasions, our own tax law has since 1918 laid down the rule that taxable income is normally to be determined "in accordance with the method of accounting regularly employed by the taxpayer in keeping his accounts," and this language remains on the statute book, although it must be admitted that the Bureau of Internal Revenue has done its best to make it nugatory.

So today it is, I think, clear that upon both principle and authority, accounting must be regarded as a process involving the recognition of custom and convention and the use of judgment, rather than as the application of rigid and un-varying rules. It follows that rules may, and sometimes must be, changed as conditions change. This is of course true of law; and it may serve to emphasize the point in relation to accounting if I refer here to certain legal decisions on an accounting question with which I expect to deal in a later article.

In 1876 the Supreme Court said that the public "rarely ever took into account the depreciation of the buildings in which the business is carried on," and in 1878 it supported the government in its claim that a railroad company should not be allowed to include a depreciation charge in operating expenses, holding that "only such expenditures as are actually made can with any propriety be claimed as a deduction from earnings." In 1909, however, we find the Court saying: "Before coming to the question of profit at all, the company is entitled to earn a sufficient sum annually to provide not only for current repairs but for making good the depreciation and replacing the parts of the property when they come to the end of their life." *

Now, once it is recognized that accounting is largely a matter of convention, it is easy to perceive that the nature of the conventions adopted may greatly influence the development of an economy. This is particularly apparent under a system of free enterprise, under which the hope of profit is the main reliance for the upbuilding of the industry of the community; for what is profit in the commercial sense here involved is not only an accounting question but is, indeed, the central question of modern accounting.

In the simplest forms of organized life, accounting problems arise, and the way in which they are decided influences action. The administrators of even a non-profit institution —a club, for instance—are called upon to account to its members. Shall they limit the accounts to actual receipts and disbursements? Must they not at least exclude or deal sepa-

* *Eyster* v. *Centennial Board of Finance,* 94 U. S. (1876); *U. S.* v. *Kansas Pacific Ry. Co.,* 99 U. S., 459 (1878); *City of Knoxville* v. *Knoxville Water Company,* 212 U. S., 13 (1909).

rately with borrowings and repayments; and if they ignore unpaid bills, may there not be a temptation to delay payments that ought to be made in order to present a more favorable showing? If bills owing by the club but unpaid are to be brought into account, should amounts owing to the club also be taken into consideration? In technical language, should not the account be one of income and expenditure rather than one of receipts and disbursements? Taking a further step—in order to reduce the cost thereof, insurance has been written for three years; should the whole cost be charged against the one year and the next two years be relieved of any corresponding charge? Or, an automobile has been bought—should the cost be charged against the year or distributed over the probable useful life of the car? Speaking technically again, should not some accrual basis of accounting be employed?

From this example, it is easy to see how considerations of policy may influence accounting, or how the form of accounting may influence the course of events. One form of accounting may show a balance for the year in favor of the club, with the result that the dues may be left unchanged or even reduced; another might show a balance against the club and lead to an increase of dues. Reluctance to put an increase in force may lead the administrators to choose the method which gives the seemingly more favorable result. Indeed, to leave bills unpaid at the end of an administration, thus unfairly relieving the accounts of the outgoing and unfairly burdening those of the incoming administration, is a well-known device of dishonest politicians.

Apart from such crude devices as this, what would have been the effects if our municipalities had adopted the accounting practice of providing for future pensions in the years in which the service which gave rise to the right thereto was rendered? It is by no means abnormal that the actuarial value of the pension benefits attaching to municipal employment should be equal to twenty per cent of the nominal compensation of the employee. If, therefore, municipal budgets provided currently for the deferred compensation as well as for that immediately paid, and if the present value of the future liability were treated as a part of the indebtedness of the municipality, both the budgets and the borrowing capacity of the municipality might be very largely affected. In the City of New York, some of the funds are maintained on at least a quasi-actuarial basis, while in other cases no provision is made for future liabilities, the present value of which today runs into several hundred millions of dollars. As against the advantages of a more accurate disclosure of the costs of government and of the financial position of a municipality which would be derived from the inclusion of the provision for deferred pensions liabilities, there would no doubt have to be considered the possibilities of abuse that would be created if funds to meet such liabilities were currently set aside and entrusted to city officials for investment in order to provide for the obligations as they become due.

The most important group of problems which the accountant has to consider relates to the distinction between capital and income. In some cases, the question is whether amounts receivable or payable shall be carried once and for all to the income account or to the capital account. In other cases, the issue is how and when amounts which have been carried in the first instance to the capital account shall be transferred to the income account.

At this point it seems desirable to emphasize the fact that accounting is not essentially a process of valuation, as some writers on accounting and some economists conceive it to be. Professor C. R. Rorem's *Accounting Method* * seems to me to suffer from this misconception, and it is hardly too much to say that Professor Canning's book (to which I have already referred) is built up on it. Primarily, accounting is historical in its approach, with valuation entering into it at times as a safeguard. The emphasis is on cost, though where an asset is intended for sale and its selling value is known to be less than cost, the lower figure may be substituted for cost. The

* Cf. below, pp. 365-70.

outstanding illustration of this practice is the almost universal custom of valuing goods on hand at cost or market, whichever is lower.*

Capital assets, in particular, have traditionally been recorded by the accountant at cost or at cost less deduction for depreciation. To the accountant it has seemed to be neither a practicable nor a useful undertaking to attempt to determine the value of assets not intended to be sold and for which there is no ready market, especially as the concepts of value differ (and it has been said that in one English act the word "value" is used in twenty-seven different senses †). If the accountant accepts the economic measure of value as being the discounted value of a prospective income stream, it seems to him futile to attempt to reflect fluctuations of the income prospects and the discount rate on the books of a corporation which has no thought of attempting to realize its capital or of doing anything except receive and deal with the income stream as it comes in. He would rather concentrate on the more useful task of measuring—with what accuracy is attainable—the income stream as it flows.

True, during the 1920's, accountants fell from grace and took to readjusting capital values on the books of companies to an extent never before attempted. In extenuation, they might plead that unsound laws, unpractical economics, and a widespread, if unfounded, belief in a new order of things combined to recommend such a course, but the wiser policy is to admit the error and to determine not to be misled into committing it again.

The accounting function in relation to capital assets is to measure and record not the fluctuations in their value but the extent to which their usefulness is being exhausted through age or use, and to make proper charges against income in respect of such exhaustion, based on the cost of the

---

* Incidentally, the growing emphasis on the income account as an index of earning capacity, and hence of capital value, may make desirable some modification of the treatment commonly adopted in this matter.

† See *Proceedings of the International Congress on Accounting*, London (1933), p. 135.

property exhausted, with the intent that the property shall stand on the books at its salvage value when the term of its usefulness is ended. Conversely, when money is borrowed to be repaid at a premium (as, for instance, when a bond is sold at a discount), the amount borrowed forms the basis of the accounting, with sums added thereto and charged to income periodically as the obligation is maturing, so that at maturity the full amount repayable will stand on the books as a liability.

In practice, two accounts are frequently used in dealing with either capital assets or capital liabilities. In the case of an asset, one will record the original cost and the other the accumulated provision for exhaustion. In the case of a liability, one will record the ultimate amount repayable and the other the proportion of the discount which is carried forward to be charged against the unexpired period of the loan; but this subdivision of the account into two parts is merely a technique employed for the sake of convenience.

The fact that cost rather than present value is thus commonly used in the accounting upon which published balance sheets are based is by no means universally recognized; and, when recognized, it is sometimes criticized on the ground that the main purpose of a balance sheet is to enlighten the investor, and that what the investor is interested in is the value of property, not its cost. The misunderstanding and the criticism are so common, and reflect so many disputable assumptions, that it seems desirable to discuss them briefly.

The misunderstanding appears to arise mainly from the looseness in the use of language which is responsible for so much of the existing confusion of thought in relation to accounts. I have already mentioned the fact that in a single act of the English parliament the word "value" is alleged to have been used in at least twenty-seven senses, and it would certainly not be difficult to match this record in our own experience.

Any thoughtful student of finance must have been struck by the fact that one constantly encounters the word "value" with a qualifying adjective attached to it which in every case limits and in some cases negatives the meaning of the noun. Thus we have the phrases—"book value," "cost value," "replacement value," "assessed value," "going concern value," "liquidation value," "market value," "intrinsic value," "fair value," "sound value," "discovery value" (perhaps the most fantastic of all), etc., etc. Almost any asset will be found to be stated in the balance sheet at one or other of these so-called values.

These expressions, no doubt, have a certain usefulness, though in some instances the concept they are used to describe is remote from the concept of value. The real trouble is, that since the word "value" forms a part of each phrase, and since all of them represent things that are expressed in money, essential dissimilarities in their significance are apt to be overlooked. Hence people who would not dream of adding together a cart-horse and a saw-horse and speaking of the result as two horses, have no compunction at all about adding together a book figure (or, as they call it, a book "value") and a market value, and speaking of the result as a "value," even in the case of a stock the selling price of which is a mere fraction of that "value." Oscar Wilde defined a cynic as a man who knew the price of everything and the value of nothing.* It would be well if some of those who talk glibly of value would develop enough cynicism to keep the test of salability (and earning capacity) more constantly in mind.

The fact is that the word "value" has come to be used to describe what is often really a mere figure—"book figure" would be more accurate than "book value," and the "figure" at which an asset is carried more accurate than the "value" at which an asset is carried. It must be admitted that ac-

* Cecil Graham: What is a cynic?
Lord Darlington: A man who knows the price of everything and the value of nothing.
Cecil Graham: And a sentimentalist, my dear Darlington, is a man who sees an absurd value in everything and doesn't know the market price of any single thing.
Lady Windermere's Fan, Act III.

countants have themselves some responsibility for the misunderstanding that exists, and academic writers, regulatory
bodies and appraisers have also largely contributed to it.
However, what has come to be called "wishful thinking" is
probably mainly responsible for it. The transition from the
thought that it would be convenient and helpful if balance
sheets did represent realizable values to the thought that
they do has been all too easy.

A similar misunderstanding is not altogether uncommon
in England, though there is little or no real justification for
it there. In the case of railroads and public utilities, to
which what is known as the "double account" system has applied (as prescribed, for instance, in the Regulation of Railways Act of 1868), capital assets have not appeared as such
in any balance sheet—instead, the expenditures thereon have
been recorded in a statement of receipts and expenditures on
account of capital, only the balance of which has entered
into the general balance sheet of the company. In the case
of companies incorporated under the general incorporation
law, the model balance sheet embodied in *Table A* of the Act
of 1862 contained an instruction in respect of not only capital assets but also stock in trade, reading as follows: "The
cost to be stated with deductions for deterioration in value
as charged to the reserve fund or profit-and-loss account." I
have even seen an opinion by eminent counsel, now on the
English bench, to the effect that it was no part of the purpose
of a balance sheet to reflect the values of assets, though directors might, in their discretion, see fit to embody in it information which would throw light on those values.

Turning now to the objection that if balance sheets do not
reflect values they ought to do so, because that is what the
investor is interested in—a number of minor exceptions to
the position thus asserted might be taken, but the answer to
the objection is that it is utterly impracticable to ascertain
the values of capital assets in the case of businesses of any
magnitude, and that the figures would be of no real interest
to the investor if they could be ascertained. What the in-

vestor is actually interested in is, obviously, the value of his investment; and the objection therefore presupposes that the value of an investment may be computed by adding up the values of the assets which represent that investment and deducting from the total any liabilities to which they are subject.

Now, only brief consideration is necessary to show that this assumption is valid in the case of a profitable business only upon the further assumption that the value of the assets essential to the business and not intended for sale is simply the difference between the value of the business as a whole and the realizable value of the assets which can be separately sold without sacrifice. By the hypothesis and in fact, what the investor or speculator is interested in is the value of the business as a whole, and that is dependent mainly on what it will produce in the future and is not determinable by any purely accounting process. Not only so, but if the accountant were to assume the task of valuing the business as a whole, he would have met the assumed need, and it would be entirely supererogatory for him to attempt to allocate that value as between the different assets of the business.

How great the difficulties presented by such an allocation would be may be indicated by stating generally the character of the problem presented, as follows: How shall we compute the value of a producing unit which has been in use for a term of years, assuming that another type of unit could be bought new today for substantially less than the cost of reproducing the existing unit and would effect an economy in operation; assuming, further, that there is a strong probability that still another type will be developed within a few years which will cost less and be more efficient than any now available, and making due allowance for the fact that the existing unit is in actual operation and that a period of time more or less considerable would be needed for the installation of a new unit?

There may be other elements in the problem to be considered, but certainly any so-called valuation which ignores those I have suggested cannot be claimed to represent the value of the asset. The easy solutions, termed "replacement values" or "sound values," beg the question. While it is impossible to say what percentage of the capital equipment of the country would be replaced even substantially where and as it is, it is quite certain that the percentage is small. It is well known, also, that correct timing of major replacements is one of the most important factors in determining whether a given industrial enterprise shall succeed or fail.

To carry consideration of the question one step further— inasmuch as the value of a successful business is dependent mainly on its earning capacity, it follows that to anyone interested in determining that value the greatest service which accounts can render is to throw light on earning capacity— not on the so-called values of assets which are not intended to be sold. And, so far as the records of the past can be an aid to the estimation of future earning capacity, an account which ignores fluctuations in the value of capital assets is likely to be far more useful than one that attempts to reflect them.

Accounts have other important uses, possibly not less important than that of throwing light on the value of the evidences of ownership in a business. The determination of realized profits, and of the income subject to taxation, and the presentation of fairly comparable statements of operating results for successive periods, would all be made more difficult and more complex if at the same time the accounts were being adjusted periodically so as to reflect the fluctuations in the value of the assets held for use and not for sale.

The canon of sound accounting, that fluctuations in the value of capital assets not only may but should be ignored, rests on surer ground and is more realistic than the contention that balance sheets should aim to reflect values. In this, as in so many other fields, error has resulted from attempts at oversimplification. What the equation: "Assets minus liabilities equals proprietorship" and the phrase "net worth" gain in simplicity, they sacrifice in significance. A balance sheet, in which one asset is stated at book value, another at replacement value, a third at liquidation value and a fourth at going-concern value, and the liabilities at their face value, does not yield a figure that can be described as net worth expressed in a single measure of value any more than a figure in which were mingled American and Chinese dollars and Mexican and Chilean pesos, all preceded by the same familiar dollar sign, could produce a net worth expressed in any one of those currencies.

Of those who decline to recognize the impossibility of determining capital value by the methods commonly proposed, few have suggested annual or anything more than periodical adjustment of the balances on property accounts to conform with so-called valuations. The Interstate Commerce Commission, while insisting on the need for valuation as a basis for a revision of the property accounts of the carriers, has indicated quite clearly that, once the revision had been effected, it contemplated cost as the basis for all subsequent accounting; and it has treated as axiomatic the proposition that charges against income for property exhaustion should be based on cost.

The question may no doubt fairly be raised whether, even if value is eliminated as a possible basis for arriving at the figures at which capital assets shall be carried (due allowance being made for exhaustion of useful life), there is any other basis which is preferable to cost. The alternative most favored is estimated cost of replacement; but while the usefulness of computations of cost of replacement for a wide variety of administrative purposes may be admitted, the regular use thereof as the basis for the restatement of the book figures is not, I think, one of them.

Any adequate discussion of this question would involve consideration of all the manifold purposes for which accounts are used and go far beyond the scope of such an article as this. In my judgment, however, it will as a rule be wiser to retain the virtues of continuity and reality in the book records which the cost basis affords and, in appropriate cases, to furnish to stockholders a supplementary statement based on replacement cost (which must in any event be hypothetical and ephemeral). Whatever course is followed, it is necessary to relinquish the hope that balance sheets can be made to reflect the value of capital assets, if that word is to be used without any qualifying phrase that destroys the substance and leaves only the shadow of its meaning.

Cases will arise—as, for instance, that presented by a devaluation such as occurred in Germany—in which cost figures lose their significance to such an extent as to make some different treatment necessary, but such cases are exceptional and their existence merely emphasizes the fundamental importance of honest and competent judgment in accounting.

This does not mean that the balance sheet is valueless, but only that it is a highly technical production the significance of which is severely limited and has in the past often been greatly over-rated. In origin the balance sheet is an account; in England it still commonly bears the headings "Dr" and "Cr" instead of the "assets" and "liabilities" to which we have become accustomed. These facts were recognized by the Committee on Coöperation with Stock Exchanges of the American Institute of Accountants in its report to the New York Exchange of September 28, 1932, in which it included as among the objects which the Exchange ought to pursue:

1. To bring about a better recognition by the investing public of the fact that the balance sheet of a large modern corporation does not and should not be expected to represent an attempt to show present values of the assets and liabilities of the corporation.

2. To emphasize the fact that balance sheets are necessarily to a large extent historical and conventional in character, and to encourage the adoption of revised forms of balance sheets which will disclose more clearly than at present on what basis assets of various kinds are stated.

3. To emphasize the cardinal importance of the income account, such importance being explained by the fact that the value of a business is dependent mainly on its earning capacity.

In recent years it has become increasingly apparent that for the large modern corporation, at least, the balance sheet is not in itself an adequate supplement to the income and surplus accounts, and it is not surprising that the regulations of the Securities and Exchange Commission have called for additional statements. The schedules filed under those regulations, and the explanations, often voluminous, which commonly accompany them, should do much to create a juster appreciation of both the significance and the limitations of a balance sheet. There will still be those who will clamor for an unattainable combination of completeness, precision and simplicity and for a uniformity which would be superficial and illusory. The demand for predigested preparations which will meet all needs, without any exercise of selective judgment or intelligence, is encountered in the fields of accounting and finance as elsewhere.

II

CAPITAL VALUE AND ANNUAL INCOME *

ONE of the most striking contrasts between American and English financial and accounting practice is to be found in the fact that here we regard gains or losses on the sale of capital assets as finding a place in the income account, while in England they are regarded as increasing or decreasing capital. In this article I propose to consider some of the economic policies which may be in part, at least, attributable to the habit of mind which our practice reflects.

Unquestionably, the difference in practice does reflect a difference in habit of mind. Anyone who has lived both here and in England will recognize the truth of the statement that here we think in terms of capital value and there they think in terms of annual income. Inquire whether a man is well-to-do here and you will be told he is probably worth so many dollars; ask a similar question in England and the answer (if you get one at all) will certainly be that he is probably worth so much a year. It is not difficult to understand why this should be so. In England, modern business developed in a community in which previously the predominant interest had been in land and which already thought in terms of annual produce. The opening sentence of Adam Smith's *The Wealth of Nations* (1776) reads:

The annual labor of every nation is the fund which originally supplies it with all the necessaries and conveniencies of life which it annually consumes, and which consist always either in the immediate produce of that labor, or in what is purchased with that produce from other nations.

Cannan, in his edition of the work, comments on this passage as follows:

* *The Journal of Accountancy* (February, 1936).

319

This word [*i.e.*, "annual"], with 'annually' just below, at once marks the transition from the old British economists' ordinary practice of regarding the wealth of a nation as an accumulated fund (Note 1, p. 1).

He says, further, that:

The conception of the wealth of nations as an annual produce, annually distributed, . . . has been of immense value (Introduction, p. xxxiii).

With us, business developed in a new country: the great opportunities for gain lay in sharing in the growth of the country rather than in securing a part of its current annual yield.

Three fields in which the effects of the difference in the point of view may be discovered at once suggest themselves —those of local taxation, rate regulation, and income taxation.

In colonial days, according to Seligman, there were many cases in which, while the tax was imposed on property, the assessment was made on the basis of annual value. This was true of Massachusetts, Rhode Island, New Hampshire, New York, Delaware and Virginia.* Bullock, in discussing the local general property tax, also mentions that Massachusetts as a province levied taxes on the basis of the annual value of property, but that the second tax law passed after the adoption of the Constitution of 1780 changed to the basis of capital value, which is today, in general, the basis of local taxation throughout the United States.† Whether the causes of the change were in any way related to those which produced the more momentous political developments of that time, I am not sufficiently versed in history to say.

When we turn to rate regulation, it is apparent that the principles we have adopted were based upon the Federal Constitution as interpreted by the Supreme Court in a series of cases of which the most important was perhaps *Smyth* v.

---

* *The Income Tax*, 2nd ed., p. 380.
† C. J. Bullock, *Selected Readings in Public Finance*, 3rd ed., p. 311.

Ames (1898). So, too, the enactment of what was really an income tax law in 1909, and of an avowed income tax law in 1913, brought definitions of income in conformity with the same habit of mind in the cases of *Stratton's Independence* v. *Howbert, Doyle* v. *Mitchell Bros. Co.*, and *Eisner* v. *Macomber*.

In *Smyth* v. *Ames* the Supreme Court decided for the first time that the basis for all calculations as to the reasonableness of rates must be the "fair value" of the property being used for the convenience of the public. Giving only the most general indication of how this value was to be determined by reciting some of the factors that must be considered, without any expression of opinion as to the weight to be assigned to each, and making the clear reservation that there might be still other factors to be considered, the Court started that pursuit of the will-o'-the-wisp of fair value which is still being carried on with no greater success than was to be anticipated. The charge made by Jevons against Ricardo, that he "shunted the car of economic science on to a wrong line," might perhaps with more justice be made against those who were responsible for bringing about the decision in *Smyth* v. *Ames*.

In *Doyle* v. *Mitchell* the Court held, first, that the value, at the date of the passage of the taxing act, of capital assets converted into manufactured articles and sold, must be deducted from the proceeds of sale before anything to be taxed as income could be arrived at; and, secondly, that the proceeds of sale or conversion in excess of that basic value were income.

On the first point, there is at least some appearance of inconsistency between this decision and that in *Stratton's Independence*, in which the Court held that the proceeds of mining could be taxed as income without any allowance for the exhaustion of the mine which was a necessary incident of the operation. However, no distinction between the two cases was made in the decision in *Eisner* v. *Macomber* which provided what has become the accepted legal definition of income in our Courts:

After examining dictionaries in common use (Bouvier's Law; Standard; Webster's International and the Century), we find little to add to the succinct definition adopted in two cases arising under the corporation tax act of 1909 (*Stratton's Independence* v. *Howbert*, 231 U. S., 399, 415; *Doyle* v. *Mitchell Bros. Co.*, 247 U. S., 179, 185): 'Income may be defined as the gain derived from capital, from labor, or from both combined,' provided it be understood to include profit gained through a sale or conversion of capital assets, to which it was applied in the Doyle case. (252 U. S., 207.)

It may be noted that in presenting the Income Tax Bill of 1913 Congressman (now Secretary) Hull expressed the view that an occasional purchase not for immediate resale, followed after a substantial interval by sale at a higher price, would not produce taxable income thereunder. It would have been well, perhaps, if his view had prevailed.

The decision in *Smyth* v. *Ames* forced the question of present value of capital assets upon the attention of all public utility companies. The income tax decisions made the value of capital assets at March 1, 1913, a question of cardinal importance for all corporations owning capital assets at that date. The attention thus focused on the subject of present fair value, and the marked change in price levels which took place during the war period, together constitute an adequate explanation of the extent to which the practice of readjusting book values of capital assets to so-called present values was carried in the 1920's, which was criticized in the previous article of this series.

That the principles and practices, established as I have outlined, have met with scant approval in economic circles is indicated by examination of the works of economists of high standing. Upon the question of local taxation, Bullock says:

> After forty years' discussion, the United States has the most crude, inequitable, and unsatisfactory system of local taxation—if, indeed, we can call 'system' that which more resembles chaos—that can be found in any important country in the civilized world.*

* Bullock, *op. cit.*, p. 289.

And T. S. Adams speaks of the system as "a hypocritical pretense, a source of wholesale lawbreaking and chronic inequality, a by-word for inefficiency and injustice." *

Undeterred by this experience, we enacted Federal capital stock tax laws which required taxpayers to report annually under oath the "fair value" of property for which no market existed or was desired, and any real valuation of which would have involved the difficulties and complexities mentioned in my previous article and would have been useless for any other purpose than compliance with the law. Needless to say, in practice no real attempt to fix fair value was made—instead, the tax being relatively small, the taxing authority was usually able to collect substantially more than was justly due because the additional tax was less than would have been the cost of demonstrating its injustice.

This tax was abolished in 1926, but in 1933 it was revived in the particularly obnoxious form of the linked capital tax and excess-profits tax—the corporate taxpayer was first permitted (and required) to fix the taxable fair value itself, with the knowledge that placing the taxable value low would increase its liability to excess-profits tax on its income. The two taxes were imposed at the bottom of a depression, when the market value of capital invested in industry was generally far below the amount actually invested—thus the taxpayer was faced with the choice of paying a capital stock tax on a value that did not exist, or an excess-profits tax on profits which were not excessive upon the test set forth in the law of what constituted an excess. It is hard to conceive of a tax device better calculated to bring the taxing system into disrepute.

In England, local taxation has for centuries been based on the annual value of property.† In national taxation the influence of the landowning classes was for a long time dominant, and prior to 1894 even death duties on land were levied only on the capitalized value of an annuity equal to the net

* Bullock, *op. cit.*, p. 982.
† Cf. Cannan, *History of Local Rates in England, passim.*

rental value of the land for the life of the heir. In that year, however, land was subjected to death duties (estate duty) on the basis of its full capital value, at progressive rates which have since been greatly increased.* In 1909, a further step was taken. A system of taxation on the increment in land value was initiated, but the administrative difficulties proved so great that this experiment was abandoned. Thus, apart from transaction taxes, such as stamp duties on the transfer of property, death duties remain as the one case (of course, an important case) in which English taxes are levied on the basis of capital values.

The estimation of the capital value of land from the annual value, which is fostered by the English practice, serves a useful purpose in checking too optimistic valuation. Had this method of approach been general here, the disastrous Florida land boom could hardly have occurred, and fewer of our farmers would have found themselves ruined through acquiring by the use of borrowed money additional lands at prices out of proportion to the annual yield obtainable therefrom. A writer in the *University of Pennsylvania Law Review* for December, 1935, has suggested that there is a tendency today to give more weight to current annual value in establishing valuations of real property for purposes of local taxation.†

Economic opinion on the theory of value in relation to rate regulation scarcely calls for comment, if that opinion is, as I believe it to be, accurately summed up in the following quotation from J. C. Bonbright:

* These provisions were the subject of a sharp difference of opinion between the Prime Minister (Lord Rosebery) and the Chancellor of the Exchequer (Sir William Harcourt) who had been the rival candidates for the succession to Mr. Gladstone. It is interesting to find in the Chancellor's reply to the Prime Minister's criticism this comment:

"Your observations upon the American attempt at a *property tax* are well founded, but everybody admits the objections to a *property tax*, which is levied annually on the possessors do not apply to a *death duty* which occurs only once in a generation on the transmission of estates into other hands."

Cf. A. G. Gardiner, *Life of Sir William Harcourt*, Vol. II, p. 285.

† A bill to amend the tax law, in relation to the assessment of real property, has recently been introduced in the New York State Senate. It would require that all real property: "Shall be assessed at the full *annual income* value thereof."

I think I am speaking the truth when I say that every economist without a single exception agrees that whatever is the proper basis of rate control . . . that basis cannot logically be the value of the property . . . this country alone of all the countries in the world attempts to use valuation as a basis of rate control.*

I shall, however, discuss some special phases of the problem of regulation in my final article.

In the third field already mentioned, that of income taxation, economic opinion has not, I think, generally approved the taxation of capital gains as income, even though the practice has escaped the wholesale condemnation which has been visited on our systems of local taxation and rate regulation. For myself, I have long felt that though it may seem unfair that unearned increment should escape taxation while earned income is heavily taxed, the weight of the argument is against the taxation of capital gains. And I am still more opposed to the treatment of capital gains as income for purposes other than those of taxation—indeed, one of the minor objections to the taxation of such gains as income is that it encourages the taxpayer to treat them as income in ordering his own affairs, instead of adding them to his capital or holding them in reserve against the all too probable future capital loss.

In an article written in 1922,† I recited some of the reasons that led me to the conclusions which I still hold, and I shall now do no more than consider what further light on the question the events of the intervening years have afforded. They have shown that the tax operates to produce artificial markets for securities, by preventing sales which, but for the tax, would be made, and thus has tended to make the fall more violent when it comes. They have also demonstrated with disconcerting completeness the validity of the argument that an equitable tax, designed to give relief in respect of losses commensurate with the tax on gains will, on balance, adversely affect the revenue, and that the adverse effect will be

* J. C. Bonbright, *Accounting Review*, Vol. V (1930), pp. 111, 122.
† See above, Part V, Chap. II.

felt when the revenue is least able to bear it. As a result, changes have been made in the law which implicitly admit that capital gains are not income but leave them subject to tax as if they were, changes which sacrifice justice to immediate revenue, through the continuation of the tax on net gains and the practical denial of relief in respect of net losses.

The new provisions, by which a portion of the gain on sale of assets held for a period of years is taxed as income at rates which are reached by adding that portion of the gain to what happens to be the income of the year in which the gain is realized, are difficult to justify upon any theory of ability to pay or equality of sacrifice, or upon any of the canons of sound taxation. The denial of allowances for losses on property sold is manifestly unjust and results in such absurdities as taxpayers being led to sacrifice substantial salvage values in order to preserve the right to take deductions for losses which are allowable if property is abandoned but not if it is sold. There is, moreover, something repugnant to one's sense of justice in the sight of a Government deliberately devaluing the currency and taxing as a gain the difference between the price received in depreciated currency and the price paid prior to devaluation in the undepreciated currency, and at the same time denying to taxpayers relief in respect of losses occasioned by the fall in prices which is pleaded in justification of the devaluation.

The provisions of the law relating to non-taxable reorganizations and exchanges, and other provisions necessitated by the taxation of capital gains, are constantly adding to the complexities and uncertainties of taxation. Meanwhile, the great argument for the taxation of capital gains—that without it unearned increment would go untaxed—has been greatly weakened by the enactment of high gift and estate taxes.

The amount of capital gains spent as income, though large in itself, is small in comparison with the aggregate of such gains. If gains are offset by later losses, it is grossly unjust that heavy taxes should be levied on the gains with no compensating relief in respect of the losses; if they are added to capital, that capital is heavily taxed whenever it is transferred by gift or bequest.

Students of taxation have agreed that an income tax at high rates cannot long continue to be successfully levied unless the law is generally regarded as broadly just in its form and administration. It cannot, I think, be maintained that this is true of our existing income tax system, and those who deny its justice can point to the provisions respecting capital gains and losses as striking evidence in support of their position. It is inevitable that provisions which the taxpayer regards as deliberately unfair shall encourage deliberate evasion; and, even if it is true that evasion existed prior to the enactment of these unjust provisions, this hardly seems sufficient ground for a policy of deliberate injustice on the part of the Legislature. Congress would be well advised to abandon the policy of taxing capital gains—or, if that is deemed to be politically impossible, to tax them as something other than income at a flat rate not high enough to act as a deterrent to the taking of profits. This could be done without awaiting the general revision of our Federal tax system, which it so urgently needed.

Sooner or later, however, we must broaden the scheme of Federal taxation, and particularly the basis of the income tax. Not until this has been done can we hope to enjoy the relative stability of revenue which England has experienced in spite of the depression and of the magnitude of its tax burden.

Turning from the tax aspect of the question of capital gain, I would draw attention to a danger against which some safeguards are, I think, urgently required. This danger arises from the alarming habit which seems to be developing of regarding every annual report as a new edition of a prospectus. Even those who contend that realized capital gains are a form of income must concede that such gains and recurrent income have no common relationship to earning capacity, except to the small extent that capital gains may represent recurring income that has not been distributed. Apart from this item, which for practical purposes may be disregarded, the gain normally represents either (a) the capitalized value of a change in capacity to earn recurring income (demonstrated or assumed); or (b) a change in the rate of capitalization applied to an unchanged earning capacity; or (c) a combination of the two. This being so, such a capital gain cannot properly be added to a recurring earning capacity (which has not already been capitalized) to form the basis from which, by multiplication, a capital value may be determined. To my mind, few points are of more importance in connection with the problem of presenting illuminating reports to investors than that of taking some steps which will tend to prevent investors from including capital gains with current income in one sum, from which they will compute capital value by a single multiplication.

The treatment of capital gains as income reached its most pernicious development during the boom period in the practice of regarding stock dividends as income in an amount equal to the market value of the stock, the evil being especially marked in the case of pyramided holding companies. To the extent that the amount included in income exceeded the amount of earnings which formed the basis of the distribution by the company declaring the dividend, the credit to income by the receiving company represented nothing except an unrealized capital appreciation. Another unsound practice is that of requiring investments of insurance companies to be carried in their reports at "market value" even if above cost.* When market prices rise to dizzy heights, as in 1928-29, the assets of such companies as reported under the regulations rise with them. When prices fall too precipitately, however, the evidence of the market is rejected and artificial market prices are constructed by the Commissioners. The result in practice is, therefore, that the portfolios of what should be our safest and soundest institutions are carried at quoted market prices if those are very high but above

---

* It should be noted, however, that in the case of bonds "amortized value" is permitted and freely used as an alternative.

market prices if those are very low. The fact that resort to artificial prices was deemed necessary three times within a quarter of a century suggests that the Commissioners should at least recognize the limited significance of market quotations when they are high as well as when they are low.

From the point of view of the technical accountant, it is a curious contradiction that we, who have gone further than any other country in refining double-entry bookkeeping and distributing charges over successive periods by elaborate systems of accrual, should in our thinking have, in effect, adhered to the old single-entry method of determining gain or income by deducting worth at the end of the period from worth at the beginning thereof.

Some of our economists and statisticians have even undertaken to include fluctuations in the value of the "national" capital in computations of the "national" income. In doing so, they have exaggerated the growth of wealth in boom periods and its decline in periods of depression with, as I think, unfortunate results. In a recent article, Sir Josiah Stamp commented on this procedure as follows:

American writers have included the rise in the market value of capital assets under income (or the fall as a deduction), but the practice is not generally accepted in other countries.*

He went on to express the opinion that this was "all of a piece with the strange compound of capital charges and income in the American system of taxation." In fairness to American economists, however, it may be questioned whether the views which he criticized are shared by more than a small minority of them. In publishing his paper, he printed the following interesting footnote:

On the day of reading, the latest official publication was received from Washington.† In this, the whole method has been abandoned: 'the inclusion of gains and losses yielded

* "Methods Used in Different Countries for Estimating National Income," *Journal of the Royal Statistical Society* (1934), pp. 449-50.
† *National Income, 1929-1932*, Department of Commerce in coöperation with the National Bureau of Economic Research, Inc.

by such changes in asset values would be either a duplication, since it would amount to counting both a change in net income, and the change in capitalization of that income, or a distortion of the national income estimate as a measure of the economic system's end product.' It seems clear that the publication to the nation of figures of national income already heavily diminished, but reduced to a minus quantity by the special deduction of the huge shrinkage in capital values for 1932-3, was too much for any realistic official statisticians to face.

The preoccupation with capital and capital gains is also to be found in the securities legislation passed under the present administration, which is obviously, if unconsciously, framed in the interest of the short-time speculator for the rise rather than of the long-time investor for the yield. Even the members of the Securities Commission seem to have developed doubts on the question whether the Acts were really necessary or will prove beneficial in relation to issues of securities by seasoned corporations. Further, some of the information which is required by the Commission in registration statements and annual reports would seem possibly to be helpful to speculators (though more clearly to competitors), but more likely to injure than to benefit the long-time investors, whose interests surely deserve special consideration.

It has seemed to me particularly unfortunate that at a time when devaluation, inflation, and apprehension of further experimentation with our fiscal system were impairing confidence in what had been regarded as high-grade securities and tempting small savers to gamble in equities, the whole emphasis of the Administration and of Congress should be upon efforts to diminish slightly the hazards of stock gambling, and none upon the magnitude of the hazards that were bound to remain.

Granting the desirability of telling the public that great losses had been caused by the misdeeds of issuers and vendors of securities, it was at least equally desirable to tell the public that these losses were but a small fraction of those resulting from the financial, industrial and political hazards to which all business is subject, and that enormous losses on investment in enterprise and invention are a part of the price we must pay for progress.* The two Securities Acts are calculated to create expectations which they cannot satisfy; and although they may perhaps be made to serve a useful purpose, the hope would be stronger if the Acts had been less theoretical and punitive in conception, and had had more regard to what is remedial and practical. It lies in continued wise administration and judicious amendment rather than in the Acts themselves. Indeed, one of the dangers of the admitted excellence of administration by the Securities Commission up to the present time is that it may tend to blind us to the inherent defects of the law.

The same emphasis on capital value is, I think, also in large measure responsible for the laws passed in recent years making the propriety of dividends dependent on there being an excess of assets over liabilities and capital, thus displacing the old rule under which the source of income to a stockholder was the earning of a profit by the corporation in which he held stock, and the declaration of a dividend merely fixed the time when it became income to him. This change, whether desirable or undesirable, may obviously have very important economic consequences, particularly in conjunction with the no par value stock laws. If generally adopted, it would rob the word "dividend" of its old significance, since under it the payment of a dividend does not imply the previous earning of a profit and a dividend may be, in every real sense, a distribution of capital. Though perhaps the new law represents only an attempt to escape from the difficulties

---

* I expressed substantially these views when securities legislation was pending, both in 1933 and 1934. In my testimony before the Senate Committee on Banking and Currency in 1934, I said:

"My feeling on this subject, I think, must be very much that which the committee feels in regard to the larger subject. You want to do everything that you can to make buying and selling securities, particularly by the small man, safer and surrounded with more information. But you must realize that all you can do will not reduce the risks that he is bound to run very greatly, and there is always the danger that by legislating you create a feeling of confidence in the securities that are offered which legislation cannot possibly impart to them" (*Hearings*, p. 7176).

with which we are familiar without adequate thought of the new difficulties which may be encountered, to me it seems to be fraught with great possibilities of evil.

There was doubtless a time when the assets test was regarded as protecting the interests of creditors and necessary for that purpose; but with the law and common practice permitting legal capital to be fixed at nominal figures, such a rule adds little or nothing to the common proviso that no dividends shall be paid when a corporation is insolvent or when payment of the dividend would make it so. It is noteworthy that even this last provision is deemed unnecessary in England; it was in the English law of 1855, but was eliminated in 1862. Since then, apart from the general Statute of Frauds, the sole reliance in England for protection against improper dividends (and also against the acquisition by a corporation of its own capital stock) has been the section which sets forth the way, and the only way, in which the share capital may be reduced. This protection seems to have been adequate; no doubt its effectiveness has been increased by vigorous declarations such as that of Lord Campbell in *Burnes* v. *Pennell* (1849): "Dividends are supposed to be paid out of profits only, and when directors order a dividend, to any given amount, without expressly saying so, they impliedly declare to the world that the company has made profits which justify such a dividend." This dictum is commonly reflected in articles of association in the form of a terse declaration that: "No dividend shall be paid otherwise than out of profits."

In its new form (*e.g.,* in Delaware), the assets test is, of course, nothing more than a device to permit directors to declare dividends when there are no profits. The power conferred by that law to make the legal capital of a corporation only a fraction of its economic capital makes such dividend declaration possible without insuring any substantial margin of protection to creditors.

An anomalous situation is presented by the New York law as at present construed by the courts of that state (the construction and the constitutionality of the provision, however, are at present involved in cases pending in the Court of Appeals of the State). It makes directors of a business corporation liable if they declare a dividend unless, after the declaration of the dividend, the value of the remaining assets is at least equal to the liabilities and the legal capital of the corporation. The elusive term "value" is not further defined, and as the law is at present construed, no defense of good faith or reasonable care will protect the director if it is subsequently found by a court of competent jurisdiction that upon some theory of value accepted by it the value of the assets fell short of the required standard.

Now, in any such legislation, the relationship between the theories governing the definition of capital and the restriction of dividends is of the first importance. A rigid rule regarding dividends may be made tolerable by liberal rules defining capital. If the law seeks to make legal capital and actual capital correspond closely, then a dividend rule like New York's becomes unreasonably harsh.

It is obvious that in the case of a company whose legal capital is approximately the same as its actual capital, such a law would subject directors to a hazard which they would not be warranted in assuming; a director could vote only at his peril for the distribution by way of dividends of unquestioned current earnings. New York, which took the leading part in adopting the questionable device of stocks without par value has, however, afforded domestic corporations an opportunity to make their legal capital a purely nominal figure which may be only a fraction of the true capital. This provision, while open to many objections, does afford a way in which the hazards of the dividend rule may be avoided.

However, the New York law goes further than to establish a rule applicable to domestic corporations—it imposes the same liability on directors of foreign corporations which transact business in New York. Now, outside the State of New York, and particularly outside the United States, there are many jurisdictions in which either the law or custom makes the legal capital substantially the true capital of the corporation and in which the law permits the distribution of current profits without regard to fluctuations in the value of capital assets not intended to be sold. Such an approach to the question is at least as reasonable as that of the State of New York, but it will be observed that the directors of a company formed in such a jurisdiction, but transacting business in New York, are placed in a peculiarly unhappy position. For the capital of the corporation will be determined by the laws of the jurisdiction in which it is incorporated, but the question whether a dividend paid was warranted will be determined by a New York court, under New York law, and upon New York theories of value. The law so construed seems to constitute an obnoxious attempt to impose New York ideas of questionable soundness upon corporations formed in other jurisdictions but transacting business within the state. If the Court of Appeals sustains the current construction, modification of the law would seem to be called for.

In each of the several fields which have been considered, the habit of thinking in terms of capital value seems to me to have encouraged economic tendencies which are harmful to the community. It is clear, also, that while it is seldom possible to determine annual income precisely, and sometimes difficult to arrive at even an approximation thereto, the problem of determining income is easier than that of establishing capital value. This for the simple reason that value, itself, must be dependent mainly on the income prospects; and in order to measure it, we must first estimate earnings. Then we still have to face the difficulty of determining what is the capital value of an earning capacity of the kind with which we are dealing.

Economists, teachers, legislators and accountants should all do what is in their power to bring home to our people the truth of Adam Smith's doctrine that the annual produce constitutes the wealth of the country; and to encourage them to rely for economic security on the income derived from their work and their property, rather than upon the hope of enhancement of capital value, which may seem to offer the easy road to affluence but more often proves a lure to disaster. Then the *Economist* may no longer be able to say, as it did on October twelfth last, that:

Even today, in spite of depression and Securities Acts, the capital profit is still as completely monarch in Wall Street as the income yield is in Throgmorton Street.

III

RAILROAD RETIREMENTS AND DEPRECIATION *

IN this article I propose to consider briefly some economic and historical aspects of the problem of accounting for the exhaustion of the useful life of fixed properties (not including equipment) of railroads.

I have chosen this question for discussion for a number of reasons. Undoubtedly, the way in which it has been dealt with has had a marked effect on the economic development of our country; it lies in the field in which, as I pointed out in my first article, the most important problems arise which the accountant has to consider; it has a close relation to the question of regulation of rates on the basis of capital values on which I touched in my second article; and the Interstate Commerce Commission has, in recent years, decreed a revolutionary change in the practice of carriers under its control. An examination of past practice and of suggested alternatives raises sharply the question of the nature of accounting conventions and of the justification therefor.

Methods of providing for the expense represented by the exhaustion of property, though varying greatly in detail, fall into two broad classifications: those which aim to distribute the charge as uniformly as possible over the period of usefulness of the particular unit of property, and those according to which the time for making the charge is fixed by the actual or impending retirement of a unit. The former are commonly referred to as depreciation methods and the latter as retirement methods, and these convenient designations will be employed in this article.

In order to keep the discussion within appropriate limits, it seems desirable to restrict it narrowly to the fixed properties of railroads and to refrain from dealing either with

* *The Journal of Accountancy* (March, 1936).

equipment, which constitutes the other main division of the capital assets of railroads, or with the case of other public utilities. The cases of fixed property and equipment differ in the fundamental fact that so long as operations are continued, fixed property must either be reasonably maintained or replaced, while so long as an adequate supply of newer equipment is available to do the work of the road, obsolete equipment can be kept in nominal service and under a retirement system of accounting carried at cost in the accounts, indefinitely. It was doubtless this consideration which led the Interstate Commerce Commission to require the railroads in 1907 to adopt a system of depreciation charges in respect of equipment, but not in respect of track and other fixed properties.

Up to the present, railroads both here and abroad have generally adopted retirement methods. The question whether railroads should adopt some depreciation method does not appear to have been extensively considered in our country at least until the railroad system was largely built up. The word "depreciation" does not appear in the Instructions in regard to the keeping of Railway Accounts, issued by the Railroad Commissioners of Massachusetts in 1876, or in the index of Hadley's *Railroad Transportation* (1885), or in the decision of the Supreme Court in *Smyth* v. *Ames* (1898). Our practice, however, was undoubtedly greatly influenced by English practice, and in that country the issue was hotly discussed as early as the middle of the last century, following the collapse of the great railroad boom of the forties. A select committee of the House of Lords in 1849 took testimony on the subject (including, incidentally, that of an accountant who stated that he had been carrying on his profession in London for more than twenty years) and in its report favored the creation of depreciation reserves:

It must be obvious [it said] that for the maintenance of railways in a due state of efficiency, as relating to the way, the buildings, the rolling stock and other property, an adequate provision ought to be made, as a matter of necessary precaution and prudence. The creation of a Reserve or Depreciation Fund for such purposes, as contemplated by Parliament (Companies Clauses Act of 1845, 8 Vict. c. 16, s. 122),* seems now to be generally admitted as necessary, and in some instances, the Committee rejoice to observe, it is practically adopted. Without such fund there is a constant temptation to misapply capital, where capital still exists; and where capital is exhausted, the progressive deterioration of the line can hardly be avoided, greatly to the risk of the public, and to the inevitable sacrifice of the ultimate interests of the company itself. It would be difficult to prescribe by law the exact amount to be carried annually to this fund; but the fact of the creation or the non-existence of a Reserve or Depreciation Fund, together with its amount, where it exists, should always appear upon the face of the accounts. The receipts and expenditure of such fund, where it has been established, should in all cases be kept and exhibited, separate and distinct, should be examined and certified by the auditors, and should be annually submitted, as well as left open to the inspection of the shareholders.†

The controversy continued for many years until the passage of the Regulation of Railways Act of 1868. That act provided a special form of accounting for railways, which came to be known as the double account system. Under that system, all capital outlays were carried in an account entitled "Receipts and expenditures on account of capital"; only the balance of this account appeared in the general balance sheet of the company. Rejecting the pleas that depreciation reserves should be made mandatory, Parliament contented itself with requiring certificates that the properties had been adequately maintained and that the dividends proposed to be declared were, in the opinion of the auditors, properly pay-

* The provision seems to have been permissive rather than mandatory. Section 122, the section cited, provides that:
"Before apportioning the profits to be divided among the shareholders the directors may, if they think best, set aside thereout such sum as they may think proper to meet contingencies, or for enlarging, repairing, or improving the works connected with the undertaking, or any part thereof, and may divide the balance only among the shareholders."

† *Third Report, Select Committee on Audit of Railway Accounts*, X *Parliamentary Papers* (1849), p. ix.

able after making all charges against revenue which in their opinion ought to be made thereagainst.

Thus, while directors were free to make provisions for depreciation if they saw fit to do so, the question whether such provisions had to be made turned ultimately on whether the auditors regarded such depreciation as one of the expenses which ought to be provided out of revenue; and leading accountants both here and in England took the view that this was not a necessary expense.*

I turn now to consider what the effect on the development of our country would have been if the depreciation method of accounting had been put into effect in the early days of railroad enterprise. I raised this question in a memorandum which was submitted in 1927 to the Interstate Commerce Commission and in an article which appeared in the *Quarterly Journal of Economics* of February, 1929, and from which I may, perhaps, quote:

The result of a depreciation plan is obviously to throw an added charge for use and exhaustion of property upon the earliest years of operation, years in which the traffic development would be in progress and in which consequently the charge would be more burdensome than in later years. Such a condition would seem to be exactly the reverse of that which would be economically desirable from the standpoint of the community. Its interests would be served by keeping the charges in the early years down to the minimum consistent with maintaining the efficiency of the property, thus enlarging the volume of the commodities that could profitably be transported, and building up both the traffic and the community more rapidly than would otherwise be possible. The best interests of the community in such a situation would be served, it would seem, by a mutual agreement to ignore the depreciation on the property in so far as it could never be made good while the property was being operated; the owners of the railroad agreeing that this depreciation should not be treated as a part of cost of operation, and the community agreeing on the other hand

---

* Cf. H. R. Hatfield, *Accounting*, p. 142.

that in computing return no deduction should be made from the original investment therefor.*

From a financial standpoint, with depreciation charges treated as a part of operating cost, only a small proportion of the enterprises proposed could have been claimed to present the prospect of being able to earn their fixed charges within a reasonable period after being opened for traffic. The published results of the ventures of those who had been bold enough to proceed would have discouraged others from attempting similar enterprises. On the basis of the accounting methods then employed, which ignored accruing depreciation, Hadley estimated in 1885 that the railroads as a whole were earning not more than five per cent on the actual capital invested. To my mind, it is incontestable that the effect of the application of such depreciation accounting would have been that the construction of a large part of our railway mileage would at least have been greatly delayed—if, indeed, some part would ever have been constructed at all. Such a result would have been exactly the opposite of that sought at the time by legislatures and the public.

Hadley begins his chapter on railroad legislation with the statement:

The early railroad legislation in the United States was devised for the object of securing railroad construction. The only fear was that railroads would not be built as fast as they were needed. †

And, as late as 1907, the Interstate Commerce Commission was complaining:

It may conservatively be stated that the inadequacy of transportation facilities is little less than alarming. ‡

Since the development of other public utilities and commercial enterprises followed naturally on the development of railroads, this portion of the growth of our capital equip-

* Vol. XLIII, p. 211.
† A. T. Hadley, *Railroad Transportation* (1885), p. 125.
‡ *Annual Report of the Interstate Commerce Commission* (1907), p. 9.

ment would also have been greatly retarded. It has been said that we owe our great railroad facilities and the developments which they made possible, in a large measure, to unsound finance; but if it be held that depreciation provisions are an essential element of sound railroad accounting, then unsound accounting must share with unsound finance in the responsibility for the tremendous economic development that has taken place since railroad enterprises were first begun. I do not here undertake to consider whether the growth may have been too rapid to be healthy—I make only the point that the accounting practice affected the economic development of the country; whether for better or for worse, others may dispute.

It is no doubt true that as a result of the accounting methods followed, large amounts of capital have been lost by investors. How large such losses in the aggregate must have been is brought home to us when we consider enterprises such as street railways, in respect of which capital has been furnished by investors—first, for the cost of an original installation of horse-cars; then for the cost of equipping the lines for electrical operation (with, in some cases, an intermediate cable development); and, finally, as we have recently seen in New York and elsewhere, the electrically operated street cars have been displaced by buses. This, however, merely emphasizes the truth too often ignored by unfriendly critics of the existing economic order—who see only the large gains made by a relatively small number of fortunate individuals from the development of the capital equipment of the nation—that in the aggregate, the community pays only a relatively small return to capital for the amount invested, and that it is the community that is the one sure gainer therefrom. However legitimate the project, however honest the finance, however conservative and scrupulous the accounting, and however competent the management may be, the losses in industry are bound to be enormous, and the community can well afford to allow the few who meet with unusual success to receive and retain substantial rewards as a part of the price it pays for *all* the capital invested.*

I should perhaps anticipate here an objection that the methods of accounting adopted may have been an effect rather than a cause: the objection that this may be a case in which methods of accounting have been influenced by other than accounting considerations, rather than one in which accounting judgment has influenced the economic development. True, the methods followed here and in Great Britain might represent the giving of effect to an opinion deliberately reached as to what was economically desirable, or they might be the reflection of the views (born, perhaps, of the wishes) of those who were interested in the creation of such enterprises. There is, however, nothing to suggest that the depreciation method was regarded by those responsible for the enabling legislation, either here or in England, as sounder, but was deliberately ignored because it was believed that the development and welfare of the country would be aided by ignoring it. Nor do I believe that those who were responsible for finding the capital for railroad enterprises in England or here, or those auditors in England who were required under the Act of 1868 to certify that dividends were *bona fide* due after providing for the charges which ought to be made against revenue, believed that sound finance or good accounting called for depreciation provisions which would ultimately provide for the amortization of outlays on all property except that which was indestructible and could never become obsolete, and deliberately refrained from requiring such provisions.

The policy that omitted any provisions for depreciation was, in England, entirely consistent with the policy which omitted any provision for amortization of obviously wasting assets such as mines, ships, or annuities. It was consistent with the whole theory of the determination of income under the English income tax laws (which had been revived in 1842

* Failure to recognize frankly these simple truths seems to me to be a major ground for criticism of measures for control of security issues which have been put forward in the last year or two.

before railroad development in England had proceeded very far). American practice in the early days was undoubtedly determined largely by English precedents, which was natural in view of the fact that the capital for our railroad enterprises came largely from abroad, and particularly from England.

I believe that in dealing, or omitting to deal, with depreciation the railroads merely followed the general accounting practice of the times. In my first article I referred to the change of attitude on the question on the part of the Supreme Court between 1878 and 1909. It was not until the present century that depreciation charges became general even in industrial accounting practice in our country—in fact, full recognition of the necessity therefor might almost be said to date from the enactment of the first corporation income tax law in 1909, under which depreciation was an allowable deduction which corporations generally were anxious to secure, and which was allowed only if taken up on the books.

The first serious proposal to apply depreciation methods to fixed properties of railroads appears to have been made as the result of the study of the question of railroad valuation by the Interstate Commerce Commission under the Valuation Act of 1913, though, as already noted, the Commission had in 1907 taken steps looking to the application of a depreciation method to railroad equipment. In its valuations under the authority of the Act, the Commission consistently deducted from the gross value depreciation on what is known as the straight line method—that is to say, the method which aims to distribute the ultimate loss of value evenly over the service life of a unit of property. The Supreme Court in its decisions on valuation questions has consistently rejected the straight line method, and the deductions it has recognized have resembled more nearly what has been called observed depreciation.

By an amendment to the Interstate Commerce Act in 1920

(Section 20, § 5), the Commission was given authority to prescribe the classes of property for which depreciation charges might properly be included under operating expenses and the percentages of depreciation which should be charged with respect to the uses of such classes of property. After much consideration of the question and extended hearings, the Commission handed down a report in November, 1926; * but, as a result of objections to its conclusions, granted a rehearing which eventually resulted in a new report dated July 28, 1931.† This varied in some important respects from the earlier one, but adhered to the theory of straight line depreciation which the railroads were ordered to put into force as from July 1, 1933. The effective date has since been changed by executive order and now stands indefinitely postponed.

Shortly before the second report, the Supreme Court in the United Railways case ‡ had laid down the principle that for the purposes of rate cases any depreciation charge must be based upon present value and not upon original cost, as was contemplated by the Commission. Clearly, however, a system of depreciation charges based upon a fluctuating present value was altogether impracticable for the purposes of current accounting by the railroads. If the Commission was for such current purposes to require depreciation charges, they could hardly be based on anything except cost. At the same time, with the Commission insisting on straight line depreciation and original cost, and the Court insisting on observed depreciation and present value, there was no apparent prospect of the Commission's attaining the objective which it had stressed of placing railroad accounts on such a basis as to make them equally useful for the purposes of current accounting and rate-case determination.

In the report of 1931 the Commission, after citing the

* No. 14700, *Depreciation Charges of Telephone Companies;* No. 15100, *Depreciation Charges of Steam Railroad Companies.*
† Same title.
‡ *United Railways and Electric Company of Baltimore* v. *West et al.,* 280 U. S. (1930), 234.

varied views of carriers and the need for uniformity, concluded that a depreciation method was preferable to a retirement method. Observing that in regulating accounts the Commission was performing its administrative function, and that so long as the regulation was not arbitrary in the sense of being without reasonable basis, there was no ground for judicial interference, it proceeded to consider various depreciation methods. It recognized that the arguments in favor of the sinking fund and annuity methods had force, going so far as to say, "It may be that from a scientific and theoretical standpoint the annuity method is the soundest of all," but concluded that the balance of the argument was in favor of the straight-line method. Its discussion of this question concludes thus:

We are disposed to abide by the finding in our prior report in favor of the straight-line method. It is the method which has consistently been used in our valuation proceedings. On the record before us, indeed, we would hardly be justified in reaching any other conclusion.

This conclusion, it should also be said, is associated with the confidence we entertain that the courts, when the issues and facts are made entirely clear to them, will recognize the connection and interrelation between depreciation in accounting and in valuation which have been pointed out hereinbefore (p. 413).

Here we have what are at once the weakest and the determining arguments of the Commission on the question at issue. While unquestionably straight line depreciation is commonly used for current accounting purposes, particularly in the industrial field, its use for valuation purposes does not find support either in theory, in practice, or in court decisions. The Commission's own view of fixed property is that it represents a given number of years of service value. If this view be accepted, the unit which has at the beginning of a year 100 years of useful life, has at the end thereof 99 years of such life left in it, and the reduction in value during the year is measured by the difference between the value of an annuity for 100 years and that of an annuity for 99 years. This difference is not 1%, but less than 1% of 1%.

Continuing, the Commission found that (to use the language of the syllabus), "Depreciation accounting becomes a necessary measure of self-protection to the carriers, in view of the decisions of the Supreme Court of the United States to the effect that accrued depreciation must be taken into consideration in ascertaining the rate-base value" (§ 34, p. 353). This argument would be more convincing if the views of the Commission had been shared generally by the carriers, which, however, regarded the Commission's proposals as "neither practicable nor wise" (p. 382), or if the methods of computing depreciation prescribed by the Commission had been more in harmony with the past decisions of the Supreme Court. Perhaps a more accurate statement of the argument would be that depreciation accounting will become necessary for the self-protection of the carriers if the Supreme Court justifies the confidence of the Commission, recognizes the connection and interrelation between valuation and depreciation accounting, and does so in such a way as to substitute the Commission's ideas upon depreciation for those which it has heretofore expressed.

Referring again to the syllabus, while paragraph 22 reads: "It is not essential that the accounts should correspond in all respects with the facts which may be controlling in a confiscation case," we find in paragraph 43 the statement: "It is a matter of vital importance to harmonize the requirements for valuation and depreciation accounting purposes, so that unnecessary duplication of effort will be avoided."

Reading the order as a whole, one is left with a very definite impression that the Commissioners participating in it are thoroughly convinced that straight line depreciation should be deducted from gross value in any determination of the rate base, and that depreciation computed on the same basis should be charged against income. In order to secure recognition for the first of these two points, they are willing to make large concessions on secondary questions.

Encouraged by *dicta* in minority opinions of the Court, they hope by the exercise of their authority in the matter of current accounts to induce the Supreme Court at long last to come around to their point of view. In presenting their case they make effective use of the arguments and practices of the telephone companies in support of straight line depreciation as an operating charge, though declining to accept the contention of those companies that unexpended depreciation reserves are in the nature of surplus.*

In 1934 an opportunity was afforded to judge how far the reasoning of the Commission had made progress with the Supreme Court. The opportunity did not come in a railroad case, in which the proponents of straight line depreciation would have had to face the argument that their proposal ran counter to the practice of railroads generally, here and abroad since the earliest days of operation, including nearly a quarter of a century during which railroad accounting had been under the jurisdiction of the Interstate Commerce Commission—it came up in the case of a telephone company †
which had followed a straight line depreciation plan after the Commission's own heart. As a result, the depreciation reserve had grown to be from 26% to 28% of the cost of property, including land. The court below had found the proper deduction for depreciation for valuation purposes to be from 15% to 16%, and the telephone company had claimed the proper deduction for this purpose to be from 8% to 9%.

The Supreme Court's decision against the telephone company was based on the ground that it had failed to sustain the burden of showing that the amounts charged to operating expenses for depreciation had not been excessive. It spoke of the "striking contrast" between the reserve that had been accumulated and the existing depreciation as indicated by

* For efforts to enlist the support of the Congress, see letter of January 21, 1931, reprinted in the *Annual Report of the Interstate Commerce·Commission* (1931), pp. 347-57.
† *Lindheimer et al.* v. *Illinois Bell Telephone Co.,* 292 U. S. (1934), 151.

"proof which the Company strongly emphasizes as complete and indisputable in its sharp criticism of the amount of accrued depreciation found by the District Court in valuing the property."

Mr. Justice Butler, in a concurring opinion, indicated that he was not a convert to the view of the Interstate Commerce Commission. In doing so, he stated in clear language one of the objections which has been most strongly urged against the depreciation method:

From the foregoing it justly may be inferred that charges made according to the principle followed by the company create reserves much in excess of what is needed for maintenance. The balances carried by the company include large amounts that never can be used for the purposes for which the reserve was created. In the long run the amounts thus unnecessarily taken from revenue will reach about one-half the total cost of all depreciable parts of the plant. The only legitimate purpose of the reserve is to equalize expenditures for maintenance so as to take from the revenue earned in each year its fair share of the burden. To the extent that the annual charges include amounts that will not be required for that purpose, the account misrepresents the cost of the service.

The company's properties constitute a complex and highly developed instrumentality containing many classes of items that require renewal from time to time. But, taken as a whole, the plant must be deemed to be permanent. It never was intended to be new in all its parts. It would be impossible to make it so. Expenditures in an attempt to accomplish that would be wasteful. Amounts sufficient to create a reserve balance that is the same percentage of total cost of depreciable items as their age is of their total service life cannot be accepted as legitimate additions to operating expenses (pp. 181-82).

The argument thus admirably stated raises two important questions pertinent to the present discussion. The narrower one is whether any economic advantage is to be gained by adopting a system which calls for the creation today of a reserve of the character described by Mr. Justice Butler as "unnecessary"—a reserve which if created at all should have been created in the past, but which has not been called for under the system of railroad accounting heretofore in force. The second is whether there is any principle higher than that of general economic advantage and justice by which accounting practices must be governed and judged.

It is interesting to note the way in which the Commission has dealt with the first point. In its report of November, 1926, it ordered that a reserve account equal to the amount of depreciation which under its new system was deemed to have accrued in the past could be set up on the books of the carriers, and a suspense account of equal amount set up on the asset side. It asserted, quite unjustly I think, that the theoretically correct way would be to make the charge to profit and loss, on the ground that it represented a failure to accrue depreciation charges in the past; but recognizing the impracticability of this course, proposed that it should remain in suspense until extinguished by charges against profit and loss in the future. Strong exception was taken to these proposals, and in the revised order of 1931 the Commission decreed that the amount of the accrued depreciation at the date when the new system was to become effective should be computed and broken down into component parts corresponding to the primary investment accounts—but that no cognizance of the sum so computed should be taken in the books.

This solution was more realistic than the Commission's previous proposal and was calculated to avert in the case of the carriers such criticism as that expressed later by Mr. Justice Butler in respect to the telephone company. Coupled with a change which required depreciation accounting by groups of units instead of by units (as previously contemplated), it provided a way out of the difficulty of dealing, when retirement occurs in the future, with the depreciation deemed to have accrued in the past on the unit retired. In effect, this depreciation is to be charged against the reserve that is to be created to provide for depreciation in the future.

The procedure as laid down is open to several criticisms: it is illogical; it involves the abandonment of a large part of the Commission's theory; and it results in charging against a reserve expenses for which no corresponding credit has previously been made to that reserve. However, the only alternative would have been to require the accumulation of a reserve out of future earnings at the expense either of the shippers or of the security-holders, a course for which there would be no economic justification. Of the two alternative courses, that adopted by the Commission was doubtless the wiser.

Our railroads having reached a state of maturity, there is reason to expect that a depreciation plan on the modified basis would over a period of years produce charges to operation not greatly different from those which would result from the application of a sound retirement method. With the objection to the earlier plan that it added greatly to the burdens upon the carriers' future earnings largely removed, the major question now is whether any advantages sufficient to justify such a change in the general railroad practice of the past, here and abroad, are likely to result from the adoption of the Commission's plan.

A serious demerit of the scheme is its complexity, and the enormous amount of bookkeeping which it would entail. Outside the Commission probably no great virtue will be seen in the fact that with the aid of the extra-accounting statistical record of accrued depreciation at the date when the system becomes effective, it would bring about some sort of coördination between the accounting and the *Commission's* theory of valuation. A further advantage claimed by the Commission was that the procedure would insure more uniform charges for upkeep against operating in good times as well as in bad. Events since 1931 have already proved the vanity of this hope. We find the Commission itself reporting in 1934 that, although depreciation remained on a pre-depression basis, it had allowed carriers to charge not only certain retirements but also certain repairs against profit and loss instead of against operating expenses.*

Unless the order does bring about a change in the attitude of the Supreme Court as the Commission hopes, and of this there is no present indication, it will, I think, have to be conceded that the results of the activities of the Commission in the matter have not justified the expense they have occasioned. Moreover, the importance of the rate base in the case of the railroads as a whole has steadily diminished as competitive methods of transport have reduced their revenues. Recapture of earnings has gone by the board and railroad valuation has lost most of its former importance.

I shall conclude this series of articles by discussing very briefly the question raised earlier herein, whether there are principles higher than those of general economic advantage and justice by which accounting practices must be governed and judged. Some accountants believe that there are such principles, and it has been suggested that the American Institute of Accountants, or some other body, should undertake to lay them down. It is difficult, however, to see why this should be true of accounting, when it is obviously not true in respect of law or of economics.

The better opinion is, I believe, that, as I suggested in the first of these articles, accounting is a tool of business, and the development of accounting, like the development of business law, should be determined by the best practices of business men. As stated in the report of the American Institute to the New York Stock Exchange of September 28, 1932, out of the necessities of business there has "grown up a body of conventions, based partly on theoretical and partly on practical considerations, which form the basis for the determination of income and the preparation of balance sheets today."

There is every reason to desire and to expect improvements and a constantly increasing degree of uniformity in accounting conventions. This improvement and this uniformity cannot be attained through any attempt to make

* *Annual Report* (1934), p. 2.

accounting practice a reflection of purely metaphysical concepts, but only through careful consideration of what is fair and in the best interest of those having a legitimate interest in accounts. In the case of corporate accounts, this may include stockholders and creditors—actual or potential—employees, customers, and the general public, and nice questions may arise in giving just recognition to the rights of the different groups. Clearly, however, no rule which is contrary to the interests of all of the parties should be established on the sole ground that it conforms to some abstract notion of what is sound accounting.

It is because the best accounting can be attained only through wide knowledge of business, sound judgment and mental integrity that the profession of the accountant offers today one of the most attractive fields of activity to the high-minded and clear-minded among the rising generation.

PART VII
REVIEWS AND CRITICISMS

I

REASONS FOR EXCLUDING INTEREST FROM COST *

(1916)

STANDARD schemes of accounting for various industries are receiving much consideration at the present time. This is due partly to the encouragement given such movements by the Federal Trade Commission, and partly to the work which has been carried on for some time by the Bureau of Business Research of Harvard University and other organizations, the value of which is now being recognized.

In connection with these schemes it may not be amiss to reconsider the question of the treatment of interest, particularly interest on invested capital. Many who favor including interest in expense or cost as a general principle become dubious when they are asked to specify the rate or the kind of rate they would adopt. Broadly there are three kinds of rate suggested:

(1) A rate equal to that yielded by the safest investments. (Some go further and try to eliminate the small element of risk from such a rate and call the balance pure interest or compensation solely for the use of the money.)

(2) A rate equal to that at which money can be borrowed for the particular industry.

(3) A rate sufficient to attract permanent investment into the industry.

Of the three alternatives the second is probably the most generally favored, and it will therefore be assumed as the basis of the following discussion.

At the outset it is important to consider what such a rate represents. In an industrial business commercial loans can usually be obtained up to a limit of, say, 50 per cent of the

* *The Journal of Accountancy,* Vol. XXI (June, 1916).

current assets. Money lent, therefore, has behind it 100 per cent margin of security in current assets alone, as well as plant values which may represent another 100 per cent or more. The difference between the position of the loan and that of the invested capital which stands behind it is therefore obvious.

It is suggested that it is undesirable to treat such a rate of interest on invested capital as cost in standard classification of expense or in cost of manufacture:

First, because the method is unscientific and unsound for the immediate purpose in view;

Second, because the inclusion of interest in cost produces results which are financially and economically undesirable;

Third, because in so far as the results of such methods have a bearing on the broad question of the relations between capital, labor and the public, the inclusion of interest in the manner suggested tends to mislead and thus to promote discord and social injustice.

Objection No. 1. "Because the method is unscientific and unsound for the immediate purpose in view."

The purpose in view is to arrive at the cost or expense involved in doing business in the line of industry under consideration. For such a purpose the essentials are:

First, to ascertain as far as possible all costs and to exclude anything that is not a cost;

Second, to arrive as far as possible at results that are actual and to avoid if possible the introduction of arbitrary or estimated figures;

Third, to present each element of cost as a separate item in the classification and to avoid the inclusion of any one element in more than one heading thereof.

Considering these essentials in order, whether the return on proprietor's capital is wholly or in part a cost or expense is a question on which opinions differ. As to this it is sufficient to say that if, after consideration of other essentials, it should be deemed preferable to omit the charge in respect of proprietor's capital from cost or expense, this fact would at least not impair the value of the results presented.

Turning to the second essential, it is obvious that any charge in respect of proprietor's capital must be an estimate. The next point to consider is, therefore, how accurate an estimate made in the way that is proposed will be. Now it is apparent that if the capital required in a business is provided partly in the form of a loan by A, who is given priority in respect of principal and interest, and partly by B (the proprietor) whose rights are subordinated to those of A, then without attempting to define exactly the rate of interest applicable to B's contribution, it must obviously be something different from and greater than the rate applicable to A's contribution. It appears, therefore, that the proposed rate is from its very nature inapplicable.

Further, it is apparent that some of the compensation of the proprietor's capital must be left to be provided out of the balance remaining after deducting costs, so that the procedure involves the sacrifice of the third essential above recited, namely, the presentation of each element of cost as a separate item in the classification. It may be suggested that the compensation of the proprietor's capital is not an element but a compound of *two* elements, namely, the compensation for the use of the capital and the compensation for the risk incurred. The answer to such a contention is, however, that the rate proposed to be used is itself a compound of these two elements, the defect of the rate being that it is formed in an erroneous and half-hearted manner.

At this point it may be worth while to consider roughly how far the method does provide for the two elements. The rate at which money is lent to industry, and especially small industries, is probably double the interest rate on the safest securities. The rate necessary to attract investments (not loans) into such an industry is not less than three times the rate on the safest investments.* If, say, one-third of the

---

* If the safe investment rate be taken at, say, 3 per cent, this gives a borrowing rate of 6 per cent and an investment rate of 9 per cent, which happens to be almost exactly the average rate earned on the amount invested (capital and surplus) in all the national banks of the country for the seven years ending June 30, 1914.

capital be raised by borrowing, the rate to be applied to the proprietor's capital would on these assumptions be three and a half times the safe investment rate.

For, taking the total capital invested at 300 and r as annual interest on a safe investment of 100:

the interest on 300 at r would be.................. 9 r

the interest on 100 borrowed at 2 r................ 2 1

leaving for interest on 200 proprietor's capital of 3½

   r per cent..................................... 7 r

Now if the rate on safest investment (r) be taken as the compensation for use of capital, the borrowing rate of 2 r provides 1 r for risk. If the proper rate for proprietor's capital be taken at 3½ r, of which 1 r represents compensation for use and 2½ r compensation for risk, it may be said that the method provides for the "use" element and about 40 per cent of the "risk" element contained in the "cost" of proprietor's capital.

To sum up, the position is that whether the first essential is fulfilled is a controversial question, and that the second and third essentials are clearly sacrificed. It would seem that in these circumstances the first objection urged is fully sustained. This objection would not be fatal if the method produced good results when viewed from a broader standpoint, and it is therefore desirable to proceed to a consideration of the next objection.

Objection No. 2. Because the inclusion of interest in cost produces results which are financially and economically undesirable.

The evil effects from an administrative, financial and accounting standpoint of including interest in cost have been pointed out in previous articles in *The Journal of Accountancy,* and no attempt will therefore be made to deal with this subject exhaustively here. Briefly the main objections are:

First, plant investment which yields only a rate which is admittedly less than commensurate with the risk attending investment in the industry is commercially and economically unsound.

A method which purports to allow for cost of increased capital by means of a rate determined by the rate at which money can be borrowed, therefore, tends to encourage unwise plant expenditure.

If the money is obtained, not by borrowing, but by a permanent increase of capital, then the return on that capital will have to be far greater than the loan rate. If the money is obtained by borrowing, then, quite apart from the rate, the policy is unwise—excessive investment in fixed assets of capital obtained by borrowing being one of the commonest causes of failure.

Second, there is no sense or advantage in including in cost interest on investment in fixed assets unless interest on investment in current assets employed in manufacture is also considered.

The attempt to introduce correctly computed interest allowances on both classes of investments involves difficulties out of all proportion to any possible benefits.

These objections may seem strange in view of the fact that the principal argument advanced in favor of including interest in cost is that it takes capital investment into account in comparative costs. But it is submitted that it is better to leave capital investment out of account altogether than to take it into account on a basis that does not even purport to represent the true cost of capital. There are theoretical grounds for the claim that interest on some logical basis should be included in cost, though it is not worth while in practice to attempt to do it. There would seem to be no basis in theory and far more danger than advantage in practice in including a rate determined as the rate now under discussion would be determined.

Third, the method leads to less conservative valuation of inventories and to showing as profits available for dividends amounts which have not been realized or even earned.

It may be asked why, if these views are correct, so many people do favor including such a rate of interest in cost. The answer is perhaps found partly in the following considerations:

First, the great extent to which capital is obtained by borrowing in this country;

Second, the very general use and acceptance of 6 per cent as an interest rate;

Third, the general failure to appreciate the true rates of return earned in industry. This is in a measure the natural result of the "watering" of capital in the past for the purpose of concealing the true rates of profits being earned;

Fourth, anxiety to do anything that tends to reduce underselling;

Fifth, the hope that, by including part of its claim to compensation as cost and a part as profit, capital may be able to secure more than it otherwise would obtain. Later reasons will be advanced for concluding that such a hope is ill-founded;

Sixth, the influence of bankers, based on a false analogy from their own business.

A man who has never considered the problem of fair return regards 6 per cent as a well-recognized rate, applies it often where it has no proper application, and accepts it when it is charged against him.

The executive head of a business who charges 6 per cent on capital employed against each department of his business may or may not be conscious that he would never invest money in a department at that rate. He knows, however, that the department head will recognize and accept that rate, but would not probably understand or willingly accept a charge of a higher rate and feels that by charging 6 per cent he gets at least that much protection against underselling. The same comment applies to trade associations which combine to put out accounting schemes, the underlying purpose of which is as a rule the reduction of destructive competition.

Whether or not the result accomplished in this direction is good or bad from an economic standpoint is an open question. In the case of a man who does not realize what a selling price ought to include, it is probably helpful both to him and to his competitors. But at its best the method is a hybrid and a makeshift, and taking all effects together the evil effects preponderate.

Objection No. 3. "Because in so far as the results of such methods have a bearing on the broad question of the relations between capital, labor and the public, the inclusion of interest in the manner suggested tends to mislead and thus to promote discord and social injustice."

The relation of the problem to the broad question of the proper distribution of the fruits of organized industry between labor and capital is apparent, and nothing could be more essential than that the practice adopted should avoid anything likely to add to misconceptions of one another's equitable claims which are largely responsible for the bitterness of the controversy between the two.

Upon any great question the tendency must be to reduce the issue to the simplest terms. The fair disposition of the results of organized industry is one of the greatest of questions, and the issue here is reduced in the public mind to one between labor and capital—everything that does not go to labor is regarded as going to capital. The elements other than labor entitled to compensation may in the economic mind be subdivided, and the economist may attempt to differentiate between pure interest, compensation for risk, the reward of the entrepreneur, etc., but in the public mind and for practical purposes these elements are combined in capital. Moreover, in general, once an enterprise is launched these elements are vested in the same body of individuals, so that the fact that the isolation of the elements is not possible except in theory does not cause any difficulty in practice.

If so-called interest on capital is deducted as expense, the general disposition will be to assert claims to a part or the whole of the balance. The public (especially in the case of public service companies) will attribute the net profit shown to over-exaction from the public. Labor will claim that it is attributable to underpayment of labor or at least to the results of combined effort in which labor should participate.

If, however, the results are presented without including anything in expense for return on capital, it will be clearly recognized that if capital is not entitled to all the residuum, at least capital has a claim on it which must first be satisfied. That claim would seem to be for an amount standing as nearly as possible in the same relation to capital as the amounts included in expense in respect of labor stand to labor.

The elements included in the compensation to labor include some or all of the following:

(a) A minimum wage;
(b) Payment for special skill;
(c) Compensation for special conditions of employments including risk, responsibility and inconvenience;
(d) Compensation paid on account of specially favorable financial conditions (such as the two 10 per cent additions to wages by the Steel Corporation recently);
(e) A share of the final residuum (paid in the form of wage dividends or otherwise);

All these items except (e) are treated as expense, under the head of wages.

Turning now to capital—pure interest may be said to correspond roughly to minimum wage in the case of labor. There is no element in capital corresponding to the special skill in the case of labor. There are, however, in the case of capital, elements corresponding exactly to the items (c), (d) and (e).

But while the items (a) to (d) are included in expense in respect of labor, only item (a) and an indefinite fraction * of (c) are proposed to be included in expense in respect of capital.

The ordinary reader of the figures (and certainly also the enemies of capital) will, however, assume that the interest included in expense stands to capital in the same relation as the wages included in expense do to labor, and no amount of explanation will be very effective in avoiding or removing such a misconception. Nor can such an explanation be effectively made, since it involves explaining that while the

* Possibly 40 per cent.

amount included under wages does represent compensation based on the conditions under which the labor is employed, the compensation assigned capital under interest does not even purport to be the compensation to which it is fairly entitled under the conditions under which it is invested, but what it would fairly earn if employed in some different and much safer way.

An analysis of the amounts paid or due to labor and capital such as is suggested above is outside the scope of a classification of expenses, though it would be a positive contribution towards the proper treatment of the problem of the relations between the two bodies. It is, however, in the highest degree important that classifications should not present figures in such a one-sided and erroneous way as to add another misconception to those that already keep labor and capital apart. If accounts cannot actually promote harmony between the two, at least let every possible step be taken to insure that they shall not add to the discord.

It may be asked whether interest should not be included in expense on some other basis if not on the one proposed. The alternatives are apparently the "pure interest" rate (or the rate on the safest investments which approximates thereto) or else the rate that will attract investment into the industry. To adopt the pure interest basis means providing for compensation for the *use* of money, but not for the risk to which it is subjected; and as the risk is by far the more important element, there would seem to be little or no practical advantage in following this course, nor indeed any probability of being generally understood. The rate which will attract capital into an industry would seem to be one of the things which accounts should help to determine rather than anything which could be assumed as an element of cost.

II

COST ACCOUNTING *

(1925)

This term embraces methods of cost determination which are either a part of, or coördinated with, the general accounting of the enterprise as distinguished from estimates of costs not so controlled or checked. Cost accounting methods have probably been developed more extensively in the United States than in any other country. This development has taken place mainly in the period since 1895, and it may be regarded as a natural phase of the general industrial development in that period. The same conditions which have stimulated the use of labour-saving methods and mass production have naturally lent new importance to the determination and analysis of costs, and have made it imperative that the substantial accuracy of the statistics of cost used shall be beyond question. This can only be assured by linking up cost statistics with general financial and accounting records and results.

In the problem of cost accounting there may be said to be usually three main objects to be achieved, three main classifications to be followed and three major considerations governing the scope of the methods to be employed. These nine elements are necessarily to some extent interrelated, and it may therefore be well to state them at the outset.

The main objects referred to are: (1) To afford a sound basis for selling policy; (2) To provide tests of operating efficiency; (3) To establish a basis for accounting records and financial policy. The classifications of cost are broadly, (1) labor, (2) material, (3) overhead expenses. The character and scope of the methods to be employed must be deter-

* From an article written for *The Encyclopædia Britannica*, 13th edition (1926).

364

mined largely by considerations of (1) speed, (2) accuracy, (3) expense.

The relative importance of the objects enumerated varies with different classes of enterprise. In the case of a builder, contractor or shipbuilder, or in the case of a plant capable of producing different types of products, a cost system may be of even greater value in the determination of selling policies than in producing operating efficiency. On the other hand, in the case of a plant producing standard articles for a highly competitive market, the value of a cost system may lie almost wholly in helping to secure manufacturing or operating efficiency.

The success of any cost accounting system depends largely on correct judgment concerning the relative importance of the different elements of the problem in the particular case involved, and particularly on the success with which the naturally conflicting considerations of speed, accuracy and expense in the cost department are reconciled. If the cost system is to be of real service to those in charge of operations or sales, its results must be substantially accurate and sufficiently specific to enable those officers to localize waste and the responsibility therefor. Such results will, however, be of little value if in an attempt to secure accuracy the ascertainment of the results is unduly delayed, or an expense is incurred greater than the possible benefits to be derived from the greater accuracy ultimately secured. The recognition of this fact and the consequent resort to simpler, though perhaps less scientific and less meticulously accurate methods, have perhaps been the most marked characteristics of the development of cost accounting in the United States in recent years. The growth of interest in cost accounting, which began about 1895, was greatly stimulated by the consolidations which were effected about the year 1900.

Among the results of these consolidations were the transfer of ownership on a large scale from persons immediately interested in the operation of plants to the general public, and also a transfer of the general direction from small groups of operating officers to boards of directors less intimately associated with actual operations. This change resulted in a demand for more frequent and more accurate reports of operating results as a guide to financial policies and for the information of those financially interested. In the development of methods to meet the new situation the importance of the purely accounting and financial uses of costs were not infrequently overrated.

Purely accounting uses of cost records have come to be viewed in a more accurate perspective, and accounting refinements and technicalities have been increasingly subordinated to practical usefulness. At the same time, remarkable results have been achieved in expediting the compilation of costs by careful organisation, so that today large corporations frequently have completed cost figures for a month available for the operating executives within three or four days of its close.

The accountant called upon to devise a system of cost accounting will be wise to regard the accounting uses of the system as entirely secondary, and to aim at making the system as valuable as possible to those controlling the policies and operations of the business. The sales manager, in fixing prices, must estimate costs in advance of sale, and the value to him of a system which records actual costs lies mainly in the check it affords on the correctness of his estimates, and the extent to which it permits and facilitates the use of actual costs of the past as a basis for estimates of cost in the future under changing conditions.

The operating or production manager's requirements are more extensive and more varied. He must be in a position to determine whether fluctuations in cost are due to conditions within the control of the management or not, and if so, to localise the responsibility. He must, for instance, be in a position to determine such questions as whether a higher cost of material at one plant than at another is attributable to less efficiency in purchasing, or to the use or the waste of more material, and how far apparent high costs of production are really costs of production, and how far they are attributable to lack of production, *i.e.,* to idle time and such causes. Every effort should therefore be made to frame a cost accounting system so as to afford as much light as is practicable on manufacturing operations and make that light available at the earliest possible moment.

Broadly, there are three main types of cost accounting systems. The first undertakes to determine the cost for each *production order,* which may cover either a single unit of production where units are large, or a batch of units where they are smaller. The second takes account of costs by separate *processes or operations*—thus determining a unit cost for each process or operation and leaving the cost of any article produced to be determined by bringing together the costs of several processes or operations through which it passes. The third seeks to determine costs by *products or classes of products* and to compute the costs of the units produced by dividing the total costs incurred in producing similar units in any period by the number of units produced in that period. Multiple products from a common raw material, as in the case of petroleum and packing industries, constitute a separate and difficult problem.

An important question is the relation of the cost accounting to the general accounting records of the enterprise. From the standpoint of accounting technique the cost system, which forms an integral part of a general accounting system, possesses a unity and completeness which cannot be achieved in any other way. It is, however, easy to pay too great a price for this artistic completeness, and there has been a marked disposition to employ methods under which the cost accounting is less closely tied to the general accounting.

The value of cost figures is greatly enhanced by comparisons either with past achievements or with an "ideal" or standard of cost. Much attention has been given to methods of cost accounting in complex industries, based on standard costs for specific articles, processes or operations, supplemented by methods for adjusting these standard costs for changes in conditions, and for ensuring that the aggregate costs allocated as the results of these adjustments are in actual or substantial agreement with the aggregate costs incurred as shown by the general books. For discussion of the subdivision of costs, the reader must be referred to text-books. A warning may be given that accounting text-books are apt to over-rate and engineering text-books to under-rate general accounting and financial *desiderata*. In particular, the importance may be emphasised of avoiding use of a cost system in a way which would involve inventorying goods at more than true cost through the inclusion in costs of either (*a*) interdepartmental profits (and for this purpose wholly-owned subsidiary companies should be regarded as departments), (*b*) profits in the form of interest or otherwise, or (*c*) selling costs. All these items may, however, be included in appropriate ways in costs compiled for executive use in formulating policies.

Overhead costs per unit (up to the limit of economical production) decrease as the output increases, and vice versa. Sales may therefore be advantageous, even though they do not reimburse direct costs and a rateable proportion of overhead expenses. The cost accountant should therefore do all in his power, especially where profit margins are narrow, to segregate overhead costs, to analyse them and to interpret them to the executive, so as to ensure that they will be given due, but not undue, weight in the formulation of policies. The allocations of overhead are, at best, rough approximations, but much has been done to secure more accurate allocations by computing overhead for individual departments, machines or tools, by adopting bases of apportionment, more carefully selected and more closely related to the actual facts of production than previously, and in similar ways.

In some systems, standard rates of burden rather than actual rates are charged into cost, being credited to clearing accounts to which actual overhead expenses are charged. Where this is done, watchfulness and judgment in dealing with these clearing accounts are imperative. This is, however, only one illustration of the most important of all truths in cost accounting, that skill and judgment in applying, adjusting and interpreting cost methods in actual use are even more important than ingenuity in devising a system in the first instance.

III

AN EXAMINATION OF AFFIDAVITS IN

De Koven et al. v. *The Lake Shore & Michigan Southern Railway Company*

(1923)

THE case of the plaintiff rests substantially on Mr. Thompson's affidavit, as Professor Friday simply restates what Mr. Thompson has said. In his first affidavit Mr. Thompson propounded a method of determining the relative values of Lake Shore and Consolidated Company stock, based on the theory that, in income, expectation has a value graduated according to the extent of mortgages ranking ahead of it. . . .

Mr. Thompson takes one element which admittedly affects to some extent the market value of earning capacity (the extent of the fixed charges or mortgages to which income is subject); assigns to that element a weight fixed by himself; calculates the relative values of the respective income capitalizations with reference to this element alone; and then briefly dismisses all other elements of value by calling attention to certain elements which he claims would on comparison be favorable to the Lake Shore, arguing that therefore, if he took into account these other favorable factors, he would necessarily reach still higher values.

The fundamental importance to this method of the correctness *of the weight assigned to the one element* taken into consideration and the fallacy of the statement as to the other elements of value may be illustrated as follows: Suppose the problem were to determine the relation in areas between two rectangles, A, 14 feet long and 5 feet broad, and B, 6 feet long and 4½ feet broad; and suppose the proposition were advanced that it was a well-known mathematical fact that the areas of rectangles were to some extent dependent on their length and that therefore the areas of the two rectangles were to one another at least as the squares of their lengths, *i.e.,* as 196 to 25; that in reality this conclusion understated the relative size of rectangle A because the breadths had not been considered and the breadth of rectangle A is 5 feet and of B only 4½ feet. It is at once clear that the crucial question involved in this proposition is the propriety of the step by which the method proceeds from the undoubtedly correct statement that the area of rectangles is affected by their length to the precise measurement of such effect. If the proponent of the method cannot demonstrate that this relation is correctly expressed by the squares of the length, or if his opponents can disprove this claim, then no amount of evidence that areas of rectangles are affected by their length, or that the areas are affected by their breadth, or that where the length and breadth are equal the area is the square of the length, can be of any avail.

In Mr. Thompson's calculation the corresponding crucial step is that in which he undertakes to measure precisely the effect of the influence of prior fixed charges or mortgages on the value of an income expectation. If this step cannot be successfully defended, no mass of evidence to show that market values are affected to some extent by the proportion of fixed charges to corporate income, or to show that estimates of future earnings are made in financial practice, or any of the like propositions to which so much of Mr. Thompson's second affidavit is devoted, can save his method from complete rejection.

Let us consider what the reply affidavits show and how far Mr. Thompson has been able to combat them.

The reply affidavits show clearly that the method employed by Mr. Thompson is not one generally recognized or commonly employed for similar purposes.

They show that the method is fundamentally defective because amongst other errors:

(1) Mr. Thompson, whilst making the extent of the mortgages to which the final net income is subject the

crucial test of value, has ignored the mortgages upon the income before it reaches the Lake Shore or the combined companies as the case may be; and

(2) The method by which Mr. Thompson arrives at the rate of capitalization of 15% of 46% of the net corporate income in each case is incorrect, and that rate is not warranted upon a fair consideration of the facts.

They show that the error in the conclusion resulting from these two errors alone is so great that a correction thereof would lead to the conclusion on Mr. Thompson's own method that the basis of consolidation is fair and equitable to the Lake Shore minority stockholders.

They further show that, tested by application to other cases, the results derived from Mr. Thompson's method are incorrect.

Messrs. May, Porter and White (all having wide experience in matters involving the determination of the absolute and relative values of stocks) all testify that they have never known Mr. Thompson's method or any method at all similar thereto employed for such purposes. Mr. Thompson in his reply says:

I submit that my method is novel only in this, that it reduced to concrete form a principle universally recognized in the financial world; and as evidence of that fact I submit herewith, out of a great number of citations from financial works and investors' manuals, the following quotations.

The citation which comes nearest to supporting his method is from Sakolski:

Considered in relation to the funded obligations outstanding, this item determines *to some extent* the investment values of these securities.

As well might Mr. Thompson quote Sakolski as authority for the undoubtedly correct statement that the area of a field depends to some extent on its perimeter as supporting a novel method invented by himself for determining areas from perimeters without regard to shape. The whole world of finance and the world of physics are full of influences whose existence is recognized but which have never been measured.

In effect Mr. Thompson concedes the novel and untried quality of the method—and the fact that it is new is not without significance. If the method were reliable the opportunities for its use would be innumerable; and its simplicity renders it extremely unlikely that the method would have remained so long undiscovered, seeing that the problem of determining relative values of securities has engaged for many years some of the keenest minds engaged in business.

IV

THE DEPARTMENT OF COMMERCE *Versus* MR. HOOVER *

(1926)

Summing up the impression one derives from an examination of the report † and the evidence, the Secretary was evidently keenly alive to the fact that a rubber shortage was impending, and to the desirability of bringing to the attention of the American people, in a striking way, the need of some action to forestall this condition. This he has undoubtedly done.

If in doing so he has advanced theories and contentions which upon the evidence of his department seem incapable of being sustained, this merely confirms what some of the most ardent admirers of his ability and achievements have reluctantly concluded: that his undeniably great gifts lie rather in the fields of organization of effort and of public opinion than in the fields of economics and the dispassionate analysis of controversial facts. His plea for a policy of freedom of raw materials from governmental control suffers from a too strongly nationalistic approach, from an overstatement of the case in specific instances, and from a failure to anticipate the obvious retort upon our own protectionist policies and to set forth the economic grounds upon which he distinguishes between the two policies and bases his appeal.

The evidence fails to demonstrate that the restriction scheme was either very beneficial to growers or highly injurious to consumers. It rather raises doubt whether the

---

* Excerpt from "Rubber: The Inquiry and the Facts," *The Atlantic Monthly* (June, 1926).

† *Plantation Rubber in the East Indies*, Department of Commerce (1925). See also *Hearings Before the Committee on Interstate and Foreign Commerce*, House of Representatives, 69th Congress, 1st Session on H. R. 59 (1926).

374

benefits to those whom it was intended to help were sufficient to justify its adoption.

The continuance of control after the rise of last summer may legitimately be criticized, but nothing in the nature of a serious grievance against the growers seems to be established. They have, of course, conducted their operations with a view to gain, and not from altruistic motives; but, viewing the whole subject in perspective, and taking one year with another, it is evident that they have provided the raw materials upon which a major development of our industry and comfort is based, at prices which would not have been attractive to our own capital.

The problem of rubber supply is a serious one and may be said to have entered into a new phase during 1925. It is fortunate that the change should have come at a time of prosperity so that its effects were not of serious consequence to our manufacturers or to our consumers.

Our people have a genius for economy in production, and our national vice is extravagance in consumption. Stimulation of the one and a slight curb on the other should suffice to bring about a satisfactory relation between demand and supply during the years immediately ahead, in which no great increase of production can be expected. The rise in prices will afford such a stimulation and such a check, and should at the same time encourage the plantation of new areas which will in the course of years provide for the natural expansion of demand.

If Americans find in the field an attractive opportunity for the employment of some of the country's abundant supply of capital, well and good; the record certainly establishes no case for our entering the field on an uncommercial basis.

V

REPORT OF THE ADVISORY COMMITTEE ON CORPORATE RELATIONS, G. O. MAY, CHAIRMAN, TO THE SOCIAL SCIENCE RESEARCH COUNCIL

(1927)

Your committee believes that modern developments in the field of corporate relations have great social significance and importance and constitute a field in which valuable research may be undertaken. They suggest that any project should be so framed as to form part of a general review of the corporation of today in connection with the broader problems of the relations in industry between capital, management, labor and the public interest. Such a general review would include:

I. An inquiry into the extent to which the business activities of the country are carried on by corporations or quasi-corporations, in the aggregate and in specified fields, including comparisons with the past to indicate the trend and rate of change

II. A survey of the existing corporations in the United States with a view to classification according to—
   - (a) Character of activities
   - (b) Character of beneficial ownership *
   - (c) Effective control
   - (d) Size

* The general type of classification contemplated under the second sub heading is somewhat as follows:
(1) Investor owned (directly or through holding company)
   Widely distributed
   Closely held
   Personally owned
(2) Customer owned
(3) Banker owned
(4) Management owned
(5) Employee owned
(6) Coöperatively owned
(7) Charitably or publicly owned

III. A study of the trends of recent corporate developments:

(a) The nature of the trends including the tendencies to develop new types of corporate stocks, towards employee ownership, management ownership, etc., and including particularly an examination of the relations between beneficial ownership and effective control and management of corporations the ownership of which is widely distributed

(b) The *intended and actual* effects of the methods being developed on the relations of those interested or engaged in the activity (beneficial owners, management and labor)

    1. *Inter se*

    2. With the rest of the community

(c) The relative social importance of the principal trends noted

IV. A consideration of existing corporation laws and practice with a view to determining in what ways they tend to promote or interfere with the development of the industrial economy of the country along socially desirable lines.

For the first head of inquiry the bulk of the necessary material is, it is believed, available in the records of the National Bureau of Economic Research.

The second head of inquiry your committee regards as of very great importance. The corporations of the country are not a homogeneous group but differ widely in their essential character. The corporation which is owned by a single stockholder is different in almost every respect from a corporation like the American Telephone & Telegraph Company, whose stock is widely distributed.

Your committee believes, however, that before an effective survey under this head can be undertaken there should be secured a substantial improvement in the statistical material available. It believes that, in particular, the Bureau of Internal Revenue is in a position to secure statistical data which would be of great value to the tax administration and at the same time would be of great value for broader economic purposes. The question has been discussed with the

Treasury and it is hoped that steps in the desired direction may be undertaken. Your committee recommends that this head of the inquiry be left in abeyance until this phase is further developed.

The fourth head of the inquiry covers a very wide field and your committee does not believe that more should be undertaken at this time than perhaps a general survey of the situation such as would enable the lines of a more extensive subsequent survey to be formulated.

The main recommendation of your committee is, therefore, a project covering subjects included under the third head of the inquiry as above outlined.

A suggested outline of the scope of such a project follows:

I. The ownership, direction and management of corporations and the trends and rates of change therein:

   A. The extent to which property is held by publicly financed (as contrasted with personal, family or close) corporations in the United States:
      1. In gross
      2. In particular fields
      3. The trend and rate of change in this respect

   B. The nature and distribution of beneficial ownership in such property:
      1. By ownership of obligations or redeemable preferred stocks entitling the holders to fixed dividends or distributions
      2. By ownership of non-redeemable preferred stocks and securities entitling the holders to participation in profits, other than fixed dividends or distributions

   C. The sources from which the personnel of direction and management is drawn—the object being to ascertain to what extent such personnel bears a relation to:
      1. The group of beneficial owners as a whole
      2. Particular divisions of that group
      3. Groups otherwise interested in the corporations

D. The extent to which direction and management is virtually separated from beneficial ownership:
  1. Through legal devices
  2. Factually, through mere size or otherwise

E. The methods and motives regulating the selection of direction and management, regard being had to fact rather than form

II. The situation considered from the standpoint of those interested in the enterprise, as beneficial owners, managers or employees:

A. Considering the group as a whole—the effectiveness of the modern public corporation tested by:
  1. Business success
  2. Relations to other entities in the industry
  3. Industrial conditions within the entity

B. Between owners and managers:
  The cost—and rewards—of management

C. Between owners and managers and employees:
  1. The merger of beneficial ownership and employees' interest
  2. The development of community of interest between employees and management (rather than owners)

III. The situation considered from the standpoint of economic welfare and the public interest:

A. The effectiveness of the modern corporation from the standpoint of:
  1. Service to customers—quality and adequacy
  2. The trend towards or from monopoly
  3. Public relations

IV. Development of the social regulatory machinery to meet the existing and prospective situation:

A. As between those in control and beneficial owners:
  1. Legally through the creation of new or the extension of old legal rights and obligations and relationships
  2. Through economic machinery such as regulatory functions of stock exchanges or other business bodies

The reasons for making such a study are sufficiently clear to require little discussion. Manifestly, separation of management responsibility from beneficial ownership has already taken place in large measure, and is continuing to take place with great rapidity. Apparently, at the same time, new legal and economic relationships are being built up both within the corporate entity and between it and its public, its employees, and the state. These relationships are being forged partly on a basis of experience and partly as a result of underlying concepts of lawyers, business men, economists and statesmen. Old safeguards have become insufficient; new ones, if improvidently worked out, may harass economic development, and fail to protect. Even a new psychology is growing up as the United States becomes increasingly an investing creditor nation. Law, banking methods, business standards, all are involved. Underlying any philosophy there must be a sound understanding of the facts.

VI

SOME MEMORANDA

(1) CONSOLIDATED RETURNS

(1929)

LIKE most such questions, the question of consolidated returns presents different phases in the case of public utilities and commercial businesses, respectively. The question of reflecting interests in companies controlled, but not substantially wholly owned, arises in relation to the earnings statement and the balance sheet. The problem as regards the earnings statement can, I think, be met without very much difficulty, the most important point being that the amount of the earnings accruing from companies in which there is a substantial minority interest should be shown separately. In the case of the balance sheet, the pronounced difference between public utilities and commercial concerns is that in the case of the latter the quick asset position is of crucial importance, while this point is relatively a minor one in the case of public utilities. In the case of commercial companies, I do not think a balance sheet is adequate if it shows a very large minority interest outstanding and gives no indication whether that minority interest is mainly in the capital assets or in the current assets.

As a matter of fact, I have had some doubts about the suitability of the consolidated balance sheet to public utility accounting. The basic idea of consolidated accounting was that the subsidiary companies were essentially parts of the same business and that the allocations between them were almost entirely in the discretion of the management. The position in regard to public utilities which, though under the same ownership, are subject to regulation, is materially different; and I am by no means sure that the best form of

381

reporting for a group consisting of a holding company and a number of public utilities has yet been evolved.

I do not think it is desirable to minimize the difference between substantial ownership and mere control. Those who control but do not wholly own a corporation have a fiduciary obligation to the minority which is very real in equity and probably also in law, though not always fully observed. I think the application to companies barely controlled of methods based originally on substantial ownership is open to objection on this broad ground. Of course, each case differs in detail; a 25% minority interest may be only a means of giving one or more people an interest in the business similar to that which might be given a branch manager, or it may represent an important and possibly justly disgruntled body of stockholders.

One comes back as usual to the conclusion that there can be no satisfactory arbitrary rule of universal application nor any substitute for judgment. The one essential is to reveal fairly the effective position, and this may be done in different ways in different circumstances. I am inclined to think that one should aim to establish broad limits and allow discretion within those limits, satisfying oneself by inquiries from time to time that an honest and competent discretion is being exercised in particular cases.

Our own feeling is that roughly the burden of proof shifts at somewhere about 90%—above that point the presumption becomes increasingly strong in favor of consolidation; below that point the reverse is true.

I think the view correct that where companies are controlled but not consolidated, the holding companies' equity in their earnings and assets should be fairly disclosed in its annual reports in some way; in many cases this can best be done in a statistical statement.

(2) THE CORPORATION LAW OF DELAWARE *

(1929)

DEAR ——:

I have read with much interest the document containing suggested changes in the corporation law of Delaware. I do not see at the moment how greater license could be conferred on promoters and directors and at the same time any semblance of rights preserved to stockholders or the State. I am particularly interested to note the conclusion that the discretion of the directors is such a perfect substitute for all other forms of protection to stockholders, and that the distinction between capital and income can be obliterated by legislation. Possibly some of our "manufacturers of securities" will find that the law as amended still unduly fetters corporate development, but there will be time enough to strike off these fetters if and when they are discovered. In the meantime no one can, I think, deny that a substantial advance has been made along the primrose path.

Personally and unofficially yours,

GEORGE O. MAY

P.S. I suppose there is no possible chance of a court holding that the granting of such freedom of action to directors implies corresponding responsibility.

(3) CAPITAL STOCK OF NO PAR VALUE

(1929)

The one substantial advantage which we recognize in capitalization through capital stock without par value is that which was stressed by the promoters of the first law, namely, that it facilitates the financing of corporations which have met with misfortunes and therefore would, as a practical matter, be unable to sell stock having par value at or above par, and would be legally unable to sell it at a price below par.

A second and psychological advantage is that the payment of dividends on stock without par value in some cases carries

---

* A letter written March 4, 1929.

less suggestion of excessive profits than would a similar distribution on stock having par value. This consideration, it seems to us, would have weight in the case of companies which are large employers of labor and carry on an unregulated business with the general public.

Against these advantages we feel that there are substantial disadvantages, and that these are particularly important in the case of companies incorporated in Delaware whose financial policy includes the regular payment of stock dividends.

We do not feel that the development of the no par value stock laws up to the present has been very sound or satisfactory; particularly in the State of Delaware the changes in the law which have been made from time to time seem to us to have been determined by the exigencies of particular situations rather than by any clear and complete understanding of the problem. As the law now stands the distinctions between capital and income are almost obliterated, and the freedom granted to treat what is essentially a capital contribution as surplus, and to pay dividends either from such surplus or from earnings, would, if generally availed of, soon destroy the significance of dividends. We think a reaction is to be expected and that signs of this reaction are to be found in such statutes as those of Ohio and Louisiana, which require a formal notification to stockholders in case a dividend is paid from any source except profits earned—not to mention more rigid statutes such as that of Wisconsin.

It may be also that the removal of practically all restraint on directors in the statutes of a state may result in their being held to a higher degree of responsibility under the common law than if the statutes were more restrictive. We have heard this view expressed by lawyers of high standing, though it is perhaps not the majority view.

In what is perhaps one of the earliest of the English dividend cases Lord Campbell said:

Dividends are supposed to be paid out of profits only, and when directors order a dividend, to any given amount, without expressly saying so, they impliedly declare to the world that the company has made profits, which justify such a dividend.

This is clearly not today an accurate statement of the law in most states, or particularly in the State of Delaware, but it does seem to state the position fairly from the standpoints of financial morality and good practice. Cases may arise, especially in connection with mergers or consolidations, in which distributions from something not technically profits of the paying corporation may be justified, but these cases are exceptional and rare. The provisions of the Delaware law to which we have referred were probably drafted to meet such situations, and if their application were restricted to such cases no great harm would be done; experience, however, suggests that this will not be the case.

Under the Delaware law a dividend may perhaps be defined as an allocation to stockholders of funds which are not capital. Such an allocation may be satisfied either in money, property, or additional stock of the corporation declaring the dividend; in the last-mentioned case the dividend becomes a stock dividend, the funds allocated become capitalized. In every case the amount of the allocation is necessarily, we think, the amount of the dividend. Though these propositions seem to us almost self-evident, we are aware that they have not been uniformly followed in actual practice. Issues of capital stock which have been termed "stock dividends" have been made without any contemporaneous allocation to capital, and stock dividends have been described in terms inconsistent with the conclusions above reached. In our judgment, however, when additional shares of capital stock without par value are issued without any contemporaneous allocation to capital of funds not previously a part of the capital of the corporation, the transaction is a splitting of stock or multiplication of stock, rather than a stock dividend. Further, we think that a description of a stock dividend paid on capital stock without par value in stock without par value as a dividend of so much per cent is erroneous and essentially meaningless. The amount of the dividend is the amount allocated to capital in respect thereof. Where stock has a par value the rate of dividend may be indicated either explicitly as a dividend of so many dollars a share, or implicitly as a dividend of so much per cent, which, the value being known, is readily susceptible of expression in dollars a share. Where stock has no par value the latter alternative is not available.

Under the Delaware statute the amount allocated to capital in respect of a stock dividend appears to be in the absolute discretion of the directors. It would apparently be permissible to capitalize, say, 5 cents a share in respect of the stock issued as a dividend even though contemporaneously other stocks were being sold for cash at $100 a share. The effect of this liberality of the law seems to us to be twofold: First, that it imposes on directors a moral responsibility to capitalize a reasonable sum in respect of the dividends which they may declare; secondly, that it imposes on the responsible officers and directors of the corporation the obligation to describe the dividend clearly in terms of the amount a share capitalized in respect thereof. No rules regarding the amount to be capitalized have been formulated, so far as we are aware, either by authority or by custom. In some cases amounts derived from previous practice while par stock was outstanding have been continued though the logic of the figure has ceased to exist; in other cases merely nominal figures have been capitalized. The Listing Committee of the New York Stock Exchange has indicated its view that the amount capitalized should be substantial, but has not, we think, given any more definite indication of its position. Our feeling is that the burden is normally on directors to justify their action in so far as they capitalize a sum less than the minimum price at which they would consider selling the stock to subscribers, though we recognize that there may be ample justification for such a course in individual cases. The conversion of common stock to stock of no par value would, as we see it, add to the responsibilities of the directors and involve the sacrifice of certain psychological advantages in relation to dividend policy without compensating benefits. For these reasons we would advise against such a change unless there are important advantages in other directions, of which we have no knowledge, which tend to make the change expedient.

(4) ACCOUNTING FOR STOCK DIVIDENDS RECEIVED

(1929)

The periodical stock dividend policy is, as I understand it, predicated on the belief that in such businesses there is a continuous opportunity to invest new money at more than the going rate of return on comparable investments, and that the method of withholding cash dividends and declaring stock dividends conserves this benefit to the stockholders to the full extent of the annual earnings in a most advantageous way. Those who advocate this practice usually insist that it is legitimate only if it is reasonably expected that the earnings a share will not be reduced by the procedure adopted.

Even upon these assumptions I am convinced that it is wholly incorrect to treat such dividends received as income to the extent of the market value of the stock received at the time of its receipt. I say that it is wholly incorrect because I am convinced that it is incorrect on the basis of established accounting practice, is incorrect on the basis of any other consistent and reasonable scheme of accounting that can be suggested, is incorrect as a matter of economics, and should be incorrect as a matter of law.

The first point requires little or no discussion. Accounting for profits is, as I have frequently before said, not a matter of logical definition but a matter of established practice; but while practice varies, still, among all the varieties, one principle is almost universally observed, namely, that profits should not be taken credit for until realized. In the stock dividend cases the Supreme Court held that in common usage and therefore in law the term "income" included only realized gains and not unrealized increment. Nothing is *realized* when a stock dividend is received.

It may be argued, however, that new conditions and new financial systems call for new principles of accounting, and it is, therefore, desirable to consider the question from the standpoint of one attempting to lay down sound rules of accounting to fit a new financial system in which the declaration of such dividends is assumed to be an integral part. The question then arises, What basic principle could be substituted?

Three possible alternatives suggest themselves. The first, which would involve the least departure from the accepted practice of the past, would be to treat a legitimate periodical stock dividend as being income in the amount of the income of the paying corporation during the period covered thereby. It might be more nearly correct to limit the amount credited by the recipient to the amount capitalized by the payor in respect of the dividend, but no great harm should result from the more liberal policy of allowing a credit to the full extent of the realized income of the payor, though of course there would be need for safeguards against later duplication of the credit in respect of the part of realized income not capitalized on the declaration of the stock dividend.

The second alternative is the complete abandonment of the now practically universal rule that unrealized increment should not be treated as income or profit, and to determine profits by a single-entry method involving complete revaluation at the close of every fiscal period. If this method were adopted, the stock dividend point would become immaterial because all assets, whether acquired by purchase or through stock dividends, would be revalued. It may be that there are some arguments for such a method of determination of profits; personally, I should be extremely sorry to see it adopted, and I do not think it is likely to command the support of any large section of the legal, business, banking, accounting, or economic opinion of the country. Further discussion of this point would be irrelevant to the present issue because, as I have pointed out, if this method were adopted the treatment of stock dividends would become immaterial.

The third possible basis seems to me to be a recognition of the economic fact that a dividend, whether paid in cash or stock, is not a real source of gain to a stockholder; the real source of gain to him is the earning of a profit by the corporation in which he holds stock. A dividend is merely a realization (and is a credit to income under the existing methods of accounting simply because it is a realization). It is upon such considerations that the use of the consolidated balance sheet and income account in the case of parent and subsidiary is based. So far as the present question is concerned, the effect of its adoption would be the same as would follow from the adoption of the first suggestion considered. The credit to income could not exceed the earnings of the corporation paying the dividend.

It seems to me that the same conclusion is reached from an analysis of the nature of a share of stock. If a stockholder holding ten shares of a corporation receives during a year one share of stock as a stock dividend, he cannot properly treat this as income except to the extent that the eleven shares held at the end of the year represent something which was not represented by the ten shares held at the beginning of the year. A share of stock in a public company represents essentially a right to participate in the benefits of future earnings and opportunities; physical assets are important only so far as the proceeds thereof may be distributable or as they constitute instrumentalities for the production of earnings and opportunities. Among the things represented by the ten shares at the beginning of the year was a share of the benefits derivable from the opportunity to invest additional capital in the business on terms more advantageous than the going rate of return on such investments. It is obvious that the eleven shares held at the end of the year represent no larger right under this head than the ten shares represented at the beginning of the year. Such part of the value of the eleventh share, therefore, as is based upon this right or opportunity has merely been transferred from the ten shares to the eleventh.

Assuming the market appraisal of this right or opportunity as a whole to be the same at the end as at the beginning of the year, the market value a share will fall to the extent of one-eleventh of the value a share assigned to the right in the market at the beginning of the year, though of course this effect may be offset by the effect of other changes in conditions during the year.   It may be that the psychological effect of the dividend action will be to raise the market valuation of future opportunities; but upon a rigid analysis it is apparent that the right to benefit from psychological effects of the action of the directors attached to the stock held at the beginning of the year.   The new stock does not represent any new property created during the year except that created by the investment of the income of the year.

The Supreme Court has held categorically that stock dividends are not income.   Admittedly the periodical stock dividend (the kind here under discussion) is different in its nature from the stock dividend that was before the Court in *Eisner* v. *Macomber,* but the line of reasoning contained in the last preceding paragraph of this memorandum leads to the conclusion that if the question were re-presented, the Court would be likely to extend its previous decision to cover periodical stock dividends, a conclusion reinforced by a reading of the Court's decision.   In any case it would be most unlikely to hold that such periodical stock dividends were income in an amount exceeding the amount of income earned and not distributed in cash by the distributing corporation during the period covered by the stock dividend.

It is not without significance that in *Eisner* v. *Macomber* the Act under consideration provided that stock dividends should be considered income to the amount of their cash value when received, and that the Government made no effort to support this position, apparently recognizing the impossibility of doing so successfully.   It merely claimed that the dividends were income to the extent of the profits upon which they were based. In the synopsis of the Attorney-General's argument he is reported as arguing as follows:

The substance of the Act of 1916 is that no corporate earnings are taxed as distributed gains which might not have been taxed as undivided profits when they accrued, and all such earnings which might have been taxed as undivided profits are taxed when distributed.

And as ending with the following:

His gain comes, not from the declaration of a dividend of any kind, but from what his capital has earned. The only effect of the dividend is to fix the date upon which, under the law, his share of corporate earnings, previously accrued, becomes taxable.

The only remaining point to be considered is whether the treatment of stock dividend as income to the amount of the value of the stock when received would be in the general interest. I feel sure that it would not.

Market values are affected by innumerable conditions, one of the most important of which may be monetary inflation. The result of this practice is to treat an increase in value due to monetary inflation as current income, analogous to interest and dividends based on actual earnings; and where the practice is adopted by a series of corporations, each one of which, except the first, holds stock in preceding companies, this effect of inflation is increased in geometrical progression. The practice seems to me to be fraught with the greatest danger to the whole financial structure. It involves inserting the thin edge of the wedge of unrealized increment into the income account. If such increment is to be treated as income, profits or earnings, it should be recognized frankly that a fundamental revision of existing business accounting practice is being effected.

(5) THE PROPRIETY OF A CORPORATION'S TRADING IN ITS OWN
STOCK

(1929)

The question of the propriety of a corporation's trading
in its own stock may be considered from three points of view:

1. From the standpoint of corporations in general.
2. From the standpoint of a corporation which has invited
the public to trade in its stock by listing that stock on
a public exchange.
3. From the standpoint of the exchange on which such
stock is listed.

Considered from the first of these standpoints, the question
may be a difficult one and the conclusion doubtful. The objection to the practice seems to me to become clearer when
the question is considered from the second standpoint and
quite clear when considered from the third, which is the one
in which the Committee on Stock Lists of the Exchange is
interested.

As is usually the case in the ethics of stock dealing, the
objections to corporations' trading in their own stock are
more clearly manifest on consideration of the sale than of
the purchase of stock. It may well be in the interests of all
concerned for a corporation to purchase its own stock in
certain circumstances; it seems to be doubtful whether it is
ever right for a corporation to sell its own stock over the exchanges.

Certainly this seems objectionable from the standpoint of
the Exchange, which is as much concerned with the rights
of potential purchasers of stock as it is with the rights of
existing stockholders. The main purpose of the Exchange
is to offer opportunities for trading in securities under conditions as nearly fair to both parties as can be secured. It
should be, and is, always on its guard to prevent insiders'
gaining an undue advantage over the general public. In
doing so, it is naturally handicapped by the impossibility
of framing any precise rule to define insiders; but a corpo-

ration, itself, clearly falls in such a category, and the Exchange should not countenance the corporation's dealing with the general public in relation to its own stock over the exchanges.

Probably in the majority of cases no detriment to the general public would result from the corporation's being permitted to buy its own stock over the Exchange. The only people who might conceivably have a right to object would be the vendors of such stock and possible purchasers of the stock. The vendors could hardly have a complaint, since the presence of the corporation in the market would tend to raise the price; nor could the potential purchasers have any serious cause of complaint, assuming always that the purchases by the corporation were in good faith, because the corporation might be assumed to buy only when the stock was selling below what the management conceived to be its intrinsic value.

When, however, the case of the sale of stock by the corporation is considered, the position is different. In such cases, the possible complainants would be the stockholders and the potential purchasers. The former would seem to have cause for complaint if the stock were sold below its true value, and the latter if it were sold above the true value.

Pursuing this line of thought, it seems to me clear that merely upon the consideration of abstract principles the Exchange is fully warranted in refusing to list stock of companies which do not agree to refrain from trading in their own stock, and in reserving the right to make reasonable regulations governing any occasional purchases or sales. Obviously, the arguments on the basis of abstract reasoning in favor of such a rule are fortified by consideration of the abuses in which the trading by corporations in their own stock is likely to result. Such abuses are illustrated by the many cases in which corporations bought their own stock during the market collapse of 1929, primarily for the purpose of supporting the value of the stock in the interest of insiders whose stock was pledged for loans.

VII

SOME BOOK REVIEWS

(1)

INTEREST AS A COST

by *Clinton H. Scovell*

New York (1924) *

MR. SCOVELL'S book contains an attempt, which is not wholly consistent or convincing, to reconcile economic theory and practical cost accounting, as well as a discussion of the general accounting and legal phases of the subject. Commencing with the statement that the "margin between selling price and cost is profit," the author considers different kinds of cost, such as sacrifice cost and consumers' cost, and ultimately decides that the objective of the cost accountant should be "entrepreneur's cost." At this point having perhaps, as we have, referred to two dictionaries and found as the primary definition of "entrepreneur": "One who gets up a musical entertainment," he wisely undertakes to define "entrepreneur." His definition is embodied in the following sentence:

By 'entrepreneur' is meant the person or persons— whether single proprietor, partners, or body of common stockholders—who own the capital goods and the product, hold control, and undertake the risks of operation.

Clearly there are here included qualifications which may or may not be united in the same individual or group. The defining paragraph, however, ends with the following sentence:

An entrepreneur may receive managerial wages or salary as laborer, interest as capitalist and profit as entrepreneur.

* *The Journal of Accountancy*, Vol. XXXVII (June, 1929).

Further, in his appendix the author quotes with approval Taylor's statement:

> In strict economic analysis, however, profits ought to be limited to the third element, the taking of responsibility and the making of final decisions.

This evidence leads to the inference that the term "entrepreneur" is used in the common economic sense of someone standing back of labor, capital and management alike. If so, it may be questioned whether the standpoint of this somewhat shadowy individual is the most useful one from which to consider "cost" for practical purposes. Certainly also from this standpoint the cost of capital includes compensation for risk as well as for use, just as it includes accident insurance as well as wages.

Frequently, however, the author seems to regard profits as including, if not indeed being the compensation to, capital for risk (though not for use), and expresses it in terms of a percentage on the capital employed. As he also quotes and italicizes a reference by Taussig to "earnings of management or business profits," it would seem that he is unwilling to make a definite choice between three materially different concepts of profit and consequently of cost.

The uncertainty thus created is not dissipated by his discussion of specific rates, for he proposes a rate of 5%, 6% or 7%; that is, a rate substantially higher than is necessary as pure compensation for use of capital but substantially less than is required to cover both use and risk.

On the accounting phase the author quotes Simpson's *Economics for the Accountant* to the following effect:

> Obviously he (the accountant) is not making his statements for anyone other than the common stockholders. On the balance sheet, for example, the surplus is not described as the common stockholders' surplus, but it so evidently belongs to them that no specific mention is necessary. Every accounting statement is made for the common stockholders, who may or may not be entrepreneur-capitalists but who are always entrepreneurs.

We are not prepared to accept either of the arguments here advanced without question. The second point lies in the field of economics and may turn on the definition of "entrepreneur." On the accounting point the author is clearly in error; surplus does not necessarily belong to common stockholders. It may, for instance, be used to pay dividends on preferred stock in respect of either a past or a future period.

The review of court decisions does not lead to any very significant conclusions one way or the other, and indeed this is not a question upon which the courts could be expected to furnish guidance.

The author makes a valiant effort on behalf of his favorite theory, but it cannot be said that he has succeeded in putting it beyond the reach of controversy.

(2)

THE ECONOMICS OF INSTALMENT SELLING (2 vols.)

by *Edwin R. A. Seligman*

New York (1927) *

Professor Seligman's two volumes, *The Economics of Instalment Selling,* illustrate in a striking way the new tendency in business to secure a broad basis of fact for business decisions rather than to rely on "hunches" and inspirations. Evidence abounds of the increasing use of basic statistics and special studies in the development of business policies. The tendency, like most other tendencies, is not without its dangers. There is the danger of predicating policies too largely on statistics; there is also the danger of predicating statistics too largely on policies. As Sir Josiah Stamp emphasized in a recent address, statistics are an invaluable aid to intelligence but never a substitute for it.

Nothing is further from our thought than to suggest that Professor Seligman's work illustrates the dangers as well as the tendency. Without regarding it as the last word on the

---

* *The Journal of Accountancy,* Vol. XLV (January, 1928).

subject and without accepting even Professor Seligman's view that "an entirely new chapter is opening up in both theory and business life" and that "we now stand on the brink of another revolution in economic science and economic life, scarcely inferior to its predecessor," this publication must be recognized as an invaluable contribution to the study of a subject which is of undeniably great social importance.

The first volume discusses the economic aspects of the problem, states the broad results of the studies undertaken, and formulates conclusions. The second gives statistics of the volume of instalment selling and retail selling, and also gives five separate studies entitled:

The consumers' study
The merchandise study
The dealer study
The repossession study
The depression study

The reader is thus given the choice of accepting the conclusions or re-examining the problem for himself on the basis of a substantial amount of authentic statistics.

To the layman the discussion of the economic meaning of the terms production and consumption will have little interest. He will, however, readily agree that credit cannot be adjudged good or bad merely by labeling it production credit or consumption credit. Consumption is necessary to production since, in order to live, producers must consume, and if what they consume adds more than an equivalent to production such consumption is economically justified.

Probably instalment purchases of automobiles in comparatively few cases come within that most desirable category of short-time credits, the self-liquidating transaction; the automobile will seldom earn currently for its owner enough to pay the deferred instalments. The evidence seems to indicate, however, that the credits arising from such purchases are usually in the class of secured credits.

The question that is uppermost in many minds is how

instalment sales of automobiles would be affected by a serious, and particularly a sudden, depression; and therefore many will turn at once to the "depression study" which deals with business in the anthracite region during the strike period, September, 1925—February, 1926. A study of the data suggests, however, that it does not afford an adequate basis for any very definite conclusions. Apparently the acceptance company whose records were studied only began buying paper in the district in August, 1924, and its purchases suggest that its policy was conservative, perhaps because the strike was in prospect.

The purchases are given for a period of 24 months, of which 13 preceded and 5 followed the strike. The comparative purchases for successive periods are significant, bearing in mind that normally the months from early spring to early summer would be those of heaviest business.

Sep.-Feb., 1924-25.................... $114,000
Mar.-Aug., 1925..................... 244,000
Sep.-Feb., 1925-26 (strike period)....... 226,000
Mar.-July, 1926 (five months)......... 1,029,000

The purchases during six spring and summer months of 1925 were scarcely more than those during an equal period covering fall and winter months and the strike period, and were about equal to one month's purchases in the summer following the strike.

The effect of depression on automobile instalment sales still remains to be measured. It would be interesting to have a more exhaustive study than the volumes contain of the effect of depression on the piano and other classes of instalment business for which longer records and more ample material is available.

The dangers involved in the policy of taking used property in part payment for new are emphasized. This is a point on which accounting can exercise a real and helpful influence. Clearly property taken in trade should not be valued on the basis of the trade-in prices. In the past, adoption of this practice even with some reserve has been known to result in used property being valued at higher figures than similar new units which were valued at manufacturing cost. The sound rule is that the used unit when made ready for resale should not stand at a higher percentage of its probable sale price than the new unit. Adoption of such a rule tends to keep the trade-in business on a financially sound basis.

Though Professor Seligman began his study with an open mind, he was fully convinced of the economic value of instalment selling before it ended. His discussion may at times seem to suggest the advocate rather than the judge, but it is clearly the expression of honest conviction, not special pleading. In general his conclusions seemed well founded. A large amount of desirable buying is facilitated by instalment selling. In desirable buying is included not only buying for directly productive uses, but buying which lightens the burden of heavy toil, shortens unduly long hours of labor, or in other ways adds to the efficiency or the just contentment of the purchaser.

There is good and bad instalment selling of automobiles; good and bad buying. The nature of the buying is less susceptible of analysis, but in general the selling seems to be as economically sound as most selling. Down payments are substantial; the periods over which instalments are spread are reasonably short. The method is still on trial and the rapidity of its development cannot fail to cause some concern, but the study seems to show that at least the worst fears are ill founded. Certainly all interested in the subject owe a debt to Professor Seligman for his thorough and able analysis of the problem.

(3)

ACCOUNTING METHOD

by *C. Rufus Rorem*

Chicago (1928) *

The interest to the legal profession of such books as that of Professor Rorem, and others written for the use of stu-

* *American Bar Association Journal* (November, 1929).

dents, is twofold. They have a narrower usefulness as indicating the commonly accepted rules covering the treatment of particular items; examination suggests that the general practice is as a rule fairly stated in Professor Rorem's volume. They have, however, a broader interest in so far as they convey an understanding of the underlying philosophy of accounting, which is by no means generally understood by lawyers. Upon this phase the first part of Professor Rorem's book, which deals with "the rôle of accounting in modern economic life," should be interesting to lawyers who have come to recognize the rapidly growing importance of that rôle. As the author points out, accounting today concerns itself not merely with the formal recording of business transactions but with their analysis and interpretation also, and in the complex business life of today has become an economic tool of the first importance. Upon the proper use of that tool, or in other words upon the correct interpretation of the facts recorded, depends in large measure the success or failure of business enterprises.

The book will not perhaps be entirely successful in clearing up existing confusion regarding the principles and objectives of general corporate accounting—a confusion for which accountants are themselves largely responsible. They commonly state that a balance sheet is intended to be a statement, as nearly accurate as possible, of financial position, but when the question is pursued it becomes clear that this is not the case. On the contrary a corporate balance sheet is usually a congeries of figures, some historical, some conventional, and some reflecting actual current values, and its importance is subordinated to that of the profit and loss account.

What are profits and when do they emerge? is the question most frequently asked of accounts by lawyers, and indeed also by bankers, business men and economists. Now, profit earning is in general a process that is continuous and often drawn out, and the attribution of profits to particular short periods of time, though a practical business necessity, does violence to fact and must therefore be arbitrary. The oft-stated rule that a profit should not be taken up until realized does not altogether meet the case, for not only is there the question, what constitutes realization, but there is the obvious fact that a profit is usually a balance of a number of items, some positive, some negative, which cannot all be realized simultaneously. The determination of profits is, then, the result of method and opinion, not of logical definition, and the question arises how method and opinion are to be controlled,—the ultimate purpose being, as already stated, to attribute to a particular day, month or year a profit which is the result of interrelated transactions extending over much longer periods of time. The answer is that principles have in fact been evolved which seem in general to work satisfactorily, and that such rules have acquired authority and to some extent the force of law. The courts in England have held, for instance, when called upon to interpret statutes taxing profits without defining them, that the answer to the question, What are profits and when may they be deemed to have emerged? must be found in the practices of responsible business men. But business practices are not uniform or unchanging, consequently there is usually more than one correct answer to the question, What are the profits of a given business for a given period? Our own statutes have recognized this condition and every Revenue Act since that of 1918 has provided that income shall be determined "in accordance with the method of accounting regularly employed by the taxpayer" unless that method does not correctly reflect income, in which case it is to be determined in accordance with such method as in the opinion of the Commissioner does clearly reflect income.

Both lawyers and economists have been bothered by the lack of fixed rules for determining profits and by the fact that two equally legitimate methods of accounting may give widely different results for a given period. It is possible that the tendency to make the declaration of dividends less dependent upon profits, which characterizes some new corporation laws, is in part due to legal dissatisfaction with the uncertainty attaching to the determination of profits.

Some economists have favored the determination of profits by periodical valuations; the increase in net worth plus the amount distributed representing the profit for the period intervening between any two valuations; accounting being relied on only for a record of the assets and liabilities to be valued and for the analysis of the profits and not for the determination of the amount thereof. This method does not, however, in practice give satisfactory results.

Professor Rorem explains the established accounting method as a continuous process of evaluation, with the proviso that for certain purposes and in the case of certain assets and liabilities the valuations are conventionalized. While this view is interesting and often expressed, it may be doubted whether it is either particularly helpful or historically correct. When the accountant records an asset acquired at cost and retains it at that figure even though its value is greater than cost, he does so because it is the cost that is significant to him, not because he desires to value the asset and accepts cost as the measure of value, in default of any better. The point may be illustrated from the case of valuation of inventories at cost where the market value is clearly in excess thereof. Dickinson, in his *Accounting Practice and Procedure,* page 93, says:

The object of the profit and loss account of a manufacturing or merchandising concern is to ascertain as closely as possible the profits which have been realized on sales actually made; and for this reason raw materials on hand, and products partly or wholly manufactured, but not sold, should be entirely eliminated. In practice this result is obtained by valuing them at cost, no more and no less, and so exactly offsetting the charges to manufacturing account for materials, labor and expenses, in so far as the result of their combination in manufacturing processes is still uncompleted and unsold.

This reflects the philosophy of accounting more accurately than Professor Rorem's explanation of the use of cost in the case cited as being a conventional valuation. Historically, it may be noted that the form of balance sheet under the English Companies Act of 1862 (the general corporation law) called for the inclusion therein of plant and stock in trade "at cost with deduction for deterioration in value as charged to the reserve fund or profit and loss." The provisions regarding accounts contained in the Act (which were to govern unless the articles of association of a company expressly provided otherwise) are interesting for their emphasis on the Income and Expenditure (or Profit and Loss) Account:

§ 79. Once at the least in every year the Directors shall lay before the Company in General Meeting a Statement of the Income and Expenditure for the past year, made up to a date not more than three months before such meeting.

§ 80. The Statement so made shall show, arranged under the most convenient heads, the amount of gross income, distinguishing the several sources from which it has been derived, and the amount of gross expenditure, distinguishing the expense of the establishment, salaries, and other like matters: Every item of expenditure fairly chargeable against the year's income shall be brought into account, so that a just balance of profit and loss may be laid before the meeting; and in cases where any item of expenditure which may in fairness be distributed over several years has been incurred in any one year the whole amount of such item shall be stated, with the addition of the reasons why only a portion of such expenditure is charged against the income of the year.

§ 81. A balance sheet shall be made out in every year, and laid before the Company in general meeting, and such balance sheet shall contain a summary of the property and liabilities of the Company arranged under the heads appearing in the form annexed to this table, or as near thereto as circumstances admit.

In practice the provisions of § 80 were often modified in the articles of association of companies, and frequently only a balance sheet was required to be furnished; but there is no doubt that the amount and nature of the earnings and the manner in which they are computed are the facts of paramount importance to investors in reasonably successful companies, as the present market abundantly witnesses.

The constantly widening diffusion of corporate securities makes more important than ever before a proper disclosure to stockholders of corporate affairs, and this in turn requires that broad rules relating to the determination of corporate profits should be clearly established and given legal effect. To accomplish this result coöperation between theorists, practicing accountants, and lawyers experienced in business affairs is necessary.

Chapters 21 and 22 of Professor Rorem's book contain a statement of working rules which is generally clear and accurate, though this reviewer prefers to describe them as working rules of accounting rather than as working rules of accounting valuation, as Professor Rorem terms them. These chapters are brief and illuminating and should be of real interest and value to the legal or general reader.

(4)

IRVING FISHER'S DEFINITION OF INCOME *

The method by which Professor Fisher attempted to convince his European readers (the article was apparently first published in German in Vienna) that legislatures and courts were coming round to his views is more interesting than convincing. He takes a few specific corollaries that would follow from his general propositions and treats approval of those corollaries as implying at least a degree of concurrence in the basic proposition. Thus one of these corollaries is that stock dividends are not income. Hence *Eisner* v. *Macomber,* in which the Supreme Court so held, is quoted. But the quotation does not include the paragraph in which the Court, after referring to economic concepts, popular usages and dictionaries, approved an earlier definition of the Court: "In-

* From an editorial discussion in *The Journal of Accountancy*, Vol. XLV (February, 1928), of Irving Fisher's *The Income Concept in the Light of Experience.*

come may be defined as the gain derived from capital, from labor, or from both combined"—with the proviso that—"it be understood to include profits gained through a sale or conversion of capital assets," which incidentally is not income upon Professor Fisher's theory. He sums up his legal discussion by saying that it shows "how the true theory of capital and income seems to be slowly working itself out." But until the language just quoted is reversed, the theory that is being worked out cannot be claimed to bear any strong resemblance to that which Professor Fisher seeks to thrust upon us. By similar methods he even seeks to make it appear that his concept is in accord with popular usage, though the mere fact that upon his theory such phrases as "spending more than his income" and "saving half his income" are meaningless is sufficient to demonstrate the contrary. It is difficult to see what good such articles accomplish beyond producing psychic income to their authors.

(5)

THE ECONOMICS OF ACCOUNTANCY

by *John B. Canning*

New York (1929) *

In a review of this work in *The American Economic Review* for December, 1930, Professor Fisher says: "It would not seem an exaggeration to say that *The Economics of Accountancy: A Critical Analysis of Accounting Theory*, by John B. Canning marks an epoch in the two branches of knowledge to which it relates—economics and accountancy."

Even those who deem this praise extravagant must welcome the evidence that professors of economics do not carry the insensibilities of the economic man into their own work, but are human beings with genial human failings. The relation between the two professors is gracefully acknowledged in Professor Canning's preface. If he is the father of the work, Professor Fisher is the grandfather; and the indulgence

* Written in 1929; not previously published.

of grandparents is proverbial. Naturally enough, also, it is the family traits in the grandchild that particularly gratify the grandparent.

Not that it is necessary that one's mind should be bound by family ties to that of Professor Canning in order to see value in his book. It is painstaking, informed, interesting, and stimulating. Least of all should accountants be unduly critical of the work, for Professor Canning displays a sympathy with accountants and a knowledge and an appreciation of their work that is not common in other than purely professional writers.

It may, however, be questioned whether the relation between accountancy and economics is exactly that which Professor Canning suggests—as, for instance, where he says: "The economist will be quick to note that the accountant's conception of assets is economic rather than legal." It is fairly clear that accounting practices have not been consciously influenced by economic thought to any considerable extent. The simple fact is that accounting is a tool of business, and the development of accounting, like the development of business law, has been determined by the practices of business men.

Professor Canning's suggestion that the viewpoint of the accountant is not legal is based on inadequate premises. In the argument from which a sentence is quoted above, his conclusion is based on the fact that accountants are not governed by legal title in determining whether or not property is an asset of the corporation or enterprise with whose accounts they are concerned. True; but property title is only one branch of law, and there are other branches which take cognizance of and aim to protect beneficial interests and effective ownerships where those are vested in other than the holders of the legal title.

Generally speaking, where accounting and economic thought run along parallel lines, they do so because both are running parallel to business practice. Where accounting treatment diverges from economic theory, it is usually because economic theory has diverged from business practice. To accountants, as to business men, income is essentially a money concept, and the idea of psychic income leaves them cold. A definition of income which will make an income tax identical with a tax on expenditures seems to them a misuse of terminology, however interesting the underlying concept may be.

(6)

CORPORATION PROFITS

by *Laurence H. Sloan*

New York (1929) *

In this book the author presents some statistics of the larger industrial corporations and some criticisms of the present contents of corporate reports. We may assume that the statistics are the best of the kind readily available, but if so we must recognize how unsafe it is to draw inferences from them without a careful study of each individual company.

To the fact that the data cover only two years the author points as the chief deficiency of the volume. A more important if less easily remedied deficiency is the lack of homogeneity in the material. This defect impairs the significance of all the statistics, most seriously, perhaps, where computations are based wholly or largely on book values of capital, as, for instance, in Chapter IV, in which percentages of depreciation charges are discussed, and Chapter VII dealing with the percentage of earnings on invested capital.

In any such discussions it is essential to understand how varied are the bases on which the capital assets of industrial corporations are carried. The point is particularly important just now because in the last quarter of a century we have had radical changes both in the practice relating to incorporation and in price levels. Capital assets may be stated on the basis of cost or on the basis of a valuation. It may be a pre-war or a post-war basis. The cost may be a cost in cash

* *Journal of the American Statistical Association* (December, 1929).

or a cost in securities. If the latter, it may be a legal cost measured by a par value of a grossly inflated stock issue if the corporation was formed early in the century, or it may be greatly understated if the assets were acquired by a recent issue of stock without par value.

A computation which ignores such differences can scarcely be regarded as more significant than one showing the average consumption of food by a group of animals in which mice, rabbits and elephants are included in undisclosed proportions. The difficulty of securing a really satisfactory grouping is undoubtedly great, but the reader is at least entitled to a clear statement of the defective character of the material used. It may be that the author appreciates fully the varied character of his material, and has satisfied himself that after making due allowance therefor his conclusions are valid and significant. He does not, however, succeed in creating such an impression.

The criticisms of present practice and the suggestions for improvement are of a rather perfunctory and elementary character, though put forward with an air of daring innovation. The form of ideal report suggested bears a strong resemblance to the standard forms set forth in the first general corporation act in England, that of 1862.

The author reveals no understanding of the complexities of accounting in a large business corporation of today or of the philosophy of accounting. Those who hope to find in this work an important contribution to the solution of a question of great and growing importance will be disappointed.

(7)

THE GENERAL THEORY OF EMPLOYMENT, INTEREST AND MONEY

by *J. M. Keynes*

London (1936)

DEAR MR. KEYNES:

I have been examining with interest your new book. Your explorations lead into fields in which I can scarcely claim to follow you, much less to criticize, and therefore I am not go ing to make any general comment except that I gather the impression that you have at times deliberately overdrawn the picture in order to arrest attention. Your discussion of the influences which determine security prices, though acute and admirably presented, seems to me a case in point; but I have welcomed it as a useful corrective to the views of people like Mr. Frankfurter, who think that prices are determined mainly, if not solely, by intelligent analysis of the statistical information which is given to potential traders.

At page 103, however, you enter a field where I can feel reasonably at home, and here I will venture, if I may, to criticize. In your table based on Kuznets, the deductions clearly relate only to business capital formation, and there is no corresponding deduction in respect of state and private capital formation. Consequently, your "net" figure remains a gross figure in respect of these last-mentioned items (which constitute by far the larger part of the aggregate with which you are dealing) and is net only in respect of one part (considerably less than half) of the whole. It follows that comments based on that net figure rest on unsound premises. For instance, your point that Kuznets must have underestimated the rate of depreciation and depletion is surely not well taken, since your percentage is arrived at by comparing the deduction in respect of business capital with the total amount of capital formation of all kinds.

In casting about for an explanation of the apparent statistical error, I noted that your discussion of the Kuznets figures began with the statement that his figures gave results similar to those given by the English figures of Mr. Colin Clark. I have been interested to find that, using only the figures for business capital formation for the four years, this statement is fully borne out, the percentage of net to gross capital formation being approximately 30% in one case and 33% in the other, whereas on the figures in your table the percentages are 70 and 33, which cannot be said to be strikingly similar. This has led me to wonder whether at least a part of your text may not have been written originally in relation to a table derived from Kuznets but dealing only with the formation of business capital.

I have found your book stimulating, and recognize the penetrating character of much of your analysis, though I have a feeling that you fail to distinguish adequately between what is theoretically possible and perhaps ideally desirable in the way of a planned economy and what is actually attainable under modern political conditions.

Yours very truly,

GEORGE O. MAY

February 25, 1936.

INDEX

INDEX

416